A CHRONOLOGICAL
OUTLINE OF
AMERICAN LITERATURE

A CHRONOLOGICAL OUTLINE OF AMERICAN LITERATURE

Samuel J. Rogal

Bibliographies and Indexes in American Literature, Number 8

GREENWOOD PRESS
NEW YORK • WESTPORT, CONNECTICUT • LONDON

Library of Congress Cataloging-in-Publication Data

Rogal, Samuel J.
  A chronological outline of American literature.

  (Bibliographies and indexes in American literature,
ISSN 0742-6860 ; no. 8)
  Bibliography: p.
  Includes index.
    1. American literature—Chronology. 2. American
literature—Outlines, syllabi, etc. I. Title.
II. Series.
PS92.R67 1987   810.2'02   86-33472
ISBN 0-313-25471-0 (lib. bdg. : alk. paper)

Library of Congress Catalog Card Number: 86-33472
ISBN: 0-313-25471-0
ISSN: 0742-6860

First published in 1987

Greenwood Press, Inc.
88 Post Road West, Westport, Connecticut 06881

Printed in the United States of America

∞

The paper used in this book complies with the
Permanent Paper Standard issued by the National
Information Standards Organization (Z39.48-1984).

10 9 8 7 6 5 4 3 2 1

Contents

Introduction

As the title indicates, the <u>Chronological Outline of American Literature</u> is intended, principally, to assist scholars, students, and general readers of American literature in determining the extent of literary activity and of events related to literature in the United States during a specific year, decade, or even century. As such, this volume should not be considered a repository for literary trivia, wherein mental gymnasts may leap over one another in their efforts to memorize dates, authors, and titles that, in and by themselves, have little meaning and even less value. Rather, the entries upon the pages of this reference book will enable the serious reader to comprehend the significance of events and activities as they have affected and contributed to the literary history of the United States.

For example, consider the centennial of the nation, 1876, a year embedded in the minds and notebooks of historians essentially because of Alexander Graham Bell's first transmission, Colorado's admission to the Union as the thirty-eighth state, the Battle of the Little Big Horn, the formation of the National Baseball League, and the James' brother raid on Northfield, Minnesota. In that same year, the American Chemical Society came into being, while the Boston Public Library and the Johns Hopkins University both flung open new doors. Ira David Sankey composed his collection of <u>Gospel Hymns</u> (a series extending to 1891); General Henry Martin Robert published his <u>Rules of Order</u>; Thomas Y. Crowell founded his publishing firm; and young Melville Dewey set forth a new system for the classification of library books.

Yet, neither we nor the historians should fail to remember that Americans living in 1876 could have witnessed, if interested, the publication of Louisa May Alcott's <u>Rose in Bloom</u> and <u>Silver Pitchers and Independence</u>; Mark Twain's <u>Adventures of Tom Sawyer</u>; Ralph Waldo Emerson's <u>Letters and Social Aims</u>; <u>Brete Harte's Gabriel Conroy</u> and <u>Two Men of Sandy Bar</u>; the first publication of Nathaniel Hawthorne's <u>The Dolliver Romance</u>; Henry James' <u>Roderick Hudson</u>; Herman Melville's poem, <u>Clarel</u>; Charles Dudley Warner's <u>My Winter on the Nile</u>; Walt Whitman's <u>Two Rivulets</u>; and John Greenleaf Whittier's <u>Mabel Martin</u>. Sherwood Anderson and Jack London came into the world in 1876, while the likes of Orestes August Brownson, Horace Bushnell, Samuel Benjamin Helbert Judah, and John Neal all departed life and letters. Thus, from little more than a list of authors, titles, and events, we may perceive a clear example of a year alive with literary energy--a moment, as it were, in the history of the nation, in which political, scientific, and social advancements fired the imaginations of America's writers and fed the appetites of a newly formed but nonetheless growing reading public.

However, still other reasons arise for observing literary productivity from a chronological perspective, particularly when a specific moment in history produces unexpected variety and identifies the complex alliance necessarily formed by transition and new developments. What are we to conclude, for instance, from an examination of the nation's bicentennial, 1976, and a focus upon the literary events of that year? Wherein lie the common bonds of chronology and theme, of purpose and audience, of form and structure between Isaac Asimov and James Baldwin? Donald Barthelme and Ann Beattie? Saul Bellow and Peter Benchley? Edward Berrigan and John Berryman? Elizabeth Bishop and Philip Booth? How are we, as students and readers, to judge the impact upon a readership that, within a single year, was asked to partake of such a varied menu as Vance Bourjaily's Now Playing at Canterbury, Gerald Brace's Days That Were, Richard Brautigan's Loading Mercury with a Pitchfork, James Cain's The Institute, or Erskine Caldwell's Afternoons in Mid-America? How may we focus clearly upon a year that produced a narrative by Truman Capote, a novel by R.V. Cassill, an autobiography by Elizabeth Coatsworth, and a play by Donald Coburn? Surely, such questions, and the almost endless avenues upon which one may discover some answers, constitute the real purpose for examining literary details and events related to literature within the United States from a year-by-year viewpoint and structure.

Nevertheless, the Chronological Outline of American Literature is in no way intended to serve as a substitute for such multi-dimensional reference works as Lyle Wright's three-volume American Fiction; W.J. Burke and W.D. Howe's American Authors and Books; H.H. Clark's American Literature: Poe through Garland and R.B. Davis's American Literature through Bryant; Jacob Blanck's Bibliography of American Literature; the Cambridge History of American Literature; Robert E. Spiller's A Literary History of the United States; or the Oxford Companion to American Literature. Thus, this Chronological Outline contains neither a complete list of all American writers and their works nor a complete bibliography for any single writer whose name appears therein. Rather, the attempt has been to inject variety and representation, as well as literary diversity, into the literary events of a given year and to satisfy as many readers as possible (though knowing full well that a number of them will never be satisfied concerning the inclusion of one writer and the exclusion of another). Further, the term literature has been employed in the broadest meaning of that word; therefore, writers representing a large number of areas and disciplines--drama, poetry, fiction, history, theology, science, philosophy, medicine, sport, fine arts, psychology, politics, economics, and juvenilia--have been hung upon the numerous pages (or pegs) of this Outline.

Obviously, in a reference volume such as the Chronological Outline of American Literature, readers may well wish to inquire about the selection process that determines the particular items to be included (as well as those that have been excluded). Essentially, the selection criteria for this particular project have been significance and representativeness--terms that do not always present clear and objective boundaries. Those two qualities pose no serious problems when one considers major literary figures and their principal works. The student of the Romantic period in American literature, for example, will have little difficulty casting the likes of Irving, Cooper, Bryant, Poe, Emerson, Hawthorne, Melville, Thoreau, Longfellow, Whittier, or Lowell into the

major molds. Does that mean, however, that those literati of the period between (approximately) 1820 and 1860 who never quite reached their
artistic "majority" should be excluded from such reference projects as
this Chronological Outline? Certainly not! What it does mean, though,
is that the so-called lesser lights of a given period in American lite-
rature--the minor figures, as they are known--need to be studied care-
fully, both in terms of their specific contributions to that period and
the relationships of their literary efforts to the works of their major
contemporaries.

The labels secondary and minor need not necessarily be considered
derogatory or synonymous with artistic obscurity or sterility. For example, the novelists Lew Wallace and Francis Marion Crawford attempted
to inject the spirit of American Romanticism into the mundane lives of
the masses; such poets as Thomas Bailey Aldrich, George Henry Boker,
Richard Watson Gilder, Edmund Clarence Stedman, Richard Henry Stoddard,
and Bayard Taylor attempted to imitate the British Romantics of the early nineteenth century and came to be recognized, on a limited basis, as
representing the Continental traditions of European Romanticism. Such
literary figures cannot be identified or stamped as minor writers simply
because they lacked imagination or genius or artistic responsibility;
rather, their fiction, poetry, drama, or nonfiction prose intentionally
directed ideas and themes to specialized and sometimes limited audiences. Nevertheless, those audiences cannot be ignored if one is deter-
mined to consider the overall context of intellectual, literary, and
even social history of what we know as American Romanticism. The novelists and poets mentioned above constituted a vital part of that history, and they contributed significantly to it.

Of course, the issue is not that simple (or clear, perhaps) when
one observes the immediate present. The order and the neatness that literary historians seek (and eventually find) in antiquity have not set-
tled in upon the 1960s, the 1970s, and the 1980 s. Thus, the works of
writers from those decades (from this decade, especially) have not been
tested by time, by the tastes of a terribly diverse reading public, or
by the criteria of critical commentators and scholars--all necessary for
final determination of actual and enduring literary merit. The almost
unlimited variety of literary exercises, in addition to a host of literary demands, create problems whenever one attempts to raise the dis-
tinctions between literary artistry and pure popularity. Despite those
problems, decisions concerning the immediate moment must come forth; to
turn one's back upon the present--to avoid the literature of the United
States from 1966 through 1986--means to turn away from intellectual and
cultural reality, to erase (without justification) almost three decades
from the face of this nation's artistic productivity. Therefore, the
criteria for including contemporary writers in the Chronological Outline
remain essentially the same as for those of the more clearly defined
past literary periods. Significance and representativeness remain pri-
mary considerations, but they have been seasoned with liberal doses of
educated guesswork, the critical reactions of those competent to judge
the literary activity flurrying about them, and what may be known in
polite circles as editorial prerogative.

The format for the Chronological Outline of American Literature is
simple and self-explanatory: it goes forward upon the vehicles of chronological and alphabetical order. The necessary symbols and abbrevia-
tions employed throughout the main body of the text appear in the "Key
to Symbols" that follows. Also, the reader will find a list of "Refe-
rences," easily available texts that might be consulted for further re-

search.

Finally, the compiler of this outline wishes to dedicate the project to the students and the faculty of Illinois Valley Community College.

Key to Symbols

affl = affiliated

auto = autobiography

bib = bibliography

biog = biography

c = ceased

ded = dedicated

des = description

dia = dialogue

dr = drama

e = prose essay

ed = edition/edited by

enl = enlarged

est = established

f = founded

fic = fiction

hist = history

hum = humor

illus = illustrations

juv = juvenile

let = letters

med = meditations

misc = miscellany

nar = narrative

per = periodical

po = poetry

pra = prayers

pub = published

ref = reference

rev = revised

sat = satire

ser = sermon

trans = translation

trav = travel

vol(s) = volume(s)

NOTE: The name in parentheses following the name of the author --e.g., William Edward March Campbell (William March)--indicates pseudonym; the Index provides both legal name and pseudonym.

References

Academy of American Poets. Fifty Years of American Poetry: Anniversary Volume for the Academy of American Poets. Intro. Robert Penn Warren. New York: Harry N. Abrams, Publishers, 1984.

Blanck, Jacob N. Bibliography of American Literature. 6 vols. New Haven, Connecticut: Yale University Press, 1955-1973.

Bryer, Jackson R. (ed.). Fifteen Modern American Authors. A Survey of Research and Criticism. Durham, North Carolina: Duke University Press, 1969.

Burke, W.J., Will D. Howe, Irving Weiss, and Anne Weiss (eds.). American Authors and Books: 1640 to the Present Day. 3rd ed., rev. New York: Crown Publishers, 1972.

Cambridge History of American Literature. 4 vols. New York: Putnam, 1917-1921.

Clark, Harry Hayden. American Literature: Poe through Garland. New York: Appleton-Century-Crofts, 1971.

Contemporary Authors: A Bio-Bibliographical Guide to Current Authors and Their Works. Detroit: Gale Research Company, 1964----.

Cowart, David (ed.). Twentieth-Century American Science Fiction Writers. 2 vols. Detroit: Gale Research Company, 1981.

Davis, Richard Beale. American Literature through Bryant. New York: Appleton-Century-Crofts, 1969.

Gohdes, Clarence. Bibliographical Guide to the Study of Literature of the U.S.A. 4th ed. Durham, North Carolina: Duke University Press, 1976.

Hall, Halbert W. (ed.). Science Fiction Book Review Index, 1923-1973. Detroit: Gale Research Company, 1975.

----. Science Fiction Book Review Index, 1974-1979. Detroit: Gale Research Company, 1981.

Hart, James D. (ed.). The Oxford Companion to American Literature. 5th ed. New York: Oxford University Press, 1983.

Heyen, William (ed.). The Generation of 2000: Contemporary American Poets. Princeton, New Jersey: Ontario Review Press, 1984.

Kunitz, Stanley J., and Howard Haycraft (eds.). American Authors, 1600-1900. New York: H.W. Wilson Company, 1938.

----. Twentieth-Century Authors. New York: H.W. Wilson Company, 1942.

----. Twentieth-Century Authors, Supplement. New York: H.W. Wilson Company, 1955.

Leary, Lewis G. (ed.). Articles on American Literature, 1900-1950.

Durham, North Carolina: Duke University Press, 1954.

Matthews, Geraldine O. (ed.). Black American Writers, 1773-1949. A Bibliography and Union List. Boston: G.K. Hall, 1975.

McMichael, George (ed.). Anthology of American Literature. 3rd. ed. 2 vols. New York: Macmillan Publishing Company, 1985.

MLA International Bibliography. New York: Modern Language Association, 1921----.

New York Theatre Reviews, 1870-1919. 6 vols. New York: New York Times and Arno Press, 1975.

New York Theatre Reviews, 1920-1970. 10 vols. New York: New York Times, 1971.

Nicholls, Peter (ed.). The Science Fiction Encyclopaedia. Garden City, New York: Doubleday and Company, 1979.

Richards, Robert Fulton (ed.). Concise Dictionary of American Literature. New York: Greenwood Press, Publishers, 1955.

Rush, Theressa G., et al (eds.). Black American Writers, Past and Present: A Bibliographical and Biographical Dictionary. 2 vols. Metuchen, New Jersey: Scarecrow Press, 1975.

Spiller, Robert E., et al (eds.). Literary History of the United States. 4th ed. 3 vols. New York: Macmillan Publishing Company, 1974.

Vendler, Helen (ed.). The Harvard Book of Contemporary American Poetry. Cambridge, Massachusetts: The Belknap Press of Harvard University Press, 1985.

Vinson, James (ed.). Contemporary Dramatists. 2nd ed. London: St. James Press, 1977.

----. Contemporary Novelists. 2n ed. London: St. James Press, 1976.

----. Contemporary Poets. 2nd ed. London: St. James Press, 1975.

----. Great Writers of the English Language: Poets, Novelists and Prose Writers, Dramatists. 3 vols. New York: St. Martin's Press, 1979.

Woodress, James L. (ed.). American Literary Scholarship. Durham, North Carolina: Duke University Press, 1963----.

Wright, Lyle. American Fiction, 1774-1850. 2nd ed. San Marino, California: Huntington Library, 1969.

----. American Fiction, 1851-1875. San Marino, California: Huntington Library, 1957.

----. American Fiction, 1876-1900. San Marino, California: Huntington Library, 1966.

A CHRONOLOGICAL
OUTLINE OF
AMERICAN LITERATURE

1   *The Sixteenth Century*

1507

EVENTS

Martin Waldseemuller notes the term "America" on one of his maps

1578

BIRTHS

Nathaniel Ward

1580

BIRTHS

John Smith

1584

BIRTHS

John Cotton

1585

BIRTHS

Alexander Whitaker

1586

BIRTHS

Thomas Hooker

1588

BIRTHS

John Winthrop

1590

BIRTHS

William Bradford
Thomas Morton

1591

BIRTHS

John Wilson

1592

BIRTHS

Samuel Gorton
John Wheelwright

1594

BIRTHS

Stephen Daye

1595

BIRTHS

Thomas Parker
Edward Winslow

1596

BIRTHS

Richard Mather

1597

BIRTHS

John Davenport
John Underhill

1598

BIRTHS

Edward Johnson

2 The Seventeenth Century

1602

BIRTHS

    Samuel Maverick
    Samuel Stone

1603

BIRTHS

    Roger Williams

1604

BIRTHS

    John Eliot

1605

BIRTHS

    Thomas Shepard

1606

BIRTHS

    John Norton

1607

EVENTS

Captain John Smith establishes a colony at Jamestown, Virginia

1608

EVENTS

Puritans settle in Holland

LITERATURE

John Smith. A True Relation of Occurrences and Accidents in Virginia
(nar)

1609

BIRTHS

John Clarke

1610

EVENTS

Thomas West, Baron De La Warr, first colonial governor of Virginia,
to 1618

1612

BIRTHS

Anne Bradstreet

1613

BIRTHS

Nathaniel Morton

LITERATURE

Alexander Whitaker. Good News from Virginia (ser)

1616

LITERATURE

John Smith. A Description of New England (des)

1617

BIRTHS
   Peter Folger

DEATHS
   Alexander Whitaker

1620

EVENTS

   Puritans establish the Plymouth Colony

1621

BIRTHS

   William Hubbard
   Thomas Mayhew

1624

LITERATURE

   John Smith. The General History of Virginia (hist)
   Edward Winslow. Good News from New England (nar)

1626

LITERATURE

   John Wilson. A Song, or Story, for the Lasting Remembrance of Divers
      Famous Works (po)

1629

EVENTS

   The Company of Massachusetts Bay in New England (est)
   John Winthrop, governor of Massachusetts Bay, to 1639

1630

EVENTS

   The Arbella arrives at Salem, Massachusetts, with 600-700 Puritans
      from England

LITERATURE

    William Bradford. History of Plymouth Plantation, to 1650 (hist)
    John Winthrop. A Modell of Christian Charity (e)

1631

BIRTHS

    Urian Oakes
    William Stoughton
    Michael Wigglesworth

DEATHS
    John Smith

1635

BIRTHS

    Mary White Rowlandson

EVENTS

    Concord, Massachusetts (f)

1636

EVENTS

    Harvard College (f)
    Providence Plantations (f)

1637

LITERATURE

    Thomas Morton. New English Canaan, Containing an Abstract of New
        England (des)

1638

BIRTHS

    George Alsop
    George Keith

LITERATURE

    John Underhill. Newes from America (nar)

1639

BIRTHS

Increase Mather

EVENTS

The Particular Baptists establish a church in Rhode Island

LITERATURE

William Pierce. An Almanack for New England for the Year 1639 (ref)

1640

BIRTHS

Samuel Willard

LITERATURE

John Cotton, Richard Mather, John Eliot, and Thomas Weld. The Whole
   Booke of Psalmes, Faithfully Translated, into Englishe Metre--
   "The Bay Psalm Book" (trans)

1641

LITERATURE

Thomas Shepard. The Sincere Convert (e)
Nathaniel Ward. The Body of Liberties (e)

1642

BIRTHS

Edward Taylor
Benjamin Tompson

EVENTS

Sir William Berkeley, colonial governor of Virginia, to 1652

1643

BIRTHS

Solomon Stoddard

LITERATURE

Richard Mather. Aplolgie of the Churches of New-England for Church Covenant (e)

_____. Church-Government and Church-Covenant Discussed (e)

Roger Williams. A Key to the Language of America (ref)

1644

BIRTHS

Edward Taylor

LITERATURE

John Cotton. The Keys of the Kingdom of Heaven (e)
Thomas Parker. True Copy of a Letter Written by Mr. T. Parker (e)
Roger Williams. The Bloudy Tenent of Persecution (e)
_____. Mr. Cotton's Letter Lately Printed, Examined and Answered (e)
_____. Queries of Highest Consideration (e)
John Winthrop. Arbitrary Government (e)

1645

LITERATURE

John Cotton. The Way of the Churches of Christ in New-England (e)
John Wheelwright. Mercurius Americanus (e, hist)
Roger Williams. Christenings Make Not Christians (e)

1646

LITERATURE

John Cotton. Milk for Babes, Drawn Out of the Breasts of Both Testaments (e)
Samuel Gorton. Simplicities Defense against Seven-Headed Policie (e)
Thomas Parker. The Visions and Prophecies of Daniel Expounded (e)
Edward Winslow. Hypocrisie Unmasked (e)

1647

DEATHS

Thomas Hooker
Thomas Morton

LITERATURE

John Cotton. The Bloudy Tenent Washed and Made White in the Bloud of the Lamb (e)

Nathaniel Ward. The Simple Cobbler of Aggawam (sat)
Edward Winslow. New Englands Salamander Discovered by an Irreligious
    and Scornfull Pamphlet (e)

1648

BIRTHS

John Rogers

LITERATURE

John Cotton. A Survey of the Summe of Church-Discipline, vol. 2
    (e)
_____. The Way of the Congregational Churches (e)
Thomas Hooker. A Survey of the Summe of Church Discipline, vol. 1
    (e)
John Norton. Responsio ad Gubiel (e)
Thomas Shepard. The Clear Sun-shine of the Gospel Breaking Forth
    upon the Indians (e)

1649

DEATHS

Thomas Shepard
John Winthrop

LITERATURE

Richard Mather. A Platform of Church-Discipline (e)
Thomas Mayhew and John Eliot. The Glorious Progress of the Gospel
    (e)
Thomas Shepard. Theses Sabbaticae (e)

1650

LITERATURE

Anne Bradstreet. The Tenth Muse Lately Sprung Up in America (po)

1651

BIRTHS

Francis Daniel Pastorius

1652

BIRTHS

Samuel Sewall
John Wise

DEATHS

John Cotton
Nathaniel Ward

LITERATURE

John Clarke. Ill News from New England (e)
Thomas Mayhew and John Eliot. Tears of Repentance (e)
Samuel Stone. A Congregational Church Is a Catholike Visible Church
(e)
Roger Williams. The Bloudy Tenent Yet More Bloudy (e)
_____. The Hireling Ministry None of Christs (e)

1653

LITERATURE

John Norton. A Discussion of That Great Point in Divinity, the Suf-
ferings of Christ (e)

1654

LITERATURE

William Bradford. Dialogue between Some Young Men Born in New Eng-
land and Sundry Ancient Men That Came Out of Holland (po)
John Eliot. Catechism (trans)
Edward Johnson. The Wonder-Working Providence of Sions Saviour in
New England (hist)

1655

BIRTHS

James Blair

DEATHS

Edward Winslow

1656

LITERATURE

John Hammond. Leah and Rachel; or, the Two Fruitfull Sisters, Virginia and Maryland (e)

1657

DEATHS

William Bradford
Thomas Mayhew

LITERATURE

Samuel Gorton. An Antidote against the Common Plague of the World
(e)

1658

BIRTHS

Francis Makemie

LITERATURE

John Norton. Abel Being Dead Yet Speaketh; or, the Life and Death of
John Cotton (biog)

1659

LITERATURE

John Eliot. The Christian Commonwealth (e)
John Norton. The Heart of New England Rent at the Blasphemes of the
Present Generation (e)

1660

EVENTS

Sir William Berkeley, second term as governor of Virginia, to 1677

LITERATURE

Samuel Maverick. A Brief Description of New England and the Severall
Townes Therein (des)
Thomas Shepard. The Parable of the Ten Virgins Opened and Applied
(e, pub)

1661

EVENTS

John Eliot's translation of the New Testament into the language of
the Massachuset Indians

1662

LITERATURE

Michael Wigglesworth. The Day of Doom (po)

1663

BIRTHS

Cotton Mather

DEATHS

John Norton
Samuel Stone

EVENTS

John Eliot's translation of the Old Testament into the language of
the Massachuset Indians

LITERATURE

John Davenport. A Discourse about Civil Government in a New Presen-
tation Whose Design Is Religion (e)

1664

BIRTHS

John Williams

LITERATURE

Anne Bradstreet. Meditations Divine and Moral (e)

1665

BIRTHS

Samuel Penhallow

LITERATURE

Samuel Gorton. Saltmarsh Returned from the Dead (e)
Cornelius Watkinson, Philip Howard, and William Darby. Ye Beare and
Ye Club (dr)

1666

LITERATURE

George Alsop. A Character of the Province of Mary-land (des, po)
Michael Wigglesworth. The Day of Doom, rev. ed (po)

1667

DEATHS

John Wilson

1668

DEATHS

Stephen Daye

1669

DEATHS

Richard Mather

LITERATURE

John Eliot. The Indian Primer (ref, pub)
Nathaniel Morton. New Englands Memorial (hist)

1670

BIRTHS

Hugh Jones

DEATHS

John Davenport

LITERATURE

Increase Mather. The Life and Death of That Reverend Man of God, Mr.
    Richard Mather (biog)
William Stoughton. New Englands Time Interest (ser)
Michael Wigglesworth. Meat Out of the Eater (po)

1672

BEATHS

Anne Bradstreet

Edward Johnson
John Underhill

1673

BIRTHS

Robert Beverley
Thomas Church
Benjamin Colman
Experience Mayhew

1674

BIRTHS

William Byrd II
James Logan
Samuel Niles

1675

EVENTS

"King Philip's" War begun

1676

DEATHS

John Clarke
Samuel Maverick

EVENTS

Nathaniel Bacon's rebellion
"King Philip's" War ended

LITERATURE

Peter Folger. A Looking-Glass for the Times (po)
William Hubbard. The Happiness of a People in the Wisdome of Their
    Rulers (ser)
Increase Mather. A Brief History of the War with the Indians (hist)
Benjamin Tompson. New Englands Crisis. Or, a Brief Narrative of New
    Englands Lamentable Estate at Present (po, sat)
        . New-Englands Tears for Her Present Miseries (po)
Roger Williams. George Fox Digg'd Out of His Burrowes (e)

1677

DEATHS

Samuel Gorton
Thomas Parker

LITERATURE

William Hubbard. Narrative of the Troubles with the Indians in New-
England (nar)
Increase Mather. A Relation of the Troubles Which Have Hapned in
New-England by Reasons of the Indians There (nar, e)
Urian Oakes. Elegie (po)

1678

DEATHS

Mary White Rowlandson

LITERATURE

Anne Bradstreet. Poems, 2nd ed. (po, pub)

1679

BIRTHS

Roger Wolcott

DEATHS

John Wheelwright

1680

LITERATURE

John Wilson. A Song of Deliverance (po, pub)

1681

DEATHS

Urian Oakes

EVENTS

William Penn awareded a charter for land in the New World

1682

LITERATURE

Cotton Mather. A Poem to the Memory of Urian Oakes (po)
Mary White Rowlandson. The Sovereignty and Goodness of God, Together
    with the Faithfulness of His Promises Displayed; being a Narrative
    of the Captivity and Restauration of Mrs. Mary Rowlandson (nar,
    pub)
Edward Taylor. Preparatory Meditations, to 1725 (po)

1683

DEATHS

Roger Williams

LITERATURE

Benjamin Harris. The New England Primer (ref, pub)

1684

LITERATURE

Richard Mather. An Essay for the Reading of Illustrious Providences
    (e)

1685

LITERATURE

Thomas Budd. Good Order Established in Pennsylvania and New Jersey
    (e, nar)
Edward Taylor. God's Determinations Touching His Elect (po)

1686

DEATHS

Nathaniel Morton

1687

BIRTHS

Thomas Prince

1688

BIRTHS

Cadwallader Colden
Samuel Keimer

1689

LITERATURE

Samuel Green (publisher). The Present State of the New-English Af-
    fairs (e)
Cotton Mather. The Declaration of the Gentlemen, Merchants, and In-
    habitants of Boston (e)
_____. Memorable Provinces, Relating to Witchcraft and Pos-
    sessions (e, nar)
Michael Wigglesworth. Riddles Unriddled; or, Christian Paradoxes (po)

1690

DEATHS

John Eliot
Peter Folger

LITERATURE

Cotton Mather. The Present State of New England (e)

1691

EVENTS

Plymouth absorbed into the Massachusetts Bay colony

LITERATURE

Samuel Sewall and Edward Rawson. The Revolution in New England Jus-
    tified (e)

1692

LITERATURE

Cotton Mather. Political Fables (fic)

1693

EVENTS

The College of William and Mary (f)

LITERATURE

George Keith. Exhortation and Caution to Friends (e)
Cotton Mather. The Wonders of the Invisible World (nar)
Increase Mather. Cases of Conscience Concerning Evil Spirits (nar,
     e)

1694

LITERATURE

Francis Mackemie. An Answer to George Keith's Libel (e)
Edward Taylor. Treatise Concerning the Lord's Supper (ser)

1695

BIRTHS

Aquila Rose

1696

BIRTHS

Thomas Walter

1697

BIRTHS

John Peter Zenger

LITERATURE

James Blair, Henry Hatwell, and Edward Chilton. The Present State
     of Virginia and the College (nar, des)
Cotton Mather. Pietas in Patriam (biog)
Francis Daniel Pastorius. Four Boasting Disputers of This World
     Briefly Rebuked (e)
Samuel Sewall. Phaenomena Quaedam Apocalyptica (e)

1698

DEATHS

Thomas Budd

LITERATURE

Cotton Mather. Eleutheria: Or, an Idea of the Reformation in England
     (e)
Francis Daniel Pastorius. A New Primer of English (ref)

1699

BIRTHS

John Bartram
Richard Lewis

LITERATURE

George Keith. The Deism of William Penn and His Brethren (e)
Francis Makemie. Truths in a True Light (e)
Cotton Mather. A Family Well-Ordered (e)
_____. La Fe del Christiano (e)

3 The Eighteenth Century

LITERATURE

Cotton Mather. Reasonable Religion (e)
Samuel Sewall. The Selling of Joseph (e)
Solomon Stoddard. The Doctrine of Institutional Churches (e)

1701

DEATHS

William Stoughton

EVENTS

Yale College (f)

LITERATURE

Cotton Mather. Some Few Remarks upon a Scandalous Book by One Robert
   Calef (e)
Edward Taylor. Christographia, to 1703 (ser)

1702

LITERATURE

Cotton Mather. Magnalia Christi Americana (hist)

1703

BIRTHS

Jonathan Edwards

1704

BIRTHS

Rev. John Adams

DEATHS

William Hubbard

EVENTS

Boston News-Letter, to 1776 (per)

LITERATURE

Cotton Mather. Le Vrai Patron des Saines Paroles (e)

1705

BIRTHS

Charles Chauncy
James Ralph

DEATHS

Michael Wigglesworth

LITERATURE

Robert Beverley. The History and Present State of Virginia (hist)
Francis Makemie. A Plain and Friendly Persuasive to the Inhabitants
   of Virginia and Maryland for Promoting Towns and Cohabitation (e)

1706

BIRTHS

Benjamin Franklin
Samuel Mather

LITERATURE

George Keith. A Journal of Travels from New-Hampshire to Caratuck
   (trav)
Cotton Mather. The Negro Christianized (e)

1707

BIRTHS

Mather Byles

Stephen Hopkins
William Smith

DEATHS

Samuel Willard

LITERATURE

Benjamin Colman. Elijah's Translation (po)
_____. The Government and Improvement of Mirth (ser)
Francis Makemie. A Narrative of a New and Unusual American Impri-
    sonment (nar, e)
John Williams and Cotton Mather. The Redeemed Captive, Returning
    to Zion (nar)

1708

BIRTHS

John Seccomb
Jane Colman Turell

DEATHS

Francis Makemie

LITERATURE

Ebenezer Cook. The Sot-Weed Factor (po)
Cotton Mather. The Good Education of Children (e)
Solomon Stoddard. The Inexcusableness of Neglecting the Worship of
    God, under a Pretense of Being in an Unconverted Condition (e)

1709

BIRTHS

James Adair

LITERATURE

Experience Mayhew. Massachusee Psalter (trans)

1710

BIRTHS

Richard Bland
Jonathan Carver

LITERATURE

Cotton Mather. Bonifacius: An Essay upon the Good (e)
John Wise. The Churches Quarrel Espoused (e)

1711

BIRTHS

Thomas Hutchinson
Eleazar Wheelock

1713

BIRTHS

Anthony Benezet

LITERATURE

Samuel Sewall. Proposals Touching the Accomplishment of Prophecies
  (e)
Solomon Stoddard. The Efficacy of the Fear of Hell to Restrain Men
  from Sin (e)

1714

DEATHS

Benjamin Tompson

LITERATURE

Robert Hunter. Androboros (fic)
Solomon Stoddard. A Guide to Christ (e)

1716

DEATHS

George Keith

LITERATURE

Thomas Church. Entertaining Passages Relating to Philip's War (nar)

1717

LITERATURE

John Wise. A Vindication of the Government of New-England Churches
  (e)

1718

BIRTHS

David Brainerd

LITERATURE

Cotton Mather. Psalterium Americanum (trans)

1719

BIRTHS

Joseph Belamy

EVENTS

The American Weekly Mercury, to 1746 (per)
The Boston Gazette, to 1741 (per)

1720

BIRTHS

Jupiter Hammon
Jonathan Mayhew
Samuel Smith
John Woolman

DEATHS

Francis Daniel Pastorius

LITERATURE

John Rogers. The Book of the Revelation of Jesus Christ (e)
Thomas Walter. A Choice Dialogue between John Faustus, a Conjuror,
   and Jack Tory, His Friend (e)

1721

BIRTHS

Samuel Hopkins

EVENTS

Hell-Fire Club, Boston, to 1724
The New-England Courant, to 1726 (per)

DEATHS

John Rogers

LITERATURE

Cotton Mather. The Christian Philosopher (e)
_____. Sentiments on the Small Pox Inoculated (e)
Samuel Sewall. A Memorial Relating to the Kennebeck Indians (e)
Thomas Walter. The Grounds and Rules of Musick Explained; or, an
   Introduction to the Art of Singing by Note (e, ref)
John Wise. A Word of Comfort to a Melancholy Country (e)

1722

BIRTHS

Samuel Adams
Humphrey Marshall

DEATHS

Robert Beverley

LITERATURE

Robert Beverley. The History and Present State of Virginia, enl.
   ed. (hist)
James Blair. Our Saviour's Divine Sermon on the Mount, 5 vols.
   (ser, pub)
Cotton Mather. An Account of Inoculating the Small Pox (nar, e)
_____. The Angel of Bethesda (ref)
Experience Mayhew. Observations on the Indian Language (e)
Solomon Stoddard. An Answer to Some Cases of Conscience Respecting
   the Country (e)
Thomas Walter. The Sweet Psalmist of Israel (po)

1723

BIRTHS

Samson Occom
John Witherspoon

DEATHS

Increase Mather
Aquila Rose

LITERATURE

Benjamin Colman. God Deals with Us As Rational Creatures (ser)
Samuel Keimer. Elegy on the Much Lamented Death of Aquila Rose (po)

1724

BIRTHS

Isaac Backus
Henry Laurens

LITERATURE

Hugh Jones. An Accidence to the English Tongue (ref)
_____. The Present State of Virginia (des)
Cotton Mather. Parentator (biog)

1725

BIRTHS

James Otis

DEATHS

Thomas Walter
John Wise

EVENTS

New York Gazette, to 1744 (per)

LITERATURE

Nathaniel Ames. Astronomical Diary and Almanack, to 1775 (ref)
Benjamin Franklin. A Dissertation on Liberty and Necessity, Plea-
    sure and Pain (e)
Roger Wolcott. Poetical Meditations (po)

1726

DEATHS

Samuel Penhallow

LITERATURE

Cotton Mather. Manuductio ad Ministerium (e)
_____. Ratio Disciplinae (e)
Samuel Penhallow. History of the Wars of New England with the
    Eastern Indians (hist)
Samuel Willard. Compleat Body of Divinity (ser, pub)

1727

BIRTHS

William Smith (of Pennsylvania)
Ezra Stiles

EVENTS

The Junto Club, Philadelphia, to 1767
The Maryland Gazette, to 1839 (per)
New England Weekly Journal, to 1741 (per)

LITERATURE

Cadwallader Colden. History of the Five Indian Nations (hist)
Experience Mayhew. Indian Converts (e)

1728

BIRTHS

Robert Proud
William Smith (of New York)
Mercy Otis Warren

DEATHS

Cotton Mather

EVENTS

The Universal Instructor and Pennsylvania Gazette, to 1729 (per)

LITERATURE

James Franklin. The Rhode Island Almanack, to 1758 (ref)
Richard Lewis. Musiculpa (sat, trans)

1729

BIRTHS

Samuel Seabury

DEATHS

Solomon Stoddard
Edward Taylor
John Williams

EVENTS

The Pennsylvania Gazette, to 1815 (per)

LITERATURE

Samuel Mather. The Life of the Very Reverend and Learned Cotton

Mather (biog)

1730

BIRTHS

Robert Munford

DEATHS

Samuel Sewall

EVENTS

Literary and Philosophical Society of Newport, to 1747

LITERATURE

Anthony Aston. _The Fool's Opera; or, the Taste of the Age_ (dr)
Ebenezer Cook. _Sotweed Redivivus_ (po)
James Ralph. _The Fashionable Lady_ (dr)

1731

BIRTHS

Joseph Galloway

EVENTS

The Weekly Rehearsal, Boston, to 1735 (per)

LITERATURE

Ebenezer Cook. _The History of Colonel Nathaniel Bacon's Rebellion_
    (po)
Jonathan Edwards. _God Glorified in Man's Dependence upon Him_ (e)
John Seccomb. _Father Abbey's Will_ (po)

1732

BIRTHS

John Dickinson

LITERATURE

Richard Lewis. _Carmen Saeculare_ (po)
_____. _Description of Spring_ (po)
_____. _A Rhapsody_ (po)

1733

BIRTHS

Nathan Fiske
Benjamin Youngs Prime

DEATHS

Richard Lewis

EVENTS

New York Weekly Journal, to 1752 (per)

LITERATURE

Benjamin Franklin. Poor Richard's Almanack, to 1758 (nar, fic, ref)

1734

BIRTHS

Benjamin Church

LITERATURE

Jonathan Edwards. Divine and Supernatural Light (ser)

1735

BIRTHS

John Adams
Myles Cooper
Michel-Guillaume Jean de Crevecoeur
John Morgan
Samuel Andrew Peters
Benjamin Trumbull

DEATHS

Jane Colman Turell

EVENTS

Boston Evening Post, to 1775 (per)

LITERATURE

James Logan. Cato's Moral Distichs (trans, pub)
Jane Colman Turell. Reliquiae Turellae (po)

1736

BIRTHS

Thomas Godfrey

EVENTS

Virginia Gazette, to 1766 (per)

LITERATURE

Thomas Prince. Chronological History of New England in the Form of
  Animals (hist)
John Peter Zenger. A Brief Narrative of the Case and Tryal of John
  Peter Zenger (nar)

1737

BIRTHS

Jacob Duche
Francis Hopkinson
Jonathan Odell
Thomas Paine
James Smith

LITERATURE

Jonathan Edwards. A Faithful Narrative of the Surprising Work of
  God (e)

1738

BIRTHS

Ethan Allen
Jonathan Boucher

LITERATURE

Jonathan Edwards. Charity and Its Fruits (ser)

1739

BIRTHS

William Bartram
John Maylem

DEATHS

Samuel Keimer

1740

BIRTHS

Arthur Lee

DEATHS

Rev. John Adams

EVENTS

James Blair, governor of Virginia, to 1741

LITERATURE

Aquila Rose. Poems on Several Occasions (pub)

1741

BIRTHS

Benedict Arnold

EVENTS

The American Magazine, to 1741 (per)
The General Magazine, to 1741 (per)

LITERATURE

William Byrd. History of the Dividing Line (hist)
Jonathan Edwards. The Distinguishing Marks of a Work of the Spirit
    of God (e)
_____. Sinners in the Hands of an Angry God (ser)
Patrick Tailfer. A True and Historical Narrative of the Colony of
    Georgia (hist)

1742

BIRTHS

Thomas Atwood Digges
Nathaniel Evans

LITERATURE

Jonathan Edwards. Some Thoughts Concerning the Present Revival of
    Religion in New England (e)

1743

DEATHS

James Blair

EVENTS

American Philosophical Society (f)
New York Gazette, or, the Weekly Post-boy, to 1773 (per)
Pennsylvania Journal and Weekly Advertiser, to 1797 (per)

LITERATURE

Charles Chauncy. Seasonable Thoughts on the State of Religion in
    New England (e)
Benjamin Franklin. A Proposal for Promoting Useful Knowledge (e)

1744

BIRTHS

Abagail Adams
Jeremy Belknap
Enos Hitchcock
Josiah Quincy the elder

DEATHS

William Byrd II

LITERATURE

Mather Byles. Poems on Several Occasions (pub)
Benjamin Franklin. Account of the New Invented Pennsylvania Fire
    Place (des)
James Logan. M.T. Cicero's Cato Major (trans)
Experience Mayhew. Grace Defended
Thomas Prince. The Christian History, to 1745 (e)

1745

EVENTS

Tuesday Club of Annapolis, to 1756

LITERATURE

Rev. John Adams. Poems on Several Occasions: Original and Transla-
    ted (po, pub)
Cadwallader Colden. Explication of the First Causes of Action in
    Matter, and, of the Causes of Gravitation (e)
Samuel Niles. A Brief and Plain Essay on God's Wonder Working Pro-
    vidence in the Reduction of Louisburg (po)   .
_____. Tristitiae Ecclesiarum (e)

1746

BIRTHS

William Billings

DEATHS

John Peter Zenger

EVENTS

Princeton University (f)

LITERATURE

David Brainerd. Divine Grace Displayed (nar)
_____. Mirabilia Dei Inter Indicos (nar)
Jonathan Edwards. A Treatise Concerning Religious Affections (e)
_____. A Vindication of the Gospel Doctrine of Justifying
    Faith (e)

1747

BIRTHS

John Filson

DEATHS

David Brainerd
Benjamin Colman

LITERATURE

Jonathan Edwards. An Humble Attempt To Promote Visible Union of
    God's People (e)
Benjamin Franklin. Plain Truth, or Serious Consideration on the Pre-
    sent State of the City of Philadelphia (e)
Thomas Shepard. Three Valuable Pieces (e, nar, pub)
William Smith. The History of the First Discovery and Settlement of
    Virginia (hist)

1748

BIRTHS

Hugh Henry Brackenridge
Jonathan Mitchell Sewald

DEATHS

Thomas Church

1749

BIRTHS

> David Ramsay
> Isaac Thomas

EVENTS

> Washington and Lee University (f)

LITERATURE

> Cadwallader Colden. Plantae Coldenghamiae, to 1751 (e)
> Jonathan Edwards. An Account of the Life of the Late Reverend Mr.
> David Brainerd (biog, nar)
> _____. An Humble Inquiry into the Rules of the Word of
> God (e)
> Benjamin Franklin. Proposals Relating to the Education of Youth in
> Pennsylvania (e)

1750

BIRTHS

> Lemuel Hopkins
> Samuel Stanhope Smith
> John Trumbull

LITERATURE

> Joseph Bellamy. True Religion Delineated (e)
> Jonathan Mayhew. Discourse Concerning Unlimited Submission and Non-
> Resistance to the Higher Powers (e)

1751

BIRTHS

> John Ledyard

DEATHS

> James Logan

LITERATURE

> John Bartram. Observations on the Inhabitants, Climate, Soil. . .
> Made by Mr. John Bartram in His Travels from Pennsilvania to Lake
> Ontario (trav, nar, e)
> Jonathan Edwards. Farewell Sermon (ser)
> Benjamin Franklin. Experiments and Observations on Electricity, to
> 1754 (e)

1752

BIRTHS

Ann Eliza Bleecker
Hannah Mather Crocker
Timothy Dwight
Philip Morin Freneau
David Humphreys
Peter Markoe
St. George Tucker

EVENTS

The Independent Reflector, to 1753 (per)

1753

BIRTHS

John Taylor
Phillis Wheatley

EVENTS

Occasional Reverberator, to 1753 (per

LITERATURE

William Smith of Pennsylvania. A General Ideal of the College of
   Mirania (e)

1754

BIRTHS

Joel Barlow
Gilbert Imlay
John Parke
James Thacher

EVENTS

Columbia University (f)

LITERATURE

Jonathan Edwards. A Careful and Strict Enquiry into the Modern Pre-
   vailing Notions of Freedom of Will (e)
John Woolman. Some Considerations on the Keeping of Negroes, to
   1762 (e)

1755

BIRTHS

BIRTHS

Hannah Adams

DEATHS

William Smith

EVENTS

The Boston Gazette, to 1798 (per)
Connecticut Gazette, to 1768 (per)
Deportation of the Acadians from Nova Scotia
Instructor, to 1755 (per)
John Englishman, to 1755 (per)
University of Pennsylvania (f)

LITERATURE

Mater Byles. The Conflagration (po)

1757

BIRTHS

Caleb Bingham
Royall Tyler

EVENTS

American Magazine and Monthly Chronicle, to 1758 (per)

LITERATURE

William Smith of New York. The History of the Province of New York
    (hist)
_____. A Review of the Military Operations in
    North America, 1753-1756 (e)

1758

BIRTHS

George Richards Minot
Noah Webster

DEATHS

Jonathan Edwards
Experience Mayhew
Thomas Prince

EVENTS

Newport Mercury, to 1928 (per)

LITERATURE

Jonathan Edwards. The Great Christian Doctrine of Original Sin Defended (e)
John Maylem. The Conquest of Louisburg (po)
_____. Gallic Perfidy (po)
Thomas Prince. The Psalms, Hymns and Spiritual Songs of the Old and New Testaments (trans)
John Woolman. Considerations on Pure Wisdom and Human Policy (e)

1759

BIRTHS

Thomas Cooper
Hannah Webster Foster
Isaac Mitchell
Sarah Wentworth Morton
Sarah Sayward Barrell Keating Wood

LITERATURE

Benjamin Franklin. An Historical Review of the Constitution and Government of Pennsylvania (hist)
Thomas Godfrey. The Prince of Parthia (po)

1760

BIRTHS

Matthew Carey

DEATHS

Hugh Jones

LITERATURE

Benjamin Franklin. The Interest of Great Britain Considered with Regard to Her Colonies (e)
Jupiter Hammon. An Evening Thought (po)

1761

BIRTHS

Richard Alsop
Jedidiah Morse

LITERATURE

Francis Hopkinson. <u>Exercises</u>, to 1762 (po)
_____. <u>The Treaty</u> (po)

1762

BIRTHS

Elijah Parish
Susanna Haswell Rowson
Tabitha Gilman Tenney

DEATHS

Samuel Niles
James Ralph

LITERATURE

Thomas Godfrey. <u>The Court of Fancy</u> (po)
Francis Hopkinson. <u>Science</u> (po)
James Otis. <u>A Vindication of the House of Representatives</u> (e)

1763

BIRTHS

Amasa Delano
Abiel Holmes

DEATHS

Thomas Godfrey

LITERATURE

Eleazar Wheelock. <u>Plain and Faithful Narrative of the Indian Cha-
    rity School at Lebanon</u>, to 1775 (nar, hist)
John Woolman. <u>A Plea for the Poor</u> (e)

1764

BIRTHS

Morris Birkbeck
Joseph Brown Ladd

EVENTS

<u>Hartford Courant</u>, to 1837 (per)
Rhode Island College, later Brown University (f)
Stamp Act infuriates Bostonians and leads to the burning of the
    governor's palace

LITERATURE

John Dickinson. <u>Protest against the Appointment of Benjamin Franklin</u> (e)
Benjamin Franklin. <u>Cool Thoughts on the Present Situation of Our Public Affairs</u> (e)
_____. <u>Preface to the Speech of Joseph Galloway</u> (e)
Thomas Hutchinson. <u>History of the Colony of Massachusetts Bay, from Its First Settlement in 1628 to the Year 1750</u>, 2 vols, to 1767 (hist)
Jonathan Mayhew. <u>Letter of Reproof to Mr. John Cleaveland</u> (e)
James Otis. The <u>Rights of the British Colonies</u> (e)
Benjamin Youngs Prime. The <u>Patriot Muse</u> (po)

1765

BIRTHS

William Hill Brown

EVENTS

The <u>Constitutional Courant</u>, to 1765 (per)

LITERATURE

Benjamin Church. The <u>Times</u> (po)
John Dickinson. <u>The Late Regulations Respecting the British Colonies on the Continent of America</u> (e)
Jonathan Edwards. <u>Two Dissertations</u> (e, pub)
Thomas Godfrey. <u>Juvenile Poems on Various Subjects. With the Prince of Parthia, a Tragedy</u> (po, pub)
Stephen Hopkins. <u>The Rights of Colonies Examined</u> (e)
Martin Howard. A <u>Defense of the Letter from a Gentleman at Halifax to His Friend in Rhode Island</u> (e)
_____. A <u>Letter from a Gentleman at Halifax to His Friend in Rhode Island</u> (e)
John Morgan. A <u>Discourse upon the Institution of Medical Schools in America</u> (e)
Samuel Smith. <u>The History of the Colony of Nova-Caesaria, or New Jersey, to the Year 1721</u> (hist)

1766

BIRTHS

William Dunlap
Alexander Wilson

DEATHS

Jonathan Mayhew

EVENTS

Rutgers University (f)
Virginia Gazette, 2nd series, to 1773 (per)

LITERATURE

Anthony Benezet. A Caution to Great Britain and Her Colonies (e)
Richard Bland. An Enquiry into the Rights of the British Colonies
   (e)
Jonathan Mayhew. The Snare Broken (ser)
John Morgan. Dissertation on the Reciprocal Advantages of a Perpetu-
   al Union between Great Britain and Her American Colonies (e)

1767

BIRTHS

John Quincy Adams

DEATHS

Nathaniel Evans

EVENTS

Pennsylvania Chronicle, to 1773 (per)

LITERATURE

Thomas Forrest (Andrew Barton). The Disappointment; or, the Force
   of Credulity (dr)
John Trumbull. An Essay on the Uses and Advantages of the Fine Arts
   (e)

1768

BIRTHS

William Littell

LITERATURE

John Dickinson. Letters from a Farmer in Pennsylvania (e)
Arthur Lee. The Monitor's Letters (e)

1769

BIRTHS

Joseph Doddridge
Anne Newport Royall

EVENTS

Dartmouth College (f)

LITERATURE

Henry Laurens. Some General Observations on American Custom House Officers and Courts of Vice-Admiralty (e)

1770

EVENTS

Massachusetts Spy, to 1781 (per)

LITERATURE

William Billings. The New-England Psalm Singer (po, trans)
Robert Mumford. The Candidates (dr)
John Woolman. Considerations on the True Harmony of Mankind (e)

1771

BIRTHS

Hosea Ballou
Charles Brockden Brown
Margaretta Fangeres
Thomas Green Fessenden
Peter Irving
Elihu Hubbard Smith

EVENTS

Francis Asbury sent to America by John Wesley as bishop to the American Methodists
Pennsylvania Packet or General Advertiser, to 1795 (per)

LITERATURE

Anthony Benezet. An Historical Account of Guinea (hist, nar)
Charles Chauncy. A Compleat View of Episcopacy (e)
Benjamin Franklin. Autobiography, to 1790 (auto)
Philip Morin Freneau and Hugh Henry Brackenridge. The Rising Glory of America (po)

1772

BIRTHS

James Cheetham
William Cliffton
Josiah Quincy the younger
William Wirt

DEATHS

John Woolman

LITERATURE

Nathaniel Evans. Poems on Several Occasions, with Some Other Compo-
    sitions (pub)
Francis Hopkinson. Dirtilla (po)
Thomas Paine. The Case of the Officers of Exise (e)
John Trumbull. The Progress of Dulness, to 1773 (po)
John Woolman. An Epistle (e)

1773

BIRTHS

Nathaniel Bowditch
Robert Treat Paine

EVENTS

The Boston Tea Party
Rivington's New-York Gazetteer, to 1775 (per)

LITERATURE

Benjamin Church. An Oration to Commemorate the Bloody Tragedy of
    the Fifth of March, 1770 (e)
Samuel Mather. Attempt to Shew That America Must Be Known to the
    Antients (e)
            . The Sacred Minister (po)
Mercy Otis Warren. The Adulateur (dr)
Phillis Wheatley. Poems on Various Subjects, Religious and Moral
    (pub)

1774

BIRTH

Isaac Story

EVENTS

Thomas Paine arrives in America
The Royal American Magazine, to 1775 (per)

LITERATURE

Anthony Benezet. The Mighty Destroyer Displayed (e)
Hugh Henry Brackenridge. A Poem on Divine Revelation (po)
Myles Cooper. The American Querist (e)
            . A Friendly Address to All Reasonable Americans (e)
John Dickinson. Essay upon the Constitutional Power of Great Britain

(e)
Jacob Duche. Observations; or, Caspipina's Letters (des)
The First Book of the American Chronicles of the Times, to 1775 (sat)
Joseph Galloway. Plan of a Proposed Union between Great Britain and
    the Colonies (e)
Francis Hopkinson. A Pretty Story (sat)
Arthur Lee. An Appeal to the Justice and Interests of the People of
    Great Britain (e)
Samson Occom. A Choice Collection of Hymns and Spiritual Songs (po,
    ed)
Josiah Quincy the elder. Observations on the Boston Port-Bill (e)
Samuel Seabury. The Congress Canvassed (e)
_____. Free Thoughts on the Proceedings of the Continental
    Congress (e)
_____. A View of the Controversy between Great Britain and
    Her Colonies (e)
John Trumbull. An Elegy on the Times (po)
John Woolman. Journal (nar, pub)

1775

BIRTHS

    Paul Allen
    John Daly Burk
    John Davis
    William Munford
    James Ogilvie
    George Tucker

DEATHS

    Josiah Quincy the elder

EVENTS

    Pennsylvania Magazine, to 1776 (per)
    Second Continental Congress in session

LITERATURE

    James Adair. The History of the American Indians (hist)
    John Dickinson. A Declaration by the Representatives of the United
        Colonies (e)
    Thomas Atwood Digges. Adventures of Alonso: Containing Some Striking
        Anecdotes of the Present Prime Minister of Portugal (fic)
    Philip Morin Freneau. General Gage's Confession (po)
    _____. General Gage's Soliloquy (po)
    Joseph Galloway. A Candid Examination of the Mutual Claims of Great
        Britain and the Colonies (e)
    Arthur Lee. A Second Appeal to the Justice and Interests of the Peo-
        ple of Great Britain (e)
    Samuel Seabury. An Alarm to the Legislature of the Province of New
        York (e)
    William Smith of Pennsylvania. Sermon on the Present Situation of

American Affairs (ser)
Mercy Otis Warren. The Group (dr)

1776

DEATHS

Richard Bland
Benjamin Church
Cadwallader Colden
Samuel Smith

EVENTS

Adoption of the Declaration of Independence
Independent Chronicle, Boston, to 1819 (per)
Phi Beta Kappa Society (f)
Virginia Declaration of Rights

LITERATURE

John Adams. Thoughts on Government (e)
Hugh Henry Brackenridge. The Battle of Bunkers-Hill (dr)
Nathan Fiske. Historical Discourse (hist)
Francis Hopkinson. A Prophecy (e)
_____. Two Letters (e)
John Leacock (Joseph Leacock). The Fall of British Tyranny; or, American Liberty Triumphant (dr)
John Morgan. A Recommendation of Inoculation (e)
Robert Munford. The Patriots (dr)
Jonathan Odell. A Birthday Song (po)
Thomas Paine. The American Crisis, to 1783 (e)
_____. Common Sense (e)
John Witherspoon. The Dominion of Providence over the Passions of Men (ser)

1777

BIRTHS

John Blair Linn
John Pickering

EVENTS

Aitken Bible, to 1782 (pub)
Rivington's New-York Loyal Gazette, to 1783 (per)

LITERATURE

Isaac Backus. History of New England, with Particular Reference to the Denomination of Christians Called Baptists, 3 vols, to 1796 (hist)
Hugh Henry Brackenridge. The Death of General Montgomery (dr)

Francis Hopkinson. Answer to General Burgoyne's Proclamation (sat)
_____. Letter Written by a Foreigner on the Character of
the English Nation (sat)
_____. A Political Catechism (sat)

1778

BIRTHS

William Austin
James Kirke Paulding
Margaret Bayard Smith

LITERATURE

Hugh Henry Brackenridge. Six Political Discourses (ser)
Jonathan Carver. Travels through the Interior Part of North America
(nar, des)
Benjamin Franklin. The Ephemera (e)
Francis Hopkinson. The Battle of the Kegs (po, sat)
_____. Date Obolum Bellisario (po)
_____. Letter to Joseph Galloway (e)

1779

BIRTHS

Washington Allston
Francis Scott Key
Clement Clarke Moore
William Tudor

DEATHS

Eleazar Wheelock

EVENTS

The United States Magazine, Philadelphia, to 1779 (per)

LITERATURE

Ethan Allen. Narrative of Colonel Ethan Allen's Captivity (nar)
Jacob Duche. Discourses on Various Subjects (ser)
Benjamin Franklin. The Morals of Chess (hum)
_____. The Whistles (hum)
Jonathan Odell. Word of Congress (po)
Mercy Otis Warren. The Motley Assembly (dr)

1780

BIRTHS

William Ellery Channing the elder
Timothy Flint

DEATHS

Jonathan Carver
Thomas Hutchinson

LITERATURE

Anthony Benezet. Short Account of the People Called Quakers (hist)
Benjamin Franklin. The Dialogue between Franklin and the Gout (hum)
David Humphreys. A Poem Addressed to the Armies of the United States
    (po)
_____. A Poem on the Happiness of America (po)
Jonathan Odell. The American Times (po)
Thomas Paine. Public Good (e)

                              1781

BIRTHS

George Washington Parke Custis
Robert Hare

DEATHS

Martin Howard

EVENTS

Thomas's Massachusetts Spy; or, the Worcester Gazette, to 1785 (per)

LITERATURE

Philip Morin Freneau. The British Prison Ship (po)
Francis Hopkinson. The Temple of Minerva (po dr)
Samuel Andrew Peters. General History of Connecticut, by a Gentleman
    of the Province (hist)
John Witherspoon. The Druid (e)

                              1782

BIRTHS

Thomas Hart Benton
Charles Jared Ingersoll

LITERATURE

Charles Chauncy. Salvation for All Men (e)
Michel-Guillaume Jean de Crevecoeur. Letters from an American Far-
    mer (nar)
John Trumbull. M'Fingal (po)

1783

BIRTHS

>Washington Irving
>John Sanderson

DEATHS

>James Adair
>Ann Eliza Bleecker
>James Otis

EVENTS

>The New York Independent Journal, or General Advertiser, to 1788
>   (per)
>Society of the Cincinnati (f)

LITERATURE

>David Humphreys.   The Glory of America; or, Peace Triumphant over
>   War (po)
>_____.   Poem on the Industry of the United States of Ame-
>   rica (po)
>John Ledyard.   A Journal of Captain Cook's Last Voyage to the Paci-
>   fic Ocean (nar)
>Noah Webster.   A Grammatical Institute of the English Language, to
>   1785 (ref)

1784

BIRTHS

>William Allen
>James Nelson Barker
>Thomas Hastings
>Nathaniel Beverley Tucker
>Joseph Emerson Worcester

DEATHS

>Anthony Benezet
>Robert Munford
>Phillis Wheatley

EVENTS

>Francis Asbury consecrated the first bishop of the American Metho-
>   dist Episcopal Church
>Massachusetts Centinel and the Republican Journal, to 1790 (per)

LITERATURE

>Hannah Adams.   Alphabetical Compendium of the Various Sects. . .

from the Beginning of the Christian Era to the Present Day (ref)
Ethan Allen. Reason the Only Oracle of Man (e)
Jeremy Belknap. A History of New Hampshire, 3 vols, to 1792 (hist)
Anthony Benezet. Some Observations on the Indian Natives of This
    Continent (des, e)
Charles Chauncy. The Mystery Hid from Ages and Generations (e)
John Filson. The Discovery, Settlement, and Present State of Ken-
    tucke (hist)
Francis Hopkinson. Modern Learning Exemplified (e)
Peter Markoe. The Patriot Chief (dr)

1785

BIRTHS

John James Audubon
Peter Cartwright
James McHenry
Mordecai Manuel Noah
John Pierpont
David Walker
Samuel Woodworth

DEATHS

Myles Cooper
Stephen Hopkins
Samuel Mather

EVENTS

The Friendly Club, to 1807
The Worcester Magazine, to 1788 (per)

LITERATURE

Timothy Dwight. The Conquest of Canaan (po)
Thomas Jefferson. Notes on the State of Virginia (e)
Humphrey Marshall. Arbustrum Americanum: The American Grove (e,ref)
David Ramsay. History of the Revolution of South Carolina, 2 vols
    (hist)
Ezra Stiles. An Account of the Settlement of Bristol, Rhode Island
    (nar)
Isaiah Thomas. A Specimen of Types (ref)
Noah Webster. Sketches of American Policy (e)

1786

BIRTHS

Nicholas Biddle
Henry Marie Brackenridge

DEATHS

Joseph Brown Ladd

EVENTS

The Columbian Magazine, to 1792 (per)

LITERATURE

The Anarchiad, to 1787 (po)
Philip Morin Freneau. Poems (pub)
_____. Poems Written Chiefly during the Late War
   (po, pub)
Francis Hopkinson. A Plan for the Improvement of the Art of Paper
   War (e, sat)
Joseph Brown Ladd. The Poems of Arouet (po, pub)
Thomas Paine. Dissertations on Government (e)
John Parke. The Lyric Works of Horace, to Which Are Added, a Number
   of Original Poems (trans, po)
_____. Virginia (dr)
John Witherspoon. Essay on Money (e)

1787

BIRTHS

William Crafts
Richard Henry Dana, Sr.
Eliza Leslie
Caroline Matilda Warren
Emma Hart Willard

DEATHS

Charles Chauncy

EVENTS

The American Magazine, to 1788 (per)
The American Museum, to 1792 (per)
United States Constitution framed by the Federal Constitutional Con-
   vention
University of Pittsburgh (f)

LITERATURE

John Adams. Defence of the Constitutions of Government of the Uni-
   ted States of America against the Attack of Mr. Turgot (e)
Joel Barlow. The Vision of Columbus (po)
Alexander Hamilton, James Madison, John Jay. The Federalist, to
   1788 (e)
Jupiter Hammon. An Address to the Negroes of the State of New York
   (e)
Peter Markoe. The Algerine Spy in Pennsylvania (fic)
Royall Tyler. The Contrast (dr)
_____. May Day in Town; or, New York in an Uproar (dr)

1788

BIRTHS

William John Grayson
Sarah Josepha Buell Hale

DEATHS

Mather Byles
John Filson

EVENTS

Calliopean Society, New York, to 1831
The Philological Society, New York, to 1789

LITERATURE

John Dickinson. Letters of Fabius, First Series (e)
Timothy Dwight. The Triumph of Infidelity (po)
Philip Morin Freneau. Miscellaneous Works (pub)
David Humphreys. An Essay on the Life of the Honourable Major-General Israel Putnam (e, biog)
Samuel Low. The Politician Outwitted (dr)
Peter Markoe. The Storm (po)
_____. The Times (po, sat)
George Richards Minot. The History of the Insurrection in Massachusetts in the Year 1786 (hist)
St. George Tucker. Liberty, a Poem on the Independence of America (po)

1789

BIRTHS

James Fenimore Cooper
Asa Greene
James Abraham Hillhouse
Catharine Maria Sedgwick
Susan Ridley Sedgwick
Richard Henry Wilde

DEATHS

Ethan Allen
John Ledyard
John Morgan
John Parke

EVENTS

Annals of Congress, to 1824 (per)
Friendly Club of New York (f)
Gazette of the United States, to 1847 (per)

The Massachusetts Magazine, to 1796 (per)
University of North Carolina, Chapel Hill (f)
George Washington, 1st President of the United States, to 1797

LITERATURE

William Hill Brown. The Power of Sympathy (fic)
William Dunlap. Darby's Return (dr)
_____. The Father; or, American Shandyism (dr)
Noah Webster. Dissertations on the English Language (e)

1790

BIRTHS

Alexander Hill Everett
Fitz-Greene Halleck
Augustus Baldwin Longstreet

DEATHS

Joseph Bellamy
Benjamin Franklin

EVENTS

The General Advertiser, to 1794 (per)
The Columbian Centinel, to 1840 (per)
The New York Magazine, to 1797 (per)

LITERATURE

Enos Hitchcock. Memoirs of the Bloomsgrove Family (fic)
David Humphreys. The Widow of Malabar (dr)
Sarah Wentworth Morton. Ouabi; or, the Virtues of Nature (po)
Mercy Otis Warren. Poems Dramatic and Miscellaneous (pub)
John Winthrop. Journal, Parts I-II (nar, pub)

1791

BIRTHS

Peter Cooper
Nathaniel Deering
James Athearn Jones
John Howard Payne
Lydia Huntley Sigourney

DEATHS

Francis Hopkinson
Benjamin Youngs Prime

EVENTS

The Bill of Rights
Massachusetts Historical Society (f)
National Gazette, to 1793 (per)

LITERATURE

John Adams. Discourses on Davila (e)
William Bartram. Travels through North and South Carolina, Georgia,
    East and West Florida, the Cherokee Country, the Extensive Terri-
    tories of the Muscogulges, or Creek Confederacy, and the Country
    of the Chactaws (nar, des)
Thomas Paine. The Rights of Man, to 1792 (e)
Benjamin Youngs Prime. Columbia's Glory (po)
Samuel Seabury. Discourses on Several Subjects, 3 vols, to 1798 (e)

1792

BIRTHS

Hew Ainslie
James Gillespie Birney
James Ewell Heath
William Leete Stone

DEATHS

Henry Laurens
Arthur Lee
Peter Markoe
Samson Occom
John Seccomb

LITERATURE

Joel Barlow. Advice to the Privileged Orders (e)
_____. A Letter to the National Convention in France (e)
Jeremy Belknap. The Foresters (nar)
Hugh Henry Brackenridge. Modern Chivalry, to 1815 (fic)
Francis Hopkinson. The Miscellaneous Essays and Occasional Writings
    (pub)
Gilbert Imlay. A Topographical Description of the Western Territory
    of North America (des)

1793

BIRTHS

Henry Charles Carey
John Neal

DEATHS

William Hill Brown
William Smith of New York

EVENTS

American Minerva, to 1797 (per)
The Eagle; or, Dartmouth Centinel, to 1799 (per)
Farmer's Almanack (per, f)
Farmer's Weekly Museum, to 1810 (per)
Hamilton College, Clinton, New York (f)
The Mercury, Boston, to 1797 (per)
Williams College, Williamstown, Massachusetts (f)

LITERATURE

Richard Alsop. American Poems (po)
Ann Eliza Bleecker. The Posthumous Works of Ann Eliza Bleeker (pub)
Margaretta Fangeres. A Collection of Essays--Prose and Poetical (e, po)
The Hapless Orphan; or, Innocent Victim of Revenge (fic)
Enos Hitchcock. The Farmer's Friend; or, the History of Mr. Charles Worthy (fic)
Samuel Hopkins. Systems of Doctrines Contained in Divine Revelation (e)
Gilbert Imlay. The Emigrants, 3 vols (fic)
Elihu Hubbard Smith. American Poems (po, ed)

1794

BIRTHS

Maria Gowen Brooks
William Cullen Bryant
Edwin Clifford Holland
Carlos Wilcox

DEATHS

John Witherspoon

EVENTS

Aurora, to 1835 (per)
Bowdoin College (f)
Federal Orrery, to 1796 (per)

LITERATURE

Jeremy Belknap. American Biography, 2 vols, to 1798 (biog, hist)
Caleb Bingham. The American Preceptor (ref)
William Dunlap. Fatal Deception (dr)
Timothy Dwight. Greenfield Hill (po)
Thomas Paine. The Age of Reason, to 1795 (e)
Susanna Haswell Rowson. Slaves in Algiers (dr)
Ezra Stiles. A History of Three of the Judges of King Charles I (hist, biog)

1795

BIRTHS

Joseph Rodman Drake
John Pendleton Kennedy
James Gates Percival
Daniel Pierce Thompson

DEATHS

Ezra Stiles

EVENTS

Claypoole's American Daily Advertiser, to 1800 (per)
Walpole Literary Club, New Hampshire, to 1800

LITERATURE

Hugh Henry Brackenridge. Incidents of the Insurrection in the Wes-
   tern Part of Pennsylvania (nar)
Ebenezer Bradford. The Art of Courting (fic)
William Dunlap. Fountainville Abbey (dr)
Philip Morin Freneau. Poems Written between the Years 1768 and 1794
   (po)
Robert Treat Paine. The Invention of Letters (po)
Susanna Haswell Rowson. The Female Patriot (dr)
_____. Trials of the Human Heart (dr)
_____. The Volunteers (dr)
Isaac Story. Liberty (po)

1796

BIRTHS

Junius Brutus Booth
John Gardiner Calkins Brainard
Thomas Bulfinch
Charles Follen
John Gorham Palfrey
William Hickling Prescott

DEATHS

Samuel Seabury

LITERATURE

Joel Barlow. Hasty Pudding (po)
Matthew Carey. The Porcupiniad: A Hudibrastic Poem (po)
William Cliffton. The Group; or, an Elegant Representation (e)
William Dunlap. The Archers (dr)
Lemuel Hopkins. The Guillotina, or a Democratic Dirge (po)
John Blair Linn. The Poetical Wanderer (po)

Robert Treat Paine. The Ruling Passion (po)
Thomas Paine. Letter to George Washington (e)
Susanna Haswell Rowson. Americans in England (dr)
Elihu Hubbard Smith. Edwin and Angelina (po, dr)
Isaac Story. All the World's a Stage (po)
St. George Tucker. Dissertation on Slavery (e)
_____. The Probationary Odes of Jonathan Pindar (po, sat)

1797

BIRTHS

Walter Colton
James Wallis Eastburn
Nicnolas Marcellus Hentz
Samuel Joseph May
Henry Junius Nott
William Ware

EVENTS

John Adams, 2nd President of tne United States, to 1801
The Commercial Advertiser, to 1905 (per)
The Massachusetts Mercury, to 1801 (per)
Porcupine's Gazette and Daily Advertiser, to 1799 (per)

LITERATURE

Caleb Bingham. The Columbian Orator (ref)
Ann Eliza Bleecker. The History of Maria Kittle (fic, pub)
Jonathan Boucher. A View of the Causes ana Consequences of the American Revolution (e)
William Hill Brown. West Point Preserved (dr, pub)
John Daly Burk. Bunker Hill, or the Death of General Warren (po, dr)
John Dickinson. Letters of Fabius, Second Series (e)
Hannah Webster Foster. The Coquette (fic)
John Blair Linn. Bourville Castle (dr)
Sarah Wentworth Morton. Beacon Hill: A Local Poem, Historic and Descriptive (po)
Robert Proud. The History of Pennsylvania, 2 vols, to 1798 (hist)
Benjamin Trumbull. A Complete History of Connecticut (hist)
Royall Tyler. The Algerine Captive (fic)
_____. The Georgia Spec; or, Land in the Moon (dr)

1798

BIRTHS

William Apes
McDonald Clarke
Baynard Rush Hall
Joseph C. Hart
George Moses Horton

Mirabeau Buonaparte Lamar
Ralph Ingersoll Lockwood

DEATHS

Jeremy Belknap
Jacob Duche
Elihu Hubbard Smith

EVENTS

Ulster County Gazette, to 1822 (per)

LITERATURE

William Austin. Strictures on Harvard University (nar)
Charles Brockden Brown. Alcuin: A Dialogue (e)
_____. Wieland (fic)
John Daly Burke. Female Patriotism, or the Death of Joan d'Arc (po,
    dr)
William Dunlap. Andre (dr)
Hannah Webster Foster. The Boarding School; or, Lessons of a Precep-
    tress to Her Pupils (e)
Abiel Holmes. The Life of Ezra Stiles (biog)
William Milns. All in a Bustle; or, the New House (dr)
Robert Munford. A Collection of Plays and Poems (pub)
William Munford. Prose on Several Occasions (pub)
Robert Treat Paine. Adams and Liberty (po)
Susanna Haswell Rowson. Reuben and Rachel; or, Tales of Old Times
    (fic)
Jonathan Mitchell Sewall. Versification of President Washington's
    Excellent Farewell Address (po)

1799

BIRTHS

Amos Bronson Alcott
James Lawson
Grenville Mellen
Robert Charles Sands
Richard Penn Smith

DEATHS

William Cliffton
Nathan Fiske

EVENTS

The Monthly Magazine and American Review, to 1801 (per)

LITERATURE

Hannah Adams. A Summary History of New England (hist)

Charles Brockden Brown. Arthur Mervyn (fic)
_____. Edgar Huntley (fic)
_____. Ormond (fic)
Thomas Cooper. Political Essays (pub)
William Dunlap. The Italian (dr)
Philip Morin Freneau. Letters on Various Interesting and Important
    Subjects (e)
Sarah Wentworth Morton. The Virtues of Society (po)
James Smith. An Account of Remarkable Occurrences in the Life and
    Travels of Col. James Smith (nar)
Helena Wells. The Stepmother (fic)

4   The Nineteenth Century: 1800–1850

1800

BIRTHS

George Bancroft
Catharine Esther Beecher
Charles James Cannon
Caroline Lee Whiting Hentz
Samuel Kettell
William Holmes McGuffey
John Augustus Stone

DEATHS

William Billings
Jupiter Hammon

EVENTS

Library of Congress (est)
National Intelligencer and Washington Advertiser, to 1870 (per)
Poulson's American Daily Advertiser, to 1839 (per)
Tuesday Club of Philadelphia, to 1804

LITERATURE

William Cliffton. Poems (pub)
John Davis. The Farmer of New Jersey (fic)
John Blair Linn. The Death of Washington: A Poem (po)
Susanna Haswell Rowson. The Columbian Daughter (dr)
Jonathan Mitchell Sewall. Eulogy on the Late General Washington (po)
Helena Wells. Constantia Neville; or, the West Indian (fic)
Sarah Sayward Barrell Keating Wood. Julia and the Illuminated Baron
   (fic)

1801

BIRTHS

Robert Dale Owen
Brigham Young

DEATHS

Benedict Arnold
Margaretta Fangeres
Lemuel Hopkins
Humphrey Marshall

EVENTS

The American Review and Literary Journal, to 1802 (per)
Hudson Balance, Hudson, New York, to 1809 (per)
Thomas Jefferson, 3rd President of the United States, to 1809
New York Evening Post (per, f)
The Port Folio, to 1827 (per)

LITERATURE

Paul Allen. Original Poems, Serious and Entertaining (po)
Charles Brockden Brown. Clara Howard (fic)
_____. Jane Talbot (fic)
Michel-Guillaume Jean de Crevecoeur. Voyage dans la Haute Pensylva-
    nie et dans l'etat de New York (trav)
John Davis. The Wanderings of William (fic)
Nathan Fiske. The Moral Monitor (e, pub)
Charles Jared Ingersoll. Edwy and Elgiva (dr)
John Blair Linn. The Powers of Genius (po)
Jonathan Mitchell Sewall. Miscellaneous Poems (pub)
Isaac Story. A Parnassean Shop, Opened in the Pindaric Stile; by
    Peter Quince, Esq. (po, sat)
Tabitha Gilman Tenney. Female Quixotism (fic)
Sarah Sayward Barrell Keating Wood. Dorval; or, the Speculator (fic)

1802

BIRTHS

Horace Bushnell
William Alexander Caruthers
Lydia Maria Child
Alonzo Delano
William Leggett
George Pope Morris
Edward Coote Pinkney
George Dennison Prentice

DEATHS

George Richards Minot

EVENTS

The United States Military Academy, West Point, New York (f)

LITERATURE

Nathaniel Bowditch. The New American Practical Navigator (ref)
James Cheetham. View of the Political Conduct of Aaron Burr (e)
Washington Irving. Letters of Jonathan Oldstyle, Gent., to 1803,
    (sat)
Sarah Sayward Barrell Keating Wood. Amelia; or, the Influence of
    Virtue (fic)

1803

BIRTHS

Jacob Abbott
Adin Ballou
Orestes Augustus Brownson
George Henry Calvert
Rufus Dawes
Ralph Waldo Emerson
Sumner Lincoln Fairfield
Sarah Helen Power Whitman

DEATHS

Samuel Adams
Joseph Galloway
Enos Hitchcock
Samuel Hopkins
William Smith of Pennsylvania
Isaac Story

EVENTS

The Literary Magazine and American Register, to 1807 (per)
Monthly Anthology and Boston Review, to 1811 (per)

LITERATURE

John Davis. Travels of Four Years and a Half in the United States
    (des)
Thomas Green Fessenden. Terrible Tractoration (po)
William Wirt. Letters of the British Spy (e)

1804

BIRTHS

Charles Frederick Briggs
Nathaniel Hawthorne
Samuel Benjamin Helbert Judah
William Joseph Snelling

DEATHS

Jonathan Boucher
John Blair Linn

EVENTS

Anthology Club, Boston, to 1811
Harmony Society, to 1903

LITERATURE

Hanna Adams. The Truth and Excellence of the Christian Religion (e)
John Quincy Adams. Letters on Silesia (e)
William Austin. Letters from London (nar)
Hosea Ballou. Notes on the Parables (e)
John Daly Burk. History of Virginia, to 1816 (hist)
Thomas Green Fessenden. Original Poems (pub)
Isaac Mitchell. The Asylum: or, Alonzo and Melissa (fic)
Elijah Parish and Jedidiah Morse. A Compendious History of New Eng-
    land (hist)
Susanna Haswell Rowson. Miscellaneous Poems (pub)
William Wirt. The Rainbow (e)
Sarah Sayward Barrell Keating Wood. Ferdinand and Elmira: A Russian
    Story (fic)

1805

BIRTHS

John Turvill Adams
William Gannaway Brownlow
Charles Etienne Arthur Gayarre

EVENTS

Boston Atheneaum (f)
Thespian Mirror, to 1806 (per)

LITERATURE

Hosea Ballou. A Treatise on Atonement (e)
Joel Barlow. Prospectus of a National Institution To Be Established
    in the United States (e)
John Davis. The First Settlers of Virginia (fic)
_____. The Post Captain (fic)
Thomas Green Fessenden. Democracy Unveiled (e)
William Ioor. Independence; or, Which Do You Like Best, the Peer or
    the Farmer? (dr)
John Blair Linn. Valerian (po)
Caroline Matilda Warren. The Gamesters; or, Ruins of Innocence (fic)
Mercy Otis Warren. History of the Rise, Progress, and Termination
    of the American Revolution, 3 vols (hist)
Alexander Wilson. The Foresters (po)

1806

BIRTHS

Robert Montgomery Bird
Horatio Bridge
Emma Catherine Embury
Charles Fenno Hoffman
Cornelius Ambrosius Logan
Isaac McLellan
William Gilmore Simms
Elizabeth Oakes Smith
Frederick William Thomas
Nathaniel Parker Willis

DEATHS

Isaac Backus

LITERATURE

William Littell. Epistles of William, Surnamed Littell, to the People of the Realm of Kentucky (e, sat)
John Howard Payne. Julia; or, the Wanderer (dr)
Noah Webster. Compendious Dictionary of the English Language (ref)

1807

BIRTHS

Charles Francis Adams the elder
William Bayle Bernard
Elizabeth Margaret Chandler
Theodore Sedgwick Fay
Henry William Herbert
Richard Hildreth
Henry Wadsworth Longfellow
Joseph Clay Neal
John Greenleaf Whittier

EVENTS

The American Register, to 1810 (per)
The Pastime, to 1808 (per)

LITERATURE

James Nelson Barker. Tears and Smiles (dr)
Joel Barlow. The Columbiad (po)
William Hill Brown. Ira and Isabella; or, the Natural Children (fic, pub)
William Dunlap. Leicester (dr)
William Ioor. The Battle of Eutaw Springs (dr)
Washington Irving. Salmagundi; or, the Whim-Whams and Opinions of Launcelot Langstaff, Esq., and Others, to 1808 (sat)

Samuel Andrews Peters. A History of the Reverend Hugh Peters (biog)

1808

BIRTHS

William Davis Gallagher
Ray Palmer
Edmund Quincy
Samuel Francis Smith

DEATHS

John Daly Burk
John Dickinson
Jonathan Mitchell Sewall

LITERATURE

James Nelson Barker. The Indian Princess; or, La Belle Sauvage (dr)
William Cullen Bryant. The Embargo (po)
John Davis. Walter Kennedy (fic)

1809

BIRTHS

Timothy Shay Arthur
Albert Brisbane
Thomas Holley Chivers
Philip St. George Cooke
Oliver Wendell Holmes
Joseph Holt Ingraham
Joseph Stevens Jones
Laughton Osborn
Albert Pike
Edgar Allan Poe

DEATHS

Thomas Paine

EVENTS

The Balance and New York Journal, Albany, New York (per, f)
The Literary Gazette, to 1821 (per)
James Madison, 4th President of the United States, to 1817

LITERATURE

William Allen. American Biographical and Historical Dictionary (ref)
James Cheetham. Life of Thomas Paine (biog)
Philip Morin Freneau. Collected Poems, 2 vols (pub)
Washington Irving. A History of New York. . .by Diedrich Knicker-

bocker (sat)
John Howard Payne. Lovers' Vows (dr)
David Ramsay. History of South Carolina, from Its First Settlement in 1670 to 1808, 2 vols (hist)
Samuel Stanhope Smith. Lectures on the Evidences of the Christian Religion (e)
Royall Tyler. Yankey in London (sat, fic)

1810

BIRTHS

Alfred W. Arrington (Charles Summerfield)
John Brougham
James Freeman Clarke
Robert Taylor Conrad
James Sloan Gibbons
John Beauchamp Jones
Mary Sargeant Nichols
Ann Sophia Stephens

DEATHS

Charles Brockden Brown
James Cheetham

LITERATURE

William Crafts. The Raciad and Other Occasional Poems (po)
Charles Jared Ingersoll. Inchiquin, the Jesuit's Letters (e)
Isaiah Thomas. History of Printing in America, 2 vols (hist)

1811

BIRTHS

Delia Salter Bacon
William Starbuck Mayo
Frances Sargeant Locke Osgood
Harriet Elizabeth Beecher Stowe
Alfred Billings Street
Sara Payson Willis (Fanny Fern)

DEATHS

Robert Treat Paine

EVENTS

Niles' Weekly Register, Baltimore, to 1849 (per)

1812

BIRTHS

Stephen Pearl Andrews
Thomas Gold Appleton
George Ticknor Curtis
Martin Robinson Delany
John Treat Irving
Peter Hamilton Myers
William Tappan Thompson

DEATHS

Joel Barlow
Isaac Mitchell

EVENTS

American Antiquarian Society (f)
The General Repository and Review, to 1813 (per)

LITERATURE

Hannah Adams. The History of the Jews (hist)
Mordecai Manuel Noah. Paul and Alexis (dr)
James Kirke Paulding. The Diverting History of John Bull and Bro-
    ther Jonathan (sat)
John Pierpont. The Portrait (po)
Rebecca Rush. Kelroy (fic)
James Smith. A Treatise on the Mode and Manner of Indian War (e)
Samuel Stanhope Smith. Lectures on the Subjects of Moral and Poli-
    tical Philosophy, 2 vols (e)
William Wirt. The Old Bachelor (e)

1813

BIRTHS

Nathaniel Harrington Bannister
Henry Ward Beecher
Charles Timothy Brooks
Susan Fenimore Cooper
Christopher Pearse Cranch
Sylvester Judd
Elijah Kellogg
Daniel Ricketson
Epes Sargent
Henry Theodore Tuckerman
Jones Very

DEATHS

Michel-Guillaume Jean de Crevecouer
Robert Proud
Alexander Wilson

EVENTS

Boston Daily Advertiser, to 1929 (per)
The Christian Disciple, Boston, to 1823 (per)

LITERATURE

Washington Allston. The Sylphs of the Seasons (po)
Edwin Clifford Holland. Odes, Naval Songs, and Other Occasional
    Poems (po)
James Kirke Paulding. The Lay of the Scottish Fiddle (po, sat)
Susanna Haswell Rowson. Sarah; or, the Exemplary Wife (fic)

1814

BIRTHS

Jeremiah Clemens
Eliza Ann Dupuy
George Washington Harris
William Howe Cuylor Hosmer
Alexander Beaufort Meek
John Lathrop Motley

DEATHS

James Smith
Mercy Otis Warren

EVENTS

New Harmony Society, to 1828

LITERATURE

Nicholas Biddle and Paul Allen (eds.). History of the Expedition of
    Captains Lewis and Clark (nar)
Henry Marie Brackenridge. Views of Louisiana (des)
Hugh Henry Brackenridge. Law Miscellanies (e)
Mathew Carey. The Olive Branch (e)
David Humphreys. The Yankee in England (dr)
Francis Scott Key. The Star-Spangled Banner (po)
William Littell. Festoons of Fancy: Consisting of Compositions Ama-
    tory, Sentimental, and Humorous in Verse and Prose (sat)
John Taylor. An Inquiry into the Principles and Policy of the Govern-
    ment of the United States (e)

1815

BIRTHS

Joseph Glover Baldwin
Richard Henry Dana, Jr.
Johnson Jones Hooper

Thomas Low Nichols
Elizabeth Stuart Phelps
Frederick William Shelton

DEATHS

Richard Alsop
David Ramsay

EVENTS

The North American Review, to 1939 (per)

LITERATURE

Hannah Mather Crocker. Series of Letters on Free Masonry (e)
William Dunlap. Life of Charles Brockden Brown (biog)
Philip Morin Freneau. Collected Poems (pub)
James Kirke Paulding. The United States and England (e)
Lydia Huntley Sigourney. Moral Pieces in Prose and Verse (pub)

1816

BIRTHS

Samuel Austin Allibone
William Wells Brown
Philip Pendleton Cooke
Evert Augustus Duyckinck
Samuel Adams Hammett (Philip Paxton)
Richard Burleigh Kimball
Robert Traill Spence Lowell
John Godfrey Saxe

DEATHS

Hugh Henry Brackenridge

EVENTS

Delphian (Literary) Club (f)
The Portico, Baltimore, to 1818 (per)

LITERATURE

Hosea Ballou. A Series of Letters in Defense of Divine Revelation
    (e)
James Ogilvie. Philosophical Essays (e)
John Pickering. Vocabulary of Words and Phrases Peculiar to the Uni-
    ted States (ref)
John Pierpont. Airs of Palestine (po)
David Ramsay and Samuel Stanhope Smith. History of the United States
    3 vols, to 1817 (hist, pub)
George Tucker. Letters from Virginia (e)
Alexander Wilson. Poems; Chiefly in the Scottish Dialect (po)

Samuel Woodworth. The Champions of Freedom, 2 vols (fic)

1817

BIRTHS

    John Bigelow
    Harriet Farley
    James Thomas Fields
    Henry Beck Hirst
    Gideon Hiram Hollister
    Emily Chubbock Judson (Fanny Forester)
    Cornelius Mathews
    Nathan Cook Meeker
    Henry David Thoreau

DEATHS

    Caleb Bingham
    Timothy Dwight

EVENTS

    University of Michigan (f)
    James Monroe, 5th President of the United States, to 1825

LITERATURE

    James Nelson Barker. How To Try a Lover (dr)
    Morris Birkbeck. Notes on a Journey to the Territory of Illinois
      (nar)
    Henry Marie Brackenridge. South America (e)
    William Cullen Bryant. Thanatopsis (po)
    Amasa Delano. Narrative Voyages and Travels (nar, des)
    John Neal. Keep Cool (fic)
    James Kirke Paulding. Letters from the South, 2 vols (e)

1818

BIRTHS

    Charlotte Mary Sanford Barnes
    William Ellery Channing the younger
    George Copway
    Frederick Swartwout Cozzens (Richard Haywarde)
    Mary Henderson Eastman
    Elizabeth Payson Prentiss
    Thomas Mayne Reid

DEATHS

    Abagail Adams
    David Humphreys
    Jonathan Odell

LITERATURE

Morris Birkbeck. Letters from Illinois (nar)
Hannah Mather Crocker. Observations on the Rights of Women (e)
Timothy Dwight. Theology, Explained and Defended, 5 vols, to 1819
    (ser)
Edwin Clifford Holland. Corsair (dr)
John Pendleton Kennedy. The Red Book, to 1819 (fic, nar)
John Neal. Battle of Niagara (po)
_____. Goldau, or, the Maniac Harper (po)
James Kirke Paulding. The Backwoodsman (po)
John Howard Payne. Brutus; or, the Fall of Tarquin (dr, po)
Benjamin Trumbull. A Complete History of Connecticut, rev. ed.
        (hist)

1819

BIRTHS

John Bidwell
Joseph Beckham Cobb
Alexander Crummell
Thomas Dunn English
Josiah Gilbert Holland
Julia Ward Howe
William Wilberforce Lord
James Russell Lowell
Herman Melville
Anna Cora Mowatt
Charles Jacobs Peterson
Emma Dorothy Eliza Nevitte Southworth
William Westmore Story
William Ross Wallace
Charles Wilkins Webber
Edwin Percy Whipple
Walt Whitman
Henry Augustus Wise

DEATHS

James Wallis Eastburn
Samuel Stanhope Smith

EVENTS

Colgate University (f)
The National Recorder, to 1821 (per)
New York American, to 1845 (per)
University of Virginia (f)
The Zoar Community, Ohio, to 1898

LITERATURE

Henry Marie Brackenridge. Voyage to South America (nar)
William Ellery Channing the elder. Baltimore Sermon (ser, pub)

Joseph Rodman Drake and Fitz-Greene Halleck. The Croaker Papers (po)
Fitz-Greene Halleck. Fanny, to 1821 (po)
James Abraham Hillhouse. Percy's Masque (po, dr)
Washington Irving. The Sketch Book, to 1820 (e, fic)
John Neal. Otho (po, dr)
Mordecai Manuel Noah. She Would Be a Soldier (dr)
James Kirke Paulding. Salmagundi, 2nd series (sat, po)
David Ramsay. Universal History Americanized, 12 vols (hist)
Richard Henry Wilde. The Lament of the Captive (po)

1820

BIRTHS

Susan Brownell Anthony
John Bartlett
Dion Boucicault
Henry Howard Brownell
Alice Cary
Lucretia Peabody Hale
Margaret Junkin Preston

DEATHS

Joseph Rodman Drake
James Ogilvie
Benjamin Trumbull

EVENTS

The Charleston Mercury, South Carolina, to 1868 (per)
The Providence Journal, Rhode Island (per, f)

LITERATURE

Maria Gowen Brooks. Judith, Esther, and Other Poems (po)
William Ellery Channing the elder. The Moral Argument against Cal-
    vinism (ser)
James Fenimore Cooper. Precaution (fic)
William Crafts. Sullivan's Island, the Raciad, and Other Poems (po)
James Wallis Eastburn and Robert Charles Sands. Yamoyden (po)
Peter Irving. Giovanni Sbogarro (fic)
Samuel Benjamin Helbert Judah. The Mountain Torrent (dr)
Henry Wadsworth Longfellow. The Battle of Lovewell's Pond (po)
Mordecai Manuel Noah. The Siege of Tripoli (dr)
Robert Charles Sands and James Wallace Eastburn. Yamoyden (po)
John Taylor. Constriction Construed and Constitutions Vindicated
    (e)
William Tudor. Letters on the Eastern States (e)

1821

BIRTHS

John Ross Browne
William Frederick Poole
Frederick Goddard Tuckerman

EVENTS

Amherst College, Amherst, Massachusetts (f)
The Saturday Evening Post, to 1969 (per)
The Saturday Magazine, to 1822 (per)

LITERATURE

John Quincy Adams. Report on Weights and Measures (e)
Paul Allen. Noah (po)
William Cullen Bryant. Poems (pub)
James Fenimore Cooper. The Spy (fic)
Richard Henry Dana, Sr. (ed.). The Idle Man, to 1822 (per)
Joseph Doddridge. Logan (dr)
Timothy Dwight. Travels in New England and New York, 4 vols, to 1822
   (trav, pub)
Mordecai Manuel Noah. Marion; or, the Hero of Lake George (dr)
James Gates Percival. Poems (pub)
William Tudor. Miscellanies (e)

1822

BIRTHS

Emerson Bennett
Benjamin Paul Blood
Edward Everett Hale
Richard Malcolm Johnston
George Lippard
Donald Grant Mitchell
Thomas Buchanan Read

DEATHS

Thomas Atwood Digges

EVENTS

Bread and Cheese Club, New York, to 1827
The Museum of Foreign Literature and Science, to 1842 (per)

LITERATURE

Hew Ainslie. A Pilgrimage to the Land of Burns (po)
McDonald Clarke. Elixir of Moonshine by the Mad Poet (po)
Sumner Lincoln Fairfield. The Siege of Constantinople (po)
Fitz-Greene Halleck. Alnwick Castle (po)
Washington Irving. Bracebridge Hall (fic, e)
Samuel Benjamin Helbert Judah. Odofriede (po, dr)
James Lawson. Ontwa, the Son of the Forest (po, nar)
James McHenry. The Pleasures of Friendship (po)

John Neal. Logan, a Family History, 2 vols (fic)
Mordecai Manuel Noah. The Grecian Captive (dr)
James Kirke Paulding. A Sketch of Old England, by a New England Man
    2 vols (e, des)
James Gates Percival. Clio, 3 vols, to 1827 (po)
Catharine Maria Sedgwick. A New England Tale (fic)
John Taylor. Tyranny Unmasked (e)

1823

BIRTHS

Sidney Frances Bateman
George Henry Boker
Sylvanus Cobb, Jr.
Charles Carleton Coffin
Augustine Joseph Hickey Duganne
George Long Duyckinck
Thomas Wentworth Higginson
Edward Zane Carroll Judson (Ned Buntline)
Henry Morford
Francis Parkman
Elizabeth Drew Barstow Stoddard
Lydia Louise Ann Very

DEATHS

William Bartram
Amasa Delano

EVENTS

The Christian Examiner, Boston, to 1869 (per)
New York Mirror, to 1842 (per)

LITERATURE

James Fenimore Cooper. The Pilot (fic)
_____. The Pioneers (fic)
Samuel Benjamin Helbert Judah. Gotham and the Gothamites (po, sat)
_____. The Rose of Arragon (dr)
_____. A Tale of Lexington (dr)
James McHenry. The Spectre of the Forest (fic)
_____. Waltham (po)
_____. The Wilderness; or, Braddock's Times (fic)
Clement Clarke Moore. 'Twas the Night before Christmas (po)
Sarah Wentworth Morton. My Mind and Its Thoughts (e, po)
John Neal. Errata; or, the Works of Will Adams, 2 vols (fic)
_____. Randolph (fic)
_____. Seventy-Six, 2 vols (fic)
James Kirke Paulding. Koningsmarke, the Long Finne (fic)
John Howard Payne. Clari; or, the Maid of Milan (dr)
John Taylor. New Views of the Constitution (e)
James Thacher. A Military Journal during the American Revolutionary
    War (nar)

Henry Tudor. The Life of James Otis of Massachusetts (biog)

1824

BIRTHS

Phoebe Cary
William Turner Coggleshall
George William Curtis
Charles Godfrey Leland
Sarah Anna Lewis
George Henry Miles
Mary Hayden Green Pike
William Henry Thomes

DEATHS

Edwin Clifford Holland
William Littell
Susanna Haswell Rowson
John Taylor

EVENTS

The Springfield Republican, Massachusetts (per, f)
United States Literary Gazette, Boston, to 1826 (per)

LITERATURE

William Austin. Peter Rugg, the Missing Man (fic)
James Nelson Barker. Superstition (dr)
John Gardiner Calkins Brainard. Letters Found in the Ruins of Fort
    Bradford (fic)
Lydia Maria Child. Hobomok (fic)
Joseph Doddridge. Notes on the Settlement and Indian Wars of the
    Western Parts of Virginia and Pennsylvania, from 1766 to 1783
    (hist)
Washington Irving. Tales of a Traveller (fic, e)
John Howard Payne. Charles the Second (dr)
Catharine Maria Sedgwick. Redwood (fic)
Margaret Bayard Smith. A Winter in Washington (fic)
George Tucker. The Valley of Shenandoah (fic)
Royall Tyler. The Chestnut Tree (po)
Samuel Woodworth. LaFayette (dr)

1825

BIRTHS

William Mumford Baker
Francis James Child
William Cuthbert Falkner
Mary Jane Hawes Holmes
Harriet Jane Hanson Robinson

Richard Henry Stoddard
James Bayard Taylor
Francis Henry Underwood

DEATHS

Morris Birkbeck
William Munford
Elijah Parish

EVENTS

John Quincy Adams, 6th President of the United States, to 1829
Biblical Repertory, to 1888 (per)
The New Harmony Gazette, Indiana, to 1829 (per)
New York Review and Athenaeum Magazine, to 1826 (per)
Register of Debates, Washington, D.C., to 1837 (per)

LITERATURE

John Gardiner Calkins Brainard. Occasional Pieces of Poetry (pub)
Lydia Maria Child. The Rebels; or, Boston before the Revolution
   (fic)
James Fenimore Cooper. Lionel Lincoln (fic)
Charles Follen. Hymns for Children (po)
Fitz-Greene Halleck. Marco Bozzaris (po)
Nicholas Marcellus Hentz. Tadeskund, the Last King of the Lenape
   (fic)
James Abraham Hillhouse. Hadad (po, dr)
James Athearn Jones. The Refugee (fic)
William Leggett. Leisure Hours at Sea (po)
John Neal. American Writers (e, hist)
_____. Brother Jonathan, 3 vols (fic)
James Kirke Paulding. John Bull in America; or, the New Munchausen
   (e)
Edward Coote Pinkney. Poems (pub)
Richard Penn Smith. The Divorce (dr)
John Winthrop. The History of New England, 2 vols, to 1826 (nar,
   pub)
Samuel Woodworth. The Forest Rose (dr)
_____. The Widow's Son (dr)

                              1826

BIRTHS

Samuel Bowles
John William DeForest
Frances Fuller Victor

DEATHS

John Adams
Paul Allen
William Crafts

Joseph Doddridge
Jedidiah Morse
Samuel Andrew Peters
Royall Tyler

EVENTS

Atkinson's Casket, to 1839 (per)
National Academy of Design (f)
United States Review and Literary Gazette, to 1826 (per)
Western Reserve College, Cleveland, Ohio, to 1967

LITERATURE

William Ellery Channing the elder. Unitarian Christianity Most Fa-
    vorable to Piety (ser)
James Fenimore Cooper. The Last of the Mohicans (fic)
Timothy Flint. Francis Berrian; or, the Mexican Patriot (fic)
_____. Recollections of the Last Ten Years (nar)
Abiel Holmes. The Annals of America (hist, ref)
Oliver Wendell Holmes. Songs in Many Keys (po)
William Leggett. Journals of the Ocean (po)
George Pope Morris. Brier Cliff (dr)
James Kirke Paulding. The Merry Tales of the Three Wise Men of Go-
    tham (fic)
John Howard Payne. Richelieu (dr)
John Pickering. Comprehensive Lexicon of the Greek Language (ref)
Samuel Woodworth. Melodies, Duets, Songs, and Ballads (po)

1827

BIRTHS

Ethel Lynn Beers
Rose Terry Cooke
Maria Susanna Cummins
Francis Miles Finch
John Rollin Ridge
John Townsend Trowbridge
Lewis Wallace

DEATHS

St. George Tucker
Carlos Wilcox

EVENTS

The Token, Boston, to 1842 (per)
The Western Monthly Review, to 1830 (per)
The Youth's Companion, Boston, to 1929 (per)

LITERATURE

John James Audubon. The Birds of America, to 1838 (illus, nar)
James Fenimore Cooper. The Prairie (fic)
_____. The Red Rover (fic)
George Washington Parke Custis. The Indian Prophecy, a National
    Drama in Two Acts, Founded on the Life of George Washington (dr)
Sumner Lincoln Fairfield. The Cities of the Plain (po)
Sarah Josepha Buell Hale. Northwood: A Tale of New England (fic)
Fitz-Greene Halleck. Alnwick Castle, with Other Poems (po)
Samuel Benjamin Helbert Judah. The Buccaneers (fic)
Edgar Allan Poe. Tamerlane and Other Poems (po)
Anne Newport Royall. The Tennessean (fic)
Catharine Maria Sedgwick. Hope Leslie; or, Early Times in the Massa-
    chusetts (fic)
George Tucker. A Voyage to the Moon (fic)
Nathaniel Parker Willis. Sketches (po)
Sarah Sayward Barrell Keating Wood. Tales of the Night (fic)

                            1828

BIRTHS

    Oliver Bell Bunce
    Horatio Franklin Moore
    Fitz-James O'Brien
    Frederick Beecher Perkins
    Henry Timrod
    Theodore Winthrop

DEATHS

    John Gardiner Calkins Brainard
    Gilbert Imlay
    Edward Coote Pinkney

EVENTS

    Cherokee Phoenix, to 1835 (per)
    Old Corner Bookstore, Boston (est)
    The Southern Review, Charleston, South Carolina, to 1832 (per)

LITERATURE

    Robert Montgomery Bird. The City Looking Glass (dr)
    James Fenimore Cooper. Notions of the Americans (e)
    Emma Catherine Embury. Guido (fic)
    Timothy Flint. The Life and Adventures of Arthur Clenning (fic)
    Nathaniel Hawthorne. Fanshawe (fic)
    James Ewell Heath. Edge-Hill (fic)
    Washington Irving. History of the Life and Voyages of Christopher
        Columbus (hist, biog)
    Grenville Mellen. Sad Tales and Glad Tales (fic)
    John Neal. Rachel Dyer (fic)
    Susanna Haswell Rowson. Charlotte's Daughter; or, the Three Orphans
        (fic, pub)
    Margaret Bayard Smith. What Is Gentility? (fic)

James Thacher. American Medical Biography (biog)
Noah Webster. An American Dictionary of the English Language, 2 vols
  (ref)
Carlos Wilcox. Remains (ser, po, pub)

1829

BIRTHS

Jane Cunningham Croly
Philander Deming
Silas Weir Mitchell
Charles Dudley Warner

EVENTS

American Monthly Magazine, Boston, to 1831 (per)
Encyclopaedia Americana (ref)
The Free Enquirer, Indiana, to 1835 (per)
Andrew Jackson, 7th President of the United States, to 1837

LITERATURE

William Apes. A Son of the Forest (nar)
Mathew Carey. Autobiographical Sketches (auto, pub)
James Fenimore Cooper. The Wept of Wish-ton-Wish (fic)
Timothy Flint. George Mason, the Young Backwoodsman (fic)
Sarah Josepha Buell Hale. Sketches of American Character (fic)
Washington Irving. A Chronicle of the Conquest of Granada (fic)
James Athearn Jones. Tales of an Indian Camp, 3 vols (fic)
Samuel Kettell. Specimens of American Poetry, 3 vols (ed)
William Leggett. Tales and Sketches. By a Country Schoolmaster (fic)
James Kirke Paulding. Tales of the Good Woman (fic)
Edgar Allan Poe. Al Araaf (po)
Richard Penn Smith. The Disowned (dr)
_____. The Eighth of January (dr)
_____. The Sentinels; or, the Two Sergeants (dr)
_____. William Penn; or, the Elm Tree (dr)
John Augustus Stone. Metamora; or; the Last of the Wampanoags (dr)
William Tudor. Gebel Teir (fic)
David Walker. Walker's Appeal (e)

1830

BIRTHS

Noah Brooks
John Esten Cooke
Emily Elizabeth Dickinson
Paul Hamilton Hayne
Helen Maria Hunt Jackson
Joseph Kirkland
Mary Virginia Terhune

DEATHS

William Tudor
David Walker

EVENTS

Boston Daily Evening Transcript, to 1941 (per)
Daily Journal, Louisville, Kentucky, to 1868 (per)
Godey's Lady's Book, to 1892 (per)
Illinois Monthly Magazine, to 1832 (per)

LITERATURE

Amos Bronson Alcott. Observations on the Principles and Methods of
    Infant Instruction (e)
Robert Montgomery Bird. Pelopidas (dr)
John Gardiner Calkins Brainard. Fugitive Tales (fic, pub)
Mathew Carey. Miscellaneous Essays (pub)
William Ellery Channing the elder. Remarks on American Literature
    (e)
James Fenimore Cooper. The Water-Witch (fic)
George Washington Parke Custis. Pocahontas (dr)
_____. The Railroad (dr)
Timothy Flint. The Shoshonee Valley (fic)
Sarah Josepha Buell Hale. Poems for Our Children (po, pub)
Oliver Wendell Holmes. Old Ironsides (po)
James Lawson. Tales and Sketches, by a Cosmopolite (fic)
George Pope Morris. Woodman, Spare That Tree! (po)
John Neal. Authorship (fic)
James Kirke Paulding. The Lion of the West (fic)
Catharine Maria Sedgwick. Clarence; or, a Tale of Our Own Times
    (fic)
Richard Penn Smith. The Deformed (po, dr)
_____. The Triumph at Plattsburg (dr)
_____. The Water Witch (dr)
William Joseph Snelling. Tales of the Northwest; or, Sketches of
    Indian Life and Character (nar, fic)
Joseph Emerson Worcester. Comprehensive Pronouncing and Explanatory
    Dictionary of the English Language (ref)

1831

BIRTHS

Jane Goodwin Austin
Amelia Edith Huddleston Barr
James Phinney Baxter
Rebecca Blaine Harding Davis
Mary Elizabeth Mapes Dodge
Ignatius Donnelly
Metta Victoria Victor

DEATHS

Hannah Adams
Isaiah Thomas
John Trumbull

EVENTS

The first singing, on 4 July, of the patriotic hymn "America"
The Independent Messenger, to 1839 (per)
The Liberator, Boston, to 1865 (per)
The New England Anti-Slavery Society (f)
The New England Magazine, to 1835 (per)
New York University (f)
Spirit of the Times, New York, to 1861 (per)

LITERATURE

Delia Salter Bacon. Tales of the Puritans (fic)
William Bayle Bernard. The Dumb Belle (dr)
Robert Montgomery Bird. The Gladiator (dr)
Charles Timothy Brooks. William Tell (trans)
James Fenimore Cooper. The Bravo (fic)
_____. A Letter to General Lafayette (e)
Nathaniel Deering. Carabasset (dr)
Thomas Hastings and Lowell Mason. Spiritual Songs for Social Wor-
    ship (po, ed)
Caroline Lee Whiting Hentz. De Lara; or, the Moorish Bride (fic)
Charles Jared Ingersoll. Julian (dr)
James Athearn Jones. Haverhill; or, Memoirs of an Officer in the
    Army of Wolfe (fic)
Laughton Osborn. Sixty Years of the Life of Jeremy Levis, 2 vols
    (fic)
James Kirke Paulding. The Dutchman's Fireside (fic)
Edgar Allan Poe. Poems by Edgar A. Poe (pub)
Richard Penn Smith. Caius Marius (dr, po)
_____. The Forsaken (fic)
Samuel Francis Smith. America (po)
William Joseph Snelling. Truth: A New Year's Gift for Scribblers
    (po, sat)
John Augustus Stone. The Demoniac; or, the Prophet's Bride (dr)
_____. Tancred: King of Sicily (dr)
John Taylor. Arator (e, pub)
John Greenleaf Whittier. Legends of New-England in Prose and Verse
    (fic, po)
_____. Moll Pitcher (po)
Emma Hart Willard. The Fulfillment of a Promise (po)

1832

BIRTHS

Elizabeth Chase Akers
Louisa May Alcott
Horatio Alger
Hubert Howe Bancroft
Moncure Daniel Conway   Mary Ashley Van Voorhees Townsend

DEATHS

Philip Morin Freneau
Robert Charles Sands

EVENTS

The Western Monthly Magazine, Cincinnati, Ohio, to 1837 (per)

LITERATURE

Jacob Abbott. The Young Christian (fic)
William Bayle Bernard. Rip Van Winkle (dr)
Robert Montgomery Bird. Oralloosa (dr)
William Cullen Bryant. Poems (pub)
Thomas Holley Chivers. The Path of Sorrow (po)
Robert Taylor Conrad. Conrad, King of Naples (dr)
James Fenimore Cooper. The Heidenmauer (fic)
William Dunlap. The History of the American Theatre (hist)
Sumner Lincoln Fairfield. The Last Night of Pompeii (po)
Theodore Sedgwick Fay. Dreams and Reveries of a Quiet Man (e)
Caroline Lee Whiting Hentz. Werdenberg; or, the Forest League (fic)
Washington Irving. The Alhambra (fic, des)
Joseph Stevens Jones. The Liberty Tree (dr)
John Pendleton Kennedy (Mark Littleton). Swallow Barn (fic, nar)
James Kirke Paulding. Westward Ho! (fic)

1833

BIRTHS

Jane Andrews
Mary Abigail Dodge (Gail Hamilton)
Edwin Thomas Booth
David Ross Locke (Petroleum V. Nasby)
Rowland Evans Robinson
Edmund Clarence Stedman
Denman Thompson

EVENTS

The American Anti-Slavery Society (f)
The American Monthly Magazine, to 1838 (per)
Haverford College, Pennsylvania (f)
The Knickerbocker Magazine, New York, to 1865 (per)
New York Sun, to 1966 (per)
Oberlin College, Ohio (f)

LITERATURE

William Apes. The Experiences of Five Christian Indians (nar)
William Bayle Bernard. The Kentuckian; or, a Trip to New York (dr)
Elias Boudinot. Poor Sarah; or, the Indian Woman (fic)
Maria Gowen Brooks. Zophiel (po)
Lydia Maria Child. Appeal in Favor of That Class of American Called

Africans (e)
James Fenimore Cooper. The Headman (fic)
George Washington Parke Custis. North Point (dr)
Richard Henry Dana, Sr. Poems and Prose Writings (pub)
Timothy Flint. Memoir of Daniel Boone (biog)
Asa Greene. The Life and Adventures of Dr. Dodimus Duckworth (fic)
_____. Travels in America by George Fibbleton (fic)
_____. A Yankee among the Nullifiers (fic)
Ralph Ingersoll Lockwood. Rosine Laval (fic)
Henry Wadsworth Longfellow. Outre-Mer:A Pilgrimage beyond the Sea
    to 1834 (fic)
Grenville Mellen. The Martyr's Triumph (po)
John Neal. The Down-Easters (fic)
William Gilmore Simms. Martin Faber (fic)
Richard Penn Smith. Is She a Brigand? (dr)
John Augustus Stone. The Ancient Briton (dr)
Frederick William Thomas. The Emigrant (po)

1834

BIRTHS

George Arnold (McArone)
Charles Farrar Browne (Artemus Ward)
Richard Realf
Francis Richard Stockton
Charles Henry Webb

DEATHS

Elizabeth Margaret Chandler
John Augustus Stone
William Wirt

EVENTS

Congressional Globe, Washington, D.C., to 1873 (per)
The Ladies' Companion, New York, to 1844 (per)
Southern Literary Messenger, Richmond, Virginia, to 1864 (per)

LITERATURE

George Bancroft. History of the United States, to 1876, 1885 (hist)
Robert Montgomery Bird. The Broker of Bogota (dr)
_____. Calavar; or, the Knight of the Conquest
    (fic)
Henry Marie Brackenridge. Recollections of Persons and Places in the
    West (nar, des)
William Alexander Caruthers. The Cavalier of Virginia, to 1835 (fic)
_____. The Kentuckian in New York (fic)
Thomas Holley Chivers. Conrad and Eudora (po, dr)
James Fenimore Cooper. A Letter to His Countrymen (e)
George Washington Parke Custis. The Eighth of January (dr)
William Dunlap. History of the Rise and Progress of the Arts of De-
    sign in the United States, 2 vols (hist)

Asa Greene. The Perils of Pearl Street (fic)
Joseph C. Hart. Miriam Coffin; or, the Whale-Fishermen (fic)
Francis Scott Key. The Power of Literature and Its Connection with
    Religion (e)
William Leggett. Naval Stories (fic)
Cornelius Ambrosius Logan. Yankee Land; or, the Foundling of the
    Apple Orchard (dr)
Henry Junius Nott. Novelettes of a Traveller; or, Odds and Ends from
    the Knapsack of Thomas Singularity, Journeyman Printer, 2 vols
    (fic)
Albert Pike. Prose Sketches and Poems, Written in the Western Coun-
    try (nar, fic, po)
Susan Ridley Sedgwick. Allan Prescott; or, the Fortunes of a New
    England Boy (fic)
William Gilmore Simms. Guy Rivers (fic)
William Leete Stone. Tales and Sketches, 2 vols (fic, nar, des)

                              1835

BIRTHS

    Lyman Abbott
    Charles Francis Adams the younger
    Phillips Brooks
    Andrew Carnegie
    Samuel Langhorne Clemens (Mark Twain)
    Augusta Jane Evans
    Adah Isaacs Menken
    Ellen Louise Chandler Moulton
    Harriet Elizabeth Prescott Spofford
    William Osborn Stoddard
    Celia Laighton Thaxter
    Theodore Tilton
    Moses Coit Tyler

EVENTS

    New York Herald, to 1924 (per)
    Southern Literary Journal and Monthly Magazine, Charleston, South
        Carolina, to 1838 (per)
    The Western Messenger, Cincinnati, Ohio; Louisville, Kentucky, to
        1841 (per)

LITERATURE

    Jacob Abbott. The Rollo Series, to 1877 (fic)
    Amos Bronson Alcott. Record of a School, Exemplifying the General
        Principles of Spiritual Culture, ed. Elizabeth Peabody (e, nar)
    Robert Montgomery Bird. The Hawks of Hawk-Hollow (fic)
    _____. The Infidel; or, the Fall of Mexico (fic)
    Henry Charles Carey. Essay on the Rate of Wages (e)
    Robert Taylor Conrad. Jack Cade (dr)
    James Fenimore Cooper. The Monikens (sat)
    Joseph Rodman Drake. The Culprit Fay and Other Poems (po)
    Theodore Sedgwick Fay. Norman Leslie: A Tale of the Present Times

(fic)
William Davis Gallagher. Erato, 3 vols, to 1837 (po)
Henry William Herbert. The Brothers: A Tale of the Fronde (fic)
Washington Irving. A Tour on the Prairies (nar, trav)
John Pendleton Kennedy. Horse-Shoe Robinson (fic)
Ralph Ingersoll Lockwood. The Insurgents (fic)
Cornelius Ambrosius Logan. The Wag of Maine (dr)
Augustus Baldwin Longstreet. Georgia Scenes, Characters, and Inci-
    dents (fic)
Edgar Allan Poe. Politian, a Tragedy, to 1836 (po, dr)
Catharine Maria Sedgwick. The Linwoods; or, Sixty Years Since in
    America (fic)
William Gilmore Simms. The Partisan (fic)
_____. The Yemassee (fic)
William Leete Stone. The Mysterious Bridal and Other Tales, 3 vols
    (fic)
Frederick William Thomas. Clinton Bradshaw; or, the Adventures of a
    Lawyer (fic)
Daniel Pierce Thompson. May Martin; or, the Money Diggers (fic)
_____. Timothy Peacock, Esq. (sat)
Nathaniel Parker Willis. Melanie and Other Poems (po)
_____. Pencillings by the Way, 3 vols (nar)
Joseph Emerson Worcester. A Gross Literary Fraud Exposed (e)

1836

BIRTHS

    Henry Mills Alden
    Thomas Bailey Aldrich
    Francis Brett Harte
    Fitz Hugh Ludlow
    Jane Marsh Parker
    Mary Spear Tiernan
    William Winter

DEATHS

    Hannah Mater Crocker

EVENTS

    Battle of the Alamo, San Antonio, Texas
    Mount Holyoke College, South Hadley, Massachusetts (f)
    Philadelphia Public Ledger, to 1934 (per)
    Transcendental Club, Concord, Massachusetts, to 1844

LITERATURE

    Amos Bronson Alcott. Conversations with Children on the Gospels,
        2 vols, to 1837 (nar, e)
    _____. The Doctrine and Discipline of Human Culture
        (e)
    William Apes. Eulogy on King Philip (e)
    Robert Montgomery Bird. Metamora (dr)

_____. Sheppard Lee (fic)
Orestes Augustus Brownson. New Views of Christianity, Society, and
    the Church (e)
Elizabeth Margaret Chandler. Essays, Philosophical and Moral (e)
_____. Poetical Works (pub)
Lydia Maria Child. Philothea (fic)
William Dunlap. Thirty Years Ago; or, the Memoirs of a Water Drin-
    ker (fic)
Ralph Waldo Emerson. Nature (e)
Richard Hildreth. The Slave; or, Memoirs of Archy Moore (fic)
Oliver Wendell Holmes. Poems (pub)
Joseph Holt Ingraham. Lafitte: The Pirate of the Gulf (fic)
Washington Irving and Pierre Munro Irving. Astoria (hist)
William Holmes McGuffey. Eclectic Readers, 6 vols, to 1857 (ed, ref)
James Kirke Paulding. The Book of St. Nicholas (fic)
Susan Ridley Sedgwick. The Young Emigrants (juv fic)
William Gilmore Simms. Mellichampe (fic)
Richard Penn Smith. The Actress of Padua (dr)
_____. The Actress of Padua and Other Tales (fic)
_____. The Daughter (dr)
Frederick William Thomas. East and West (fic)
Nathaniel Beverley Tucker. George Balcombe (fic)
_____. The Partisan Leader (fic)
John Greenleaf Whittier. Mogg Megone (po)
Nathaniel Parker Willis. Inklings of Adventure (nar)

1837

BIRTHS

    Daniel Garrison Brinton
    John Burroughs
    Edward Eggleston
    William Dean Howells
    Henry Martyn Robert

DEATHS

    Thomas Green Fessenden
    Asa Greene
    Abiel Holmes
    Henry Junius Nott
    Tabitha Gilman Tenney

EVENTS

    Baltimore Sun (per, f)
    The Gentleman's Magazine, Philadelphia, to 1840 (per)
    Hartford Daily Courant, to 1887 (per)
    New Orleans Picayune, to 1914 (per)
    United States Magazine and Democratic Review, Washington, D.C., to
        1849 (per)
    Martin Van Buren, 8th President of the United States, to 1841

LITERATURE

Nathaniel Harrington Bannister. England's Iron Days (dr)
Catharine Esther Beecher. An Essay on Slavery and Abolitionism (e)
Robert Montgomery Bird. Nick of the Woods; or, the Jibbenainosay
    (fic)
Henry Charles Carey. Principles of Political Economy, 3 vols, to
    1840 (e)
Thomas Holley Chivers. Nacoochee (po, e)
James Fenimore Cooper. Gleanings in Europe, to 1838 (des, e, nar)
William Dunlap. History of New York for Schools (e, hist)
Ralph Waldo Emerson. The American Scholar (e)
Nathaniel Hawthorne. Peter Parley's Universal History (ed)
_____. Twice-Told Tales, to 1842 (fic)
John Treat Irving. The Hawk Chief: A Tale of the Indian Country
    (fic)
Washington Irving. The Adventures of Captain Bonneville, U.S.A.
    (fic)
Robert Dale Owen. Pocahontas (dr)
Epes Sargent. The Bride of Genoa (dr)
_____. Velasco (dr)
Frederick William Shelton. The Trollopiad; or, Traveling Gentlemen
    in America (po)
Richard Penn Smith. The Bravo (dr)
William Joseph Snelling. The Rat-Trap; or, Cogitations of a Convict
    in the House of Correction (nar)
William Ware. Letters from Palmyra (fic)
John Greenleaf Whittier. Poems Written during the Progress of the
    Abolition Question, 1830-1838 (po)
Nathaniel Parker Willis. Bianca Visconti (po)

1838

BIRTHS

Henry Brooks Adams
John Wilkes Booth
John Augustin Daly
John Milton Hay
Thomas Raynesford Lounsbury
Edward Payson Roe
Abram Joseph Ryan
Francis Hopkinson Smith
Albion Winegar Tourgee

DEATHS

Nathaniel Bowditch
Peter Irving

EVENTS

The Boston Quarterly Review, to 1842 (per)
Duke University (f)
Transactions and Proceedings of the American Philosophical Society
    (per, f)

LITERATURE

Robert Montgomery Bird. Peter Pilgrim; or, a Rambler's Recollections (fic)
James Fenimore Cooper. The American Democrat (e)
_____. Chronicles of Cooperstown (nar)
_____. Home As Found (fic)
_____. Homeward Bound (fic)
Emma Catherine Embury. Constance Latimer; or, the Blind Girl (fic)
Joseph Holt Ingraham. Burton; or, the Sieges (fic)
John Pendleton Kennedy. Rob of the Bowl (fic)
James Russell Lowell. Class Poem (po)
George Pope Morris. The Deserted Bride and Other Poems (po)
Joseph Clay Neal. Charcoal Sketches; or, Scenes in a Metropolis (sat)
Laughton Osborn. The Vision of Rubeta (fic)
Edgar Allan Poe. The Narrative of Arthur Gordon Pym, of Nantucket (fic)
William Hickling Prescott. The History of Ferdinand and Isabella, 3 vols (hist, biog)
John Sanderson. Sketches of Paris: In Familiar Letters to His Friends (nar, des)
William Gilmore Simms. Pelayo (fic)
_____. Richard Hurdis (fic)
William Ware. Probus (fic)
John Greenleaf Whittier. Poems (pub)

1839

BIRTHS

George Cary Eggleston
James A. Herne
Olive Logan
James Ryder Randall

DEATHS

Matthew Carey
Thomas Cooper
William Dunlap
William Leggett

EVENTS

Graham's Magazine, Philadelphia, to 1858 (per)
The Liberty Bell, Boston, to 1858 (misc)
New World, ed. Park Benjamin, to 1845 (per)

LITERATURE

Delia Salter Bacon. The Bride of Fort Edward (dr)
Robert Montgomery Bird. The Adventures of Robin Day (fic)
Charles Frederick Briggs. The Adventures of Harry Franco (fic)
James Gillespie Burney. Letters on the Political Obligations of Abo-

litionists (e)
James Fenimore Cooper. History of the Navy (hist)
Rufus Dawes. Miscellaneous Poems (po)
_____. Nix's Mate (fic)
William Dunlap. History of the New Netherlands, Province of New York, and State of New York, 2 vols, to 1840 (hist)
Theodore Sedgwick Fay. Sydney Clifton; or, Vicissitudes in Both Hemispheres (fic)
Charles Follen. Poems (po, pub)
James Ewell Heath. Whigs and Democrats (fic)
James Abraham Hillhouse. Demetria (po, dr)
Joseph Stevens Jones. The People's Lawyer (dr)
Henry Wadsworth Longfellow. Hyperion (fic, po)
_____. Voices of the Night (po)
Cornelius Mathews. Behemoth: A Legend of the Mound-Builders (fic)
George Pope Morris. The Little Frenchman and His Water Lots, with Other Sketches of the Times (nar, fic)
John Lothrop Motley. Morton's Hope (fic)
Edgar Allan Poe. The Fall of the House of Usher (fic)
William Gilmore Simms. The Damsel of Darien (fic)
Daniel Pierce Thompson. The Green Mountain Boys (fic)
Jones Very. Essays and Poems (pub)
Nathaniel Parker Willis. A L'Abri; or, the Tent Pitch'd (nar)
_____. Tortesa the Usurer (po)

1840

BIRTHS

Adolph Francis Alphonse Bandelier
Thomas Davidson
Edward Sylvester Ellis
Ralph Olmstead Keeler
George Wilbur Peck
John Clark Ridpath
Constance Fenimore Woolson

DEATHS

Timothy Flint
Charles Follen
Hannah Webster Foster

EVENTS

The Dial (New England Transcendentalists), Boston, to 1844 (per)
National Anti-Slavery Standard, New York, to 1872 (per)

LITERATURE

Abagail Adams. Letters of Mrs. Adams (nar, pub)
Amos Bronson Alcott. Orphic Sayings (pub)
Albert Brisbane. Social Destiny of Man (e)
Orestes Augustus Brownson. Charles Elwood, or the Infidel Converted (fic)

Philip Pendleton Cooke. Florence Vane (po)
James Fenimore Cooper. Mercedes of Castile (fic)
_____. The Pathfinder (fic)
Richard Henry Dana, Jr. Two Years before the Mast (nar)
Theodore Sedgwick Fay. The Countess Ida: A Tale of Berlin (fic)
Charles Fenno Hoffman. Greyslaer (fic)
Washington Irving. Oliver Goldsmith (biog)
Joseph Stevens Jones. The Carpenter of Rouen (dr)
John Pendleton Kennedy. Quodlibet: Containing Some Annals Thereof
    by Solomon Second-Thoughts, Schoolmaster (sat)
Cornelius Ambrosius Logan. The Vermont Wool Dealer (dr)
Cornelius Mathews. The Politicians (dr)
Frances Sargent Locke Osgood. The Casket of Fate (po)
Edgar Allan Poe. Tales of the Grotesque and Arabesque (fic)
Josiah Quincy the younger. The History of Harvard University, 2 vols
    (hist)
William Gilmore Simms. Border Beagles (fic)
Frederick William Thomas. Howard Pickney (fic)
Noah Webster. An American Dictionary of the English Language, 2 vols
    rev ed (ref)
John Greenleaf Whittier. Moll Pitcher, rev ed (po)
_____. Moll Pitcher and the Minstrel Girl (po)
Nathaniel Parker Willis. American Scenery, 2 vols (nar)
_____. Loiterings of Travel, 3 vols (trav)

1841

BIRTHS

Charles Heber Clark
Cincinnatus Hiner Miller (Joaquin Miller)
Edward Rowland Sill
George Alfred Townsend

DEATHS

William Austin
James Abraham Hillhouse
Grenville Mellen

EVENTS

Arcturus, Boston, to 1842 (per)
Brook Farm Cooperative Community, West Roxbury, Massachusetts, to
    1847
The Brooklyn Eagle, to 1955 (per)
Fordham University, New York (f)
William Henry Harrison, 9th Prrsident of the United States, to 1841
The Ladies' Repository, Cincinnati, Ohio, to 1876 (per)
New York Tribune, to 1924 (per)
John Tyler, 10th President of the United States, to 1845

LITERATURE

Washington Allston. Monaldi (fic)

John Bidwell. Echoes of the Past (nar)
William Byrd II. History of the Dividing Line (nar, pub)
_____. A Journey to the Land of Eden (nar, pub)
_____. A Progress to the Mines (nar, pub)
James Fenimore Cooper. The Deerslayer (fic)
Richard Henry Dana, Jr. The Seaman's Friend (e, ref)
Ralph Waldo Emerson. Essays (pub)
Sumner Lincoln Fairfield. Poems and Prose Writings (pub)
William Davis Gallagher. Selections from the Poetical Literature of
    the West (ed)
Nathaniel Hawthorne. Famous Old People (juv)
_____. Grandfather's Chair (juv)
_____. Liberty Tree (juv)
John Beauchamp Jones. Wild Western Scenes (fic)
Henry Wadsworth Longfellow. Ballads and Other Poems (po)
James Russell Lowell. A Year's Life and Other Poems (po)
Frances Sargent Locke Osgood. The Poetry of Flowers and Flowers of
    Poetry (po)
Edgar Allan Poe. The Murders in the Rue Morgue (fic)
William Gilmore Simms. The Kinsmen (fic)
William Ware. Julian (fic)

1842

BIRTHS

Charles Follen Adams
Ambrose Gwinett Bierce
Edwin Lassetter Bynner
Charles Edward Carryl
Ina Donna Coolbrith
John Habberton
Bronson Crocker Howard
Sidney Lanier
Charles Bertrand Lewis (M. Quad)
James Morrison Steele MacKaye

DEATHS

William Ellery Channing the elder
McDonald Clarke
Samuel Woodworth

EVENTS

Boston Miscellany of Literature and Fashion, to 1843 (per)
Hopedale Community, Milford, Massachusetts, to 1856
Lowell Offering, Lowell Massachusetts, to 1845 (per)
New Mirror, New York, to 1844 (per)
The Southern Quarterly Review, Charleston, South Carolina, to 1857
    (per)

LITERATURE

John Bidwell. A Journey to California (nar, trav)

Charles Timothy Brooks. Songs and Ballads (trans)
Orestes Augustus Brownson. The Mediatorial Life of Jesus (biog, e)
William Cullen Bryant. The Fountain (po)
James Fenimore Cooper. The Two Admirals (fic)
_____. Wing-and-Wing (fic)
Nathaniel Hawthorne. Biographical Stories for Children (juv)
Charles Fenno Hoffman. The Vigil of Faith (po)
John Trent Irving (John Quod). The Quod Correspondence (fic)
Henry Wadsworth Longfellow. Poems on Slavery (po)
Cornelius Mathews. The Career of Puffer Hopkins (fic)
Edgar Allan Poe. The Masque of the Red Death (fic)
William Gilmore Simms. Beauchampe (fic)
Elizabeth Oakes Smith. The Western Captive (fic)
Alfred Billings Street. The Burning of Schenectady (po)
Walt Whitman. Franklin Evans; or, the Inebriate: A Tale of the
    Times (fic)

1843

BIRTHS

    Bartley Campbell
    Constance Cary Harrison
    Prentiss Ingraham
    Henry James
    Frank Hitchcock Murdoch
    Charles Warren Stoddard

DEATHS

    Washington Allston
    Francis Scott Key
    Noah Webster

EVENTS

    The Eclectic Museum, New York, Philadelphia, Boston, to 1844 (per)
    Miss Leslie's Magazine, to 1844 (per)
    The Pioneer, to 1843 (per)
    The Present, to 1844 (per)

LITERATURE

    Timothy Shay Arthur. Temperance Tales (fic)
    Maria Gowen Brooks. Idomen; or, the Vale of Yumuri (fic)
    William Ellery Channing the younger. Poems (pub)
    James Fenimore Cooper. Le Mouchoir (fic)
    _____. Ned Myers (fic, biog)
    _____. Wyandotte (fic)
    Thomas Dunn English. Ben Bolt (po)
    Theodore Sedgwick Fay. Hoboken (fic)
    Baynard Rush Hall (Robert Carlton). The New Purchase; or, Seven and
        a Half Years in the Far West (fic)
    Henry Wadsworth Longfellow. The Spanish Student (po, dr)
    Cornelius Mathews. Poems on Man in His Various Aspects under the

American Republic (po)
Joseph Clay Neal. In Town and About (nar, sat)
Thomas Low Nichols. Ellen Ramsay (fic)
James Gates Percival. The Dream of a Day (po)
John Pierpont. The Anti-Slavery Poems of John Pierpont (po, pub)
Edgar Allan Poe. The Rationale of Verse (e)
William Hickling Prescott. History of the Conquest of Mexico, 3 vols
    (hist)
Ann Sophia Stephens (Jonathan Slick). High Life in New York (fic)
William Tappan Thompson. Major Jones's Courtship, to 1844 (fic)
John Greenleaf Whittier. Lays of My Home and Other Poems (po)
_____. The Song of the Vermonters (po)

1844

BIRTHS

George Washington Cable
Richard Watson Gilder
Charles King
Harriet Mulford Stone Lothrop (Margaret Sidney)
John Boyle O'Reilly
James Maurice Thompson
Elizabeth Stuart Phelps Ward

DEATHS

Nicholas Biddle
Sumner Lincoln Fairfield
John Sanderson
Margaret Bayard Smith
William Leete Stone
James Thacher
Caroline Matilda Warren

EVENTS

Bethel (Missouri) Community, to 1880
Brownson's Quarterly Review, Boston, to 1875 (per)
The Christian Citizen, to 1851 (per)
Columbian Lady's and Gentleman's Magazine, New York, to 1849 (per)
The Eclectic Magazine, New York, Philadelphia, Boston, to 1907 (per)
Evening Mirror, New York, to 1860 (per)
The Ladies' Magazine, to 1845 (per)
The Living Age, Philadelphia, to 1941 (per)

LITERATURE

Nathaniel Harrington Bannister. Putnam (dr)
Charles Frederick Briggs. Working a Passage (fic)
William Cullen Bryant. The White-Footed Deer (po)
Charles James Cannon. Mora Carmody; or, Woman's Influence (fic)
James Freeman Clarke (ed). Hymn Book for the Church of the Disciples
    to 1852 (po)
James Fenimore Cooper. Afloat and Ashore (fic)

_____. Miles Wallingford (fic)
Charles Fenno Hoffman. The Echo (po)
William Howe Cuyler Hosmer. Yonnondio, or Warriors of the Genesee
     (po)
Sarah Anna Lewis. Records of the Heart (po)
George Lippard. The Monks of Monk Hall (dr)
James Russell Lowell. Poems (pub)
Clement Clark Moore. Poems (pub)
Anna Cora Mowatt. The Fortune Hunter (fic)
Joseph Clay Neal. Peter Ploddy and Other Oddities (sat)
Thomas Low Nichols. The Lady in Black (fic)
Edgar Allan Poe. The Raven (po)
Susan Ridley Sedgwick. Alida; or, Town and Country (fic0
Ann Sophia Stephens. Alice Copley: A Tale of Queen Mary's Time (fic)
James Bayard Taylor. Ximena (po)
John Greenleaf Whittier. Ballads and Other Poems (po)
_____. Miscellaneous Poems (pub)

                         1845

BIRTHS

     Will Carleton
     John Ames Mitchell
     John Banister Tabb

DEATHS

     Maria Gowen Brooks
     James McHenry

EVENTS

     American Whig Review, to 1852 (per)
     Arthur's Ladies Magazine, to 1846 (per)
     Broadway Journal, New York, to 1846 (per)
     Dwight's American Magazine, to 1852 (per)
     The Harbinger, Brook Farm and New York, to 1849 (per)
     The National Police Gazette, New York, to 1937 (per)
     James Knox Polk, 11th President of the United States, to 1849
     The Southern and Western Monthly Magazine and Review, Charleston,
          South Carolina, to 1864 (per)

LITERATURE

     Emerson Bennett. The League of the Miami (fic)
     William Alexander Caruthers. The Knights of the Horseshoe (fic)
     Thomas Holley Chivers. The Lost Pleiad (po)
     James Fenimore Cooper. The Chainbearer (fic)
     _____. Satanstoe (fic)
     Alexander Hill Everett. Essays, Critical and Miscellaneous, to 1846
          (pub)
     Charles Etienne Arthur Gayarre. The School for Politics (fic)
     Henry Beck Hirst. The Coming of Monmouth (po)
     Johnson Jones Hooper. Some Adventures of Captain Simon Suggs, Late

of the Tallapoosa Volunteers (fic)
Sylvester Judd. Margaret (fic)
Henry Wadsworth Longfellow. The Belfry of Bruges and Other Poems
   (po)
William Wilberforce Lord. Poems (pub)
Anna Cora Mowatt. Evelyn; or, a Heart Unmasked (fic)
_____. Fashion (dr)
Thomas Low Nichols. Raffle for a Wife (fic)
Edgar Allan Poe. The Imp of the Perverse (fic)
_____. The Purloined Letter (fic)
_____. The Raven and Other Poems (po, pub)
_____. The Pit and the Pendulum (fic)
_____. Tales (if, pub)
William Hickling Prescott. Biographical and Critical Miscellanies
   (biog, e)
Epes Sargent. Change Makes Change (sat)
_____. Fleetwood; or, the Stain of Birth (fic)
William Gilmore Simms. Count Julian (fic)
_____. Helen Halsey; or, the Swamp State of Conela-
   chita (fic)
_____. The Wigwam and the Cabin, to 1846 (fic)
William Tappan Thompson. Chronicles of Pineville (fic)
John Greenleaf Whittier. The Stranger in Lowell (po)
Nathaniel Parker Willis. Dashes at Life with a Free Pencil (fic)

1846

BIRTHS

   Anna Katharine Green
   Julian Hawthorne
   Lloyd Mifflin
   Edward Noyes Westcott

DEATHS

   William Alexander Caruthers
   Sarah Wentworth Morton
   John Pickering

EVENTS

   De Bow's Review, New Orleans; Columbia, South Carolina; Nashville,
      Tennessee; Washington, D.C., to 1880 (per)
   The Home Journal, New York, to 1901 (per)

LITERATURE

   Catharine Esther Beecher. The Evils Suffered by American Women and
      Children (e)
   John Ross Browne. Etchings of a Whaling Cruise (trav)
   James Fenimore Cooper. Lives of Distinguished American Naval Offi-
      cers (biog)
   _____. The Redskins (fic)
   Nathaniel Hawthorne. Mosses from an Old Manse (fic)

Henry Williams Herbert (Frank Forester). My Shooting Box (fic)
Joseph Holt Ingraham. Leisler; or, the Rebel and the King's Man
    (fic)
George Lippard. Blanche of Brandywine (fic)
Cornelius Mathews. Witchcraft, or the Martyrs of Salem (dr, po)
Samuel Joseph May. The Rights and Condition of Women (ser)
Herman Melville. Typee (fic)
Henry Morford. The Rest of Don Juan (po)
William Munford. The Iliad (trans, pub)
James Kirke Paulding. The Old Continental; or, the Price of Liberty
    (fic)
Edgar Allan Poe. The Cask of Amontillado (fic)
_____. The Philosophy of Composition (e)
John Godfrey Saxe. Progress: A Satirical Poem (po)
Ann Sophia Stephens. The Diamond Necklace, and Other Tales (fic)
Henry Theodore Tuckerman. Thoughts on the Poets (e)
John Greenleaf Whittier. Voices of Freedom (po)

1847

BIRTHS

John Peter Altgeld
Henry Augustus Beers
Borden Parker Browne
Mary Hartwell Catherwood
John Wallace Crawford
Edgar Fawcett
Mary Hallock Foote
Archibald Clavering Gunter
Arthur Sherburne Hardy
Blanche Willis Howard
Julia A. Moore
Joseph Pulitzer

DEATHS

Nathaniel Harrington Bannister
Alexander Hill Everett
Joseph Clay Neal
Richard Henry Wilde

EVENTS

Century Association, New York (f)
Chicago Tribune (per, f)
The Literary World, New York, to 1853 (per)
The Massachusetts Quarterly Review, to 1850 (per)
The Merchants' Ledger, New York, to 1855 (per)
National Era, Washington, D.C., to 1860 (per)
New England Offering, Lowell, Massachusetts, to 1850 (per)
North Star, Rochester, New York, to 1864 (per)
The Union Magazine, New York, to 1852 (per)

LITERATURE

Alfred W. Arrington. The Desperadoes of the Southwest (fic)
Charles Frederick Briggs. The Trippings of Tom Pepper, 2 vols, to
    1850 (fic)
John Brougham. Metamora; or, the Last of the Pollywoags (dr)
William Wells Brown. Narrative (auto)
Horace Bushnell. Christian Nurture (e)
William Ellery Channing the younger. Poems, Second Series (pub)
Philip Pendleton Cooke. Froissart's Ballads (po)
George Copway. Life, History, and Travels (auto, nar)
Ralph Waldo Emerson. Poems (pub)
Harriet Farley. Shells from the Strand of the Sea of Genius (e, fic)
Charles Fenno Hoffman. Love's Calendar (po)
Emily Chubbuck Judson. Alderbrook (po, fic)
_____. Allen Lucas, the Self-Made Man (fic)
George Lippard. Legends of Mexico (fic)
Henry Wadsworth Longfellow. Evangeline (po)
Herman Melville. Omoo (fic)
Anna Cora Mowatt. Armand, the Child of the People (dr, po)
James Kirke Paulding. The Bucktails; or, Americans in England (dr)
William Hickling Prescott. History of the Conquest of Peru, 2 vols
    (hist)
Epes Sargent. Songs of the Sea, with Other Poems (po)
William Wetmore Story. Poems (pub)
Daniel Pierce Thompson. Locke Amsden; or, the Schoolmaster (fic)

1848

BIRTHS

    Brooks Adams
    Frances Courtenay Baylor
    Hjalmar Hjorth Boyesen
    John Vance Cheney
    Sarah Barnwell Elliot
    Joel Chandler Harris
    James Otis Kaler

DEATHS

    John Quincy Adams
    William Joseph Snelling

EVENTS

    The College of the City of New York (f)
    The Independent, New York, to 1928 (per)
    The Lily, to 1854 (per)
    Oneida Community, New York (est)
    University of Wisconsin, Madison (f)

LITERATURE

    John Quincy Adams. Poems of Religion and Society (po)
    Timothy Shay Arthur. Agnes; or, the Possessed: A Revelation of Mes-
        merism (fic)

Charlotte Mary Sanford Barnes. The Forest of Princes (dr)
_____ . Octavia Brigaldi (po, dr)
Emerson Bennett. Mike Fink (fic)
William Wells Brown. Anti-Slavery Harp (po)
Oliver Bell Bunce. The Morning of Life (dr)
Henry Charles Carey. The Past, the Present, and the Future (e)
Thomas Halley Chivers. Search after Truth; or, a New Revelation of
    the Psycho-Physiological Nature of Man (e)
James Fenimore Cooper. The Crater (fic)
_____ . Jack Tier (fic)
_____ . The Oak Openings (fic)
_____ . The Sea Lions (fic)
Joseph C. Hart. The Romance of Yachting (e)
Henry Beck Hirst. Endymion (po)
Eliza Leslie. Amelia, or a Young Lady of Vicissitudes (fic)
Sarah Anna Lewis. Child of the Sea and Other Poems (po)
James Russell Lowell. The Biglow Papers (po)
_____ . A Fable for Critics (po)
_____ . Poems : Second Series (po, pub)
_____ . The Vision of Sir Launfal (po)
Cornelius Mathews. Jacob Leisler (dr)
Peter Hamilton Myers. The First of the Knickerbockers (fic)
Joseph Clay Neal. Charcoal Sketches, Second Series (sat, pub)
Edgar Allan Poe. Eureka (po)
William Frederick Poole. Alphabetical Index to Subjects Treated in
    Periodicals (ref)
Elizabeth Oakes Smith. The Salamander: A Legend for Christmas (fic)
Daniel Pierce Thompson. Lucy Hosmer; or, the Guardian and the Ghost
    (fic)
_____ . The Shaker Lovers, and Other Tales (fic)
William Tappan Thompson. Major Jones's Sketches of Travel (fic)
William Ross Wallace. Alban the Pirate (po)
Charles Wilkins Webber. Old Hicks, the Guide (fic)
Edwin Percy Whipple. Essays and Reviews, 2 vols, to 1849 (e)

1849

BIRTHS

    James Lane Allen
    Frances Eliza Hidgson Burnett
    Thomas Allibone Janvier
    Sarah Orne Jewett
    Emma Lazarus
    Katherine Sherwood Bonner MacDonald
    James Whitcomb Riley
    Ruth McEnery Stuart

DEATHS

    Edgar Allan Poe

EVENTS

    The Spirit of the Age, New York, to 1850 (per)

Zachary Taylor, 12the President of the United States, to 1850

LITERATURE

Emerson Bennett. Leni-Leoti (fic)
_____. Prairie Flower (fic)
George Henry Boker. Calaynos (dr, po)
John Brougham. Temptation, or the Irish Immigrant (dr)
Horace Bushnell. God in Christ (e)
Alice Cary and Phoebe Cary. Poems (po, pub)
William Ellery Channing the younger. The Woodman (po)
Ralph Waldo Emerson. Addresses and Lectures (e)
Henry William Herbert (Frank Forester). The Deerstalkers (fic)
Henry Beck Hirst. The Penance of Roland (po)
Washington Irving. A Book of the Hudson (fic, e)
_____. Mahomet and His Successors, 2 vols, to 1850
   (biog)
John Beauchamp Jones. The Western Merchant (fic)
Cornelius Ambrosius Logan. Chloroform; or, New York a Hundred Years
   Hence (dr)
Henry Wadsworth Longfellow. Kavanagh (fic)
_____. The Seaside and Fireside (po)
James Russell Lowell. Poems, 2 vols (pub)
William Starbuck Mayo. Kaloolah; or, Journeyings to the Djebel Kum-
   ri (fic)
Herman Melville. Mardi (fic)
_____. Redburn (fic)
John Lothrop Motley. Merry Mount (fic)
Peter Hamilton Myers. The Young Patroon (fic)
Francis Parkman. The Orgeon Trail (nar)
James Kirke Paulding. The Puritan and His Daughter (fic)
Charles Jacobs Peterson. Grace Dudley; or, Arnold at Saratoga (fic)
Edgar Allan Poe. Annabel Lee (po)
_____. The Bells (po)
Emma Dorothy Eliza Nevitte Southworth. Retribution (fic)
Alfred Billings Street. Frontenac (po)
James Bayard Taylor. Rhymes of Travel, Ballads and Poems (po)
Frederick William Thomas. Sketches of Character, and Tales Founded
   on Fact (e)
Henry David Thoreau. Civil Disobedience (e)
_____. A Week on the Concord and Merrimack Rivers
   (nar)
Henry Theodore Tuckerman. Characteristics of Literature (e)
Charles Wilkins Webber. The Gold Mines of Gila (fic)
John Greenleaf Whittier. Poems (pub)
Henry Augustus Wise. Los Gringos; or, an Inside View of Mexico and
   California (fic)

1850

BIRTHS

Herbert Baxter Adams
Arlo Bates
Edward Bellamy

Henry B. Brewster
Eugene Field
Alice French
Lafcadio Hearn
Joseph Hergesheimer
Henry Francis Keenan
Mary Noailles Murfree
Ella Wheeler Wilcox

DEATHS

Philip Pendleton Cooke
Frances Sargent Locke Osgood

EVENTS

Millard Fillmore, 13th Presedient of the United States, to 1853
Harper's Monthly Magazine, New York, to 1900 (per)
The International Monthly Magazaine of Literature, Art, and Science,
   New York, to 1852 (per)

LITERATURE

Charles Francis Adams the elder. The Works of John Adams, to 1856
   (ed, pub)
Washington Allston. Lectures on Art (e, pub)
Timothy Shay Arthur. The Debtor's Daughter; or, Life and Its Changes
   (fic)
George Henry Baker. The Betrothal (dr)
William Cullen Bryant. Letters of a Traveller, to 1859 (e)
Oliver Bell Bunce. Marco Bozzaris (dr)
Charles James Cannon. The Oath of Office (dr)
Joseph Beckham Cobb. The Creole; or, Siege of New Orleans (fic)
Walter Colton. Deck and Port (nar)
_____. Three Years in California (nar)
James Fenimore Cooper. The Ways of the Hour (fic)
Susan Fenimore Cooper. Rural Hours (nar)
George Copway. The Ojibway Conquest (po)
_____. Traditional History of the Ojibway Nation (hist)
Richard Henry Dana, Sr. Poems and Prose Writings, 2nd ed (pub)
Eliza Ann Dupuy. The Conspirator (fic)
Ralph Waldo Emerson. Representative Men (e)
Robert Hare. Standish the Puritan (fic)
Thomas Hastings. Devotional Hymns and Religious Poems (po, ed)
Nathaniel Hawthorne. The Scarlet Letter (fic)
Caroline Lee Withing Hentz. Linda (fic)
Sylvester Judd. Philo, and Evangeliad (po)
_____. Richard Edney and the Governor's Family (fic)
William Starbuck Mayo. The Berber (fic)
Herman Melville. White-Jacket (fic)
George Henry Miles. Mohammed, the Arabian Prophet (dr, po)
Donald Grant Mitchell. Reveries of a Bachelor (fic, e)
Peter Hamilton Myers. The King of the Hurons (fic)
Edgar Allan Poe. The Poetic Principle (e, pub)
Thomas Mayne Reid. The Rifle Rangers (fic)
John Godfrey Saxe. Humorous and Satirical Poems (pub)

Frederick William Shelton. Salander and the Dragon, a Romance of the Hartz Prison (fic)
Henry Theodore Tuckerman. The Optimist (e)
Edwin Percy Whipple. Lectures on Subjects Connected with Literature and Life (e)
John Greenleaf Whittier. Songs of Labor and Other Poems (po)
Nathaniel Parker Willis. Life, Here and There (fic)

5 *The Nineteenth Century:*
1851–1899

BIRTHS

William Crary Brownell
Kat O'Flaherty Chopin
Grace Elizabeth King
Albery Allson Whitman

DEATHS

John James Audubon
Walter Colton
James Fenimore Cooper
Mordecai Manuel Noah
Nathaniel Beverley Tucker

EVENTS

The Carpet-Bag, Boston, to 1853 (per)
Gleason's Pictorial Drawing-Room Companion, Boston, to 1854 (per)
The New York Times (per, est)
Northwestern University, Evanston, Illinois (f)

LITERATURE

Stephen Pearl Andrews. Cost the Limit of Price (e)
Benjamin Paul Blood. The Philosophy of Justice (e)
George Henry Boker. The World a Mask (dr)
Horace Bushnell. The Age of Homespun (des)
Thomas Holley Chivers. Eonchs of Ruby (po)
Joseph Beckham Cobb. Mississippi Scenes (nar, fic)
Sylvanus Cobb, Jr. The King's Talisman (fic)
George William Curtis. Nile Notes of a Howadji (trav)
Nathaniel Deering. Bozzaris (po, dr)
John William DeForest. History of the Indians of Connecticut (hist)
Augustine Joseph Hickey Duganne. Parnassus in Pillory (e)
Theodore Sedgwick Fay. Ulric; or, the Voices (po)
Charles Etienne Arthur Gayarre. History of Louisiana, 4 vols, to

1866 (hist)
Nathaniel Hawthorne. The House of Seven Gables (fic)
_____. The Snow-Image and Other Twice-Told Tales (fic)
Gideon Hiram Hollister. Mount Hope (fic)
Johnson Jones Hooper. The Widow Rugby's Husband. A Night at the Ugly
    Man's, and Other Tales of Alabama (fic)
Henry Wadsworth Longfellow. The Golden Legend (po, dr)
William Wilberforce Lord. Christ in Hades (po)
William Starbuck Mayo. Romance Dust from the Historic Placer (fic)
Herman Melville. Moby Dick; or, the Whale (fic)
Donald Grant Mitchell. Dream Life (e, fic)
Elizabeth Stuart Phelps. The Sunny Side; or, the Country Minister's
    Wife (fic)
Thomas Mayne Reid. The Scalp Hunters (fic)
William Gilmore Simms. Katharine Walton (fic)
Elizabeth Oakes Smith. Woman and Her Needs (e)
James Bayard Taylor. A Book of Romances, Lyrics, and Songs (po)
Daniel Pierce Thompson. The Rangers; or, the Tory's Daughter (fic)
Henry Theodore Tuckerman. Characteristics of Literature, rev ed (e)
_____. Poems (pub)
Frances Fuller Victor and Metta Victoria Victor. Poems of Sentiment
    and Imagination (po)
William Ross Wallace. Meditations in America and Other Poems (po)
Charles Dudley Warner. The Book of Eloquence (e)

1852

BIRTHS

    Nathan Haskell Dole
    Mary Eleanor Wilkins Freeman
    Robert Grant
    Edwin Charles Markham
    James Brander Matthews
    Henry Van Dyke
    Charles Erskine Scott Wood

DEATHS

    Hosea Ballou
    Junius Brutus Booth
    John Howard Payne
    Elizabeth Stuart Phelps
    William Ware

EVENTS

    American Geographical Society (f)
    Boston Public Library (f)
    Dwight's Journal of Music, Boston, to 1881 (per)
    The Golden Era, San Francisco, California, to 1893 (per)

LITERATURE

    William Wells Brown. My Three Years in Europe (nar, trav)

Alice Cary. Clovernook; or, Recollections of Our Neighborhood in the
   West (fic)
George William Curtis. The Howadji in Syria (trav)
                    . Lotus-Eating (nar)
Martin Robinson Delany. The Condition, Elevation, Emigration, and
   Destiny of the Colored People in the United States (e)
Mary Henderson Eastman. Aunt Phillis's Cabin; or, Southern Life As
   It Is (fic)
Harriet Farley. Happy Nights at Hazel Nook (e, fic)
Baynard Rush Hall. Frank Freeman's Barber Shop (fic)
Nathaniel Hawthorne. The Blithedale Romance (fic)
                  . A Wonder Book (fic)
Henry William Herbert (Frank Forester). The Quorndon Hounds; or, a
   Virginian at Melton Mowbray (fic)
Joseph Stevens Jones. The Silver Spoon (dr)
Herman Melville. Pierre (fic)
George Washington Miles. Hernando de Soto (dr)
Charles Jacobs Peterson. History of the United States Navy (hist)
Elizabeth Stuart Phelps. The Angel over the Right Shoulder (fic)
               . A Peep at Number Five (fic)
Richard Realf. Guesses at the Beautiful (po)
Thomas Mayne Reid. The Boy Hunters (fic)
Emma Dorothy Eliza Nevitte Southworth. The Curse of Clifton (fic)
Richard Henry Stoddard. Poems (pub)
Harriet Elizabeth Beecher Stowe. Uncle Tom's Cabin (fic)
Frederick William Thomas. An Autobiography of William Russell (fic)
Charles Wilkins Webber. Tales of the Southern Border (fic)

1853

BIRTHS

   Alice Morse Earle
   Ernest Francisco Fenollosa
   Edgar Watson Howe
   Robert Underwood Johnson
   Thomas Nelson Page
   Paul Meredith Potter
   Irwin Russell

DEATHS

   Sylvester Judd
   Cornelius Ambrosius Logan

EVENTS

   Antioch College, Yellow Springs, Ohio (f)
   Franklin Pierce, 14th President of the United States, to 1857
   Putnam's Monthly Magazine, New York, to 1857 (pub, per)

LITERATURE

   Joseph Glover Baldwin. The Flush Times of Alabama and Mississippi
      (nar, hist)

George Henry Boker. Leonor de Guzman (dr)
William Wells Brown. Clotelle; or, the President's Daughter (fic)
John Ross Browne. Yusef; or, a Crusade in the East (nar, trav)
George William Curtis. The Potiphar Papers (e)
Alonzo Delano. Pen-Knife Sketches, or Chips of the Old Blocks (fic)
Augustine Joseph Hickey Duganne. Art's True Mission in America (e)
──────────────────────. A Sound Literature the Safeguard of
  Our National Institutions (e)
Samuel Adams Hammett (Philip Paxton). A Stray Yankee in Texas (fic)
Nathaniel Hawthorne. Tanglewood Tales (fic, juv)
George Lippard. New York: Its Upper Ten and Lower Million (fic)
Frederick William Shelton. The Rector of St. Bardolph's (fic)
──────────────────────. Up the River (des)
William Gilmore Simms. The Sword and the Distaff (fic)
──────────────────────. Vasconselos (fic)
Harriet Elizabeth Beecher Stowe. A Key to Uncle Tom's Cabin (ref)
Henry Theodore Tuckerman. Leaves from the Diary of a Dreamer (nar,
  fic)
Sarah Helen Power Whitman. Hours of Life (po)
John Greenleaf Whittier. The Chapel of the Hermits and Other Poems
  (po)
──────────────────────. Poetical Works (pub)
Sara Payson Willis (Fanny Fern). Fern Leaves from Fanny's Portfolio
  (fic)

1854

BIRTHS

  Francis Marion Crawford
  Maud Howe Elliott
  Edith Matilda Thomas

DEATHS

  Robert Montgomery Bird
  John Davis
  James Athearn Jones
  Emily Chubbuck Judson (Fanny Forester)
  George Lippard
  Anne Newport Royall
  Richard Penn Smith

EVENTS

  Ballou's Pictorial Drawing-Room Companion, Boston, to 1859 (per)
  Chicago Times, to 1918 (per)
  United States Magazine, New York, to 1858 (per)

LITERATURE

  Louisa May Alcott. Flower Fables (fic)
  Adin Ballou. Practical Christian Socialism (e)
  Thomas Hart Benton. Thirty Years' View, to 1856 (auto)
  Timothy Shay Arthur. Ten Nights in a Barroom and What I Saw There

(fic)
Benjamin Paul Blood. The Bride of the Iconoclast (po)
Orestes Augustus Brownson. The Spirit-Rapper (fic)
James Freeman Clarke. The Christian Doctrine of Prayer (e)
John Esten Cooke. Leather Stocking and Silk (fic)
_____. The Virginia Comedians (fic)
Maria Susanna Cummins. The Lamplighter (fic)
Alonzo Delano. Life on the Plains and among the Diggings (nar)
William John Grayson. The Hireling and the Slave (po)
Sarah Josepha Buell Hale. Woman's Record (hist)
Caroline Lee Whiting Hentz. The Planter's Northern Bride (fic)
William Howe Cuyler Hosmer. Poetical Works, 2 vols (pub)
Julia Ward Howe. Passion Flowers (po)
John Beauchamp Jones. Freaks of Fortune; or, the History of Ned Lorn
    (fic)
Ellen Louise Chandler Moulton. This, That, and the Other (nar, fic,
    des)
John Neal. One Word More (e)
Fitz-James O'Brien. The Gentleman from Ireland (dr)
Albert Pike. Nugae (po)
Mary Hayden Green Pike. Ida May (fic)
Edmund Quincy. Wensley, a Story without a Moral (fic)
John Rollin Ridge. The Life and Adventures of Joaquin Murieta, the
    Celebrated California Bandit (fic)
Epes Sargent. The Priestess (dr)
William Gilmore Simms. The Scout (fic)
_____. Woodcraft (fic)
Elizabeth Oakes Smith. Bertha and Lily (fic)
_____. The Newsboy (fic)
Ann Sophia Stephens. Fashion and Famine (fic)
Harriet Elizabeth Beecher Stowe. Sunny Memories of Foreign Lands
    (nar, trav)
James Bayard Taylor. Poems of the Orient (po)
Mary Virginia Terhune. Alone (fic)
Henry David Thoreau. Slavery in Massachusetts (e)
_____. Walden; or Life in the Woods (nar)
John Greenleaf Whittier. A Sabbath Scene (po)
Brigham Young. Journal of Discourses, 26 vols, to 1886 (ser, pub)

1855

BIRTHS

    Oscar Fay Adams
    LeBaron Russell Briggs
    Henry Cuyler Bunner
    Harry Stillwell Edwards
    William Gillette
    Josiah Royce
    Edgar Evertson Saltus
    Frederic Jesup Stimson
    Edward Waterman Townsend
    George Edward Woodberry

DEATHS

Joseph C. Hart
Samuel Kettell
Sarah Sayward Barrell Keating Wood

EVENTS

New York Ledger, to 1903 (per)
The Saturday Club, Boston (f)

LITERATURE

Hew Ainslie. Scottish Songs, Ballads, and Poems (po)
Thomas Bailey Aldrich. The Bells (po)
Joseph Glover Baldwin. Party Leaders (e, hist)
George Bancroft. Literary and Historical Miscellanies (e)
John Bartlett. Familiar Quotations, 1st ed (ref)
George Henry Baker. Francesca da Rimini (dr, po)
John Brougham. Po-ca-hon-tas! or, Ye Gentle Savage (dr)
Thomas Bulfinch. The Age of Fable (hist)
Charles James Cannon. Ravellings from the Web of Life (fic)
Francis James Child (ed). The Works of Edmund Spenser, 5 vols (pub)
William Turner Coggleshall. Oakshaw (fic)
Augustine Joseph Hickey Duganne. Poetical Works (pub)
Evert Augustus Duyckinck and George Long Duyckinck. Cyclopaedia of
    American Literature (ref)
Augusta Jane Evans. A Tale of the Alamo (fic)
Samuel Adams Hammett (Philip Paxton). The Wonderful Adventures of
    Captain Priest (fic)
Paul Hamilton Hayne. Poems (pub)
Joseph Holt Ingraham. The Prince of the House of David (fic)
Washington Irving. Life of Washington, 5 vols, to 1859 (biog)
_____. Wolfert's Roost (fic, e)
Charles Godfrey Leland. Meister Karl's Sketch-Book (fic)
Henry Wadsworth Longfellow. The Song of Hiawatha (po)
Cornelius Mathews. False Pretences; or, Both Sides of Good Society
    (dr)
Herman Melville. Israel Potter (fic)
Ellen Louise Chandler Moulton. Juno Clifford (fic)
Mary Sergeant Nichols. Mary Lyndon; or, Revelations of a Life (fic)
Charles Jacobs Peterson. Kate Aylesford, a Story of the Refugees
    (fic)
William Hickling Prescott. History of the Reign of Philip the Second
    3 vols, to 1858 (hist)
Frederick William Shelton. Peeps from a Belfry; or, the Parish
    Sketch Book (des)
William Gilmore Simms. The Forayers (fic)
Emma Dorothy Eliza Nevitte Southworth. The Missing Bride (fic)
James Bayard Taylor. Poems of Home and Travel (po)
Walt Whitman. Leaves of Grass (po)
Sara Payson Willis (Fanny Fern). Ruth Hall (fic)
Henry Augustus Wise. Tales for the Marines (fic)

1856

BIRTHS

Lyman Frank Brown
Harriot Stanton Blatch
Louis Dembitz Brandeis
Henry Guy Carleton
Edward Channing
Harold Frederic
Frank Harris
Elbert Hubbard
Charles Major
Sarah Pratt McLean
Lizette Woodworth Reese
Mabel Loomis Todd
Kate Douglas Wiggin
Thomas Woodrow Wilson

DEATHS

Caroline Lee Whiting Hentz
Nicholas Marcellus Hentz
James Gates Percival
Charles Wilkins Webber

EVENTS

Aurora (Oregon) Community, to 1881
Porter's Spirit of the Times, New York, to 1861 (per)

LITERATURE

John Turvill Adams. The Lost Hunter (fic)
Richard Alsop. The Charms of Fancy (po, pub)
Alfred W. Arrington. The Rangers and Regulators of the Tanaha (fic)
Sidney Frances Bateman. Self (dr)
Thomas Hart Benton. Abridgement of the Debates of Congress, from
    1789 to 1856 (e, hist, ed)
John Bigelow. The Life of John Charles Fremont (biog)
George Henry Boker. Plays and Poems (pub)
Charles Timothy Brooks. Faust (trans)
George Henry Calvert. Introduction to Social Science (e)
Jeremiah Clemens. Bernard Lile (fic)
Frederick Swartwout Cozzens (Richard Haywarde). The Sparrowgrass
    Papers (e)
Christopher Pearse Cranch. The Last of the Huggermuggers (juv)
George William Curtis. Prue and I (e)
_____. The Duty of the American Scholar to Politics
    and the Times (e)
John William DeForest. Oriental Acquaintance: or, Letters from Syria
    (nar)
_____. Witching Times, to 1857 (fic)
Eliza Ann Dupuy. The Huguenot Exiles (fic)
William John Grayson. Chicora (po)
Alonzo Delano. Old Block's Sketch Book (fic, nar)
Ralph Waldo Emerson. English Traits (e)
Caroline Lee Whiting Hentz. Ernest Linwood (fic)
Mary Jane Hawes Holmes. Lena Rivers (fic)
William Wilberforce Lord. Andre (po)

Nathan Cook Meeker. The Adventures of Captain Armstrong (fic)
Herman Melville. Bartleby the Scrivener (fic)
_____. Benito Cereno (fic)
_____. The Piazza Tales (fic)
Horatio Franklin Moore. Songs and Ballads of the American Revolution
    (po, ed)
John Lothrop Motley. The Rise of the Dutch Republic, 3 vols (hist)
Anna Cora Mowatt. Mimic Life (nar)
Joseph Clay Neal. The Misfortunes of Peter Faber, and Other Sketches
    (sat, nar, pub)
Francis Parkman. Vassall Morton (fic)
Mary Hayden Green Pike. Caste (fic)
Margaret Junkin Preston. Silverwood: A Book of Memories (nar)
Thomas Mayne Reid. The Quadroon (dr)
William Gilmore Simms. Charlemont (fic)
_____. Eutaw (fic)
Harriet Elizabeth Beecher Stowe. Dred: A Tale of the Great Dismal
    Swamp (fic)
James Bayard Taylor. Poems (pub)
Lydia Louise Ann Very. Poems (pub)
Walt Whitman. Leaves of Grass, 2nd ed (po)
John Greenleaf Whittier. The Panorama and Other Poems (po)

1857

BIRTHS

Gertrude Franklin Atherton
Alice Brown
Samuel McCord Crothers
Frank Hamilton Cushing
Clarence Seward Darrow
Margaretta Wade Campbell Deland
Henry Blake Fuller
Emerson Hough
James Gibbons Huneker
Thomas William Lawson
Charles Monroe Sheldon
Frank Lebby Stanton
Ida Minerva Tarbell
Augustus Thomas

DEATHS

James Gillespie Burney
George Washington Parke Custis

EVENTS

Atlantic Monthly, Boston (per, f)
James Buchanan, 15th President of the United States, to 1861
Harper's Weekly, New York, to 1916 (per)
Russell's Magazine, Charleston, South Carolina, to 1860 (per)

LITERATURE

Delia Salter Bacon. Philosophy of the Plays of Shakespeare Unfolded
    (e)
Dion Boucicault. The Poor of New York (dr)
John Brougham. Columbus (dr)
Orestes Augustus Brownson. The Convert (auto)
Oliver Bell Bunce. Love in '76 (dr)
Peter Cartwright. Autobiography (pub)
Philip St. George Cooke. Scenes and Adventures in the Army (nar)
Christopher Pearse Cranch. Kobboltozo (juv)
Maria Susanna Cummins. Mabel Vaughan (fic)
Alonzo Delano. A Live Woman in the Mines (dr)
Paul Hamilton Hayne. Sonnets and Other Poems (pub)
Josiah Gilbert Holland. The Bay-Path (fic)
Francis Scott Key. Poems (pub)
Mirabeau Buonaparte Lamar. Verse Memorials (po)
James Lawson. Poems (pub)
Charles Godfrey Leland. Hans Breitmann's Party (fic)
Fitz Hugh Ludlow. The Hasheesh Eater (nar, fic)
Alexander Beaufort Meek. Songs and Poems of the South (po)
Herman Melville. The Confidence Man (fic)
Anna Cora Mowatt. Twin Roses (nar)
Catharine Maria Sedgwick. Married or Single? (fic)
Richard Henry Stoddard. Songs of the Summer (po)
Daniel Pierce Thompson. Gaut Gurley; or, the Trappers of Umbabog
    (fic)
Mary Ashley Van Voorhis Townsend. The Brother Clerks (fic)
John Townsend Trowbridge. Neighbor Jackwood (fic)
John Greenleaf Whittier. The Poetical Works, 2 vols (pub)
                        . The Sycamores (po)
Nathaniel Parker Willis. Paul Fane (fic)

1858

BIRTHS

    Franz Boas
    Charles Waddell Chesnutt
    Hiram Martin Chittenden
    Sam Walter Foss
    William Nathaniel Harben
    Edward Mandell House
    Alfred Henry Lewis (Dan Quin)
    John Trotwood Moore
    Agnes Repplier

DEATHS

    James Nelson Barker
    Thomas Hart Benton
    Thomas Holley Chivers
    Joseph Beckham Cobb
    Robert Taylor Conrad
    Robert Hare
    Henry William Herbert
    Eliza Leslie

Ralph Ingersoll Lockwood

EVENTS

Saturday Press, New York, to 1860 (per)

LITERATURE

Samuel Austin Allibone. A Critical Dictionary of English Literature
   and British and American Authors, 3 vols, to 1871 (ref)
John Brougham. The Mustard Ball; or, Love at the Academy (dr)
William Wells Brown. The Escape (dr)
Thomas Bulfinch. The Age of Chivalry (hist)
Horace Bushnell. Nature and the Supernatural (e)
Henry Charles Carey. The Principles of Social Science, 3 vols, to
   1859 (e)
Peter Cartwright. Backwoods Preacher (auto, nar)
William Ellery Channing the younger. Near Home (po)
Joseph Beckham Cobb. Leisure Labors (e)
John William DeForest. European Acquaintance: Being Sketches of
   People (nar)
James Thomas Fields. A Few Verses for a Few Friends (po)
William John Grayson. The Country (po)
Samuel Adams Hammett (Philip Paxton). Piney Woods Tavern, or Sam
   Slick in Texas (fic)
Josiah Gilbert Holland. Bitter-Sweet (po)
Oliver Wendell Holmes. The Autocrat of the Breakfast Table (e, po)
_____. The Deacon's Masterpiece; or, the Wonderful
   One Hoss Shay (po)
Johnson Jones Hooper. Dog and Gun, a Few Loose Chapters on Shooting
   (fic)
John Beauchamp Jones. The War Path (fic)
Henry Wadsworth Longfellow. The Courtship of Miles Standish (po)
Robert Traill Spence Lowell. The New Priest in Conception (fic)
John Gorham Palfrey. History of New England, 5 vols, to 1890 (hist)
Mary Hayden Green Pike. Agnes (fic)
William Tappan Thompson. Scenes of Georgia (fic)

1859

BIRTHS

Andy Adams
Irving Addison Bacheller
David Belasco
Solomon Rabinowitz (Sholom Aleichem)

DEATHS

Delia Salter Bacon
Rufus Dawes
Washington Irving
Mirabeau Buonaparte Lamar
William Hickling Prescott

EVENTS

Cooper Union, New York, New York (f)
Spirit of the Times, 2nd series, New York, to 1902 (per)
Vanity Fair, New York, to 1863 (per)

LITERATURE

John Turvill Adams. The White Chief among the Red Men; or, Knight of
   the Golden Melice (fic)
Sidney Frances Bateman. Geraldine (dr)
Dion Boucicault. The Octoroon; or, Life in Louisiana (dr)
Daniel Garrison Brinton. Notes on the Floridian Peninsula (des)
Sylvanus Cobb, Jr. The Patriot Cruiser (fic)
William Turner Coggleshall. The Protective Policy in Literature (e)
John Esten Cooke. Henry St. John, Gentleman (fic)
George Washington Parke Custis. Recollections and Private Memoirs of
   Washington, to 1860 (nar, biog, pub)
Richard Henry Dana, Jr. To Cuba and Back (nar)
John William DeForest. Seacliff; or, the Mystery of the Westervelts
   (fic)
Martin Robinson Delany. Blake: or, the Huts of America, to 1862 (fic)
Augusta Jane Evans. Beulah (fic)
Joseph Holt Ingraham. The Pillar of Fire (fic)
George Henry Miles. Senor Valiente (dr)
John Neal. True Womanhood (fic)
William Gilmore Simms. The Cassique of Kiawah (fic)
Emma Dorothy Eliza Nevitte Southworth. The Hidden Hand (fic)
Harriet Elizabeth Beecher Stowe. The Minister's Wooing (fic)
Henry David Thoreau. A Plea for Captain John Brown (e)

1860

BIRTHS

Jane Addams   Harriet Monroe
Abraham Cahan
Hannibal Hamlin Garland
Charlotte Perkins Gilman
Louise Imogen Guiney
Charles Hale Hoyt
George Lyman Kittredge
Clinton Scollard
Frank Dempster Sherman
Daniel Berkeley Updike
Owen Wister

DEATHS

Charles James Cannon
Joseph Holt Ingraham
James Kirke Paulding

EVENTS

The Dial, Cincinnati, Ohio, to 1860 (per)
The Southern Literary Messenger, Richmond, Virginia, to 1864 (per)

LITERATURE

Sidney Frances Bateman. Evangeline (dr)
Benjamin Paul Blood. Optimism (e)
Dion Boucicault. The Colleen Bawn (dr)
William Cullen Bryant. A Forest Hymn (po)
Lydia Maria Child. Correspondence (pub)
Jeremiah Clemens. The Rivals (fic)
William Turner Coggleshall. The Poets and Poetry of the West (po, e
   ed)
Maria Susanna Cummins. El Fureidis (fic)
Ralph Waldo Emerson. The Conduct of Life (e)
Francis Brett Harte. M'liss (fic)
Nathaniel Hawthorne. The Marble Faun (fic)
Paul Hamilton Hayne. Avolio (po)
Josiah Gilbert Holland. Miss Gilbert's Career (fic)
Oliver Wendell Holmes. The Professor at the Breakfast Table (e, po)
William Dean Howells and John James Piatt. Poems of Two Friends (po)
Joseph Holt Ingraham. The Throne of David (fic)
John Lothrop Motley. The History of the United Netherlands, 4 vols,
   to 1867 (hist)
Jane Marsh Parker. Barley Wood (fic)
George Dennison Prentice. Prenticeana (nar, e)
Harriet Elizabeth Prescott Spofford. Sir Robin's Ghost (fic)
Ann Sophia Stephens. Malaeska: The Indian Wife of the White Hunter
   (fic)
Daniel Pierce Thompson. The Doomed Chief (fic)
Henry David Thoreau. After the Death of John Brown (e)
_____. The Last Days of John Brown (e)
Henry Timrod. Poems (pub)
Frederick Goddard Tuckerman. Poems (pub)
Walt Whitman. Leaves of Grass, rev ed (po)
John Greenleaf Whittier. Home Ballads and Other Poems (po)
Joseph Emerson Worcester. A Dictionary of the English Language (ref)

1861

BIRTHS

Charles Wolcott Balestier
William Bliss Carman
Henry Harland
Albert Bigelow Paine
John Herbert Quick
Morgan Andrew Robertson
Frederick Jackson Turner

DEATHS

George Tucker
Theodore Winthrop

EVENTS

Abraham Lincoln, 16th President of the United States, to 1865
Vassar College, Poughkeepsie, New York (f)

LITERATURE

Thomas Bailey Aldrich. Pampinea (po)
The Anarchiad: A New England Poem (po, pub)
Jane Andrews. The Seven Little Sisters Who Live in the Round Ball
    That Floats in the Air (fic)
Henry Charles Carey. Harmony of Interests (e)
George William Curtis. Trumps (fic)
Lucretia Peabody Hale and Edward Everett Hale. Struggle for Life
    (fic)
Oliver Wendell Holmes. Elsie Venner (fic)
Albert Pike. Dixie (po)
James Ryder Randall. Maryland, My Maryland (po)
Theodore Winthrop. Cecil Dreeme (fic, pub)

                              1862

BIRTHS

John Kendrick Bangs
Albert Jeremiah Beveridge
Nicholas Murray Butler
John Jay Chapman
Wilbur Lucius Cross
Josephus Daniels
John William Fox, Jr.
Langdon Elwyn Mitchell
William Sydney Porter (O. Henry)
Morris Rosenfeld
Edwin Milton Royle
Edith Newbold Jones Wharton

DEATHS

James Ewell Heath
Johnson Jones Hooper
Charles Jared Ingersoll
Fitz-James O'Brien
Henry David Thoreau

LITERATURE

William Gannaway Brownlow. Sketches of the Rise, Progress, and De-
    cline of Secession (nar, e)
Alexander Crummell. The Future of Africa (e)
Rebecca Blaine Harding Davis. Margaret Howth (fic)
Mary Abigail Dodge (Gail Hamilton). Country Living and Country Think-
    ing (e)
James Sloan Gibbons. We Are Coming, Father Abraham, Three Hundred
    Thousand More (po)

Julia Ward Howe. The Battle-Hymn of the Republic (po)
Richard Burleigh Kimball. Under-Currents of Wall-Street (fic)
James Russell Lowell. The Biglow Papers, Second Series, 3 vols (po)
_____ and Francis James Child. Il Pesceballo: Opera
   Seria (dr)
Albert Pike. Letter to the President of the Confederate States (e)
Thomas Buchanan Read. The Wagoner of the Alleghanies (po)
Elizabeth Drew Barstow Stoddard. The Morgesons (fic)
Harriet Elizabeth Beecher Stowe. Agnes of Sorrento (fic)
_____. The Pearl of Orr's Island (fic)
James Bayard Taylor. The Poet's Journal (po)
Metta Victoria Victor. Maum Guinea and Her Plantation Children (fic)
William Ross Wallace. The Liberty Bell (po)
Theodore Winthrop. Edwin Brothertoft (fic, pub)
_____. John Brent (fic, pub)

1863

BIRTHS

   Charles McLean Andrews
   Gamaliel Bradford
   Ernest Lacy
   Alfred Edward Newton
   Amelie Rives
   George Santayana
   Geneva Stratton-Porter

DEATHS

   Charlotte Mary Sanford Barnes
   George Copway
   George Long Duyckinck
   Emma Catherine Embury
   William John Grayson
   Baynard Rush Hall
   Clement Clarke Moore

EVENTS

   Abraham Lincoln delivers the "Gettysburg Address"
   The Round Table, New York, to 1864 (per)

LITERATURE

   Louisa May Alcott. Hospital Sketches (nar)
   William Wells Brown. The Black Man: His Antecedents, His Genius, and
      His Achievements (hist)
   George Henry Calvert. The Gentleman (e)
   Francis James Child. Observations on the Language of Chaucer (e)
   John Esten Cooke. Life of Stonewall Jackson (biog)
   Nathaniel Hawthorne. Our Old Home (e)
   Henry Wadsworth Longfellow. Tales of a Wayside Inn, First Series
      (po)
   Henry Morford. The Days of Shoddy (fic)

_____. Shoulder-Straps (fic)
Harriet Elizabeth Prescott Spofford. The Amber Gods and Other Stories (fic)
Ann Sophia Stephens. The Rejected Wife (fic)
James Bayard Taylor. Hannah Thurston (fic)
Henry David Thoreau. Excursions (e, pub)
_____. Life without Principle (e, pub)
Theodore Winthrop. The Canoe and the Saddle (trav, nar, pub)
_____. Life in the Open Air (nar, trav, pub)

1864

BIRTHS

Richard Harding Davis
Thomas Dixon
Richard Hovey

DEATHS

Joseph Glover Baldwin
Nathaniel Hawthorne
George Pope Morris
Josiah Quincy the younger

EVENTS

Oneida Circular, Oneida Community, New York State, to 1876 (per)
The Radical Club, Boston, to 1880

LITERATURE

John Ross Browne. Crusoe's Island (trav)
Henry Howard Brownell. Lyrics of a Day; or, Newspaper-Poetry (po)
William Cullen Bryant. Thirty Poems (po)
George Henry Calvert. Arnold and Andre (dr)
Sylvanus Cobb, Jr. Ben Hamed (fic)
Maria Susanna Cummins. Haunted Hearts (fic)
Mary Elizabeth Mapes Dodge. Irvington Stories (fic)
Augusta Jane Evans. Macaria; or, Altars of Sacrifice (fic)
Oliver Wendell Holmes. Soundings from the Atlantic (e)
Richard Malcolm Johnston. Georgia Sketches (fic)
Richard Burleigh Kimball. Was He Successful? (fic)
Dacid Ross Locke (Petroleum V. Nasby). The Nasby Papers (e, sat, pub)
Henry Wadsworth Longfellow. Divina Commedia, to 1867 (po)
Augustus Baldwin Longstreet. Master William Mitten (fic)
Robert Traill Spence Lowell. Poems (pub)
Henry Morford. The Coward (fic)
_____. Red-Tape and Pigeon-Hole Generals As Seen from the Ranks (nar)
Thomas Low Nichols. Forty Years of American Life, 1821-1861 (nar, des)
Margaret Junkin Preston. Beechenbrook: A Rhyme of the War (po)
Epes Sargent. Peculiar; a Tale of the Great Transition (fic)

Elizabeth Oakes Smith. Black Hollow (fic)
Harriet Elizabeth Prescott Spofford. Azarian: An Episode (fic)
James Bayard Taylor. John Godfrey's Fortunes (fic)
————————————————. The Poems (po)
William Henry Thomes. The Gold Hunters' Adventures; or, Life in Aus-
    tralia (fic)
Henry David Thoreau. The Maine Woods (nar, pub)
John Townsend Trowbridge. Cudjo's Cave (fic, pub)
Frederick Goddard Tuckerman. Poems (pub)
John Greenleaf Whittier. In War Time and Other Poems (po)

1865

BIRTHS

Irving Babbitt
John Bennett
Bernard Berenson
Stephen Bonsal
James Henry Breasted
Madison Julius Cawein
Robert William Chambers
William Clyde Fitch
Paul Leicester Ford
Lucy Fitch Perkins
William Lyon Phelps
Elizabeth Robins
Lloyd Logan Pearsall Smith

DEATHS

George Arnold (McArone)
John Wilkes Booth
Jeremiah Clemens
Samuel Adams Hammett (Philip Paxton)
Richard Hildreth
Alexander Beaufort Meek
Lydia Huntley Sigourney
Joseph Emerson Worcester

EVENTS

The Catholic World, to 1971 (per)
Cornell University, Ithaca, New York (f)
Free Religious Association (f)
Andrew Johnson, 17th President of the United States, to 1869
The Nation, New York (per, f)
The Radical, Boston, to 1872 (per)
Saturday Press, 2nd series, New York, to 1866 (per)

LITERATURE

Amos Bronson Alcott. Ralph Waldo Emerson, to 1882 (e)
Louisa May Alcott. Moods (fic)
Dion Boucicault and Joseph Jefferson. Rip van Winkle (dr)

Samuel Bowles. Across the Continent (nar, des)
Thomas Bulfinch. Shakespeare Adapted for Reading Classes (ref)
Jeremiah Clemens. Tobias Wilson (fic)
Mary Abigail Dodge (Gail Hamilton). A New Atmosphere (e)
Mary Elizabeth Mapes Dodge. Hans Brinker; or, the Silver Skates (fic)
Augustine Joseph Hickey Duganne. Camps and Prisons (nar)
Edward Everett Hale. The Man without a Country (fic)
Francis Brett Harte. Outcroppings (po)
George Moses Horton. Naked Genius (po)
James Russell Lowell. Ode Recited at the Commemoration of the Living
    and Dead Soldiers of Harvard University (po)
Joseph Clay Neal. Charcoal Sketches: Three Books Complete in One
    (sat, nar, pub)
Ray Palmer. Hymns and Sacred Pieces (po)
Thomas Buchanan Read. A Summer Story, Sheridan's Ride, and Other
    Poems (po, pub)
John Godfrey Saxe. Clever Stories of Many Nations Rendered in Rhyme
    (po)
Elizabeth Drew Barstow Stoddard. Two Men (fic)
Richard Henry Stoddard. Abraham Lincoln: An Horatian Ode (po)
Henry David Thoreau. Cape Cod (des, pub)
Walt Whitman. Drum-Taps (po)
_____. Sequel to Drum-Taps (po)
John Greenleaf Whittier. National Lyrics (po)

1866

BIRTHS

    George Ade
    Gelett Frank Burgess
    Richard LeGallienne
    George Barr McCutcheon
    Meredith Nicholson
    William Gilbert Patten (Burt L. Standish)
    Joseph Lincoln Steffens
    Edward Lucas White

DEATHS

    Maria Susanna Cummins
    John Beauchamp Jones
    John Pierpont
    Frederick William Thomas

EVENTS

    Every Saturday, Boston, to 1874 (per)
    Fisk University, Nashville, Tennessee (f)
    The Galaxy, New York, to 1878 (per)
    New York World, to 1931 (per)
    The Richmond Eclectic, to 1868 (per)
    The Round Table, 2nd series, New York, to 1869 (per)

LITERATURE

Elizabeth Chase Akers. Poems (po, pub)
George Arnold. Drift: A Sea-Shore Idyl and Other Poems, ed. William
     Winter (po)
Henry Howard Brownell. War-Lyrics and Other Poems (pub)
George F. Harrington (William Mumford Baker). Inside: A Chronicle of
     Secession (fic)
Thomas Bulfinch. Oregon and Eldorado (hist)
Horace Bushnell. The Vicarious Sacrifice (e)
John Esten Cooke. Surry of Eagle's Nest (fic)
Richard Henry Dana, Jr. Elements of International Law by Wheaton (e,
     ed)
Charles Etienne Arthur Gayarre. Philip II of Spain (biog)
Gideon Hiram Hollister. Thomas a Becket (po, dr)
Julia Ward Howe. Later Lyrics (po)
William Dean Howells. Venetian Life (trav)
Herman Melville. Battle-Pieces and Aspects of War (po)
George Henry Miles. Christine (po)
Donald Grant Mitchell. Dr. Johns (fic)
Silas Weir Mitchell. The Case of George Dedlow (fic)
Thomas Buchanan Read. Poetical Works, 3 vols (pub)
James Bayard Taylor. The Picture of St. John (po)
_____. The Story of Kennett (fic)
Mary Virginia Terhune. Sunnybank (fic)
William Henry Thomes. The Bushrangers (fic)
John Townsend Trowbridge. Coupon Bonds (fic)
Henry Theodore Tuckerman. The Criterion (e)
Henry David Thoreau. A Yankee in Canada (trav, pub)
Charles Henry Webb. Liffith Lank (hum)
_____. St. Twel'mo (hum)
John Greenleaf Whittier. Prose Works, 2 vols (pub)
_____. Snow-Bound: A Winter Idyl (po)

1867

BIRTHS

     John Spencer Bassett
     Finley Peter Dunne
     Charles Klein
     David Graham Phillips
     Laura Ingalls Wilder
     Harry Leon Wilson

DEATHS

     Alfred W. Arrington (Charles Summerfield)
     Charles Farrar Browne (Artemus Ward)
     Thomas Bulfinch
     William Turner Coggleshall
     Fitz-Greene Halleck
     John Rollin Ridge
     Catharine Maria Sedgwick
     Susan Ridley Sedgwick
     Henry Timrod
     Nathaniel Parker Willis

EVENTS

Harper's Bazar (Bazaar), New York (per, f)
Howard University, Washington, D.C. (f)
Johns Hopkins University, Baltimore, Maryland (f)
The Southern Review, Baltimore, to 1879 (per)

LITERATURE

George Arnold. Poems, Grave and Gay (po, pub)
Henry Ward Beecher. Norwood; or, Village Life in New England (fic)
John Burroughs. Notes on Walt Whitman As Poet and Person (e)
Samuel Langhorne Clemens. The Celebrated Jumping Frog of Calaveras
    County and Other Sketches (fic)
Frederick Swartwout Cozzens (Richard Haywarde). The Sayings of Dr.
    Bushwacker and Other Learned Men (e)
John Augustin Daly. Under the Gaslight (dr)
John William DeForest. Miss Ravenel's Conversion from Secession to
    Loyalty (fic)
Ralph Waldo Emerson. May-Day and Other Pieces (po)
Augusta Jane Evans. St. Elmo (fic)
George Washington Harris. Sut Lovingood Yarns (fic)
Francis Brett Harte. Condensed Novels and Other Papers (fic, sat)
        . The Lost Galleon (po)
Josiah Gilbert Holland. Kathrina, Her Life and Mine in a Poem (po)
Oliver Wendell Holmes. The Guardian Angel (fic)
William Dean Howells. Italian Journeys (trav)
Elijah Kellogg. Good Old Times (fic, juv)
Sidney Lanier. Tiger-Lilies (fic)
Fitz Hugh Ludlow. Little Brother and Other Genre Pictures (fic)
Henry Morford and John Brougham. The Bells of Shandron (dr)
William Gilmore Simms. Joscelyn: A Tale of the Revolution (fic)
Elizabeth Oakes Smith. Bald Eagle (fic)
Charles Warren Stoddard. Poems (pub)
Elizabeth Drew Barstow Stoddard. Temple House (fic)
Harriet Elizabeth Beecher Stowe. Religious Poems (po)
Walt Whitman. Leaves of Grass, rev ed (po)
John Greenleaf Whittier. The Tent on the Beach and Other Poems (po)
Richard Henry Wilde. Hesperia (po)

1868

BIRTHS

Mary Hunter Austin
William Edward Burghardt DuBois
Robert Herrick
Edgar Lee Masters
Eleanor Hodgman Porter
Philip Henry Savage
Mary Stanbery Watts
William Allen White

DEATHS

William Allen
Adah Isaacs Menken
Daniel Pierce Thompson

EVENTS

The Aldine: A Journal of Art and Typography, New York, to 1879 (per)
Atlanta Constitution (per, f)
University of California at Berkeley (f)
Courier-Journal, Louisville, Kentucky (per, f)
Hearth and Home, to 1875 (per)
Lippincott's Magazine, Philadelphia, to 1915 (per)
New Eclectic, Baltimore, to 1871 (per)
Overland Monthly, San Francisco, to 1875 (per)
Putnam's Magazine, New York, to 1906 (per)
Vanity Fair, New York, to 1936 (per)

LITERATURE

Amos Bronson Alcott. Tablets (e)
Louisa May Alcott. Little Women, to 1869 (fic)
John Bigelow (ed). The Autobiography of Benjamin Franklin (auto)
Benjamin Paul Blood. The Colonnades (po)
John Esten Cooke. Fairfax (fic)
Rebecca Blaine Harding Davis. Waiting for the Verdict (fic)
A Dictionary of Books Relating to America, from Its Discovery to the
     Present Time, 29 vols, to 1936 (ref)
Mary Abigail Dodge (Gail Hamilton). Woman's Wrongs: A Counter-Irri-
     tant (e)
Edward Everett Hale. If, Yes, and Perhaps (fic)
Richard Burleigh Kimball. Henry Powers, Banker (fic)
Sarah Anna Lewis. Sappho (po, dr)
Adah Isaacs Menken. Infelicia (po)
Cincinnatus Hiner Miller (Joaquin Miller). Specimens (po)
Ray Palmer. Hymns of My Holy Hours (po)
John Rollin Ridge. Poems (pub)
Edward Rowland Sill. The Hermitage and Other Poems (po, pub)
Elizabeth Oakes Smith. The Sagamore of Saco (fic)
William Wetmore Story. Graffiti d'Italia (po)
James Bayard Taylor. The Golden Wedding: A Masque (po)
Elizabeth Stuart Phelps Ward. The Gates Ajar (fic)

1869

BIRTHS

George Randolph Chester
Herbert David Croly
Olive Tilford Dargan
Chester Bailey Fernald
Hutchins Hapgood
Carl Sadakichi Hartman
Frank Bird Linderman
William Vaughan Moody
Joseph Percival Pollard

Eugene Manlove Rhodes
Edwin Arlington Robinson
George Sterling
Newton Booth Tarkington
Brand Whitlock

DEATHS

Frederick Swartwout Cozzens (Richard Haywarde)
George Washington Harris
Henry Augustus Wise

EVENTS

Appleton's Journal, New York, to 1881 (per)
Ulysses Simpson Grant, 18th President of the United States, to 1877

LITERATURE

Samuel Bowles. The Switzerland of America (nar, des)
John Ross Browne. Adventures in Apache Country (trav, nar)
William Cullen Bryant. Hymns (po)
Samuel Langhorne Clemens. The Innocents Abroad (nar)
John Esten Cooke. Hilt to Hilt (fic)
_____. Mohun (fic)
Mary Elizabeth Mapes Dodge. A Few Friends and How They Amused Them-
    selves (fic)
Emma Catherine Embury. Selected Poems (pub)
Edward Everett Hale. Sybaris and Other Homes (sat)
Thomas Wentworth Higginson. Malbone (fic)
Henry James. Pyramus and Thisbe (dr)
Ralph Olmstead Keeler. Gloverson and His Silent Partners (fic)
James Russell Lowell. Poetical Works (pub)
_____. Under the Willows and Other Poems (pub)
Samuel Joseph May. Some Recollections of Our Anti-Slavery Conflict
    (nar)
Cincinnatus Hiner Miller (Joaquin Miller). Joaquin et al (po)
John Neal. Wandering Recollections of a Somewhat Busy Life (auto)
Elizabeth Payson Prentiss. Stepping Heavenward (fic)
William Gilmore Simms. Voltmeier; or, the Mountain Men (fic)
Emma Dorothy Eliza Nevitte Southworth. The Fatal Marriage (fic)
Edmund Clarence Stedman. The Blameless Prince (po)
Harriet Elizabeth Beecher Stowe. Old-town Folks (fic)
Frederick Goddard Tuckerman. Poems (pub)
Edwin Percy Whipple. Literature of the Age of Elizabeth (e, hist)
John Greenleaf Whittier. Among the Hills and Other Poems (po)

1870

BIRTHS

Ray Stannard Baker
Herbert Eugene Bolton
Mary Johnston
Joseph Crosby Lincoln

Robert Morss Lovett
Benjamin Franklin Norris
Alice Caldwell Hegan Rice

DEATHS

John Pendleton Kennedy
Augustus Baldwin Longstreet
Fitz Hugh Ludlow
Anna Cora Mowatt
George Dennison Prentice
William Gilmore Simms
Emma Hart Willard

EVENTS

The American Anti-Slavery Society, Philadelphia (c)
The Christian Union, New York, to 1893 (per)
The Index, affl. the Free Religious Association, to 1886 (per)
The Literary World, Boston, to 1904 (per)
Lotos Club, New York, New York (f)
Scribner's Monthly, New York, to 1881 (per)
Woodhull and Clafflin's Weekly, New York, to 1876 (per)

LITERATURE

Louisa May Alcott. The Old-Fashioned Girl (fic)
Thomas Baily Aldrich. The Story of a Bad Boy (fic)
William Mumford Baker. The New Timothy (fic)
Adin Ballou. Primitive Christianity and Its Corruptions (e)
John Bigelow. Beaumarchais the Merchant (biog, hist)
William Cullen Bryant. Iliad (po, trans)
John Esten Cooke. The Heir of Gaymount (fic)
Ralph Waldo Emerson. Society and Solitude (e)
Francis Brett Harte. The Luck of Roaring Camp and Other Stories (fic
    pub)
Bronson Crocker Howard. Saratoga (dr)
Helen Maria Hunt Jackson. Verses by H.H. (po)
Ralph Olmstead Keeler. Vagabond Adventures (nar)
Richard Burleigh Kimball. Today in New York (fic)
Olive Logan. Surf (dr)
James Russell Lowell. The Cathedral (po)
Fitz Hugh Ludlow. The Heart of the Continent (fic)
Cincinnatus Hiner Miller (Joaquin Miller). Pacific Poems (po)
John Neal. Great Mysteries and Little Plagues (nar)
Robert Dale Owen . Beyond the Breakers (fic)
Margaret Junkin Preston. Old Song and New (po)
Epes Sargent. The Woman Who Dared (po)
Emma Dorothy Eliza Nevitte Southworth. The Maiden Widow (fic)
Francis Richard Stockton. Ting-a-Ling (juv, fic)
Harriet Elizabeth Beecher Stowe. Lady Byron Vindicated (biog, e)
James Bayard Taylor. The Ballad of Abraham Lincoln (juv, po)
_____. Joseph and His Friend (fic)
George Alfred Townsend. Poems (pub)
Francis Fuller Victor. The River of the West (fic)
Elizabeth Stuart Phelps Ward. Hedged In (fic)

Charles Dudley Warner. My Summer in a Garden (e)
John Greenleaf Whittier. Ballads of New England (po)
_____. Poetical Works, 2 vols (pub)

1871

BIRTHS

Samuel Hopkins Adams
Winston Churchill
Stephen Crane
Thomas Augustine Daly
Theodore Herman Albert Dreiser
Charles Macomb Flandrau
James Forbes
Arthur Guiterman
James Weldon Johnson
Charles Rann Kennedy
Harold MacGrath
John Thomas McIntyre
Vernon Louis Parrington
Melville Davisson Post
Lola Ridge
Winchell Smith
Jesse Lynch Williams

DEATHS

Henry Marie Brackenridge
Alice Cary
Phoebe Cary
Samuel Joseph May
George Henry Miles
Henry Theodore Tuckerman

EVENTS

Smith College, Northampton, Massachusetts (f)
Southern Magazine, Charleston, South Carolina, to 1875 (per)

LITERATURE

Charles Francis Adams the younger and Henry Adams. Chapters of Erie
    and Other Essays (e)
Louisa May Alcott. Little Men (fic)
Catharine Esther Beecher. Women Suffrage (e)
Henry Ward Beecher. The Life of Jesus, the Christ (bio)
John Bigelow. France and Hereditary Monarchy (hist)
William Cullen Bryant. Odyssey, to 1872 (po, trans)
John Burroughs. Wake-Robin (e)
Peter Cartwright. Fifty Years As a Presiding Elder (auto)
William Ellery Channing the younger. The Wanderer (po)
James Freeman Clarke. Ten Great Religions, to 1883 (e)
John Esten Cooke. Hammer and Rapier (fic)
John Augustin Daly. Divorce (dr)

_____. Horizon (dr)
John William DeForest. Overland (fic)
Edward Eggleston. The Hoosier Schoolmaster (fic)
Edward Everett Hale. Ten Times One Is One (fic)
John Milton Hay. Castilian Days (e)
_____. Pike County Ballads (po)
Henry James. A Passionate Pilgrim (fic)
Richard Malcolm Johnston. Dukesborough Tales (fic)
Emma Lazarus. Admetus and Other Poems (po)
Cincinnatus Hiner Miller (Joaquin Miller). Songs of the Sierras (po)
George Wilbur Peck. Adventures of One Terence McGrant (fic, nar)
Harriet Elizabeth Prescott Spofford. New-England Legends (fic)
Harriet Elizabeth Beecher Stowe. My Wife and I (fic, e)
_____. Pink and White Tyranny (fic, sat)
Elizabeth Stuart Phelps Ward. The Silent Partner (fic)
Walt Whitman. Democratic Vistas (e)
_____. Leaves of Grass, rev ed (po)
_____. Passage to India (po)
John Greenleaf Whittier. Miriam and Other Poems (po)

1872

BIRTHS

Eleanor Hallowell Abbott
Maude Adams (Maude Kiskadden)
Paul Laurence Dunbar
Zane Grey
Rupert Hughes
Lenora Speyer
Albert Payson Terhune
Harold Bell Wright

DEATHS

Henry Howard Brownell
Peter Cartwright
Thomas Hastings
Frank Hitchcock Murdoch
Thomas Buchanan Read
Sara Payson Willis (Fanny Fern)

EVENTS

Publishers' Weekly, New York (per. f)

LITERATURE

Amos Bronson Alcott. Concord Days (nar)
Louisa May Alcott. Aunt Jo's Scrap-Bag, 6 vols, to 1882 (fic)
Stephen Pearl Andrews. Basic Outline of Universology (e)
Thomas Gold Appleton. Faded Leaves (po)
Amelia Edith Huddleton Barr. Romance and Reality (fic)
Henry Ward Beecher. Yale Lectures on Preaching, to 1874 (e)
Samuel Langhorne Clemens. Roughing It (nar, fic)

Christopher Pearse Cranch. The Aeneid (trans)
John William DeForest. Kate Beaumont (fic)
Edward Eggleston. The End of the World (fic)
James Thomas Fields. Yesterday with Authors (nar)
Charles Etienne Arthur Gayarre. Fernando deLemos (fic)
Archibald Clavering Gunter. Found the True Vein (dr)
Lucretia Peabody Hale and Edward Everett Hale. Six of One by Half a
    Dozen of the Other (fic)
Nathaniel Hawthorne. Septimus Felton (fic, pub)
Paul Hamilton Hayne. Legends and Lyrics (po)
Oliver Wendell Holmes. The Poet at the Breakfast Table (e, po)
William Dean Howells. Their Wedding Journey (fic)
Prentiss Ingraham. The Masked Spy (fic)
Henry Wadsworth Longfellow. Christus, a Mystery (dr, po)
_____. Tales of a Wayside Inn, 2nd series (po)
Frank Hitchcock Murdoch. Bohemia; or, the Lottery of Art (dr, sat)
_____. Davy Crockett (dr)
Albert Pike. Hymns to the Gods (po)
Edward Payson Roe. Barriers Burned Away (fic)
Harriet Elizabeth Beecher Stowe. Sam Lawson's Oldtown Fireside Sto-
    ries (fic)
James Bayard Taylor. Beauty and the Beast, and Tales of Home (fic)
_____. The Masque of the Gods (dr)
Celia Laighton Thaxter. Poems (pub)
William Henry Thomes. A Slaver's Adventures (fic)
_____. The Whaleman's Adventures (fic)
Charles Dudley Warner. Saunterings (trav)
John Greenleaf Whittier. The Pennsylvania Pilgrim and Other Poems
    (po)
Ella Wheeler Wilcox. Drops of Water (po)

1873

BIRTHS

    Carl Lotus Becker
    Guy Wetmore Carryl
    Willa Sibert Cather
    George Cram Cook
    Dane Coolidge
    Benjamin DeCasseres
    William Henry Irwin
    George Cabot Lodge
    Emily Post
    Anne Douglas Sedgwick
    Stewart Edward White
    William E. Woodward

DEATHS

    Ralph Olmstead Keeler
    William Holmes McGuffey
    Frederick Goddard Tuckerman

EVENTS

The Delineator, New York, to 1937 (per)
St. Nicholas, to 1940 (juv per)
Woman's Home Companion, Cleveland, Ohio, to 1886 (per)

LITERATURE

Louisa May Alcott. Work (fic)
Thomas Bailey Aldrich. Marjorie Daw and Other People (fic)
Ambrose Gwinett Bierce (Dod Grile). The Fiend's Delight (nar)
_____. Nuggets and Dust Panned Out in
    California (nar)
William Cullen Bryant. The Little People of the Snow (po)
_____. Orations and Addresses (e, pub)
Will Carleton. Farm Ballads (po)
William Ellery Channing the younger. Thoreau, the Poet-Naturalist
    (biog)
Samuel Langhorne Clemens and Charles Dudley Warner. The Gilded Age
    (fic)
John Esten Cooke. Her Majesty the Queen (fic)
John William DeForest. The Wetherel Affair (fic)
Edward Eggleston. The Mystery of Metropolisville (fic)
George Cary Eggleston. A Man of Honour (fic)
Edgar Fawcett. Purple and Fine Linen (fic)
Francis Brett Harte. Mrs. Skagg's Husbands (fic)
Julian Hawthorne. Bressant (fic)
Thomas Wentworth Higginson. Oldport Days (nar, des)
Josiah Gilbert Holland. Arthur Bonnicastle (fic)
William Dean Howells. Chance Acquaintance (fic)
Edward Zane Carroll Judson (Ned Buntline). The Scouts of the Plains
    (dr)
William Starbuck Mayo. Never Again (fic)
Frank Hitchcock Murdoch. Only a Jew (dr, pub)
John Boyle O'Reilly. Songs from Southern Seas (po)
Daniel Ricketson. The Factory Bell and Other Poems (po, pub)
Samuel Sewall. Talitha Cumi (e, pub)
Edmund Clarence Stedman. Poetical Works (pub)
Charles Warren Stoddard. South-Sea Idyls (nar)
Harriet Elizabeth Beecher Stowe. Palmetto-Leaves (nar, des)
James Bayard Taylor. Lars: A Pastoral of Norway (po)
Henry Timrod. Poems (pub)
Lewis Wallace. The Fair God (fic)
Charles Dudley Warner. Backlog Studies (e)

1874

BIRTHS

Charles Auslin Beard
Thornton Waldo Burgess
Owen Davis
Clarence Shepard Day
Robert Lee Frost
Zona Gale
Ellen Glasgow
Amy Lawrence Lowell

Josephine Preston Peabody
Gertrude Stein
Joseph Trumbull Stickney
Mary Marvin Heaton Vorse
Eugene Walter

DEATHS

Alonzo Delano
Henry Beck Hirst

EVENTS

The Anti-Monopolist, Minnesota, to 1879 (per)
Congressional Record, Washington, D.C. (per, est)

LITERATURE

Charles Francis Adams the elder (ed). Memoirs of John Quincy Adams,
    to 1877 (auto, nar)
Thomas Bailey Aldrich. Cloth of Gold (po)
_____. Prudence Palfrey (fic)
Hubert Howe Bancroft. The Native Races, 5 vols, to 1875 (hist)
Benjamin Paul Blood. The Anaesthetic Revelation and the Gist of
    Philosophy (e)
Catherine Esther Beecher. Educational Reminsicences and Suggestions
    (nar, e)
Ambrose Gwinett Bierce (Dod Grile). Cobwebs from an Empty Skull
    (nar)
Hjalmar Hjorth Boyesen. Gunnar (fic)
William Wells Brown. The Rising Son (hist)
William Cullen Bryant. Among the Trees (po)
Charles Heber Clark. Out of the Hurly-Burly (fic)
James Freeman Clarke. Common Sense in Religion (e)
Rebecca Blaine Harding Davis. John Andross (fic)
Mary Elizabeth Mapes Dodge. Rhymes and Jingles (po)
Edward Eggleston. The Circuit Rider (fic)
George Cary Eggleston. A Rebel's Recollections (auto)
Edward Everett Hale. His Name (fic)
James Lawson. Liddlesdale (po, dr)
Emma Lazarus. Alide (fic)
Henry Wadsworth Longfellow. Tales of a Wayside Inn, 3rd series (po)
Robert Traill Spence Lowell. Anthony Brade, a Story of a School
    (fic)
John Neal. Portland Illustrated (des)
Frederic Beecher Perkins. Scope; or, the Lost Library (fic)
Edward Payson Roe. Opening a Chestnut Burr (fic)
Charles Warren Stoddard. Summer Cruising in the South Seas (nar,
    des)
James Bayard Taylor. The Prophet (dr)
Theodore Tilton. Tempest-Tossed (fic)
Albion Winegar Tourgee. 'Toinette (fic)
Mary Ashley Van Voorhis Townsend. The Captain's Story (po)
Charles Dudley Warner. Baddeck (e)
Charles Henry Webb. John Paul's Book (hum)

1875

BIRTHS

Percy Holmes Boynton
Anna Hempstead Branch
Wallace Admah Irwin
Percy Wallace MacKaye
Emery Bemsley Pottle (Gilbert Emery)
Arthur Hobsob Quinn
Joel Elias Spingarn
Frederic Ridgely Torrence
Arthur Cheney Train
Henry Kitchell Webster

DEATHS

William Bayle Bernard
John Ross Browne

EVENTS

Chicago Daily News, to 1978 (per)
Wellesley College, Wellesley, Massachusetts (f)

LITERATURE

Louisa May Alcott. Eight Cousins (fic)
Thomas Gold Appleton. A Sheaf of Leaves (e)
Will Carleton. Farm Legends (po)
Christopher Pearse Cranch. The Bird and the Bell (po)
Jane Cunningham Croly. For Better or Worse: A Book for Some Men and
    All Women (e)
John William DeForest. Honest John Vane (fic)
_____. Playing the Mischief (fic)
Richard Watson Gilder. The New Day (po)
Francis Brett Harte. Tales of the Argonauts (fic, pub)
Josiah Gilbert Holland. Sevenoaks (fic)
Oliver Wendell Holmes. Songs of Many Seasons (po)
William Dean Howells. A Foregone Conclusion (fic)
_____. Private Theatricals, to 1876 (fic)
Henry James. A Passionate Pilgrim and Other Tales (fic)
_____. Transatlantic Sketches (fic, des)
Joseph Stevens Jones. Paul Revere and the Sons of Liberty (dr)
Henry Wadsworth Longfellow. The Masque of Pandora (po)
_____. Morituri Salutamus (po)
Margaret Junkin Preston. Cartoons (po)
John Godfrey Saxe. Leisure-Day Rhymes (po)
Harriet Elizabeth Beecher Stowe. We and Our Neighbors (fic, e)
James Bayard Taylor. Home Pastorals, Ballads, and Lyrics (po)
James Maurice Thompson. Hoosier Mosaics (fic)
Walt Whitman. Memoranda during the War (nar)
John Greenleaf Whittier. Hazel-Blossoms (po)
Constance Fenimore Woolson. Castle Nowhere (fic)

1876

BIRTHS

Sherwood Anderson
Mary Ritter Beard
Irvin Shrewsbury Cobb
William Ellery Leonard
John (Jack) Griffith London
Mary Roberts Rinehart
Jean Webster

DEATHS

Orestes Augustus Brownson
Horace Bushnell
Samuel Benjamin Helbert Judah
John Neal

EVENTS

Frank Leslie's Popular Monthly, New York, to 1906 (per)
The Library Journal (per, f)
The National Repisitory, to 1880 (per)

LITERATURE

Charles Follen Adams. Leedle Yawcob Strauss (po)
John Adams and Abagail Adams. Familiar Letters of John Adams and
  His Wife. . .during the Revolution (let, pub)
Louisa May Alcott. Rose in Bloom (fic)
_____. Silver Pitchers and Independence (fic)
Thomas Gold Appleton. A Nile Journey (nar)
William Mumford Baker. Carter Quarterman (fic)
Albert Brisbane. General Introduction to the Social Sciences (e)
Charles Heber Clark. Elbow-Room (fic)
Samuel Langhorne Clemens. The Adventures of Tom Sawyer (fic)
Charles Carleton Coffin. The Boys of '76 (fic)
Ralph Waldo Emerson. Letters and Social Aims (e)
John Habberton. Helen's Babies (fic)
Francis Brett Harte. Gabriel Conroy (fic)
_____. Two Men of Sandy Bar (dr)
Nathaniel Hawthorne. The Dolliver Romance (fic, pub)
Helen Maria Hunt Jackson. Mary Philbrick's Choice (fic)
Henry James. Roderick Hudson (fic)
Herman Melville. Clarel (po)
Julia A. Moore. The Sweet Singer of Michigan Salutes the Public (po)
Henry Morford. The Spur of Monmouth (fic)
George Dennison Prentice. Poems (pub)
Henry Martyn Robert. Robert's Rules of Order, to 1915, 1943 (ref)
Edward Payson Roe. Near to Nature's Heart (fic)
Emma Dorothy Eliza Nevitte Southworth. Self-Raised (fic)
Charles Dudley Warner. My Winter on the Nile (trav)
Charles Henry Webb. Parodies: Prose and Verse (hum, pub)
Walt Whitman. Two Rivulets (e, po)

John Greenleaf Whittier. Mabel Martin: A Harvest Idyl (po)

1877

BIRTHS

Rex Ellingwood Beach
Charles William Beebe
John Barry Benefield
William Stearns Davis
Lloyd Cassel Douglas
Gordon Hall Gerould
Alice Babette Toklas
Richard Walton Tully

DEATHS

Charles Frederick Briggs
William Gannaway Brownlow
William Howe Cuyler Hosmer
Joseph Stevens Jones
John Lothrop Motley
Robert Dale Owen
Edmund Quincy
Brigham Young

EVENTS

Rutherford Birchard Hayes, 19th President of the United States, to
1881
Puck, New York, to 1918 (per)

LITERATURE

Amos Bronson Alcott. Table Talk (e)
Louisa May Alcott. A Modern Mephistopheles (fic)
Thomas Bailey Aldrich. Flower and Thorn (po)
                          . The Queen of Sheba (fic)
Noah Brooks. The Boy Emigrants (fic)
Phillips Brooks. Lectures on Preaching (e)
Frances Eliza Hodgson Burnett. That Lass o' Lowrie's (fic)
John Burroughs. Birds and Poets (e)
John Esten Cooke. Canolles (fic)
James Thomas Fields. Underbrush (e)
Edward Everett Hale. Philip Nolan's Friends (fic)
Francis Brett Harte and Samuel Langhorne Clemens. Ah Sin (dr)
Julian Hawthorne. Garth (fic)
Josiah Gilbert Holland. Nicholas Minturn (fic)
Henry James. The American (fic)
Sarah Orne Jewett. Deephaven (fic)
Sidney Lanier. Poems (pub)
James Lawson. The Maiden's Oath (dr)
James Russell Lowell. Three Memorial Poems (po)
Cincinnatus Hiner Miller (Joaquin Miller). The Dantes in the Sier-
ras (dr)

Frederic Beecher Perkins. Devil Puzzlers and Other Stories (fic)
Edward Payson Roe. A Knight of the Nineteenth Century (fic)
James Bayard Taylor. The National Ode (po)
Denman Thompson. Joshua Whitcomb (dr)
Lewis Wallace. Commodus (dr)
Elizabeth Stuart Phelps Ward. The Story of Avis (fic)
Charles Dudley Warner. In the Levant (trav)
Albery Allson Whitman. Not a Man and Yet a Man (po)
John Greenleaf Whittier. Favorite Poems (po, pub)

1878

BIRTHS

James Truslow Adams
Claude Gernade Bowers
William Stanley Beaumont Braithwaite
Henry Seidel Canby
Grace Hazard Conkling
Adelaide Crapsey
Rachel Crothers
James Oliver Curwood
Owen MaMahon Johnson
Donald Robert Perry Marquis
Carl August Sandburg
Upton Beall Sinclair

DEATHS

Hew Ainslie
Catharine Esther Beecher
Samuel Bowles
William Cullen Bryant
Evert Augustus Duyckinck
Peter Hamilton Myers
Laughton Osborn
Elizabeth Payson Prentiss
Richard Realf
James Bayard Taylor
Sarah Helen Power Whitman

EVENTS

The Princeton Review, to 1884 (per)

LITERATURE

Charles Francis Adams the younger. Railroads: Their Origin and Prob-
    lems (hist, e)
Louisa May Alcott. Under the Lilacs (fic)
William Mumford Baker. The Virginians in Texas (fic)
_____. A Year Worth Living (fic)
Edward Bellamy. Six to One: A Nantucket Idyl (fic)
William Cullen Bryant. The Flood of Years (po)
James Freeman Clarke. Essentials and Non-Essentials in Religion (e)

Philip St. George Cooke. Conquest of New Mexico and California (hist, nar)
John William DeForest. Justine's Lovers (fic)
Martin Robinson Delany. Principia of Ethnology (e)
Edward Eggleston. Roxy (fic)
Anna Katharine Green. The Leavenworth Case (fic)
Francis Brett Harte. An Heiress of Red Dog and Other Sketches (fic, pub)
Bronson Crocker Howard. Old Love Letters (dr)
Henry James. The Europeans (fic)
_____. French Poets and Novelists (e)
_____. Watch and Ward (fic)
Henry Wadsworth Longfellow. Keramos (po)
Robert Traill Spence Lowell. A Story or Two from an Old Dutch Town (fic)
Katherine Sherwood Bonner MacDowell. Like unto Like (fic)
Julia A. Moore. A Few Words to the Public, with New and Original Poems by Julia A. Moore (po)
John Boyle O'Reilly. Songs, Legends, and Ballads (po)
Samuel Sewall. Diary, 3 vols, to 1882 (nar, pub)
Harriet Elizabeth Beecher Stowe. Poganuc People (fic)
James Bayard Taylor. Prince Deukalion (dr)
Moses Coit Tyler. History of American Literature during the Colonial Time, 1607-1765, 2 vols (hist)
Charles Dudley Warner. Being a Boy (e)
_____. In the Wilderness (trav)
John Greenleaf Whittier. The Vision of Echard and Other Poems (po)

1879

BIRTHS

Ernest Sutherland Bates
James Branch Cabell
Melville Henry Cane
John Erskine
Janet Ayer Fairbank
Dorothy Canfield Fisher
Katharine Fullerton Gerould
Nicholas Vachel Lindsay
Felix Riesenberg
Elsie Singmaster
Constance Lindsay Skinner
Wallace Stevens

DEATHS

Jacob Abbott
Ethel Lynn Beers
Henry Charles Carey
Richard Henry Dana, Sr.
Sarah Josepha Buell Hale
Nathan Cook Meeker
Irwin Russell

EVENTS

Radcliffe College, Cambridge, Massachusetts (f)

LITERATURE

Henry Brooks Adams. The Life of Albert Gallatin (biog)
Ethel Lynn Beers. All Quiet along the Potomac, and Other Poems (po,
 pub)
David Belasco and James A. Herne. Hearts of Oak (dr)
Edward Bellamy. The Duke of Stockbridge (fic)
Hjalmar Hjorth Boyesen. Goethe and Schiller (e)
Phillips Brooks. The Influence of Jesus (e)
Henry Cuyler Bunner and Brander Matthews. In Partnership (fic)
John Burroughs. Locusts and Wild Honey (e)
George Washington Cable. Old Creole Days (fic)
John Wallace Crawford. The Poet Scout (po)
Bartley Campbell. My Partner (dr)
John William DeForest. Irene the Missionary (fic)
Sarah Barnwell Elliott. The Felmeres (fic)
William Dean Howells. The Lady of the Aroostook (fic)
Henry James. Daisy Miller (fic)
_____. Hawthorne (e)
_____. An International Episode (fic)
_____. The Madonna of the Future, and Other Tales (fic)
Olive Logan. Newport (dr)
Thomas Raynesford Lounsbury. A History of the English Language
 (hist)
John Boyle O'Reilly. Moondyne (fic)
Abram Joseph Ryan. Father Ryan's Poems (po, pub)
Frederic Jesup Stimson. Rollo's Journey to Cambridge (fic)
Francis Richard Stockton. Rudder Grange (fic)
Celia Laighton Thaxter. Drift-Weed (po)
William Tappan Thompson. Rancy Cottem's Courtship (fic)
Albion Winegar Tourgee. Figs and Thistles (fic)
_____. A Fool's Errand (fic)

1880

BIRTHS

Sholem Asch
Joseph Warren Beach
Morris Raphael Cohen
Henry Sydnor Harrison
Peter Bernard Kyne
Henry Louis Mencken
Philip Moeller
Honore Willsie Morrow
Kathleen Norris
Julia Mood Peterkin
Channing Pollock
Ernest Poole
Carl Van Vechten

DEATHS

John Brougham
Lydia Maria Child
Mary Henderson Eastman
George Moses Horton
James Lawson
Sarah Anna Lewis
Epes Sargent
Jones Very

EVENTS

Bryn Mawr College, Bryn Mawr, Pennsylvania (f)
Case Institute of Technology, Cleveland, Ohio, to 1967
The Chautauquan, Lake Chautauqua, New York, to 1914 (per)
The Dial, Chicago, to 1929 (per)
The Springfield (Massachusetts) Daily News (per, f)

LITERATURE

Henry Brooks Adams. Democracy, an American Novel (fic)
Louisa May Alcott. Jack and Jill (fic)
Thomas Bailey Aldrich. The Stillwater Tragedy (fic)
William Mumford Baker. His Majesty: Myself (fic)
Edward Bellamy. Dr. Heidenhoff's Process (fic)
George Washington Cable. The Grandissimes (fic)
James Freeman Clarke. Self-Culture (e)
Samuel Langhorne Clemens. A Tramp Abroad (nar)
Frederick Swartwout Cozzens (Richard Haywarde). Sayings, Wise and
    Otherwise (e, misc)
Philander Deming. Adirondack Stories (fic)
Mary Abigail Dodge (Gail Hamilton). Our Common School System (e)
William Cuthbert Falkner. The White Rose of Memphis (fic)
Edgar Fawcett. The False Friend (dr)
_____. Our First Families (dr)
Lucretia Peabody Hale. The Peterkin Papers (sat)
Francis Brett Harte. Jeff Briggs's Love Story (fic)
Oliver Wendell Holmes. The Iron Gate (po)
Richard Hovey. Poems (pub)
William Dean Howells. The Undiscovered Country (fic)
Henry James. Confidence (fic)
Sidney Lanier. The Science of English Verse (e)
Henry Wadsworth Longfellow. Ultima Thule (po)
James Morrison Steele MacKaye. Hazel Kirke (dr)
Charles Warren Stoddard. Mashallah! (nar)
Richard Henry Stoddard. Poems (pub)
Albion Winegar Tourgee. Bricks without Straw (fic)
George Alfred Townsend. Tales of the Chesapeake (fic)
Lewis Wallace. Ben Hur: A Tale of the Christ (fic)
Constance Fenimore Woolson. Rodman the Keeper: Southern Sketches
    (fic)

1881

BIRTHS

Franklin Pierce Adams
Bess Streetor Aldrich
Harold Witter Bynner
John Cournos
Charles Caldwell Dobie
Edgar Albert Guest
Alice Corbin Henderson
Clarence Budington Kelland
William Morley Punshon McFee
John Gneisenau Neihardt
Charles Gilman Norris
Elizabeth Madox Roberts
Thomas Sigismund Stribling
Austin Strong
Stark Young

DEATHS

Sidney Franes Bateman
Nathaniel Deering
Eliza Ann Dupuy
James Thomas Fields
Josiah Gilbert Holland
Gideon Hiram Hollister
Sidney Lanier
Henry Morford
John Gorham Palfrey
Frederick William Shelton
Alfred Billings Street
William Ross Wallace

EVENTS

Chester Alan Arthur, 21st President of the United States, to 1885
The Century Illustrated Monthly Magazine, New York, to 1930 (per)
The Critic, to 1906 (per)
James Abram Garfield, 20th President of the United States, to 1881
Judge, New York, to 1939 (per)
Tuskegee Institute, Tuskegee, Alabama (f)

LITERATURE

Thomas Bailey Aldrich. Friar Jerome's Beautiful Book (po)
Susan Brownell Anthony. History of Woman Suffrage, 4 vols, to 1887,
    1900 (hist, e)
Jane Goodwin Austin. A Nameless Nobleman (fic)
Oliver Bell Bunce. The Opinions and Disputations of Bachelor Bluff
    (e)
Frances Eliza Hodgson Burnett and William Gillette. Esmeralda (dr)
Frances Eliza Hodgson Burnett. A Fair Barbarian (fic)
George Washington Cable. Madame Delphine (fic)
Charles Carleton Coffin. The Boys of '61 (fic)

Rose Terry Cooke. Somebody's Neighbors (fic)
Ina Donna Coolbrith. A Perfect Day (po)
John William DeForest. The Bloody Chasm (fic)
Edgar Fawcett. Americans Abroad (dr)
William Davis Gallagher. Miami Woods (po)
William Gillette. The Private Secretary (dr)
Joel Chandler Harris. Uncle Remus: His Songs and His Sayings (po,
    (misc)
Bronson Crocker Howard. Baron Rudolph (dr)
William Dean Howells. Dr. Breen's Practice (fic)
_____. A Fearful Responsibility (fic)
Helen Maria Hunt Jackson. A Century of Dishonor (hist)
Henry James. The Portrait of a Lady (fic)
_____. Washington Square (fic)
James Otis Kaler (James Otis). Toly Tyler; or, Ten Weeks with a Cir-
    cus (fic)
Harriet Mulford Stone Lothrop (Margaret Sidney). Five Little Peppers
    and How They Grew (juv)
Sarah Pratt McLean. Cape Cod Folks (fic)
Fitz-James O'Brien. Poems and Stories (po, fic, pub)
Edward Payson Roe. Without a Home (fic)
Francis Richard Stockton. The Floating Prince and Other Fairy Tales
    (juv, fic)
James Maurice Thompson. A Tallahassee Girl (fic)
Henry David Thoreau. Early Spring in Massachusetts (nar, pub)
Mary Spear Tiernan. Homoselle (fic)
Albion Winegar Tourgee. A Royal Gentleman (fic)
Charles Dudley Warner. American Men of Letters Series, to 1904
    (biog, e, ed)
_____. Captain John Smith (biog)
_____. Washington Irving (biog)
Walt Whitman. Leaves of Grass, rev ed, to 1882 (po)
John Greenleaf Whittier. The King's Missive, and Other Poems (po)

1882

BIRTHS

Konrad Bercovici
Maxwell Struthers Burt
Jesse Redmon Fauset
Susan Glaspell
Herman Hagedorn
Avery Hopwood
Ludwig Lewisohn
Mina Gertrude Lowry (Mina Loy)
George Jean Nathan
James Oppenheim
Olive Higgins Prouty
Hendrik Willem Van Loon
Margaret Wilson

DEATHS

John Turvill Adams

Richard Henry Dana, Jr.
Ralph Waldo Emerson
Henry Wadsworth Longfellow
William Tappan Thompson

EVENTS

The Arkansas Traveler, to 1892 (per
The Authors' Club, New York, New York (f)

LITERATURE

Henry Brooks Adams. John Randolph (biog)
Amos Bronson Alcott. Sonnets and Canzonets (po)
Louisa May Alcott. Proverb Stories (fic)
George Bancroft. History of the Formation of the Constitution (hist)
Hubert Howe Bancroft. History of the Pacific States, 34 vols, to
    1890 (hist)
John Bigelow. Molinos the Quietist (biog, e)
Daniel Garrison Brinton. Library of Aboriginal American Literature,
    8 vols, to 1890 (ref, ed)
Bartley Campbell. The White Slave (dr)
Samuel Langhorne Clemens. The Prince and the Pauper (fic)
Francis Marion Crawford. Mr. Isaacs, a Tale of Modern India (fic)
Frank Hamilton Cushing. Myths of Creation (trans)
Thomas Davidson. The Philosophical System of Antonio Rosimini-Ser-
    bati (e)
William Cuthbert Falkner. The Little Brick Church (fic)
Paul Hamilton Hayne. Collected Poems (pub)
Lafcadio Hearn. One of Cleopatra's Nights (fic)
Gideon Hiram Hollister. Kenley Hollow (fic)
Bronson Crocker Howard. Young Mrs. Winthrop (dr)
William Dean Howells. A Modern Instance (fic)
Emma Lazarus. Songs of a Semite (po)
Charles Bertrand Lewis (M. Quad). Brother Gardener's Lime Kiln (fic)
Henry Wadsworth Longfellow. In the Harbor (po)
Thomas Raynesford Lounsbury. James Fenimore Cooper (biog)
Theodore Tilton. Swabian Stories (po)
Albion Winegar Tourgee. John Eax and Mamelon (fic)
Mary Ashley Van Voorhis Townsend. Down the Bayou and Other Poems
    (po)
Elizabeth Stuart Phelps Ward. Dr. Zay (fic)
Walt Whitman. Specimen Days and Collect (nar)
Constance Fenimore Woolson. Anne (fic)

1883

BIRTHS

Charles Badger Clark
Max Forrester Eastman
Arthur Davison Ficke
Martin Archer Flavin
Francis Hackett
Hatcher Hughes

Hibbard (Harry) Kemp
Alfred Kreymborg
Clarence Edward Mulford
William Carlos Williams
Austin Tappan Wright

DEATHS

William Mumford Baker
Charles Timothy Brooks
Peter Cooper
Thomas Mayne Reid

EVENTS

The Ladies' Home Journal (per, f)
Life, to 1936 (per)
Overland Monthly, San Francisco, 2nd series, to 1935 (per)

LITERATURE

Thomas Bailey Aldrich. From Ponkapong to Pesth (e)
Arlo Bates. Mr. Jacobs (fic)
Francis James Child. English and Scottish Popular Ballads, 5 vols,
   to 1898 (po, ed)
Samuel Langhorne Clemens. Life on the Mississippi (nar)
John Esten Cooke. Fanchette (fic)
_____. Virginia (hist)
Peter Cooper. Ideas for a Science of Good Government (e)
Francis Marion Crawford. Dr. Claudius (fic)
Mary Elizabeth Mapes Dodge. Donald and Dorothy (fic)
Edward Eggleston. The Hoosier Schoolboy (fic)
Mary Hallock Foote. The Led-Horse Claim (fic)
Robert Grant. An Average Man (fic)
Arthur Sherburne Hardy. But Yet a Woman (fic)
Joel Chandler Harris. Nights with Uncle Remus (po, fic)
Nathaniel Hawthorne. The Ancestral Footstep (fic, pub)
_____. Dr. Grimshawe's Secret (fic, pub)
Oliver Wendell Holmes. Medical Essays (e)
_____. Pages from an Old Volume (e)
Blanche Willis Howard. Guenn: A Wave on the Breton Coast (fic)
Edgar Watson Howe. The Story of a Country Town (fic)
William Dean Howells. A Woman's Reasons (fic)
Henry James. Daisy Miller (dr)
_____. Portraits of Places (des)
_____. The Siege of London (fic)
Charles King. The Colonel's Daughter (fic)
Sidney Lanier. The English Novel (e, pub)
Katherine Sherwood Bonner MacDowell. Dialect Tales (fic)
Sarah Pratt McLean. Towhead (fic)
George Wilbur Peck. Peck's Bad Boy and His Pa (fic, nar)
George Dennison Prentice. Poems (pub)
James Whitcomb Riley. The Old Swimmin'-Hole and 'Leven More Poems
   (po)
Edward Rowland Sill (Andrew Hedbrooke). The Venus of Milo and Other
   Poems (po)

William Henry Thomes. On Land and Sea (trav)
James Maurice Thompson. His Second Campaign (fic)
_____. Songs of Fair Weather (po)
William Tappan Thompson. John's Alive, and Other Sketches (fic, pub)
Albion Winegar Tourgee. Hot Plowshares (fic)
Jones Very. Poems (pub)
Elizabeth Stuart Phelps Ward. Beyond the Gates (fic)
Charles Dudley Warner. A Roundabout Journey (trav)
John Greenleaf Whittier. The Bay of Seven Islands, and Other Poems
    (po)
Ella Wheeler Wilcox. Poems of Passion (po)
Constance Fenimore Woolson. For the Major (fic)

1884

BIRTHS

    Earl Derr Biggers
    Donald Evans
    Edith Summers Kelley
    Alfred Damon Runyon
    Odell Shepard
    Charles Wilbert Snow
    Sara Teasdale
    George Sylvester Viereck
    Margaret Widdemer
    Elinor Hoyt Wylie

DEATHS

    Thomas Gold Appleton
    William Wells Brown
    Augustine Joseph Hickey Duganne
    Charles Fenno Hoffman
    Mary Sergeant Nichols

EVENTS

    American Historical Association (f)
    Grolier Club, New York, New York (f)

LITERATURE

    Henry Brooks Adam. Esther (fic)
    Louisa May Alcott. Spinning-Wheel Stories (fic)
    Thomas Bailey Aldrich. Mercedes and Later Lyrics (po)
    John Peter Altgeld. Our Penal Machinery and Its Victims (e)
    Arlo Bates. The Pagans (fic)
    Edward Bellamy. Miss Ludington's Sister (fic)
    Henry Cuyler Bunner. Airs from Arcady and Elsewhere (po)
    Edwin Lassetter Bynner. Penelope's Suitors (fic)
    Henry Guy Carleton. The Thompson Street Poker Club (dr)
    Samuel Langhorne Clemens. The Adventures of Huckleberry Finn (fic)
    Francis Marion Crawford. An American Politician (fic)
    _____. A Roman Singer (fic)

_____. To Leeward (fic)
William Cuthbert Falkner. Rapid Ramblings in Europe (trav)
Edgar Fawcett. The Buntling Ball (po, dr)
Louise Imogen Guiney. Songs at the Start (po)
Edward Everett Hale. The Fortunes of Rachel (fic)
Joel Chandler Harris. Mingo and Other Sketches in Black and White (fic)
Julian Hawthorne. Archibald Malmaison (fic)
_____. Nathaniel Hawthorne and His Wife (biog)
John Milton Hay. The Bread-Winners (fic)
Lafcadio Hearn. Stray Leaves from Strange Literature (fic)
Helen Maria Hunt Jackson. Ramona (fic)
Henry James. Tales of Three Cities (fic)
Sarah Orne Jewett. A Country Doctor (fic)
Richard Malcolm Johnston. Old Mark Langston, a Tale of Duke's Creek (fic)
Sidney Lanier. Poems (pub)
Katherine Sherwood Bonner MacDowell. Suwanee River Tales (fic)
James Brander Matthews. Margery's Lovers (dr)
Mary Noailles Murfree. In the Tennessee Mountains (fic)
_____. Where the Battle Was Fought (fic)
Frederic Jesup Stimson. The Crime of Henry Vane (fic)
Francis Richard Stockton. The Lady or the Tiger? (fic)
William Henry Thomes. Lewey and I (fic)
Henry David Thoreau. Summer (nar, pub)
Henry Timrod. Katie (po, pub)
George Alfred Townsend. The Entailed Hat (fic)
Albery Allson Whitman. The Rape of Florida (po)

1885

BIRTHS

Thomas Bertram Costain
DuBose Heyward
Ringgold Wilmer Lardner
Harry Sinclair Lewis
Ezra Weston Loomis Pound
Kenneth Lewis Roberts
Louis Untermeyer
Carl Clinton Van Doren
Anzia Yezierska

DEATHS

Timothy Shay Arthur
Martin Robinson Delany
Helen Hunt Maria Jackson

EVENTS

Stephen Grover Cleveland, 22nd President of the United States, to 1889
Stanford University, Palo Alto, California (f)

LITERATURE

Amelia Edith Huddleston Barr. Jan Vedder's Wife (fic)
Arlo Bates. A Wheel of Fire (fic)
Henry Ward Beecher. Evolution and Religion (e)
John Bigelow. The Writings of Samuel Jones Tilden (misc, ed)
Daniel Garrison Brinton. The Lenape and Their Legends (hist, e)
George Washington Cable. Dr. Sevier (fic)
Will Carleton. City Ballads (po)
William Ellery Channing the younger. Eliot (po)
John Esten Cooke. My Lady Pokahontas (fic)
Rose Terry Cooke. Root-Bound (fic)
Francis Marion Crawford. Zoroaster (fic)
Philander Deming. Tompkins and Other Folks (fic)
Henry Harland (Sidney Luska). As It Was Written: A Jewish Musician's
    Story (fic)
Oliver Wendell Holmes. A Mortal Antipathy (fic)
Bronson Crocker Howard. One of Our Girls (dr)
William Dean Howells. The Rise of Silas Lapham (fic)
Henry James. A Little Tour in France (fic)
_____. Stories Revived, 3 vols (fic, pub)
Thomas Allibone Janvier. Color Studies (fic)
Sarah Orne Jewett. A Marsh Island (fic)
Henry Francis Keenan. The Money-Makers (fic)
James Russell Lowell. Under the Elm and Other Poems (po)
Langdon Elwyn Mitchell. Sylvian (dr)
Silas Weir Mitchell. In War Time (fic)
Mary Noailles Murfree. Down the Ravine (fic)
_____. The Prophet of the Great Smoky Mountains
    (fic)
Edmund Quincy. The Haunted Adjutant (fic, pub)
Josiah Royce. The Religious Aspect of Philosophy (e)
Edmund Clarence Stedman. The Poets of America, 2 vols (po, ed)
Charles Warren Stoddard. The Lepers of Molokai (nar, des)
James Maurice Thompson. At Love's Extremes (fic)
Mary Spear Tiernan. Suzette (fic)
John Greenleaf Whittier. Early Poems (po, pub)
Thomas Woodrow Wilson. Congressional Government (e)

1886

BIRTHS

Zoe Akins
Margaret Ayer Barnes
William Rose Benet
Randolph Silliman Bourne
Van Wyck Brooks
Hilda Doolittle
John Gould Fletcher
Douglas Southall Freeman
Alfred Joyce Kilmer
Edward Brewster Sheldon
Shaemas Shields (Shaemas O'Sheel)
Wilbur Daniel Steele

Rex Todhunter Stout
Jean Starr Untermeyer
John Hall Wheelock

DEATHS

Charles Francis Adams the elder
Stephen Pearl Andrews
John Esten Cooke
Emily Elizabeth Dickinson
Paul Hamilton Hayne
Edward Zane Carroll Judson (Ned Buntline)
Abram Joseph Ryan
Ann Sophia Stephens
Metta Victoria Victor
Edwin Percy Whipple

EVENTS

Cosmopolitan, Rochester, New York; New York, New York (per, f)
The Forum, to 1950 (per)
Ladies' Home Companion, to 1957 (per)
The New Princeton Review, to 1888 (per)

LITERATURE

Oscar Fay Adams. Through the Years with the Poets, 12 vols (ref)
Louisa May Alcott. Jo's Boys (fic)
            . Lulu's Library, 3 vols, to 1889 (fic)
Amelia Edith Huddleston Barr. The Bow of Orange Ribbon (fic)
Henry Cuyler Bunner. The Midge (fic)
Frances Eliza Hodgson Burnett. Little Lord Fauntleroy (fic)
Edwin Lassetter Bynner. Agnes Surriage (fic)
Andrew Carnegie. Triumphant Democracy (e)
Charles Edward Carryl. Davy and the Goblin (fic)
William Ellery Channing the younger. John Brown and the Heroes of
    Harper's Ferry (po)
Rose Terry Cooke. The Sphinx's Children and Other People's (fic)
Edward Sylvester Ellis. Seth Jones; or, the Captives of the Frontier
    (fic)
William Gillette. Held by the Enemy (dr)
Robert Grant. Face to Face (fic)
Archibald Clavering Gunter. Prince Karl (dr)
Lucretia Peabody Hale. The Last of the Peterkins (sat)
Arthur Sherburne Hardy. The Wind of Destiny (fic)
Henry Harland (Sidney Luska). Mrs. Peixada (fic)
William Dean Howells. Indian Summer (fic)
Helen Maria Hunt Jackson. Sonnets and Lyrics (po, pub)
Henry James. The Bostonians (fic)
            . The Princess Casamassima (fic)
Sarah Orne Jewett. A White Heron (fic)
Isaac McLellan. Poems of the Rod and Gun (pub)
Silas Weir Mitchell. Roland Blake (fic)
Jane Marsh Parker. The Midnight Cry (fic)
Rowland Evans Robinson. Forest and Stream Fables (fic)
Edward Payson Roe. He Fell in Love with His Wife (fic)

Frederic Jesup Stimson. The Sentimental Calendar (fic)
Francis Richard Stockton. The Casting Away of Mrs. Lecks and Mrs.
    Aleshine (fic)
_____. The Late Mrs. Null (fic)
William Osborn Stoddard. The Lives of the Presidents, 10 vols, to
    1889 (biog)
Celia Laighton Thaxter. Idyls and Pastorals (po)
Denman Thompson. The Old Homestead (dr)
Jones Very. Poems and Essays (po, e, pub)
Elizabeth Stuart Phelps Ward. The Madonna of the Tubs (fic)
John Greenleaf Whittier. Poems of Nature (po)
Constance Fenimore Woolson. East Angels (fic)

1887

BIRTHS

George Abbott
Leonard Bacon
Ernest Boyd
Walter Stanley Campbell (Stanley Vestal)
Mary Ellen Chase
Floyd Dell
Edna Ferber
Norman Foerster
James Norman Hall
John Robinson Jeffers
George Edward Kelly
Marianne Craig Moore
Samuel Eliot Morrison
Charles Bernard Nordhoff

DEATHS

Jane Andrews
Henry Ward Beecher
Sylvanus Cobb, Jr.
Emma Lazarus
Ray Palmer
Charles Jacobs Peterson
John Godfrey Saxe
Edward Rowland Sill

EVENTS

Hartford (Connecticut) Courant (per, est)
Newberry Library, Chicago (f)
Scribner's Magazine, New York, to 1939 (per)

LITERATURE

Brooks Adams. The Emancipation of Massachusetts (hist)
Herbert Baxter Adams. The Study of History in American Colleges and
    Universities (e)
Amos Bronson Alcott. New Connecticutt (po)

Arlo Bates. Sonnets in Shadow (po)
James Phinney Baxter. British Invasion from the North (hist)
Frances Courtenay Baylor. Behind the Blue Ridge (fic)
John Bigelow. The Works of Benjamin Franklin, 10 vols, to 1888
   (misc, ed)
Henry B. Brewster. The Theories of Anarchy and Law (e)
Alice Brown. Fools of Nature (fic)
Henry Cuyler Bunner. The Story of a New York House (fic)
John Vance Cheney. Thistle-Drift (po)
Charles Carleton Coffin. Drum-Beat of the Nation, to 1891 (hist)
Moncure Daniel Conway. Pine and Palm (fic)
Francis Marion Crawford. Marzio's Crucifix (fic)
                      . Saracinesca (fic)
Sarah Barnwell Elliot. A Simple Heart (fic)
Harold Frederic. Seth's Brother's Wife (fic)
Mary Eleanor Wilkins Freeman. A Humble Romance (fic)
Alice French. Knitters in the Sun (fic)
Archibald Clavering Gunter. Mr. Barnes of New York (fic)
Edward Everett Hale. Franklin in France, 2 vols, to 1888 (hist)
Henry Harland (Sidney Luska). The Yoke of the Thorah (fic)
Joel Chandler Harris. Free Joe and Other Georgian Sketches (fic)
Bronson Crocker Howard. The Henrietta (dr)
William Dean Howells. The Minister's Charge (fic)
Joseph Kirkland. Zury: The Meanest Man in Spring County (fic)
Richard LeGallienne. My Ladies' Sonnets (po)
Amy Lawrence Lowell, Elizabeth Lowell, Katherine Bigelow Lowell.
   Dream Drops; or, Stories from Fairy Land (fic)
James Morrison Steele MacKaye. Paul Kauvar (dr)
Herman Melville. Billy Budd, to 1891, 1924 (fic)
Thomas Nelson Page. In Ole Virginia (fic)
George Wilbur Peck. How Private Geo. W. Peck Put Down the Rebellion
   (nar)
Lizette Woodworth Reese. A Branch of May (po)
James Whitcomb Riley. Afterwhiles (po)
Harriet Jane Hanson Robinson. Captain Mary Miller (dr)
Rowland Evans Robinson. Uncle Lisha's Shop: Life in a Corner of
   Yankeeland (fic)
Edward Payson Roe. The Earth Trembled (fic)
Josiah Royce. The Feud of Oakfield Creek (fic)
Edgar Evertson Saltus. Mr. Incoul's Misadventure (fic)
Francis Richard Stockton. The Bee Man of Orn, and Other Fanciful
   Tales (juv, fic)
Edith Matilda Thomas. Lyrics and Sonnets (po)
Elizabeth Stuart Phelps Ward. The Gates Between (fic)
                          . Jack, the Fisherman (fic)
Edwin Percy Whipple. American Literature, and Other Papers (e, pub)
                  . Recollections of Eminent Men (e, pub)
Kate Douglas Wiggin. The Birds' Christmas Carol (juv, fic)

                              1888

BIRTHS

   Maxwell Anderson
   James Boyd

Heywood Campbell Broun
Raymond Chandler
Stuart Chase
Thomas Stearns Eliot
Aline Kilmer
Clare Kummer
Eugene Gladstone O'Neill
Anne Parrish
John Crowe Ransom
Lew Sarett
Alan Seeger
Willard Huntington Wright

DEATHS

Amos Bronson Alcott
Louisa May Alcott
Bartley Campbell
James Freeman Clarke
David Ross Locke (Petroleum V. Nasby)
Edward Payson Roe

EVENTS

American Folk-Lore Society (f)
Collier's, to 1957 (per)
The Players Club, New York (f)
Temple University, Philadelphia, Pennsylvania (f)

LITERATURE

Herbert Baxter Adams. Thomas Jefferson and the University of Virginia (e, hist)
Louisa May Alcott. A Garland for Girls (fic)
Hubert Howe Bancroft. California Pastoral (e, nar)
                    . California Inter Pocula (e, hist)
John Kendrick Bangs and Frank Dempster Sherman. New Waggings of Old Tales (fic)
Amelia Edith Huddleston Barr. Remember the Alamo (fic)
Arlo Bates and Harriet L. Vose. Prince Vance (fic)
Frances Courtenay Baylor. Juan and Juanita (fic)
David Belasco and Henry C. DeMille. Lord Chumley (dr)
Edward Bellamy. Looking Backward: 2000-1887 (fic)
John Bigelow. France and the Confederate Navy (hist)
Frances Eliza Hodgson Burnett. Editha's Burglar (fic)
                    . Sara Crewe (fic)
George Washington Cable. Bonaventure (fic)
John Vance Cheney. Wood Blooms (po)
Sylvanus Cobb, Jr. The Gunmaker of Moscow (fic, pub)
Margaretta Wade Campbell Deland. John Ward, Preacher (fic)
Edward Eggleston. The Graysons (fic)
Henry Harland (Sidney Luska). My Uncle Florimond (fic)
Oliver Wendell Holmes. Before the Curfew (po)
Bronson Crocker Howard. Shenandoah (dr)
William Dean Howells. April Hopes (fic)
Henry James. The Art of Fiction (e)

_____. The Aspern Papers (fic)
_____. Partial Portraits (e)
_____. The Reverberator (fic)
Sarah Orne Jewett. The King of Folly Island (fic)
Richard Malcolm Johnston. Mr. Absalom Billingslea, and Other Georgia Folk (fic)
Charles King. A War-Time Wooing (fic)
Grace Elizabeth King. Monsieur Motle (fic)
Joseph Kirkland. The McVeys (fic)
James Russell Lowell. Heartease and Rue (po)
Herman Melville. John Marr and Other Sailors (po)
Thomas Nelson Page. Befo' de War (po)
Agnes Repplier. Books and Men (e)
James Whitcomb Riley. Pipes o' Pan at Zekesbury (po)
Amelie Rives. A Brother to Dragons (fic)
_____. Herod and Mirianne (po, dr)
_____. The Quick and the Dead? (fic)
_____. Virginia of Virginia (fic)
Irwin Russell. Poems by Irwin Russell, ed. Joel Chandler Harris (po, pub)
Edgar Evertson Saltus. The Truth about Tristrem Varick (fic)
Edmund Clarence Stedman and Ellen M. Hutchinson. A Library of American Literature, 11 vols, to 1890 (misc, ed)
Francis Richard Stockton. The Dusantes (fic)
Mary Virginia Terhune. A Gallant Fight (fic)
Ernest Lawrence Thayer. Casey at the Bat (po)
Henry David Thoreau. Winter (nar, pub)
Lewis Wallace. The Boyhood of Christ (nar)
Charles Dudley Warner. On Horseback (e)
Walt Whitman. November Boughs (po)
John Greenleaf Whittier. Narrative and Legendary Poems (po)

1889

BIRTHS

Conrad Porter Aiken
William Hervey Allen
Harry Elmer Barnes
Thomas Beer
Robert Charles Benchley
Donn Byrne
John Colton
Erle Stanley Gardner
Howard Lindsay
Waldo David Frank
Fannie Hurst
George Simon Kaufman
Ben Ames Williams

DEATHS

Samuel Austin Allibone
George Henry Calvert
William Cuthbert Falkner

Cornelius Mathews

EVENTS

The Arena, Boston, to 1909 (per)
Benjamin Harrison, 23rd President of the United States, to 1893
Hull House, Chicago (f)
Munsey's, New York, to 1929 (per)

LITERATURE

Henry Brooks Adams. History of the United States during the Adminis-
    tration of Jefferson and Madison, 9 vols, to 1891 (hist)
Jane Andrews. Stories Mother Nature Told Her Children (fic, pub)
Jane Goodwin Austin. Standish of Standish (fic)
Arlo Bates. The Philistines (fic)
James Phinney Baxter. Early Voyages to America (hist)
William Crary Brownell. French Traits, an Essay in Comparative Cri-
    ticism (e)
Andrew Carnegie. The Gospel of Wealth (e)
Mary Hartwell Catherwood. The Romance of Dollard (fic)
Samuel Langhorne Clemens. A Connecticut Yankee in King Arthur's
    Court (fic)
Francis Marion Crawford. Greifenstein (fic)
_____. Sant' Ilario (fic)
George Ticknor Curtis. Constitutional History of the United States
    to the Close of the Civil War, to 1896 (hist)
_____. John Charaxes (fic)
Edgar Fawcett. Agnosticism and Other Essays (e)
Eugene Field. A Little Book of Profitable Tales (fic, pub)
_____. A Little Book of Western Verse (po, pub)
Arthur Sherburn Hardy. Passe Rose (fic)
Henry Harland. Grandison Mather (fic)
_____. A Latin-Quarter Courtship (fic)
Lafcadio Hearn. Chita: A Memory of Last Island (fic)
Richard Hovey. The Laurel: An Ode to Mary Day Lanier (po)
William Dean Howells. Annie Kilburn (fic)
Henry James. A London Life (fic)
Emma Lazarus. Poems (pub)
Charles Bertrand Lewis (M. Quad). Trials and Troubles of the Bowser
    Family (fic)
Sarah Pratt McLean. Last Chance Junction (fic)
Amelie Rives. The Witness of the Sun (fic)
Harriet Jane Hanson Robinson. The New Pandora (dr)
Rowland Evans Robinson. Sam Lovel's Camps: Uncle Lisha's Friends un-
    der Bark and Canvas (fic)
Edgar Evertson Saltus. The Pace That Kills (fic)
_____. A Transient Guest, and Other Episodes (fic)
Francis Richard Stockton. The Great War Syndicate (fic)
Augustus Thomas. The Burglar (dr)
Charles Dudley Warner. A Little Journey in the World (fic)
Walt Whitman. Leaves of Grass, re ed (po)
Thomas Woodrow Wilson. The State: Elements of Historical and Practi-
    cal Politics (e)
Constance Fenimore Woolson. Jupiter Lights (fic)

1890

BIRTHS

Frederick Lewis Allen
Barrett Harper Clark
Marcus Cook Connelly
Elmer Holmes Davis
Harvey Fergusson
Frances Noyes Hart
Manuel Komroff
Josephine Lawrence
Claude McKay
Christopher Darlington Morley
Katherine Anne Porter
Conrad Michael Richter
Paul Rosenfeld

DEATHS

Adin Ballou
George Henry Boker
Dion Boucicault
Albert Brisbane
Oliver Bell Bunce
John Boyle O'Reilly

EVENTS

University of Chicago (f)
Literary Digest, to 1938 (per)
The Smart Set, New York, to 1930 (per)

LITERATURE

Charles Francis Adams the younger. Richard Henry Dana (biog)
Henry Mills Alden. God in His World (e)
Thomas Bailey Aldrich. Wyndham Towers (po)
Hubert Howe Bancroft. Literary Industries (auto)
Adolph Francis Alphonse Bandelier. The Delight Makers (hist)
James Phinney Baxter. Sir Ferdinando Gorges (biog)
Edwin Lassetter Bynner. The Begum's Daughter (fic)
Mary Hartwell Catherwood. The Story of Tonty (fic)
Madison Julius Cawein. Lyrics and Idyls (po)
Kate O'Flaherty Chopin. At Fault (fic)
Susan Fenimore Cooper. William West Skiles: A Sketch of Missionary
    Life (biog)
Francis Marion Crawford. A Cigarette Maker's Romance (fic)
Margaretta Ward Campbell Deland. Sidney (fic)
Emily Elizabeth Dickinson. Poems (pub)
William Clyde Fitch. Beau Brummel (dr)
Harold Frederic. In the Valley (fic)
_____. The Lawton Girl (fic)
Alice French. Expiation (fic)
Henry Blake Fuller (Stanton Page). The Chevalier of Pensieri-Vani
    (fic)

Archibald Clavering Gunter. Miss Nobody of Nowhere (fic)
Henry Harland. Two Voices (fic)
_____. Two Women or One (fic)
Constance Cary Harrison. The Anglomaniacs (fic)
John Milton Hay. Abraham Lincoln: A History, 10 vols (biog, hist)
Lafcadio Hearn. Karma (fic)
_____. Youma (fic)
James A. Herne. Margaret Fleming (dr)
Richard Hovey. Harmonics (po)
William Dean Howells. A Boy's Town (fic)
_____. A Hazard of New Fortunes (fic)
Charles Hale Hoyt. A Texas Steer (dr)
Henry James. The Tragic Muse (fic)
Thomas Allibone Janvier. The Aztec Treasure-House (fic)
Richard Malcolm Johnston. Widow Guthrie (fic)
Paul Meredith Porter. The Ugly Duckling (dr)
James Whitcomb Riley. Rhymes of Childhood (po)
Edgar Evertson Saltus. Love and Lore (e)
Frank Dempster Sherman. Lyrics for a Lute (po)
Francis Richard Stockton. Ardis Claverden (fic)
Richard Henry Stoddard. The Lion's Club and Other Poems (po)
Edith Matilda Thomas. The Inverted Torch (po)
Albion Winegar Tourgee. Pactolus Prime (fic)
Lydia Louise Ann Very. Poems and Prose Writings (pub)
John Greenleaf Whittier. Legends and Lyrics (po)
George Edward Woodberry. The North Shore Watch (po)
_____. Studies in Letters and Life (e)

1891

BIRTHS

Margaret Culkin Banning   Anne Nichols
Samuel Flagg Bemis
Octavus Roy Cohen
Esther Forbes
Maurice Gerschon Hindus
Sidney Coe Howard
Percy Marks
Henry Miller
Elliot Harold Paul
Jim Tully
Harold Vinal

DEATHS

Charles Wolcott Balestier
George Bancroft
James Russell Lowell
Robert Traill Spence Lowell
Herman Melville
Albert Pike
Mary Spear Tiernan

EVENTS

The New Nation (per, f)
Review of Reviews, to 1937 (per)

LITERATURE

James Lane Allen. Flute and Violin (fic)
Jane Goodwin Austin. Betty Alden (juv, fic)
Hubert Howe Bancroft. Chronicles of the Builders, 7 vols, to 1892
  (hist)
John Kendrick Bangs. Tiddledywink Tales (fic)
Ambrose Gwinett Bierce. Tales of Soldiers and Civilians (fic)
Hjalmar Hjorth Boyesen. The Mammon of Unrighteousness (fic)
Henry B. Brewster. The Prison (fic)
Daniel Garrison Brinton. The American Race (e, des)
Henry Cuyler Bunner. Short Sixes (fic)
_____. Zadoc Pine (fic)
Mary Hartwell Catherwood. The Lady of Fort St. John (fic)
Rose Terry Cooke. Huckleberries Gathered from New England Hills
  (fic)
Richard Harding Davis. Gallegher and Other Stories (fic)
Emily Elizabeth Dickinson. Poems: Second Series (pub)
Ignatius Donnelly. Caesar's Column: A Story of the Twentieth Century
  (fic)
Alice Morse Earle. The Sabbath in Puritan New England (hist)
Edward Eggleston. The Faith Doctor (fic, sat)
George Cary Eggleston and Dorothy Marbourg. Juggernaut (fic)
Sarah Barnwell Elliott. Jerry (fic)
Edgar Fawcett. Songs of Doubt and Dream (po)
Mary Eleanor Wilkins Freeman. A New England Nun (fic)
Hannibal Hamlin Garland. Main-Travelled Roads (fic)
Henry Harland. Mea Culpa (fic)
Francis Brett Harte. A Sappho of Green Springs and Other Stories
  (fic, pub)
Oliver Wendell Holmes. Over the Teacups (e, po)
Richard Hovey. Launcelot and Guenevere: A Poem in Dramas (po, dr)
Edgar Watson Howe. The Confession of John Whitlock (fic)
Charles Hale Hoyt. A Trip to Chinatown (dr)
Thomas Allibone Janvier. Stories of Old New Spain (fic)
_____. The Uncle of an Angel (fic)
Joseph Kirkland. The Captain of Company K (fic)
David Ross Locke (Petroleum V. Nasby). The Demagogue (fic, pub)
Herman Melville. Timoleon (po)
Harriet Monroe. Valeria and Other Poems (pub)
Thomas Nelson Page. Elsket and Other Stories (fic)
_____. On Newfound River (fic)
Lizette Woodworth Reese. A Handful of Lavender (po)
Agnes Repplier. Points of View (e)
Amelie Rives. According to St. John (fic)
Francis Hopkinson Smith. Colonel Carter of Cartersville (fic)
Francis Richard Stockton. The Rudder Grangers Abroad (fic)
William Osborn Stoddard. Little Smoke: A Tale of the Sioux (juv,
  fic)
Augustus Thomas. Alabama (dr)
Charles Dudley Warner. As We Were Saying (e)
_____. Our Italy (trav)
Walt Whitman. Good-Bye, My Fancy (po, e)

_____ . Leaves of Grass, rev ed, to 1892 (po)

1892

BIRTHS

Djuna Barnes
John Peale Bishop
Pearl Sydenstricker Buck
James Mallahan Cain
Robert Peter Tristram Coffin
Janet Flanner
Josephine Frey Herbst
Archibald MacLeish
Edna St. Vincent Millay
Elmer Reizenstein (Elmer Rice)
Thorne Smith
James Floyd Stevens
Ruth Suckow

DEATHS

Rose Terry Cooke
Christopher Pearse Cranch
George William Curtis
James Sloan Gibbons
Richard Burleigh Kimball
Walt Whitman
John Greenleaf Whittier

EVENTS

Godey's Magazine, New York, to 1898 (per)
Sewanee Review, Sewanee, Tennessee (per, f)

LITERATURE

Charles Francis Adams the younger. Three Episodes of Massachusetts
    History (nar, hist)
James Lane Allen. The Blue Grass Region of Kentucky (des)
Charles Wolcott Balestier. Benefits Forgot (fic, pub)
Ambrose Gwinett Bierce. Black Beetles in Amber (po)
_____ . The Monk and the Hangman's Daughter (fic,
    trans)
Hjalmar Hjorth Boyesen. The Golden Calf (fic)
Phillips Brooks. Essays and Addresses (e, pub)
William Crary Brownell. French Art (e)
Edwin Lassetter Bynner. The Chase of the Meteor (fic)
_____ . Zachary Phips (fic)
Henry Guy Carleton. The Gilded Fool (dr)
Charles Edward Carryl. The Admiral's Caravan (fic, po)
John Vance Cheney. The Golden Guess (e)
Samuel Langhorne Clemens. The American Claimant (fic)
Francis Marion Crawford. Don Orsino (fic)
_____ . The Three Fates (fic)

Alexander Crummell. Africa and America (e)
Thomas Davidson. Aristotle and Ancient Educational Ideals (e)
Rebecca Blaine Harding Davis. Silhouettes of American Life (fic)
Richard Harding Davis. Van Bibber and Others (fic)
_____. The West from a Car Window (nar, trav)
Eugene Field. A Second Book of Verse (po, pub)
_____. With Trumpet and Drum (po)
_____ and Roswell Martin Field. Echoes from the Sabine Farm
    (trans, po)
Mary Hallock Foote. The Chosen Valley (fic)
Sam Walter Foss. Back Country Poems (po, pub)
Harold Frederic. The Return of the O'Mahony (fic)
Henry Blake Fuller. The Chatelaine of La Trinitee (fic)
Hannibal Hamlin Garland. Jason Edwards: An Average Man (fic)
_____. A Little Norsk (fic)
_____. A Member of the Third House (fic)
_____. A Spoil of Office (fic)
Edward Everett Hale. East and West (fic)
Joel Chandler Harris. Uncle Remus and His Friends (fic)
Constance Cary Harrison. Belhaven Tales (fic)
Francis Brett Harte. Colonel Starbottle's Client and Some Other Peo-
    ple (fic, pub)
James A. Herne. Shore Acres (dr)
Bronson Crocker Howard. Aristocracy (dr)
William Dean Howells. Quality of Mercy (fic)
Henry James. The Lesson of the Master (fic)
Richard Malcolm Johnston. Mr. Billy Downs and His Likes (fic)
Grace Elizabeth King. Tales of a Time and Place (fic)
Silas Weir Mitchell. Characteristics (fic)
Harriet Monroe. Columbian Ode (po)
Benjamin Franklin Norris. Yvernelle, a Tale of Feudal France (po)
Agnes Repplier. Essays in Miniature (e)
Amelie Rives. Barbara Dering (fic)
Josiah Royce. The Spirit of Modern Philosophy (e)
Frank Dempster Sherman. Little Folk Lyrics (po)
Francis Hopkinson Smith. A Day at Laguerre's and Other Days (fic)
James Maurice Thompson. Poems (pub)
Henry David Thoreau. Autumn (nar, pub)

1893

BIRTHS

    Faith Baldwin
    Carleton Beals
    Samuel Nathaniel Behrman
    Morris Gilbert Bishop
    Maxwell Bodenheim
    William Edward March Campbell (William March)
    Carl Lamson Carmer
    Elizabeth Jane Coatsworth
    James Bryant Conant
    Russel Crouse
    Donald Grady Davidson
    Irving Fineman

Herbert Sherman Gorman
Samuel Bernard Greenberg
Joseph Wood Krutch
Margaret Kernochan Leech
Anita Loos
John Phillips Marquand
Dorothy Rothschild Parker
Evelyn Scott
Gilbert Vivian Seldes
Israel Joshua Singer
John Van Alstyn Weaver
Thyra Samter Winslow

DEATHS

Edwin Thomas Booth
Horatio Bridge
Phillips Brooks
Edwin Lassetter Bynner
Katherine Sherwood Bonner MacDowell
Francis Parkman
Elizabeth Oakes Smith

EVENTS

Stephen Grover Cleveland, 24th President of the United States, to
    1897
McClure's Magazine, to 1929 (per)
The Outlook, to 1932 (per)

LITERATURE

Henry Brooks Adams. Memoirs of Marau Taaroa, Last Queen of Tahiti
    (nar)
Thomas Bailey Aldrich. An Old Town by the Sea (e)
Adolph Francis Alphonse Bandelier. The Gilded Man (fic)
David Belasco and Franklin Fyles. The Girl I Left Behind Me (dr)
Ambrose Gwinett Bierce. Can Such Things Be? (fic)
Hjalmar Hjorth Boyesen. The Social Struggles (fic)
Frances Eliza Hodgson Burnett. The One I Know the Best of All (auto)
William Bliss Carman. Low Tide on Grand Pre: A Book of Lyrics (po)
Mary Hartwell Catherwood. Old Kaskaskia (fic)
Stephen Crane. Maggie: A Girl of the Street (fic)
Francis Marion Crawford. The Novel--What It Is (e)
                        . Pietro Ghisleri (fic)
Nathan Haskell Dole. Not Angels Quite (fic)
Paul Laurence Dunbar. Oak and Ivy (po)
Alice Morse Earle. Customs and Fasions in Old New England (hist)
Sarah Barnwell Elliot. John Paget (fic)
Emma Catherine Embury. Selected Prose Writings (e, pub)
Ralph Waldo Emerson. Natural History of Intellect (e, pub)
Ernest Francisco Fenellosa. The Discovery of America, and Other Poems
    (po)
Eugene Field. The Holy Cross, and Other Tales (fic, pub)
Harold Frederic. The Copperhead (fic)
Mary Eleanor Wilkins Freeman. Giles Corey, Yeoman (dr)

_____. Jane Field (fic)
Alice French. Stories of a Western Town (fic)
Henry Blake Fuller. The Cliff-Dwellers (fic)
Hannibal Hamlin Garland. Prairie Folks (fic)
Louise Imogen Guiney. A Roadside Harp (po)
Edward Everett Hale. A New England Boyhood (auto)
Henry Harland. Mademoiselle Miss (fic)
Constance Cary Harrison. Sweet Bells Out of Tune (fic)
Richard Hovey. Seward: An Elegy on the Death of Thomas William Par-
    sons (po)
William Dean Howells. The Coast of Bohemia (fic)
_____. An Imperative Duty (fic)
_____. The World of Chance (fic)
Henry James. Essays in London and Elsewhere (e)
_____. Picture and Text (e)
_____. The Private Life (fic)
_____. The Real Thing, and Other Tales (fic)
_____. The Wheel of Time (fic)
Sarah Orne Jewett. A Native of Winby (fic)
Grace Elizabeth King. Balcony Stories (fic)
William Lyon Phelps. The Beginnings of the English Romantic Movement
    (e)
Agnes Repplier. Essays in Idleness (e)
James Whitcomb Riley. Poems Here at Home (po)
Amelie Rives. Athelwold (dr, po)
Edgar Evertston Saltus. Madame Sapphira (fic)
Ruth McEnery Stuart. A Golden Wedding, and Other Tales (fic)
Augustus Thomas. In Mizzoura (dr)
Francis Henry Underwood. Quabbin: The Story of a Small Town (fic)
Lewis Wallace. The Prince of India (fic)
John Greenleaf Whittier. A Legend of the Lake (po)
Thomas Woodrow Wilson. Division and Reunion, 1829-1889 (hist)
_____. An Old Master, and Other Political Essays (e)

1894

BIRTHS

    Justin Brooks Atkinson
    Edward Estlin Cummings
    Clyde Brion Davis
    Rachel Lyman Field
    Louis Fraina (Lewis Corey)
    Paul Eliot Green
    Samuel Dashiell Hammett
    Ben Hecht
    George Rolfe Humphries
    Robert Gruntal Nathan
    Charles Reznikoff
    Chard Powers Smith
    Laurence Stallings
    Donald Ogden Stewart
    Genevieve Taggard
    James Grover Thurber
    Eunice Tietjens

Jean Toomer
Mark Albert Van Doren
Thames Ross Williamson

DEATHS

Jane Goodwin Austin
Susan Fenimore Cooper
George Ticknor Curtis
William Davis Gallagher
Oliver Wendell Holmes
Joseph Kirkland
James Morrison Steele MacKaye
William Frederick Poole
Celia Laighton Thaxter
Francis Henry Underwood
Constance Fenimore Woolson

EVENTS

The Chap Book, Cambridge, Massachusetts; Chicago, to 1898 (per)

LITERATURE

Thomas Bailey Aldrich. Two Bites at a Cherry with Other Tales (fic)
James Lane Allen. A Kentucky Cardinal (fic)
Gertrude Franklin Atherton. Before the Gringo Came (fic)
James Phinney Baxter. The Pioneers of New France in New England
   (hist)
Frances Courtenay Baylor. Claudia Hyde (fic)
Bernard Berenson. Venetian Painters of the Renaissance (hist)
Noah Brooks. Tales of the Maine Coast (fic)
Henry Cuyler Bunner. More Short Sixes (fic)
George Washington Cable. John March, Southerner (fic)
Henry Guy Carleton. The Butterflies (dr)
William Bliss Carman and Richard Hovey. Songs from Vagabondia (po)
Robert William Chambers. In the Quarter (fic)
Kate O'Flaherty Chopin. Bayou Folk (fic)
Samuel Langhorne Clemens. Tom Sawyer Abroad (fic)
_____. The Tragedy of Pudd'nhead Wilson (fic)
Moncure Daniel Conway. The Writings of Thomas Paine, to 1896 (misc,
   ed)
Ina Donna Coolbrith. The Singer of the Sea (po)
Francis Marion Crawford. Katherine Lauderdale (fic)
Thomas Davidson. Education of the Greek People (e)
Richard Harding Davis. The Exiles (fic)
_____. Our English Cousins (trav)
_____. The Rulers of the Mediterranean (trav)
Margaretta Wade Campbell Deland. Philip and His Wife (fic)
Mary Elizabeth Mapes Dodge. The Land of Pluck (fic)
Mary Hallock Foote. Coeur d'Alene (fic)
Paul Leicester Ford. The Honorable Peter Stirling (fic)
Harold Frederic. Marsena, and Other Stories (fic)
Mary Eleanor Wilkins Freeman. Pembroke (fic)
Hannibal Hamlin Garland. Crumbling Idols (e)
William Gillette. Too Much Johnson (dr)

Louise Imogen Guiney. A Little English Gallery (biog)
Archibald Clavering Gunter. A Princess of Paris (fic)
Frank Harris. Elder Conklin (fic)
William Dean Howells. A Traveler from Altruria (fic)
Henry James. Theatricals, 2 vols, to 1895 (dr)
Charles King. Under Fire (fic)
Ernest Lacy. Chatterton (po, dr)
James Brander Matthews. Vignettes of Manhattan (fic)
Thomas Nelson Page. The Burial of the Guns (fic)
Agnes Repplier. In the Dozy Hours (e)
Rowland Evans Robinson. Danvis Folks (fic)
Edgar Evertson Saltus. Enthralled (fic)
George Santayana. Sonnets and Other Pieces (po)
Harriet Elizabeth Prescott Spofford. A Scarlet Poppy, and Other Sto-
   ries (fic)
Frederic Jesup Stimson. Mrs. Knollys, and Other Stories (fic)
Francis Richard Stockton. Pomona's Travels (fic)
John Banister Tabb. Poems (pub)
Frederick Jackson Turner. The Significance of the Frontier in Ameri-
   can History (e)
Elizabeth Stuart Phelps Ward. A Singular Life (fic)
Charles Dudley Warner. The Golden House (fic)
John Greenleaf Whittier. The Demon Lady (po)
Constance Fenimore Woolson. Horace Chase (fic)

1895

BIRTHS

Margaret Frances Bacon
Ben Lucien Burman
Babette Deutsch
Vardis Alvero Fisher
Caroline Gordon
Robert Silliman Hillyer
John Howard Lawson
Charles MacArthur
George Rippey Stewart
Hans Otto Storm
Dan Totheroh
Edmund Wilson

DEATHS

Hjalmar Hjorth Boyesen
Philip St. George Cooke
Eugene Field
Charles Etienne Arthur Gayarre
William Starbuck Mayo
Samuel Francis Smith
William Wetmore Story
William Henry Thomes

EVENTS

American Historical Review (per, f)
The Bibelot, to 1915 (e, po, fic, per)
The Bookman, to 1933 (per)
The Lark, San Francisco, to 1897 (per)
New York Public Library (est)

LITERATURE

Brooks Adams. Law of Civilization and Decay (e)
Henry Mills Alden. A Study of Death (e)
John Kendrick Bangs. The Idiot (fic)
_____. Mr. Bonaparte of Corsica (fic)
David Belasco. The Heart of Maryland (dr)
John Bigelow. The Life of Samuel Jones Tilden (biog)
Hjalmar Hjorth Boyesen. Essays on Scandinavian Literature (e)
Henry B. Brewster. The Statuette and the Background (nar, e)
Alice Brown. Meadow-Grass (fic)
William Bliss Carman. Behind the Arras: A Book of the Unseen (po)
Robert William Chambers. The Red Republic (fic)
John Vance Cheney. The Dome in Air (e)
Hiram Martin Chittenden. Yellowstone Park (hist, des)
Ina Donna Coolbrith. Songs from the Golden Gate (po)
Stephen Crane. The Black Riders (po)
_____. The Red Badge of Courage (fic)
Francis Marion Crawford. Casa Braccio (fic)
_____. The Ralstons (fic)
Richard Harding Davis. About Paris (trav)
Nathan Haskell Dole. The Hawthorn Tree, and Other Poems (po)
Paul Laurence Dunbar. Majors and Minors (po)
Henry Blake Fuller. With the Procession (fic)
Hannibal Hamlin Garland. Rose of Dutcher's Coolly (fic)
William Gillette. Secret Service (dr)
Henry Harland. Grey Roses (fic)
Joel Chandler Harris. Mr. Rabbit at Home (fic)
Carl Sadakichi Hartmann. Conversations with Walt Whitman (nar)
Lafcadio Hearn. Out of the East (fic)
Emerson Hough. The Singing Mouse Stories (fic)
Henry James. Terminations (fic)
Sarah Orne Jewett. The Life of Nancy (fic)
Ernest Lacy. Rinaldo (po, dr)
James Russell Lowell. Last Poems (pub)
James Brander Matthews. His Father's Son (fic)
John Ames Mitchell. Amos Judd (fic)
Mary Noailles Murfree. The Mystery of Witch-Face Mountain (fic)
Paul Meredith Potter. Trilby (dr)
Philip Henry Savage. First Poems and Fragments (po, pub)
Lloyd Logan Pearsall Smith. The Youth of Parnassus (fic)
Samuel Francis Smith. Poems of Home and Country (po)
Elizabeth Drew Barstow Stoddard. Poems (pub)
Augustus Thomas. The Capitol (dr)
Edith Matilda Thomas. In Sunshine Land (po)
Henry David Thoreau. Poems of Nature (po, pub)
Theodore Tilton. Sonnets to the Memory of Frederick Douglas (po)
Edward Waterman Townsend. Chimmie Fadden Explains (fic)
_____. Chimmie Fadden, Major Max, and Other Sto-
ries (fic)

Moses Coit Tyler. Three Men of Letters (e)
Henry Van Dyke. Little Rivers (e)
Jesse Lynch Williams. Princeton Stories (fic)
Constance Fenimore Woolson. The Front Yard (fic)

1896

BIRTHS

Philip Barry
Roark Bradford
Louis Bromfield
Harold Lenoir Davis
John Roderigo Dos Passos
Thomas Hornsby Ferril
Francis Scott Key Fitzgerald
Robert McAlmon
Marjorie Kinnan Rawlings
Mari Sandoz
Robert Emmet Sherwood
Grace Zaring Stone

DEATHS

Henry Cuyler Bunner
Francis James Child
Charles Carleton Coffin
Mary Abigail Dodge (Gail Hamilton)
Harriet Elizabeth Beecher Stowe

LITERATURE

Lyman Abbott. Christianity and Social Problems (e)
Thomas Bailey Aldrich. Judith and Holofernes (po)
James Lane Allen. Aftermath (fic)
_____. A Summer in Arcady (fic)
John Kendrick Bangs. A Houseboat on the Styx (fic)
Bernard Berenson. Florentine Painters of the Renaissance (hist)
Abraham Cahan. Yekel, a Tale of the New York Ghetto (fic)
William Bliss Carman and Richard Hovey. More Songs from Vagabondia
   (po)
Robert William Chambers. A King and a Few Dukes (fic)
Samuel Langhorne Clemens. The Personal Recollections of Joan of Arc
   (fic)
_____. Tom Sawyer, Detective (fic)
Stephen Crane. The Little Regiment (fic)
Francis Marion Crawford. Corleone (fic)
Frank Hamilton Cushing. Outlines of Zuni Creation Myths (trans)
Richard Harding Davis. Three Gringos in Venezuela and Central Ameri-
   ca (trav)
Emily Elizabeth Dickinson. Poems: Third Series (po, pub)
Paul Laurence Dunbar. Lyrics of Lowly Life (po)
_____. The Uncalled (fic)
Harry Stillwell Edwards. Sons and Fathers (fic)
Chester Bailey Fernald. The Cat and the Cherub (fic)

Paul Leicester Ford. The True George Washington (e)
John William Fox, Jr. Cumberland Vendetta (fic)
Harold Frederic. The Damnation of Theron Ware (fic)
_____. March Hares (fic)
Joel Chandler Harris. Sister Jane: Her Friends and Acquaintances
   (fic)
Julian Hawthorne. A Fool of Nature (fic)
Lafcadio Hearn. Kokoro (fic)
Henry James. Embarrassments (fic)
_____. The Other House (fic)
Sarah Orne Jewett. The Country of the Pointed Firs (fic)
Richard LeGallienne. The Quest of the Golden Girl (fic)
Isaac McLellan. Haunts of Wild Game (po)
William Gilbert Patten (Burt L. Standish). Frank Merriwell (fic)
Lizette Woodworth Reese. A Quiet Road (po)
Edwin Arlington Robinson. The Torrent and the Night Before (po)
Rowland Evans Robinson. In New England Fields and Woods (nar, fic)
George Santayana. The Sense of Beauty (e)
Charles Monroe Sheldon. In His Steps (fic)
Francis Hopkinson Smith. Tom Grogan (fic)
Frederic Jesup Stimson. King Noanett (fic)
Ruth McEnery Stuart. Sonny (fic)
William Henry Thomes. The Ocean Rovers (fic, pub)
Mabel Loomis Todd. A Cycle of Sonnets (po)
Henry Van Dyke. The Story of the Other Wise Man (ser, e)
Charles Dudley Warner. The Relation of Literature to Life (e)
William Allen White. The Real Issue, and Other Stories (fic)
Thomas Woodrow Wilson. Mere Literature, and Other Essays (e)
Owen Wister. Red Men and White (fic)
Constance Fenimore Woolson. Dorothy (fic)

1897

BIRTHS

   Herbert Sebastian Agar
   Joseph Auslander
   Stringfellow Barr
   Louise Bogan
   Catherine Shober Drinker Bowen
   Kenneth Duva Burke
   William Henry Chamberlain
   Robert Myron Coates
   Merle Eugene Curti
   Bernard Augustine DeVoto
   William Harrison Faulkner
   Joseph Freeman
   Christopher LeFarge
   David Thompson Watson McCord
   Horace McCoy
   Lillian Eugenia Smith
   Thornton Niven Wilder

DEATHS

Margaret Junkin Preston

EVENTS

William McKinley, 25th President of the United States, to 1901
Survey Graphic, New York, to 1944 (per)

LITERATURE

Lyman Abbott. The Theology of an Evolutionist (e)
Oscar Fay Adams. A Dictionary of American Authors (ref)
James Lane Allen. The Choir Invisible (fic)
John Kendrick Bangs. The Pursuit of the Houseboat (fic)
Frances Courtenay Baylor. Miss Nina Barrow (fic)
Edward Bellamy. Equality (fic)
John Bennett. Master Skylark (fic)
Bernard Berenson. Central Italian Painters of the Renaissance (hist)
John Bigelow. The Mystery of Sleep (e)
Daniel Garrison Brinton. Religions of Primitive People (e)
Alice Brown. The Day of His Youth (fic)
William Bliss Carman. Ballads of Lost Haven: A Book of the Sea (po)
Mary Hartwell Catherwood. The Spirit of an Illinois Town (fic)
Kate O'Flaherty Chopin. A Night in Arcadie (fic)
Samuel Langhorne Clemens. Following the Equator (nar)
Stephen Crane. The Third Violet (fic)
Richard Harding Davis. Cuba in War Time (nar)
_____. Soldiers of Fortune (fic)
Alice Morse Earle. Colonial Days in Old New York (hist)
Charles Macomb Flandrau. Harvard Episodes (fic)
John William Fox, Jr. Hell fer Sartain (fic)
Mary Eleanor Wilkins Freeman. Jerome, a Poor Man (fic)
Alice French. The Missionary Sheriff (fic)
Hannibal Hamlin Garland. Wayside Courtships (fic)
Ellen Glasgow. The Descendant (fic)
Louise Imogen Guiney. Patrins, to 1901 (e)
Constance Cary Harrison. A Son of the Old Dominion (fic)
Carl Sadakichi Hartmann. Buddha (dr)
_____. Christ (po, dr)
Robert Herrick. The Man Who Wins (fic)
Emerson Hough. The Story of the Cowboy (hist)
William Dean Howells. The Landlord at Lion's Head (fic)
_____. An Open-Eyed Conspiracy (fic)
Henry James. The Spoils of Poynton (fic)
_____. What Maisie Knew (fic)
Richard Malcolm Johnston. Old Times in Middle Georgia (fic)
James Otis Kaler (James Otis). At the Siege of Quebec (fic)
Alfred Henry Lewis (Dan Quin). Wolfville (fic)
James Brander Matthews. Outlines in Local Color (fic)
Silas Weir Mitchell. Hugh Wynne, Free Quaker (fic)
John Trotwood Moore. Songs and Stories from Tennessee (fic, po)
Mary Noailles Murfree. The Young Mountaineers (fic)
Thomas Nelson Page. The Old Gentleman of the Black Stock (fic)
Melville Davisson Post. The Man of Last Resort (fic)
Edwin Arlington Robinson. The Children of the Night (po)
Rowland Evans Robinson. Uncle Lisha's Outing (fic)
Josiah Royce. The Conception of God (e)

Ruth McEnery Stuart. In Sumpkinsville: Character Tales (fic)
John Banister Tabb. Lyrics (po)
Moses Coit Tyler. The Literary History of the American Revolution,
    1763-1783, 2 vols (hist)
Henry Van Dyke. The First Christmas Tree (ser, e)
Lydia Louise Ann Very. Sayings and Doings among the Insects and Flo-
    wers (fic)

                              1898

BIRTHS

    Ludwig Bemelmans
    Stephen Vincent Benet
    Thomas Alexander Boyd
    Malcolm Cowley
    Horace Victor Gregory
    Donald Culross Peattie

DEATHS

    Edward Bellamy
    Alexander Crummell
    Theodore Sedgwick Fay
    Harold Frederic
    Blanch Willis Howard
    Richard Malcolm Johnston
    Daniel Ricketson
    Edward Noyes Westcott

EVENTS

    National Institute of Arts and Letters (f)

LITERATURE

    Gertrude Franklin Atherton. The Californians (fic)
    Arlo Bates. The Puritans (fic)
    David Belasco. Zaza (dr)
    Edward Bellamy. Blindman's World, and Other Stories (fic)
    Nicholas Murray Butler. The Meaning of Education (e)
    Abraham Cahan. The Imported Bridegroom, and Other Stories (fic)
    Guy Wetmore Carryl. Fables for the Frivolous (po)
    Mary Hartwell Catherwood. Heroes of the Middle West: The French
        (hist)
    Robert William Chambers. Ashes of Empire (fic)
    _____. Lorraine (fic)
    John Jay Chapman. Emerson, and Other Essays (e)
    Winston Churchill. The Celebrity: An Episode (fic)
    Stephen Crane. The Open Boat (fic)
    Francis Marion Crawford. Via Crucis (fic)
    Jane Cunningham Croly. The History of the Women's Club Movement in
        America (hist)
    Clarence Seward Darrow. A Persian Pearl (e)
    Thomas Davidson. Rousseau and Education According to Nature (e)

Richard Harding Davis. The Cuban and Porto Rican Campaigns (nar)
_____. The King's Jackal (fic)
_____. A Year from a Reporter's Note-Book (nar)
John William DeForest. A Lover's Revolt (fic)
Margaretta Wade Campbell Deland. Old Chester Tales (fic)
Finley Peter Dunne. Mr. Dooley in Peace and War (hum)
Sarah Barnwell Elliott. The Durket Sperret (fic)
John William Fox, Jr. The Kentuckians (fic)
Harold Frederic. Gloria Mundi (fic)
Louise Imogen Guiney. England and Yesterday (po)
Henry Harland. Comedies and Errors (fic)
Joel Chandler Harris. Tales of the Home Folks in Peace and War (fic)
Constance Cary Harrison. Good Americans (fic)
Robert Herrick. The Gospel of Freedom (fic)
Richard Hovey. Along the Trail (po)
_____. The Birth of Galahad (dr)
Henry James. In the Cage (fic)
_____. The Turn of the Screw (fic)
_____. The Two Magics (fic)
Richard Malcolm Johnston. Pearce Amerson's Will (fic)
George Cabot Lodge. The Song of the Wave (po)
Charles Major. When Knighthood Was in Flower (fic)
Edgar Lee Masters. A Book of Verse (po, pub)
Sarah Pratt McLean. The Moral Imbeciles (fic)
Lloyd Mifflin. The Slopes of Helicon (po)
Silas Weir Mitchell. The Adventures of Francois (fic)
Benjamin Franklin Norris. Moran of the Lady Letty (fic)
Thomas Nelson Page. Red Rock (fic)
Lottie Blair Parker. Way Down East (dr)
Josephine Preston Peabody. The Wayfarers (po)
Richard Realf. Poems by Richard Realf--Poet, Soldier, Workman (po,
     pub)
John Clark Ridpath. The Ridpath Library of Universal Literature, 25
     vols (misc, ed)
Morgan Andrew Robertson. Spun-Yarn (fic)
Rowland Evans Robinson. A Hero of Ticonderoga (fic)
Morris Rosenfeld. Songs from the Ghetto (po, pub)
Philip Henry Savage. Poems (pub)
Harriet Elizabeth Prescott Spofford. Hester Stanley's Friends (fic)
Frank Lebby Stanton. Comes One with a Song (po)
Francis Richard Stockton. Buccaneers and Pirates of Our Coast (fic)
_____. The Great Stone of Sardis (fic)
Charles Warren Stoddard. A Cruise under the Crescent (nar)
Lydia Louise Ann Very. The Better Path (fic)
_____. A Strange Disclosure (fic)
Lewis Wallace. The Wooing of Malkatoon (po)
Edward Noyes Westcott. David Harum, a Story of American Life (fic)
Owen Wister. Lin McLean (fic)

1899

BIRTHS

     Louis Adamic
     Leonie Fuller Adams

Archie Binns
William Riley Burnett
Ellsworth Prouty Conkle
John Wesley Conroy
Harold Hart Crane
Ann Green
Ernest Miller Hemingway
Janet Lewis
Joseph Moncure March
Vladimir Nabokov
Lynn Riggs
James Vincent Sheean
Philip Duffield Stong
John Orley Allen Tate
Elwyn Brooks White

DEATHS

Horatio Alger
Daniel Garrison Brinton
John Augustin Daly
Isaac McLellan
Frederic Beecher Perkins
Philip Henry Savage
Emma Dorothy Eliza Nevitte Southworth

EVENTS

Everybody's, New York, to 1928 (per)
Gideon Society (f)
Pearson's Magazine, New York, to 1925 (per)

LITERATURE

George Ade. Fables in Slang (fic)
Henry Augustin Beers. History of English Romanticism, 2 vols, to
    1901 (hist)
Ambrose Gwinett Bierce. Fantastic Tables (fic)
Alice Brown. Tiverton Tales (fic)
George Washington Cable. Strong Hearts (fic)
Mary Hartwell Catherwood. Spanish Peggy (fic)
Charles Waddell Chesnutt. The Conjure Woman (fic)
_____. The Wife of His Youth (fic)
Kate O'Flaherty Chopin. The Awakening (fic)
Winston Churchill. Richard Carvell (fic)
Stephen Crane. Active Service (fic)
_____. The Monster (fic)
_____. War Is Kind (po)
Richard Harding Davis. The Lion and the Unicorn (fic)
Nathan Haskell Dole. Omar, the Tent Maker (fic)
Paul Laurence Dunbar. Lyrics of the Hearthside (po)
Alice Morse Earle. Child Life in Colonial Days (hist)
Chester Bailey Fernald. Chinatown Stories (fic)
William Clyde Fitch. Barbara Frietchie (dr)
_____. Nathan Hale (dr)

Paul Leicester Ford. Janice Meredith (fic)
John William Fox, Jr. A Mountain Europa (fic)
Harold Frederic. The Market Place (fic)
Alice French. The Captured Dream (fic)
Hannibal Hamlin Garland. Boy Life on the Prairie (fic)
Louise Imogen Guiney. The Martyrs' Idyl (po)
Lafcadio Hearn. In Ghostly Japan (fic)
James A. Herne. The Reverend Griffith Davenport (dr)
_____. Sag Harbor (dr)
Thomas Wentworth Higginson. Old Cambridge (nar, des)
William Dean Howells. Ragged Lady (fic)
_____. Their Silver Wedding Journey (fic)
Elbert Hubbard. A Message to Garcia (nar)
Henry James. The Awkward Age (fic)
James Otis Kaler (James Otis). With Perry on Lake Erie (fic)
Ernest Lacy. The Ragged Earl (po, dr)
Edwin Charles Markham. The Man with the Hoe, and Other Poems (po)
Lloyd Mifflin. Echoes of Greek Idyls (po)
Langdon Elwyn Mitchell. Becky Sharp (dr)
Mary Noailles Murfree. The Story of Old Fort Loudon (fic)
Benjamin Franklin Norris. Blix (fic)
_____. McTeague (fic)
Morgan Andrew Robertson. Where Angels Fear To Tread (fic)
George Santayana. Lucifer: A Theological Tragedy (dr, po)
Joel Elias Spingarn. A History of Literary Criticism in the Renais-
sance (hist)
Francis Richard Stockton. A Vizier of the Two Horned Alexander (fic)
Newton Booth Tarkington. The Gentleman from Indiana (fic)
Augustus Thomas. Arizona (dr)
Henry Timrod. Complete Poems (pub)
Henry Van Dyke. Fisherman's Luck (e)
Lydia Louise Ann Very. A Strange Recluse (fic)
Charles Dudley Warner. That Fortune (fic)
Henry Kitchell Webster and Samuel Merwin. The Short-Line War (fic)
Edith Newbold Jones Wharton. The Greater Inclination (fic)
William Allen White. The Court of Boyville (fic)
George Edward Woodberry. Heart of Man (e)

6 The Twentieth Century: 1900–1940

1900

BIRTHS

Sara Mahala Redway Smith Benson
Myron Brinig
John Mason Brown
Janet Taylor Caldwell
Edward Dahlberg
Julian Green
Albert Hackett
Richard Halliburton
Laura Zametkin Hobson
Arthur Kober
Meridel LeSeuer
Margaret Mitchell
Martha Ostenso
Melvin Beaunorus Tolson
William Lindsay White
Arthur Yvor Winters
Frances Winwar
Thomas Clayton Wolfe

DEATHS

John Bidwell
Stephen Crane
Frank Hamilton Cushing
Thomas Davidson
Lucretia Peabody Hale
Richard Hovey
Charles Hale Hoyt
John Clark Ridpath
Rowland Evans Robinson
Moses Coit Tyler
Charles Dudley Warner

EVENTS

Harper's New Monthly Magazine, New York, to 1925 (per)
World's Work. to 1932 (per)

LITERATURE

Herbert Baxter Adams. Public Libraries and Popular Education (e)
James Lane Allen. The Reign of Law (fic)
Irving Addison Bacheller. Eben Holden (fic)
Lyman Frank Baum. The Wonderful Wizard of Oz (fic)
David Belasco and John L. Long. Madame Butterfly (dr)
Gelett Frank Burgess. Goops, and How To Be Them (fic, po)
John Burroughs. Squirrels and Other Fur-Bearers (e)
Guy Wetmore Carryl. Mother Goose for Grown-Ups (po)
Charles Waddell Chesnutt. The House behind the Cedars (fic)
Samuel Langhorne Clemens. The Man That Corrupted Hadleyburg (fic)
Stephen Crane. Whilomville Stories (fic)
_____. Wounds in the Raid (nar, fic)
Francis Marion Crawford. In the Palace of the King (fic)
Richard Harding Davis. With Both Armies in South Africa (nar)
William Stearns Davis. A Friend of Caesar (fic)
Theodore Herman Albert Dreiser. Sister Carrie (fic)
Paul Laurence Dunbar. The Love of Landry (fic)
_____. Uncle Eph's Christmas (dr)
John William Fox, Jr. Crittenden (fic)
Mary Eleanor Wilkins Freeman. The Heart's Highway (fic)
Henry Blake Fuller. The Last Refuge (fic)
Ellen Glasgow. The Voice of the People (fic)
Robert Grant. Unleavened Bread (fic)
Henry Harland. The Cardinal's Snuff-Box (fic)
Frank Harris. Montes the Matador (fic)
_____. Mr. and Mrs. Daventry (dr)
Lafcadio Hearn. Shadowings (fic)
Robert Herrick. The Web of Love (fic)
Richard Hovey. Taliesin: A Masque (dr)
Henry James. The Soft Side (fic)
Mary Johnston. To Have and To Hold (fic)
James Otis Kaler (James Otis). The Minute Boys of the Wyoming Valley
    (fic)
Alfred Henry Lewis (Dan Quin). Sandburrs (fic)
John (Jack) Griffith London. The Son of the Wolf (fic)
Sarah Pratt McLean. Vesty of the Basins (fic)
Lloyd Mifflin. The Fields of Dawn (po)
Langdon Elwyn Mitchell. The Adventures of Francois (dr)
Silas Weir Mitchell. Dr. North and His Friends (fic)
William Vaughan Moody. The Masque of Judgment (po, dr)
Benjamin Franklin Norris. A Man's Woman (fic)
Josephine Preston Peabody. Fortune and Men's Eyes (dr, po)
Channing Pollock. The Pit (dr)
Rowland Evans Robinson. A Danvis Pioneer (fic)
Josiah Royce. The World and the Individual, 2 vols, to 1901 (e)
George Santayana. Interpretations of Poetry and Religion (e)
Edward Rowland Sill. Prose (pub)
Hester Elizabeth Prescott Spofford. Old Madame, and Other Tragedies
    (fic)
Frank Lebby Stanton. Songs from Dixie Land (po)
Clarence Edmund Stedman. An American Anthology (misc, ed)

Ida Minerva Tarbell. Life of Abraham Lincoln, 2 vols (biog)
Newton Booth Tarkington. Monsieur Beaucaire (fic)
Lydia Louise Ann Very. An Old-Fashioned Garden, and Walks and Musings
    Therein (nar)
Albert Payson Terhune and Mary Virginia Terhune. Dr. Dale: A Story
    without a Moral (fic)
James Maurice Thompson. Alice of Old Vincennes (fic)
Frederic Ridgely Torrence. The House of a Hundred Lights (po)
Henry Kitchell Webster. The Banker and the Bear (fic)
Edith Newbold Jones Wharton. The Touchstone (fic)
Owen Wister. The Jimmyjohn Boss (fic)
George Edward Woodberry. Makers of Literature (e)

1901

BIRTHS

    Gerald Warner Brace
    Sterling Allan Brown
    Alfred Bertram Guthrie, Jr.
    Walter Edwin Havighurst
    Granville Hicks
    Zora Neale Hurston
    Oliver Hazard Perry LaFarge
    Theodore Morrison
    Louis Paul
    Laura Reichenthal (Laura Riding)
    Cornelia Otis Skinner
    John William Van Druten
    Glenway Wescott

DEATHS

    Herbert Baxter Adams
    William Ellery Channing the younger
    Jane Cunningham Croly
    Ignatius Donnelly
    James A. Herne
    Elijah Kellogg
    Thomas Low Nichols
    James Maurice Thompson
    Mary Ashley Van Voorhis Townsend
    Lydia Louise Ann Very
    Albery Allson Whitman

EVENTS

    Theodore Roosevelt, 26th President of the United States, to 1909
    Town and Country, New York (per, est)

LITERATURE

    Irving Addison Bacheller. D'ri and I (fic)
    John Spencer Bassett. The Writings of Colonel William Byrd (e, hist,
        biog)

David Belasco. DuBarry (dr)
Bernard Berenson. Study and Criticism of Italian Art, to 1902, 1915 (e)
Anna Hempstead Branch. The Heart of the Road (po)
Henry B. Brewster. L'Ame Paienne (po)
Le Baron Russell Briggs. School, College, and Character (e)
Alice Brown. Margaret Warrener (fic)
William Crary Brownell. Victorian Prose Masters (e)
George Washington Cable. The Cavalier (fic)
William Bliss Carman and Richard Hovey. Last Songs from Vagabondia (po)
Mary Hartwell Catherwood. Lazarre (fic)
Robert William Chambers. Cardigan (fic)
Charles Waddell Chesnutt. The Marrow of Tradition (fic)
Winston Churchill. The Crisis (fic)
Stephen Crane. Great Battles of the World (hist, pub)
Francis Marion Crawford. Marietta (fic)
Frank Hamilton Cushing. Zuni Folk Tales (ed, fic)
Paul Laurence Dunbar. The Fanatics (fic)
William Clyde Fitch. Captain Jinks of the Horse Marines (dr)
_____. The Climbers (dr)
Charles Macomb Flandrau. The Diary of a Freshman (fic)
Mary Eleanor Wilkins Freeman. The Portion of Labor (fic)
Henry Blake Fuller. Under the Skylights (fic)
William Nathaniel Harben. The Woman Who Trusted (fic)
Lafcadio Hearn. A Japanese Miscellany (fic)
Robert Herrick. The Real World (fic)
Henry James. The Sacred Fount (fic)
Thomas Allibone Janvier. The Passing of Thomas (fic)
Sarah Orne Jewett. The Tory Lover (fic)
Charles Klein. The Auctioneer (dr)
Thomas Raynesford Lounsbury. Shakespearean Wars, 3 vols, to 1906 (e, hist)
Edwin Charles Markham. Lincoln, and Other Poems (po)
George Barr McCutcheon. Graustark (fic)
John Ames Mitchell. The Pines of Lory (fic)
Silas Weir Mitchell. Circumstance (fic)
William Vaughan Moody. Poems (pub)
Benjamin Franklin Norris. The Octopus (fic)
Albert Bigelow Paine. The Great White Way (dr)
Josephine Preston Peabody. Marlowe (dr, po)
David Graham Phillips. The Great God Success (fic)
Joseph Percival Pollard. The Imitator (fic)
Paul Meredith Potter. Under Two Flags (dr)
Agnes Repplier. The Fireside Sphinx (e)
Alice Caldwell Hegan Rice. Mrs. Wiggs of the Cabbage Patch (juv, fic)
George Santayana. A Hermit of Carmel (po)
Upton Beall Sinclair. Springtime and Harvest (fic)
Newton Booth Tarkington. Monsieur Beaucaire (dr)
Henry Van Dyke. The Ruling Passion (fic)
Elizabeth Stuart Phelps Ward. Within the Gates (fic)
Henry Kitchell Webster and Samuel Merwin. Calumet "K" (fic)
Edward Noyes Westcott. The Teller (fic, let)
Edith Newbold Jones Wharton. Crucial Instances (fic)
Stewart Edward White. The Claim Jumpers (fic)
Albery Allson Whitman. An Idyl of the South (po)

1902

BIRTHS

Mortimore Jerome Adler
Nathan Asch
Albert Bein
Arna Wendell Bontemps
Henry Steele Commager
Jonathan Worth Daniels
Kenneth Fearing
Wolcott Gibbs
James Langston Hughes
Charles Augustus Lindbergh
Andrew Nelson Lytle
Francis Otto Matthiessen
Ogden Nash
John Ernst Steinbeck
Marya Zaturenska

DEATHS

John Peter Altgeld
Mary Hartwell Catherwood
Edward Eggleston
Thomas Dunn English
Paul Leicester Ford
Francis Brett Harte
Benjamin Franklin Norris
Francis Richard Stockton
Elizabeth Drew Barstow Stoddard
Francis Fuller Victor

EVENTS

South-Atlantic Quarterly, Durham, North Carolina (per, f)

LITERATURE

Jane Addams. Democracy and Social Ethics (e)
George Ade. The Sultan of Sulu (dr)
Elizabeth Chase Akers. The Sunset Song, and Other Verses (po)
Gertrude Franklin Atherton. The Conqueror (fic)
_____. The Splendid Idle Forties (fic)
David Belasco and John L. Long. The Darling of the Gods (dr)
Borden Parker Browne. Theism (e)
George Washington Cable. Bylow Hill (fic)
Andrew Carnegie. The Empire of Business (e)
Guy Wetmore Carryl. The Transgression of Andrew Vane (fic)
Hiram Martin Chittenden. The American Fur Trade of the Far West
  (hist)
Stephen Crane. Last Words (fic, pub)
Francis Marion Crawford. Francesca da Rimini (dr)
Richard Harding Davis. Captain Macklin (fic)
_____. Ranson's Folly (fic)

_____. The White Mice (fic)
William Stearns Davis. God Wills It (fic)
John William DeForest. Poems (pub)
Thomas Dixon. The Leopard's Spots (fic)
Paul Laurence Dunbar. The Sport of the Gods (fic)
George Cary Eggleston. Dorothy South (fic)
William Clyde Fitch. The Girl with the Green Eyes (dr)
Ellen Glasgow. The Battle-Ground (fic)
_____. The Freeman, and Other Poems (po)
Edward Everett Hale. Memories of a Hundred Years (auto)
William Nathaniel Harben. Abner Daniel (fic)
Frank Harris. The Making of a Statesman (fic)
Joel Chandler Harris. Gabriel Tolliver: A Story of Reconstruction
    (fic)
Carl Sadakichi Hartmann. A History of American Art (hist)
Lafcadio Hearn. Kotto (fic)
Emerson Hough. The Mississippi Bubble (fic)
Wallace Admah Irwin. The Love Sonnets of a Hoodlum (po)
_____. The Rubiyat of Omar Khayyam, Jr. (po)
Henry James. The Wing of the Dove (fic)
Sidney Lanier. Shakespeare and His Forerunners, 2 vols (e, pub)
Alfred Henry Lewis (Dan Quin). Wolfville Days (fic)
_____. Wolfville Nights (fic)
Joseph Crosby Lincoln. Cape Cod Ballads (po)
George Cabot Lodge. Poems (pub)
John (Jack) Griffith London. The Cruise of the Dazzler (fic)
Charles Major. Dorothy Vernon of Haddon Hall (fic)
Edgar Lee Masters. Maximilian (po, dr)
George Barr McCutcheon. Brewster's Millions (fic)
John Thomas McIntyre. The Ragged Edge (fic)
Sarah Pratt McLean. Winslow Plain (fic)
Edwin Arlington Robinson. Captain Craig (po)
Anne Douglas Sedgwick. The Rescue (fic)
Edward Rowland Sill. Poems (pub)
Francis Hopkinson Smith. The Fortunes of Oliver Horn (fic)
Lloyd Logan Pearsall Smith. Trivia (e)
Joseph Trumbull Stickney. Dramatic Verses (po)
Frederic Jesup Stimson. Jethro Bacon of Sandwich (fic)
Francis Richard Stockton. Kate Bonnet (fic)
Ruth McEnery Stuart. Napoleon Jackson: The Gentleman of the Plush
    Rocker (fic)
John Banister Tabb. Later Lyrics (po)
Augustus Thomas and Richard Harding Davis. Soldiers of Fortune (dr)
Henry Van Dyke. The Blue Flower (fic)
Charles Dudley Warner. Fashions in Literature (e, pub)
Edith Newbold Jones Wharton. The Valley of Decision (fic)
Stewart Edward White. The Blazed Trail (fic)
Brand Whitlock. The 13th District (fic)
Harry Leon Wilson. The Spenders (fic)
Thomas Woodrow Wilson. A History of the American People, 5 vols
    (hist)
Owen Wister. The Virginian (fic)

1903

BIRTHS

Kay Boyle
Erskine Preston Caldwell
Morley Callaghan
John Chamberlain
Marquis William Childs
James Gould Cozzens
Countee Cullen
Marcia Davenport
Walter Dumaux Edmonds
Dudley Fitts
Paul Horgan
Charles Reginald Jackson
Clare Boothe Luce
Caroline Miller
Merrill Moore
Anais Nin
Irving Stone
Nathan Wallenstein Weinstein (Nathaniel West)
Leane Zugsmith

DEATHS

Noah Brooks
Charles Godfrey Leland
Richard Henry Stoddard

EVENTS

American Bibliography, to 1969 (ref)

LITERATURE

Lyman Abbott. Henry Ward Beecher (biog)
Andy Adams. The Log of a Cowboy (fic)
George Ade. People You Know (fic)
Thomas Bailey Aldrich. Ponkapong Papers (e)
James Lane Allen. The Mettle of the Pasture (fic)
Mary Hunter Austin. The Land of Little Rain (nar)
Ambrose Gwinett Bierce. Shapes of Clay (po)
Guy Wetmore Carryl. Grimm Tales Made Gay (po)
_____. The Lieutenant-Governor (fic)
_____. Zut, and Other Parisians (fic)
Willa Sibert Cather. April Twilights (po)
Hiram Martin Chittenden. History of Early Steamboat Navigation on
    the Missouri River (hist)
Stephen Crane and Robert Barr. The O'Ruddy (fic)
Samuel McChord Crothers. The Gentle Reader (e)
Richard Harding Davis. The Bar Sinister (fic)
Margaretta Wade Campbell Deland. Dr. Lavendar's People (fic)
William Edward Burghardt DuBois. The Souls of Black Folk (e, po)
Paul Laurence Dunbar. Lyrics of Love and Laughter (po)
Alice Morse Earle. Two Centuries of Costume (hist)

George Cary Eggleston. The Master of Warlock (fic)
Chester Bailey Fernald. Under the Jack-Staff (fic)
John William Fox, Jr. The Little Shepherd of Kingdom Come (fic)
Mary Eleanor Wilkins Freeman. The Wind in the Rose Bush (fic)
Hutchins Hapgood. The Autobiography of a Thief (nar)
Arthur Sherburne Hardy. His Daughter First (fic)
Julian Hawthorne. Hawthorne and His Circle (biog)
Henry James. The Ambassadors (fic)
_____. The Better Sort (fic)
John(Jack) Griffith London. The Call of the Wild (fic)
_____. The People of the Abyss (nar)
Percy Wallace MacKaye. The Canterbury Pilgrims (dr)
Henry Louis Mencken. Ventures into Verse (po)
Harriet Monroe. The Passing Show (po, dr)
Mary Noailles Murfree. A Spectre of Power (fic)
Meredith Nicholson. The Main Chance (fic)
Benjamin Franklin Norris. A Deal in Wheat (fic, pub)
_____. The Pit (fic, pub)
_____. The Responsibilities of the Novelist (e,
    pub)
Thomas Nelson Page. Gordon Keith (fic)
Josephine Preston Peabody. The Singing Leaves (po)
David Graham Phillips. The Master-Rogue (fic)
Edgar Evertson Saltus. Purple and Fine Women (fic)
Upton Beall Sinclair. The Journal of Arthur Stirling (fic)
_____. Prince Hagen (fic)
Francis Hopkinson Smith. Colonel Carter's Christmas (fic)
Harriet Elizabeth Prescott Spofford. In Titian's Garden (po)
George Sterling. The Testimony of the Suns (po)
Frederic Ridgely Torrence. El Dorado (dr)
John Townsend Trowbridge. Collected Poems (pub)
Edith Newbold Jones Wharton. Sanctuary (fic)
Kate Douglas Wiggin. Rebecca of Sunnybrook Farm (juv, fic)
Harry Leon Wilson. The Lions of the Lord (fic)
Owen Wister. Philosophy 4 (fic)
George Edward Woodberry. America in Literature (hist)

1904

BIRTHS

Joseph Hamilton Basso
Richard Palmer Blackmur
Gladys Hasty Carroll
Edward Chodorov
Richard Ghormley Eberhart
James Thomas Farrell
Albert Halper
Moss Hart
MacKinlay Kantor
Louis Kronenberger
Abbott Joseph Liebling
Victoria Lincoln
Sidney Joseph Perelman
William Lawrence Shirer

Isaac Bashevis Singer
Betty Wehner Smith
Louis Zukofsky

DEATHS

Guy Wetmore Carryl
Kate O'Flaherty Chopin
Edgar Fawcett
Lafcadio Hearn
Prentiss Ingraham
Horatio Franklin Moore
Joseph Trumbull Stickney

EVENTS

American Academy of Arts and Letters (f)
Bibliography Society of America (f)

LITERATURE

Henry Brooks Adams. Mont-Saint-Michel and Chartres (e, des)
George Ade. The College Widow (dr)
Mary Hunter Austin. The Basket Woman (fic)
Amelia Edith Huddleston Barr. The Belle of Bowling Green (fic)
David Belasco and John L. Long. Adrea (dr)
William Stanley Beaumont Brathwaite. Lyrics of Life and Love (po)
LeBaron Russell Briggs. Routine and Ideals (e)
James Branch Cabell. The Eagle's Shadow (fic)
William Bliss Carman. The Friendship of Art (e)
                    . Sappho (po)
Winston Churchill. The Crossing (fic)
Moncure Daniel Conway. Autobiography (pub)
Olive Tilford Dargan. Semiramis, and Other Plays (dr)
Clarence Seward Darrow. Farmington (fic)
Richard Harding Davis. The Dictator (dr)
                    . Ranson's Folly (dr)
William Stearns Davis. Falaise of the Blessed Voice (fic)
George Cary Eggleston. Evelyn Byrd (fic)
Ellen Glasgow. The Deliverance (fic)
Robert Grant. The Undercurrent (fic)
William Nathaniel Harben. The Georgians (fic)
Henry Harland. My Friend Prospero (fic)
Joel Chandler Harris. The Tar-Baby, and Other Rhymes of Uncle Remus
    (po)
Lafcadio Hearn. Kwaidan (fic)
Robert Herrick. The Common Lot (fic)
Emerson Hough. The Law of the Land (fic)
William Dean Howells. The Son of Royal Langbrith (fic)
Wallace Admah Irwin. Nautical Lays of Landsman (po)
Henry James. The Golden Bowl (fic)
George Lyman Kittredge. The Old Farmer and His Almanack (hist)
Charles Klein. The Music Master (dr)
Joseph Crosby Lincoln. Cap'n Eri (fic)
George Cabot Lodge. Cain, a Drama (po, dr)
John (Jack) Griffith London. The Sea-Wolf (fic)

Robert Morss Lovett. Richard Gresham (fic)
Harold MacGrath. The Man on the Box (fic)
William Vaughan Moody. The Fire Bringer (po, dr)
Mary Noailles Murfree. The Frontiersmen (fic)
Thomas Nelson Page. Bred in the Bone (fic)
Josephine Preston Peabody. Pan, a Choric Idyl (po)
David Graham Phillips. The Cost (fic)
William Sydney Porter (O. Henry). Cabbages and Kings (fic)
Agnes Repplier. Compromises (e)
Elizabeth Robins. The Magnetic North (fic)
Edgar Evertson Saltus. The Pomps of Satan (fic)
Frank Dempster Sherman. Lyrics of Joy (po)
Upton Beall Sinclair. Manassas (fic)
Joseph Lincoln Steffens. The Shame of the Cities (e)
Geneva Stratton-Porter. Freckles (fic, juv)
John Banister Tabb. The Rosary in Rhyme (po)
Ida Minerva Tarbell. The History of the Standard Oil Company, 2 vols
    (hist, e)
Edith Newbold Jones Wharton. The Descent of Man (fic)
Brand Whitlock. The Happy Average (fic)
_____. Her Infinite Variety (fic)
Charles Erskine Scott Wood. A Masque of Love (po)

1905

BIRTHS

Frederic Danvay
David Cornel DeJong
Vina Delmar
John Patrick Goggan (John Patrick)
Lillian Hellman
Stanley Jasspon Kunitz
Manfred Lee
Meyer Levin
Phyllis McGinley
John Henry O'Hara
Ayn Rand
Kenneth Rexroth
Dana Trilling
Lionel Trilling
Robert Penn Warren

DEATHS

John Bartlett
Emerson Bennett
Mary Elizabeth Mapes Dodge
Henry Harland
John Milton Hay
Albion Winegar Tourgee
Lewis Wallace
Charles Henry Webb

EVENTS

The Globe and Commercial Advertiser, New York, to 1923 (per)
Taylor-Trotwood Magazine, to 1910 (per)
Variety (per, f)

LITERATURE

Andy Adams. The Outlet (fic)
George Ade. Just Out of College (dr)
Mary Hunter Austin. Isidro (fic)
Charles William Beebe. Two Bird-Lovers in Mexico (des)
David Belasco. The Girl of the Golden West (dr)
James Henry Breasted. A History of Egypt (hist)
James Branch Cabell. The Line of Love (fic)
Willa Sibert Cather. The Troll Garden (fic)
Madison Julius Cawein. Vale of Tempe (po)
Edward Channing. History of the United States, 6 vols, to 1925
    (hist)
John Vance Cheney. Poems (pub)
Charles Waddell Chesnutt. The Colonel's Dream (fic)
Hiram Martin Chittenden, and A.T. Richardson. The Life of Father
    Pierre Jean deSmet, 3 vols (biog)
Charles Heber Clark. The Quakeress (fic)
Samuel McChord Crothers. The Pardoner's Wallet (e)
Clarence Seward Darrow. An Eye for an Eye (fic)
Thomas Dixon. The Clansman (fic)
Paul Laurence Dunbar. Lyrics of Sunshine and Shadow (po)
William Clyde Fitch. Her Great Match (dr)
Alice French. The Man of the Hour (fic)
William Gillette. Clarice (dr)
Robert Grant. The Orchid (fic)
Lafcadio Hearn. The Romance of the Milky Way (fic)
Robert Herrick. The Memoirs of an American Citizen (fic)
Henry James. English Hours (e)
Nicholas Vachel Lindsay. The Tree of Laughing Bells (po)
George Cabot Lodge. The Great Adventure (po)
John (Jack) Griffith London. The Game (fic)
_____. Tales of the Fish Patrol (fic)
_____. War of the Classes (e)
Henry Lewis Mencken. George Bernard Shaw: His Plays (e)
Lloyd Mifflin. The Fleeing Nymph (po)
Silas Weir Mitchell. Constance Trescot (fic)
Mary Noailles Murfree. The Storm Centre (fic)
Meredith Nicholson. The House of a Thousand Candles (fic)
Josephine Preston Peabody. The Wings (dr, po)
David Graham Phillips. The Deluge (fic)
_____. The Plum Tree (fic)
Amelie Rives. Selene (po)
Morgan Andrew Robertson. Land-Ho! (fic)
Elizabeth Robins. A Dark Lantern (fic)
Rowland Evans Robinson. Hunting without a Gun, and Other Papers
    (nar, e, fic, pub)
_____. Out of Bondage, and Other Stories (fic, pub)
Edwin Milton Royle. The Squaw Man (dr)
Edgar Evertson Saltus. The Perfume of Eros (fic)
George Santayana. The Life of Reason, 5 vols, to 1906 (e)
Joseph Trumbull Stickney. Poems (pub)

Austin Strong and Lloyd Osbourne. The Little Father of the Wilder-
   ness (dr)
Newton Booth Tarkington. The Conquest of Canaan (fic)
Edith Newbold Jones Wharton. The House of Mirth (fic)
_____. Italian Backgrounds (trav)
John Hall Wheelock and Van Wyck Brooks. Verses by Two Undergraduates
   (po)
George Edward Woodberry. The Torch (e)

1906

BIRTHS

Hannah Arendt
Edwin Corle
George Dillon
Sidney Kingsley
Richard Lattimore
Tom Lea
Anne Morrow Lindbergh
Clifford Odets
Allen Seager
Francis Steegmuller
Jessamyn West

DEATHS

Susan Brownell Anthony
John William DeForest
Paul Laurence Dunbar
John Treat Irving

EVENTS

American Magazine, New York, to 1956 (per)
Helicon Home Colony, Englewood, New Jersey, to 1907
Putnam's Magazine, 3rd series, New York, to 1910 (per)

LITERATURE

Andy Adams. Cattle Brands (fic)
Samuel Hopkins Adams. The Great American Fraud (e)
Henry Mills Alden. The Heart of Childhood (e)
Gertrude Franklin Atherton. Rezanov (fic)
Mary Hunter Austin. The Flock (nar)
Irving Addison Bacheller. Silas Strong (fic)
John Spencer Bassett. The Federalist System (hist)
Rex Ellingwood Beach. The Spoilers (fic)
Charles William Beebe. The Log of the Sun (des)
Henry Augustin Beers. A Short History of American Literature (hist)
Ambrose Gwinett Bierce. The Cynic's Word Book (ref)
Anna Hempstead Branch. The Shoes That Danced (po)
Gelett Frank Burgess. Are You a Bromide? (po, fic)
William Bliss Carman. Pipes of Pan (po)
Robert William Chambers. The Fighting Chance (fic)

_____. The Tracer of Lost Persons (fic)
Winston Churchill. Coniston (fic)
Samuel Langhorne Clemens. What Is Man? (e)
Rachel Crothers. The Three of Us (dr)
Thomas Augustine Daly. Canzoni (po)
Olive Tilford Dargon. Lord and Lovers, and Other Dramas (dr)
Richard Harding Davis. Miss Civilization (dr)
Margaretta Wade Campbell Deland. The Awakening of Helena Richie
    (fic)
Ellen Glasgow. The Wheel of Life (fic)
William Nathaniel Harben. Ann Boyd (fic)
Joel Chandler Harris. Uncle Remus and Br'er Rabbit (fic)
Constance Cary Harrison. Latter-Day Sweethearts (fic)
Carl Sadakichi Hartmann. Drifting Flowers of the Sea (po)
Avery Hopwood and Channing Pollock. Clothes (dr)
Wallace Admah Irwin. Random Rhymes and Odd Numbers (po)
William Ellery Leonard. Sonnets and Poems (po)
Joseph Crosby Lincoln. Mr. Pratt (fic)
John (Jack) Griffith London. Before Adam (fic)
_____. White Fang (fic)
James Russell Lowell. Four Poems (pub)
Harold MacGrath. Half a Rogue (fic)
Percy Wallace MacKaye. Jeanne d'Arc (po, dr)
Langdon Elwyn Mitchell. The New York Idea (dr)
William Vaughan Moody. A Sabine Woman (dr)
John Trotwood Moore. The Bishop of Cottontown (fic)
Mary Noailles Murfree. The Amulet (fic)
Benjamin Franklin Norris. The Joyous Miracle (fic, pub)
Joseph Percival Pollard. Nocturno (dr)
Ernest Poole. The Voice of the Street (fic)
William Sydney Porter (O. Henry). The Four Million (fic)
Amelie Rives. Augustine the Man (dr, po)
Elizabeth Robins. Votes for Women (dr)
Edgar Evertson Saltus. Vanity Square (fic)
Upton Beall Sinclair. The Jungle (fic)
Francis Hopkinson Smith. The Tides of Barnegat (fic)
Winchell Smith. Brewster's Millions (dr)
Harriet Elizabeth Prescott Spofford. Old Washington (fic)
Joseph Lincoln Steffens. The Struggle for Self-Government (e)
Frederic Jesup Stimson. In Cure of Her Soul (fic)
Henry David Thoreau. Journal, 14 vols (nar, pub)
Richard Walton Tully and David Belasco. Rose of the Rancho (dr)
Frederick Jackson Turner. Rise of the New West, 1819-1829 (hist)
George Sylvester Viereck. A Game at Love, and Other Plays (dr)
Jesse Lynch Williams. The Stolen Story (dr)
Owen Wister. Lady Baltimore (fic)
Stark Young. The Blind Man at the Window (po)
_____. Guenevere (po, dr)

1907

BIRTHS

    Benjamin Appel
    Wystan Hugh Auden

Dorothy Baker
Jacques Barzun
Rachel Carson
Mary Coyle Chase
Hiram Haydn
Robert Anson Heinlein
Helen MacInnes
James Albert Michener
Jesse Hilton Stuart
Joseph Wechsberg
John Wexley

DEATHS

Thomas Bailey Aldrich
Moncure Daniel Conway
Harriet Farley
Francis Miles Finch
Archibald Clavering Gunter
Mary Jane Hawes Holmes
William Wilberforce Lord
Theodore Tilton

LITERATURE

Andy Adams. Reed Anthony, Cowman: An Autobiography (fic)
Henry Brooks Adams. The Education of Henry Adams (auto, e)
Ray Stannard Baker (David Grayson). Adventures in Contentment (e)
Lyman Frank Baum. Ozma of Oz (fic)
Charles Austin Beard and James Harvey Robinson. The Development of
    Modern Europe, 2 vols, to 1908 (hist)
Gelett Frank Burgess. The Heart Line (fic)
Frances Eliza Hodgson Burnett. The Shuttle (fic)
Nicholas Murray Butler. True and False Democracy (e)
Harold Witter Bynner. An Ode to Harvard (po)
James Branch Cabell. Gallantry (fic)
Samuel Langhorne Clemens. Christian Science (e)
Francis Marion Crawford. Arethusa (fic)
Richard Harding Davis. The Scarlet Car (fic)
Philander Deming. The Story of a Pathfinder (fic)
Thomas Dixon. The Traitor (fic)
Nathan Haskell Dole. Six Italian Essays (e)
Arthur Davison Ficke. From the Isles (po)
                    . The Happy Princess (po)
Dorothy Canfield Fisher. Gunchild (fic)
Sam Walter Foss. Songs of the Average Man (po)
Hutchins Hopgood. The Spirit of Labor (nar)
William Nathaniel Harben. Mam' Linda (fic)
Alice Corbin Henderson. Adam's Dream and Two Other Miracle Plays for
    Children (dr)
Emerson Hough. The Story of the Outlaw (fic)
Richard Hovey. The Holy Graal (po, dr, pub)
William Dean Howells. Through the Eye of the Needle (fic)
Henry James. The American Scene (des)
Thomas William Lawson. Friday, the Thirteenth (fic)
John (Jack) Griffith London. Love of Life (fic)
Robert Morss Lovett. Winged Victory (fic)

Percy Wallace MacKaye. Sappho and Phaon (po, dr)
Silas Weir Mitchell. The Red City (fic)
Clarence Edward Mulford. Bar-20 (fic)
Meredith Nicholson. The Port of Missing Men (fic)
John Gneisenau Neihardt. The Lonesome Trail (fic)
David Graham Phillips. Light-Fingered Gentry (fic)
               . The Second Generation (fic)
Joseph Percival Pollard. The Ambitious Mrs. Alcott (dr)
Eleanor Hodgman Porter. Cross Currents (juv, fic)
William Sydney Porter (O. Henry). The Trimmed Lamp (fic)
               . Heart of the West (fic)
Paul Meredith Potter. The Honor of the Family (dr)
Elizabeth Robins. The Convert (fic)
Anne Douglas Sedgwick. A Fountain Sealed (fic)
Sara Teasdale. Sonnets to Duse, and Other Poems (po)
Augustus Thomas. The Witching Hour (dr)
Frederic Ridgely Torrence. Abelard and Heloise (dr, po)
George Sylvester Viereck. The House of Vampire (fic)
               . Ninevah (po)
Henry Kitchell Webster and Samuel Merwin. Comrade John (fic)
Edith Newbold Jones Wharton. Madame de Treymes (fic)
Brand Whitlock. The Turn of the Balance (fic)
Henry Leon Wilson and Newton Booth Tarkington. The Man from Home (dr)
Owen Wister. The Seven Ages of Washington (hist)
George Edward Woodberry. The Appreciation of Literature (e)
Harold Bell Wright. The Shepherd of the Hills (fic)

1908

BIRTHS

Harriette Arnow
Robert Emmett Cantwell
Paul Hamilton Engle
Martha Gellhorn
Nancy Hale
Joseph Kramm
Albert Maltz
William Maxwell
George Oppen
Joseph Stanley Pennell
Frederic Prokosch
Philip Rahv
Theodore Roethke
Leo Calvin Rosten
William Saroyan
Mark Schorer
Ira Wolfert
Richard Nathaniel Wright

DEATHS

Henry B. Brewster
Ernest Francisco Fenollosa
Joel Chandler Harris

Bronson Crocker Howard
Donald Grant Mitchell
Ellen Louise Chandler Moulton
Mary Hayden Green Pike
James Ryder Randall
Edmund Clarence Stedman

EVENTS

The Christian Science Monitor, Boston (per, f)

LITERATURE

Henry Mills Alden. Magazine Writing and the New Literature (e)
Mary Hunter Austin. Santa Lucia: A Common Story (fic)
Irving Babbitt. Literature and the American College (e)
Arlo Bates. The Intoxicated Ghost (fic)
Borden Parker Browne. Personalism (e)
William Stanley Beaumont Braithwaite. The House of Falling Leaves
    (po)
Anna Hempsted Branch. Rose of the World (dr)
Alice Brown. Rose MacLeod (fic)
William Bliss Carman. The Making of Personality (e)
Robert William Chambers. The Firing Line (fic)
George Randolph Chester. Get-Rich-Quick-Wallingford (fic)
Winston Churchill. Crewe's Career (fic)
John Wallace Crawford. The Broncho Book (po)
Samuel McChord Crothers. By the Christmas Fire (e)
James Oliver Curwood. The Courage of Captain Plum (fic)
Richard Harding Davis. Vera the Medium (fic)
Margaretta Wade Campbell Deland. R.J.'s Mother and Some Other People
    (fic)
Arthur Davison Ficke. The Earth Passion (po)
Charles Macomb Flandrau. Viva Mexico! (nar)
John William Fox, Jr. The Trail of the Lonesome Pine (fic)
Henry Blake Fuller. Waldo Trench and Others (fic)
Zona Gale. Friendship Village (fic)
Ellen Glasgow. The Ancient Law (fic)
Frank Harris. The Bomb (fic)
Robert Herrick. The Master of the Inn (fic)
_____. Together (fic)
Richard Hovey. To the End of the Trail (po, pub)
Henry James. The High Bid (dr)
_____. Views and Reviews (e)
Charles Rann Kennedy. The Servant in the House (dr)
_____. The Winterfeast (dr)
Alfred Henry Lewis (Dan Quin). Wolfville Folks (fic)
Ludwig Lewisohn. The Broken Snare (fic)
George Cabot Lodge. Herakles (po)
John (Jack) Griffith London. The Iron Heel (fic)
Percy Wallace MacKaye. Mater (dr)
_____. The Scarecrow (dr)
Henry Louis Mencken. The Philosophy of Friedrich Nietzsche (e)
David Graham Phillips. Old Wives for New (fic)
_____. The Worth of a Woman (dr)
William Sydney Porter (O. Henry). The Gentle Grafter (fic)

_____. The Voice of the City (fic)
Ezra Weston Loomis Pound. A Lumo Spento (po)
Mary Roberts Rinehart. The Circular Staircase (fic)
Amelie Rives. The Golden Rose (fic)
Elizabeth Robins. Come and Find Me (fic)
Josiah Royce. The Philosophy of Loyalty (e)
Anne Douglas Sedgwick. Amabel Channice (fic)
Edward Brewster Sheldon. Salvation Nell (dr)
Upton Beall Sinclair. The Metropolis (e)
Lloyd Logan Pearsall Smith. Sonnets (po)
Eugene Walter. Paid in Full (dr)
Edith Newbold Jones Wharton. The Hermit and the Wild Woman (fic)
_____. A Motor-Flight through France (trav)
Thomas Woodrow Wilson. Constitutional Government in the United
    States (e)
William Winter. Other Days (nar)

1909

BIRTHS

    James Agee
    Nelson Algren
    Walter Van Tilburg Clark
    August William Derleth
    Daniel Fuchs
    Chester Bomar Himes
    Elia Kazan
    Elder James Olson
    Selden Rodman
    Gladys Schmitt
    Wallace Earle Stegner
    Eudora Welty

DEATHS

    Francis Marion Crawford
    Augusta Jane Evans
    William Clyde Fitch
    Richard Watson Gilder
    Edward Everett Hale
    Sarah Orne Jewett
    George Cabot Lodge
    Olive Logan
    Charles Warren Stoddard
    John Banister Tabb

EVENTS

    National Association for the Advancement of Colored People (f)
    William Howard Taft, 27th President of the United States, to 1913
    Twentieth-Century Magazine, Boston, to 1913 (per)

LITERATURE

James Lane Allen. The Bride of the Mistletoe (fic)
Mary Hunter Austin. Lost Borders (fic)
Arlo Bates. A Mother's Meeting (dr)
Lyman Frank Baum. The Road to Oz (fic)
Rex Ellingwood Beach. The Silver Horde (fic)
John Bigelow. Retrospections of an Active Life, 5 vols, to 1913 (nar, auto)
Ambrose Gwinett Bierce. Collected Works, to 1912 (misc, pub)
_____. The Shadow on the Dial (e)
Borden Parker Browne. Studies in Christianity (e)
Van Wyck Brooks. The Wine of the Puritans (e)
Alice Brown. The Story of Thyrza (fic)
William Crary Brownell. American Prose Masters (e)
James Branch Cabell. Chivalry (fic)
_____. The Cords of Vanity (fic)
William Bliss Carman. The Rough Riders, and Other Poems (po, pub)
Samuel Langhorne Clemens. Is Shakespeare Dead? (e)
Francis Marion Crawford. The White Sister (fic)
Herbert David Croly. The Promise of American Life (e)
Wilbur Lucius Cross. The Life and Times of Laurence Sterne (biog)
Rachel Crothers. A Man's World (dr)
Thomas Augustine Daly. Carmina (dr)
Francis Miles Finch. The Blue and the Gray, and Other Verses (po, pub)
William Clyde Fitch. The City (dr)
Ellen Glasgow. The Romance of a Plain Man (fic)
Susan Glaspell. The Glory of the Conquered (fic)
Robert Grant. The Chippendales (fic)
Louise Imogen Guiney. Happy Ending (po)
Hutchins Hapgood. An Anarchist Woman (nar)
Frank Harris. The Man Shakespeare (biog, e)
Emerson Hough. 54-40 or Fight! (fic)
Wallace Admah Irwin. Letters of a Japanese Schoolboy (e)
Henry James. The Altar of the Dead (fic)
Clare Kummer. Bible Rimes for the Not Too Young (po)
Nicholas Vachel Lindsay. The Tramp's Excuse, and Other Poems (po)
George Cabot Lodge. The Soul's Inheritance (po)
John (Jack) Griffith London. Martin Eden (fic)
Lloyd Mifflin. Flower and Thorn (po)
William Vaughan Moody. The Faith Healer (dr)
Ellen Louise Chandler Moulton. Poems and Sonnets (po, pub)
Meredith Nicholson. The Lords of High Decision (fic)
Benjamin Frank Norris. The Third Circle (fic, pub)
James Oppenheim. Dr. Rast (fic)
_____. Monday Morning (po)
Thomas Nelson Page. John Marvel, Assistant (fic)
David Graham Phillips. The Fashionable Adventures of Joshua Craig (fic)
_____. The Hungry Heart (fic)
Joseph Percival Pollard. Their Day in Court (e)
William Sydney Porter (O. Henry). Options (fic)
_____. Roads of Destiny (fic)
Melville Davisson Post. Corrector of Destinies (fic)
Ezra Weston Loomis Pound. Exultations (po)
_____. Personae (po)
Lizette Woodworth Reese. A Wayside Lute (po)

Mary Roberts Rinehart. The Man in Tower Ten (fic)
Edward Brewster Sheldon. The Nigger (dr)
Lloyd Logan Pearsall Smith. Songs and Sonnets (po)
Joseph Lincoln Steffens. Upbuilders (e)
Gertrude Stein. Three Lives (fic)
George Sterling. A Wine of Wizardry (po)
Geneva Stratton-Porter. A Girl of the Limberlost (fic)
Ruth McEnery Stuart. Aunt Amity's Silver Wedding, and Other Stories
    (fic)
Augustus Thomas. The Harvest Moon (dr)
Eugene Walter. The Easiest Way (dr)
Edith Newbold Jones Wharton. Artemis to Actaeon (po)
William Allen White. A Certain Rich Man (fic)
William Carlos Williams. Poems (pub)
William Winter. Old Friends (nar)
_____. Poems (pub)
Harold Bell Wright. The Calling of Dan Matthews (fic)

1910

BIRTHS

    Paul Bowles
    Hilda Conkling
    Peter DeVries
    Robert Stuart Fitzgerald
    Ketti Frings
    Ernest Kellogg Gann
    Josephine Winslow Johnson
    Wright Morris
    Charles Olson
    Kenneth Patchen
    Winfield Townley Scott

DEATHS

    Borden Parker Browne
    Henry Guy Carleton
    Samuel Langhorne Clemens (Mark Twain)
    Rebecca Blaine Harding Davis
    Julia Ward Howe
    William Vaughan Moody
    William Sydney Porter (O. Henry)

EVENTS

    The Baltimore Evening Sun (per, f)
    The Harvard Classics (misc, pub, est)

LITERATURE

    Eleanor Hallowell Abbott. Molly Make-Believe (fic)
    Charles Follen Adams. Yawcob Strauss, and Other Poems (po)
    Jane Addams. Twenty Years at Hull House (nar)
    James Lane Allen. The Doctor's Christmas Eve (fic)

Irving Babbitt. The New Laokoon (e)
Hubert Howe Bancroft. Retrospection, Political and Personal (auto)
Charles William Beebe. Our Search for a Wilderness (nar)
Anna Hempstead Branch. Rose of the Wind (po)
Borden Parker Browne. The Essence of Religion (e)
Thornton Waldo Burgess. Old Mother West Wind (fic)
Nicholas Murray Butler. Education in the United States (e)
John Jay Chapman. The Treason and Death of Benedict Arnold (dr)
Winston Churchill. A Modern Chronicle (fic)
Dane Coolidge. Hidden Water (fic)
Samuel McChord Crothers. Among Friends (e)
Richard Harding Davis. Notes of a War Correspondent (nar)
William Stearns Davis. Influence of Wealth in Imperial Rome (hist)
Arthur Davison Ficke. The Breaking of Bonds (po)
Hannibal Hamlin Garland. Other Main-Traveled Roads (fic)
Charlotte Perkins Gilman. What Diantha Did (fic)
Hutchins Hapgood. Types from City Streets (nar)
Frank Harris. Sheakespeare and His Love (dr)
Robert Herrick. A Life for a Life (fic)
Henry James. The Finer Grain (fic)
Owen McMahon Johnson. The Varmint (fic)
Robert Underwood Johnson. Saint-Gaudens, an Ode (po)
Richard LeGallienne. Orestes (dr)
John (Jack) Griffith London. Burning Daylight (fic)
                        . Lost Face (fic)
Harold MacGrath. A Splendid Hazard (fic)
Percy Wallace MacKaye. Anti-Matrimony (dr)
John Trotwood Moore. Uncle Wash, His Stories (fic)
Clarence Edward Mulford. Hopalong Cassidy (fic)
Meredith Nicholson. Siege of the Seven Suitors (fic)
Josephine Preston Peabody. The Piper (dr, po)
David Graham Phillips. The Husband's Story (fic)
William Sydney Porter (O. Henry). Strictly Business (fic)
                        . Whirligigs (fic)
Ezra Weston Loomis Pound. Gaudier-Brzeska (biog)
                        . Nohor, Accomplishment (ed)
                        . Provenca (po)
                        . The Spirit of Romance (e)
James Ryder Randall. Poems (pub)
Eugene Manlove Rhodes. Good Men and True (fic)
Amelie Rives. Pan's Mountain (fic)
Edwin Arlington Robinson. The Town Down the River (po)
George Santayana. Three Philosophical Poets (e)
Anne Douglas Sedgwick. Franklin Winslow Kane (fic)
Mary Stanbery Watts. Nathan Burke (fic)
Edith Newbold Jones Wharton. Tales of Men and Ghosts (fic)
Stuart Edward White. The Rules of the Game (fic)
Jesse Lynch Williams. The Married Life of the Frederic Carrolls (fic)

1911

BIRTHS

William Attaway
Ben Belitt

Elizabeth Bishop
Hortense Calisher
Jerome Chodorov
James Vincent Cunningham
Pietro DiDonato
John Fante
Paul Goodman
Alfred Hayes
Ruth McKenney
Josephine Miles
Czeslaw Milosz
Ann Petry
Thomas Lanier (Tennessee) Williams
Audrey Wurdemann

DEATHS

Elizabeth Chase Akers
John Bigelow
Alice Morse Earle
Goerge Cary Eggleston
Sam Walter Foss
Thomas Wentworth Higginson
David Graham Phillips
Joseph Percival Pollard
Joseph Pulitzer
Harriet Jane Hanson Robinson
Denman Thompson
Elizabeth Stuart Phelps Ward

EVENTS

The Masses, New York, to 1918 (per)

LITERATURE

Charles Francis Adams the younger. Studies: Military and Diplomatic
    (e)
Franklin Pierce Adams. Tobogganing on Parnassus (po)
Henry Brooks Admas. The Life of George Cabot Lodge (biog)
Mary Hunter Austin. The Arrow Maker (dr)
John Spencer Bassett. Life of Andrew Jackson (biog)
Joseph Warren Beach. The Comic Spirit in George Meredith (e)
Rex Ellingwood Beach. The Ne'er-do-Well (fic)
David Belasco and Cecil B. DeMille. The Return of Peter Grimm (dr)
Ambrose Gwinett Bierce. The Devil's Dictionary (ref)
Franz Boas. The Mind of Primitive Man (e)
Frances Eliza Hodgson Burnett. The Secret Garden (fic)
Francis Marion Crawford. Wandering Ghosts (fic, pub)
Rachel Crothers. He and She (dr)
Margaretta Wade Campbell Deland. The Iron Woman (fic)
Theodore Herman Albert Dreiser. Jennie Gerhardt (fic)
Edna Ferber. Dawn O'Hara (fic)
Charles Macomb Flandrau. Prejudices (e)
Alice French. Stories That End Well (fic)
Charlotte Perkins Gilman. The Crux (fic)

Ellen Glasgow. The Miller of Old Church (fic)
Susan Glaspell. The Visioning (fic)
Frank Harris. The Women of Shakespeare (e)
Constance Cary Harrison. Recollections Grave and Gay (auto)
Henry Sydnor Harrison. Queed (fic)
Robert Herrick. The Healer (fic)
Owen McMahon Johnson. Stover at Yale (fic)
_____. The Tennessee Shad (fic)
Mary Johnston. The Long Roll (fic)
Alfred Joyce Kilmer. Summer of Love (po)
John (Jack) Griffith London. South Sea Tales (fic)
George Barr McCutcheon. Mary Midthorne (fic)
Silas Weir Mitchell. John Sherwood, Iron Master (fic)
Kathleen Norris. Mother (fic)
Thomas Nelson Page. Robert E. Lee, Man and Soldier (biog)
Lucy Fitch Perkins. The Dutch Twins (juv, fic)
David Graham Phillips. The Conflict (fic)
Eleanor Hodgman Porter. Miss Billy (juv, fic)
William Sydney Porter (O. Henry). Sixes and Sevens (fic, pub)
Ezra Weston Loomis Pound. Canzoni (po)
Anne Douglas Sedgwick. Tante (fic)
Edward Brewster Sheldon. The Boss (dr)
_____. The Princess Zim-Zim (dr)
Shaemas Shields (Shaemas O'Sheel). The Blossomy Bough (po)
Francis Hopkinson Smith. Kennedy Square (fic)
Joel Elias Spingarn. The New Criticism (e)
_____. The New Hesperides (po)
George Sterling. The House of Orchids (po)
Geneva Stratton-Porter. The Harvester (fic)
Sara Teasdale. Helen of Troy, and Other Poems (po)
Augustus Thomas. As a Man Thinks (dr)
Edith Newbold Jones Wharton. Ethan Frome (fic)
John Hall Wheelock. The Human Fantasy (po)
Kate Douglas Wiggin. Mother Carey's Chickens (juv, fic)
William Winter. Shakespeare on the Stage, 2 vols, to 1915 (e)
Harold Bell Wright. The Winning of Barbara Worth (fic)
Eugene Walter. Fine Feathers (dr)

1912

BIRTHS

John Cheever
Norman Cousins
William Everson (Brother Antoninus)
Frederick Feikema (Frederick Manfred/Feike Feikema)
Garson Kanin
Mary Therese McCarthy
Willard Motley
Eleanor May Sarton
Virginia Sorensen
Robert Lewis Taylor
Studs Louis Terkel
Barbara Wertheim Tuchman

DEATHS

Will Carleton
James Otis Kaler

EVENTS

Authors' League of America (f)
Loeb Classif Library (misc, series, trans)
Poetry: A Magazine of Verse, Chicago (per, f)

LITERATURE

Jane Addams. A New Conscience and an Ancient Evil (e)
Gertrude Franklin Atherton. Julia France and Her Times (fic)
Mary Hunter Austin. A Woman of Genius (fic)
Franz Boas. Changes in Bodily Form of Descendants of Immigrants (e)
Gamaliel Bradford. Lee, the American (biog)
James Henry Breasted. The Development of Religion and Thought in
    Ancient Egypt (hist)
Dorothy Canfield Fisher. The Squirrel-Cage (fic)
William Bliss Carman. Echoes from Vagabondia (po)
Willa Sibert Cather. Alexander's Bridge (fic)
Irvin Shrewsbury Cobb. Cobb's Anatomy (hum)
Samuel McChord Crothers. Humanly Speaking (e)
Thomas Augustine Daly. Madrigali (po)
Olive Tilford Dargan. Mortal Gods and Other Plays (dr)
William Stearns Davis. Friar of Wittenberg (fic)
Theodore Herman Albert Dreiser. The Financier (fic)
Donald Evans. Discords (po)
Dorothy Canfield Fisher. The Squirrel-Cage (fic)
Susan Glaspell. Lifted Masks (fic)
Zane Grey. Riders of the Purple Sage (fic)
Hermann Hagedorn. Poems and Ballads (pub)
Alice Corbin Henderson. The Spinning Woman of the Sky (po)
Edward Mandell House. Philip Dru, Administrator: A Story of Tomorrow,
    1920-1935 (fic)
Thomas Allibone Janvier. From the South of France (fic)
John Robinson Jeffers. Flagons and Apples (po)
James Weldon Johnson. The Autobiography of an Ex-Colored Man (fic)
Mary Johnston. Cease Firing (fic)
Charles Rann Kennedy. The Terrible Meek (dr)
William Ellery Leonard. The Vaunt of Man (po)
Joseph Crosby Lincoln. The Poetmaster (fic)
Nicholas Vachel Lindsay. Rhymes To Be Traded for Bread (po)
John (Jack) Griffith London. Smoke Bellew (fic)
Amy Lawrence Lowell. A Dome of Many-Colored Glass (po)
Percy Wallace MacKaye. Yankee Fantasies (dr)
James Brander Matthews. Vistas of New York (fic)
Claude McKay. Songs of Jamaica (po)
Henry Louis Mencken, and George Jean Nathan. The Artist (dr)
Edna St. Vincent Millay. Renascence (po)
William Vaughan Moody. The Death of Eve (po, dr, pub)
_____. Poems and Plays, 2 vols (pub)
Meredith Nicholson. A Hoosier Chronicle (fic)
David Graham Phillips. George Helm (fic, pub)

_____. The Price She Paid (fic)
Melville Davisson Post. The Nameless Thing (fic)
Ezra Weston Loomis Pound. Patria Mia (e)
_____. Ripostes (po)
_____. The Sonnets and Ballate of Guido Cavalcan-
    ti (trans)
Agnes Repplier. Americans and Others (e)
Amelie Rives. Hidden House (fic)
Edgar Evertson Saltus. The Monster (fic)
Edward Brewster Sheldon. Egypt (dr)
_____. The High Road (dr)
Richard Walton Tully. The Bird of Paradise (dr)
Henry Van Dyke. The Unknown Quantity (fic)
Jean Webster. Daddy Long-Legs (juv, fic)
Edith Newbold Jones Wharton. The Reef (fic)
John Hall Wheelock. The Beloved Adventure (po)
Edwin Percy Whipple. Charles Dickens, the Man and His Work (biog, e,
    (pub)
Elinor Hoyt Wylie. Incidental Numbers (po)

1913

BIRTHS

James Richard Broughton
Norman Oliver Brown
Eleanor Clark
Nathalia Crane
Robert Hayden
William Inge
Walter Francis Kerr
John Frederick Nims
Tillie Olsen
Muriel Rukeyser
Delmore Schwartz
Karl Jay Shapiro
Irwin Shaw
Lewis Thomas
Jerome Weidman
Mitchell Wilson

DEATHS

Thomas Allibone Janvier
Charles Major
Cincinnatus Hiner Miller (Joaquin Miller)
Jane Marsh Parker

EVENTS

Armory Art Show, New York, New York (est)
Thomas Woodrow Wilson, 18th President of the United States, to 1921

LITERATURE

Brooks Adams. Theory of Social Revolution (e)
Mary Hunter Austin. The Green Bough (fic)
_____. The Lovely Lady (fic)
Amelia Edith Huddleston Barr. All the Days of My Life (auto)
Rex Ellingwood Beach. The Iron Trail (fic)
Charles Austin Beard. An Economic Interpretation of the Constitution
    (e)
William Rose Benet. Merchants from Cathay (po)
Earl Derr Biggers. Seven Keys to Baldpate (fic)
Randolph Silliman Bourne. Youth and Life (e)
William Stanley Beaumont Braithwaite. Year Book of American Poetry,
    to 1929 (po, ed)
Alice Brown. Vanishing Points (fic)
James Branch Cabell. The Soul of Melicent (fic)
William Bliss Carman. The Kinship of Nature (e)
Willa Sibert Cather. O Pioneers! (fic)
John Jay Chapman. William Lloyd Garrison (e)
Winston Churchill. The Inside of the Cup (fic)
Rachel Crothers. Ourselves (dr)
Theodore Herman Albert Dreiser. A Traveler at Forty (auto)
Max Forrester Eastman. Enjoying Poetry (e)
Edna Ferber. Roast Beef, Medium (fic)
Arthur Davison Ficke. Mr. Faust (po, dr)
Alice French. A Step on the Stair (fic)
Robert Lee Frost. A Boy's Will (po)
Zona Gale. When I Was a Little Girl (auto, nar)
Ellen Glasgow. Virginia (fic)
Frank Harris. Unpath'd Waters (fic)
Henry Sydnor Harrison. V.V.'s Eyes (fic)
Joseph Hergesheimer. Sheridan (biog)
Robert Herrick. His Great Adventure (fic)
_____. One Woman's Life (fic)
William Dean Howells. New Leaf Mills (nar)
Wallace Admah Irwin. Mr. Togo, Maid of All Work (e)
Clarence Budington Kelland. Mark Tidd (fic)
Charles Rann Kennedy. The Necessary Evil (dr)
Richard LeGallienne. The Lonely Dancer (po)
Alfred Henry Lewis (Dan Quin). Faro Nell and Her Friends (fic)
Nicholas Vachel Lindsay. General William Booth Enters into Heaven,
    and Other Poems (po)
John (Jack) Griffith London. John Barleycorn (fic)
_____. The Valley of the Moon (fic)
Percy Wallace MacKaye. Tomorrow (dr)
Silas Weir Mitchell. Westways (fic)
Honore Willsie Morrow. The Heart of the Desert (fic)
George Jean Nathan. The Eternal Mystery (e)
Josephine Preston Peabody. The Wolf of the Gubbio (dr, po)
Eleanor Hodgman Porter. Pollyanna (juv, fic)
William Sydney Porter (O. Henry). Rolling Stones (fic, pub)
Josiah Royce. The Problem of Christianity, 2 vols (e)
George Santayana. Winds of Doctrine (e)
Anne Douglas Sedgwick. The Nest (fic)
Edward Brewster Sheldon. Romance (dr)
Constance Lindsay Skinner. Builder of Men (fic)
Mary Stanbery Watts. Van Cleve (fic)
Edith Newbold Jones Wharton. The Custom of the Country (fic)

John Hall Wheelock. Love and Liberation (po)
Stewart Edward White. Gold (fic)
William Carlos Williams. The Tempers (po)
Harry Leon Wilson. Bunker Bean (fic)
Thomas Woodrow Wilson. The New Freedom (e)
William Winter. The Wallet of Time (e)

1914

BIRTHS

John Berryman
Daniel J. Boorstin
William Seward Burroughs
Ralph Waldo Ellison
Howard Melvin Fast
Jean Garrigue
William Gibson
Albert Joseph Guerard
John Richard Hersey
Barbara Howes
David Ignatow
Randall Jarrell
Ross Franklin Lockridge, Jr.
Bernard Malamud
Budd Wilson Schulberg
William Edgar Stafford

DEATHS

Adolph Francis Alphonse Bandelier
Ambrose Gwinett Bierce
Madison Julius Cawein
Adelaide Crapsey
Alfred Henry Lewis (Dan Quin)
Silas Weir Mitchell
George Alfred Townsend

EVENTS

The Little Review, Chicago, to 1929 (per)
The New Orleans Times-Picayune, to 1980 (per)
The New Republic (per, f)
The Unpopular Review, to 1919 (per)

LITERATURE

Conrad Potter Aiken. Earth Triumphant (po)
James Lane Allen. The Last Christmas Tree (po)
Mary Hunter Austin. California, the Land of the Sun (e)
_____. Love and the Soul Maker (e)
Rex Ellingwood Beach. The Auction Block (fic)
William Rose Benet. The Falconer of God (po)
Gamaliel Bradford. Confederate Portraits (biog)
Louis Dembitz Brandeis. Other People's Money (e)

William Crary Brownell. Criticism (e)
Charles Heber Clark. By the Bend of the River (fic)
George Cram Cook and Susan Glaspell. Suppressed Desire (dr)
Herbert David Croly. Progressive Democracy (e)
Rachel Crothers. Young Wilson (dr)
Olive Tilford Dargan. Path Flower, and Other Verses (po)
Richard Harding Davis. With the Allies (nar)
Emily Elizabeth Dickinson. The Single Hound (po, pub)
Theodore Herman Albert Dreiser. The Titan (fic)
Donald Evans. Sonnets from the Patagonian (po)
Edna Ferber. Personality Plus (fic)
Arthur Davison Ficke. Sonnets of a Portrait Painter (po)
Robert Lee Frost. North of Boston (po)
Katharine Fullerton Gerould. Vain Oblations (fic)
Susan Glaspell, and George Cram Cook. Suppressed Desire (dr)
Arthur Sherburne Hardy. Diane and Her Friends (fic)
Frank Harris. Great Days (fic)
Joseph Hergesheimer. The Lay Anthony (fic)
Robert Herrick. Clark's Field (fic)
Rupert Hughes. What Will People Say? (fic)
Fannie Hurst. Just around the Corner (fic)
Henry James. Notes of a Son and Brother (auto)
_____. Notes on Novelists (e)
Thomas Allibone Janvier. At the Casa Napoleon (fic, pub)
Hibbard (Harry) Kemp. The Cry of Youth (po)
Charles Rann Kennedy. The Idol-Breaker (dr)
Alfred Joyce Kilmer. Trees, and Other Poems (po)
Alfred Kreymborg. Erna Vitek (fic)
Charles Godfrey Leland. Hans Breitmann's Ballads (po, pub)
Harry Sinclair Lewis. Our Mr. Wrenn (fic)
Nicholas Vachel Lindsay. The Congo, and Other Poems (po)
_____. Adventures While Preaching the Gospel of
   Beauty (nar)
Robert Morss Lovett. Cowards (dr)
Amy Lawrence Lowell. Sword Blades and Poppy Seed (po)
_____. Weeping Pierrot and Laughing Pierrot (dr)
William Morley Punshon McFee. Aliens (fic)
John Gneisenau Neihardt. Life's Lure (fic)
Benjamin Franklin Norris. Vandover and the Brute (fic, pub)
Eugene Gladstone O'Neill. The Web (dr)
James Oppenheim. Songs for the New Age (po)
Elmer Reizenstein (Elmer Rice). On Trial (dr)
Eugene Manlove Rhodes. Bransford in Arcadia (fic)
Amelie Rives. World's End (fic)
Edwin Arlington Robinson. Van Zorn (dr)
Ann Douglas Sedgwick. The Encounter (fic)
Edward Brewster Sheldon. The Garden of Paradise (dr)
_____. The Song of Songs (dr)
Elsie Singmaster. Katy Gaumer (fic)
Wilbur Daniel Steele. Storm (fic)
Gertrude Stein. Tender Buttons (po)
Newton Booth Tarkington. Penrod (juv, fic)
Richard Walton Tully. Omar the Tentmaker (dr)
Mary Stanbery Watts. The Rise of Jennie Cushing (fic)
Jesse Lynch Williams. And So They Were Married (dr)
George Edward Woodberry. North Africa and the Desert (trav)

1915

BIRTHS

Saul Bellow   Helen Yglesias
Nathaniel Benchley
Isabella Stewart Gardner
Charles William Goyen
Alfred Kazin
Thomas Merton
Kenneth Millar
Arthur Miller
Alice H.B. Sheldon
Jean Stafford
Theodore Harold White
Herman Wouk

DEATHS

Charles Francis Adams the younger
Charles Heber Clark
Philander Deming
Elbert Hubbard
Charles Klein
Thomas Raynesford Lounsbury
Morgan Andrew Robertson
Francis Hopkinson Smith

EVENTS

Ina Donna Coolbrith, 1st Poet Laureate of California, to 1928
The Midland, Iowa City, Iowa, to 1933 (per)
McBride's Magazine, to 1916 (per)
The Province (Massachusetts) Players (est)
The Washington Square Players, New York, New York, to 1918

LITERATURE

Lyman Abbott. Reminiscences (nar)
James Lane Allen. The Sword of Youth (fic)
Charles Austin Beard. Economic Origins of Jeffersonian Democracy
Carl Lotus Becker. Beginnings of the American People (hist)
Stephen Vincent Benet. Five Men and Pompey (po)
Herbert Eugene Bolton. Texas in the Middle Eighteenth Century (hist)
Van Wyck Brooks. America's Coming-of-Age (e)
Alice Brown. Children of Earth (dr)
John Burroughs. The Breath of Life (e)
James Branch Cabell. The Rivet in Grandfather's Neck (fic)
Willa Sibert Cather. The Song of the Lark (fic)
Robert William Chambers. Police!!! (fic)
John Jay Chapman. Greek Genius, and Other Essays (e)
                 . Memories and Milestones (e)
Winston Churchill. A Far Country (fic)
Barrett Harper Clark. British and American Drama of Today (e)
Charles Badger Clark. Sun and Saddle Leather (po)
Irvin Shrewsbury Cobb. Old Judge Priest (fic)

Grace Hazard Conkling. Afternoons of April (po)
Adelaide Crapsey. Verse (po, pub)
Benjamin DeCasseres. The Shadow-Eater (po)
Margaretta Wade Campbell Deland. Around Old Chester (fic)
Theodore Herman Albert Dreiser. The "Genius" (fic)
Maud Howe Elliott and Laura E. Richards. Julia Ward Howe (biog)
Edna Ferber. Emma McChesney and Co. (fic)
Arthur Davison Ficke. The Man on the Hilltop (po)
Dorothy Canfield Fisher. The Bent Twig (fic)
_____. Hillsboro People (fic)
John Gould Fletcher. Irradiations: Sands and Spray (po)
Katharine Fullerton Gerould. The Great Tradition (fic)
Susan Glaspell. Fidelity (fic)
Robert Grant. The High Priestess (fic)
Arthur Guiterman. The Laughing Muse (po)
Frank Harris. Contemporary Portraits, 5 vols, to 1927 (biog, nar)
_____. The Veils of Isis (fic)
Joseph Hergesheimer. Mountain Blood (fic)
James Weldon Johnson. Goyescas: or, the Rival Lovers (dr)
George Lyman Kittredge. Chaucer and His Poetry (e)
Ringgold Wilmer Lardner. Bib Ballads (po)
Harry Sinclair Lewis. The Trail of the Hawk (fic)
Ludwig Lewisohn. The Modern Drama (e)
Donald Robert Perry Marquis. Dreams and Dust (po)
Edgar Lee Masters. Spoon River Anthology (po)
Julia A. Moore. Sunshine and Shadow (fic)
Honore Willsie Morrow. Still Jim (fic)
John Gneisenau Neihardt. The Song of Hugh Glass (po)
William Lyon Phelps. Browning: How To Know Him (e)
Ernest Poole. The Harbor (fic)
Eleanor Hodgman Porter. Pollyanna Grows Up (juv, fic)
Ezra Weston Loomis Pound. Cathay (po, trans)
Elizabeth Madox Roberts. In the Great Steep's Garden (po)
Edwin Arlington Robinson. The Porcupine (dr)
Shaemas Sheilds (Shaemus O'Sheel). The Light Feet of Goats (po)
Newton Booth Tarkington. The Turmoil (fic)
Sara Teasdale. Rivers to the Sea (po)
Edith Matilda Thomas. The Flower from the Ashes (po)
Edith Newbold Jones Wharton. Fighting France, from Dunkerque to
    Belfort (nar)
Stewart Edward White. The Gray Dawn (fic)
Margaret Widdemer. The Factories, with Other Lyrics (po)
Harry Leon Wilson. Ruggles of Red Gap (fic)
Charles Erskine Scott Wood. The Poet in the Desert (po)

1916

BIRTHS

    John Malcolm Brinnin
    John Horne Burns
    John Ciardi
    Shelby Foote
    Elizabeth Hardwick
    Shirley Hardie Jackson

James Farl Powers
Albert Murray
Walker Percy
Anya Seton
Peter Viereck
Irving Wallace
Frank Garvin Yerby

DEATHS

Richard Harding Davis
Edward Sylvester Ellis
Henry James
Ernest Lacy
John (Jack) Griffith London
George Wilbur Peck
James Whitcomb Riley
Josiah Royce
Alan Seeger
Solomon Rabinowitz (Sholom Aleichem)
Frank Dempster Sherman
John Townsend Trowbridge
Jean Webster

EVENTS

The Seven Arts, to 1917 (per)
Theatre Arts, to 1964 (per)

LITERATURE

Conrad Potter Aiken. The Jig of Forslin: A Symphony (po)
_____. Turns and Movies (po)
Sherwood Anderson. Windy McPherson's Son (fic)
William Rose Benet. The Great White Wall (po)
Bernard Berenson. Venetian Paintings in America (e)
Albert Jeremiah Beveridge. Life of John Marshall, 4 vols, to 1919
    (biog, hist)
Randolph Silliman Bourne. The Gary Schools (e)
Gamaliel Bradford. Portraits of Women (biog)
James Henry Breasted and James Harvey Robinson. Ancient Times: The
    History of the Ancient World, rev 1934 (hist)
Alice Brown. The Prisoner (fic)
Harold Witter Bynner (Emanuel Morgan). Spectra (po)
_____ and Arthur Davison Ficke (Anne
    Kish). Spectra (po, sat)
James Branch Cabell. The Certain Hour (fic)
_____. From the Hidden Way (po)
William Bliss Carman. April Airs: A Book of New England Lyrics (po)
Samuel Langhorne Clemens. The Mysterious Stranger (fic, pub)
Irving Shrewsbury Cobb. Speaking of Operations (hum)
Samuel McChord Crothers. The Pleasures of an Absentee Landlord (e)
James Oliver Curwood. The Grizzly King (fic)
Olive Tilford Dargan. The Cycle's Rim (po)
Richard Harding Davis. With the French in France and Salonika (nar)
Margaretta Wade Campbell Deland. The Rising Tide (fic)

Hilda Doolittle. Sea Garden (po)
Theodore Herman Albert Dreiser. A Hoosier Holiday (auto)
_____. Plays of the Natural and Supernatu-
ral (dr)
Donald Evans. Nine Poems from a Valetudinarium (po)
_____. Two Deaths in the Bronx (po)
Dorothy Canfield Fisher. The Real Motive (fic)
John Gould Fletcher. Goblins and Pagodas (po)
Robert Lee Frost. Mountain Interval (po)
Ellen Glasgow. Life and Gabriella (fic)
Susan Glaspell. Trifles (dr)
Edgar Albert Guest. A Heap o' Livin' (po)
Hutchins Hapgood. Enemies (fic)
Arthur Sherburne Hardy. Helen (fic)
Frank Harris. Love in Youth (fic)
_____. Oscar Wilde: His Life and Confessions, 2 vols (biog)
William Dean Howells. The Leatherwood God (fic)
Fannie Hurst. Every Soul Hath Its Song (fic)
William Henry Irwin and Bayard Veiller. The Thirteenth Chair (dr)
John Robinson Jeffers. Californians (po)
Sarah Orne Jewett. Verses (pub)
Grace Elizabeth King. The Pleasant Ways of St. Medard (fic)
George Lyman Kittredge. Shakespeare (biog, e)
_____. A Study of Gawain and the Green Knight (e)
Alfred Kreymborg. Mushrooms (po)
Clare Kummer. Good Gracious, Annabelle! (dr)
Peter Bernard Kyne. Cappy Ricks (fic)
Ernest Lacy. The Bard of Mary Redcliffe (dr, pub)
Ringgold Wilmer Lardner. You Know Me, Al: A Busher's Letters (fic)
Nicholas Vachel Lindsay. A Handy Guide for Beggars, Especially Those
of the Poetic Fraternity (e, nar)
Amy Lawrence Lowell. Men, Women, and Ghosts (po)
Percy Wallace MacKaye. Poems and Plays, 2 vols (pub)
Donald Robert Percy Marquis. Hermione and Her Little Group of Seri-
ous Thinkers (sat)
Edgar Lee Masters. The Great Valley (po)
_____. Songs and Satires (po)
William Morley Punshon McFee. Casuals of the Sea (fic)
Henry Louis Mencken. A Book of Burlesques (sat)
Langdon Elwyn Mitchell. Major Pendennis (dr)
Philip Moeller. Helena's Husband (dr)
Eugene Gladston O'Neill. Bound East for Cardiff (dr)
James Oppenheim. War and Laughter (po)
Josephine Preston Peabody. Harvest Moon (po)
Ezra Weston Loomis Pound. Certain Noble Plays of Japan (dr, ed)
_____. Lustra (po)
Agnes Repplier. Counter-Currents (e)
Eugene Manlove Rhodes. The Desire of the Moth (fic)
Edwin Arlington Robinson. The Man against the Sky (po)
Josiah Royce. The Hope of the Great Community (e)
Carl August Sandburg. Chicago Poems (po, pub)
George Santayana. Egotism in German Philosophy (e)
Alan Seeger. I Have a Rendezvous with Death (po)
_____. Poems (pub)
Winchell Smith. Turn to the Right (dr)
Austin Strong. Bunny (dr)

Newton Booth Tarkington. Penrod and Sam (fic, juv)
_____. Seventeen (fic, juv)
Richard Walton Tully. The Flame (dr)
Mark Albert Van Doren. Henry David Thoreau: A Critical Study (e)
George Sylvester Viereck. Songs of Armageddon (po)
Edith Newbold Jones Wharton. Xingu, and Other Stories (fic)
Edward Lucas White. El Supremo (fic)
Harold Bell Wright. When a Man's a Man (fic)

1917

BIRTHS

Robert Woodruff Anderson
Louis Stanton Auchincloss
Jane Bowles
Gwendolyn Brooks
Leslie Aaron Fiedler
Peter McNab, Jr. (Harry Brown)
William Eastlake
Robert Traill Spence Lowell, Jr.
Carson Smith McCullers
Peter Hillsman Taylor

DEATHS

Hiram Martin Chittenden
John Wallace Crawford
Samuel Bernard Greenberg
Ruth McEnery Stuart
William Winter

EVENTS

Pulitzer Prize in Journalism and Letters (est)

LITERATURE

Conrad Potter Aiken. Nocturne of Remembered Spring (po)
Sherwood Anderson. Marching Men (fic)
Sholem Asch. Mottke, the Thief (dr)
Mary Hunter Austin. The Ford (fic)
John Spencer Bassett. The Middle Group of American Historians (e)
Lyman Frank Baum. The Lost Princess of Oz (fic)
Konrad Bercovici. Crimes of Charity (nar)
John Peale Bishop. Green Fruit (po)
Randolph Silliman Bourne. Education and Living (e)
Ernest Boyd. Contemporary Drama of Ireland (e)
Gamaliel Bradford. A Naturalist of Souls (auto)
Alice Brown. Bromley Neighborhood (fic)
William Crary Brownell. Standards (e)
Frances Eliza Hodgson Burnett. The White People (fic)
Nicholas Murray Butler. A World in Ferment (e)
Harold Witter Bynner. Grenstone Poems (po, pub)
James Branch Cabell. The Cream of Jest (fic)

Abraham Cahan. The Rise of Devid Levinsky (fic)
The Cambridge History of American Literature, 4 vols, to 1921 (hist)
Winston Churchill. The Dwelling Place of Light (fic)
Charles Badger Clark. Grass-Grown Trails (po)
Thomas Stearns Eliot. Ezra Pound: His Metric and Poetry (e)
_____ . Prufrock and Other Observations (po)
Edna Ferber. Fanny Herself (fic)
Arthur Davison Ficke. An April Elegy (po)
Mary Hallock Foote. Edith Bonham (fic)
Waldo David Frank. The Unwelcome Man (fic)
Hannibal Hamlin Garland. A Son of the Middle Border (auto)
Gordon Hall Gerould. Peter Sanders, Retired (fic)
Katharine Fullerton Gerould. A Change of Air (fic)
Susan Glaspell. Close the Book (dr)
Edgar Albert Guest. Just Folks (po)
Joseph Hergesheimer. The Three Black Penneys (fic)
Robert Silliman Hillyer. Sonnets and Other Lyrics (po)
Henry James. The Ivory Tower (fic)
_____ . The Middle Years (auto)
_____ . The Sense of the Past (fic)
James Weldon Johnson. Fifty Years, and Other Poems (po)
Alfred Joyce Kilmer. Main Street (po)
Ringgold Wilmer Lardner. Gullible's Travels (fic)
Harry Sinclair Lewis. The Innocents (fic)
_____ . The Job (fic)
Nicholas Vachel Lindsay. The Chinese Nightingale, and Other Poems
   (po)
John (Jack) Griffith London. The Human Drift (e, pub)
_____ . Jerry of the Islands (fic, pub)
Archibald MacLeish. Tower of Ivory (po)
Henry Louis Mencken. A Book of Prefaces (e)
Edna St. Vincent Millay. Renascence, and Other Poems (pub)
Philip Moeller. Madame Sand (dr)
Christopher Darlington Morley. Parnassus on Wheels (fic)
Honore Willsie Morrow. Lydia of the Pines (fic)
George Jean Nathan. Mr. George Jean Nathan Presents (e)
Charles Gilman Norris. Salt (fic)
James Oppenheim. The Book of Self (po)
David Graham Phillips. Susan Lenox: Her Fall and Rise, 2 vols (fic,
   pub)
Ernest Poole. His Family (fic)
William Sydney Porter (O. Henry). Waifs and Strays (fic, pub)
Elmer Reizenstein (Elmer Rice). Morningside Plays (dr, pub)
Eugene Manlove Rhodes. West Is West (fic)
Edwin Arlington Robinson. Merlin (po)
Upton Beall Sinclair. King Coal (fic)
Constance Lindsay Skinner. Good-Morning, Rosamond (fic)
Joel Elias Spingarn. Creative Criticism (e)
George Stirling. Thirty-Five Sonnets (po)
Frederic Jesup Stimson. My Story (fic)
Charles Warren Stoddard. Poems (po, pub)
Sara Teesdale. Love Songs (po)
Eunice Tietjens. Profiles from China (po)
Frederic Ridgely Torrence. Granny Maumee, the Rider of Dreams, and
   Simon the Cyrenian (dr)
Edith Newbold Jones Wharton. Summer (fic)

Jesse Lynch Williams. Why Marry? (dr)
William Carlos Williams. Al Que Quiere! (po)
George Edward Woodberry. Ideal Passion (po)

1918

BIRTHS

Walter Jackson Bate
Louis Osborne Coxe
Allen Stuart Drury
George Paul Elliott
Arthur Laurents
Edwin O' Connor
William Jay Smith
Frank Morrison (Mickey) Spillane

DEATHS

Charles Follen Adams
Henry Brooks Adams
Hubert Howe Bancroft
Randolph Silliman Bourne
Alfred Joyce Kilmer
John Ames Mitchell

EVENTS

The Stars and Stripes, to 1919 (per)
The Theatre Guild (f)

LITERATURE

Conrad Potter Aiken. The Charnel Rose; Senlin, a Biography; and
    Other Poems (po)
Sherwood Anderson. Mid-American Chants (po)
Mary Hunter Austin. The Trail Book (fic)
_____. The Young Woman Citizen (e)
Amelia Smith Huddleston Barr. The Paper Cap (fic)
Joseph Warren Beach. The Method of Henry James (e)
Carl Lotus Becker. Eve of the Revolution (hist)
Charles William Beebe. Jungle Peace (des)
Stephen Vincent Benet. Young Adventure (po)
William Rose Benet. The Burglar of the Zodiac (po)
Bernard Berenson. Sienese Paintings (e)
Harriot Stanton Blatch. Mobilizing Woman-Power (e)
Maxwell Bodenheim. Minna and Myself (po)
_____ and Ben Hecht. The Master-Poisoner (dr)
Ernest Boyd. Appreciations and Depreciations (e)
Van Wyck Brooks. Letters and Leadership (e)
Heywood Campbell Broun. A.E.F. (nar)
Maxwell Struthers Burt. John O'May, and Other Stories (fic)
Willa Sibert Cather. My Antonia (fic)
Robert William Chambers. The Restless Sex (fic)
George Cram Cook and Susan Glaspell. Tickless Time (dr)

Dane Coolidge. The Fighting Fool (fic)
Floyd Dell. The Angel Intrudes (dr)
Theodore Herman Albert Dreiser. Free (fic)
_____. The Hand of the Potter (dr)
Dorothy Canfield Fisher and John Redwood Fisher. Home Fires in
    France (fic)
Mary Eleanor Wilkins Freeman. Edgewater People (fic)
Henry Blake Fuller. On the Stairs (fic)
Zona Gale. Birth (fic)
Susan Glaspell and George Cram Cook. Tickless Time (dr)
_____. A Woman's Honor (dr)
Arthur Guiterman. The Mirthful Lyre (po)
Joseph Hergesheimer. Gold and Iron (fic)
Emerson Hough. The Passing of the Frontier (hist)
Fannie Hurst. Gaslight Sonatas (fic)
Henry James. Within the Rim, and Other Essays (e, pub)
Alfred Kreymborg. Plays for Poem-Mimes (dr, po)
Ringgold Wilmer Lardner. Treat 'Em Rough (fic)
Amy Lawrence Lowell. Can Grande's Castle (po)
Edgar Lee Masters. Toward the Gulf (po)
Henry Lewis Mencken. In Defense of Women (e)
Edna St. Vincent Millay. The Princess Marries the Page (dr)
Philip Moeller. Five Somewhat Historical Plays (dr, pub)
George Jean Nathan. The Popular Theatre (e)
Alfred Edward Newton. The Amenities of Book Collecting and Kindred
    Affections (e)
Eugene Gladstone O'Neill. The Moon of the Caribbees (dr)
Lucy Fitch Perkins. The French Twins (juv, fic)
Ernest Poole. The Dark People (fic)
_____. His Second Wife (fic)
_____. The Village (fic)
Melville Davisson Post. Uncle Abner: Master of Mysteries (fic)
Ezra Weston Loomis Pound. Pavannes and Divisions (e)
Lola Ridge. The Ghetto, and Other Poems (po)
Amelie Rives. The Ghost Garden (fic)
Carl August Sandburg. Cornhuskers (po)
George Santayana. Philosophical Opinions in America (e)
Upton Beall Sinclair. The Profits of Religion (e)
Thorne Smith. Biltmore Oswald: The Diary of a Hapless Recruit (fic)
Winchell Smith and Frank Bacon. Lightnin' (dr)
Wilbur Daniel Steele. Land's End (fic)
Austin Strong. Three Wise Fools (dr)
Newton Booth Tarkington. The Magnificent Ambersons (fic)
Augustus Thomas. The Copperhead (dr)
Hendrik Willem Van Loon. A Short History of Discovery (hist)
Mary Marvin Heaton Vorse. The Prestons (fic)
Mary Stanbery Watts. The Boardman Family (fic)
Edith Newbold Jones Wharton. The Marne (fic)
John Hall Wheelock. Alan Seeger (e)
Margaret Widdemer. Old Road to Paradise (po)
Charles Erskine Scott Wood. Maia (po)

                              1919

BIRTHS

Ronald Verlin Cassill
Robert Edward Duncan
Thomas Orlo Heggen
Robert James Collas Lowry
Robie Mayhew Macauley
William Morris Meredith
Jerome David Salinger
Edward Reed Whittemore II

DEATHS

Oscar Fay Adams
Henry Mills Alden
Amelia Edith Huddleston Barr
Lyman Frank Baum
Benjamin Paul Blood
Andrew Carnegie
John William Fox, Jr.
William Nathaniel Harben
Ella Wheeler Wilcox

EVENTS

University of California at Los Angeles (f)
The Liberator, New York, to 1924 (per)
The New School for Social Research, New York, New York (f)
The Unpartisan Review, to 1921 (per)
Yale Series of Younger Poets (po, pub, est)

LITERATURE

Brooks Adams. The Degradation of the Democratic Dogma (e)
Conrad Potter Aiken. Scepticisms (e)
Zoe Akins. Declassee (dr)
Sherwood Anderson. Winesburg, Ohio (fic)
Mary Hunter Austin. Outland (fic)
Irving Babbitt. Rousseau and Romanticism (e)
Irving Addison Bacheller. A Man for the Ages (fic)
Konrad Bercovici. Dust of New York (fic)
Randolph Silliman Bourne. Untimely Papers (e, pub)
Thornton Waldo Burgess. The Burgess Bird Book for Children (fic)
Donn Byrne. The Stranger's Banquet (fic)
James Branch Cabell. Beyond Life (e)
_____. Jurgen (fic)
John Jay Chapman. Songs and Poems (po, pub)
Winston Churchill. Dr. Jonathan (fic)
John Cournos. The Mask (fic)
James Oliver Curwood. Nomads of the North (fic)
Thomas Augustine Daly. McAroni Ballads (po)
Josephus Daniels. The Navy and the Nation (hist, e)
Floyd Dell. Were You Ever a Child? (e)
Babette Deutsch. Banners (po)
Theodore Herman Albert Dreiser. Twelve Men (biog)
Finley Peter Dunne. Mr. Dooley on Making a Will (hum)
Harry Stillwell Edwards. Aeneas Africanus (fic)
Donald Evans. Ironica (po)

Mary Hallock Foote. Ground-Swell (fic)
James Forbes. The Famous Mrs. Fair (dr)
Waldo David Frank. Our America (e)
Henry Blake Fuller. Bertram Cope's Year (fic)
Ellen Glasgow. The Builders (fic)
Susan Glaspell. Bernice (dr)
Zane Grey. Tales of Fishing (fic)
Hutchins Hapgood. The Story of a Lover (fic)
Avery Hopwood. The Gold Diggers (dr)
Joseph Hergesheimer. The Happy End (fic)
_____. Java Head (fic)
_____. Linda Condon (fic)
Emerson Hough. The Sagebrusher (fic)
Fannie Hurst. Humoresque (fic)
Hibbard (Harry) Kemp. The Passing God (po)
Aline Kilmer. Candles That Burn (po)
John (Jack) Griffith London. On the Makaloa Flat (fic, pub)
Amy Lawrence Lowell. Pictures of the Floating World (po)
Edgar Lee Masters. Starved Rock (po)
John Thomas McIntyre. A Young Man's Fancy (dr)
Henry Lewis Mencken. The American Language, rev ed 1921, 1923, 1936,
    1945, 1948 (ref, e)
_____. Prejudices, rev ed 1920, 1922, 1924, 1926, 1927
    (e)
Edna St. Vincent Millay. Aria da Capo (dr)
Philip Moeller. Moliere (dr)
_____. Sophie (dr)
Christopher Darlington Morley. The Haunted Bookshop (fic)
_____. The Rocking Horse (po)
Honore Willsie Morrow. The Forbidden Trail (fic)
Robert Gruntal Nathan. Peter Kindred (fic)
John Gneisenau Neihardt. The Song of Three Friends (po)
Ezra Weston Loomis Pound. Quia Pauper Amavi (po)
John Crowe Ransom. Poems about God (po)
Edgar Evertson Saltus. The Paliser Case (fic)
Carl August Sandburg. The Chicago Race Riots (nar)
Upton Beall Sinclair. Jimmie Higgins (fic)
Newton Booth Tarkington. Clarence (dr)
Sara Teasdale. Vignettes of Italy: A Cycle of Nine Songs for High
    Voice (po)
Albert Payson Terhune. Lad: A Dog (fic)
Louis Untermeyer. Modern American Poetry, 1st ed (po, ed)
Mary Stanbery Watts. From Father to Son (fic)
John Hall Wheelock. Dust and Light (po)
Ben Ames Williams. All the Brothers Were Valiant (fic)

                        1920

BIRTHS

    Roger Angell
    Isaac Asimov
    Ray Douglas Bradbury
    John Brooks
    Charles Bukowski

Amy Clampitt
Lawrence Ferlinghetti
Oakley Hall
Irving Howe
Howard Nemerov
Harvey Swados

DEATHS

Frances Courtenay Baylor
Charles Edward Carryl
Louise Imogen Guiney
Constance Cary Harrison
William Dean Howells
Julia A. Moore
Eleanor Hodgman Porter

EVENTS

The Freeman, to 1924 (per)
The Frontier, to 1939 (per)
Grabhorn Press, San Francisco, to 1968

LITERATURE

George Ade. Hand-Made Fables (fic)
Conrad Potter Aiken. The House of Dust: A Symphony (po)
Sherwood Anderson. Poor White (fic)
Mary Hunter Austin. No. 26 Jayne Street (fic)
Margaret Culkin Banning. This Marrying (fic)
Mary Ritter Beard. A Short History of the American Labor Movement,
    rev ed 1925 (hist)
Henry Augustin Beers. The Connecticut Wits, and Other Essays (e)
Stephen Vincent Benet. Heavens and Earth (po)
William Rose Benet. Moons of Grandeur (po)
Harriot Stanton Blatch. A Woman's Point of View (e)
Benjamin Paul Blood. Pluriverse (po, pub)
Maxwell Bodenheim. Advice (po)
Randolph Silliman Bourne. The History of a Literary Radical, ed. Van
    Wyck Brooks (e, pub)
Van Wyck Brooks. The Ordeal of Mark Twain (e, biog)
Alice Brown. Homespun Gold (fic)
_____. The Wind between the Worlds (fic)
John Burroughs. Accepting the Universe (e)
Harold Witter Bynner. A Canticle of Pan (po)
Donn Byrne. The Foolish Matrons (fic)
James Branch Cabell. Domnei (fic)
Andrew Carnegie. Autobiography (pub)
Willa Sibert Cather. Youth and the Bright Medusa (fic)
Grace Hazard Conkling. Wilderness Songs (po)
Hilda Conkling. Poems by a Little Girl (po)
Rachel Crothers. Nice People (dr)
Samuel McChord Crothers. The Dame School of Experience (e)
James Oliver Curwood. The Valley of Silent Men (fic)
Clarence Shepard Day. The Simian World (e)
Floyd Dell. Moon-Calf (fic)

John Roderigo Dos Passos. One Man's Initiation--1917 (fic)
Theodore Herman Albert Dreiser. Hey Rub-a-Dub-Dub (e)
William Edward Burghardt DuBois. Darkwater (po, e)
Thomas Stearns Eliot. Poems (pub)
_____. The Sacred Wood (e)
Francis Scott Key Fitzgerald. Flappers and Philosophers (fic)
_____. This Side of Paradise (fic)
John William Fox, Jr. Erskine Dale, Pioneer (fic, pub)
Waldo David Frank. The Dark Mother (fic)
Zona Gale. Miss Lulu Bett (fic, dr)
Gordon Hall Gerould. Youth in Harley (fic)
Arthur Guiterman. Chips of Jade (po)
Frank Harris. A Mad Love (fic)
Alice Corbin Henderson. Red Earth (po)
Avery Hopwood and Mary Roberts Rinehart. The Bat (dr)
Joseph Hergesheimer. San Cristobal de la Habana (fic)
Robert Sulliman Hillyer. Alchemy: A Symphonic Poem (po)
_____. The Five Books of Youth (po)
James Gibbons Huneker. Painted Veils (fic)
Clarence Budington Kelland. Conflict (fic)
Hibbard (Harry) Kemp. Chanteys and Ballads (po)
Alfred Kreymborg. Plays for Merry Andrews (po, dr)
Clare Kummer. Rollo's Wild Oat (dr)
William Ellery Leonard. The Lynching Bee (po)
Harry Sinclair Lewis. Main Street (fic)
Frank Bird Linderman. On a Passing Frontier (e, fic)
Nicholas Vachel Lindsay. The Daniel Jazz, and Other Poems (po)
_____. The Golden Book of Springfield. Being a Re-
    view of a Book That Will Appear in 2018 (fic)
_____. The Golden Whales of California and Other
    Rhymes in the American Language (po)
Percy Wallace MacKaye. Washington, the Man Who Made Us (dr)
Edgar Lee Masters. Doomesday Book (po)
_____. Mitch Miller (fic)
William Morley Punshon McFee. Captain Macedoine's Daughter (fic)
Henry Louis Mencken and George Jean Nathan. Heliogabalus (dr)
Edna St. Vincent Millay. A Few Figs from Thistles (po)
Eugene Gladstone O'Neill. Beyond the Horizon (dr)
_____. Chris Christopherson (dr)
_____. Diff'rent (dr)
_____. The Emperor Jones (dr)
Ernest Poole. Blind (fic)
Ezra Weston Loomis Pound. Hugh Selwyn Mauberley (po)
_____. Instigations (e)
_____. Umbra (po)
Lizette Woodworth Reese. Spicewood (po)
Lola Ridge. Sum-Up (po)
Edwin Arlington Robinson. Launcelot (po)
_____. The Three Taverns (po)
Carl August Sandburg. Smoke and Steel (po)
George Santayana. Character and Opinion in the United States (e)
Lew Sarett. Many Many Moons (po)
Evelyn Scott. Love (dr)
_____. Precipitations (po)
Anne Douglas Sedgwick. Christmas Roses (fic)
_____. The Third Window (fic)

Upton Beall Sinclair. 100%, the Story of a Patriot (fic)
Elsie Singmaster. Basil Everman (fic)
Harriet Elizabeth Prescott Spofford. The Elder's People (fic)
Sara Teasdale. Flame and Shadow (po)
Albert Payson Terhune. Bruce (fic)
Arthur Cheney Train. Tutt and Mr. Tutt (fic)
Frederick Jackson Turner. The Frontier in American History (hist)
Mark Albert Van Doren. The Poetry of John Dryden (e)
Hendrik William Van Loon. Ancient Man (hist)
Glenway Wescott. The Bitterns (po)
Edith Newbold Jones Wharton. The Age of Innocence (fic)
_____. In Morocco (trav)
Stewart Edward White. The Rose Dawn (fic)
Walt Whitman. The Gathering of the Forces, 2 vols (e, pub)
William Carlos Williams. Kora in Hell (po)
George Edward Woodberry. The Roamer (po)
Anzia Yezierska. Hungry Hearts (fic)

1921

BIRTHS

Hayden Carruth
Alex Palmer Haley
James Jones
James Rodney McConkey
Elizabeth Spencer
Richard Purdy Wilbur

DEATHS

James Phinney Baxter
John Burroughs
Donald Evans
John Habberton
James Gibbons Huneker
Lloyd Mifflin
Paul Meredith Potter
Edgar Evertson Saltus
Harriet Elizabeth Prescott Spofford

EVENTS

Broom, to 1932 (per)
Warren Gamaliel Harding, 29th President of the United States, to
    1923
The Reviewer, Richmond, Virginia, to 1925 (per)

LITERATURE

Lyman Abbott. What Christianity Means to Me (e)
James Truslow Adams. The Founding of New England (hist)
Samuel Hopkins Adams. Success (fic)
Conrad Potter Aiken. Punch: The Immortal Liar (po)
Zoe Aikens. Daddy's Gone A-Hunting (dr)

_____. The Varying Shore (dr)
Sherwood Anderson. The Triumph of the Egg (fic, po)
Gertrude Franklin Atherton. The Sisters-in-Law (fic)
Faith Baldwin. Mavis of Green Hill (fic)
Harry Elmer Barnes. The Social History of the Western World (hist)
Robert Charles Benchley. Of All Things (nar)
Stephen Vincent Benet. The Beginning of Wisdom (fic)
Konrad Bercovici. Ghitza (fic)
Harriot Stanton Blatch. Elizabeth Cady Stanton (biog)
Herbert Eugene Bolton. The Spanish Borderlands (hist)
Heywood Campbell Broun. Seeing Things at Night (e)
Maxwell Struthers Burt. Chance Encounters (fic)
Donn Byrne. Messer Marco Polo (fic)
James Branch Cabell. Figures of Earth (fic)
_____. Joseph Hergesheimer (e)
Marcus Cook Connelly and George Simon Kaufman. Dulcy (dr)
John Cournos. The Wall (fic)
Stephen Crane. Men, Women, and Boats (fic, pub)
Rachel Crothers. Everyday (dr)
Elmer Holmes Davis. The History of the New York Times (hist)
Owen Davis. The Detour (dr)
Clarence Shepard Day. The Crow's Nest (e)
Floyd Dell. The Briary-Bush (fic)
Hilda Doolittle. Hymen (po)
John Roderigo Dos Passos. Three Soldiers (fic)
Harry Stillwell Edwards. Aeneas Africanus, Defendant (fic)
Edna Ferber. The Girls (fic)
Harvey Fergusson. Blood of the Conquerors (fic)
Dorothy Canfield Fisher. The Brimming Cup (fic)
John Gould Fletcher. Breakers and Granite (po)
_____. Paul Gauguin (biog, e)
Zona Gale. The Secret Way (po)
Hannibal Hamlin Garland. A Daughter of the Middle Border (auto, nar)
Susan Glaspell. The Inheritors (dr)
_____. The Verge (dr)
Ben Hecht. Erik Dorn (fic)
Avery Hopwood and Wilson Collison. Getting Gertie's Garter (dr)
Sidney Coe Howard. Swords (dr, po)
Hatcher Hughes and Elmer Reizenstein (Elmer Rice). Wake-Up, Jonathan
    (dr)
James Langston Hughes. The Gold Piece (dr)
Fannie Hurst. Star-Dust (fic)
Wallace Admah Irwin. Seed of the Sun (fic)
Henry James. Notes and Reviews (e, pub)
Clarence Budington Kelland. Scattergood Baines (fic)
Aline Kilmer. Vigils (po)
Ringgold Wilmer Lardner. The Big Town (fic)
Joseph Crosby Lincoln. Galusha the Magnificent (fic)
Frank Bird Linderman. Bunch-Grass and Blue Joint (po)
Amy Lawrence Lowell. Legends (po)
Donald Robert Perry Marquis. Carter and Other People (sat)
_____. Noah an' Jonathan an' Captain John Smith
    (po)
_____. The Old Soak (sat)
Robert McAlmon. Explorations (po)
William Morley Punshon McFee. Harbours of Memory (nar, fic)

Edna St. Vincent Millay. The Lamp and the Bell (po, dr)
_____ . Second April (po)
_____ . Two Slatterns and a King (dr)
Marianne Craig Moore. Poems (pub)
Christopher Darlington Morley. Chimney-smoke (po)
Honore Willsie Morrow. The Enchanted Canyon (fic)
George Jean Nathan. The Theatre, the Drama, the Girls (e)
Robert Gruntal Nathan. Autumn (fic)
John Gneisenau Neihardt. Two Mothers (dr)
Alfred Edward Newton. A Magnificent Farce and Other Diversions of a
    Book Collector (e, nar)
Charles Gilman Norris. Brass (fic)
Eugene Gladstone O'Neill. Anna Christie (dr)
_____ . Gold (dr)
_____ . The Straw (dr)
James Oppenheim. The Mystic Warrior (po, auto)
Ernest Poole. Beggars' Gold (fic)
Emery Bemsley Pottle (Gilbert Emery). The Hero (dr)
_____ . Queed (dr)
Elmer Reizenstein (Elmer Rice), and Hatcher Hughes. Wake Up, Jonathan
    (dr)
Eugene Manlove Rhodes. Stepsons of Light (fic)
Edwin Arlington Robinson. Avon's Harvest (po)
_____ . Collected Poems (pub)
Rowland Evans Robinson. Silver Fields and Other Sketches of a Farmer-
    Sportsman (nar, fic, pub)
Evelyn Scott. The Narrow-House (fic)
Lloyd Logan Pearsall Smith. More Trivia (e, misc)
Leonora Speyer. A Canopic Jar (po)
Donald Ogden Stewart. A Parody Outline of History (sat)
Newton Booth Tarkington. Alice Adams (fic)
Carl Clinton Van Doren. The American Novel (e)
Hendrik Willem Van Loon. The Story of Mankind (hist)
John Van Alstyn Weaver. In American (po)
Edward Lucas White. Andivius Hedulio (fic)
Walt Whitman. The Uncollected Poetry and Prose of Walt Whitman, 2
    vols (pub)
Ben Ames Williams. Evered (fic)
William Carlos Williams. Sour Grapes (po)
Arthur Yvor Winter. The Immobile Wind (po)
Elinor Hoyt Wylie. Nets to Catch the Wind (po)

                              1922

BIRTHS

    William Alfred
    Vance Nye Bourjaily
    William Demby
    Mark Harris
    Jack Kerouac
    George Frederick Morgan
    Howard Moss
    Grace Paley
    Kurt Vonnegut, Jr.

Calder Baynard Willingham, Jr.

DEATHS

Lyman Abbott
John Kendrick Bangs
John Vance Cheney
Mary Noailles Murfree
Thomas Nelson Page
Josephine Preston Peabody
Mary Virginia Terhune

EVENTS

The Fugitive, Nashville, Tennessee, to 1925 (per)
The Reader's Digest, Pleasantville, New York (per, est)
Secession, New York, New York, to 1924 (per)

LITERATURE

Conrad Potter Aiken. Priapus and the Pool (po)
Jane Addams. Peace and Bread in Time of War (e)
Zoe Akins. The Texas Nightingale (dr)
William Hervey Allen and DuBose Heyward. Carolina Chansons (po)
Ray Stannard Baker. Woodrow Wilson and World Settlement, 3 vols
   (hist)
Joseph Warren Beach. The Technique of Thomas Hardy (e)
Charles Austin Beard. The Economic Basis of Politics (e)
Carl Lotus Becker. The Declaration of Independence (e, hist)
Thomas Beer. The Fair Rewards (fic)
Robert Charles Benchley. Love Conquers All (nar)
Stephen Vincent Benet. Young People's Pride (fic)
John Peale Bishop and Edmund Wilson. The Undertaker's Garland (po)
Maxwell Bodenheim. Introducing Irony (po)
Claude Gernade Bowers. The Party Battle of the Jackson Period (hist)
Ernest Boyd. Ireland's Literary Renaissance (e)
Gamaliel Bradford. American Portraits (biog)
Heywood Campbell Broun. The Boy Grew Older (fic)
_____. Pieces of Hate, and Other Enthusiasms (e)
Alice Brown. Old Crow (fic)
John Burroughs. My Boyhood (auto)
Harold Witter Bynner. A Book of Plays (dr, pub)
Donn Byrne. The Wind Bloweth (fic)
Willa Sibert Cather. One of Ours (fic)
John Colton and Clemence Randolph. Rain (dr)
Hilda Conkling. Shoes of the Wind (po)
Marcus Cook Connelly and George Simon Kaufman. Merton of the Movies
   (dr)
John Cournos. Babel (fic)
Edward Estlin Cummings. The Enormous Room (nar)
Josephus Daniels. Our Navy at War (hist)
Olive Tilford Dargan. Lute and Furrow (po)
Clarence Seward Darrow. Crime: Its Cause and Treatment (hist, e)
William Stearns Davis. A Short History of the Near East (hist)
Benjamin DeCasseres. Chameleon--Being the Book of My Selves (e)
Margaretta Wade Campbell Deland. The Vehement Flame (fic)

John Roderigo Dos Passos. A Pushcart at the Curb (po)
_____. Rosinante to the Road Again (e)
Theodore Herman Albert Dreiser. A Book about Myself (auto)
Thomas Stearns Eliot. The Waste Land (po)
Dorothy Canfield Fisher. Rough-Hewn (fic)
Francis Scott Key Fitzgerald. The Beautiful and the Damned (fic)
_____. Tales of the Jazz Age (fic)
James Forbes. The Endless Chain (dr)
Waldo David Frank. City Block (fic)
_____. Rahab (fic)
Katharine Fullerton Gerould. Lost Valley (fic)
_____. Valiant Dust (fic)
Ellen Glasgow. Old Man in His Time (fic)
Ben Hecht. Fantazius Mallare (fic)
_____. Gargoyles (fic)
_____. 1001 Afternoons in Chicago (fic)
Joseph Hergesheimer. The Bright Shawl (fic)
_____. Cytherea (fic)
DuBose Heyward and William Hervey Allen. Carolina Chansons (po)
Emerson Hough. The Covered Wagon (fic)
Sidney Coe Howard. S.S. Tenacity (dr)
Rupert Hughes. Souls for Sale (fic)
Fannie Hurst. The Vertical City (fic)
George Edward Kelly. The Torch-Bearers (dr)
Hibbard (Harry) Kemp. Tramping on Life (po)
Peter Bernard Kyne. The Go-Getter (fic)
William Ellery Leonard. Two Lives (po)
Harry Sinclair Lewis. Babbitt (fic)
Janet Lewis. The Indians in the Woods (po)
Ludwig Lewisohn. The Drama and the Stage (e)
Frank Bird Linderman. Lige Mounts, Free Trapper (fic)
Amy Lawrence Lowell. A Critical Fable (po)
John Phillips Marquard. The Unspeakable Gentleman (fic)
Donald Robert Perry Marquis. The Revolt of the Oyster (fic)
_____. Poems and Portraits (po, des)
_____. Sonnets to a Red-Haired Lady (by a Gen-
tleman with a Blue Beard) and Famous Love Affairs (po)
Edgar Lee Masters. Children of the Market Place (fic)
William Morley Punshon McFee. Command (fic)
Claude McKay. Harlem Shadows (po)
Christopher Darlington Morley. Where the Blue Begins (fic)
Honore Willsie Morrow. Judith of the Godless Valley (fic)
George Jean Nathan. The Critic and the Drama (e)
Robert Gruntal Nathan. Youth Grows Old (po)
Anne Nichols. Abie's Irish Rose (dr)
Eugene Gladstone O'Neill. The First Man (dr)
_____. The Hairy Ape (dr)
Elliot Harold Paul. Indelible (fic)
Josephine Preston Peabody. Portrait of Mrs. W. (dr)
Channing Pollock. The Fool (dr)
Ernest Poole. Millions (fic)
Emily Post. Etiquette (e, ref)
Olive Higgins Prouty. Stella Dallas (fic)
John Herbert Quick. Vandemark's Folly (fic)
Eugene Manlove Rhodes. Copper Streak Trail (fic)
Elizabeth Madox Roberts. Under the Tree (po)

Carl August Sandburg. Slabs of the Sunburnt West (po)
_____. Rootabaga Stories (juv)
George Santayana. Soliloquies in England (e)
Lew Sarett. The Box of God (po)
Evelyn Scott. Narcissus (fic)
Anne Douglas Sedgwick. Adrienne Toner (fic)
Upton Beall Sinclair. They Call Me Carpenter (fic)
Gertrude Stein. Geography and Plays (dr)
Thomas Sigismund Stribling. Birthright (fic)
Austin Strong. Seventh Heaven (dr)
Genevieve Taggard. For Eager Lovers (po)
Sara Teasdale. Helen of Troy, and Other Poems, rev ed (po)
Dan Totheroh. Wild Birds (dr)
Jim Tully. Emmett Lawler (fic)
Daniel Berkeley Updike. Printing Types: Their History, Forms, and
    Use, 2 vols (hist, ref)
Carl Clinton Van Doren. Contemporary American Novelists, 1900-1920
    (biog, e)
Carl Van Vechten. Peter Whiffle (fic)
Harold Vinal. White April (po)
Mary Stanbery Watts. The House of Rimmon (fic)
Edith Newbold Jones Wharton. The Glimpses of the Moon (fic)
John Hall Wheelock. The Black Panther (po)
Ben Ames Williams. Black Pawl (fic)
Jesse Lynch Williams. Why Not? (dr)
Edmund Wilson and John Peale Bishop. The Undertaker's Garland (po)
William Carlos Williams. Spring and All (po)
Harry Leon Wilson. Merton of the Movies (fic)
Margaret Wilson. The Able McLaughlins (fic)
Arthur Yvor Winters. The Magpie's Shadow (po)
Anzia Yezierska. Salome of the Tenaments (fic)

                    1923

BIRTHS

    Paddy Chayefsky
    James Lafayette Dickey
    Alan Dugan
    Paula Fox
    Joseph Hansen
    Anthony Evan Hecht
    Joseph Heller
    Daniel Gerard Hoffman
    Richard Franklin Hugo
    Jean Collins Kerr
    Denise Levertov
    John Logan
    Norman Mailer
    James Purdy
    James Marcus Schuyler
    Louis Aston Marantz Simpson
    David Derek Stacton
    Philip Whalen

DEATHS

Emerson Hough
Henry Martyn Robert
Morris Rosenfeld
Kate Douglas Wiggin

EVENTS

Chicago Literary Times, to 1924 (per)
The William L. Clements Library of Americana, University of Michigan,
    Ann Arbor (est)
Calvin Coolidge, 30th President of the United States, to 1929
Time (per, est)

LITERATURE

James Truslow Adams. Revolutionary New England (hist)
Conrad Potter Aiken. The Pilgrimage of Festus (po)
Zoe Akins. Greatness (dr)
James Lane Allen. The Alabaster Box (fic)
Maxwell Anderson. White Desert (dr)
Sherwood Anderson. Horses and Men (fic)
_____. Many Marriages (fic)
Gertrude Franklin Atherton. Black Oxen (fic)
Mary Hunter Austin. The American Rhythm (e, po)
Leonard Bacon. Uleg Beg (po)
Margaret Culkin Banning. Country Club People (fic)
Djuna Barnes. A Book (dr, fic, po)
Philip Barry. You and I (dr)
Carleton Beals. Rome or Death--the Story of Fascism (e)
Thomas Beer. Stephen Crain (biog)
Samuel Flagg Bemis. Jay's Treaty (hist)
Stephen Vincent Benet. A Ballad of William Sycamore (po)
_____. Jean Huguenot (fic)
_____. King David (po)
Konrad Bercovici. Costa's Daughter (dr)
_____. Murdo (fic)
Maxwell Bodenheim. Against This Age (po)
_____. The Sardonic Arm (po)
Louise Bogan. Body of This Death (po)
Thomas Alexander Boyd. Through the Wheat (fic)
Gamaliel Bradford. Damaged Souls (biog)
Donn Byrne. The Changeling (fic)
James Branch Cabell. The High Place (fic)
Willa Sibert Cather. A Lost Lady (fic)
Robert William Chambers. The Hi-Jackers (fic)
Charles Badger Clark. Spike (fic)
Elizabeth Jane Coatsworth. Fox Footprints (po)
Rachel Crothers. Mary the Third (dr)
Edward Estlin Cummings. Tulips and Chimneys (po)
Owen Davis. Icebound (dr)
William Stearns Davis. Life on a Medieval Barony (hist)
Floyd Dell. Janet March (fic)
John Roderigo Dos Passos. Streets of Night (fic)
Theodore Herman Albert Dreiser. The Color of a Great City (des)

Janet Ayer Fairbank. The Cortlands of Washington Square (fic)
Harvey Fergusson. Capitol Hill (fic)
Francis Scott Key Fitzgerald. The Vegetable; or, from President to
    Postman (sat, dr)
Martin Archer Flavin. Children of the Moon (dr)
Norman Foerster. Nature in American Literature (e)
Waldo David Frank. Holiday (fic)
Robert Lee Frost. New Hampshire (po)
Zona Gale. Faint Perfume (fic)
Katharine Fullerton Gerould. Conquistador (fic)
Ellen Glasgow. The Shadowy Third (fic)
Arthur Guiterman. The Light Guitar (po)
Frank Harris. My Life and Loves, 3 vols, to 1927 (auto, biog, nar)
Carl Sadakichi Hartmann. Confucius (dr)
Ben Hecht. The Florentine Dagger (fic)
Ernest Miller Hemingway. Three Stories and Ten Poems (fic, po, pub)
Robert Herrick. Homely Lilla (fic)
Robert Silliman Hillyer. The Hills Give Promise (po)
Emerson Hough. North of 36 (fic)
Sidney Coe Howard. Casanova (dr)
_____. Sancho Panza (dr)
Fannie Hurst. Lummox (fic)
Wallace Admah Irwin. More Letters of a Japanese Schoolboy (nar, e)
Edith Summers Kelley. Weeds (fic)
Alfred Kreymborg. Less Lonely (po)
_____. Puppet Plays (po, dr)
John Howard Lawson. Roger Bloomer (dr)
William Ellery Leonard. Red Bird (dr)
Ludwig Lewisohn. Don Juan (fic)
Nicholas Vachel Lindsay. Collected Poems (pub)
_____. Going-to-the-Sun (po)
Mina Gertrude Lowy (Mina Loy). Lunar Baedecker (po)
Percy Wallace MacKaye. The Fine-Pretty World (dr)
Edgar Lee Masters. Skeeters Kirby (fic)
John Thomas McIntyre. Blowing Weather (fic)
Edna St. Vincent Millay. The Ballad of the Harp Weaver (po)
Christopher Darlington Morley. Parson's Pleasure (po)
Honore Willsie Morrow. The Exile of the Lariat (fic)
Robert Gruntal Nathan. The Puppet Master (fic)
Alfred Edward Newton. Doctor Johnson (dr)
Meredith Nicholson. Hope of Happiness (fic)
Charles Gilman Norris. Bread (fic)
James Oppenheim. Golden Bird (po)
Elliot Harold Paul. Impromptu (fic)
Ernest Poole. Danger (fic)
William Sydney Porter (O. Henry). Postscripts (fic, pub)
Emery Bemsley Pottle (Gilbert Emery). Tarnish (dr)
Ezra Weston Loomis Pound. Indiscretions (e)
John Herbert Quick. The Hawkeye (fic)
Arthur Hobson Quinn. A History of the American Drama, 3 vols, to
    1927 (hist)
Lizette Woodworth Reese. Wild Cherry (po)
Elmer Reizenstein (Elmer Rice). The Adding Machine (dr)
Edwin Arlington Robinson. Roman Bartholow (po)
Carl August Sandburg. Rootabaga Pigeons (juv)
George Santayana. Poems (pub)

_____. Skepticism and Animal Faith (e)
Evelyn Scott. Escapade (nar)
Upton Beall Sinclair. The Goose-Step (e)
Charles Wilbert Snow. Maine Coast (po)
Wilbur Daniel Steele. Isles of the Blest (fic)
_____. The Shame Dance (fic)
George Stirling. Selected Poems (pub)
Wallace Stevens. Harmonium (po)
Donald Ogden Stewart. Aunt Polly's Story of Mankind (sat)
Thomas Sigismund Stribling. Fombombo (fic)
Genevieve Taggard. Hawaiian Hilltop (po)
Newton Booth Tarkington. The Midlander (fic)
Jean Toomer. Cane (fic, po, dr)
Louis Untermeyer. Roast Leviathan (po)
Hendrik Willem Van Loon. The Story of the Bible (hist, nar)
Carl Van Vechten. The Blind Bow-Boy (fic)
Lula Vollmer. The Shame Woman (dr)
_____. Sun-Up (dr)
Mary Stanbery Watts. Luther Nichols (fic)
John Van Alstyn Weaver. Finders (po)
Ben Ames Williams. Thrifty Stock (fic)
Edith Newbold Jones Wharton. A Son at the Front (fic)
Brand Whitlock. J. Hardin and Son (fic)
Margaret Widdemer. A Tree with a Bird in It (po)
Jesse Lynch Williams. Not Wanted (fic)
William Carlos Williams. The Great American Novel (e)
Thyra Samter Winslow. Picture Frames (fic)
William E. Woodward. Bunk (fic)
Elinor Hoyt Wylie. Black Armour (po)
_____. Jennifer Lorn (fic)
Anzia Yezierska. Children of Loneliness (fic)
Stark Young. The Flower in Drama (e)

1924

BIRTHS

    James Baldwin
    Thomas Louis Berger
    Truman Capote
    Evan Shelby Connell, Jr.
    Sidney (Cid) Corman
    William Howard Gass
    Herbert Gold
    William Humphrey
    Leon Uris

DEATHS

    Frances Eliza Hodgson Burnett
    George Randolph Chester
    George Cram Cook
    Charles Bertrand Lewis (M. Quad)
    Harriet Mulford Stone Lothrop (Margaret Sidney)
    Geneva Stratton-Porter

Thomas Woodrow Wilson

EVENTS

The American Mercury (per, est)
Commonweal (per, f)
New York Herald Tribune, to 1966 (per)
The Pierpont Morgan Library, New York, New York (est)
The Saturday Review, to 1982 (per)

LITERATURE

Maxwell Anderson and Laurence Stallings. What Price Glory? (dr)
Sherwood Anderson. A Story Teller's Story (fic)
Joseph Auslander. Sunrise Trumpets (po)
Irving Babbitt. Democracy and Leadership (e)
Philip Barry. The Youngest (dr)
Charles William Beebe. Galapagos: World's End (des)
Thomas Beer. Sandoval (fic)
Konrad Bercovici. Iliana (fic)
Maxwell Bodenheim. Crazy Man (fic)
Ernest Boyd. Portraits: Real and Imaginary (e, biog)
Percy Holmes Boynton. Some Contemporary Americans (e)
Louis Bromfield. The Green Bay Tree (fic)
Heywood Campbell Broun. Sitting on the World (e)
William Crary Brownell. The Genius of Style (e)
Kenneth Duva Burke. The White Oxen (fic)
Maxwell Struthers Burt. The Diary of a Dude Wrangler (fic)
_____. The Interpreter's House (fic)
Nicholas Murray Butler. The Faith of a Liberal (e)
Donn Byrne. Blind Raftery (fic)
James Branch Cabell. Straws and Prayer-Books (e)
John Jay Chapman. Letters and Religion (e)
Elizabeth Jane Coatsworth. Atlas and Beyond (po)
Marcus Cook Connelly and George Simon Kaufman. Beggar on Horseback
   (dr)
John Cournos. The New Candide (fic)
James Gould Cozzens. Confusions (fic)
Nathalia Crane. The Janitor's Boy (po)
Herbert David Croly. Willard Straight (biog)
Rachel Crothers. Expressing Willie (dr)
Josephus Daniels. The Life of Woodrow Wilson (biog)
Margaretta Wade Campbell Deland. New Friends in Old Chester (fic)
Bernard Augustine DeVoto. The Crooked Mile (fic)
Hilda Doolittle. Heliodora, and Other Poems (po)
Thomas Stearns Eliot. Homage to John Dryden (e)
William Harrison Faulkner. The Marble Faun (po)
Jessie Redmon Fauset. There Is Confusion (fic)
Edna Ferber. So Big (fic)
_____ and George Simon Kaufman. Minick (dr)
Arthur Davison Ficke. Out of Silence, and Other Poems (po)
Waldo David Frank. Chalk Face (fic)
_____. Salvos (e)
Zona Gale. Mr. Pitt (dr)
Arthur Guiterman. A Poet's Proverbs (po)
Frank Harris. Undream'd of Shores (fic)

Ben Hecht. Broken Necks (fic)
_____. Humpty Dumpty (fic)
_____. The Kingdom of Evil (fic)
_____. Tales of Chicago Streets (fic)
Joseph Hergesheimer. Balisand (fic)
Robert Herrick. Waste (fic)
DuBose Heyward. Skylines and Horizons (po)
Emerson Hough. Mother of Gold (fic)
Sidney Coe Howard. They Knew What They Wanted (dr)
_____, and Edward Sheldon. Bewitched (dr)
Hatcher Hughes. Hell-Bent for Heaven (dr)
John Robinson Jeffers. Tamar and Other Poems (po)
George Edward Kelly. The Show-Off (dr)
Hibbard (Harry) Kemp. Boccacio's Untold Tale, and Other One-Act
    Plays (dr)
Ringgold Wilmer Lardner. How To Write Short Stories (sat, fic)
Margaret Kernochan Leech. The Back of the Book (fic)
William Ellery Leonard. Tutankhamen and After (po)
Ludwig Lewisohn. The Creative Life (e)
Joseph Crosby Lincoln. Rugged Water (fic)
Archibald MacLeish. The Happy Marriage (po)
Percy Marks. The Plastic Age (fic)
Donald Robert Perry Marquis. The Dark Hours (dr)
_____. The Old Soak's History of the World
    (fic)
Edgar Lee Masters. Mirage (fic)
_____. The New Spoon River (po)
Robert McAlmon. Village: As It Happened through a Fifteen-Year Pe-
    riod (fic)
William Morley Punshon McFee. Race (fic)
Edna St. Vincent Millay. Distressing Dialogues (nar)
Marianne Craig Moore. Observations (po)
Honore Willsie Morrow. The Devonshers (fic)
Clarence Edward Mulford. Hopalong Cassidy Returns (fic)
George Jean Nathan. Materia Critica (e)
Eugene Gladstone O'Neill. All God's Chillun Got Wings (dr)
_____. Desire under the Elms (dr)
James Oppenheim. The Sea (po)
Anne Parrish. Semi-Attached (fic)
Julia Mood Peterkin. Green Thursday (nar, fic)
Ernest Poole. The Avalanche (fic)
Ezra Weston Loomis Pound. Antheil and the Treatise on Harmony (po)
John Herbert Quick. The Invisible Woman (fic)
John Crowe Ransom. Chills and Fever (po)
_____. Grace after Meat (po)
Agnes Repplier. Under Dispute (e)
Edward Arlington Robinson. The Man Who Died Twice (nar, po)
Paul Rosenfeld. Port of New York (e)
Anne Douglas Sedgwick. The Little French Girl (fic)
Edward Brewster Sheldon and Sidney Coe Howard. Bewitched (dr)
Upton Beall Sinclair. The Goslings (e, nar)
Joel Elias Spingarn. Poems (po, pub)
Laurence Stallings. Plumes (fic)
_____ and Maxwell Anderson. What Price Glory? (dr)
Donald Ogden Stewart. Mr. and Mrs. Haddock Abroad (sat)
Thomas Sigismund Stribling. Red Sand (fic)

Ruth Suckow. Country People (fic)
Sara Teasdale. Flame and Shadow, rev ed (po)
Jim Tully. Beggars of Life (auto)
Daniel Berkeley Updike. In the Day's Work (e)
Mark Albert Van Doren. Spring Thunder (po)
Carl Van Vechten. The Tattooed Countess (fic)
Mary Stanbery Watts. The Fabric of the Loom (fic)
Glenway Wescott. The Apple of the Eye (fic)
Edith Newbold Jones Wharton. Old New York (fic)
Ben Ames Williams. Audacity (fic)
Thomas Woodrow Wilson. Robert E. Lee (hist, pub)
William E. Woodward. Lottery (fic)
Stark Young. The Colonnade (dr)
_____. The Three Fountains (fic)

1925

BIRTHS

Philip Booth   Bob Kaufman
Theodore Vernon Enslin
Frank Daniel Gilroy
John Clendennin Burne Hawkes, Jr.
Donald Rodney Justice
Kenneth Jay Koch
Maxine Winokur Kumin
Flannery O'Connor
Jack Spicer
William Styron
Gore Vidal
John Alfred Williams

DEATHS

James Lane Allen
George Washington Cable
Thomas William Lawson
Amy Lawrence Lowell
John Herbert Quick
William Osborn Stoddard
Edith Matilda Thomas

EVENTS

American Speech (per, f)
Bennington (Vermont) College (f)
John Simon Guggenheim Memorial Foundation, New York (f)
Harper's Magazine (per, f)
The New Yorker (per, f)
This Quarter, to 1932 (per)
The Virginia Quarterly Review, University of Virginia, Charlottes-
    ville (per, f)

LITERATURE

George Abbott. The Fall Guy (dr)
Leonie Fuller Adams. Those Not Elect (po)
Conrad Potter Aiken. Bring! Bring! (fic)
James Lane Allen. The Landmark (fic)
Maxwell Anderson. You Who Have Dreams (po)
_____ and Laurence Stallings. The Buccaneer (dr)
                                         . First Flight (dr)
Sherwood Anderson. Dark Laughter (fic)
_____. The Modern Writer (nar)
Nathan Asch. The Office (fic)
Mary Hunter Austin. Everyman's Genius (e)
Leonard Bacon. Ph. D's (po)
Harry Elmer Barnes. The New History and the Social Studies (e)
Philip Barry. In a Garden (dr)
John Spencer Bassett. The Plantation Owner As Revealed in His Let-
   ters (hist, nar)
Charles William Beebe. Jungle Days (nar)
Robert Charles Benchley. Pluck and Luck (nar)
John Barry Benefield. The Chicken-Wagon Family (fic)
Stephen Vincent Benet. Tiger Joy (po)
Konrad Bercovici. The Marriage Guest (fic)
_____. On New Shoes (nar)
Maxwell Bodenheim. Replenishing Jessica (fic)
Claude Gernade Bowers. Jefferson and Hamilton (biog)
Ernest Boyd. H.L. Mencken (e, biog)
_____. Studies from Ten Literatures (e)
James Boyd. Drums (fic)
Thomas Alexander Boyd. Points of Honor (fic)
Gamaliel Bradford. Wives (biog)
Le Baron Russell Briggs. Men, Women, and Colleges (e)
Louis Bromfield. Escape (fic)
_____. Possession (fic)
Van Wyck Brooks. The Pilgrimage of Henry James (e, biog)
Harold Witter Bynner. Young Harvard (po)
Willa Sibert Cather. The Professor's House (fic)
Stuart Chase. The Tragedy of Waste (e)
Barrett Harper Clark. A Study of the Modern Drama (e)
Robert Peter Tristram Coffin. Book of Crowns and Cottages (e)
Dane Coolidge. The Fighting Danites (fic)
John Cournos. Sport of Gods (dr)
James Gould Cozzins. Michael Scarlett (fic)
Nathalia Crane. Lava Lane (po)
Rachel Crothers. A Lady's Virtue (dr)
Countee Cullen. Color (po)
Edward Estlin Cummings. & (po)
_____. XLI Poems (po, pub)
Olive Tilford Dargan. Highland Annals (fic)
Benjamin DeCasseres. Forty Immortals (e)
_____. James Gibbons Huneker (e)
Floyd Dell. Intellectual Vagabondage: An Apology for the Intelligen-
   tsia (e)
_____. Runaway (fic)
Babette Deutsch. Honey Out of the Rock (po)
Hilda Doolittle. Collected Poems (pub)
John Roderigo Dos Passos. Manhattan Transfer (fic)
Theodore Herman Albert Dreiser. An American Tragedy (fic)

Thomas Stearns Eliot. The Hollow Men (po)
John Erskine. The Private Lives of Helen of Troy (fic)
Janet Ayer Fairbank. The Smiths (fic)
Francis Scott Key Fitzgerald. The Great Gatsby (fic)
Gordon Hall Gerould. A Midsummer Mystery (fic)
Ellen Glasgow. Barren Ground (fic)
Robert Grant. The Bishop's Granddaughter (fic)
Paul Eliot Green. The Lord's Will, and Other Carolina Plays (dr)
Richard Halliburton. The Royal Road to Romance (trav, nar)
Ernest Miller Hemingway. In Our Time (fic)
Joseph Hergesheimer. From an Old House (nar)
DuBose Heyward. Porgy (fic)
Robert Silliman Hillyer. The Halt in the Garden (po)
Sidney Coe Howard. Lucky Sam McCarver (dr)
Hatcher Hughes. Ruint (dr)
John Robinson Jeffers. Roan, Stallion, Tamar, and Other Poems (po)
Clarence Budington Kelland. Rhoda Fair (fic)
George Edward Kelly. Craig's Wife (dr)
Charles Rann Kennedy. The Salutation (dr)
Manuel Komroff. The Grace of Lambs (fic)
Wilmer Ringgold Lardner. What Of It? (fic)
John Howard Lawson. Processional (dr)
Harry Sinclair Lewis. Arrowsmith (fic)
Nicholas Vachel Lindsay. Collected Poems (pub)
Anita Loos. Gentlemen Prefer Blondes (fic)
Robert Morss Lovett. Edith Wharton (e)
Amy Lawrence Lowell. What's O'Clock (po, pub)
Archibald MacLeish. The Pot of Earth (po)
Percy Marks. Martha (fic)
John Phillips Marquand. The Black Cargo (fic)
John Thomas McIntyre. A Young Man's Fancy (fic)
Christopher Darlington Morley. Thunder on the Left (fic)
Honore Willsie Morrow. We Must March (fic)
Robert Gruntal Nathan. Jonah (fic)
John Gneisenau Neihardt. Poetic Values (e)
_____. The Song of the Indian Wars (po)
Alfred Edward Newton. The Greatest Book in the World, and Other Papers (e)
Charles Gilman Norris. Pig Iron (fic)
Eugene Gladstone O'Neill. The Fountain (dr)
Martha Ostenso. Wild Geese (fic)
Anne Parrish. The Perennial Bachelor (fic)
Channing Pollock. The Enemy (dr)
Ernest Poole. The Hunter's Moon (fic)
_____. The Little Dark Man (fic)
Emery Bemsley Pottle (Gilbert Emery). Episode (dr)
Ezra Weston Loomis Pound. A Draft of XVI Cantos (po)
John Herbert Quick. One Man's Life (auto)
Edwin Arlington Robinson. Dionysus in Doubt (po)
Paul Rosenfeld. Men Seen (e)
George Santayana. Dialogues in Limbo (e)
Lew Sarett. Slow Smoke (po)
Evelyn Scott. The Golden Door (fic)
Constance Lindsay Skinner. The Search Relentless (fic)
Chard Powers Smith. Along the Wind (po)
Laurence Stallings and Maxwell Anderson. The Buccaneer (dr)

_____. First Flight (dr)
Wilbur Daniel Steele. Taboo (fic)
_____. The Terrible Woman (dr)
Gertrude Stein. The Making of Americans (fic)
James Floyd Stevens. Paul Bunyan (fic)
Donald Ogden Stewart. The Crazy Fool (sat)
Ruth Suckow. The Odyssey of a Nice Girl (fic)
Eunice Tietjens. Profiles from Home (po)
Frederic Ridgely Torrence. Hesperides (po)
Jim Tully. Jarnegan (fic)
Carl Clinton Van Doren. James Branch Cabell (biog, e)
Mark Albert Van Doren and Carl Clinton Van Doren. American and British Literature Since 1890 (hist, e)
John William Van Druten. Young Woodley (dr)
Hendrik Willem Van Loon. Tolerance (hist)
Carl Van Vechten. Firecrackers (fic)
_____. Red (e)
Lula Vollmer. The Dunce Boy (dr)
John Van Alstyne Weaver. More "In American" (po)
Glenway Wescott. Natives of Rocks (po)
Edith Newbold Jones Wharton. The Mother's Recompense (fic)
_____. The Writing of Fiction (e)
Margaret Widdemer. Ballads and Lyrics (po)
Jesse Lynch Williams. Lovely Lady (dr)
William Carlos Williams. In the American Grain (e)
Thames Ross Williamson. Run, Sheep, Run (fic)
Margaret Wilson. The Kenworthys (fic)
William E. Woodward. Bread and Circuses (fic)
Elinor Hoyt Wylie. The Venetian Glass Nephew (fic)
Stark Young. Glamour (e)
_____. The Saint (dr)

1926

BIRTHS

Alice Adams
Archie Randolph Ammons
Paul Blackburn
Robert Elwood Bly
Carl Frederick Buechner
Robert White Creeley
James Patrick Donleavy
William Price Fox
Allen Ginsberg
Charles Gordone
John Clellon Holmes
Harold Louis Humes
John Knowles
Nelle Harper Lee
Alison Lurie
Wallace Markfield
James Ingram Merrill
Frank O'Hara
William DeWitt Snodgrass

David Russell Wagoner
Edward Lewis Wallant

DEATHS

Henry Augustin Beers
George Stirling

EVENTS

Book-of-the-Month-Club (est)
New Masses, New York, to 1948 (per)

LITERATURE

George Abbott. Broadway (dr)
James Truslow Adams. New England in the Republic (hist)
Samuel Hopkins Adams. Revelry (fic)
William Hervey Allen. Israfel (biog)
_____. Toward the Flame (fic)
Sherwood Anderson. Sherwood Anderson's Notebook (nar)
_____. Tar, a Midwest Childhood (fic)
John James Audubon. Delineations of American Scenery and Character
   (nar, pub)
Joseph Auslander. Cyclops' Eye (po)
Irving Addison Bacheller. Opinions of a Cheerful Yankee (nar)
Margaret Culkin Banning. The Women of the Family (fic)
Harry Elmer Barnes. The Genesis of the World War (hist)
Philip Barry. White Wings (dr)
Charles William Beebe. The Arcturus Adventure (nar)
Thomas Beer. The Mauve Decade (hist)
Samuel Flagg Bemis. Pinckney's Treaty (hist)
John Barry Benefield. Short Turns (fic)
Stephen Vincent Benet. Spanish Bayonet (fic)
Konrad Bercovici. Singing Winds (fic)
_____. The Volga Boatman (fic)
Earl Derr Biggers. The Chinese Parrot (fic)
Ernest Boyd. Guy deMaupassant (biog)
James Henry Breasted. The Conquest of Civilization (hist)
Louis Bromfield. Early Autumn (fic)
Heywood Campbell Broun. Gandle Follows His Nose (fic)
Donn Byrne. Hangman's House (fic)
James Branch Cabell. The Music from Behind the Moon (fic)
_____. The Silver Stallion (fic)
Melville Henry Cane. January Garden (po)
Willa Sibert Cather. My Mortal Enemy (fic)
Barrett Harper Clark. Eugene O'Neill (e, biog)
John Colton. The Shanghai Gesture (dr)
John Cournos. Miranda Masters (fic)
Harold Hart Crane. White Buildings (po)
Nathalia Crane. The Singing Crow (po)
_____. The Sunken Garden (hist)
Edward Estlin Cummings. is 5 (po)
Merle Eugene Curti. Austria and the United States, 1848-1852 (hist)
Margaretta Wade Campbell Deland. The Kays (fic)
Floyd Dell. An Old Man's Folly (fic)

_____. The Outline of Marriage (e)
Babette Deutsch. A Brittle Heaven (fic)
Bernard Augustine DeVoto. The Chariot of Fire (fic)
Hilda Doolittle. Palimpset (fic)
John Roderigo Dos Passos. The Garbage Man (dr)
Theodore Herman Albert Dreiser. Moods, Cadenced and Declaimed (po)
John Erskine. Galahad (fic)
William Harrison Faulkner. Soldiers' Pay (fic)
Edna Ferber. Show Boat (fic)
Dorothy Canfield Fisher. Her Son's Wife (fic)
Francis Scott Key Fitzgerald. All the Sad Young Men (fic)
Janet Flanner. The Cubical City (fic)
John Gould Fletcher. Branches of Adam (po)
Esther Forbes. O, Genteel Lady (fic)
Waldo David Frank. Virgin Spain (trav)
Zona Gale. Preface to a Life (fic)
Hannibal Hamlin Garland. Trail Makers of the Middle Border (nar,
    fic)
Ellen Glasgow. The Romantic Comedians (fic)
Susan Glaspell. The Road to the Temple (biog)
Herbert Sherman Gorman. A Victorian American: Henry Wadsworth Long-
    fellow (biog)
Julian Green. Avarice House (fic)
Paul Eliot Green. Lonesome Road (dr)
Arthur Guiterman. I Sing the Pioneer (po)
Frank Harris. Joan la Ramee (dr)
Ben Hecht. Count Bruga (fic)
Ernest Miller Hemingway. The Sun Also Rises (fic)
_____. The Torrents of Spring (fic)
Joseph Hergesheimer. Tampico (fic)
Robert Herrick. Chimes (fic)
Sidney Coe Howard. Ned McCobb's Daughter (dr)
_____. The Silver Cord (dr)
James Langston Hughes. The Weary Blues (po)
Rupert Hughes. George Washington, 3 vols, to 1930 (biog)
Fannie Hurst. Mannequin (fic)
George Edward Kelly. Daisy Mayme (dr)
Hibbard (Harry) Kemp. More Miles (po)
_____. The Sea and the Dunes (po)
Joseph Wood Krutch. Edgar Allan Poe: A Study in Genius (biog, e)
Ringgold Wilmer Lardner. The Love Nest (fic)
Margaret Kernochan Leech. Tin Wedding (fic)
Ludwig Lewisohn. The Case of Mr. Crump (fic)
Nicholas Vachel Lindsay. The Candle in the Cabin: A Weaving Together
    of Script and Singing (po)
_____. Going-to-the-Stars (po)
Amy Lawrence Lowell. East Wind (po, pub)
Charles MacArthur and Edward Brewster Sheldon. Lulu Belle (dr)
Percy Wallace MacKaye. Tall Tales of the Kentucky Mountains (dr)
Archibald MacLeish. Nobodaddy (po, dr)
_____. Streets in the Moon (po)
Percy Marks. Which Way Parnassus? (fic)
Edgar Lee Masters. Lee, dr, po)
Robert McAlmon. The Portrait of a Generation (po)
David Thompson Watson McCord. Oddly Enough (e)
John Thomas McIntyre. Shot Towers (fic)

Henry Lewis Mencken. Notes on Democracy (e)
Harriet Monroe. Poets and Their Arts (e)
John Trotwood Moore. Hearts of Hickory (fic)
Clarence Edward Mulford. Bar-20 Rides Again (fic)
Vladimir Nabokov. Mary (fic)
Robert Gruntal Nathan. The Fiddler in Barley (fic)
John Gneisenau Neihardt. Collected Poems (pub)
_____. Indian Tales, and Others (fic)
Eugene Gladstone O'Neill. The Great God Brown (dr)
Martha Ostenso. The Dark Dawn (fic)
Dorothy Rothschild Parker. Enough Rope (po)
Vernon Lewis Parrington. The Connecticut Wits (e)
Anne Parrish. Tomorrow Morning (fic)
Ernest Poole. With Eastern Eyes (fic)
Emery Bemsley Pottle (Gilbert Emery) and Amelie Rives. Love-in-a-
    Mist (dr)
Lizette Woodworth Reese. Selected Poems (pub)
Elizabeth Madox Roberts. My Heart and My Flesh (fic)
Carl August Sandburg. Abraham Lincoln: The Prairie Years, 2 vols
    (biog)
Elsie Singmaster. Keller's Anna Ruth (fic)
Thorne Smith. Topper (fic)
Charles Wilbert Snow. The Inner Harbor (po)
Leonora Speyer. Fiddler's Farewell (po)
Wilbur Daniel Steele. Urkey Island (fic)
Gertrude Stein. Composition As Explanation (e)
George Sterling. Robinson Jeffers, the Man and the Artist (biog, e)
James Floyd Stevens. Brawnyman (fic)
Thomas Sigismund Stribling. Teeftallow (fic)
Austin Strong. The Drums of Oude (dr)
Ruth Suckow. Iowa Interiors (fic)
Genevieve Taggard. Words for the Chisel (po)
Sara Teesdale. Dark of the Moon (po)
Louis Untermeyer. Collected Parodies (po)
Mark Albert Van Doren. 7 P.M., and Other Poems (po)
Carl Van Vechten. Excavations (e)
_____. Nigger Heaven (fic)
Mary Marvin Heaton Vorse. Passaic (fic)
John Van Alstyn Weaver and George Abbott. Love 'Em and Leave 'Em
    (dr)
Glenway Wescott. Like a Lover (fic)
Edith Newbold Jones Wharton. Here and Beyond (fic)
_____. Twelve Poems (pub)
Brand Whitlock. Uprooted (fic)
Margaret Widdemer. The Singing Wood (po, dr)
Thornton Niven Wilder. The Bridge of San Luis Rey (fic)
_____. The Cabala (fic)
_____. The Trumpet Shall Sound (dr)
Ben Ames Williams. The Silver Forest
Thames Ross Williamson. Gypsy Down the Lane (fic)
_____. The Man Who Cannot Die (fic)
Edmund Wilson. Discordant Encounters (dr)
Thyra Samter Winslow. Show Business (fic)
William E. Woodward. George Washington: The Image and the Man (biog)
Willard Huntington Wright (S.S. Van Dine). The Benson Murder Case
    (fic)

Elinor Hoyt Wylie. The Orphan Angel (fic)
Stark Young. Heaven Trees (fic)

1927

BIRTHS

John Lawrence Ashbery
David Brion Davis
James Leo Herlihy
Roger Kahn
Galway Kinnell
Judith Krantz
Philip Lamantia
Robert Ludlam
Peter Matthiessen
William Stanley Merwin
May Swenson
James Arlington Wright

DEATHS

Brooks Adams
Albert Jeremiah Beveridge
Samuel McChord Crothers
James Oliver Curwood
Frank Lebby Stanton

EVENTS

American Caravan, to 1936 (per)
Hound and Horn, Cambridge, Massachusetts; New York, New York, to
     1934 (per)
The Literary Guild (f)
The Prairie Schooner, Lincoln, Nebraska (per, f)

LITERATURE

George Abbott. Coquette (dr)
James Truslow Adams. Provincial Society, 1690-1763 (hist)
Conrad Potter Aiken. Blue Voyage (fic)
Maxwell Anderson. Saturday's Children (dr)
Sherwood Anderson. A New Testament (po)
Nathan Asch. Love in Chartres (fic)
Justin Brooks Atkinson. Henry Thoreau: Cosmic Yankee (e)
Ray Stannard Baker. Woodrow Wilson: Life and Letters, 8 vols, to
     1939 (biog, hist, nar, ed)
Philip Barry. John (dr)
_____. Paris Bound (dr)
Carleton Beals. Brimstone and Chili (e)
Charles Austin Beard and Mary Ritter Beard. The Rise of American Ci-
     vilization, 2 vols (hist, e)
Charles William Beebe. Pheasant Jungles (des)
Samuel Nathaniel Behrman. The Second Man (dr)
Robert Charles Benchley. 20,000 Leagues under the Sea; or, David

Copperfield (nar)
William Rose Benet. Man Possessed (po)
Franz Boas. Primitive Art (e)
Maxwell Bodenheim. Returning to Emotion (po)
Ernest Boyd. Literary Blasphemies (e)
James Boyd. Marching On (fic)
Percy Holmes Boynton. More Contemporary Americans (e)
Heywood Campbell Broun and Margaret Leech. Anthony Comstock: Rounds-
     man of the Lord (biog)
Louis Bromfield. A Good Woman (fic)
_____. The House of Women (dr)
Van Wyck Brooks. Emerson and Others (e, biog)
Alice Brown. Dear Old Templeton (fic)
William Crary Brownell. Democratic Distinction in America (e)
_____. The Spirit of Society (e)
Maxwell Struthers Burt. The Delectable Mountains (fic)
Donn Byrne. Brother Saul (fic)
James Branch Cabell. Something about Eve (fic)
Walter Stanley Campbell (Stanley Vestal). Fandango: Ballads of the
     Old West (po)
Willa Sibert Cather. Death Comes to the Archbishop (fic)
Robert William Chambers. The Drums of Aulone (fic)
Barrett Harper Clark. OEdipus or Pollyanna (e)
Countee Cullen. The Ballad of the Brown Girl (po)
_____. Caroling Dusk (po, ed)
_____. Copper Sun (po)
Edward Estlin Cummings. him (dr, po)
Donald Grady Davidson. The Tall Men (po)
Elmer Holmes Davis. Show Window (e)
William Stearns Davis. Gilman of Redford (fic)
Floyd Dell. An Unmarried Father (fic)
_____. Upton Sinclair (biog)
Babette Deutsch. In Such a Night (fic)
George Dillon. Boy in the Wind (po)
Hilda Doolittle. Hippolytus Temporizes (po, dr)
John Roderigo Dos Passos. Orient Express (trav, nar)
Theodore Herman Albert Dreiser. Chains (fic)
Thomas Stearns Eliot. Shakespeare and the Stoicism of Seneca (e)
John Erskine. Adam and Eve (fic)
Janet Ayer Fairbank. Idle Hands (fic)
William Harrison Faulkner. Mosquitoes (fic)
Edna Ferber. Mother Knows Best (fic)
_____ and George Simon Kaufman. The Royal Family (dr)
Harvey Fergusson. Wolf Song (fic)
Rachel Lyman Field. The Cross-Stitch Heart and Other Plays (dr)
Vardis Alvero Fisher. Sonnets to an Imaginary Madonna (po)
Zona Gale. Yellow Gentians and Blue (fic)
Herbert Sherman Gorman. Hawthorne: A Study in Solitude (biog)
Julian Green. The Closed Garden (fic)
_____. The Pilgrims on the Earth (fic)
Paul Eliot Green. In Abraham's Bosom (dr)
_____. The Field God (dr)
Arthur Guiterman. Wildwood Fables (po)
Herman Hagedorn. The Rough Riders (fic)
Richard Halliburton. The Glorious Adventure (trav, nar)
Frances Noyes Hart. The Bellamy Trial (fic)

Ernest Miller Hemingway. Men without Women (fic)
Robert Silliman Hillyer. The Happy Episode (po)
James Langston Hughes. Fine Clothes to a Jew (po)
Fannie Hurst. Song of Life (fic)
John Robinson Jeffers. The Women at Point Star (po)
James Weldon Johnson. God's Trombones: Seven Negro Sermons in Verse
     (po)
George Edward Kelly. Behold the Bridegroom (dr)
Hubbard (Harry) Kemp. The Bronze Treasury: An Anthology of Eighty-
     One Obscure Poets (po, ed)
Manuel Komroff. Juggler's Kiss (fic)
Alfred Kreymborg. Funnybone Alley (juv)
John Howard Lawson. Loud Speaker (dr)
Harry Sinclair Lewis. Elmer Gantry (fic)
Janet Lewis. The Wheel in Midsummer (po)
Ludwig Lewisohn. Roman Summer (fic)
Charles Augustus Lindbergh. We (nar)
Amy Lawrence Lowell. Ballads for Sale (po, pub)
_____. The Madonna of Carthagena (po, pub)
Charles MacArthur and Sidney Coe Howard. Salvation (dr)
Percy Marks. Lord of Himself (fic)
Donald Robert Perry Marquis. The Almost Perfect State (fic)
_____. Archy and Mehitabel (po)
_____. Out of the Sea (dr)
John Thomas McIntyre. Slag (fic)
Langdon Elwyn Mitchell. Understanding America (e)
Samuel Eliot Morison. The Oxford History of the United States, 1783-
     1917, 2 vols (hist)
Honore Willsie Morrow. Forever Free (fic)
Robert Gruntal Nathan. The Woodcutter's House (fic)
Charles Gilman Norris. Zelda Marsh (fic)
Eugene Gladstone O'Neill. Lazarus Laughed (dr)
Martha Ostenso. The Mad Carews (fic)
Vernon Louis Parrington. Main Currents in American Thought, 3 vols,
     to 1930 (e, hist)
_____. Sinclair Lewis, Our Own Diogenes (e)
Julia Mood Peterkin. Black April (fic)
Ernest Poole. Silent Storms (fic)
John Crowe Ransom. Two Gentlemen in Bonds (po)
Lizette Woodworth Reese. Little Henrietta (po)
Laura Reichenthal (Laura Riding) and Robert Graves. A Survey of Mo-
     dernist Poetry (e)
Eugene Manlove Rhodes. Once in the Saddle (fic)
Lola Ridge. Red Flag (po)
Felix Riesenberg. East Side, West Side (fic)
Lynn Riggs. Big Lake (dr)
Amelie Rives and Emery Bemsley Pottle (Gilbert Emery). Love-in-a-
     Mist (dr)
Edwin Arlington Robinson. Tristram (po)
Carl August Sandburg. The American Songbag (po, ed)
George Santayana. Platonism and the Spiritual Life (e)
_____. The Realm of Essence (e)
Evelyn Scott. Ideals (fic)
_____. Migrations: An Arabesque in Histories (fic)
Anne Douglas Sedgwick. The Old Countess (fic)
James Vincent Sheean. The Anatomy of Virtue (fic)

Robert Emmet Sherwood. The Love Nest (dr)
_____. The Road to Rome (dr)
Upton Beall Sinclair. Oil! (fic)
Frank Lebby Stanton. Frank L. Stanton's Just from Georgia (e, po, pub)
James Floyd Stevens. Mattock (fic)
Newton Booth Tarkington. The Plutocrat (fic)
Dan Totheroh. Wild Orchard (fic)
Jim Tully. Circus Parade (nar)
Jean Starr Untermeyer. Steep Ascent (po)
Mark Albert Van Doren. Edward Arlington Robinson (e)
Hendrik Willem Van Loon. America (hist)
Lula Vollmer. Trigger (dr)
Glenway Wescott. The Grandmothers (fic)
Edith Newbold Jones Wharton. Twilight Sleep (fic)
John Hall Wheelock. The Bright Doom (po)
Stuart Edward White. Story of California (fic)
Brand Whitlock. Transplanted (fic)
Walt Whitman. The Half-Breed, and Other Stories (pub)
Ben Ames Williams. Immortal Longings (fic)
Thames Ross Williamson. Stride of Man (fic)
Thyra Samter Winslow. People Round the Corner (fic)
Arthur Yvor Winters. The Bare Hills (po)
Charles Erskine Scott Wood. Heavenly Discourse (sat)
Audrey Wurdemann. The House of Silk (po)
Anzia Yezierska. Arrogant Beggar (fic)
Stark Young. The Theatre (e)

1928

BIRTHS

Edward Franklin Albee
Peter Hubert Davison
Jessie Hill Ford
Donald Andrew Hall
Marguerite Johnson (Maya Angelou)
William Kennedy
Philip Levine
Cynthia Ozick
Hubert Selby
Richard Selzer
Anne Sexton
Richard Gustave Stern
Kate Wilhelm

DEATHS

John Spencer Bassett
William Crary Brownell
Donn Byrne
Ina Donna Coolbrith
Sarah Barnwell Elliot
Avery Hopwood
Henry Francis Keenan

George Barr McCutcheon
Elinor Hoyt Wylie

EVENTS

Dictionary of American Biography (biog, ref)
English Language Institute of America (est)
Mercury and Weekly News, Newport, Rhode Island (per, est)
The New England Quarterly (per, est)

LITERATURE

Conrad Potter Aiken. Costumes by Eros (fic)
Bess Streeter Aldrich. Lantern in Her Hand (fic)
Maxwell Anderson and Harold Hickerson. Gods of the Lightning (dr)
Mary Hunter Austin. Children Sing in the Far West (po)
Irving Addison Bacheller. Coming Up the Road (nar)
Leonard Bacon. The Legend of Quincibald (po)
Djuna Barnes. Ryder (fic)
Margaret Ayer Barnes. The Age of Innocence (dr)
Philip Barry. Holiday (dr)
_____ and Elmer Reizenstein (Elmer Rice). Cock Robin (dr)
Ernest Sutherland Bates. The Friend of Jesus (e)
Charles William Beebe. Beneath Tropic Seas (des)
Thomas Beer. The Road to Heaven (fic)
John Barry Benefield. A Little Clown Lost (fic)
Stephen Vincent Benet. John Brown's Body (po)
Konrad Bercovici. Alexander (biog)
_____. Peasants (fic)
_____. Story of the Gypsies (nar)
Albert Jeremiah Beveridge. Life of Abraham Lincoln, 2 vols (biog, pub)
Earl Derr Biggers. Behind That Curtain (fic)
Franz Boas. Materials for the Study of Inheritance in Man (e)
Maxwell Bodenheim. The King of Spain, and Other Poems (po)
Thomas Alexander Boyd. Shadow of the Long Knives (fic)
_____. Simon Girty, the White Savage (biog)
Gamaliel Bradford. Life and I (auto)
Roark Bradford. Ol' Man Adam and His Children (fic)
William Stanley Beaumont Baraithwaite. Frost on the Green Tree (fic)
Louis Bromfield. The Strange Case of Miss Annie Spragg (fic)
John Burroughs. The Heart of John Burroughs's Journals (nar, pub)
Maxwell Struthers Burt. They Could Not Sleep (fic)
Donn Byrne. Crusade (fic)
_____. Destiny Bay (fic)
James Branch Cabell. The White Robe (fic)
Morley Callaghan. Strange Fugitive (fic)
Walter Stanley Campbell (Stanley Vestal). Happy Hunting Grounds (fic)
_____. Kit Carson (biog)
Octavus Roy Cohen. Florian Slappey Goes Abroad (fic)
Ellsworth Prouty Conkle. Crick Bottom Plays (dr, pub)
John Cournos. A Modern Plutarch (biog)
James Gould Cozzens. Cock Pit (fic)
Nathalia Crane. Venus Invisible (po)
Clarence Shepard Day. Thoughts without Words (e)

Vina Delmar. Bad Girl (fic)
Bernard Augustine DeVoto. The House of Sun-Goes-Down (fic)
Hilda Doolittle. Hedylus (fic)
Theodore Albert Dreiser. Dreiser Looks at Russia (e)
William Edward Burghardt DuBois. The Dark Princess (fic)
Thomas Stearns Eliot. For Lancelot Andrewes (e)
Vardis Alvero Fisher. Toilers of the Hills (fic)
John Gould Fletcher. The Black Rock (po)
_____. John Smith--Also Pocahontas (biog)
Norman Foerster. American Criticism (e)
Esther Forbes. A Mirror for Witches (fic)
Waldo David Frank. The Rediscovery of America (e)
Robert Lee Frost. West-Running Brook (po)
Zona Gale. Portage, Wisconsin (auto, nar)
Hannibal Hamlin Garland. Back-Trailers from the Middle Border (fic,
    nar)
Susan Glaspell. Brook Evans (fic)
Paul Eliot Green. In the Valley (dr)
_____. Wide Fields (fic)
Julian Hawthorne. Shapes That Pass (auto)
Ben Hecht and Charles MacArthur. Front Page (dr)
Josephine Frey Herbst. Nothing Is Sacred (fic)
Joseph Hergesheimer. Quiet Cities (fic)
Robert Silliman Hillyer. The Seventh Hill (po)
Sidney Coe Howard. Olympia (dr)
_____, and Charles MacArthur. Salvation (dr)
Fannie Hurst. A President Is Born (fic)
John Robinson Jeffers. An Artist (po)
_____. Cawdor, and Other Poems (po)
_____. Poems (pub)
Alfred Kreymborg. The Lost Sail (po)
John Howard Lawson. The International (dr)
William Ellery Leonard. A Song of Earth (po)
Harry Sinclair Lewis. The Man Who Knew Coolidge (fic)
Ludwig Lewisohn. The Island Within (fic)
Nicholas Vachel Lindsay. Johnny Appleseed, and Other Poems (po)
Anita Loos. But Gentlemen Marry Brunettes (fic)
Charles MacArthur and Ben Hecht. The Front Page (dr)
Percy Wallace MacKaye. Gobbler of God (po)
_____. Kentucky Mountain Fantasies (dr)
Archibald MacLeish. The Hamlet of A. MacLeish (po)
Joseph Moncure March. The Set-Up (po, nar)
_____. The Wild Party (po, nar)
Donald Robert Perry Marquis. Love Sonnets of a Cave Man (po)
Edgar Lee Masters. Jack Kelso (dr, po)
David Thompson Watson McCord. Stirabout (e)
William Morley Punshon McFee. Pilgrims of Adversity (fic)
John Thomas McIntyre. Stained Sails (fic)
Claude McKay. Home to Harlem (fic)
Edna St. Vincent Millay. The Buck in the Snow (po)
Honore Willsie Morrow. With Malice toward None (fic)
Vladimir Nabokov. King, Queen, Knave (fic)
George Jean Nathan. Art of the Night (e)
Robert Gruntal Nathan. The Bishop's Wife (fic)
Alfred Edward Newton. This Book Collecting Game (e, nar)
Meredith Nicholson. The Cavalier of Tennessee (fic)

Eugene Gladstone O'Neill. Marco Millions (dr)
_____. Strange Interlude (dr)
Dorothy Rothschild Parker. Sunset Gun (po)
Anne Parrish. All Kneeling (fic)
Donald Culross Peattie and Louise Redfield Peattie. Up Country (fic)
Julia Mood Peterkin. Scarlet Sister Mary (fic)
Channing Pollock. Mr. Moneypenny (dr)
Emery Bemsley Pottle (Gilbert Emery). Thank You, Doctor (dr)
Ezra Weston Loomis Pound. A Draft of Cantos XVII to XXVII (po)
Laura Reichenthal (Laura Riding). Contemporaries and Snobs (e)
Elmer Reizenstein (Elmer Rice) and Philip Barry. Cock Robin (dr)
Feliz Riesenberg. Red Horses (fic)
Lynn Riggs. A Lantern To See By (dr)
_____. Sump'n Like Wings (dr)
Elizabeth Madox Roberts. Jingling in the Wind (fic)
Elizabeth Robins. Ibsen and the Actress (nar)
Edwin Arlington Robinson. Sonnets, 1889-1927 (po, pub)
Paul Rosenfeld. The Boy in the Sun (fic)
_____. By Way of Art (e)
Carl August Sandburg. Good Morning, America (po)
Robert Emmet Sherwood. The Queen's Husband (dr)
Shaemas Shields (Shaemas O'Sheel). Jealous of Dead Leaves (po)
Upton Beall Sinclair. Boston (fic)
James Floyd Stevens. Homer in the Sagebrush (fic)
Thomas Sigismund Stribling. Bright Metal (fic)
Ruth Suckow. The Bonney Family (fic)
Genevieve Taggard. Travelling Standing Still (po)
Newton Booth Tarkington. The World Does Move (nar)
John Orley Allen Tate. Mr. Pope, and Other Poems (po)
Albert Payson Terhune. Lad of Sunnybank (fic)
Eunice Tietjens. Poetry of the Orient (po, trans)
Jim Tully. Shanty Irish (fic)
Louis Untermeyer. Burning Bush (po)
_____. Moses (nar, trans)
Mark Albert Van Doren. Now the Sky, and Other Poems (po)
Hendrik Willem Van Loon. The Life and Times of Pieter Stuyvesant
    (biog, hist)
_____. Man, the Miracle Maker (hist)
Carl Van Vechten. Spider Boy (fic)
Mary Marvin Heaton Vorse. Second Cabin (fic)
Glenway Wescott. Goodbye, Wisconsin (fic)
Edith Newbold Jones Wharton. The Children (fic)
Brand Whitlock. Big Matt (fic)
Thornton Niven Wilder. The Angel That Troubled the Waters (dr)
Ben Ames Williams. The Dreadful Night (fic)
William Carlos Williams. A Voyage to Pagany (fic)
Margaret Wilson. Daughters of India (fic)
William E. Woodward. Meet General Grant (biog)
Elinor Hoyt Wylie. Mr. Hodge and Mr. Hazard (fic)
_____. One Person (po)
_____. Trivial Breath (po)
Stark Young. The Torches Flare (fic)

1929

BIRTHS

James (Jimmy) Breslin
Edward Merton Dorn
Marilyn French
George Palmer Garrett, Jr.
Shirley Ann Grau
John Hollander
Richard Joseph Howard
Ursula K. LeGuin
Ira Levin
Robert Pack
Adrienne Rich
Howard Sackler
Michael Joseph Shaara, Jr.
Gilbert Sorrentino

DEATHS

William Bliss Carman
Henry Blake Fuller
James Brander Matthews
John Trotwood Moore
Vernon Louis Parrington
Jesse Lynch Williams

EVENTS

Herbert Clark Hoover, 31st President of the United States, to 1933

LITERATURE

Leonie Fuller Adams. High Falcon (po)
Herbert Sebastian Agar. The Garment of Praise (e)
Conrad Potter Aiken. Selected Poems (pub)
Sherwood Anderson. Hello Towns! (nar)
_____. Nearer the Grass Roots (e)
Benjamin Appel. Mixed Vintage (po)
John James Audubon. Journal (nar, pub)
Joseph Auslander. Hell in Harness (po)
_____. Letters to Women (po)
Djuna Barnes. A Night among the Horses (dr, fic, po)
Harry Elmer Barnes. The Twilight of Christianity (hist)
Margaret Ayer Barnes. Jenny (dr)
Joseph Hamilton Basso. Relics and Angels (fic)
Thomas Beer. Hanna (biog, hist)
Samuel Nathaniel Behrman. Meteor (dr)
_____. Serena Blandish (dr)
Albert Bein (Charles Walt). Love in Chicago (fic)
_____. Road Out of Hell (fic)
Earl Derr Biggers. The Black Camel (fic)
Maxwell Bodenheim. Sixty Seconds (fic)
Louise Bogan. Dark Summer (po)
Claude Gernade Bowers. The Tragic Era: The Revolution after Lincoln

(hist)
Thomas Alexander Boyd. Mad Anthony Wayne (biog)
Gamaliel Bradford. As God Made Them (biog)
Roark Bradford. This Side of Jordan (fic)
Anna Hempsted Branch. Sonnets from a Lock Box (po)
Myron Brinig. Madonna without Child (fic)
_____. Singermann (fic)
Louis Bromfield. Awake and Rehearse (fic)
John Mason Brown. The Modern Theatre in Revolt (e)
Thornton Waldo Burgess. The Burgess Sea Shore Book for Children
   (fic)
Ben Lucien Burman. Mississippi (fic)
William Riley Burnett. Little Caesar (fic)
Harold Witter Bynner. The Jade Mountain (po)
Donn Byrne. Field of Honor (fic)
James Branch Cabell. Sonnets from Antan (po)
_____. The Way of Ecben (fic)
Morley Callaghan. A Native Argosy (fic)
Walter Stanley Campbell (Stanley Vestal). 'Dobe Walls (fic)
William Bliss Carman. Wild Garden (po)
Stuart Chase. Men and Machines (e)
_____. Prosperity: Fact or Myth? (e)
Robert Myron Coates. The Eater of Darkness (fic)
Elizabeth Jane Coatsworth. Compass Rose (po)
Robert Peter Tristram Coffin. An Attic Room (e)
Malcolm Cowley. Blue Juniata (po)
James Gould Cozzens. The Son of Perdition (fic)
Nathalia Crane. An Alien from Heaven (fic)
Rachel Crothers. Let Us Be Gay (dr)
Countee Cullen. The Black Christ (po)
Merle Eugene Curti. The American Peace Crusade (hist)
Edward Dahlberg. Bottom Dogs (fic)
Frederic Dannay and Manfred Lee (Ellery Queen). The Roman Hat Mys-
   tery (fic)
William Stearns Davis. The Whirlwind (fic)
Benjamin DeCasseres. The Superman in America (e)
Vina Delmar. Kept Woman (fic)
_____. Loose Ladies (fic)
Babette Deutsch. Potable Gold: Some Notes on Poetry and This Age (e)
Emily Elizabeth Dickinson. Further Poems (pub)
John Roderigo Dos Passos. Airways, Inc. (dr)
Lloyd Cassel Douglas. Magnificent Obsession (fic)
Theodore Herman Albert Dreiser. A Gallery of Women, 2 vols (fic)
_____. My City (des)
Walter Dumaux Edmonds. Rome Haul (fic)
Thomas Stearns Eliot. Dante (e)
William Harrison Faulkner. Sartoris (fic)
_____. The Sound and the Fury (fic)
Jessie Redmon Fauset. Plum Bun (fic)
Kenneth Fearing. Angel Arms (po)
Harvey Fergusson. In Those Days (fic)
Arthur Davison Ficke. Mountain against Mountain (po)
Rachel Lyman Field. Hitty, Her First Hundred Years (fic)
Martin Archer Flavin. Broken Dishes (dr)
_____. The Criminal Code (dr)
Norman Foerster. The American Scholar (e)

Waldo David Frank. New Year's Eve (dr)
Henry Blake Fuller. Gardens of This World (fic)
Zona Gale. Borgia (fic)
Ellen Glasgow. They Stooped to Folly (fic)
Susan Glaspell. The Fugitive's Return (fic)
Herbert Sherman Gorman. The Incredible Marquis (biog)
Julian Green. Leviathan (fic)
Paul Eliot Green. Tread the Green Grass (dr)
Arthur Guiterman. Song and Laughter (po)
Francis Hackett. Henry the Eighth (biog)
Richard Halliburton. New Worlds To Conquer (trav, nar)
Samuel Dashiell Hammett. Red Harvest (fic)
Frances Noyes Hart. Hide in the Dark (fic)
Ernest Miller Hemingway. A Farewell to Arms (fic)
Josephine Frey Herbst. Money for Love (fic)
Joseph Hergesheimer. Swords and Roses (e)
DuBose Heyward. Mamba's Daughters (fic)
Fannie Hurst. Five and Ten (fic)
_____. Procession (fic)
John Robinson Jeffers. Dear Judas, and Other Poems (po)
George Simon Kaufman and Ringgold Wilmer Lardner. June Moon (dr)
George Edward Kelly. Maggie the Magnificent (dr)
George Lyman Kittredge. Witchcraft in Old and New England (hist)
Manuel Komroff. Coronet, 2 vols (fic)
Alfred Kreymborg. Manhattan Men (po)
_____. Our Singing Strength (hist)
Louis Kronenberger. The Grand Manner (fic)
Joseph Wood Krutch. The Modern Temper (e)
Oliver Hazard Perry LaFarge. Laughing Boy (fic)
Ringgold Wilmer Lardner. Round Up (fic)
Meyer Levin. Reporter (fic)
Harry Sinclair Lewis. Dodsworth (fic)
Joseph Crosby Lincoln and Freeman Lincoln. Blair's Attic (fic)
Nicholas Vachel Lindsay. Every Soul Is a Circus (po)
_____. The Litany of Washington Street (e)
Percy Marks. The Unwilling God (fic)
Donald Robert Perry Marquis. A Variety of People (fic)
Edgar Lee Masters. The Fate of the Jury (po)
Robert McAlmon. North America, Continent of Conjecture (po)
William Morley Punshon McFee. Sailors of Fortune (fic)
Claude McKay. Banjo (fic)
Philip Moeller. Camel through the Needle's Eye (dr)
Merrill Moore. The Noise That Time Makes (po)
Honore Willsie Morrow. The Splendor of God (fic)
Robert Gruntal Nathan. A Cedar Box (po)
_____. There Is Another Heaven (fic)
Eugene Gladstone O'Neill. Dynamo (dr)
Martha Ostenso. The Young May Moon (fic)
Anne Parrish. The Methodist Faun (fic)
Elliott Harold Paul. Lava Rock (fic)
_____. Low Run Tide (fic)
Sidney Joseph Perelman. Dawn Ginsbergh's Revenge (nar, sat)
Lizette Woodworth Reese. A Victorian Village (nar)
Elmer Reizenstein (Elmer Rice). See Naples and Die (dr)
_____. Street Scene (dr)
_____. The Subway (dr)

_____ and Dorothy Rothschild Parker. <u>Close</u>
<u>Harmony</u> (dr)
Agnes Repplier. <u>Pere Marquette</u> (biog)
Lola Ridge. <u>Firehead</u> (po)
Edwin Arlington Robinson. <u>Cavender's House</u> (po)
Carl August Sandburg. <u>Steichen the Photographer</u> (biog)
Evelyn Scott. <u>The Wave</u> (fic)
Anne Douglas Sedgwick. <u>Dark Hester</u> (fic)
Gilbert Vivian Seldes. <u>The Wings of the Eagle</u> (fic)
Edward Brewster Sheldon and Margaret Ayer Barnes. <u>Jenny</u> (dr)
Constance Ludwig Skinner. <u>Red Willows</u> (fic)
Joel Elias Spingarn. <u>A Spingarn Enchiridion</u> (e)
Wilbur Daniel Steele. <u>Tower of Sand</u> (fic)
John Ernst Steinbeck. <u>Cup of Gold</u> (fic)
Donald Ogden Stewart. <u>Father William</u> (sat)
Grace Zaring Stone. <u>The Heaven and Earth of Dona Elena</u> (fic)
Rex Todhunter Stout. <u>How Like a God</u> (fic)
Thomas Sigismund Stribling. <u>Clues of the Caribbees</u> (fic)
_____. <u>Strange Moon</u> (fic)
Ruth Suckow. <u>Cora</u> (fic)
Newton Booth Tarkington. <u>Penrod Jashber</u> (juv, fic)
James Grover Thurber and Elwyn Brooks White. <u>Is Sex Necessary?</u> (sat)
Eunice Tietjens. <u>Leaves in Windy Weather</u> (po)
Dan Totheroh. <u>Men Call Me Fool</u> (fic)
Jim Tully. <u>Shadows of Men</u> (nar)
John William Van Druten. <u>Young Woodley</u> (fic)
Robert Penn Warren. <u>John Brown: The Making of a Martyr</u> (biog)
Edith Newbold Jones Wharton. <u>Certain People</u> (fic)
_____. <u>Hudson River Bracketed</u> (fic)
Elwyn Brooks White. <u>The Lady Is Cold</u> (po)
_____ and James Grover Thurber. <u>Is Sex Necessary?</u> (sat)
Jesse Lynch Williams. <u>They Still Fall in Love</u> (fic)
Thames Ross Williamson. <u>Hunky</u> (fic)
Edmund Wilson. <u>I Thought of Daisy</u> (fic)
_____. <u>Poets, Farewell!</u> (po)
Margaret Wilson. <u>Trousers of Taffeta</u> (fic)
Thomas Clayton Wolfe. <u>Look Homeward, Angel</u> (fic)
Charles Erskine Scott Wood. <u>Poems from the Ranges</u> (po)
Elinor Hoyt Wylie. <u>Angels and Earthly Creatures</u> (po, pub)
Stark Young. <u>River House</u> (fic)
Leane Zugsmith. <u>All Victories Are Alike</u> (fic)

1930

BIRTHS

    John Barth
    Gregory Nunzio Corso
    Stanley Lawrence Elkin
    Peter Steinham Feibleman
    Bruce Jay Friedman
    Lorraine Hansberry
    Maureen Howard
    Mary Gray Hughes
    Elain Lobl Konigsburg

Harry Matthews
Wilfred John Joseph Sheed
Gary Sherman Snyder

DEATHS

Herbert David Croly
William Stearns Davis
Mary Eleanor Wilkins Freeman
Arthur Sherburne Hardy
Henry Sydnor Harrison
Melville Davisson Post
George Edward Woodberry

EVENTS

The Encyclopaedia of the Social Sciences, to 1935 (ref)
Fortune (per f)
The New Freeman, to 1931 (per)

LITERATURE

James Truslow Adams. The Adams Family (biog)
Samuel Hopkins Adams. The Godlike Daniel (biog)
Jane Addams. The Second Twenty Years at Hull House (nar)
Conrad Potter Aiken. John Deth (po)
Zoe Akins. The Greeks Had a Word for It (dr)
Maxwell Anderson. Elizabeth the Queen (po, dr)
Nathan Asch. Pay Day (fic)
Sholem Asch. The Mother (fic)
Wystan Hugh Auden. Poems (pub)
John James Audubon. Letters (nar, pub)
Irving Addison Bacheller. A Candle in the Wilderness (fic)
Faith Baldwin. Office Wife (fic)
Margaret Culkin Banning. Mixed Marriage (fic)
Margaret Ayer Barnes. Dishonored Lady (dr)
_____. Years of Grace (fic)
Philip Barry. Hotel Universe (dr)
Ernest Sutherland Bates. This Land of Liberty (e)
Charles Austin Beard and William Beard. The American Leviathan (e)
Albert Bein. Youth in Hell (fic)
Robert Charles Benchley. No Poems (nar)
Maxwell Bodenheim. Bringing Jazz (po)
Ernest Boyd. The Virtue of Vices (e)
James Boyd. Long Hunt (fic)
Kay Boyle. Wedding Day (fic)
Gamaliel Bradford. Daughters of Eve (biog)
Roark Bradford. Ol' King David an' the Philistine Boys (fic)
Louis Bromfield. Twenty-four Hours (fic)
John Mason Brown. Upstage (e)
Pearl Sydenstricker Buck. East Wind, West Wind (fic)
William Riley Burnett. Iron Man (fic)
Nicholas Murray Butler. The Path to Peace (e)
James Branch Cabell. Some of Us (e)
Erskine Preston Caldwell. The Bastard (fic)
_____. Poor Fool (fic)
Morley Callaghan. It's Never Over (fic)

Melville Henry Cane. Behind Dark Spaces (po)
Carl Lamson Carmer. Deep South (po)
William Henry Chamberlain. Soviet Russia (e)
Robert Myron Coates. The Outlaw-Years (hist)
Elizabeth Jane Coatsworth. The Cat Who Went to Heaven (juv)
Irvin Shrewsbury Cobb. To Be Taken before Sailing (hum)
Henry Steele Commager and Samuel Eliot Morison. The Growth of the
    American Republic (hist)
Marcus Cook Connelly. The Green Pastures (dr)
John Cournos. Wandering Women (fic)
Harold Hart Crane. The Bridge (po)
William Stearns Davis. Life in Elizabethan Days (hist)
Benjamin DeCasseres. Mencken and Shaw (e)
Babette Deutsch. Fire for the Night (po)
Emily Elizabeth Dickinson. Poems: Centenary Edition (po, pub)
John Roderigo Dos Passos. The 42nd Parallel (fic)
Richard Ghormley Eberhart. A Bravery of Earth (po)
Walter Dumaux Edmonds. The Big Barn (fic)
Thomas Stearns Eliot. Ash-Wednesday (po)
Janet Ayer Fairbank. The Lion's Den (fic)
William Harrison Faulkner. As I Lay Dying (fic)
Edna Ferber. Cimarron (fic)
Harvey Fergusson. Footloose McGarnigal (fic)
Irving Fineman. The Pure Young Man (fic)
Dorothy Canfield Fisher. The Deepening Stream (fic)
John Gould Fletcher. The Two Frontiers (e)
Norman Foerster. Toward Standards (e)
Louis Fraina (Lewis Corey). The House of Morgan: A Social Biography
    of the Masters of Money (biog, hist)
Joseph Freeman. Voices of October: Soviet Literature and Art (e)
Robert Lee Frost. Collected Poems (pub)
Henry Blake Fuller. Not on the Screen (fic, sat)
Zona Gale. Bridal Pond (fic)
Hannibal Hamlin Garland. Roadside Meetings (nar)
Susan Glaspell. Alison's House (dr)
Anne Green. The Selbys (fic)
Julian Green. Christine, and Other Stories (fic)
Horace Victor Gregory. Chelsea Rooming House (po)
Samuel Dashiell Hammett. The Maltese Falcon (fic)
Frank Harris. My Reminiscences As a Cowboy (nar)
Moss Hart and George Simon Kaufman. Once in a Lifetime (dr)
Ben Hecht. A Jew in Love (fic)
Joseph Hergesheimer. The Party Dress (fic)
Robert Silliman Hillyer. The Gates of the Compass (po)
Sidney Coe Howard. Marseilles (dr)
Hatcher Hughes and Alan Williams. It's a Grand Life (dr)
James Langston Hughes. Not without Laughter (fic)
William Henry Irwin and Sidney Coe Howard. Lute Song (dr)
John Robinson Jeffers. Apology for Bad Dreams (po)
_____. Stars (po)
James Weldon Johnson. Saint Peter Relates an Incident of the Resur-
    rection Day (po)
Clarence Budington Kelland. Hard Money (fic)
Alfred Kreymborg. Lyric America (po, ed)
_____. Prologue in Hell (po)
Joseph Wood Krutch. Five Masters: A Study of the Mutations of the

    Novel (e)
Stanley Jasspon Kunitz. Intellectual Things (po)
William Ellery Leonard. This Midland City (po)
Meyer Levin. Frankie and Johnny (fic)
Ludwig Lewisohn. Stephen Escott (fic)
Frank Bird Linderman. American (fic)
Robert Morss Lovett. A Preface to Fiction (e)
Archibald MacLeish. New Found Land (po)
John Phillips Marquand. Warning Hill (fic)
Donald Robert Perry Marquis. Off the Arm (fic)
Edgar Lee Masters. Lichee Nuts (e)
William Morley Punshon McFee. North of Suez (fic)
Henry Lewis Mencken. Treatise on the Gods (e)
Samuel Eliot Morison and Henry Steele Commager. The Growth of the
    American Republic, 2 vols (hist)
Honore Willsie Morrow. The Last Full Measure (fic)
Vladimir Nabokov. The Defense (fic)
Alfred Edward Newton. Mr. Strahan's Dinner Party (dr)
_____. A Tourist in Spite of Himself (nar)
Charles Gilman Norris. Seed (fic)
Martha Ostenso. The Waters under the Earth (fic)
Dorothy Rothschild Parker. Laments for the Living (fic)
Elliot Harold Paul. The Amazon (fic)
_____. The Governor of Massachusetts (fic)
Sidney Joseph Perelman. Parlor, Bedlam, and Bath (sat, nar)
Ernest Poole. The Car of Croesus (fic)
Katherine Anne Porter. Flowering Judas (fic)
John Crowe Ransom. God without Thunder: An Unorthodox Defense of
    Unorthodoxy (e)
Lizette Woodworth Reese. White April (po)
Elmer Reizenstein (Elmer Rice). A Voyage to Puriba (fic)
Lynn Riggs. The Iron Dish (po)
_____. Roadside (dr)
Amelie Rives. Firedamp (fic)
Elizabeth Madox Roberts. The Great Meadow (fic)
_____. Under the Tree, rev ed (po)
Kenneth Lewis Roberts. Arundel (fic)
Edwin Arlington Robinson. The Glory of the Nightingales (po, nar)
Carl August Sandburg. Potato Face (juv)
George Santayana. The Realm of Matter (e)
Evelyn Scott. Blue Rum (fic)
_____. The Winter Alone (fic)
Anne Douglas Sedgwick. Philippa (fic)
James Vincent Sheean. Gog and Magog (fic)
Edward Brewster Sheldon and Margaret Ayer Barnes. Dishonored Lady
    (dr)
Robert Emmet Sherwood. This Is New York (dr)
_____. Waterloo Bridge (dr)
Upton Beall Sinclair. Mountain City (fic)
Chard Powers Smith. Hamilton: A Poetic Drama (po, dr)
_____. The Quest of Pan (po)
Thorne Smith. Did She Fall? (fic)
Winchell Smith. The Vinegar Tree (dr)
Gertrude Stein. Lucy Church Amiably (fic)
Donald Ogden Stewart. Rebound (dr)
Grace Zaring Stone. The Bitter Tea of General Yen (fic)

Rex Todhunter Stout. Seed on the Wind (fic)
Thomas Sigismund Stribling. Backwater (fic)
Genevieve Taggard. The Life and Mind of Emily Dickinson (biog, e)
John Orley Allen Tate. Three Poems (pub)
Sara Teasdale. Stars To-Night: Verses New and Old for Boys and
    Girls (juv, po)
Arthur Cheney Train. The Adventures of Ephraim Tutt (fic)
Carl Clinton Van Doren. Swift (biog, e)
Hendrik Willem Van Loon. R. v. R. (fic, biog)
Carl Van Vechten. Parties (fic)
Mary Marvin Heaton Vorse. Strike! (fic)
Glenway Wescott. The Babe's Bed (fic)
John Wexley. The Last Mile (dr)
Thornton Niven Wilder. The Woman of Andros (fic)
Ben Ames Williams. Great Oaks (fic)
Jesse Lynch Williams. She Knew She Was Right (fic, pub)
Thames Ross Williamson. The Earth Told Me (fic)
Arthur Yvor Winters. The Proof (po)
Owen Wister. Roosevelt, the Story of a Friendship, 1880-1919 (biog,
    nar)
Stark Young. The Street of the Islands (fic)

1931

BIRTHS

Jane Augustine
Leonard Stanley Baker
Donald Barthelme
Mary Higgins Clark
Edgar Lawrence Doctorow
Shirley Hazzard
Ella Lefland
Toni Morrison
Jane Rule
Reg Saver
George Edwin Starbuck

DEATHS

David Belasco
Edward Channing
Frank Harris
Nicholas Vachel Lindsay
Austin Tappan Wright

EVENTS

The Group Theatre, New York, New York, to 1941
Guide to Historical Literature (per, est)
New York World Telegram, to 1967 (per)
"The Star Spangled Banner" adopted as the national anthem of the
    United States
Story, Vienna, Austria; Mallorca; New York, New York, to 1953 (per)

LITERATURE

Louis Adamic. Dynamite: The Story of Class Violence in America (nar, hist)
Franklin Pierce Adams. Christopher Columbus (po)
James Truslow Adams. The Epic of America (hist)
Conrad Potter Aiken. The Coming Forth by Day of Osiris Jones (po)
_____. Preludes for Memnon (po)
Bess Streeter Aldrich. White Bird Flying (fic)
Frederick Lewis Allen. Only Yesterday (hist)
Sherwood Anderson. Perhaps Women (e)
Justin Brooks Atkinson. East of the Hudson (nar)
Philip Barry. Tomorrow and Tomorrow (dr)
Carleton Beals. Mexican Maze (e)
Mary Ritter Beard. On Understanding Women (e)
Samuel Nathaniel Behrman. Brief Moment (dr)
Stephen Vincent Benet. Ballads and Poems, 1915-1930 (po, pub)
John Peale Bishop. Many Thousands Gone (fic)
Maxwell Bodenheim. Naked on Roller Skates (fic)
Herbert Eugene Bolton. Outpost of Empire (hist)
Arna Wendell Bontemps. God Sends Sunday (fic)
Thomas Alexander Boyd. Light-horse Harry Lee (biog)
Kay Boyle. Plagued by the Nightingale (fic)
Percy Holmes Boynton. The Rediscovery of the Frontier (e)
Gamaliel Bradford. The Quick and the Dead (biog, hist)
Roark Bradford. John Henry (fic)
Myron Brinig. Wide Open Town (fic)
Heywood Campbell Broun and George Britt. Christians Only (e)
Pearl Sydenstricker Buck. The Good Earth (fic)
Kenneth Duna Burke. Counterstatement (e)
William Riley Burnett. The Silver Eagle (fic)
Erskine Preston Caldwell. American Earth (fic)
Morley Callaghan. No Man's Meat (fic)
Henry Seidel Canby. Classic Americans (e, biog)
Robert Emmett Cantwell. Laugh and Lie Down (fic)
Willa Sibert Cather. Shadows on the Rock (fic)
William Henry Chamberlain. The Soviet Planned Economic Order (e)
Stuart Chase. Mexico (e)
Irvin Shrewsbury Cobb. Incredible Truth (hum)
Robert Peter Tristram Coffin. Portrait of an American (biog)
Morris Raphael Cohen. Reason and Nature (e)
James Gould Cozzens. S.S. San Pedro (fic)
Rachel Crothers. As Husbands Go (dr)
Edward Estlin Cummings. Vi Va (po)
Merle Eugene Curti. Bryan and World Peace (hist)
Thomas Augustine Daly. McAroni Medleys (po)
Max Forrester Eastman. The Literary Mind: Its Place in the Age of Science (e)
Dorothy Canfield Fisher. Basque People (fic)
Owen Davis. I'd Like To Do It Again (auto)
Babette Deutsch. Epistle to Prometheus (po)
George Dillon. The Flowering Stone (po)
Theodore Herman Albert Dreiser. Dawn (auto)
_____. Newspaper Days (auto)
_____. Tragic America (e)
William Harrison Faulkner. Idyll in the Desert (fic)

_____. Sanctuary (fic)
_____. These 13 (fic)
Jessie Redmon Fauset. The Chinaberry Tree (fic)
Edna Ferber. American Beauty (fic)
Vardis Alvero Fisher. Dark Bridwell (fic)
Charles Macomb Flandrau. Loquacities (e)
Waldo David Frank. America Hispana (e)
Hannibal Hamlin Garland. Companions on the Trail (nar)
Katharine Fullerton Gerould. The Light That Never Was (fic)
Susan Glaspell. Ambrose Holt and Family (fic)
Caroline Gordon. Penhally (fic)
Robert Grant. The Dark Horse (fic)
Anne Green. Reader, I Married Him (fic)
Paul Eliot Green. The House of Connelly (dr)
Frank Harris. Bernard Shaw (biog)
Ben Hecht. The Champion from Far Away (fic)
Joseph Hergesheimer. The Limestone Tree (fic)
DuBose Heyward. Jasbo Brown (po)
James Langston Hughes. Dear Lovely Death (po)
_____. The Negro Mother, and Other Dramatic Recita-
   tions (po)
Rupert Hughes. No One Man (fic)
Fannie Hurst. Back Street (fic)
Wallace Admah Irwin. The Days of Her Life (fic)
John Robinson Jeffers. Descent to the Dead: Poems Written in Ireland
   and Great Britain (po)
Robert Underwood Johnson. Poems of Fifty Years (po, pub)
George Simon Kaufman, Morrie Ryskind, and George Gershwin. Of Thee I
   Sing (dr)
George Edward Kelly. Philip Goes Forth (dr)
Manuel Komroff. Two Thieves (fic)
Oliver Hazard Perry LaFarge. Sparks Fly Upward (fic)
Meyer Levin. Yehuda (fic)
Nicholas Vachel Lindsay. Selected Poems (pub)
Edgar Lee Masters. Godbey (dr, po)
_____. Lincoln, the Man (biog)
William Morley Punshon McFee. The Harbourmaster (fic)
Edna St. Vincent Millay. Fatal Interview (po)
Philip Moeller and J.L.A. Burrell. Fata Morgana (dr)
Theodore Morrison. The Serpent in the Cloud (po)
Ogden Nash. Free Wheeling (po)
_____. Hard Lines (po)
_____. Selected Verse (pub)
Eugene Gladstone O'Neill. Mourning Becomes Electra (dr)
Dorothy Rothschild Parker. Death and Taxes (po)
Channing Pollock. The House Beautiful (dr)
Ernest Poole. The Destroyer (fic)
Lizette Woodworth Reese. The York Road (nar)
Elmer Reizenstein (Elmer Rice). Counsellor-at-Law (dr)
_____. The Left Bank (dr)
Agnes Repplier. Mere Marie of the Ursulines (biog)
Lynn Riggs. Green Grow the Lilacs (dr)
Elizabeth Madox Roberts. A Buried Treasure (fic)
Kenneth Lewis Roberts. The Lively Lady (fic)
Edwin Arlington Robinson. Matthias at the Door (po, nar)
George Santayana. The Genteel Tradition at Bay (e)

Lew Sarett. Wings against the Moon (po)
Evelyn Scott. A Calendar of Sin (fic)
Robert Emmet Sherwood. Reunion in Vienna (dr)
_____. The Virtuous Knight (fic)
Upton Beall Sinclair. The Wet Parade (fic)
Lloyd Logan Pearsall Smith. Afterthoughts (e)
Thorne Smith. The Night Life of the Gods (fic)
_____. Turnabout (fic)
Leonora Speyer. Naked Heel (po)
Gertrude Stein. How To Write (ref, ed)
Wallace Stevens. Harmonium, enlarged ed (po)
Grace Zaring Stone. The Almond Tree (fic)
Thomas Sigismund Stribling. The Forge (fic)
Ruth Suckow. Children and Older People (fic)
James Grover Thurber. The Owl in the Attic, and Other Perplexities
    (hum)
Jean Toomer. Essentials (e)
Dan Totheroh. One-Act Plays for Everyone (dr)
Frederick Goddard Tuckerman. Sonnets (po, pub)
Mark Albert Van Doren. Jonathan Gentry (po, nar)
_____. The Poetry of John Dryden, rev ed (e)
George Sylvester Viereck. My Flesh and Blood; a Lyric Autobiography,
    with Indiscreet Annotations (po)
John Van Alstyn Weaver. Trial Balance (po)
Nathan Wallenstein Weinstein (Nathaniel West). The Dream Life of
    Balso Snell (fic)
John Wexley. Steel (dr)
Thornton Niven Wilder. The Long Christmas Dinner (dr)
Thames Ross Williamson. In Krusack's House (fic)
Edmund Wilson. Axel's Castle (e)
Margaret Wilson. The Crime of Punishment (fic)
Arthur Yvor Winters. The Journey (po)
Leane Zugsmith. Goodbye and Tomorrow (fic)

1932

BIRTHS

David Antin
Don Berry
Burt Blechman
Robert Lowell Coover
John Gregory Dunne
Jack Gelber
Edward Hoagland
Rona Jaffe
Michael Thomas McClure
Linda Pastan
Sylvia Plath
Ronald Sukenick
John Hoyer Updike

DEATHS

Gamaliel Bradford

Charles Waddell Chesnutt
Harold Hart Crane
Grace Elizabeth King
 Harold McGrath
James Oppenheim
Clinton Scollard
Mabel Loomis Todd
Frederick Jackson Turner
Henry Kitchell Webster

EVENTS

The American Scholar (per, est)
The American Spectator, to 1937 (per)
Common Sense, to 1946 (per)
Folger Shakespeare Memorial Library, Washington, D.C. (est)
The New Outlook, to 1935 (per)

LITERATURE

Louis Adamic. Laughing in the Jungle (auto)
James Truslow Adams. The March of Democracy, 2 vols, to 1933 (hist)
Maxwell Anderson. Night over Taos (po, dr)
Sherwood Anderson. Beyond Desire (fic)
Gertrude Franklin Atherton. Adventures of a Novelist (auto)
Wystan Hugh Auden. The Orators (po, e)
Mary Hunter Austin. Earth Horizon (auto)
Irving Babbitt. On Being Creative (e)
Philip Barry. The Animal Kingdom (dr)
Jacques Barzun. The French Race (e)
Joseph Warren Beach. The Twentieth-Century Novel (e)
Charles Austin Beard. A Charter for the Social Sciences (e)
Carl Lotus Becker. The Heavenly City of the Eighteenth-Century Phi-
    losophers (hist, e)
Charles William Beebe. Nonsuch: Land of Water (des)
Samuel Nathaniel Behrman. Biography (dr)
William Rose Benet. Rip Tide (po, fic)
Konrad Bercovici. The Incredible Balkans (nar, des)
Claude Gernade Bowers. Beveridge and the Progressive Era (hist)
Kay Boyle. Year Before Last (fic)
Myron Brinig. This Man Is My Brother (fic)
Van Wyck Brooks. Sketches in Criticism (e)
Sterling Allan Brown. Southern Road (po)
Pearl Sydenstricker Buck. The House of Earth (fic)
_____. Sons (fic)
Kenneth Duva Burke. Towards a Better Life (e)
William Riley Burnett. The Giant Swing (fic)
James Branch Cabell. These Restless Heads (fic)
Erskine Preston Caldwell. Tobacco Road (fic)
Morley Callaghan. A Broken Journey (fic)
Walter Stanley Campbell (Stanley Vestal). Sitting Bull (biog)
Willa Sibert Cather. Obscure Destinies (fic)
John Chamberlain. Farewell to Reform (e)
John Jay Chapman. New Horizons in American Life (e)
Mary Ellen Chase. A Goodly Heritage (auto)
Stuart Chase. A New Deal (e)

Edward Chodorov. Wonder Boy (dr)
Rachel Crothers. When Ladies Meet (dr)
Countee Cullen. One Way to Heaven (fic)
Edward Dahlberg. From Flushing to Calvary (fic)
Olive Tilford Dargon (Fielding Burke). Call Home the Heart (fic)
Clarence Seward Darrow. The Story of My Life (auto)
Marcia Davenport. Mozart (biog)
Clarence Shepard Day. God and My Father (auto)
Margaretta Wade Campbell Deland. Captain Archer's Daughter (fic)
Bernard Augustine DeVoto. Mark Twain's America (e)
John Roderigo Dos Passos. 1919 (fic)
Lloyd Cassel Douglas. Forgive Us Our Trespasses (fic)
Thomas Stearns Eliot. John Dryden: The Poet, the Dramatist, the Critic (e)
Janet Ayer Fairbank. The Bright Land (fic)
James Thomas Farrell. Young Lonigan (fic)
William Harrison Faulkner. Light in August (fic)
_____. Miss Zilphia Gant (fic)
_____. Salmagundi (e, po)
Edna Ferber and George Simon Kaufman. Dinner at Eight (dr)
Irving Fineman. Lovers Must Learn (fic)
Vardis Alvero Fisher. In Tragic Life (fic)
Waldo David Frank. Dawn in Russia (trav)
Joseph Freeman. The Soviet Worker (e)
Hannibal Hamlin Garland. My Friendly Contemporaries (nar)
Ellen Glasgow. The Sheltered Life (fic)
Herbert Sherman Gorman. Scottish Queen (biog)
Anne Green. Marietta (fic)
Julian Green. The Strange River (fic)
Paul Eliot Green. Your Fiery Furnace (dr)
Nancy Hale. The Good Die Young (fic)
Richard Halliburton. The Flying Carpet (trav)
Samuel Dashiell Hammett. The Thin Man (fic)
Ben Hecht and Charles MacArthur. 20th Century (dr)
Ernest Miller Hemingway. Death in the Afternoon (fic)
Robert Herrick. The End of Desire (fic)
DuBose Heyward. Peter Ashley (fic)
Robert Silliman Hillyer. Riverhead (fic)
Sidney Coe Howard. The Late Christopher Bean (dr)
James Langston Hughes. The Dream-Keeper, and Other Poems (po)
_____. Scottsboro Limited: Four Poems and a Play in Verse (po, dr)
John Robinson Jeffers. Thurso's Landing, and Other Poems (po)
Manuel Komroff. A New York Tempest (fic)
Alfred Kreymborg. The Little World (po)
Joseph Wood Krutch. Experience and Art (e)
John Howard Lawson. Success Story (dr)
Janet Lewis. The Invasion (fic)
Ludwig Lewisohn. Expression in America (e)
Frank Bird Linderman. Red Mother (fic)
Grace Lumpkin. To Make My Bread (fic)
Charles MacArthur and Ben Hecht. 20th Century (dr)
Archibald MacLeish. Conquistador (po)
Albert Maltz and George Sklar. Merry-Go-Round (dr)
John Thomas McIntyre. Drums in the Dawn (fic)
Claude McKay. Gingerbread (fic)

Henry Louis Mencken. Making a President (e, nar)
Harriet Monroe and Alice Corbin Henderson. The New Poetry (po, ed)
Christopher Darlington Morley. Human Being (fic)
_____. The Swiss Family Manhattan (fic)
Vladimir Nabokov. Glory (fic)
Anais Nin. D.H. Lawrence: An Unprofessional Study (e)
Charles Bernard Nordhoff and James Normal Hall. Mutiny on the Bounty (fic)
Anne Parrish. Loads of Love (fic)
Donald Culross Peattie. Port of Call (fic)
_____. Sons of the Martian (fic)
Julia Mood Peterkin. Bright Skin (fic)
Ernest Poole. Nurses on Horseback (fic)
Elmer Reizenstein (Elmer Rice). Black Sheep (dr)
Agnes Repplier. To Think of Tea! (e)
Elizabeth Madox Roberts. The Haunted Mirror (fic)
Edwin Arlington Robinson. Nicodemus (po)
Alfred Damon Runyon. Guys and Dolls (fic)
Carl August Sandburg and Paul M. Angle. Mary Lincoln, Wife and Widow (biog)
Upton Beall Sinclair. American Outpost (auto)
George Sklar and Albert Maltz. Merry-Go-Round (dr)
Thorne Smith. The Bishop's Jaegers (fic)
_____. Topper Takes a Trip (fic)
Charles Eilbert Snow. Down East (po)
Gertrude Stein. A Long Gay Book (fic)
John Ernst Steinbeck. The Pastures of Heaven (fic)
James Floyd Stevens. The Saginaw Paul Bunyan (fic)
Philip Duffield Stong. State Fair (fic)
Thomas Sigismund Stribling. The Store (fic)
John Orley Allen Tate. Poems, 1928-1931 (pub)
Sara Teasdale. A Country House (po)
James Grover Thurber. The Seal in the Bedroom, and Other Predicaments (hum)
Dan Totheroh. Distant Drums (dr)
Jim Tully. Laughter in Hell (fic)
Frederick Jackson Turner. The Significance of Sections in American History (e, pub)
Louis Untermeyer. The Donkey of God (juv, trav)
Hendrik Willem Van Loon. Van Loon's Geography (des)
Glenway Wescott. A Calendar of Saints for Unbelievers (e, nar)
_____. Fear and Trembling (e)
Edith Newbold Jones Wharton. The Gods Arrive (fic)
Stewart Edward White. The Long Rifle (fic)
Walt Whitman. I Sit and Look Out (e, pub)
Laura Ingalls Wilder. Little House in the Big Woods (juv, fic)
Ben Ames Williams. Money Musk (fic)
William Carlos Williams. The Knife of the Times (fic)
Thames Ross Williamson. Sad Indian (fic)
Edmund Wilson. The American Jitters: A Year of the Slump (nar)
Margaret Wilson. One Came Out (fic)
Thyra Samter Winslow. Blueberry Pie (fic)
Thomas Clayton Wolfe. A Portrait of Bascom Hawke (fic)
Elinor Hoyt Wylie. Collected Poems (pub)
Anzia Yezierska. All I Could Never Be (fic)
Leane Zugsmith. Never Enough (fic)

1933

BIRTHS

Ernest J. Gaines
John Champlin Gardner, Jr.
Jerzy Nikodem Kosinski
Cormac McCarthy
Rod McKuen
Leonard Michaels
Reynolds Price
Philip Roth
Susan Sontag

DEATHS

Irving Babbitt
Earl Derr Biggers
Robert William Chambers
John Jay Chapman
Charles King
Ringgold Wilmer Lardner
Winchell Smith
Sara Teasdale
Henry Van Dyke

EVENTS

The American Review, to 1937 (per)
The Anvil, to 1937 (per)
Palinet and Union Library Catalogue of Pennsylvania, Philadelphia
    (est)
Franklin Delano Roosevelt, 32 President of the United States, to 1945

LITERATURE

James Truslow Adams. Henry Adams (biog)
Leone Fuller Adams. This Measure (po)
Herbert Sebastian Agar. The People's Choice (hist)
Conrad Potter Aiken. Great Circle (fic)
William Hervey Allen. Anthony Adverse (fic)
Maxwell Anderson. Both Your Houses (dr)
_____. Mary of Scotland (po, dr)
Sherwood Anderson. Death in the Woods (fic)
Sholem Asch. Three Cities (fic)
Wystan Hugh Auden. The Dance of Death (po, dr)
Faith Baldwin. White Collar Girl (fic)
Margaret Ayer Barnes. Within This Present (fic)
Joseph Hamilton Basso. Beauregard (biog)
Carleton Beals. The Crime of Cuba (e)
Mary Ritter Beard. America through Women's Eyes (e)
Thomas Beer. Mrs. Egg, and Other Barbarians (fic)
Albert Bein. Little Ol' Boy (dr)
John Peale Bishop. Now with His Love (po)
Herbert Eugene Bolton. New Spain and the Anglo-American West (hist)

Kay Boyle. First Lover (po)
_____ . Gentlemen, I Address You Privately (fic)
Gamaliel Bradford. Journals, ed. Van Wyck Brooks (nar, pub, ed)
James Henry Brested. The Dawn of Conscience (hist)
Myron Brinig. The Flutter of an Eye-lid (fic)
Louis Bromfield. The Farm (fic)
Pearl Sydenstricker Buck. First Wife (fic)
Ben Lucien Burman. Steamboat Round the Bend (fic)
William Riley Burnett. Dark Hazard (fic)
James Branch Cabell. Special Delivery (fic)
Erskine Preston Caldwell. God's Little Acre (fic)
_____ . We Are the Living (fic)
William Edward March Campbell (William March). Company K (fic)
Gladys Hasty Carroll. As the Earth Turns (fic)
Robert Myron Coates. Yesterday's Burdens (fic)
Morris Raphael Cohen. Law and the Social Order (e)
John Wesley Conroy. The Disinherited (fic)
James Gould Cozzens. The Last Adam (fic)
Dorothy Canfield Fisher. Bonfire (fic)
Robert Peter Tristram Coffin. Ballads of Square-Toed Americans (po)
John Colton. Nine Pine Street (dr)
Harold Hart Crane. Collected Poems (pub)
Edward Estlin Cummings. Eimi (nar, po)
Floyd Dell. Homecoming (auto)
Babette Deutsch. Mask of Silenus (fic)
Charles Caldwell Dobie. San Francisco: A Pageant (hist, des)
Walter Dumaux Edmonds. Erie Water (fic)
John Roderigo Dos Passos. Fortune Heights (dr)
Lloyd Cassel Douglas. Precious Jeopardy (fic)
Thomas Stearns Eliot. The Use of Poetry and the Use of Criticism
    (e)
James Thomas Farrell. Gas-House McGinty (fic)
Howard Melvin Fast. Two Valleys (fic)
William Harrison Faulkner. A Green Bough (po)
Harvey Fergusson. Rio Grande (hist)
Irving Fineman. Hear, Ye Sons (fic)
Zona Gale. Papa La Fleur (fic)
Erle Stanley Gardner. The Case of the Sulky Girl (fic)
_____ . The Case of the Velvet Claws (fic)
Herbert Sherman Gorman. Jonathan Bishop (fic)
Anne Green. A Marriage of Convenience (fic)
Horace Victor Gregory. No Retreat (po)
_____ . Pilgrim of the Apocalypse (e)
Edgar Albert Guest. Life's Highway (po)
Albert Halper. Union Square (fic)
Ben Hecht and Gene Fowler. The Great Magoo (dr)
Ernest Miller Hemingway. Winner Take Nothing (fic)
Alice Corbin Henderson. The Sun Turns West (po)
Josephine Frey Herbst. Pity Is Not Enough (fic)
Robert Herrick. Sometime (fic)
Robert Silliman Hillyer. Some Roots of English Poetry (e)
Paul Horgan. The Fault of Angels (fic)
Sidney Coe Howard. Alien Corn (dr)
Fannie Hurst. Imitation of Life (fic)
John Robinson Jeffers. Give Your Heart to the Hawks, and Other
    Poems (po)

George Simon Kaufman, Morrie Ryskind, and George Gershwin. Let 'Em
  Eat Cake (dr)
Clarence Budington Kelland. The Great Crooner (fic)
Sidney Kingsley. Men in White (dr)
Manuel Komroff. I, the Tiger (fic)
Alfred Kreymborg. I'm No Hero (fic)
Clare Kummer. Her Master's Voice (dr)
Oliver Hazard Perry LaFarge. Long Pennant (fic)
Meyer Levin. The New Bridge (fic)
Harry Sinclair Lewis. Ann Vickers (fic)
Frank Bird Linderman. Beyond Law (fic)
Archibald MacLeish. Frescoes for Mr. Rockefeller's City (po)
_____. Poems, 1924-1933 (pub)
Albert Maltz and George Sklar. Peace on Earth (dr)
Edgar Lee Masters. The Tale of Chicago (hist)
William Morley Punshon McFee. No Castle in Spain (fic)
_____. Reflections of Marsyas (po)
Claude McKay. Banana Bottom (fic)
Caroline Miller. Lamb in His Bosom (fic)
Christopher Darlington Morley. Mandarin in Manhattan (po)
Ogden Nash. Happy Days (po)
Robert Gruntal Nathan. One More Spring (fic)
Alfred Edward Newton. End Papers (e)
Eugene Gladstone O'Neill. Ah, Wilderness! (dr)
Martha Ostenso. There's Always Another Year (fic)
Dorothy Rothschild Parker. After Such Pleasures (fic)
Ernest Poole. Great Winds (fic)
Katherine Anne Porter. French Song-Book (trans)
Ezra Weston Loomis Pound. A.B.C. of Economics (e)
_____. A Draft of XXX Cantos (po)
Marjorie Jennan Rawlings. South Moon Under (fic)
Lizette Woodworth Reese. Pastures (po)
Elmer Reizenstein (Elmer Rice). We, the People (dr)
Agnes Repplier. Junipero Serra (biog)
Eugene Manlove Rhodes. The Trusty Knaves (fic)
Felix Riesenberg. Mother Sea (fic)
Kenneth Lewis Roberts. Rabble in Arms (fic)
Edwin Arlington Robinson. Talifer (po)
George Santayana. Some Turns of Thought in Modern Philosophy (e)
Evelyn Scott. Eva Gay (fic)
James Vincent Sheean. The Tide (fic)
Upton Beall Sinclair. Upton Sinclair Presents William Fox (e)
George Sklar and Albert Maltz. Peace on Earth (dr)
Lloyd Logan Pearsall Smith. All Trivia (e)
_____. On Reading Shakespeare (e)
Thorne Smith. Skin and Bones (fic)
Gertrude Stein. The Autobiography of Alice B. Toklas (auto)
John Ernst Steinbeck. To a God Unknown (fic)
Philip Stong. Stranger's Return (fic)
Rex Todhunter Stout. Forest Fire (fic)
Genevieve Taggard. Remembering Vaughan in New England (po)
Sara Teasdale. Strange Victory (po)
James Grover Thurber. My Life and Hard Times (nar)
Carl Clinton Van Doren. Sinclair Lewis (biog, e)
Nathan Wallenstein Weinstein (Nathaniel West). Miss Lonelyhearts
  (fic)

Edith Newbold Jones Wharton. Human Nature (fic)
Elwyn Brooks White. Alice through the Cellophane (e)
Stewart Edward White. Ranchero (fic)
Thames Ross Williamson. The Woods Colt (fic)
Margaret Wilson. One Came Out (fic)
Frances Winwar. Poor Splendid Wings (biog)
William E. Woodward. Evelyn Prentice (fic)
Elinor Hoyt Wylie. Collected Prose (pub)

1934

BIRTHS

Edmund J.M. Berrigan, Jr.
Wendell Berry
Joan Didion
Barbara Grizzuti Harrison
Diane Lain Johnson
Le Roi Jones (Imamu Amiri Baraka)
Gordon Lish
Navarre Scott Momaday
Michele Murray
John Francisco Rechy
Samuel Jay Rogal
Mark Strand
John Wieners

DEATHS

Mary Hunter Austin
Le Baron Russell Briggs
Alice French
Julian Hawthorne
Eugene Manlove Rhodes
Thorne Smith
Augustus Thomas
Edward Lucas White
Brand Whitlock

EVENTS

William Andrews Clark Memorial Library, Los Angeles, California (est)
Evening Public Ledger, to 1942 (per)
Partisan Review (per, est)

LITERATURE

Louis Adamic. The Native's Return (auto)
James Agee. Permit Me Voyage (po)
Conrad Potter Aiken. Among the Lost People (fic)
_____. Landscape West of Eden (po)
Maxwell Anderson. Valley Forge (dr)
Benjamin Appel. Brain Guy (fic)
Sholem Asch. Salvation (fic)
Margaret Frances Bacon. Off with Their Heads (po)

Philip Barry. The Joyous Season (dr)
Joseph Hamilton Basso. Cinnamon Seed (fic)
Charles Austin Beard and G.H.E. Smith. The Idea of National Interest
   (e)
                                    . The Open Door at Home (e)
Charles William Beebe. Half Mile Down (des)
Samuel Nathaniel Behrman. Rain from Heaven (dr)
Robert Charles Benchley. From Bad to Worse (nar)
Archie Binns. Lightship (fic)
Kay Boyle. My Next Bride (fic)
Roark Bradford. How Come Christmas (dr)
Louis Dembitz Brandeis. The Curse of Bigness (e, pub)
John Mason Brown. Letters from Greenroom Ghosts (e, nar)
Pearl Sydenstricker Buck. The Mother (fic)
William Riley Burnett. Goodbye to the Dust (fic)
                     . The Goodhues of Sinking Creek (fic)
James Branch Cabell. Ladies and Gentlemen (fic)
           . Smirt (fic)
James Mallahan Cain. The Postman Always Rings Twice (fic)
Morley Callaghan. Such Is My Beloved (fic)
Walter Stanley Campbell (Stanley Vestal). Warpath (fic)
William Edward March Campbell (William March). Come In at the Door
   (fic)
Henry Seidel Canby. The Age of Confidence (hist)
Robert Emmett Cantwell. The Land of Plenty (fic)
Carl Lamson Carmer. Stars Fell on Alabama (hist, fic)
William Henry Chamberlain. Russia's Iron Age (e)
Mary Ellen Chase. Mary Peters (fic)
Stuart Chase. The Economy of Abundance (e)
Robert Peter Tristram Coffin. Lost Paradise (auto)
Marcus Cook Connelly. The Farmer Takes a Wife (dr)
Edwin Corle. Mojave (fic)
Malcolm Cowley. Return: A Narrative of Ideas, to 1951 (e, auto)
James Gould Cozzens. Castaway (fic)
Merle Eugene Curti. Social Ideas of American Educators (hist)
Edward Dahlberg. Those Who Perish (fic)
Clarence Shepard Day. In the Green Mountain Country (des)
Nathaniel Deering. The Clairvoyants (dr, pub)
Bernard Augustine DeVoto. We Accept with Pleasure (fic)
John Roderigo Dos Passos. In All Countries (trav, nar)
                        . Three Plays (pub)
Walter Dumaux Edmonds. Mostly Canallers (fic)
Thomas Stearns Eliot. After Strange Gods (e)
                   . The Rock (po, e)
Maud Howe Elliott. My Cousin, F. Marion Crawford (biog)
Paul Hamilton Engle. American Song (po)
James Thomas Farrell. Calico Shoes (fic)
                   . The Young Manhood of Studs Lonigan (fic)
William Harrison Faulkner. Dr. Martino (fic)
Jessie Redmon Fauset. Comedy: American Style (fic)
Vardis Alvero Fisher. Passions Spin the Plot (fic)
Francis Scott Key Fitzgerald. Tender Is the Night (fic)
Louis Fraina (Lewis Corey). The Decline of American Capitalism (e)
Waldo David Frank. The Death and Birth of David Markand (fic)
Douglas Southall Freeman. R.E. Lee, 4 vols, to 1935 (biog, hist)
Daniel Fuchs. Summer in Williamsburg (fic)

Hannibal Hamlin Garland. Afternoon Neighbors (nar)
Caroline Gordon. Aleck Maury, Sportsman (fic)
Robert Grant. Fourscore (auto)
Anne Green. Fools Rush In (fic)
Julian Green. The Dreamer (dr)
Paul Eliot Green. Roll, Sweet Chariot (dr)
Francis Hackett. Francis the First (biog)
Nancy Hale. Never Any More (fic)
James Norman Hall. The Friends (po)
Albert Halper. The Foundry (fic)
_____. On the Shore (fic)
Francis Noyes Hart. The Crooked Lane (fic)
Carl Sadakichi Hartmann. Moses (dr)
Lillian Hellman. The Children's Hour (dr)
Josephine Frey Herbst. The Executioner Waits (fic)
Joseph Hergesheimer. The Foolscap Rose (fic)
Hatcher Hughes. The Lord Blesses the Bishop (dr)
James Langston Hughes. The Ways of White Folks (fic)
Fannie Hurst. Anitra's Dance (fic)
Zora Neale Hurston. Jonah's Gourd Vine (fic)
Josephine Winslow Johnson. Now in November (fic)
MacKinlay Kantor. Long Remember (fic)
Joseph Wood Krutch. Was Europe a Success (e)
Christopher La Farge. Hoxie Sells His Acres (fic, po)
Ringgold Wilmer Lardner. First and Last (fic, pub)
John Howard Lawson. Gentlewoman (dr)
_____. The Pure in Heart (dr)
Harry Sinclair Lewis. Work of Art (fic)
_____ and Lloyd Lewis. Jayhawker (dr)
Victoria Lincoln. February Hill (fic)
Donald Robert Perry Marquis. Chapters for the Orthodox (fic)
_____. Master of the Revels (dr)
William Maxwell. Bright Center of Heaven (fic)
Phyllis McGinley. On the Contrary (po)
Henry Louis Mencken. Treatise on Right and Wrong (e)
Edna St. Vincent Millay. Wine from These Grapes (po)
Henry Miller. Tropic of Cancer (nar)
Merrill Moore. It Is a Good Deal Later Than You Think (po)
Alfred Edward Newton. Derby Day, and Other Adventures (nar)
Charles Bernard Nordhoff and James Norman Hall. Men against the Sea
   (fic)
_____. Pitcairn's Island
   (fic)
John Henry O'Hara. Appointment in Samarra (fic)
Elder James Olson. Thing of Sorrow (po)
Eugene Gladstone O'Neill. Days without End (dr)
George Oppen. Discrete Series (po)
Anne Parrish. Sea Level (fic)
Donald Culross Peattie. The Bright Lexicon (fic)
Ernest Poole. One of Us (fic)
Katherine Anne Porter. Hacienda (fic)
Ezra Weston Loomis Pound. ABC of Reading (e)
_____. Eleven New Cantos, XXXI-XLI (po)
_____. Make It New (e)
Elmer Reizenstein (Elmer Rice). Between Two Worlds (dr)
_____. Judgment Day (dr)

Eugene Manlove Rhodes. Beyond the Desert (fic)
Kenneth Lewis Roberts. Captain Caution (fic)
Edwin Arlington Robinson. Amaranth (po, nar)
William Saroyan. The Daring Young Man on the Flying Trapeze (fic)
Clinton Scolland. The Singing Heart (po)
Evelyn Scott. Breathe upon Those Slain (fic)
Wilbur Daniel Steele and Norma Mitchell Steele. Post Road (dr)
Gertrude Stein. Four Saints in Three Acts (dr)
_____. Portraits and Prayers (nar)
Grace Zaring Stone. The Cold Journey (fic)
Irving Stone. Lust for Life (fic)
Philip Duffield Stong. Village Tale (fic)
Thomas Sigismund Stribling. Unfinished Cathedral (fic)
Jesse Hilton Stuart. Man without a Bull-Tongue Plow (po)
Ruth Suckow. The Folks (fic)
Genevieve Taggard. Not Mine to Finish (po)
Dan Totheroh. Moor Born (dr)
_____. Mother Lode (dr)
Nathan Wallenstein Weinstein (Nathaniel West). A Cool Million (fic)
John Wexley. They Shall Not Die (dr)
Elwyn Brooks White. Every Day Is Saturday (e)
Stewart Edward White. Folded Hills (fic)
William Carlos Williams. Collected Poems, 1921-1931 (pub)
Thames Ross Williamson. D Is for Dutch (fic)
Arthur Yvor Winters. Before Disaster (po)
Stark Young. So Red the Rose (fic)
Leane Zugsmith. The Reckoning (fic)
Louis Zukofsky. Le Style Apollinaire (e)

1935

BIRTHS

Richard Brautigan
Harry Crews
Ellen Gilchrist
Barbara Gordon
Ken Kesey
Allen Stuart Konigsberg (Woody Allen)
Jack Carter Richardson
Tomas Rivera
Calvin Trillin
Charles Wright

DEATHS

Andy Adams
Jane Addams
Thomas Alexander Boyd
James Henry Breasted
Clarence Shepard Day
Nathan Haskell Dole
Charlotte Perkins Gilman
Anna Katharine Green
Sarah Pratt McLean

Langdon Elwyn Mitchell
Lizette Woodworth Reese
Edwin Arlington Robinson
Anne Douglas Sedgwick

EVENTS

American Prefaces, Iowa City, Iowa, to 1943 (per)
Federal Writers' Project, to 1939
The Southern Review, Baton Rouge, Louisiana, to 1942 (per)

LITERATURE

George Abbott. Three Men on a Horse (dr)
Louis Adamic. Grandsons: A Story of American Lives (fic)
Franklin Pierce Adams. The Diary of Our Own Samuel Pepys, 2 vols
    (e, po)
Herbert Sebastian Agar. Land of the Free (e)
Conrad Potter Aiken. King Coffin (fic)
Zoe Akins. The Old Maid (dr)
Bess Streeter Aldrich. Spring Came On Forever (fic)
Nelson Algren. Boots (fic)
Frederick Lewis Allen. The Lords of Creation (hist)
Maxwell Anderson. Winterset (po, dr)
Charles McLean Andrews. The Colonial Period in American History, 2
    vols, to 1936 (hist)
Nathan Asch. The Valley (fic)
Sherwood Anderson. Puzzled America (e)
Margaret Frances Bacon. Cat-Calls (po)
Margaret Ayer Barnes. Edna, His Wife (fic)
Stringfellow Barr. Mazzini--Portrait of an Exile (biog-hist)
Philip Barry. Bright Star (dr)
Joseph Hamilton Basso. In Their Own Image (fic)
Rex Ellingwood Beach. The Wild Pastures (fic)
Carl Lotus Becker. Everyman His Own Historian (e, hist)
John Barry Benefield. Valiant Is the Word for Carrie (fic)
John Peale Bishop. Act of Darkness (fic)
Richard Palmer Blackmur. The Double Agent (e)
James Boyd. Roll River (fic)
Thomas Alexander Boyd. In Time of Peace (fic)
_____. Poor John Fitch (biog)
Myron Brinig. Out of Life (fic)
_____. Sun Sets in the West (fic)
Louis Bromfield. De Luxe (dr)
_____. The Man Who Had Everything (fic)
Pearl Sydenstricker Buck. A House Divided (fic)
Kenneth Duva Burke. Permanence and Change: An Anatomy of Purpose (e)
James Branch Cabell. Smith (fic)
Erskine Preston Caldwell. Journeyman (fic)
_____. Kneel to the Rising Sun (fic)
_____. Some American People (des)
Morley Callaghan. They Shall Inherit the Earth (fic)
William Edward March Campbell (William March). The Little Wife (fic)
Gladys Hasty Carroll. A Few Foolish Ones (fic)
Willa Sibert Cather. Lucy Gayheart (fic)
William Henry Chamberlain. The Russian Revolution, 2 vols (hist)

Albert Bein. Let Freedom Ring (dr)
Mary Ellen Chase. Silas Crockett (fic)
Edward Chodorov. Kind Lady (dr)
Charles Badger Clark. Sky Lines and Wood Smoke (po)
Robert Peter Tristram Coffin. Strange Holiness (po)
Elsworth Prouty Conkle. Loolie, and Other Short Plays (pub)
John Wesley Conroy. A World To Win (fic)
Edwin Corle. Fig Tree John (fic)
John Cournos. Autobiography (auto)
Countee Cullen. The Medea, and Some Poems (po)
Edward Estlin Cummings. No Thanks (po)
Olive Tilford Dargan. A Stone Came Rolling (fic)
Harold Lenoir Davis. Honey in the Horn (fic)
Clarence Shepard Day. Life with Father (auto)
_____. Scenes from the Mesozoic, and Other Drawings
   (des)
David Cornel DeJong. Belly Fulla Straw (fic)
Margaretta Wade Campbell Deland. If This Be I (auto)
August William Derleth. Place of Hawks (fic, ed)
Babette Deutsch. This Modern Poetry (e)
Charles Caldwell Dobie. San Francisco Tales (fic)
Lloyd Cassel Douglas. Green Light (fic)
Thomas Stearns Eliot. Murder in the Cathedral (dr)
James Thomas Farrell. Guillotine Party (fic)
_____. Judgment Day (fic)
William Harrison Faulkner. Pylon (fic)
Kenneth Fearing. Poems (pub)
Edna Ferber. Come and Get It (fic)
Rachel Lyman Field. Time Out of Mind (fic)
Vardis Alvero Fisher. The Neurotic Nightingale (e)
_____. We Are Betrayed (fic)
Dudley Fitts and Robert Stuart Fitzgerald. Alcestis (trans)
Francis Scott Key Fitzgerald. Taps at Reveille (fic)
Charles Macomb Flandrau. Sophomores Abroad (fic)
John Gould Fletcher. XXIV Elegies (po)
Louis Fraina (Lewis Corey). The Crisis of the Middle Class (e)
Joseph Freeman. Proletarian Literature in the United States (misc,
   ed)
Ellen Glasgow. Vein of Iron (fic)
Anne Green. That Fellow Perceval (fic)
Paul Eliot Green. This Body the Earth (fic)
Horace Victor Gregory. Chorus for Survival (po)
Arthur Guiterman. Death and General Putnam (po)
Richard Haliburton. Seven League Boots (trav, nar)
Walter Edwin Havighurst. Pier 17 (fic)
Ernest Miller Hemingway. Green Hills of Africa (fic)
Paul Horgan. No Quarter Given (fic)
James Langston Hughes. Little Ham (dr)
_____. Mulatto (dr)
_____. Troubled Island (dr)
Rupert Hughes. The Man without a Home (fic)
John Robinson Jeffers. Solstice, and Other Poems (po)
James Weldon Johnson. Saint Peter Relocates and Incident: Selected
   Poems (po, pub)
Josephine Winslow Johnson. Winter Orchard (fic)
MacKinlay Kantor. Turkey in the Straw (po)

——————————. The Voice of Bugle Ann (fic)
George Simon Kaufman and Katherine Dayton. First Lady (dr)
Walter Francis Kerr. Murder in Reverse (dr)
Sidney Kingsley. Dead End (dr)
Arthur Kober. Thunder over the Bronx (fic)
Oliver Hazard Perry LaFarge. All the Young Men (fic)
Josephine Lawrence. If I Had Four Apples (fic)
Harry Sinclair Lewis. It Can't Happen Here (fic)
——————————. Selected Short Stories (fic, pub)
Anne Morrow Lindbergh. North to the Orient (nar)
Clare Boothe Luce. Abide with Me (dr)
Grace Lumpkin. A Sign for Cain (fic)
Archibald MacLeish. Panic (po, dr)
Albert Maltz. Black Pit (dr)
John Phillips Marquand. Ming Yellow (fic)
Edgar Lee Masters. Invisible Landscapes (po)
——————————. Vachel Lindsay (biog)
David Thompson Watson McCord. Bay Window Ballads (po)
Horace McCoy. They Shoot Horses, Don't They? (fic)
William Morley Punshon McFee. The Beachcomber (fic)
Henry Miller. Aller Retour New York (nar)
Marianne Craig Moore. Selected Poems (pub)
Merrill Moore. Six Sides to a Man (po)
Ogden Nash. The Primrose Path (po)
Robert Gruntal Nathan. Road of Ages (fic)
John Gneisenau Neihardt. The Song of the Messiah (po)
Clifford Odets. Awake and Sing (dr)
——————————. Paradise Lost (dr)
——————————. Till the Day I Die (dr)
——————————. Waiting for Lefty (dr)
John Henry O'Hara. Butterfield 8 (fic)
——————————. The Doctor's Son (fic)
Louis Paul. The Pumpkin Coach (fic)
Ezra Weston Loomis Pound. Jefferson and/or Mussolini (e)
Frederic Prokosch. The Asiatics (fic)
Ayn Rand. The Night of January 16th (dr)
Marjorie Kinnan Rawlings. Golden Apples (fic)
Laura Reichenthal (Laura Riding). Progress of Stories (fic)
Eugene Manlove Rhodes. The Proud Sheriff (fic, pub)
Lola Ridge. Dance of Fire (po)
Elizabeth Madox Roberts. He Sent Forth a Raven (fic)
Kenneth Lewis Roberts. For Authors Only (e)
Edwin Arlington Robinson. King Jasper (po, nar)
Muriel Rukeyser. Theory of Flight (po)
Alfred Damon Runyon and Howard Lindsay. A Slight Case of Murder (dr)
Mari Sandoz. Old Jules (biog)
George Santayana. The Last Puritan (fic)
Mark Schorer. A House Too Old (fic)
Karl Jay Shapiro. Poems (pub)
Robert Emmet Sherwood. The Petrified Forest (dr)
Isaac Bashevis Singer. Satan in Goray (fic)
Chard Powers Smith. Prelude to Man (po)
Gertrude Stein. Lectures in America (e)
——————————. Narration (e)
John Ernst Steinbeck. Saint Katy the Virgin (fic)
——————————. Tortilla Flat (fic)

Wallace Stevens. Ideas of Order (po)
Philip Duffield Stong. The Farmer in the Dell (fic)
_____. Honk: The Moose (juv, fic)
_____. Week-End (fic)
Rex Todhunter Stout. The League of Frightened Men (fic)
Thomas Sigismund Stribling. The Sound Wagon (fic)
James Grover Thurber. The Middle-Aged Man on the Flying Trapeze (hum)
Frederick Jackson Turner. The United States, 1830-1850: The Nation
    and Its Sections (hist, pub)
Mark Albert Van Doren. A Winter Diary, and Other Poems (po)
_____. The Transients (fic)
Hendrik Willem Van Loon. Ships, and How They Sailed the Seven Seas
    (hist)
Robert Penn Warren. Thirty-Six Poems (po, pub)
Laura Ingalls Wilder. Little House on the Prairie (juv, fic)
Thornton Niven Wilder. Heaven's My Destination (fic)
William Carlos Williams. An Early Martyr (po)
Thames Ross Williamson. Beginning at Dusk (fic)
_____. Under the Linden Tree (fic)
Thyra Samter Winslow. My Own, My Native Land (fic)
Frances Winwar. The Romantic Rebels (biog)
Thomas Clayton Wolfe. From Death to Morning (fic)
_____. Of Time and the River (fic)
Audrey Wurdemann. The Seven Sins (po)
Stark Young. Feliciana (fic)

1936

BIRTHS

    Jean Marie Auel
    Courtlandt Dixon Barnes Bryan
    Lucille Clifton
    Stephen Dixon
    Andre Dubus
    Judith Ann Guest
    Faye Kicknosway
    Jonathan Kozol
    Marge Piercy
    Tom Robbins
    Estela Portillo Trambley
    C.K. Williams
    Bari Wood
    Paul Zindel

DEATHS

    Finley Peter Dunne
    Mary Johnston
    Harriet Monroe
    Joseph Lincoln Steffens

EVENTS

    American Theatre Association (f)

Federal Theatre Project, to 1939
Ford Foundation, New York, New York (f)
Life, to 1972 (per)
New Directions (ed, po, e)

LITERATURE

Louis Adamic. Cradle of Life: The Story of One Man's Beginnings
    (fic)
Franklin Pierce Adams. The Melancholy Lute (po)
Herbert Sebastian Agar and Allen Tate. Who Owns America? (e,ed)
Conrad Potter Aiken. Time in the Rock (po)
Bess Streeter Aldrich. The Man Who Caught the Weather (fic)
Maxwell Anderson. The Masque of Kings (po, dr)
_____. The Wingless Victory (dr)
Sherwood Anderson. Kit Brandon (fic)
Harriette Arnow. Mountain Path (fic)
Sholem Asch. The War Goes On (fic)
Leonard Bacon. Rhyme and Punishment (po)
Faith Baldwin. Men Are Such Fools (fic)
Djuna Barnes. Nightwood (fic)
Harry Elmer Barnes. The History of Sociological Thought (hist)
Philip Barry. Spring Dance (dr)
Joseph Hamilton Basso. Courthouse Square (fic)
Ernest Sutherland Bates. The Bible Designed To Be Read As Living
    Literature (trans, ed)
_____ and Oliver Carlson. Hearst, Lord of San Si-
    meon (biog)
Carleton Beals. Stones Awake (fic)
Samuel Nathaniel Behrman. End of Summer (dr)
Samuel Flagg Bemis. Diplomatic History of the United States (hist)
Robert Charles Benchley. My Ten Years in a Quandry (nar, hum)
Sara Machala Redway Smith Benson. People Are Fascinating (fic)
John Peale Bishop. Minute Particulars (po)
Herbert Eugene Bolton. Rim of Christendom (hist)
Arna Wendell Bontemps. Black Thunder (fic)
Claude Gernade Bowers. Jefferson in Power (biog)
Kay Boyle. Death of a Man (fic)
_____. The White Horses of Vienna (fic)
Percy Holmes Boynton. Literature and American Life (e)
Gerald Warner Brace. The Islands (fic)
Van Wyck Brooks. The Flowering of New England (e, hist)
John Mason Brown. The Art of Playgoing (e)
Pearl Sydenstricker Buck. The Exile (biog)
_____. Fighting Angel (biog)
William Riley Burnett. King Cole (fic)
James Branch Cabell. Preface to the Past (e)
James Mallahan Cain. Double Indemnity (fic)
Erskine Preston Caldwell. The Sacrifice of Alan Kent (fic)
Morley Callaghan. Now That April's Here (fic)
William Edward March Campbell (William March). The Tallons (fic)
Henry Seidel Canby. Alma Mater: The Gothic Age of the American Col-
    lege (hist)
Oliver Carlson and Ernest Sutherland Bates. Hearst, Lord of San Si-
    meon (biog)
Carl Lamson Carmer. Listen for a Lonesome Drum (hist, fic)

Willa Sibert Cather. Not Under Forty (e)
Mary Ellen Chase. This England (des)
Stuart Chase. Rich Land, Poor Land (e)
Marquis William Childs. Sweden: The Middle Way (e)
Henry Steele Commager. Theodore Parker (biog)
James Gould Cozzens. Men and Brethren (fic)
Clare Booth Luce. The Women (dr)
Robert Peter Tristram Coffin. John Dawn (fic)
Ellsworth Prouty Conkle. 200 Were Chosen (dr)
Nathalia Crane. Swear by the Night (po)
Edward Estlin Cummings. 1/20 (po)
Merle Eugene Curti. Peace or War: The American Struggle, 1636-1936
   (hist)
Marcia Davenport. Of Lena Geyer (fic)
Bernard Augustine DeVoto. Forays and Rebuttals (e)
Emily Elizabeth Dickinson. Unpublished Poems (pub)
Hilda Doolittle. The Hedgehog (fic)
John Roderigo Dos Passos. The Big Money (fic)
Lloyd Cassel Douglas. White Banners (fic)
Walter Damaux Edmonds. Drums along the Mohawk (fic)
Paul Hamilton Engle. Break the Heart's Anger (po)
Janet Ayer Fairbank. Rich Man, Poor Man (fic)
James Thomas Farrell. A Note on Literary Criticism (e)
_____. A World I Never Made (fic)
William Harrison Faulkner. Absalom, Absalom! (fic)
Edna Ferber and George Simon Kaufman. Stage Door (dr)
Vardis Alvero Fisher. No Villain Need Be (fic)
John Gould Fletcher. The Epic of Arkansas (po)
Joseph Freeman. An American Testament (auto)
Robert Lee Frost. A Further Range (po)
Daniel Fuchs. Homage to Blenholt (fic)
Martha Gellhorn. The Trouble I've Seen (fic)
Herbert Sherman Gorman. The Mountain and the Plain (fic)
Julian Green. Midnight (fic)
Paul Eliot Green. Hymn to the Rising Sun (dr)
Nancy Hale. The Earliest Dreams (fic)
Moss Hart and George Simon Kaufman. You Can't Take It With You (dr)
Lillian Hellman. Days to Come (dr)
Maurice Gerschon Hindus. Moscow Skies (fic)
Paul Horgan. Main Line West (fic)
James Langston Hughes and Arna Wendell Bontemps. When the Jack Hol-
   lers (dr)
Fannie Hurst. Great Laughter (fic)
John Robinson Jeffers. The Beaks of Eagles (po)
MacKinlay Kantor. Arouse and Beware (fic)
George Edward Kelly. Reflected Glory (dr)
Sidney Kingsley. Ten Million Ghosts (dr)
Manuel Komroff. Waterloo (fic)
Clare Booth Luce. The Women (dr)
Andrew Nelson Lytle. The Long Night (fic)
Archibald MacLeish. Public Speech (po)
Albert Maltz. Private Hicks (dr)
Percy Marks. A Tree Grown Straight (fic)
Edgar Lee Masters. Across the Spoon River (auto)
_____. Poems of the People (po, nar, des)
John Thomas McIntyre. Steps Going Down (fic)

Henry Miller. Black Spring (e, nar)
Margaret Mitchell. Gone with the Wind (fic)
Marianne Craig Moore. The Pangolin, and Other Verses (po)
Samuel Eliot Morison. The Puritan Pronaos (e)
Ogden Nash. The Bad Parents' Garden of Verse (po)
Anais Nin. The House of Incest (fic)
Charles Bernard Nordhoff and James Norman Hall. The Hurricane (fic)
Dorothy Rothschild Parker. Not So Deep As a Well (po)
Anne Parrish. Golden Wedding (fic)
Kenneth Patchen. Before the Brave (po)
Louis Paul. A Horse in Arizona (fic)
Frederic Prokosch. The Assassins (po)
Arthur Hobson Quinn. American Fiction (e)
Ayn Rand. We, the Living (fic)
Lizette Woodworth Reese. The Old House in the Country (po)
_____. Worleys (fic)
Conrad Michael Richter. Early Americana (fic)
Lynn Riggs. The Cherokee Night (dr)
_____. Russet Mantle (dr)
Carl August Sandburg. The People, Yes (po)
George Santayana. Obiter Scripta (e)
William Saroyan. Inhale and Exhale (fic)
_____. Three Times Three (fic)
Winfield Townley Scott. Elegy for Robinson (po)
Irwin Shaw. Bury the Dead (dr)
James Vincent Sheean. Sanfelice (fic)
Robert Emmet Sherwood. Idiot's Delight (dr)
_____. Tovarich (dr)
Israel Joshua Singer. The Brothers Ashkenazi (fic)
Lloyd Logan Pearsall Smith. Reperusals and Re-collections (e)
Joseph Lincoln Steffens. Lincoln Steffens Speaking (e, pub)
Gertrude Stein. The Geographical History of America (e)
John Ernst Steinbeck. In Dubious Battle (fic)
Wallace Stevens. Owl's Clover (po)
Philip Duffield Stong. Career (fic)
_____. No-Sitch: The Hound (juv, fic)
Jesse Hilton Stuart. Head o' W-Hollow (fic)
Ruth Suckow. Carry-Over (fic)
Genevieve Taggard. Calling Western Union (po)
John Orley Allen Tate. The Mediterranean, and Other Poems (po)
_____. Reactionary Essays on Poetry and Ideas (e)
Dan Totheroh. Searching for the Sun (dr)
Arthur Cheney Train. Mr. Tutt's Case Book (fic)
Harold Vinal. Hurricane (po)
Edith Newbold Jones Wharton. The World Over (fic)
John Hall Wheelock. Poems, 1911-1936 (po, pub)
William Carlos Williams. Adam and Eve and the City (po)
Edmund Wilson. Travels in Two Democracies (nar)
Margaret Wilson. The Law and the McLaughlins (fic)
Thomas Clayton Wolfe. The Story of a Novel (e, nar)
William E. Woodward. A New American History (nar)
Audrey Wurdemann. Splendour in the Grass (po)
Leane Zugsmith. A Time To Remember (fic)

1937

BIRTHS

Joseph Epstein
Gail Godwin
William Melvin Kelley
Arthur L. Kopit
Jeremy Larner
Morgan Llywelyn
David Meltzer
Judith Minty
Thomas Pynchon
James Scully
Robert Anthony Stone
John Kennedy Toole
Diane Wakowski
Lanford Wilson
Geoffrey Ansell Wolff

DEATHS

Anna Hempstead Branch
William Gillette
Edgar Watson Howe
Robert Underwood Johnson
Donald Robert Perry Marquis
Albert Bigelow Paine
Lucy Fitch Perkins
Edith Newbold Jones Wharton

EVENTS

Intermountain Review, to 1938 (per)

LITERATURE

Louis Adamic. The House in Antigua (hist, nar, des)
Maxwell Anderson. High Tor (dr)
_____. The Star Wagon (dr)
Benjamin Appel. Runaround (fic)
Nathan Asch. The Road (nar)
Wystan Hugh Auden. Spain (nar)
Jacques Barzun. Race: A Study in Modern Superstition (e)
Samuel Nathaniel Behrman. Amphitryon 38 (dr)
Ludwig Bemelmans. My War with the United States (nar)
Stephen Vincent Benet. The Headless Horseman (po, dr)
Archie Binns. The Laurels Are Cut Down (fic)
Richard Palmer Blackmur. From Jordan's Delight (po)
Louise Bogan. The Sleeping Fury (po)
Stephen Bonsal. Heyday in a Vanished World (nar)
Catherine Shaber Drinker Bowen. Beloved Friend (biog)
Myron Brining. The Sisters (fic)
Louis Bromfield. The Rains Came (fic)
Kenneth Duva Burke. Attitudes toward History, 2 vols (e)
James Branch Cabell. Smire (fic)
Erskine Preston Caldwell and Margaret Bourke-White. You Have Seen

Their Faces (hist, illus)
Morley Callaghan. More Joy in Heaven (fic)
Gladys Hasty Carroll. Neighbor in the Sky (fic)
William Henry Chamberlain. Collectivism: A False Utopia (e)
Mary Coyle Chase. Now You've Done It (dr)
Marquis William Childs. Washington Calling (e)
Robert Peter Tristram Coffin. Kennebec, Cradle of Americans (hist)
Ellsworth Prouty Conkle. Prologue to Glory (dr)
Edwin Corle. People on the Earth (fic)
Malcolm Cowley. After the Genteel Tradition (ed)
Merle Eugene Curti. The Learned Blacksmith: The Letters and Journals
    of Elihu Burritt (ed)
Clyde Brion Davis. The Annointed (fic)
Clarence Shepard Day. Life with Mother (auto)
Benjamin DeCasseres. Fantasia Impromptu: The Adventures of an Intel-
    lectual Faun (e)
August William Derleth. Still Is the Summer Night (fic)
Hilda Doolittle. Ion of Euripides (trans)
Richard Ghormley Eberhart. Reading the Spirit (po)
John Erskine. The Brief Hour of Francois Villon (fic)
James Thomas Farrell. Can All This Grandeur Perish? (fic)
Howard Melvin Fast. The Children (fic)
Vardis Alvero Fisher. April, a Fable of Love (fic)
John Gould Fletcher. Life Is My Song (auto)
Norman Foerster. The American State University (e)
Esther Forbes. Paradise (fic)
Waldo David Frank. In the American Jungle (e)
Daniel Fuchs. Low Company (fic)
Wolcott Gibbs. Bed of Neuroses (e)
Caroline Gordon. The Garden of Adonis (fic)
_____. None Shall Look Back (fic)
Anne Green. 16 Rue Cortambert (fic)
Paul Eliot Green. The Lost Colony (dr)
_____ and Kurt Weill. Johnny Johnson (dr)
Albert Joseph Guerard. The Past Must Alter (fic)
Albert Halper. The Chute (fic)
Moss Hart and George Simon Kaufman. I'd Rather Be Right (dr)
Walter Edwin Havighurst. The Quiet Shore (fic)
Ben Hecht. To Quito and Back (dr)
Ernest Miller Hemingway. To Have and To Have Not (fic)
Robert Silliman Hillyer. A Letter to Robert Frost and Others (po)
Paul Horgan. Lamp on the Plains (fic)
Sidney Coe Howard. The Ghost of Yankee Doodle (dr)
James Langston Hughes. Don't You Want To Be Free? (dr)
_____. Joy to My Soul (dr)
_____. Soul Gone Home (dr)
Fannie Hurst. We Are Ten (fic)
Zora Neale Hurston. Their Eyes Were Watching God (fic)
John Robinson Jeffers. Such Counsels You Gave Me, and Other Poems
    (po)
Josephine Winslow Johnson. Jordanstown (fic)
_____. Year's End (po)
MacKinlay Kantor. The Romance of Rosy Ridge (fic)
Arthur Kober. Having a Wonderful Time (dr)
Oliver Hazard Perry LaFarge. The Enemy Gods (fic)
John Howard Lawson. Marching Song (dr)

Meyer Levin. The Old Bunch (fic)
Ludwig Lewisohn. Trumpet of Jubilee (fic)
Archibald MacLeish. The Fall of the City (po, dr)
John Phillips Marquand. The Late George Apley (fic)
Edgar Lee Masters. The New World (des, nar)
_____. The Tide of Time (fic)
_____. Walt Whitman (biog)
William Maxwell. They Came Like Swallows (fic)
Robert McAlmon. Not Alone Lost (po)
Horace McCoy. No Pockets in a Shroud (fic)
John Thomas McIntyre. Ferment (fic)
Edna St. Vincent Millay. Conversation at Midnight (po)
Christopher Darlington Morley. The Trojan Horse (fic)
Vladimir Nabokov. The Gift (fic)
Clifford Odets. Golden Boy (dr)
Martha Ostenso. The Stone Field (fic)
Elliot Harold Paul. The Life and Death of a Spanish Town (nar)
Sidney Joseph Perelman. Strictly from Hunger (sat, nar)
Katherine Anne Porter. Noon Wine (fic)
Ezra Weston Loomis Pound. The Fifth Decad of Cantos (po)
_____. Polite Essays (e)
Frederic Prokosch. The Seven Who Fled (fic)
Laura Reichenthal (Laura Riding). A Trojan Ending (fic)
Elmer Reizenstein (Elmer Rice). Imperial City (fic)
Agnes Repplier. Eight Decades (e)
Conrad Michael Richter. The Sea of Grass (fic)
Kenneth Lewis Roberts. Northwest Passage (fic)
Selden Rodman. Lawrence: The Last Crusade (po)
Leo Calvin Rosten (Leonard Q. Ross). The Education of Hyman Kaplan
    (fic)
Mari Sandoz. Slogum House (fic)
George Santayana. The Realm of Truth (e)
William Saroyan. Little Children (fic)
Eleanor May Sarton. Encounter in April (po)
Evelyn Scott. Bread and a Sword (fic)
Irwin Shaw. Siege (dr)
Upton Beall Sinclair. The Flivver King (e)
Wallace Earle Stegner. Remembering Laughter (fic)
Gertrude Stein. Everybody's Autobiography (nar)
John Ernst Steinbeck. Of Mice and Men (fic)
_____. The Red Pony (fic)
Wallace Stevens. The Man with the Blue Guitar (po)
Philip Duffield Stong. Buckskin Breeches (fic)
Hans Otto Storm. Pity the Tyrant (fic)
Rex Todhunter Stout. The Hand in the Glove (fic)
John Orley Allen Tate. Selected Poems (pub)
Sara Teasdale. Collected Poems (pub)
James Grover Thurber. Let Your Mind Alone! (sat)
Louis Untermeyer. Heinrich Heine: Paradox and Poet (biog)
Hendrik Willem Van Loon. The Arts (hist)
Jerome Weidman. I Can Get It for You Wholesale (fic)
Edith Newbold Jones Wharton. Ghosts (fic)
William Carlos Williams. White Mule (fic)
Edmund Wilson. This Room and This Gin and These Sandwiches (dr)
Arthur Yvor Winters. Primitivism and Decadence (e)
Frances Winwar. Gallows Hill (fic)

Charles Erskine Scott Wood. Earthly Discourse (sat)
Audrey Wurdemann. Bright Ambush (po)
Marya Zaturenska. Cold Morning Sky (po)
Leane Zugsmith. Home Is Where You Hang Your Childhood (fic)

1938

BIRTHS

Renata Adler
Judy Sussman Blume
Raymond Carver
Donald Lee Coburn
Elizabeth Forsythe Hailey
Michael S. Harper
Norma Klein
William Kotzwinkle
Joyce Carol Oates
Robert Phillips
Ishmael Scott Read
Charles Simic
Joyce Carol Thomas

DEATHS

Clarence Seward Darrow   John Van Alstyne Weaver
Harry Stillwell Edwards
Chester Bailey Fernald
Charles Macomb Flandrau
Mary Hallock Foote
James Forbes
Zona Gale
Robert Herrick
Edward Mandell House
James Weldon Johnson
Frank Bird Linderman
Owen Wister
Thomas Clayton Wolfe

EVENTS

Contemporary Jewish Record, to 1945 (per)
Dictionary of American English, to 1944 (ref)
The Playwrights' Company (f)
Rocky Mountain Review, Salt Lake City, Utah, to 1946 (per)
Twice a Year, to 1948 (per)

LITERATURE

Herbert Baxter Adams. Historical Scholarship in the United States
    (e, nar, pub)
James Truslow Adams. Building the British Empire (hist)
Mortimer Jerome Adler. St. Thomas and the Gentiles (e)
_____. What Man Has Made of Man (e)
Herbert Sebastian Agar. The Pursuit of Happiness (hist)

William Hervey Allen. Action at Aquilla (fic)
Maxwell Anderson. The Essence of Tragedy (e)
_____. The Feast of Ortolans (dr)
_____ and Kurt Weill. Knickerbocker Holiday (dr)
Robert Ardrey. Casey Jones (dr)
Sholem Asch. Chaim Lederer's Return (fic, trans)
_____. Judge Not (fic, trans)
_____. Uncle Moses (fic, trans)
Joseph Auslander. Riders at the Gate (po)
Irving Addison Bacheller. From Stores of Memory (nar)
Leonard Bacon. Bullinger Bound (po)
Dorothy Baker. Young Man with a Horn (fic)
Margaret Culkin Banning. Too Young to Marry (fic)
Margaret Ayer Barnes. Wisdom's Gate (fic)
Philip Barry. Here Come the Clowns (dr)
_____. War in Heaven (fic)
Carleton Beals.The Coming Struggle for Latin America (e)
_____. Glass Houses: Ten Years of Freelancing (auto)
Ben Belitt. The Five-Fold Mesh (po)
Ludwig Bemelmans. Life Class (fic)
Robert Charles Benchley. After 1903--What? (nar)
William Rose Benet and Norman H. Pearson. Oxford Anthology of Ame-
    rican Literature (misc, ed)
Sara Mahala Redway Smith Benson. Emily (fic)
Kay Boyle. A Glad Day (po)
_____. Monday Night (fic)
Gerald Warner Brace. The Wayward Pilgrims (fic)
Myron Brinig. May Flavin (fic)
Cleanth Brooks and Robert Penn Warren. Understanding Poetry (e, po,
    ed)
Pearl Sydenstricker Buck. This Proud Heart (fic)
Ben Lucien Burman. Blow for a Landing (fic)
William Riley Burnett. The Dark Command (fic)
Maxwell Struthers Burt. Powder River: Let 'Er Buck (nar)
James Branch Cabell. The King Was in His Counting House (fic)
Erskine Preston Caldwell. Southways (fic)
Janet Taylor Caldwell. Dynasty of Death (fic)
Mary Ellen Chase. Dawn in Lyonesse (fic)
Stuart Chase. The Tyranny of Words (e)
Elizabeth Jane Coatsworth. Here I Stay (fic)
Robert Peter Tristram Coffin. New Poetry of New England: Frost and
    Robinson (e)
Octavus Roy Cohen. Florian Slappey (fic)
Dane Coolidge. Hell's Hip Pocket (fic)
Edwin Corle. Burro Alley (fic)
Rachel Crothers. Susan and God (dr)
Edward Estlin Cummings. Collected Poems (pub)
Jonathan Worth Daniels. A Southerner Discovers the South (e, nar)
Frederic Dannay and Manfred Lee (Ellery Queen). A Challenge to the
    Reader (fic, ed)
Donald Grady Davidson. The Attack on Leviathan (e)
_____. Lee in the Mountains (po)
Clyde Brion Davis. The Great American Novel (fic)
David Cornel DeJong. Old Haven (fic)
August William Derleth. Hawk on the Wind (po)
_____. Wind over Wisconsin (fic)

John Roderigo Dos Passos. Journey between Wars (trav, nar)
_____. U.S.A. (fic)
John Erskine. The Start of the Road (fic)
John Fante. Wait Until Spring, Bandini (fic)
James Thomas Farrell. No Star Is Lost (fic)
William Harrison Faulkner. The Unvanquished (fic)
Kenneth Fearing. Dead Reckoning (po)
Rachel Lyman Field. All This, and Heaven Too (fic)
Vardis Alvero Fisher. Forgive Us Our Virtues (fic)
John Gould Fletcher. Selected Poems (pub)
Esther Forbes. The General's Lady (fic)
Anne Green. Paris (fic)
Julian Hawthorne. The Memoirs of Julian Hawthorne (auto)
Ernest Miller Hemingway. The Fifth Column and the First Forty-Nine
    Stories (fic, pub)
Robert Sulliman Hillyer. First Principles of Verse (e)
Paul Horgan. Far from Cibola (fic)
James Langston Hughes. Front Porch (dr)
_____. A New Song (po)
John Robinson Jeffers. The Selected Poetry (pub)
MacKinlay Kantor. The Noise of Their Wings (fic)
Alfred Kreymborg. The Planets (dr)
Harry Sinclair Lewis. The Prodigal Parents (fic)
Anne Morrow Lindburgh. Listen! the Wind (nar)
William Wilberforce Lord. Complete Poetical Works (pub)
Clare Boothe Luce. Kiss the Boys Goodbye (dr)
Archibald MacLeish. Air Raid (po, dr)
Albert Maltz. The Way Things Are (fic)
Percy Marks. What's a Heaven For? (fic)
Edgar Lee Masters. Mark Twain (biog)
Horace McCoy. I Should Have Stayed Home (fic)
William Morley Punshon McFee. Derelicts (fic)
John Thomas McIntyre. Signing Off (fic)
Ruth McKenney. My Sister Eileen (fic, nar)
Henry Miller. Max and the White Phagocytes (nar)
Merrill Moore. M: One Thousand Autobiographical Sonnets (po)
Vladimir Nabokov. Invitation to a Beheading (fic)
_____. Laughter in the Dark (fic)
Ogden Nash. I'm a Stranger Here Myself (po)
George Jean Nathan. The Morning after the First Night (e)
Robert Gruntal Nathan. Journey of Tapiola (fic)
_____. Winter in April (fic)
Charles Gilman Norris. Bricks without Straw (fic)
Clifford Odets. Rocket to the Moon (dr)
John Henry O'Hara. Hope of Heaven (fic)
Martha Ostenso. The Mandrake Root (fic)
Elliot Harold Paul. Concert Pitch (fic)
Ezra Weston Loomis Pound. Guide to Kulchur (e)
Frederic Prokosch. The Carnival (po)
Ayn Rand. Anthem (fic)
John Crowe Ransom. The World's Body (e)
Marjorie Kinnan Rawlings. The Yearling (fic)
Laura Reichenthal (Laura Riding). Collected Poems (pub)
Elmer Reizenstein (Elmer Rice). American Landscape (dr)
Elizabeth Madox Roberts. Black Is My Trulove's Hair (fic)
Kenneth Lewis Roberts. March to Quebec (hist)

Muriel Rukeyser. U.S. 1 (po)
Alfred Damon Runyon. Take It Easy (fic)
William Saroyan. Love, Here Is My Hat (fic)
_____. A Native American (fic)
_____. The Trouble with Tigers (fic)
Eleanor May Sarton. The Single Hound (fic)
Delmore Schwartz. In Dreams Begin Responsibilities (po)
James Vincent Sheean. A Day of Battle (fic)
Robert Emmet Sherwood. Abe Lincoln in Illinois (dr)
Charles Wilbert Snow. Before the Wind (po)
Wilbur Daniel Steele. Sound of Rowlocks (fic)
Gertrude Stein. Picasso (e)
John Ernst Steinbeck. The Long Valley (fic)
George Rippey Stewart. East of the Giants (fic)
Irving Stone. Sailor on Horseback (fic)
Rex Todhunter Stout. Too Many Cooks (fic)
Thomas Sigismund Stribling. These Bars of Flesh (fic)
Jesse Hilton Stuart. Beyond Dark Hills (auto)
Genevieve Taggard. Collected Poems (pub)
John Orley Allen Tate. Fathers (fic)
Barbara Wertheim Tuchman. The Lost British Policy (hist)
Louis Untermeyer. Play in Poetry (e)
Carl Clinton Van Doren. Benjamin Franklin (biog)
Jerome Weidman. What's In It for Me? (fic)
John Wexley. Running Dogs (dr)
Richard Nathaniel Wright. Uncle Tom's Children (fic)
Edith Newbold Jones Wharton. The Buccaneers (fic, pub)
Elwyn Brooks White. The Fox of Peapack (po)
William Lindsay White. What People Said (fic)
Thornton Niven Wilder. The Merchant of Yonkers (dr)
_____. Our Town (dr)
William Carlos Williams. The Complete Collected Poems, 1906-1938
     (pub)
_____. Life along the Passaic River (fic)
Edmund Wilson. The Triple Thinkers (e)
Arthur Yvor Winters. Maule's Curse (e)
Audrey Wurdemann. Testament of Love (po)
Leane Zugsmith. The Summer Soldier (fic)

                              1939

BIRTHS

     Toni Cade Bambara
     Peter Soyer Beagle
     Frank Bidart
     Raymond Carver
     Clark Coolidge
     Robert Choate Darnton
     Charles Fuller
     Thomas Francis McGuane III
     Jason Miller
     Stanley Plumly
     Robert Siegel
     Albert James Young

DEATHS

Ernest Sutherland Bates
Heywood Campbell Broun
Zane Grey
Richard Halliburton
Sidney Coe Howard
Felix Riesenberg
Constance Londsay Skinner
Joel Elias Spingarn
Harry Leon Wilson
Willard Huntington Wright

EVENTS

Furioso, to 1953 (per)
Kenyon Review, Kenyon College (Ohio), to 1970 (per)
The New Anvil, to 1941 (per)
Franklin Delano Roosevelt Library, Hyde Park, New York (f)
Scribner's Commentator, to 1939 (per)
Southern Literary Messenger, Richmond, Virginia, 2nd series, to 1944
    (per)

LITERATURE

Samuel Hopkins Adams. Incredible Era (hist)
Conrad Potter Aiken. A Heart for the Gods of Mexico (fic)
Bess Streeter Aldrich. Song of Years (fic)
Maxwell Anderson. Key Largo (po, dr)
Benjamin Appel. The Powerhouse (fic)
Sholem Asch. The Nazarene (fic)
William Attaway. Let Me Breathe Thunder (fic)
Leonard Bacon. Semi-Centennial (auto)
Harry Elmer Barnes. Society in Transition (e)
Philip Barry. The Philadelphia Story (dr)
Joseph Hamilton Basso. Days before Lent (fic)
Carleton Beals. American Earth: The Biography of a Nation (hist)
Charles Austin Beard and Mary Ritter Beard. America in Mid-Passage
    (hist)
Samuel Nathaniel Behrman. No Time for Comedy (dr)
John Barry Benefield. April Was When It Began (fic)
Stephen Vincent Benet. The Devil and Daniel Webster (opera libretto)
_____. Tale before Midnight (fic)
Archie Binns. The Land Is Bright (fic)
Arna Wendell Bontemps. Drums at Dusk (fic)
Catherine Shober Drinker Bowen. Free Artist (biog)
James Boyd. Bitter Creek (fic)
Kay Boyle. The Youngest Camel (fic)
Myron Brinig. Anne Minton's Life (fic)
Louis Bromfield. It Takes All Kinds (fic)
Pearl Sydenstricker Buck. The Patriot (fic)
Nicholas Murray Butler. Across the Busy Years, 2 vols, to 1940
    (auto)
Erskine Preston Caldwell and Margaret Bourke-White. North of the
    Danube (des, illus)
William Edward March Campbell (William March). Some Like Them Short

(fic)
Henry Seidel Canby. Thoreau (biog)
Carl Lamson Carmer. The Hudson (hist)
Raymond Chandler. The Big Sleep (fic)
Dorothy Canfield Fisher. Seasoned Timber (fic)
Mary Ellen Chase. A Goodly Fellowship (auto)
Robert Peter Tristram Coffin. Captain Abby and Captain John (biog)
_____. Collected Poems (pub)
Russel Crouse and Howard Lindsay. Life with Father (dr)
Josephus Daniels. Tar Heel Editor (auto)
Clyde Brion Davis. Nebraska Coast (fic)
August William Darleth. Man Track Here (po)
_____. Restless Is the River (fic)
Babette Deutsch. One Part Love (po)
Pietro DiDonato. Christ in Concrete (fic)
John Roderigo Dos Passos. Adventures of a Young Man (fic)
Lloyd Cassel Douglas. Disputed Passage (fic)
Thomas Stearns Eliot. The Family Reunion (po, dr)
_____. Old Possum's Book of Practical Cats (po)
Paul Hamilton Engle. Corn (po)
John Fante. Ask the Dust (fic)
James Thomas Farrell. Tommy Gallagher's Crusade (fic)
Howard Melvin Fast. Conceived in Liberty (fic)
William Harrison Faulkner. The Wild Palms (fic)
Kenneth Fearing. The Hospital (fic)
Edna Ferber. A Peculiar Treasure (auto)
Arthur Davison Ficke. Mrs. Morton of Mexico (fic)
Irving Fineman. Doctor Addams (fic)
Vardis Alvero Fisher. Children of God (fic)
Waldo David Frank. The Bridegroom Cometh (fic)
Douglas Southall Freeman. The South to Posterity (hist, e)
Robert Lee Frost. Collected Poems (pub)
Zona Gale. Magna (fic)
Anne Green. The Silent Duchess (fic)
Julian Green. Personal Record (nar)
Paul Eliot Green. Out of the South (dr)
Francis Hackett. Queen Anne Boleyn (fic)
Hutchins Hapgood. A Victorian in the Modern World (auto)
Moss Hart and George Simon Kaufman. The Man Who Came to Dinner (dr)
Ben Hecht. A Book of Miracles (fic)
_____ and Charles MacArthur. Ladies and Gentlemen (dr)
Lillian Hellman. The Little Foxes (dr)
Josephine Frey Herbst. Rape of Gold (fic)
DuBose Heyward. Star Spangled Virgin (fic)
Robert Silliman Hillyer. In Time of Mistrust (po)
Paul Horgan. The Habit of Empire (fic)
Zora Neale Hurston. Moses: Man of the Mountain (fic)
Clarence Budington Kelland. Arizona (fic)
Sidney Kingsley. The World We Make (dr)
Arthur Kober. Pardon Me for Pointing (fic)
Manuel Komroff. The March of the Hundred (fic)
Joseph Wood Krutch. The American Drama Since 1918 (e)
Christopher La Farge. Each to the Other (fic, po)
Ludwig Lewisohn. For Ever Wilt Thou Love (fic)
Joseph Crosby Lincoln and Freeman Lincoln. The Ownley Inn (fic)
Howard Lindsay and Russel Crouse. Life with Father (dr)

Clare Boothe Luce. Margin for Error (dr)
Grace Lumpkin. The Wedding (fic)
Charles MacArthur and Ben Hecht. Ladies and Gentlemen (dr)
Archibald MacLeish. America Was Promises (po)
Percy Marks. The Days Are Fled (fic)
John Phillips Marquand. Wickford Point (fic)
Donald Robert Perry Marquis. Sons of the Puritans (fic, pub)
Josephine Miles. Lines at Intersection (po)
Edna St. Vincent Millay. Huntsman, What Quarry (po)
Henry Miller. The Cosmological Eye (fic, e)
_____. Tropic of Capricorn (nar)
Christopher Darlington Morley. Kitty Foyle (fic)
Honore Willsie Morrow. Demon Daughter (fic)
Anais Nin. Winter of Artifice (fic)
John Henry O'Hara. Files on Parade (fic)
Dorothy Rothschild Parker. Here Lies (fic)
Kenneth Patchen. First Will and Testament (po)
Katherine Anne Porter. Pale Horse, Pale Rider (fic)
William Sydney Porter (O Henry). O. Henry Encore (fic, pub)
Frederic Prokosch. Night of the Poor (fic)
Laura Reichenthal (Laura Riding). Lives of Wives (fic)
Muriel Rukeyser. A Turning Wind (po)
Carl August Sandburg. Abraham Lincoln: The War Years, 4 vols (biog)
Mari Sandoz. Capital City (fic)
William Saroyan. My Heart's in the Highlands (dr)
_____. Peace, It's Wonderful (fic)
_____. The Time of Your Life (dr)
Eleanor May Sarton. Inner Landscape (po)
Delmore Schwartz. A Season in Hell (po, trans)
Irwin Shaw. The Gentle People (dr)
_____. Sailor Off the Bremen (fic)
Chard Powers Smith. Artillery of Time (fic)
Leonora Speyer. Slow Wall (po)
Gertrude Stein. The World Is Round (juv)
John Ernst Steinbeck. The Grapes of Wrath (fic)
George Rippey Stewart. Doctor's Oral (fic)
Grace Zearing Stone (Ethel Vance). Escape (fic)
Philip Duffield Stong. Ivanhoe Keeler (fic)
_____. The Long Lane (fic)
Hans Otto Storm. Made in U.S.A. (fic)
Rex Todhunter Stout. Some Buried Caesar (fic)
James Grover Thurber. The Last Flower (fic)
Lionel Trilling. Matthew Arnold (e)
Mark Albert Van Doren. Collected Poems (pub)
_____. Shakespeare (e)
_____ and Carl Clinton Van Doren. American and British Literature Since 1890, rev ed (hist, e)
_____ and Theodore Spencer. Studies in Metaphysical Poetry: Two Essays and a Bibliography (e, ref)
Robert Penn Warren. Night Rider (fic)
Jerome Weidman. The Horse That Could Whistle Dixie (fic)
Nathan Wallenstein Weinstein (Nathaniel West). The Day of the Locust (fic)
Elwyn Brooks White. Quo Vadimus; or, the Case for the Bicycle (fic)
Thomas Lanier (Tennessee) Williams. American Blues (dr)
Thomas Clayton Wolfe. The Web and the Rock (fic, pub)

Stark Young. The Sea Gull (trans)

1940

BIRTHS

    Peter Bradford Benchley
    Martha Collins
    John P. Coyne
    William Heyen
    Maxine Hong Kingston
    Paul Mariani
    Bobbie Ann Mason
    Donald McCaig
    Robert Pinsky
    David William Rabe

DEATHS

    Harriot Stanton Blatch
    Dane Coolidge
    Francis Scott Key Fitzgerald
    Hannibal Hamlin Garland
    Robert Grant
    DuBose Heyward
    Edward Charles Markham
    Honore Willsie Morrow
    Alfred Edward Newton
    Nathan Wallenstein Weinstein (Nathaniel West)

EVENTS

    Accent, University of Illinois, Champagne-Urbana, to 1960 (per)
    Common Ground, Common Council for American Unity, to 1949 (per)
    Current History and Forum (per, f)
    Dictionary of American History, to 1976 (ref)
    PM, New York, New York, to 1948 (per)

LITERATURE

    George Abbott. Pal Joey (dr)
    James Truslow Adams. Dictionary of American History (ref, ed)
    _____. Empire on the Seven Seas (hist)
    Mortimore Jerome Adler. How To Read a Book (e)
    _____. Problems for Thomists (e)
    Herbert Sebastian Agar. Beyond German Victory (e)
    Conrad Potter Aiken. And in the Human Heart (po)
    _____. Conversation; or, Pilgrim's Progress (fic)
    Frederick Lewis Allen. Since Yesterday (hist)
    William Hervey Allen. It Was Like This (fic)
    Maxwell Anderson. Journey to Jerusalem (po, dr)
    _____. Off Broadway (e)
    Sherwood Anderson. Home Town (e)
    Wystan Hugh Auden. Another Time (po)
    Irving Babbitt. Spanish Character (e, pub)
    Leonard Bacon. Sunderland Capture (po)

Ernest Sutherland Bates. American Faith (e, pub)
Carleton Beals. Great Circle (auto)
_____ . Pan America (e)
Charles Austin Beard and G.H.E. Smith. The Old Deal and the New (e)
Mary Ritter Beard. Woman: Co-Maker of History (hist)
Albert Bein. Heavenly Express (dr)
Stephen Vincent Benet. Nightmare at Noon (po)
John Berryman. Twenty Poems (po, pub)
Archie Binns. Mighty Mountain (fic)
Richard Palmer Blackmur. The Expense of Greatness (e)
Harriot Stanton Blatch. Challenging Years (nar)
Franz Boas. Race, Language and Culture (e)
Claude Gernade Bowers. The Spanish Adventures of Washington Irving
    (e)
Kay Boyle. The Crazy Hunter (fic)
Percy Holmes Boynton. America in Contemporary Fiction (e)
Louis Bromfield. Night in Bombay (fic)
Van Wyck Brooks. New England: Indian Summer (hist, e)
Pearl Sydenstricker Buck. Other Gods (fic)
Ben Lucien Burman. Big River To Cross (nar)
William Riley Burnett. High Sierra (fic)
Harold Witter Bynner. Against the Cold (po)
James Branch Cabell. Hamlet Had an Uncle (fic)
Erskine Preston Caldwell. Jackpot (fic)
_____ . Trouble in July (fic)
Janet Taylor Caldwell. The Eagles Gather (fic)
Walter Stanley Campbell (Stanley Vestal). King of the Fur Traders
    (biog)
Willa Sibert Cather. Sapphira and the Slave Girl (fic)
John Chamberlain. The American Stakes (e)
William Henry Chamberlain. The Confessions of an Individualist (auto)
Raymond Chandler. Farewell, My Lovely (fic)
Stuart Chase. Idle Money, Idle Men (e)
Jerome Chadorov and Joseph Fields. My Sister Eileen (dr)
Winston Churchill. The Uncharted Way (e)
John Ciardi. Homeward to America (po)
Barrett Harper Clark. America's Lost Plays, 20 vols, to 1941 (dr, ed)
Walter Van Tilburg Clark. The Ox-Bow Incident (fic)
James Bryant Conant. Education for a Classless Society (e)
James Gould Cozzens. Ask Me Tomorrow (fic)
Edward Estlin Cummings. 50 Poems (po)
Clyde Brion Davis. The Arkansas (hist)
Elmer Holmes Davis. Not To Mention the War (e)
Clarence Shepard Day. Father and I (auto)
David Conrad DeJong. Light Sons and Dark (fic)
August William Derleth. Bright Journey (fic)
_____ . Still Small Voice (biog)
Bernard Augustine DeVoto. Minority Report (e)
Peter DeVries. But Who Wakes the Bugler? (fic)
Hilda Doolittle. Collected Poems (pub)
Lloyd Cassel Douglas. Invitation To Live (fic)
Walter Demaux Edmonds. Chad Hanna (fic)
Thomas Stearns Eliot. The Idea of a Christian Society (e)
John Erskine. Give Me Liberty (fic)
John Fante. Dago Red (fic)
James Thomas Farrell. Father and Son (fic)

William Harrison Faulkner. The Hamlet (fic)
Janet Flanner. An American in Paris (nar, des)
Martin Archer Flavin. Mr. Littlejohn (fic)
Waldo David Frank. Chart for Rough Water (e)
Ketti Frings. Hold Back the Dawn (fic)
Susan Glaspell. The Morning Is Near Us (fic)
Herbert Sherman Gorman. James Joyce (biog)
Anne Green. The Delamer Curse (fic)
Albert Halper. Sons of the Father (fic)
Moss Hart and George Simon Kaufman. George Washington Slept Here
   (dr)
Walter Edwin Havighurst. The Winds of Spring (fic)
Robert Hayden. Heart-Shape in the Dust (po)
Ernest Miller Hemingway. For Whom the Bell Tolls (fic)
Granville Hicks and Richard M. Bennett. The First To Awaken (fic)
Robert Silliman Hillyer. Pattern of a Day (po)
Maurice Gerschon Hindus. Sons and Fathers (fic)
Paul Horgan. Figures in a Landscape (fic, e)
MacKinlay Kantor. Cuba Libre (fic)
Manuel Komroff. The Magic Bow (fic)
Stanley Jasspon Kunitz. Passport to War (po)
Josephine Lawrence. But You Are Young (fic)
Meyer Levin. Citizens (fic)
Harry Sinclair Lewis. Bethel Merriday (fic)
Anne Morrow Lindbergh. The Wave of the Future (e)
Clare Boothe Luce. Europe in the Spring (dr)
_____. Margin for Error (dr)
Percy Wallace MacKaye. My Lady Dear, Arise! (po)
Archibald MacLeish. The Irresponsibles (e)
Albert Maltz. The Underground Stream (fic)
Percy Marks. No Steeper Wall (fic)
Carson Smith McCullers. The Heart Is the Lonely Hunter (fic)
William Morley Punshon McFee. Watch Below (e, fic)
Phyllis McGinley. A Pocketful of Wry (po)
Henry Louis Mencken. Happy Days, 1880-1892 (nar)
Edna St. Vincent Millay. Make Bright the Arrows (po)
Ogden Nash. The Face Is Familiar (po)
George Jean Nathan. Encyclopaedia of the Theatre (e, ref)
Robert Gruntal Nathan. Portrait of Jennie (fic)
_____. A Winter Tide (po)
Clifford Odets. Night Music (dr)
Elder James Olson. The Cock of Heaven (po)
Louis Paul. A Passion for Privacy (fic)
Sidney Joseph Perelman. Look Who's Talking (nar, sat)
Ezra Weston Loomis Pound. Cantos LII-LXXI (po)
Frederic Prokosch. Death at Sea (po)
Marjorie Kinnan Rawlings. Jacob's Ladder (fic)
_____. When the Whippoorwill (fic)
Elmer Reizenstein (Elmer Rice). Two on an Island (dr)
Kenneth Rexroth. In What Hour (po)
Conrad Michael Richter. The Trees (fic)
Elizabeth Madox Roberts. Song in the Meadow (po)
Kenneth Lewis Roberts. Oliver Wiswell (fic)
Muriel Rukeyser. The Soul and Body of John Brown (po)
Alfred Damon Runyon. My Wife Ethel (fic)
George Santayana. The Realm of Spirit (e)

William Saroyen. My Name Is Aram (fic)
Irwin Shaw. Retreat to Pleasure (dr)
Robert Emmet Sherwood. There Shall Be No Night (dr)
Upton Beall Sinclair. World's End (fic)
Charles Wilbert Snow. Maine Tides (po)
Wallace Earle Stegner. On a Darkling Plain (fic)
Gertrude Stein. Paris France (e)
Hans Otto Storm. Count Ten (fic)
Jesse Hilton Stuart. Trees of Heaven (fic)
James Grover Thurber. Fables for Our Time, and Famous Poems Illustra-
   ted (fic, po)
_____ and Elliott Nugent. The Male Animal (dr)
Arthur Cheney Train. Tassels on Her Boots (fic)
Jean Starr Untermeyer. Love and Need (po)
Carl Clinton Van Doren. The American Novel, rev ed (e)
Mark Albert Van Doren. Windless Cabins (fic)
Hendrik Willem Van Loon. The Story of the Pacific (hist)
Jerome Weidman. Letter of Credit (nar)
Nathan Wallenstein Weinstein (Nathaniel West). The Day of the Locust
   (fic, reprint)
Glenway Wescott. The Pilgrim Hawk (fic)
Stewart Edward White. Wild Geese Calling (fic)
Ben Ames Williams. Come Spring (fic)
Thomas Lanier (Tennessee) Williams. Battle of Angels (dr)
William Carlos Williams. In the Money (fic)
Edmund Wilson. To the Finland Station (e)
Arthur Yvor Winters. Poems (pub)
Frances Winwar. Oscar Wilde and the Yellow Nineties (biog)
Thomas Clayton Wolfe. You Can't Go Home Again (fic, pub)
Richard Nathaniel Wright. Native Son (fic)
_____. Uncle Tom's Children, rev (fic)

7 The Twentieth Century: 1941–1986

BIRTHS

    Max Apple
    Nora Ephron
    Robert Hass
    William Pitt Root
    Paul Edward Theroux
    Anne Tyler
    John Edgar Wideman
    Larry Alfred Woiwode

DEATHS

    Sherwood Anderson
    Louis Dembitz Brandeis
    Aline Kilmer
    Gworge Lyman Kittredge
    Lola Ridge
    Elizabeth Madox Roberts
    Hans Otto Storm
    Daniel Berkeley Updike
    Eugene Walter

EVENTS

    Ellery Queen's Mystery Magazine (per, f)
    Thoreau Society (f)

LITERATURE

    Louis Adamic. Two-Way Passage (e)
    Mortimer Jerome Adler. A Dialect of Morals (e)
    James Agee. Let Us Now Praise Famous Men (e)
    Zoe Akins. Forever Young (fic)
    Maxwell Anderson. Candle in the Wind (dr)
    Sholem Asch. What I Believe (e)
    William Attaway. Blood on the Forge (fic)

Wystan Hugh Auden. The Double Man (po)
Irving Addison Bacheller. The Winds of God (fic)
Ray Stannard Baker. Native American (auto)
Faith Baldwin. Temporary Address: Reno (fic)
Philip Barry. Liberty Jones (dr)
Jacques Barzun. Darwin, Marx, Wagner: Critique of a Heritage (e)
Joseph Hamilton Basso. Wine of the Country (fic)
Joseph Warren Beach. American Fiction, 1920-1940 (hist, e)
Rex Ellingwood Beach. Personal Exposures (fic)
Charles Austin Beard. Public Policy and the General Welfare (e)
Carl Lotus Becker. Modern Democracy (e)
_____. New Liberties for Old (e)
Thomas Beer. The Agreeable Finish (fic, pub)
Samuel Nathaniel Behrman. The Talley Method (dr)
Ludwig Bemelmans. At Your Service (fic)
_____. The Donkey Inside (nar)
_____. Hotel Splendide (fic)
William Rose Benet. The Dust Which Is God (po, fic)
Sara Mahala Redway Smith Benson. Junior Miss (fic)
Konrad Bercovici. It's the Gypsy in Me (auto)
Archie Binns. Northwest Gateway: The Story of Seattle (hist, des)
Louise Bogan. Poems and New Poems (po, pub)
Gerald Warner Brace. Light on a Mountain (fic)
William Stanley Beaumont Braithwaite. The House under Arcturus
    (auto)
Myron Brinig. All of Their Lives (fic)
Louis Bromfield. Wild Is the River (fic)
Van Wyck Brooks. On Literature Today (e)
_____. The Opinions of Oliver Allston (e)
Pearl Sydenstricker Buck. Today and Forever (fic)
Kenneth Duva Burke. The Philosophy of Literary Form (e)
William Byrd II. The Secret Diary of William Byrd of Westover (nar,
    pub, ed)
James Mallahan Cain. Mildred Pierce (fic)
Erskine Preston Caldwell and Margaret Burke-White. Say! Is This the
    U.S.A.? (des, illus)
Janet Taylor Caldwell. The Earth Is the Lord's (fic)
_____ (Max Reiner). Time No Longer (fic)
Walter Stanley Campbell (Stanley Vestal). Short Grass Country (des)
Henry Seidel Canby. The Brandywine (hist)
Carl Lamson Carmer. Genesee Fever (fic)
Rachel Carson. Under the Sea Wind (e)
William Henry Chamberlain. The World's Iron Age (e)
Mary Ellen Chase. Windswept (fic)
Stuart Chase. A Primer of Economics (e)
Jerome Chodorov and Joseph Fields. Junior Miss (dr)
Irvin Shrewsbury Cobb. Exit Laughing (auto)
Robert Peter Tristram Coffin. Thomas-Thomas-Avail-Thomas (fic)
James Bryant Conant. Speaking As a Private Citizen (e)
Edwin Corle. Desert Country (nar, des)
Edward Dahlberg. Do These Bones Live (e)
Nathalia Crane. Death of Poetry (po)
Jonathan Worth Daniels. Tar Heels (des)
Josephus Daniels. Editor in Politics (auto)
David Cornel DeJong. Day of the Trumpet (fic)
Margaretta Wade Campbell Deland. Golden Yesterdays (auto)

August William Derlith. <u>Evening in Spring</u> (fic)
John Roderigo Dos Passos. <u>The Ground We Stand On</u> (biog)
Theodore Herbert Albert Dreiser. <u>America Is Worth Saving</u> (e)
Paul Hamilton Engle. <u>Always the Land</u> (fic)
_____. <u>West of Midnight</u> (po)
James Thomas Farrell. <u>Ellen Rogers</u> (fic)
Howard Melvin Fast. <u>The Last Frontier</u> (fic)
Edna Ferber. <u>Saratoga Trunk</u> (fic)
Irving Fineman. <u>Jacob</u> (fic)
Vardis Alvero Fisher. <u>City of Illusion</u> (fic)
Francis Scott Key Fitzgerald. <u>The Last Tycoon</u> (fic)
Martin Archer Flavin. <u>Corporal Cat</u> (fic)
John Gould Fletcher. <u>South Star</u> (po)
Waldo David Frank. <u>Summer Never Ends</u> (fic)
Ellen Glasgow. <u>In This Our Life</u> (fic)
Caroline Gordon. <u>Green Centuries</u> (fic)
Julian Green. <u>Then Shall the Dust Return</u> (fic)
Paul Eliot Green. <u>The Highland Call</u> (dr)
Walter Edwin Havighurst. <u>No Homeward Course</u> (fic)
Ben Hecht. <u>1001 Afternoons in New York</u> (fic)
Lillian Hellman. <u>Watch on the Rhine</u> (dr)
Josephine Frey Herbst. <u>Satan's Sergeants</u> (fic)
Maurice Gerschon Hindus. <u>To Sing with the Angels</u> (fic)
John Robinson Jeffers. <u>Be Angry at the Sun</u> (po)
Arthur Kober. <u>My Dear Bella</u> (fic)
Christopher LaFarge. <u>Poems and Portraits</u> (pub)
Janet Lewis. <u>The Wife of Martin Guerre</u> (fic)
Joseph Crosby Lincoln and Freeman Lincoln. <u>The New Hope</u> (fic)
Andrew Nelson Lytle. <u>At the Moon's Inn</u> (fic)
Helen MacInnes. <u>Above Suspicion</u> (fic)
Archibald MacLeish. <u>The American Cause</u> (e)
_____. <u>A Time To Speak</u> (e)
Percy Marks. <u>Two Autumns</u> (fic)
John Phillips Marquand. <u>H.M. Pulham, Esq.</u> (fic)
Edgar Lee Masters. <u>Illinois Poems</u> (po)
Francis Otto Matthiessen. <u>The American Renaissance</u> (e)
Carson Smith McCullers. <u>Reflections on a Golden Eye</u> (fic)
William Morley Punshon McFee. <u>Spenlove in Arcady</u> (fic)
Peter McNab, Jr. (Harry Brown). <u>The End of a Decade</u> (po)
_____. <u>The Poem of Bunker Hill</u> (po)
Henry Louis Mencken. <u>Newspaper Days, 1899-1906</u> (nar)
Josephine Miles. <u>Poems on Several Occasions</u> (po)
Edna St. Vincent Millay. <u>Collected Sonnets</u> (po)
Henry Miller. <u>The Colussus of Maroussi</u> (nar)
_____. <u>The Wisdom of the Heart</u> (fic, e)
Marianne Craig Moore. <u>What Are Years?</u> (po)
Vladimir Nabokov. <u>The Real Life of Sebastian Knight</u> (fic)
Robert Gruntal Nathan. <u>Tapiola's Brave Regiment</u> (fic)
_____. <u>They Went On Together</u> (fic)
John Gneisenau Neihardt. <u>The Song of Jed Smith</u> (po)
Charles Bernard Nordhoff and James Norman Hall. <u>Botany Bay</u> (fic)
Clifford Odets. <u>Clash by Night</u> (dr)
Kenneth Patchen. <u>The Journal of Albion Moonlight</u> (nar, fic)
William Gilbert Patten (Burt L. Standish). <u>Mr. Frank Merriwell</u> (fic)
Frederic Prokosch. <u>The Skies of Europe</u> (fic)
John Crowe Ransom. <u>The New Criticism</u> (e)

Elmer Reizenstein (Elmer Rice). Flight to the West (dr)
Lynn Riggs. The Cream in the Well (dr)
Elizabeth Madox Roberts. Not by Strange Gods (fic)
Selden Rodman. The Airmen (po)
Theodore Roethke. Open House (po)
Lew Sarett. Collected Poems (pub)
William Saroyan. Across the Board on Tomorrow Morning (dr)
_____. The Beautiful People (dr)
_____. Fables (fic)
_____. Love's Old Sweet Song (dr)
_____. Sweeney in the Trees (dr)
Mark Schorer. The Hermit Place (fic)
Budd Wilson Schulberg. What Makes Sammy Run? (fic)
Delmore Schwartz. Shenandoah (po, dr)
Evelyn Scott. The Shadow of the Hawk (fic)
Winfield Townley Scott. Wind of the Clock (po)
Anya Seton. My Theodosia (fic)
Irwin Shaw. Welcome to the City (fic)
James Vincent Sheean. Bird of the Wilderness (fic)
William Lawrence Shirer. Berlin Diary (nar)
Upton Beall Sinclair. Between Two Worlds (fic)
Chard Powers Smith. Ladies' Day (fic)
Lloyd Logan Pearsall Smith. Milton and His Modern Critics (e)
Wallace Earle Stegner. Fire and Ice (fic)
Gertrude Stein. Ida (fic)
John Ernst Steinbeck. The Forgotten Village (dr)
_____, and Edward F. Ricketts. Sea of Cortez (nar)
Philip Duffield Stong. Miss Edeson (fic)
Jesse Hilton Stuart. Men of the Mountains (fic)
Newton Booth Tarkington. The Heritage of Hatcher Ide (fic)
John Orley Allen Tate. Reason in Madness (e)
Frederic Ridgely Torrence. Poems (pub)
Mark Albert Van Doren. The Mayfield Deer (po)
Carl Clinton Van Doren. Secret History of the American Revolution
    (hist)
Jerome Weidman. I'll Never Go There Any More (fic)
Eudora Welty. A Curtain of Green (fic)
Elwyn Brooks White and Katharine White. A Subtreasury of American
    Humor (ed)
William Lindsay White. Journey for Margaret (fic)
William Carlos Williams. The Broken Span (po)
Edmund Wilson. The Boys in the Back Room (e)
_____. The Wound and the Bow (e)
Frances Winwar. American Giant: Walt Whitman and His Times (biog)
Thomas Clayton Wolfe. The Hills Beyond (fic, pub)
Richard Nathaniel Wright. 12 Million Black Voices (hist)
Marya Zaturenska. The Listening Landscape (po)
Leane Zugsmith. Hard Times with Easy Payments (fic)

1942

BIRTHS

John Michael Crichton
John Winslow Irving

Erica Mann Jong
Garrison Keillor
William Matthews
Sharon Olds
John W. Saul III
David Smith

DEATHS

Franz Boas
Rachel Lyman Field
Alice Caldwell Hegan Rice
Edwin Milton Royle
Albert Payson Terhune
Edward Waterman Townsend

EVENTS

Carl and Lily Pforzheimer Foundation (est)
The Stars and Stripes, 2nd series (per)
Yank, to 1945 (per)

LITERATURE

Louis Adamic. What's Your Name? (e, hist)
Samuel Hopkins Adams. The Harvey Girls (fic)
Herbert Sebastian Agar. A Time for Greatness (e)
Conrad Potter Aiken. Brownstone Eclogues (po)
Bess Streeter Aldrich. Lieutenant's Lady (fic)
Nelson Algren. Never Come Morning (fic)
Maxwell Anderson. The Eve of St. Mark (po, dr)
Sherwood Anderson. Memoirs (pub)
Gertrude Franklin Atherton. Horn of Life (fic)
Margaret Culkin Banning. Women for Defense (e)
Harry Elmer Barnes. Social Institutions in an Era of World Upheaval
    (e)
Philip Barry. Without Love (dr)
Joseph Hamilton Basso. Sun in Capricorn (fic)
Charles Austin Beard and May Ritter Beard. The American Spirit (e)
Charles William Beebe. Book of Bays (des)
Samuel Nathaniel Behrman. The Pirate (dr)
Ludwig Bemelmans. I Love You, I Love You, I Love You (fic)
Samuel Flagg Bemis. Diplomatic History of the United States, rev ed
    (hist)
Robert Charles Benchley. Inside Benchley (nar)
Sara Mahala Redway Smith Benson. Meet Me in St. Louis (fic)
John Berryman. Poems (po, pub)
Archie Binns. Roaring Land (des)
Morris Gilber Bishop (W. Bolingbroke Johnson). The Widening Stain
    (fic)
Richard Palmer Blackmur. Second World (po)
Maxwell Bodenheim. Lights in the Valley (po)
Kay Boyle. Primer for Combat (fic)
Louis Dembitz Brandeis. On Zionism (e, pub)
Myron Brinig. The Family Way (fic)
John Malcolm Brinnin. The Garden Is Political (po)

————————————. The Lincoln Lyrics (po)
Louis Bromfield. Mrs. Parkington (fic)
John Mason Brown. Accustomed As I Am (e)
Maxwell Struthers Burt. Along These Streets (fic)
Pearl Sydenstricker Buck. Dragon Seed (fic)
William Byrd II. Another Secret Diary of William Byrd of Westover
    (nar, pub)
James Branch Cabell. First Gentleman of America (fic)
James Mallahan Cain. Love's Lovely Counterfeit (fic)
Erskine Preston Caldwell. All Night Long (fic)
————————————. All Out on the Road to Smolensk (nar)
Walter Stanley Campbell (Stanley Vestal). Bigfoot Wallace (biog)
Gladys Hasty Carroll. Head of the Line (fic)
Marquis William Childs. This Is Your War (e)
Robert Peter Tristram Coffin. Book of Uncles (e)
————————————. The Substance That Is Poetry (e)
————————————. There Will Be Bread and Love (po)
Thomas Bertram Costain. For My Great Folly (fic)
John Cournos. Book of Prophecy, from the Egyptians to Hitler (ed)
Norman Cousins. The Democratic Chance (e)
Malcolm Cowley. A Dry Season (po)
James Gould Cozzens. The Just and the Unjust (fic)
James Vincent Cunningham. The Helmsman (po)
Clyde Brion Davis. Follow the Leader (fic)
Harold Lenoir Davis.Proud Riders (po)
David Cornel DeJong. Benefit Street (fic)
August William Derlith. Rind of Earth (po)
————————————. Sweet Genevieve (fic)
————————————. The Wisconsin: River of a Thousand Isles
    (des)
Babette Deutsch. Rogue's Legacy (fic)
Bernard Augustine DeVoto. Mark Twain at Work (e)
Lloyd Cassel Douglas. The Robe (fic)
Richard Ghormley Eberhart. Song and Idea (po)
Walter Dumaux Edmonds. Tom Whipple (fic)
————————————. Young Ames (fic)
James Thomas Farrell. $1000 a Week (fic)
Howard Melvin Fast. The Unvanquished (fic)
William Harrison Faulkner. Go Down, Moses (fic)
Kenneth Fearing. Clark Gifford's Body (fic)
Arthur Davison Ficke. Tumultuous Shore (po)
Rachel Lyman Field. And Now Tomorrow (fic)
Esther Forbes. Paul Revere and the World He Lived In (biog, hist)
Louis Fraina (Lewis Corey). Unfinished Task: Economic Reconstruction
    for Democracy (e)
Douglas Southall Freeman. Lee's Lieutenants, a Study in Command, 3
    vols, to 1944 (hist)
Robert Lee Frost. A Witness Tree (po)
Susan Glaspell. Norma Ashe (fic)
Herbert Sherman Gorman. Brave General (fic)
Anne Green. The Lady in the Mask (fic)
Albert Joseph Guerard. Robert Bridges (e)
Francis Hackett. That Nice Young Couple (fic)
Nancy Hale. The Prodigal Women (fic)
Albert Halper. Little People (fic)
Ernest Miller Hemingway. Men at War (ed)

John Richard Hersey. Men on Bataan (fic)
Granville Hicks. Only One Storm (fic)
Robert Silliman Hillyer. My Heart for Hostage (fic)
Paul Horgan. The Common Heart (fic)
_____. Yours, A. Lincoln (dr)
James Langston Hughes. Shakespeare in Harlem (po)
_____. The Sun Do Move (dr)
Fannie Hurst. Lonely Parade (fic)
Zora Neale Hurston. Dust Tracks on a Road (auto)
Randall Jarrell. Blood for a Stranger (po)
MacKinlay Kantor. Gentle Annie (fic)
_____. Happy Land (fic)
Alfred Kazin. On Native Grounds (e)
Manuel Komroff. All in Our Day (fic)
_____. In the Years of Our Lord (fic)
Louis Kronenberger. Kings and Desperate Men (hist)
Oliver Hazard Perry LaFarge. The Copper Pot (fic)
Josephine Lawrence. There Is Today (fic)
Ludwig Lewisohn. Renegade (fic)
Helen MacInnes. Assignment in Brittany (fic)
Percy Marks. Full Flood (fic)
Edgar Lee Masters. The Sangamon (des)
Mary Therese McCarthy. The Company She Keeps (fic)
Henry Louis Mencken. A New Dictionary of Quotations, on Historical
   Principles (ref)
Edna St. Vincent Millay. The Murder of Lidice (po)
Samuel Eliot Morison. Admiral of the Ocean Sea (biog)
Christopher Darlington Morley. Thorofare (fic)
Wright Morris. My Uncle Dudley (fic)
Robert Gruntal Nathan. The Sea-Gull Cry (fic)
Charles Bernard Nordhoff and James Norman Hall. Men without Country
   (fic)
Kenneth Patchen. The Teeth of the Lion (po)
Elliot Harold Paul. The Last Time I Saw Paris (nar)
Marjorie Kinnan Rawlings. Cross Creek (nar)
Conrad Michael Richter. Tacey Cromwell (fic)
Selden Rodman. The Revolutionists (po, dr)
Muriel Rukeyser. Wake Island (po)
Carl August Sandburg. Storm over the Land (hist, biog)
William Saroyan. Razzle-Dazzle (dr)
Gladys Schmitt. The Gates of Aulis (fic)
Karl Jay Shapiro. Person, Place, and Thing (po)
_____. The Place of Love (po)
Upton Beall Sinclair. Dragon's Teeth (fic)
Israel Joshua Singer. In Die Berg (fic)
Elsie Singmaster. A High Wind Rising (fic)
Cornelia Otis Skinner and Emily Kimbrough. Our Hearts Were Young and
   Gay (nar)
Virginia Sorensen. A Little Lower Than the Angels (fic)
John   Ernst Steinbeck. Bombs Away: The Story of a Bomber Team (nar)
_____. The Moon Is Down (fic)
Wallace Stevens. Notes toward a Supreme Fiction (po)
_____. Parts of a World (po)
Grace Zaring Stone (Ethel Vance). Reprisal (fic)
Philip Duffield Stong. Iron Mountain (fic)
_____. One Destiny (fic)

Ruth Suckow. New Hope (fic)
Genevieve Taggard. Long View (po)
James Grover Thurber. My World--and Welcome to It (e, nar, fic)
_____. The Secret Life of Walter Mitty (fic)
Dan Totheroh. Deep Valley (fic)
Jim Tully. Biddy Brogan's Boy (fic)
Mark Albert Van Doren. Liberal Education (e)
_____. Our Lady Peace, and Other War Poems (po)
_____. Private Reader (e)
Robert Penn Warren. Eleven Poems on the Same Theme (po)
Eudora Welty. The Robber Bridegroom (fic)
Elwyn Brooks White. One Man's Meat (e)
Stewart Edward White. Stampede (fic)
William Lindsay White. They Were Expendable (fic)
Thornton Niven Wilder. The Skin of Our Teeth (dr)
Ben Ames Williams. Time of Peace (fic)
Edmund Wilson. Note-Books of Night (po)
Thomas Clayton Wolfe. Gentlemen of the Press (dr, pub)
Austin Tappan Wright. Islandia (fic, pub)

1943

BIRTHS

Tess Gallagher
Nikki Giovanni
Louise Gluck
James Alan McPherson
Steven Millhauser
Sandra McPherson
James Vincent Tate

Samuel Shepard Rogers, Jr. (Sam Shepard)

DEATHS

Charles McLean Andrews
Stephen Vincent Benet
Charles Caldwell Dobie
Arthur Guiterman
Frances Noyes Hart
William Lyon Phelps
Frederic Jesup Stimson

EVENTS

Institute of Early American History and Culture (est)

LITERATURE

Louis Adamic. My Native Land (e, hist)
James Truslow Adams. The American: The Making of a New Man (hist)
_____. Atlas of American History (ref, ed)
William Hervey Allen. The Forest and the Fort (fic)
Benjamin Appel. The Dark Stain (fic)
Sholem Asch. The Apostle (fic)
Joseph Auslander. The Unconquerables (po)

Leonard Bacon. Day of Fire (po)
Dorothy Baker. Trio (fic)
Faith Baldwin. He Married a Doctor (fic)
Margaret Culkin Banning. Letters from England, 1942 (nar)
Jacques Barzun. Romanticism and the Modern Age (e)
Joseph Hamilton Basso. Mainstream (e, hist, bio)
Carleton Beals. Dawn over the Amazon (fic)
_____. Rio Grande to Cape Horn (e)
Charles Austin Beard. The Republic (e)
Ludwig Bemelmans. Now I Lay Me Down To Sleep (fic)
Samuel Flagg Bemis. Latin American Policy of the United States (hist)
Robert Charles Benchley. Benchley Beside Himself (nar)
John Barry Benefield. Eddie and the Archangel Mike (fic)
Stephen Vincent Benet. Western Star (po)
Sara Mahala Redway Smith Benson. Women and Children First (fic)
Jane Bowles. Two Serious Ladies (fic)
Kay Boyle. Avalanche (fic)
Myron Brinig. The Gambler Takes a Wife (fic)
Cleanth Brooks and Robert Penn Warren. Understanding Fiction (e, ed)
John Mason Brown. To All Hands (nar)
Pearl Sydenstricker Buck. The Promise (fic)
William Riley Burnett. Nobody Lives Forever (fic)
James Branch Cabell and A.J. Hanna. The St. Johns (hist)
Janet Taylor Caldwell. The Arm and the Darkness (fic)
William Edward March Cambpell (William March). The Looking Glass
    (fic)
Henry Seidel Canby. Whitman (biog)
Gladys Hasty Carroll. Dunnybrook (fic)
William Henry Chamberlain. The Russian Enigma (e)
Raymond Chandler. The Lady in the Lake (fic)
Stuart Chase. Where's the Money Coming From? (e)
John Cheever. The Way Some People Live (fic)
Edward Chodorov. Those Endearing Young Charms (dr)
Robert Myron Coates. All the Year Round (fic)
Robert Peter Tristram Coffin. Primer for America (po)
Thomas Bertram Costain. Ride with Me (fic)
John Cournos. Treasury of Russian Life and Humor (misc, ed)
Wilbur Lucius Cross. Connecticut Yankee (auto)
Merle Eugene Curti. The Growth of American Thought (hist)
Marcia Davenport. The Valley of Decision (fic)
David Cornel DeJong. Across the Board (po)
August William Derlith. Shadow of Night (fic)
Bernard Augustine DeVoto. The Year of Decision: 1846 (hist)
Peter DeVries. The Handsome Heart (fic)
John Roderigo Dos Passos. Number One (fic)
Thomas Stearns Eliot. Four Quartets (po)
William Everson. War Elegies (po)
James Thomas Farrell. My Days of Anger (fic)
Howard Melvin Fast. Citizen Tom Paine (fic)
Kenneth Fearing. Afternoon of a Pawnbroker (po)
Vardis Alvero Fisher. Darkness and the Deep (fic)
_____. The Mothers: An American Saga of Courage (fic)
Robert Stuart Fitzgerald. A Wreath for the Sea (po)
Martin Archer Flavin. Journey in the Dark (fic)
Esther Forbes. Johnny Tremaine (fic)
Waldo David Frank. South American Journey (trav)

Joseph Freeman. Never Call Retreat (fic)
Ketti Frings. Mr. Sycamore (dr)
Ellen Glasgow. A Certain Measure (e)
Anne Green. Just before Dawn (fic)
Paul Eliot Green. The Hawthorn Tree (e)
Arthur Guiterman. Brave Laughter (po)
Francis Hackett. The Senator's Last Night (fic)
Albert Halper. Only an Inch from Glory (fic)
Moss Hart. Winged Victory (dr)
Hiram Haydn. By Nature Free (fic)
John Richard Hersey. Into the Valley (fic)
Robert Silliman Hillyer. Collected Verse (po, pub)
Laura Zametkin Hobson. The Trespassers (fic)
James Langston Hughes. Jim Crow's Last Stand (po)
Sidney Kingsley and Madge Evans. The Patriots (dr)
Harry Sinclair Lewis. Gideon Planish (fic)
Janet Lewis. Against a Darkening Sky (fic)
Joseph Crosby Lincoln. Bradshaws of Harness (fic)
Archibald MacLeish. Colloquy for the States (po)
_____. A Time To Act (e)
Percy Marks. Knave of Diamonds (fic)
John Phillips Marquand. So Little Time (fic)
David Thompson Watson McCord. On Occasion (po)
Ruth McKenney. Jake Home (fic)
Peter McNab, Jr. (Harry Brown). The Violent (po)
Henry Louis Mencken. Heathen Days, 1890-1936 (nar)
Edna St. Vincent Millay. Collected Lyrics (po)
Robert Gruntal Nathan. But Gently Day (fic)
Martha Ostenso. O River, Remember! (fic)
Kenneth Patchen. Cloth of the Tempest (po)
Sidney Joseph Perelman. The Dream Department (sat, nar)
                       and Ogden Nash. One Touch of Venus (dr)
Frederick Prokosch. The Conspirators (fic)
Ayn Rand. The Fountainhead (fic)
Elmer Reizenstein (Elmer Rice). A New Life (dr)
Conrad Michael Richter. The Free Man (fic)
Carl August Sandburg. Home Front Memo (e, po)
William Saroyan. The Human Comedy (fic)
Delmore Schwartz. Genesis (fic, po)
Allen Seager. Equinox (fic)
Upton Beall Sinclair. Wide Is the Gate (fic)
Israel Joshua Singer. The Family Carnovsky (fic)
Betty Wehner Smith. A Tree Grows in Brooklyn (fic)
Wallace Earle Stegner. The Big Rock Candy Mountain (fic)
Jesse Hilton Stuart. Taps for Private Tussie (fic)
Newton Booth Tarkington. Kate Fennigate (fic)
Henry David Thoreau. Collected Poems (pub)
James Grover Thurber. Many Moons (juv)
Arthur Cheney Train. The Autobiography of Ephraim Tutt (fic)
Lionel Trilling. E.M. Forster (e)
Carl Clinton Van Doren. Mutiny in January (hist)
John William Van Druten. The Voice of the Turtle (dr)
Hendrik Willem Van Loon. Thomas Jefferson (biog)
Robert Penn Warren. At Heaven's Gate (fic)
Eudora Welty. The Wide Net (fic)
Edmund Wilson. The Shock of Recognition (e, ed)

Arthur Yvor Winters. The Anatomy of Nonsense (e)
_____. The Giant Weapon (po)
Ira Wolfert. Tucker's People (fic)
Elinor Hoyt Wylie. Last Poems (pub)

1944

BIRTHS

Lisa Alther
Rita Mae Brown
Janet Ann Dailey
Robert Morgan
Marilynne Robinson
Alice Walker
Sherley Anne Williams

DEATHS

George Ade
John Peale Bishop
James Boyd
Irvin Shrewsbury Cobb
Katharine Fullerton Gerould
Hutchins Hapgood
Carl Sadakichi Hartmann
William Ellery Leonard
Joseph Crosby Lincoln
Israel Joshua Singer
Ida Minerva Tarbell
Eunice Tietjens
Hendrik Willem Van Loon
William Allen White
Charles Erskine Scott Wood
Harold Bell Wright

LITERATURE

Franklin Pierce Adams. Nods and Becks (e, nar, po)
James Truslow Adams. Album of American History, to 1961 (ref, ed)
_____. Frontiers of American Culture (e)
Samuel Hopkins Adams. Canal Town (fic)
Mortimore Jerome Adler. How To Think about War and Peace (e)
Conrad Potter Aiken. The Soldier (po)
William Hervey Allen. Bedford Village (fic)
Maxwell Anderson. Storm Operation (dr)
Joseph Warren Beach. Beginning with Plato (po)
_____. A Romantic View of Poetry (e)
Charles Austin Beard and Mary Ritter Beard. Basic History of the
    United States (hist)
Carl Lotus Becker. Cornell University (hist)
_____. How New Will the Better World Be? (e)
Samuel Nathaniel Behrman. Jacobowsky and the Colonel (dr)
Saul Bellow. The Dangling Man (fic)
Stephen Vincent Benet. History (hist, e, pub)

William Rose Benet. Day of Deliverance (po)
Archie Binns. Timber Beast (fic)
Stephen Bonsal. Unfinished Business (nar)
James Boyd. Eighteen Poems (po, pub)
Catherine Sober Drinker Bowen. Yankee from Olympus (biog)
Kay Boyle. American Citizen (po)
Anna Hempsted Branch. Last Poems (po, pub)
Louis Bromfield. The World We Live In (fic)
Van Wyck Brooks. The World of Washington Irving (hist, biog)
John Mason Brown. Many a Watchful Night (nar)
Erskine Preston Caldwell. Tragic Ground (fic)
Janet Taylor Caldwell. The Final Hour (fic)
William Henry Chamberlain. The Ukraine: A Submerged Nation (e)
Mary Coyle Chase. Harvey (dr)
Mary Ellen Chase. The Bible and the Common Reader (hist, trans)
Marquis William Childs. The Cabin (nar)
Elizabeth Jane Coatsworth. Country Neighborhood (fic, nar)
Robert Peter Tristram Coffin. Mainstays of Maine (e)
Edward Estlin Cummings. Anthropos: The Future of Art (e)
_____. I x I (po)
Josephus Daniels. The Wilson Era, 2 vols, to 1946 (auto, hist)
Clyde Brion Davis. The Rebellion of Leo McGuire (fic)
David Cornel DeJong. With a Dutch Accent (auto)
August William Derleth. And You, Thoreau (po)
Babette Deutsch. Take Them, Stranger (po)
Bernard Augustine DeVoto. The Literary Fallacy (e)
Hilda Doolittle. The Walls Do Not Fall (po)
John Roderigo Dos Passos. State of the Nation (trav)
William Everson. Waldport Poems (po)
James Thomas Farrell. To Whom It May Concern (fic)
Howard Melvin Fast. Freedom Road (fic)
Frederick Feikema (Frederick Manfred/Feike Feikema). The Golden
    Bowl (fic)
Vardis Alvero Fisher. Golden Rooms (fic)
Waldo David Frank. The Jew in Our Day (e)
Ketti Frings. God's Front Porch (fic)
Caroline Gordon. The Women on the Porch (fic)
Horace Victor Gregory. The Shield of Achilles (e)
Albert Joseph Guerard. The Hunted (fic)
James Norman Hall. Lost Island (fic)
Alfred Hayes. The Big Time (po)
Ben Hecht. A Guide for the Bedeviled (e)
Lillian Hellman. The Searching Wind (dr)
John Richard Hersey. A Bell for Adono (fic)
Granville Hicks. Behold Trouble (fic)
James Langston Hughes. Lament for Dark Peoples, and Other Poems (po)
Fannie Hurst. Hallelujah (fic)
Charles Reginald Jackson. The Lost Weekend (fic)
MacKinlay Kantor. Author's Choice (fic)
Joseph Wood Krutch. Samuel Johnson (biog)
Christopher LaFarge. East by Southwest (fic, po)
Ludwig Lewisohn. Breathe upon These (fic)
Victoria Lincoln. Grandmother and the Comet (fic)
Anne Morrow Lindbergh. Steep Ascent (fic)
Robert Traill Spence Lowell, Jr. Land of Unlikeness (po)
Archibald MacLeish. The American Story (fic)

Albert Maltz. The Cross and the Arrow (fic)
Percy Marks. Shade of Sycamore (fic)
William Morley Punshon McFee. Ship to Shore (fic)
Peter McNab, Jr. (Harry Brown). A Walk in the Sun (fic)
William Morris Meredith. Love Letter from an Impossible Land (po)
Kenneth Millar. The Dark Tunnel (fic)
Arthur Miller. The Man Who Had All the Luck (dr)
_____. Situation Normal (dr)
Caroline Miller. Lebanon (fic)
Henry Miller. The Air-Conditioned Nightmare (nar, e)
_____. Sunday after the War (nar, fic)
Marianne Craig Moore. Nevertheless (po)
Christopher Darlington Morley. The Middle Kingdom (po)
Theodore Morrison. The Devious Way (po)
Robert Gruntal Nathan. Darkening Meadows (po)
_____. A Morning in Iowa (po)
Anaïs Nin. Under a Glass Bell (fic)
Charles Gilman Norris. Flint (fic)
Joseph Stanley Pennell. The History of Rome Hanks (fic)
Katherine Anne Porter. The Leaning Tower (fic)
Kenneth Rexroth. The Phoenix and the Tortoise (po)
Muriel Rukeyser. Beast in View (po)
Alfred Damon Runyon. Runyon a' la Carte (fic)
William Saroyan. Dear Baby (fic)
_____. Get Away, Old Man (dr)
Anya Seton. Dragonwyck (fic)
Karl Jay Shapiro. V-Letter and Other Poems (po)
Irwin Shaw. The Assassin (dr)
_____. Sons and Soldiers (dr)
Upton Beall Sinclair. Presidential Agent (fic)
Lillian Eugenia Smith. Strange Fruit (fic)
Jean Stafford. Boston Adventure (fic)
Irving Stone. Immortal Wife (fic)
Rex Todhunter Stout. Not Quite Dead Enough (fic)
Jesse Hilton Stuart. Album of Destiny (po)
_____. Mongrel Mettle (fic)
John Orley Allen Tate. Winter Sea (po)
James Grover Thurber. The Great Quillow (juv)
Melvin Beaunorus Tolson. Rendezvous with America (po)
Mark Albert Van Doren. The Seven Sleepers, and Other Poems (po)
John William Van Druten. I Remember Mama (dr)
Harold Vinal. The Compass Eye (po)
Robert Penn Warren. Selected Poems, 1923-1943 (pub)
Elwyn Brooks White. One Man's Meat, rev ed (e)
Thomas Lanier (Tennessee) Williams. The Glass Menagerie (dr)
William Carlos Williams. The Wedge (po)
William E. Woodward. The Way Our People Lived (hist)
Marya Zaturenska. The Golden Mirror (po)

1945

BIRTHS

Annie Dillard
Michael Cristofer

Norman Dubie
Whitley Strieber

DEATHS

Carl Lotus Becker
Robert Charles Benchley
Benjamin DeCasseres
Margaretta Wade Campbell Deland
Theodore Herman Albert Dreiser
Arthur Davison Ficke
Ellen Glasgow
Hatcher Hughes
Charles Gilman Norris
William Gilbert Patten (Burt L. Standish)
Emery Bemsley Pottle (Gilbert Emery)
Amelie Rives
Arthur Cheney Train
Richard Walton Tully

EVENTS

Commentary (per, f)
Melville Society (f)
Harry S. Truman, 33rd President of the United States, to 1953
Woodrow Wilson National Fellowship Foundation (f)

LITERATURE

Louis Adamic. A Nation of Nations (e)
James Truslow Adams. Big Business in a Democracy (e)
Samuel Hopkins Adams. Alexander Woolcott: His Life and His World
    (biog)
Gertrude Franklin Atherton. Golden Gate Country (hist)
Wystan Hugh Auden. For the Time Being (po)
Margaret Frances Bacon. Starting from Scratch (po)
Ray Stannard Baker. American Chronicle (auto)
Jacques Barzun. Teacher in America (e)
Walter Jackson Bate. The Stylistic Development of Keats (e)
Charles Austin Beard. The Economic Basis of Politics, rev ed (e)
Carl Lotus Becker. Freedom and Responsibility in the American Way of
    Life (e)
Samuel Nathaniel Behrman. Dunnigan's Daughter (dr)
Franz Boas. Race and Democratic Society (e, pub)
Arna Wendell Bontemps and Jack Conroy. They Seek a City (e)
Claude Gernade Bowers. Young Jefferson. 1743-1789 (biog)
Myron Brinig. You and I (fic)
John Malcolm Brinnin. No Arch, No Triumph (po)
Louis Bromfield. Bitter Lotus (fic)
_____. Pleasant Valley (nar)
Gwendolyn Brooks. A Street in Bronzeville (po)
Pearl Sydenstricker Buck. Portrait of a Marriage (fic)
Kenneth Duva Burke. A Grammar of Motives (e)
William Riley Burnett. Tomorrow's Another Day (fic)
Maxwell Struthers Burt. Philadelphia, Holy Experiment (hist)
Walter Stanley Campbell (Stanley Vestal). The Missouri (hist)

William Edward March Campbell (William March). Trial Balance (fic)
Henry Seidel Canby. Family History (biog, auto)
Mary Coyle Chase. The Next Half Hour (dr)
Stuart Chase. Men at Work (e)
Walter Van Tilburg Clark. The City of Trembling Leaves (fic)
Robert Peter Tristram Coffin. Poems for a Son with Wings (po)
Thomas Bertram Costain. The Black Rose (fic)
Russel Crouse and Howard Lindsay. State of the Union (dr)
David Cornel DeJong. Somewhat Angels (fic)
August William Derleth. The Shield of the Valiant (fic)
Emily Elizabeth Dickinson. Bolts of Melody (po, pub)
Hilda Doolittle. Tribute to Angels (po)
John Roderigo Dos Passos. First Encounter (fic)
Paul Hamilton Engle. American Child (po)
James Thomas Farrell. The League of Frightened Philistines (e)
Frederick Feikema (Frederick Manfred/Feike Feike Feikema). Boy Al-
    mighty (fic)
Edna Ferber. Great Son (fic)
Harvey Fergusson. Home in the West (auto)
Francis Scott Key Fitzgerald. The Crack-Up (e, pub)
Robert Lee Frost. A Masque of Reason (po, dr)
Susan Glaspell. Judd Rankin's Daughter (fic)
John Patrick Goggan (John Patrick). The Hasty Heart (dr)
Caroline Gordon. The Forest of the South (fic)
Herbert Sherman Gorman. The Wine of San Lorenzo (fic)
Albert Joseph Guerard. Maquisard (fic)
Elizabeth Hardwick. The Ghostly Lover (fic)
Hiram Haydn. Manhattan Furlough (fic)
Ben Hecht. Collected Stories (pub)
Chester Bomar Himes. If He Hollers, Let Him Go (fic)
Randall Jarrell. Little Friend, Little Friend (po)
Alfred Kreymborg. Selected Poems (pub)
Christopher LaFarge. Mesa Verde (dr)
_____. The Wilsons (fic)
Arthur Laurents. Home of the Brave (dr)
William Ellery Leonard. A Man against Time, an Heroic Dream (po, pub)
Harry Sinclair Lewis. Cass Timberlane (fic)
William Maxwell. The Folded Leaf (fic)
Peter McNab, Jr. (Harry Brown). Artie Greengroin, Pfc. (fic)
Arthur Miller. Focus (fic)
Wright Morris. The Man Who Was There (fic)
Ogden Nash. Many Long Years Ago (po)
Anais Nin. This Hunger (fic)
Charles Bernard Nordhoff and James Norman Hall. High Barbaree (fic)
John Henry O'Hara. Pipe Night (fic)
Anne Parrish. Poor Child (fic)
Kenneth Patchen. An Astonished Eye Looks Out of the Air (po)
_____. The Memoirs of a Shy Pornographer (fic)
Frederic Prokosch. Age of Thunder (fic)
John Crowe Ransom. Selected Poems (pub)
Elmer Reizenstein (Elmer Rice). Dream Girl (dr)
Kark Jay Shapiro. Essay on Rime (po)
Upton Beall Sinclair. Dragon Harvest (fic)
Lloyd Logan Pearsall Smith. All Trivia, rev (e)
Wilbur Daniel Steele. That Girl from Memphis (fic)
Gertrude Stein. Brewsie and Willie (nar)

_____. Wars I Have Seen (nar)
_____. Yes Is for a Very Young Man (dr)
John Ernst Steinbeck. Cannery Row (fic)
Newton Booth Tarkington. The Image of Josephine (fic)
James Grover Thurber. The Thurber Carnival (hum, misc)
_____. The White Deer (juv)
Arthur Cheney Train. Mr. Tutt Finds a Way (fic)
Louis Untermeyer. The Wonderful Adventures of Paul Bunyan (po)
Joseph Wechsberg. Looking for a Bluebird (nar)
Glenway Wescott. Apartment in Athens (fic)
Jessamyn West. The Friendly Persuasion (fic)
Elwyn Brooks White. Stuart Little (juv, fic)
Thomas Clayton Wolfe. Mannerhouse (dr, pub)
_____. A Stone, a Leaf, a Door (po, pub)
William E. Woodward. Tom Paine: America's Godfather (biog)
Richard Nathaniel Wright. Black Boy (auto)

1946

BIRTHS

Andrea Dworkin
Gretel Ehrlich
Patricia Hampl

DEATHS

Ray Stannard Baker
Ernest Boyd
Percy Holmes Boynton
John Colton
Countee Cullen
Thomas Dixon
Channing Pollock
Paul Rosenfeld
Alfred Damon Runyon
Charles Monroe Sheldon
Edward Brewster Sheldon
Lloyd Logan Pearsall Smith
Gertrude Stein
Newton Booth Tarkington
Stewart Edward White

EVENTS

Western Review, Lawrence, Kansas; Iowa City, Iowa, to 1959 (per)

LITERATURE

Accent Anthology (po, pub)
Louis Adamic. Dinner at the White House (nar)
Maxwell Anderson. Trunkline Cafe (dr)
Sholem Asch. East River (fic)
Charles Austin Beard. American Foreign Policy in the Making, 1932-
    1940 (e, hist)

Mary Ritter Beard. Woman As a Force in History (hist)
Ludwig Bemelmans. Hotel Bemelmans (fic)
Elizabeth Bishop. North and South (po)
Arna Wendell Bontemps and Countee Cullen. St. Louis Woman (dr)
Kay Boyle. A Frenchman Must Die (fic)
_____. Thirty Stories (fic)
Louis Bromfield. A Few Brass Tacks (e)
John Mason Brown. Seeing Things (e)
Pearl Sydenstricker Buck. Pavilion of Women (fic)
James Branch Cabell. There Were Two Pirates (fic)
James Mallahan Cain. Past All Dishonor (fic)
Erskine Preston Caldwell. House in the Uplands (fic)
Janet Taylor Caldwell. This Side of Innocence (fic)
Walter Stanley Campbell (Stanley Vestal). Jim Bridger (biog)
Stuart Chase. For This We Fought (e)
Eleanor Clark. The Bitter Box (fic)
Robert Myron Coates. Bitter Season (fic)
Edwin Corle. Listen, Bright Angel (fic)
Edward Estlin Cummings. Santa Claus (dr)
Merle Eugene Curti. The Roots of American Loyalty (hist)
Donald Grady Davidson. The Tennessee, 2 vols, to 1948 (hist)
Clyde Brion Davis. The Stars Incline (fic)
David Cornel DeJong. Snow-on-the-Mountain (fic)
Hilda Doolittle. Flowering of the Rod (po)
John Roderigo Dos Passos. Tour of Duty (trav)
Theodore Herman Albert Dreiser. The Bulwark (fic)
James Thomas Farrell. Bernard Clare (fic)
_____. When Boyhood Dreams Come True (fic)
Howard Melvin Fast. The American (fic)
Kenneth Fearing. The Big Clock (fic)
Thomas Hornsby Ferril. I Hate Thursdays (e, nar)
Vardis Alvero Fisher. Imitations of Eve (fic)
John Gould Fletcher. The Burning Mountain (po)
Waldo David Frank. Island in the Atlantic (fic)
Wolcott Gibbs. Season in the Sun (e)
Paul Eliot Green. Salvation on a String (fic)
Horace Victor Gregory and Marya Zaturenska. History of American Po-
     etry, 1900-1940 (hist)
Hermann Hagedorn. The Bomb That Fell on America (po)
Mark Harris. Trumpet to the World (fic)
Alfred Hayes. All Thy Conquests (fic)
Thomas Orlo Heggen. Mr. Roberts (fic)
Lillian Hellman. Another Part of the Forest (dr)
John Richard Hersey. Hiroshima (fic)
Charles Reginald Jackson. The Fall of Valor (fic)
John Robinson Jeffers. Medea (dr, trans)
Josephine Winslow Johnson. Wildwood (fic)
Garson Kanin. Born Yesterday (dr)
George Edward Kelly. The Fatal Weakness (dr)
Christopher LaFarge. The Sudden Guest (fic)
Philip Lamantia. Erotic Poems (po)
Josephine Lawrence. Double Wedding Ring (fic)
Denise Levertov. The Double Image (po)
Janet Lewis. The Earth-Bound (po)
_____. Good-Bye, Son (fic)
Robert Traill Spence Lowell, Jr. Lord Weary's Castle (po)

Robert James Collas Lowry. Casualty (fic)
John Phillips Marquand. B.F.'s Daughter (fic)
Carson Smith McCullers. The Member of the Wedding (fic)
Phyllis McGinley. Stones from a Glass House (po)
Peter McNab, Jr. (Harry Brown). A Sound of Hunting (dr)
Thomas Merton. A Man in the Divided Sea (po)
Josephine Miles. Local Measures (po)
_____. The Vocabulary of Poetry (e)
Howard Moss. The Wound and the Weather (po)
Anais Nin. Ladders to Fire (fic)
_____. Realism and Reality (e)
Eugene Gladstone O'Neill. The Iceman Cometh (dr)
Kenneth Patchen. Selected Poems (pub)
_____. Sleepers Awake (po)
Louis Paul. Breakdown (fic)
Sidney Joseph Perelman. Keep It Crisp (nar, sat)
Ann Petry. The Street (fic)
Frederick Prokosch. The Idols of the Cave (fic)
Solomon Rabinowitz (Sholom Aleichem). The Old Country (fic, pub)
Conrad Michael Richter. The Fields (fic)
Alfred Damon Runyon. In Our Town (fic)
_____. Short Takes (fic)
George Santayana. The Idea of Christ in the Gospels (e)
William Saroyan. The Adventures of Wesley Jackson (fic)
Eleanor May Sarton. The Bridge of Years (fic)
Gladys Schmitt. David the King (fic)
Mark Schorer. William Blake: The Politics of Vision (e)
Anya Seton. The Turquoise (fic)
Irwin Shaw. Act of Faith (fic)
Odell Shepard and Willard Odell Shepard. Holdfast Gaines (fic)
Upton Beall Sinclair. A World To Win (fic)
Virginia Sorensen. On This Star (fic)
Leonora Speyer. Slow Wall, rev (po)
George Rippey Stewart. Man: An Autobiography (fic)
Grace Zaring Stone (Ethel Vance). Winter Meeting (fic)
Jesse Hilton Stewart. Foretaste of Glory (fic)
_____. Tales from the Plum Grove Hills (fic)
Genevieve Taggard. Slow Music (po)
Mark Albert Van Doren. The Country Year (po)
_____. The Noble Voice (e)
_____. John Dryden: A Study of His Poetry (e)
Gore Vidal. Williwaw (fic)
Robert Penn Warren. All the King's Men (fic)
Joseph Wechsberg. Homecoming (nar)
Jerome Weidman. Too Early To Tell (fic)
Eudora Welty. Delta Wedding (fic)
Elwyn Brooks White. The Wild Flag (e)
Edward Reed Whittemore II. Heroes and Heroines (po)
Thomas Lanier (Tennessee) Williams. 27 Wagons Full of Cotton (dr)
William Carlos Williams. Paterson, 5 vols, to 1958 (po)
Edmund Wilson. Memoirs of Hecate County (fic)
Arthur Yvor Winters. Edwin Arlington Robinson (e)
Frank Garvin Yerby. The Foxes of Harrow (fic)
Marya Zaturenska and Horace Victor Gregory. A History of American
   Poetry, 1900-1940 (hist)

1947

BIRTHS

    Florence Anthony (Ai)
    Ann Beattie
    Mark Helprin
    David Alan Mamet
    Gregory Orr

DEATHS

    Nicholas Murray Butler
    Willa Sibert Cather
    Winston Churchill
    Morris Raphael Cohen
    Richard LeGallienne
    Meredith Nicholson
    Charles Bernard Nordhoff
    Jim Tully

EVENTS

    Bibliographical Society of the University of Virginia (f)

LITERATURE

    Conrad Potter Aiken. The Kid (po)
    Nelson Algren. The Neon Wilderness (fic)
    Maxwell Anderson. Joan of Lorraine (dr)
    Benjamin Appel. But Not Yet Slain (fic)
    Louis Stanton Auchincloss. The Indifferent Children (fic)
    Margaret Culkin Banning. Clever Sister (fic)
    Harry Elmer Barnes. Historical Sociology (e, hist)
    Saul Bellow. The Victim (fic)
    Ludwig Bemelmans. Dirty Eddie (fic)
    Konrad Bercovici. The Exodus (fic)
    Archie Binns. You Rolling River (fic)
    Vance Nye Bourjaily. The End of My Life (fic)
    Gerald Warner Brace. The Garretson Chronicle (fic)
    Ray Douglas Bradbury. Dark Carnival (fic)
           . The Meadow (dr)
    Louis Bromfield. Colorado (fic)
    Van Wyck Brooks. The Times of Melville and Whitman (hist, e)
    Pearl Sydenstricker Buck. Far and Near (fic)
    John Horne Burns. The Gallery (fic)
    Harold Witter Bynner. Take Away the Darkness (po)
    James Branch Cabell. Let Me Lie (e)
    James Mallahan Cain. The Butterfly (fic)
    Erskine Preston Caldwell. The Sure Hand of God (fic)
    Henry Seidel Canby. American Memoir (hist)
    Melville Henry Cane. A Wider Arc (po)
    John Ciardi. Other Skies (po)
    James Bryant Conant. On Understanding Science (e)

Ellsworth Prouty Conkle. Five Plays (dr, pub)
Edwin Corle. Three Ways to Mecca (fic)
Thomas Bertram Costain. The Moneyman (fic)
Louis Osborne Coxe. The Sea Faring (po)
Josephus Daniels. Shirt-Sleeve Diplomat (auto)
Olive Tilford Dargan. Sons of the Stranger (fic)
Marcia Davenport. East Side, West Side (fic)
Clyde Brion Davis. Jeremy Bell (fic)
Harold Lenoir Davis. Harp of a Thousand Strings (fic)
Bernard Augustine DeVoto. Across the Wide Missouri (hist)
_____. Mountain Time (fic)
Theodore Herman Albert Dreiser. The Stoic (fic, pub)
Robert Edward Duncan. Heavenly City, Earthly City (po)
Richard Ghormley Eberhart. Burr Oaks (po)
Walter Dumaux Edmonds. In the Hands of the Senecas (fic)
_____. The Wedding Journey (fic)
James Thomas Farrell. The Life Adventurous (fic)
_____. Literature and Morality (e)
Howard Melvin Fast. Clarkton (fic)
Frederick Feikema (Frederick Manfred/Feike Feikema). This Is the
    Year (fic)
Vardis Alvero Fisher. Adam and the Serpent (fic)
Martin Archer Flavin. The Enchanted (fic)
_____. Journey in the Dark (fic)
John Gould Fletcher. Arkansas (hist)
Joseph Freeman. The Long Pursuit (fic)
Robert Lee Frost. A Masque of Mercy (po, dr)
_____. Steeple Bush (po)
Jean Garrigue. The Ego and the Centaur (po)
John Patrick Goggan (John Patrick). The Story of Mary Surratt (dr)
Anne Green. The Old Lady (fic)
Paul Eliot Green. The Common Glory (dr)
Samuel Bernard Greenberg. Poems (pub)
Albert Joseph Guerard. Joseph Conrad (e)
Alfred Bertram Guthrie, Jr. The Big Sky (fic)
Alfred Hayes. Shadow of Heaven (fic)
Josephine Frey Herbst. Somewhere the Tempest Fell (fic)
Robert Silliman Hillyer. Poems for Music (po)
Chester Bomar Himes. Lonely Crusade (fic)
Laura Zametkin Hobson. Gentleman's Agreement (fic)
James Langston Hughes. Fields of Wonder (po)
Fannie Hurst. The Hands of Veronica (fic)
William Inge. Farther Off from Heaven (dr)
Arthur Kober. That Man Is Here Again (fic)
Manuel Komroff. Feast of the Jesters (fic)
Meyer Levin. My Father's House (fic)
Harry Sinclair Lewis. Kingsblood Royal (fic)
Janet Lewis. The Trial of Soren Qvist (fic)
Abbott Joseph Liebling. The Wayward Pressman (nar)
Anita Loos. Happy Birthday (dr)
Andrew Nelson Lytle. A Name for Evil (fic)
Thomas Merton. Figures for an Apocalypse (po)
James Albert Michener. Tales of the South Pacific (fic)
Arthur Miller. All My Sons (dr)
Henry Miller. Remember to Remember (nar, e)
Willard Motley. Knock on Any Door (fic)

Vladimir Nabokov. Bend Sinister (fic)
Robert Gruntal Nathan. Mr. Whittle and the Morning Star (fic)
Howard Nemerov. Image and the Law (po)
John Frederick Nims. The Iron Pastoral (po)
Anais Nin. On Writing (e)
John Henry O'Hara. Hellbox (fic)
Kenneth Patchen. Panels for the Walls of Heaven (po)
Elliot Harold Paul. Linden on the Saugus Branch (auto)
Ann Petry. Country Life (fic)
Ezra Weston Loomis Pound. Confucius: The Unwobbling Pivot and the
     Great Digest (trans)
James Farl Powers. Prince of Darkness (fic)
Conrad Michael Richter. Always Young and Fair (fic)
Kenneth Lewis Roberts. Lydia Bailey (fic)
Selden Rodman. The Amazing Year: A Diary in Verse (po, nar)
Mari Sandoz. The Tom-Walker (fic)
William Saroyan. Jim Dandy, Fat Man in a Famine (dr)
Eleanor May Sarton. The Underground River (dr)
Gladys Schmitt. Alexandra (fic)
Mark Schorer. The State of Mind (fic)
Budd Wilson Schulberg. The Harder They Fall (fic)
Karl Jay Shapiro. Trial of a Poet (po)
James Vincent Sheean. A Certain Rich Man (fic)
William Lawrence Shirer. End of a Berlin Diary (nar)
Upton Beall Sinclair. Presidential Mission (fic)
Elsie Singmaster. I Speak for Thaddeus Stevens (fic)
William Jay Smith. Poems (pub)
Frank Morrison (Mickey) Spillane. I, the Jury (fic)
Jean Stafford. The Mountain Lion (fic)
William Edgar Stafford. Down in My Heart (po)
Wallace Earle Stegner. Second Growth (fic)
John Ernst Steinbeck. The Wayward Bus (fic)
Wallace Stevens. Transport to Summer (po)
Irving Stone. Adversary in the House (fic)
Philip Duffield Stong. Jessamy John (fic)
Robert Lewis Taylor. Adrift in a Boneyard (fic)
Lionel Trilling. The Middle of the Journey (fic)
Mark Albert Van Doren. The Careless Clock: Poems about Children in
     the Family (po)
Gore Vidal. In a Yellow Wood (fic)
Robert Penn Warren. The Circus in the Attic (fic)
Jerome Weidman. The Captain's Tiger (fic)
Richard Purdy Wilbur. The Beautiful Changes, and Other Poems (po)
Ben Ames Williams. House Divided (fic)
Thomas Lanier (Tennessee) Williams. A Streetcar Named Desire (dr)
_____, and Donald Windham. You Touched
     Me! (dr)
Calder Baynard Willingham, Jr. End As a Man (fic)
Edmund Wilson. Europe without Baedeker (trav)
Arthur Yvor Winters. In Defense of Reason (e)
Herman Wouk. Aurora Dawn (fic)

1948

BIRTHS

Marcelle Clements
Albert Goldbarth
Charles Richard Johnson
Heather McHugh

DEATHS

Gertrude Franklin Atherton
Charles Austin Beard
Roark Bradford
Alice Brown
Wilbur Lucius Cross
Thomas Augustine Daly
Josephus Daniels
Maud Howe Elliott
Susan Glaspell
William Henry Irwin
Ross Franklin Lockridge, Jr.
Claude McKay
Genevieve Taggard

EVENTS

Bollingen Prize for Poetry, Bollingen Foundation (est)
Books in Print (ref, est)
Brandeis University, Waltham, Massachusetts (f)
The Hudson Review (per, f)
Masses and Mainstream, New York, New York, to 1953 (per)

LITERATURE

William Hervey Allen. Toward the Morning (fic)
Maxwell Anderson. Anne of the Thousand Days (dr)
Wystan Hugh Auden. The Age of Anxiety: A Baroque Eclogue (po)
Joseph Auslander and Audrey Wurdemann. My Uncle Jan (fic)
Dorothy Baker. Our Gifted Son (fic)
Charles Austin Beard. President Roosevelt and the Coming of the War
   (e, hist)
Ludwig Bemelmans. The Best of Times (nar)
Bernard Berenson. Aesthetics and History in the Visual Arts (e, hist)
John Berryman. The Dispossessed (po)
John Peale Bishop. Collected Essays (pub)
_____. Collected Poems (pub)
Morris Gilbert Bishop. Champlain (biog)
Arno Wendell Bontemps. The Story of the Negro (hist)
William Stanley Beaumont Braithwaite. Selected Poems (pub)
Louis Bromfield. Malabar Farm (nar)
_____. The Wild Country (fic)
James Mallahan Cain. The Moth (fic)
Erskine Preston Caldwell. This Very Earth (fic)

Walter Stanley Campbell (Stanley Vestal). Warpath and Council Fire
     (hist)
Truman Capote. Other Voices, Other Rooms (fic)
Mary Ellen Chase. Jonathan Fisher (biog)
Stuart Chase. The Proper Study of Mankind (e)
Robert Myron Coates. Wisteria Cottage (fic)
James Gould Cozzens. Guard of Honor (fic)
Russel Crouse and Howard Lindsay. Life with Mother (dr)
Clyde Brion Davis. Temper the Wind (fic)
August William Derleth. Sac Prairie People (fic)
William Everson. The Residual Years (po)
Howard Melvin Fast. My Glorious Brothers (fic)
William Harrison Faulkner. Intruder in the Dust (fic)
Frederick Feikema (Frederick Manfred/Feike Feike Feikema). The Cho-
     kesberry Tree (fic)
Vardis Alvero Fisher. The Divine Passion (fic)
Esther Forbes. The Running of the Tide (fic)
Waldo David Frank. The Invaders (fic)
Douglas Southall Freeman. George Washington, 6 vols, to 1954 (biog)
Herbert Sherman Gorman. The Cry of Dolores (fic)
Hiram Haydn. The Time Is Noon (fic)
Barbara Howes. The Undersea Farmer (po)
Zora Neale Hurston. Seraph on the Sewanee (fic)
David Ignatow. Poems (pub)
Charles Reginald Jackson. The Outer Edges (fic)
Shirley Hardie Jackson. The Road through the Wall (fic)
Randall Jarrell. Losses (po)
John Robinson Jeffers. The Double Axe, and Other Poems (po)
Manuel Komroff. Echo of Evil (fic)
Joseph Wood Krutch. Thoreau (biog)
_____, et al. American Men of Letters Series, to 1951
     (e, ed)
Josephine Lawrence. The Pleasant Morning Light (fic)
Ludwig Lewisohn. Anniversary (fic)
Ross Franklin Lockridge, Jr. Raintree County (fic)
Robert James Collas Lowry. Find Me in Fire (fic)
Archibald MacLeish. Actfive (po)
Norman Mailer. The Naked and the Dead (fic)
William Maxwell. Time Will Darken It (fic)
David Thompson Watson McCord. About Boston (e)
Horace McCoy. Kiss Tomorrow Good-Bye (fic)
William Morris Meredith. Ships and Other Figures (po)
Thomas Merton. The Seven Storey Mountain (auto)
Henry Miller. The Smile at the Foot of the Ladder (fic)
Robert Gruntal Nathan. Long after Summer (fic)
Clifford Odets. The Big Knife (dr)
Martha Ostenso. Milk Route (fic)
Anne Parrish. A Clouded Star (fic)
Kenneth Patchen. See You in the Morning (fic)
Elliot Harold Paul. A Ghost Town on the Yellowstone (auto)
Joseph Stanley Pennell. The History of Nora Beckham (fic)
Sidney Joseph Perelman. Westward Ha! (sat, nar)
Ezra Weston Loomis Pound. The Pisan Cantos (po)
Frederic Prokosch. Storm and Echo (fic)
Theodore Roethke. The Lost Son (po)
Muriel Rukeyser. The Green Wave (po)

Carl August Sandburg. Remembrance Rock (po, fic)
Eleanor May Sarton. The Lion and the Rose (po)
Delmore Schwartz. The World Is a Wedding (fic)
Winfield Townley Scott. Mr. Whittier (po)
Allen Seager. The Inheritance (fic)
Irwin Shaw. The Young Lions (fic)
Robert Emmet Sherwood. Roosevelt and Hopkins (biog, hist)
Upton Beall Sinclair. One Clear Call (fic)
Betty Wehner Smith. Tomorrow Will Be Better (fic)
Elizabeth Spencer. Fire in the Morning (fic)
Robert E. Spiller, et al. Literary History of the United States, eds
    to 1972 (hist, ed)
John Ernst Steinbeck. The Pearl (fic)
───────────────. A Russian Journal (nar)
George Rippey Stewart. Fire (fic)
Grace Zaring Stone (Ethel Vance). The Secret Thread (fic)
John Orley Allen Tate. On the Limits of Poetry (e)
───────────────. Poems, 1922-1947 (pub)
Peter Hillsman Taylor. A Long Fourth (fic)
Robert Lewis Taylor. Doctor, Lawyer, Merchant Chief (biog)
James Grover Thurber. The Beast in Me, and Other Animals (hum)
Carl Clinton Van Doren. The Great Rehearsal (hist)
Mark Albert Van Doren. New Poems (po)
Gore Vidal. The City and the Pillar (fic)
Peter Viereck. Terror and Decorum (po)
Joseph Wechsberg. The Continental Touch (fic)
───────────────. Sweet and Sour (nar)
Thornton Niven Wilder. The Ides of March (fic)
Thomas Lanier (Tennessee) Williams. One Arm (fic)
───────────────. Summer and Smoke (dr)
Thames Ross Williamson. The Gladiator (fic)
Edmund Wilson. The Triple Thinkers, rev ed (e)
Thomas Clayton Wolfe. Mannerhouse (dr, pub)
Herman Wouk. The City Boy (fic)
Stark Young. Immortal Shadows (e)
Louis Zukofsky. A Test of Poetry (e)

1949

BIRTHS

Michael Blumenthal
Olga Broumas
Jamaica Kincaid
Mary Robison
Michael Waters

DEATHS

James Truslow Adams
William Hervey Allen
Philip Barry
Rex Ellingwood Beach
Thomas Orlo Heggen
Alice Corbin Henderson

Margaret Mitchell

EVENTS

American Heritage (per, f)
American Quarterly, Minneapolis, Minnesota; Philadelphia, Pennsylvania (per, f)
Antiquarian Booksellers' Association of America (f)
Botteghe Oscure, to 1960 (per)

LITERATURE

Conrad Potter Aiken. Skylight One (po)
Nelson Algren. The Man with the Golden Arm (fic)
Harriette Arnow. Hunter's Horn (fic)
Sholem Asch. Mary (fic)
Stringfellow Barr. Pilgrimage of Western Man (hist)
Joseph Hamilton Basso. The Green Room (fic)
Charles William Beebe. High Jungle (des)
Ludwig Bemelmans. The Eye of God (fic)
Samuel Flagg Bemis. John Quincy Adams and the Foundations of American Foreign Policy (hist)
Bernard Berenson. Sketch for a Self-Portrait (e, auto)
Paul Bowles. The Sheltering Sky (fic)
Kay Boyle. His Human Majesty (fic)
Gerald Warner Brace. A Summer's Tale (fic)
Gwendolyn Brooks. Annie Allen (po)
James Richard Broughton. The Playground (po)
Pearl Sydenstricker Buck. Kinfolk (fic)
Carl Frederick Buechner. A Long Day's Dying (fic)
William Riley Burnett. The Asphalt Jungle (fic)
John Horne Burns. Lucifer with a Book (fic)
Erskine Preston Caldwell. A Place Called Estherville (fic)
Truman Capote. Tree of Night (fic)
Carl Lamson Carmer. Dark Trees to the Wind (hist)
Gladys Hasty Carroll. West of the Hill (fic)
Mary Ellen Chase. The Plum Tree (fic)
John Ciardi. Live Another Day (po)
Walter Van Tilburg Clark. The Track of the Cat (fic)
Elizabeth Jane Coatsworth. The Creaking Stair (po)
Edwin Corle. In Winter Light (fic)
Thomas Bertram Costain. The Conqueror (hist)
                      . High Towers (fic)
Clyde Brion Davis. Playtime Is Over (fic)
Harold Lenoir Davis. Beulah Land (fic)
David Cornel DeJong. The Desperate Children (fic)
Hilda Doolittle. By Avon River (po, e)
John Roderigo Dos Passos. The Grand Design (fic)
Lloyd Cassel Douglas. The Big Fisherman (fic)
Richard Ghormley Eberhart. Brotherhood of Man (po)
Thomas Stearns Eliot. Notes toward a Definition of Culture (e)
William Everson. A Privacy of Speech (po)
James Thomas Farrell. The Road Between (fic)
William Harrison Faulkner. Knight's Gambit (fic)
Kenneth Fearing. Stranger at Coney Island (po)
Frederick Feikema (Frederick Manfred/Feike Feikema). The Primitive

(fic)
Irving Fineman. Ruth (fic)
Dudley Fitts and Robert Stuart Fitzgerald. Oedipus (trans)
Shelby Foote. Tournament (fic)
Paul Goodman. Faustina (dr)
_____. The Grand Piano (fic)
Julian Green. If I Were You (fic)
Albert Joseph Guerard. Thomas Hardy (e)
Alfred Bertram Guthrie, Jr. The Way West (fic)
Walter Edwin Havighurst. The Signature of Time (fic)
John Clendennin Burne Hawks, Jr. The Cannibal (fic)
Alfred Hayes. The Girl on Via Flaminia (fic)
Robert Silliman Hillyer. The Death of Captain Nemo (po)
James Langston Hughes. One-Way Ticket (po)
Garson Kanin. Smile of the World (dr)
MacKinlay Kantor. Wicked Water (fic)
Sidney Kingsley. Detective Story (dr)
Christopher La Farge. All Sorts and Kinds (fic)
Josephine Lawrence. My Heart Shall Not Fear (fic)
Tom Lea. The Brave Bulls (fic)
Harry Sinclair Lewis. The God Seeker (fic)
Robert James Collas Lowry. The Big Cage (fic)
_____. The Wolf That Fed Us (fic)
Percy Wallace MacKaye. The Mystery of Hamlet, King of Denmark; or,
    What We Will (dr, po)
Albert Maltz. The Journey of Simon McKeever (fic)
Percy Marks. Blair Marriman (fic)
Mary Therese McCarthy. The Oasis (fic)
John Phillips Marquand. Point of No Return (fic)
William Morley Punshon McFee. Family Trouble (fic)
Peter McNab, Jr. (Harry Brown). The Beast in His Hunger (po)
Thomas Merton. Seeds of Contemplation (e)
_____. The Waters of Siloe (e, nar)
James Albert Michener. The Fires of Spring (fic)
Arthur Miller. Death of a Salesman (dr)
Henry Miller. The Rosy Crucifixion: Sexus (nar)
Merril Moore. Clinical Sonnets (po)
Christopher Darlington Morley. The Man Who Made Friends with Himself
    (fic)
Wright Morris. The World in the Attic (fic)
Ogden Nash. Versus (po)
Robert Gruntal Nathan. The River Journey (fic)
John Gneisenau Neihardt. A Cycle of the West (po)
Howard Nemerov. The Melodramatists (fic)
John Henry O'Hara. A Rage To Live (fic)
Martha Ostenso. The Sunset Tree (fic)
Kenneth Patchen. Red Wine and Yellow Hair (po)
_____. To Say If You Love Someone (po)
Elliot Harold Paul. My Old Kentucky Home (auto)
Sidney Joseph Perelman. Listen to the Mocking Bird (sat, nar)
Ann Petry. The Drugstore Cat (juv)
Ernest Poole. The Nancy Flier (fic)
Solomon Rabinowitz (Sholom Aleichem). Tevye's Daughters (fic, pub)
Philip Rahv. Image and Idea (e)
Elmer Reizenstein (Elmer Rice). The Show Must Go On (fic)
Kenneth Rexroth. The Signature of All Things (po)

Kenneth Lewis Roberts. I Wanted To Write (nar, e)
Muriel Rukeyser. Orpheus (po)
William Saroyan. Don't Go Away Mad (dr)
Louis Aston Marantz Simpson. The Arrivistes (po)
Upton Beall Sinclair. O Shepherd, Speak! (fic)
Virginia Sorensen. The Evening and the Morning (fic)
George Rippey Stewart. Earth Abides (fic)
Jesse Hilton Stuart. The Thread That Runs So True (auto)
John Orley Allen Tate. The Hovering Fly (e)
Robert Lewis Taylor. W.C. Fields, His Follies and Fortunes (biog)
Gore Vidal. The Season of Comfort (fic)
Jerome Weidman. The Price Is Right (fic)
Eudora Welty. The Golden Apples (fic)
Elwyn Brooks White. Here Is New York (des)
Mitchell Wilson. Live with Lightning (fic)
Herman Wouk. The Traitor (dr)
Marya Zaturenska. Christina Rossetti (biog)

1950

BIRTHS

David Bradley
Jan Clausen
Jean Thompson

DEATHS

Irving Addison Bacheller
William Rose Benet
John Gould Fletcher
Charles Rann Kennedy
Edgar Lee Masters
Francis Otto Matthiessen
Edna St. Vincent Millay
Ernest Poole
Agnes Repplier
Frederic Ridgely Torrence
Carl Clinton Van Doren
William E. Woodward

EVENTS

National Book Awards (est)

LITERATURE

Herbert Sebastian Agar. The Price of Union (e)
Isaac Asimov. I Robot (fic)
_____. Pebble in the Sky (fic)
Louis Stanton Auchincloss. The Injustice Collectors (fic)
Wystan Hugh Auden. Collected Shorter Poems, 1930-1944 (pub)
Stringfellow Barr. Let's Join the Human Race (e)
Jacques Barzun. Berlioz and the Romantic Century, 2 vols (e)
Joseph Warren Beach. Involuntary Witness (po)

Catherine Shober Drinker Bowen. John Adams and the American Revolution (biog, hist)
Paul Bowles. The Delicate Prey (fic)
Ray Douglas Bradbury. The Martian Chronicles (fic)
William Stanley Beaumont Braithwaite. The Bewitched Parsonage: The Story of the Brontes (biog)
Myron Brinig. Footsteps on the Stair (fic)
James Richard Broughton. Musical Chairs (po)
Kenneth Duva Burke. A Rhetoric of Motives (e)
Erskine Preston Caldwell. Episode in Palmetto (fic)
Truman Capote. Local Color (nar)
Ronald Verlin Cassill. Eagle on the Coin (fic)
William Henry Chamberlain. America's Second Crusade (e)
Mary Ellen Chase. Abby Aldrich Rockefeller (biog)
Walter Van Tilburg Clark. The Watchful Gods (fic)
Robert Peter Tristram Coffin. Apples by Ocean (po)
_____. Maine Doings (e)
Edward Estlin Cummings. Xaipe (po)
Edward Dahlberg. Flea of Sodom (e)
Jonathan Worth Daniels. The Man of Independence (biog)
Clyde Brion Davis. The Age of Indiscretion (auto)
William Demby. Beetlecreek (fic)
John Roderigo Dos Passos. The Prospect Before Us (fic)
Robert Edward Duncan. Medieval Scenes (po)
Richard Ghormley Eberhart. An Herb Basket (po)
Thomas Stearns Eliot. The Cocktail Party (dr)
_____. Poems Written in Early Youth (po, pub)
James Thomas Farrell. An American Dream Girl (fic)
Frederick Feikema (Frederick Manfred/Feike Feikema). The Brother (fic)
Edna Ferber. Giant (fic)
Harvey Fergusson. Grant of Kingdom (fic)
Shelby Foote. Follow Me Down (fic)
Wolcott Gibbs. Season in the Sun (dr)
John Patrick Goggan (John Patrick). The Curious Savage (dr)
Paul Goodman. The Dead of Spring (fic)
Charles William Goyen. The House of Breath (fic)
Paul Eliot Green. Faith of Our Fathers (dr)
Albert Joseph Guerard. Night Journey (fic)
James Norman Hall. The Far Lands (fic)
Alfred Hayes. Welcome to the Castle (po)
Robert Anson Heinlein. The Man Who Sold the Moon (fic)
Ernest Miller Hemingway. Across the River and into the Trees (fic)
John Richard Hersey. The Wall (fic)
Laura Zametkin Hobson. The Other Father (fic)
James Langston Hughes. The Barrier (dr)
_____. Simple Speaks His Mind (fic)
Rupert Hughes. The Giant Wakes (fic)
Fannie Hurst. Anywoman (fic)
William Inge. Come Back, Little Sheba (dr)
MacKinlay Kantor. Signal Thirty-Two (fic)
Jack Kerouac. The Town and the City (fic)
Alfred Kreymborg. No More War (po)
Robert Traill Spence Lowell, Jr. Poems, 1938-1949 (pub)
Archibald MacLeish. Poetry and Opinion (e)
Albert Maltz. The Citizen Writer (e)

Mary Therese McCarthy. Cast a Cold Eye (fic)
Theodore Morrison. The Dream of Alcestis (po)
Ogden Nash. Family Reunion (po)
Robert Gruntal Nathan. The Green Leaf (po)
Howard Nemerov. Guide to the Ruins (po)
John Frederick Nims. A Fountain in Kentucky (po)
Anais Nin. The Four-Chambered Heart (fic)
Clifford Odets. The Country Girl (dr)
Ezra Weston Loomis Pound. Money Pamphlets by Pound, to 1952 (e)
Conrad Michael Richter. The Town (fic)
Carl August Sandburg. Complete Poems (pub)
William Saroyan. The Twin Adventures (fic)
Eleanor May Sarton. Shadow of a Man (fic)
Budd Wilson Schulberg. The Disenchanted (fic)
_____. Some Faces in the Crowd (fic)
Delmore Schwartz. Vaudeville for a Princess (po)
Allen Seager. The Old Man of the Mountain (fic)
Irwin Shaw. Mixed Faith (fic)
William Lawrence Shirer. The Traitor (fic)
Isaac Bashevis Singer. The Family Moskat (fic)
William Jay Smith. Celebration at Dark (po)
Frank Morrison (Mickey) Spillane. My Gun Is Quick (fic)
Wilbur Daniel Steele. Diamond Wedding (fic)
Wallace Earle Stegner. The Preacher and the Slave (fic)
_____. The Women on the Wall (fic)
John Ernst Steinbeck. Burning Bright (fic)
Wallace Stevens. The Auroras of Autumn (po)
Jesse Hilton Stuart. Hie to the Hunters (fic)
Peter Hillsman Taylor. A Woman of Means (fic)
Robert Lewis Taylor. Professor Fodorski (fic)
James Grover Thurber. The Thirteen Clocks (juv)
Lionel Trilling. The Liberal Imagination (e)
Carl Clinton Van Doren. Jane Mecom (biog)
Mark Albert Van Doren. Humanity Unlimited: Twelve Sonnets (po)
John William Van Druten. Bell, Book, and Candle (dr)
Gore Vidal. Dark Green, Bright Red (fic)
_____. A Search for the King (fic)
Peter Viereck. Strike through the Mask! (po)
Robert Penn Warren. World Enough and Time (fic)
Richard Purdy Wilbur. Ceremony, and Other Poems (po)
Thomas Lanier (Tennessee) Williams. The Roman Spring of Mrs. Stone
   (fic)
_____. The Rose Tattoo (dr)
William Carlos Williams. Make Light of It (fic)
Calder Baynard Willingham, Jr. Geraldine Bradshaw (fic)
Edmund Wilson. Classics and Commercials (e)
_____. The Little Blue Light (dr)
Richard Nathaniel Wright. The God That Failed (nar)

1951

BIRTHS

   Jorie Graham

DEATHS

Louis Adamic
Stephen Bonsal
Gelett Frank Burgess
Abraham Cahan
Lloyd Cassel Douglas
John Erskine
Janet Ayer Fairbank
James Norman Hall
Harry Sinclair Lewis
John Thomas McIntyre

EVENTS

American Studies Association (f)
Origin, to 1971 (per)

LITERATURE

George Abbott. A Tree Grows in Brooklyn (dr)
James Agee. The Morning Watch (fic)
Maxwell Anderson. Barefoot in Athens (dr)
Benjamin Appel. Fortress in the Rice (fic)
Hannah Arendt. Origins of Totalitarianism (e)
Isaac Asimov. Foundation (fic)
Justin Brooks Atkinson. Once around the Sun (e)
Wystan Hugh Auden. The Enchafed Flood: The Romantic Iconography of
    the Sea (e)
_____. Nones (po)
Joseph Auslander and Audrey Wurdemann. The Islanders (po)
Philip Barry and Robert Sherwood. Second Threshold (dr, pub)
Morris Gilbert Bishop. The Life and Adventures of LaRouchefoucauld
    (biog)
Arna Wendell Bontemps. Chariot in the Sky (nar)
_____ and John Wesley Conroy. Sam Patch (fic)
Kay Boyle. The Smoking Mountain (fic)
Ray Douglas Bradbury. The Illustrated Man (fic)
John Malcolm Brinnin. The Sorrows of Cold Stone (po)
Louis Bromfield. Mr. Smith (fic)
Pearl Sydenstricker Buck. God's Men (fic)
Carl Frederick Buechner. The Seasons' Difference (fic)
Erskine Preston Caldwell. Call It Experience (e)
Hortense Calisher. In the Absence of Angels (fic)
Morley Callaghan. The Loved and the Lost (fic)
Henry Seidel Canby. Turn West, Turn East (e)
Truman Capote. The Grass Harp (fic)
Rachel Carson. The Sea around Us (e)
John Ciardi. From Time to Time (po)
Henry Steele Commager. The American Mind (e)
James Bryant Conant. Science and Common Sense (e)
Edwin Corle. The Gila, River of the Southwest (des)
Thomas Bertram Costain. The Magnificent Century (hist)
Louis Osborne Coxe and Robert H. Chapman. Billy Budd (dr)
John Roderigo Dos Passos. Chosen Country (fic)
Paul Hamilton Engle. The Word of Love (po)

William Everson (Brother Antoninus). Triptych for the Living (po)
James Thomas Farrell. This Man, This Woman (fic)
William Harrison Faulkner. Requiem for a Nun (fic)
Frederick Feikema (Frederick Manfred/Feike Feikema). The Giant (fic)
Vardis Alvero Fisher. The Valley of Vision (fic)
Shelby Foote. Love in a Dry Season (fic)
Waldo David Frank. Birth of a World (hist)
John Patrick Goggan (John Patrick). Lo and Behold (dr)
Herbert Gold. Birth of a Hero (fic)
Caroline Gordon. The Strange Children (fic)
Albert Joseph Guerard. Andre Gide (e)
John Clendennin Burne Hawkes, Jr. The Beetle Leg (fic)
Robert Anson Heinlein. The Green Hills of Earth (fic)
Lillian Hellman. The Autumn Garden (dr)
Maurice Gerschon Hindus. Magda (fic)
Laura Zametkin Hobson. The Celebrity (fic)
Irving Howe. Sherwood Anderson: A Critical Biography (biog, e)
James Langston Hughes. Montage of a Dream Deferred (po)
Shirley Hardie Jackson. Hangsaman (fic)
Randall Jarrell. The Seven-League Crutches (po)
James Jones. From Here to Eternity (fic)
Alfred Kazin. A Walker in the City (auto)
Arthur Kober. Bella, Bella, Kissed a Fella (fic)
Manuel Komroff. Jade Star (fic)
Harry Sinclair Lewis. World So Wide (fic)
Victoria Lincoln. Out from Eden (fic)
Anita Loos. A Mouse Is Born (dr)
Clare Boothe Luce. Child of the Morning (dr)
Norman Mailer. Barbary Shore (fic)
Robert Traill Spence Lowell, Jr. The Mills of the Kavanaughs (po)
John Phillips Marquand. Melville Goodwin, U.S.A. (fic)
Carson Smith McCullers. The Ballad of the Sad Cafe (fic)
Phyllis McGinley. A Short Walk from the Station (po)
James Ingram Merrill. First Poems (po)
Thomas Merton. The Ascent to Truth (e)
James Albert Michener. Return to Paradise (fic, nar)
                      . The Voice of Asia (nar, e)
Josephine Miles. The Continuity of English Poetic Language (e)
Marianne Craig Moore. Collected Poems (pub)
Wright Morris. Man and Boy (fic)
Willard Motley. We Fished All Night (fic)
Vladimir Nabokov. Conclusive Evidence (nar, des)
Ogden Nash. Parents Keep Out (po)
Robert Gruntal Nathan. The Innocent Eve (fic)
John Gneisenau Neihardt. When the Tree Flowered (fic)
Edwin O'Connor. The Oracle (fic)
John Henry O'Hara. The Farmer's Hotel (fic)
Ezra Weston Loomis Pound. Confucian Analects (trans)
Kenneth Rexroth. Beyond the Mountains (po, dr)
Adrienne Cecile Rich. A Change of World (po)
Theodore Roethke. Praise to the End! (po)
Jerome David Salinger. The Catcher in the Rye (fic)
William Saroyan. Rock Wagram (fic)
Irwin Shaw. The Troubled Air (fic)
James Vincent Sheean. The Indigo Bunting (biog)
Odell Shepard and Willard Odell Shepard. Jenkins' Ear (fic)

Frank Morrison (Mickey) Spillane. The Big Kill (fic)
Wallace Stevens. The Necessary Angel (e)
George Rippey Stewart. Sheep Rock (fic)
Grace Zaring Stone. The Grotto (fic)
Irving Stone. The President's Lady (fic)
Philip Duffield Stong. Forty Pounds of Gold (fic)
Rex Todhunter Stout. Murder by the Book (fic)
William Styron. Lie Down in Darkness (fic)
Mark Albert Van Doren. In That Far Land (po)
John William Van Druten. I Am a Camera (dr)
Jessamyn West. The Witch Diggers (fic)
Thomas Lanier (Tennessee) Williams. I Rise in Flame, Cried the Phoe-
    nix (dr)
Calder Baynard Willingham, Jr. The Gates of Hell (fic)
_____. Reach to the Stars (fic)
Thomas Clayton Wolfe. A Western Journal of the Great Parks Trip,
    1938 (nar, pub)
William E. Woodward. Years of Madness (hist)
Herman Wouk. The Caine Mutiny (fic)
Frank Garvin Yerby. A Woman Called Fancy (fic)
Stark Young. The Pavilion (nar)

1952

BIRTHS

    Rita Dove
    Beth Henley
    Vikram Seth

DEATHS

    Owen McMahon Johnson
    Elizabeth Robins
    George Santayana
    Austin Strong

EVENTS

    New World Writing, to 1959 (per: fic, dr, e, po)

LITERATURE

    Mortimer Jerome Adler and Robert Maynard Hutchins. Great Books of
        the Western World, 54 vols (misc, ed)
    Herbert Sebastian Agar. A Declaration of Faith (e)
    Conrad Potter Aiken. Ushant (auto)
    Frederick Lewis Allen. The Big Change (hist)
    Benjamin Appel. Hell's Kitchen (fic)
    John Lawrence Ashbery. The Heroes (dr)
    Isaac Asimov. Foundation and Empire (fic)
    Louis Stanton Auchincloss. Sybil (fic)
    Wystan Hugh Auden. The Living Thoughts of Kierkegaard (e, ed)
    Margaret Frances Bacon. The Inward Eye (fic)
    Stringfellow Barr. Citizens of the World (e)

Samuel Nathaniel Behrman. Duveen (biog)
Bernard Berenson. Rumor and Reflection (e, nar)
Richard Palmer Blackmur. Language As Gesture (e)
Paul Bowles. Let It Come Down (fic)
Gerald Warner Brace. The Spire (fic)
Van Wyck Brooks. The Confident Years (hist)
James Richard Broughton. An Almanac for Amorists (po)
John Mason Brown. As They Appear (e)
Pearl Sydenstricker Buck. The Hidden Flower (fic)
Ben Lucien Burman. High Water at Catfish Bend (fic)
John Horne Burns. A Cry of Children (fic)
James Branch Cabell. Quiet, Please (nar)
Erskine Preston Caldwell. The Courting of Susie Brown (fic)
_____. A Lamp for Nightfall (fic)
Walter Stanley Campbell (Stanley Vestal). Joe Meek (biog)
_____. Queen of Cowtowns: Dodge
    City (hist)
Mary Coyle Chase. Bernardine (dr)
_____. Mrs. McThing (dr)
Eleanor Clark. Rome and a Villa (des)
Thomas Bertram Costain. The Silver Chalice (fic)
Norman Cousins. Who Speaks for Man? (e)
Robert White Creeley. Le Fou (po)
Clyde Brion Davis. Thudbury (fic)
Harold Lenoir Davis. Winds of Morning (fic)
David Cornel DeJong. Two Sofas in the Parlor (fic)
Alonzo Delano. Alonzo Delano's California Correspondence (nar, pub)
Bernard Augustine DeVoto. The Course of Empire (e)
Peter DeVries. No, But I Saw the Movie (fic)
John Roderigo Dos Passos. District of Columbia (fic)
Ralph Waldo Ellison. Invisible Man (fic)
John Fante. Full of Life (fic)
James Thomas Farrell. Yet Other Waters (fic)
Howard Melvin Fast. Spartacus (fic)
Thomas Hornsby Ferril. New and Selected Poems (pub)
Vardis Alvero Fisher. The Island of the Innocent (fic)
Shelby Foote. Shiloh (fic)
Charles William Goyen. Ghost and Flesh (fic)
Mark Harris. City of Discontent (e)
Ernest Miller Hemingway. The Old Man and the Sea (fic)
Chester Bomar Himes. Cast the First Stone (fic)
John Clellon Holmes. Go (fic)
Irving Howe. William Faulkner: A Critical Study (e)
James Langston Hughes. Laughing To Keep from Crying (fic)
Arthur Kober. Wish You Were Here (dr)
Joseph Kramm. The Shrike (dr)
Louis Kronenberger. Grand Right and Left (fic)
_____. The Thread of Laughter (e)
Arthur Laurents. The Time of the Cuckoo (dr)
Tom Lea. The Wonderful Country (fic)
Anita Loos. Gigi (dr)
Robie Mayhew Macauley. The Disguises of Love (fic)
Archibald MacLeish. Collected Poems, 1917-1952 (pub)
Bernard Malamud. The Natural (fic)
Mary Therese McCarthy. The Groves of Academe (fic)
Horace McCoy. Scalpel (fic)

William Stanley Merwin. A Mask for Janus (po)
Henry Miller. The Books in My Life (nar, e)
Wright Morris. The Works of Love (fic)
Flannery O'Connor. Wise Blood (fic)
Frank O'Hara. A City Winter (po)
Katherine Anne Porter. The Days Before (e)
Ezra Weston Loomis Pound. Guide to Kulchur (e, rev)
Kenneth Rexroth. The Dragon and the Unicorn (po, nar)
William Saroyan. The Bicycle Rider in Beverly Hills (auto)
Eleanor May Sarton. A Shower of Summer Days (fic)
Gladys Schmitt. Confessors of the Name (fic)
Elizabeth Spencer. This Crooked Way (fic)
Jean Stafford. The Catherine Wheel (fic)
Wilbur Daniel Steele. Their Town (fic)
John Ernst Steinbeck. East of Eden (fic)
Jesse Hilton Stuart. Kentucky Is My Land (po)
Ruth Suckow. Some Others and Myself (fic, nar)
Robert Lewis Taylor. Winston Churchill (biog)
Melvin Beaunorus Tolson. Black No More (dr)
_____. The Fire in the Flint (dr)
Frederic Ridgely Torrence. Poems (pub)
Gore Vidal. The Judgment of Paris (fic)
Peter Viereck. The First Morning (po)
Kurt Vonnegut, Jr. Player Piano (fic)
Elwyn Brooks White. Charlotte's Web (juv, fic)
William Carlos Williams. The Build-Up (fic)
Calder Baynard Willingham, Jr. Natural Child (fic)
Edmund Wilson. The Shores of Light (e, nar)
Arthur Yvor Winters. Collected Poems (pub)

1953

BIRTHS

Jayne Anne Phillips

DEATHS

Maude Adams (Maude Kiskadden)
Herbert Eugene Bolton
John Horne Burns
Barrett Harper Clark
Louis Fraina (Lewis Corey)
Douglas Southall Freeman
Gordon Hall Gerould
Eugene Gladston O'Neill
Marjorie Kinnan Rawlings
Ben Ames Williams

EVENTS

Discovery, to 1955 (per)
Dwight David Eisenhower, 34th President of the United States, to 1961
The Paris Review, Paris, France; New York, New York (per, f)

LITERATURE

Conrad Potter Aiken. Collected Poems (pub)
Robert Woodruff Anderson. All Summer Long (dr)
_____. Tea and Sympathy (dr)
Sherwood Anderson. Letters (pub)
Benjamin Appel. Dock Wallopers (fic)
Sholem Asch. Passage in the Night (fic)
John Lawrence Ashbery. Turandot (po)
Isaac Asimov. Second Foundation (fic)
Louis Stanton Auchincloss. A Law for the Lion (fic)
James Baldwin. Go Tell It on the Mountain (fic)
Harry Elmer Barnes. Perpetual War for Perpetual Peace (e)
Carleton Beals. Stephen F. Austin (biog)
Charles William Beebe. Unseen Life of New York (des)
Saul Bellow. The Adventures of Augie March (fic)
Ludwig Bemelmans. Father, Dear Father (nar)
Samuel Flagg Bemis. Diplomacy of the American Revolution (hist)
John Berryman. Homage to Mistress Bradstreet (po)
Archie Binns. Sea in the Forest (des)
Paul Blackburn. Proensa (po, trans)
Ray Douglas Bradbury. Fahrenheit 451 (fic)
_____. The Golden Apples of the Sun (fic)
Myron Brinig. The Street of the Three Friends (fic)
Gwendolyn Brooks. Maud Martha (fic)
Van Wyck Brooks. The Writer in America (e)
Pearl Sydenstricker Buck. Come, My Beloved (fic)
Ben Lucien Burman. The Four Lives of Mundy Tolliver (fic)
William Riley Burnett. Adobe Walls (fic)
William Seward Burroughs (William Lee). Junkie (fic)
James Mallahan Cain. Galatea (fic)
Dorothy Canfield Fisher. Vermont Tradition (e)
Paddy Chayefsky. Marty (dr)
Edwin Corle. Billy the Kid (fic)
Edward Estlin Cummings. i (e)
Harold Lenoir Davis. Team Bells Work Me (fic)
Richard Ghormley Eberhart. Undercliff (po)
Walter Dumaux Edmonds. The Boyds of Black River (fic)
James Thomas Farrell. The Face of Time (fic)
Vardis Alvero Fisher. God or Caesar? The Writing of Fiction for Be-
  ginners (e)
Shelby Foote. Jordan County (fic)
Ernest Kellogg Gann. The High and the Mighty (fic)
Jean Garrigue. The Monument Rose (po)
John Patrick Goggan (John Patrick). The Teahouse of the August Moon
  (dr)
Oakley Hall. Corpus of Joe Bailey (fic)
Albert Halper. The Golden Watch (fic)
Mark Harris. The Southpaw (fic)
Alfred Hayes. In Love (fic)
Robert Anson Heinlein. Revolt in 2100 (fic)
John Richard Hersey. The Marmot Drive (fic)
James Langston Hughes. Simple Takes a Wife (fic)
William Humphrey. The Last Husband (fic)
William Inge. Picnic (dr)
Charles Reginald Jackson. Earthly Creatures (fic)

Shirley Hardie Jackson. Life among the Savages (nar)
Randall Jarrell. Poetry and the Age (e)
George Simon Kaufman and Howard Teichmann. The Solid Gold Cadillac
    (dr)
Clarence Budington Kelland. Dangerous Angel (fic)
Kenneth Jay Koch. Poems (pub)
Joseph Wood Krutch. Modernism in Modern Drama (e)
Christopher LaFarge. Beauty for Ashes (fic, po)
Ira Levin. A Kiss before Dying (fic)
Charles Augustus Lindbergh. The Spirit of St. Louis (nar)
Robert James Collas Lowry. The Violent Wedding (fic)
Archibald MacLeish. The Music Crept by Me upon the Waters (po, dr)
Thomas Merton. The Sign of Jonas (e)
James Albert Michener. The Bridges at Toko-ri (fic)
Arthur Miller. The Crucible (dr)
Henry Miller. The Rosy Crucifixion: Plexus (nar)
Wright Morris. The Deep Sleep (fic)
Theodore Morrison. The Stones of the House (fic)
Ogden Nash. The Private Dining Room (po)
Robert Gruntal Nathan. Jezebel's Husband and the Sleeping Beauty
    (dr)
_____. The Train in the Meadow (fic)
John Gneisenau Neihardt. Eagle Voice (fic)
Charles Olson. In Cold Hell, in Thicket (po)
_____. The Maximus Poems, 1-10 (po)
_____. The Mayan Letters (e)
Dorothy Rothschild Parker and Arnaud d'Usseau. Ladies of the Corri-
    dor (dr)
Sidney Joseph Perelman. The Ill-Tempered Clavichord (sat, nar)
Ann Petry. The Narrows (fic)
Ezra Weston Loomis Pound. Section: Rock-Drill, 85-95 de los Cantares
    (po)
Solomon Rabinowitz (Shalom Aleichem). The Adventures of Mottel, the
    Cantor's Son (fic, pub)
Conrad Michael Richter. The Light in the Forest (fic)
Theodore Roethke. The Waking (po)
Jerome David Salinger. Nine Stories (fic)
Carl August Sandburg. Always the Young Strangers (nar)
Eleanor May Sarton. The Land of Silence (po)
Allen Seager. Amos Berry (fic)
Karl Jay Shapiro. Poems, 1940-1953 (pub)
_____. Beyond Criticism (e)
Upton Beall Sinclair. The Return of Lanny Budd (fic)
Jean Stafford. Children Are Bored on Sunday (fic)
William Styron. The Long March (fic)
John Orley Allen Tate. The Forlorn Demon (e)
James Grover Thurber. Thurber Country (hum, misc)
Melvin Beaunorus Tolson. Libretto for the Republic of Liberia (po)
Leon Uris. Battle Cry (fic)
Mark Albert Van Doren. Mortal Summer (po)
_____. Nobody Say a Word (fic)
_____. Spring Birth, and Other Poems (po)
David Russell Wagoner. Dry Sun, Dry Wind (po)
Robert Penn Warren. Brother to Dragons (po)
Joseph Wechsberg. Blue Trout and Black Truffles (e)
Jessamyn West. Cress Delahanty (fic)

Ben Ames Williams. The Unconquered (fic)
Thomas Lanier (Tennessee) Williams. Camino Real (dr)
Richard Nathaniel Wright. The Outsider (fic)

                              1954

DEATHS

    Bess Streeter Aldrich
    Frederick Lewis Allen
    Leonard Bacon
    Maxwell Bodenheim
    Maxwell Struthers Burt
    William Edward March Campbell (William March)
    Herbert Sherman Gorman
    Joseph Hergesheimer
    Lynn Riggs
    Lew Sarrett
    Shaemas Shields (Shaemas O'Sheels)

EVENTS

    Black Mountain Review, Asheville, North Carolina, to 1957 (per)
    National Medal for Literature (est)

LITERATURE

    Leone Fuller Adams. Poems (pub)
    William Alfred. Agamemnon (dr)
    Harriette Arnow. The Dollmaker (fic)
    Louis Stanton Auchincloss. The Romantic Egoists (fic)
    Jacques Barzun. God's Country and Mine (e)
    Joseph Hamilton Basso. The View from Pompey's Head (fic)
    Joseph Warren Beach. The Method of Henry James, rev ed (e)
    Samuel Nathaniel Behrman. The Worcester Account (fic)
                        and Joshua Logan. Fanny (dr)
    Bernard Berenson. Seeing and Knowing (e)
    Morris Gilbert Bishop. A Bowl of Bishop (po)
    Louise Bogan. Collected Poems (pub)
    Vance Nye Bourjaily. The Hound of Earth (fic)
    Claude Gernade Bowers. My Mission to Spain (nar)
    Jane Bowles. In the Summer House (fic)
    John Brooks. The Pride of Lions (e)
    Van Wyck Brooks. Scenes and Portraits: Memories of Childhood and
        Youth (auto)
    Pearl Sydenstricker Buck. My Several Worlds (auto, nar)
    Erskine Preston Caldwell. Love and Money (fic)
    William Edward March Campbell (William March). The Bad Seed (fic)
    Truman Capote. House of Flowers (dr)
    Gladys Hasty Carroll. One White Star (fic)
    John Chamberlain. MacArthur, 1941-1951 (biog)
    Raymond Chandler. The Long Goodbye (fic)
    Mary Ellen Chase. The White Gate (auto)
    Stuart Chase. The Power of Words (e)
    Paddy Chayefsky. The Bachelor Party (dr)

John Cheever. The Enormous Radio, and Other Stories (fic)
Jerome Chodorov and Joseph Fields. Anniversary Waltz (dr)
John Ciardi. Inferno (trans)
Sidney (Cid) Corman. Thanksgiving Eclogue (po)
Thomas Bertram Costain. The White and the Gold (hist)
Malcolm Cowley. The Literary Situation (e)
Robert White Creeley. The Gold Diggers, to 1965 (fic)
Edward Estlin Cummings. Poems: 1923-1954 (pub)
Jonathan Worth Daniels. The End of Innocence (biog)
Marcia Davenport. My Brother's Keeper (fic)
Clyde Brion Davis. The Newcomer (fic)
Elmer Holmes Davis. But We Were Born Free (e)
Babette Deutsch. Animal, Vegetable, Mineral (po)
_____. Poetry in Our Time (e)
Peter DeVries. Tunnel of Love (fic)
John Roderigo Dos Passos. Most Likely To Succeed (fic)
Max Forrester Eastman. Poems of Five Decades (po)
Thomas Stearns Eliot. The Confidential Clerk (dr)
James Thomas Farrell. Reflections at Fifty (e)
William Harrison Faulkner. A Fable (fic)
Frederick Feikema (Frederick Manfred/Feike Feikema). Lord Grizzly
   (fic)
Harvey Fergusson. The Conquest of Don Pedro (fic)
Dudley Fitts. Lysistrata (trans)
Esther Forbes. Rainbow on the Road (fic)
Ellen Glasgow. The Woman Within (auto, pub)
Herbert Gold. The Prospect before Us (fic)
Paul Goodman. The Structure of Literature (e)
John Clendennin Bourne Hawkes, Jr. The Goose on the Grave (fic)
_____. The Owl (fic)
Anthony Evan Hecht. A Summoning of Stones (po)
Ben Hecht. A Child of the Century (auto)
Chester Bomar Himes. Third Generation (fic)
Daniel Gerard Hoffman. An Armada of Thirty Whales (po)
Paul Horgan. Great River (hist)
Barbara Howes. In the Cold Country (po)
Shirley Hardie Jackson. The Bird's Nest (fic)
Randall Jarrell. Pictures from an Institution: A Comedy (fic)
John Robinson Jeffers. The Cretan Women (dr, trans)
_____. Hungerfield, and Other Poems (po)
Sidney Kingsley. Lunatics and Lovers (dr)
Louis Kronenberger. Company Manners (e)
Joseph Wood Krutch. The Measure of Man (e)
Robert James Collas Lowry. Happy New Year, Kamerades! (fic)
Archibald MacLeish. Songs for Eve (po)
John Phillips Marquand. Thirty Years (fic, e)
Peter Matthiessen. Race Rock (fic)
Phyllis McGinley. The Love Letters of Phyllis McGinley (po)
William Stanley Merwin. The Dancing Bears (po)
James Albert Michener. Sayonara (fic)
Edna St. Vincent Millay. Mine the Harvest (po, pub)
Marianne Craig Moore. The Fables of La Fontaine (po, trans)
Wright Morris. The Huge Season (fic)
Howard Moss. The Toy Fair (po)
Howard Nemerov. Federigo, or the Power of Love (fic)
Anais Nin. A Spy in the House of Love (fic)

Clifford Odets. The Flowering Perch (dr)
John Henry O'Hara. Sweet and Sour (e)
Elder James Olson. The Scarecrow Christ (po)
Kenneth Patchen. The Famous Boating Party (po)
Elliot Harold Paul. Desperate Scenery (auto)
Ezra Weston Loomis Pound. The Classic Anthology (trans)
_____. The Literary Essays (e, pub)
Howard Sackler. Uriel Acosta (dr)
_____. Want My Shepherd (po)
Mark Schorer. The Wars of Love (fic)
Anya Seton. Katherine (fic)
William Lawrence Shirer. Stranger Come Home (fic)
Virginia Sorensen. Many Heavens (fic)
David Derek Stacton. Dolores (fic)
_____. A Ride on a Tiger (fic)
Jean Stafford. A Winter's Tale (fic)
John Ernst Steinbeck. Sweet Thursday (fic)
Wallace Stevens. Collected Poems (pub)
Irving Stone. Love Is Eternal (fic)
May Swenson. Another Animal (po)
Peter Hillsman Taylor. The Windows of Thornton (fic)
Robert Lewis Taylor. The Bright Sands (fic)
Alice Babette Toklas. The Alice B. Toklas Cook Book (ref, nar)
Mark Albert Van Doren. Selected Poems (pub)
Gore Vidal. Messiah (fic)
David Russell Wagoner. The Man in the Middle (fic)
Eudora Welty. The Ponder Heart (fic)
Elwyn Brooks White. The Second Tree from the Corner (e, po)
Thornton Niven Wilder. The Matchmaker (dr)
Thomas Lanier (Tennessee) Williams. Hard Candy (fic)
_____. One Arm, rev (fic)
William Carlos Williams. The Desert Music (po)
_____. Selected Essays (pub)
Edmund Wilson. Five Plays (pub)
Thyra Samter Winslow. The Sex without Sentiment (fic)
Herman Wouk. The Caine Mutiny Court-Martial (dr)
Richard Nathaniel Wright. Black Power (e)
Marya Zaturenska. Selected Poems (pub)

1955

DEATHS

    James Agee
    Robert Peter Tristram Coffin
    Bernard Augustine DeVoto
    Ludwig Lewisohn
    Horace McCoy
    Robert Emmet Sherwood
    Wallace Stevens
    Lula Vollmer

EVENTS

    Daedalus, American Academy of Arts and Sciences (per, f)

LITERATURE

Samuel Hopkins Adams. Grandfather Stories (fic)
Conrad Potter Aiken. A Letter from Li Po (po)
Archie Randolph Ammons. Ommateum, with Doxology (po)
Benjamin Appel. Life and Death of a Tough Guy (fic)
Sholem Asch. The Prophet (fic)
Wystan Hugh Auden. The Shield of Achilles (po)
James Baldwin. Notes of a Native Son (nar, e)
Margaret Culkin Banning. The Dowry (fic)
Walter Jackson Bate. The Achievement of Samuel Johnson (e)
Carleton Beale. Our Yankee Heritage (e)
Mary Ritter Beard. The Making of Charles A. Beard (biog)
Ben Belitt. Wilderness Stair (po)
Archie Binns and Olive Kooken. Mrs. Fiske and the American Theatre
    (hist)
Elizabeth Bishop. Poems (pub)
Paul Blackburn. The Dissolving Fabric (po)
Richard Palmer Blackmur. The Lion and the Honeycomb (e)
Louise Bogan. Selected Criticism (e)
Claude Gernade Bowers. Making Democracy a Reality (e)
Paul Bowles. The Spider's House (fic)
Kay Boyle. Seagull on the Step (fic)
Ray Douglas Bradbury. The October Country (fic)
John Malcolm Brinnin. Dylan Thomas in America (e, nar)
Louis Bromfield. From My Experience (nar)
Van Wyck Brooks. John Sloan (biog)
Kenneth Duva Burke. Book of Moments (po)
James Branch Cabell. As I Remember It (nar)
Erskine Preston Caldwell. Gretta (fic)
Walter Stanley Campbell (Stanley Vestal). Book Lover's Southwest
    (bib)
Carl Lamson Carmer. The Susquehanna (hist, des)
Rachel Carson. The Edge of the Sea (e)
Mary Ellen Chase. Life and Language in the Old Testament (hist)
Paddy Chayefsky. The Catered Affair (dr)
_____. Television Plays (dr, pub)
Marquis William Childs. The Ragged Edge (e)
John Ciardi. As If, Poems New and Selected (po)
Robert Myron Coates. Farther Shore (fic)
Gregory Nunzio Corso. This Hang-Up Age (dr)
_____. The Vestal Lady of Brattle (po)
Thomas Bertram Costain. The Tontine (fic)
Louis Osborne Coxe. The Second Man (po)
Merle Eugene Curti. Probing Our Past (hist)
Elmer Holmes Davis. Two Minutes Till Midnight (e)
Bernard Augustine DeVoto. The Easy Chair (e)
Emily Elizabeth Dickinson. The Poems of Emily Dickinson, 3 vols
    (pub)
James Patrick Donleavy. The Ginger Man (fic)
William Harrison Faulkner. Big Woods (fic)
Lawrence Ferlinghetti. Pictures of the Gone World (po)
Dudley Fitts. The Frogs (trans)
Isabella Stewart Gardner. Birthdays from the Ocean (po)
Paul Goodman. The Young Disciple (dr)
Charles William Goyen. In a Farther Country (fic)

Shirley Ann Grau. The Black Prince (fic)
Albert Hackett. The Diary of Anne Frank (dr)
Donald Andrew Hall. Exiles and Marriages (po)
Elizabeth Hardwick. The Simple Truth (fic)
Robert Haydn. Figure of Time (po)
Chester Bomar Himes. The Primitive (fic)
David Ignatow. The Gentle Weight Lifter (po)
William Inge. Bus Stop (dr)
Randall Jarrell. Selected Poems (pub)
Garson Kanin. Do Re Mi (fic)
MacKinlay Kantor. Andersonville (fic)
Alfred Kazin. The Inmost Self (e)
Louis Kronenberger. The Republic of Letters (hist, e)
Ira Levin. No Time for Sergeants (dr)
Ludwig Lewisohn. In a Summer Season (fic)
Anne Morrow Lindbergh. Gift from the Sea (e)
John Logan. Cycle for Mother Cabrini (po)
Norman Mailer. The Deer Park (fic)
John Phillips Marquand. Sincerely, Willis Wayde (fic)
Peter Matthiessen. Partisans (fic)
William Maxwell. The Writer As Illusionist (e)
Mary Therese McCarthy. A Charmed Life (fic)
Thomas Merton. No Man Is an Island (e)
Josephine Miles. Prefabrications (po)
Arthur Miller. A View from the Bridge (dr)
Henry Miller. Nights of Love and Laughter (fic)
Marianne Craig Moore. Predilections (e)
Christopher Darlington Morley. Gentlemen's Relish (po)
Vladimir Nabokov. Lolita (fic)
Robert Gruntal Nathan. Sir Henry (fic)
Howard Nemerov. The Salt Garden (po)
Flannery O'Connor. A Good Man Is Hard To Find (fic)
John Henry O'Hara. Ten North Frederick (fic)
Ann Petry. Harriet Tubman (juv, biog)
Frederic Prokosch. A Tale for Midnight (fic)
Solomon Rabinowitz (Sholom Aleichem). The Great Fair (fic, pub)
Adrienne Cecile Rich. The Diamond Cutters (po)
Carl August Sandburg. Prairie-Town Boy (nar, juv)
Eleanor May Sarton. Faithful Are the Wounds (fic)
Gladys Schmitt. The Persistent Image (fic)
Budd Wilson Schulberg. Waterfront (fic)
Louis Aston Marantz Simpson. Good News of Death (po)
David Derek Stacton. A Fox Inside (fic)
Wilbur Daniel Steele. The Way to Gold (fic)
George Rippey Stewart. The Years of the City (fic)
Philip Duffield Stong. Blizzard (fic)
Harvey Swados. Out Went the Candle (fic)
Lionel Trilling. The Opposing Self (e)
Leon Uris. The Angry Hills (fic)
David Russell Wagoner. Money Money Money (fic)
Robert Penn Warren. Band of Angels (fic)
Joseph Wechsberg. The Self-Betrayal (fic)
Jerome Weidman. Your Daughter Iris (fic)
Eudora Welty. The Bride of the Innisfallen (fic)
John Wexley. The Judgment of Julius and Ethel Rosenberg (nar)
Richard Purdy Wilbur. The Misanthrope (dr, trans)

Thornton Niven Wilder. A Life in the Sun (dr)
Thomas Lanier (Tennessee) Williams. Cat on a Hot Tin Roof (dr)
_____. In the Winter of Cities (po)
William Carlos Williams. Journey to Love (po)
Calder Baynard Willingham, Jr. To Eat a Peach (fic)
Edmund Wilson. The Scrolls from the Dead Sea (hist)
Herman Wouk. Marjorie Morningstar (fic)

1956

DEATHS

John Barry Benefield
John Bennett
Louis Bromfield
Edwin Corle
Owen Davis
Rupert Hughes
Edith Summers Kelley
Christopher LaFarge
Robert Morss Lovett
Charles MacArthur
Percy Wallace MacKaye
Percy Marks
Robert McAlmon
Henry Louis Mencken
Clarence Edward Mulford
Leonora Speyer

EVENTS

American Society for Theatre Research (f)
Beat Movement begins in San Francisco and New York
Neon, to 1960 (per)

LITERATURE

Nelson Algren. A Walk on the Wild Side (fic)
John Lawrence Ashbery. The Compromise (dr)
_____. Some Trees (po)
Louis Stanton Auchincloss. The Great World and Timothy Colt (fic)
Wystan Hugh Auden. Making, Knowing, and Judging (e)
James Baldwin. Giovanni's Room (fic)
John Barth. The Floating Opera (fic)
Jacques Barzun. Energies of Art: Studies of Authors, Classic and
    Modern (e)
_____. Music in American Life (e)
Carleton Beals. Taste of Glory (fic)
Saul Bellow. Seize the Day (fic, dr)
Catherine Shober Drinker Bowen. The Lion and the Throne (biog)
Gwendolyn Brooks. Bronzeville Boys and Girls (po)
Van Wyck Brooks. Helen Keller: Sketch for a Portrait (biog)
John Mason Brown. Through These Men (biog)
_____. The Worlds of Robert E. Sherwood (biog)
Pearl Sydenstricker Buck. Imperial Women (fic)

Ben Lucien Burman. Seven Stars for Catfish Bend (fic)
Harold Witter Bynner. A Book of Lyrics (po)
Erskine Preston Caldwell. Gulf Coast Stories (fic)
Truman Capote. The Muses Are Heard (nar)
Russel Crouse and Howard Lindsay. The Great Sebastians (dr)
Merle Eugene Curti. The American Paradox (hist)
Clyde Brion Davis. Something for Nothing (e, hist)
Vina Delmar. Beloved (fic)
Peter DeVries. Comfort Me with Apples (fic)
Hilda Doolittle. Tribute to Freud (e)
John Roderigo Dos Passos. The Theme Is Freedom (e)
William Eastlake. Go in Beauty (fic)
James Thomas Farrell. French Girls Are Vicious (fic)
Kenneth Fearing. New and Selected Poems (pub)
Frederick Feikema (Frederick Manfred/Feike Feikema). Morning Red
    (fic)
Vardis Alvero Fisher. A Goat for Azazel (fic)
_____. Jesus Came Again (fic)
_____. Pemmican (fic)
Robert Stuart Fitzgerald. In the Rose of Time (po)
Allen Ginsberg. Howl, and Other Poems (po)
Herbert Gold. The Man Who Was Not with It (fic)
Caroline Gordon. The Malefactors (fic)
Charles William Goyen. The House of Breath (dr)
Alfred Bertram Guthrie, Jr. These Thousand Hills (fic)
Albert Halper. Atlantic Avenue (fic)
Mark Harris. Bang the Drum Slowly (fic)
John Richard Hersey. A Single Pebble (fic)
Edward Hoagland. Cat Man (fic)
Paul Horgan. Centuries of the Sante Fe (hist)
Shirley Hardie Jackson. The Witchcraft of Salem Village (juv)
Meyer Levin. Compulsion (fic)
Anne Morrow Lindbergh. The Unicorn (po)
Henry Louis Mencken. Minority Report (nar, e)
James Ingram Merrill. The Immortal Husband (dr)
William Stanley Merwin. Green with Beasts (po)
_____ and Dido Milroy. Darkling Child (dr)
Edna St. Vincent Millay. Collected Poems (pub)
Henry Miller. The Time of the Assassins (e)
Marianne Craig Moore. Like a Bulwark (po)
Wright Morris. The Field of Vision (fic)
Robert Gruntal Nathan. Rancho of the Little Loves (fic)
Edwin O'Connor. The Last Harrah (fic)
John Henry O'Hara. A Family Party (fic)
Charles Olson. The Maximus Poems, 11-23 (po)
Eugene Gladstone O'Neill. Long Day's Journey into Night (dr, pub)
Ezra Weston Loomis Pound. The Women of Trachis (dr, trans)
James Farl Powers. Presence of Grace (fic)
Kenneth Rexroth. In Defense of the Earth (po)
Kenneth Lewis Roberts. Boon Island (fic)
Lew Sarett. Covenant with Earth (po, pub)
William Saroyan. Mama, I Love You (fic)
_____. The Whole Voyald (fic)
Allen Seager. Hilda Manning (fic)
Irwin Shaw. Lucy Crown (fic)
William Lawrence Shirer. The Consul's Wife (fic)

Elizabeth Spencer. The Voice at the Back Door (fic)
David Derek Stacton. The Self-Enchanted (fic)
Wallace Earle Stegner. The City of the Living (fic)
Philip Duffield Stong. Adventures of Horse Barnsby (sat)
Jesse Hilton Stuart. Year of My Rebirth (auto)
Peter Hillsman Taylor. Tennessee Day in St. Louis (dr)
James Grover Thurber. Further Fables for Our Own Time (fic)
Lionel Trilling. Freud and the Crisis of Our Culture (e)
_____. A Gathering of Fugitives (e)
Barbara Wertheim Tuchman. Bible and Sword (hist)
Gore Vidal. A Thirsty Evil (fic)
_____. Visit to a Small Planet (dr)
Peter Viereck. The Persimmon Tree (po)
Robert Penn Warren. Segregation: The Inner Conflict in the South (e)
John Hall Wheelock. Poems Old and New (po)
Edward Reed Whittemore II. An American Takes a Walk (po)
Richard Purdy Wilbur. Things of This World (po)
Edmund Wilson. A Piece of My Mind (e)
_____. Red, Black, Blonde and Olive (hist)
Richard Nathaniel Wright. The Color Curtain (nar)

1957

DEATHS

Sholem Asch
Joseph Warren Beach
Charles Badger Clark
Walter Stanley Campbell (Stanley Vestal)
Peter Bernard Kyne
Merrill Moore
Christopher Darlington Morley
Anne Parrish
Kenneth Lewis Roberts
Philip Duffield Stong
John William Van Druten
Laura Ingalls Wilder

EVENTS

The Evergreen Review, New York, New York, to 1973 (per)
Carl H. Pforzheimer Library, New York, New York (f)
Harry S. Truman Library, Independence, Missouri (f)

LITERATURE

Herbert Sebastian Agar. Price of Power (e)
James Agee. A Death in the Family (fic, pub)
Conrad Potter Aiken. Mr. Arcularis (dr)
Joseph Warren Beach. The Making of the Auden Canon (e)
Archie Binns. The Headwaters (fic)
Philip Booth. Letter from a Distant Land (po)
Paul Bowles. Yallah (des)
Gerald Warner Brace. The Age of the Novel (e)

_____. The World of Carrick's Cove (fic)
Ray Douglas Bradbury. Dandelion Wine (fic)
Van Wyck Brooks. Days of the Phoenix (auto, nar)
Pearl Sydenstricker Buck. Letter from Peking (fic)
Mary Ellen Chase. The Edge of Darkness (fic)
John Cheever. The Wapshot Chronicle (fic)
Jerome Chadorov and Joseph Fields. The Ponder Heart (dr)
Robert Myron Coates. Hour after Westerly (fic)
Evan Shelby Connell, Jr. The Anatomy Lesson (fic)
Thomas Bertram Costain. Below the Salt (fic)
James Gould Cozzens. By Love Possessed (fic)
Edward Dahlberg. The Sorrows of Priapus (e)
Donald Grady Davidson. Still Rebels, Still Yankees (e)
Clyde Brion Davis. Unholy Uproar (fic)
Harold Lenoir Davis. Distant Music (fic)
John Roderigo Dos Passos. Men Who Made the Nation (biog)
William Edward Burghardt DuBois. The Ordeal of Mansart (fic)
Richard Ghormley Eberhart. Great Praises (po)
Thomas Stearns Eliot. On Poetry and Poets (e)
James Thomas Farrell. A Dangerous Woman (fic)
_____. My Baseball Diary (nar, e)
Howard Melvin Fast. The Naked God (nar)
William Harrison Faulkner. The Town (fic)
Frederick Feikema (Frederick Manfred/Feike Feikema). Riders of Judg-
    ment (fic)
Thomas Hornsby Ferril. And Perhaps Happiness (po, dr)
Irving Fineman. Helen Herself (fic)
Vardis Alvero Fisher. Peace Like a River (fic)
Dudley Fitts. The Birds (trans)
Janet Flanner. Men and Monuments (e)
Martin Archer Flavin. Cameron Hill (fic)
Waldo David Frank. Bridgehead (e)
Caroline Gordon. How To Read a Novel (e)
Julian Green. The Transgressor (fic)
Nancy Hale. Heaven and Hardpan Farm (fic)
Mark Harris. Something about a Soldier (fic)
_____. A Ticket for a Seamstitch (fic)
Lillian Hellman and Richard Purdy Wilbur. Candide (dr)
Robert Silliman Hillyer. The Relic (po)
Chester Bomar Himes. For Love of Imabelle (fic)
Paul Horgan. Give Me Possession (fic)
James Langston Hughes. Esther (dr)
_____. Simple Takes a Claim (fic)
_____. Simply Heavenly (dr)
William Inge. The Dark at the Top of the Stairs (dr)
Shirley Hardie Jackson. Raising Demons (nar)
James Jones. Some Came Running (fic)
Jack Kerouac. On the Road (fic)
Oliver Hazard Perry LaFarge. A Pause in the Desert (fic)
Denise Levertov. Here and Now (po)
Andrew Nelson Lytle. The Velvet Horn (fic)
Robie Mayhew Macauley. The End of Pity (fic)
Bernard Malamud. The Assistant (fic)
Albert Maltz. A Long Day in a Short Life (fic)
John Phillips Marquand. Life at Happy Knoll (fic)
Mary Therese McCarthy. Memories of a Catholic Girlhood (auto)

David Thompson Watson McCord. Selected Poems (pub)
James Ingram Merrill. The Seraglio (fic)
Thomas Merton. Silence in Heaven (e)
_____. The Silent Life (e)
William Stanley Merwin. Favor Island (dr)
Josephine Miles. Eras and Modes in English Poetry (e)
Henry Miller. Big Sur and the Oranges of Hieronymus Bosch (nar)
Wright Morris. Love among the Cannibals (fic)
Theodore Morrison. To Make a World (fic)
Howard Moss. A Swimmer in the Air (po)
Vladimir Nabokov. Pnin (fic)
Ogden Nash. You Can't Get There from Here (po)
Frank O'Hara. Meditations in an Emergency (po)
Eugene Gladstone O'Neill. A Touch of the Poet (dr, pub)
Kenneth Patchen. Hurrah for Anything (po)
Sidney Joseph Perelman. The Road to Miltown; or, Under the Spreading
   Atrophy (sat, nar)
James Purdy. The Color of Darkness (fic)
Ayn Rand. Atlas Shrugged (fic)
Conrad Michael Richter. The Lady (fic)
William Saroyan. Papa, You're Crazy (fic)
Eleanor May Sarton. The Birth of a Grandfather (fic)
_____. In Time Like Air (po)
Gladys Schmitt. A Small Fire (fic)
Irwin Shaw. Tip on a Dead Jockey (fic)
Isaac Bashevis Singer. Gimpel the Fool (fic)
Charles Wilbert Snow. Sonnets to Steve (po)
Jack Spicer. After Lorca (po)
David Derek Stacton. Remember Me (fic)
John Ernst Steinbeck. The Short Reign of Pippin IV (fic)
Wallace Stevens. Opus Posthumous (dr, e, po, pub)
Rex Todhunter Stout. If Death Ever Slept (fic)
Harvey Swados. On the Line (fic)
Studs Lewis Terkel. Giants of Jazz (biog)
James Grover Thurber. Alarms and Diversions (hum)
_____. The Wonderful O (juv)
Mark Albert Van Doren. Home with Hazel (fic)
Robert Penn Warren. Promises (po)
Jessamyn West. To See the Dream (nar)
Richard Purdy Wilbur. Poems, 1943-1956 (pub)
Thomas Lanier (Tennessee) Williams. Orpheus Descending (dr)
Arthur Yvor Winters. The Function of Criticism: Problems and Exerci-
   ses (e)
James Arlington Wright. The Green Wall (po)
Richard Nathaniel Wright. Pagan Spain (e)

1958

DEATHS

   Eleanor Hallowell Abbott
   Samuel Hopkins Adams
   Zoe Akins
   Mary Ritter Beard

Claude Gernade Bowers
James Branch Cabell
Grace Hazard Conkling
Rachel Crothers
Elmer Holmes Davis
Wolcott Gibbs
Clare Kummer
Philip Moeller
George Jean Nathan
Elliot Harold Paul
Mary Roberts Rinehart
Elsie Singmaster
Mary Stanbery Watts

EVENTS

Tri-Quarterly, Evanston, Illinois (per, f)

LITERATURE

Mortimore Jerome Adler. The Idea of Freedom (e)
James Agee. Agee on Film (e, pub)
Conrad Potter Aiken. A Reviewer's A.B.C. (e, ref)
_____. Sheepfold Hill (po)
Benjamin Appel. The Raw Edge (fic)
Hannah Arendt. The Human Condition (e)
Louis Stanton Auchincloss. Venus in Sparta (fic)
Djuna Barnes. The Antiphon (dr, po)
Stringfellow Barr. Purely Academic (fic)
John Barth. The End of the Road (fic)
Samuel Nathaniel Behrman. The Cold Wind and the Warm (dr)
Thomas Louis Berger. Crazy in Berlin (fic)
Daniel J. Boorstin. The Americans: The Colonial Experiences (hist)
Vance Nye Bourjaily. The Violated (fic)
Myron Brinig. Looking Glass Heart (fic)
John Brooks. The Man Who Broke Things (e)
Van Wyck Brooks. American Writers and Artists in Italy, 1760-1915
    (biog, hist)
_____. From a Writer's Notebook (nar, e)
Carl Frederick Buechner. The Return of Ansel Gibbs (fic)
William Byrd II. The London Diary (nar, pub)
Erskine Preston Caldwell. Claudelle Inglish (fic)
Truman Capote. Breakfast at Tiffany's (fic)
Stuart Chase. Some Things Worth Knowing: A Generalist's Guide to
    Useful Knowledge (ref)
John Cheever. The Housebreaker of Shady Hill (fic)
Marquis William Childs. Eisenhower: Captive Hero (biog)
John Ciardi. I Marry You (po)
Gregory Nunzio Corso. Bomb (po)
_____. Gasoline (po)
Thomas Bertram Costain. The Three Edwards (hist)
Louis Osborne Coxe. The Wilderness (po)
Edward Estlin Cummings. 95 Poems (pub)
Olive Tilford Dargan. Spotted Hawk (po)
Donald Grady Davidson. Southern Writers in the Modern World (e)
August William Derleth. House on the Mound (fic)

Peter DeVries. The Mackerel Plaza (fic)
Hilda Doolittle. End to Torment (nar, biog)
John Roderigo Dos Passos. The Great Days (fic)
Robert Edward Duncan. Letters (po, e)
William Eastlake. Bronc People (fic)
Thomas Stearns Eliot. The Elder Statesman (dr)
George Paul Elliott. Parktilden Village (fic)
Theodore Vernon Enslin. The Work Proposed (po)
James Thomas Farrell. It Has Come To Pass (nar, e)
Howard Melvin Fast. Moses, Prince of Egypt (fic)
William Harrison Faulkner. New Orleans Sketches (fic, pub)
Peter Steinham Feibleman. A Place without Twilight (fic)
Edna Ferber. Ice Palace (fic)
Lawrence Ferlinghetti. A Coney Island of the Mind (po)
Vardis Alvero Fisher. My Holy Satan (fic)
_____. Tale of Valor (fic)
Francis Scott Key Fitzgerald. Afternoon of an Author (fic, e, pub)
Shelby Foote. The Civil War, 3 vols, to 1973 (hist)
George Palmer Garrett, Jr. King of the Mountain (fic)
_____. The Sleeping Gypsy (po)
Martha Gellhorn. Two by Two (fic)
Wolcott Gibbs. More in Sorrow (e)
William Gibson. Two for the Seasaw (dr)
Shirley Ann Grau. The Hard Blue Sky (fic)
Paul Eliot Green. The Confederacy (dr)
_____. Drama and the Weather (e)
Horace Victor Gregory. Amy Lowell (biog, e)
Albert Joseph Guerard. The Bystander (fic)
_____. Conrad the Novelist (e)
Nancy Hale. A New England Girlhood (fic)
Donald Andrew Hall. The Dark Houses (po)
Oakley Hall. Warlock (fic)
Anthony Evan Hecht. The Seven Deadly Sins (po)
Robert Anson Heinlein. Methuselah's Children (fic)
James Leo Herlihy. Blue Denim (dr)
_____. Crazy October (dr)
John Hollander. A Crackling of Thorns (po)
John Clellon Holmes. The Horn (fic)
James Langston Hughes. Tambourines to Glory (fic)
Harold Louis Humes. Underground City (fic)
William Humphrey. Home from the Hill (fic)
Fannie Hurst. Anatomy of Me (auto)
Shirley Hardie Jackson. The Sundial (fic)
Rona Jaffe. The Best of Everything (fic)
Randall Jarrell. Uncollected Poems (pub)
Jack Kerouac. The Dharma Bums (fic)
_____. The Subterraneans (fic)
Arthur Kober. Ooh, What You Said! (fic)
Jonathan Kozol. The Fume of Poppies (fic)
Louis Kronenberger. Marlborough's Duchess (biog)
Stanley Jasspon Kunitz. Selected Poems, 1928-1958 (pub)
Denise Levertov. 5 Poems (pub)
_____. Overland to the Islands (po)
Victoria Lincoln. Dangerous Innocence (fic)
Robert James Collas Lowry. New York Call Girl (fic)
Mina Gertrude Lowry (Mina Loy). Luvar Baedecker and Time-Tables (po)

Andrew Nelson Lytle. A Novel, A Novella, and Four Stories (fic, pub)
Archibald MacLeish. J.B. (po, dr)
Bernard Malamud. The Magic Barrel (fic)
John Phillips Marquand. Women and Thomas Harrow (fic)
Carson Smith McCullers. The Square Root of Wonderful (dr)
Phyllis McGinley. Merry Christmas, Happy New Year (po)
William Morris Meredith. The Open Sea (po)
Thomas Merton. The New Man (e)
Wright Morris. The Territory Ahead (e)
Howard Moss. The Folding Green (dr)
Willard Motley. Let No Man Write My Epitaph (fic)
Robert Gruntal Nathan. So Love Returns (fic)
Howard Nemerov. Mirrors and Windows (po)
John Henry O'Hara. From the Terrace (fic)
Elder James Olson. Plays and Poems (pub)
Eugene Gladstone O'Neill. Hughie (dr, pub)
Martha Ostenso. A Man Had Tall Sons (fic)
Kenneth Patchen. Selected Poems (pub)
Ezra Weston Loomis Pound. Pavannes and Divagations (e)
Kenneth Lewis Roberts. The Battle of Cowpens (hist, pub)
Theodore Roethke. Words for the Wind (po)
Muriel Rukeyser. Body of Waking (po)
William Saroyan. The Cave Dwellers (dr)
James Marcus Schuyler. Alfred and Guinevere (fic)
Anya Seton. The Winthrop Woman (fic)
Karl Jay Shapiro. Poems of a Jew (po)
Upton Beall Sinclair. It Happened to Didymus (fic)
Betty Wehner Smith. Maggie--Now (fic)
David Derek Stacton. On a Balcony (fic)
_____. Segaki (fic)
John Ernst Steinbeck. Once There Was a War (nar, e)
Jesse Hilton Stewart. Plowshare in Heaven (fic)
May Swenson. A Cage of Spines (po)
Robert Lewis Taylor. The Travels of Jamie McPheeters (fic)
Barbara Wertheim Tuchman. The Zimmerman Telegram (hist)
Alice Babette Toklas. Aromas and Flavors of Past and Present (ref,
   hist)
John Hoyer Updike. The Carpentered Hen and Other Tame Creatures (po)
Leon Uris. Exodus (fic)
David Russell Wagoner. A Place To Stand (po)
_____. Rock (fic)
Joseph Wechsberg. Avalanche! (nar)
Jerome Weidman. The Enemy Camp (fic)
Theodore Harold White. The Mountain Road (fic)
Margaret Widdemer. The Dark Cavalier (po)
John Wieners. The Hotel Wentley Poems (po)
Thomas Lanier (Tennessee) Williams. Something Unspoken (dr)
_____. Suddenly Last Summer (dr)
Edmund Wilson. The American Earthquake (nar)
Herman Wouk. Nature's Way (dr)
Richard Nathaniel Wright. The Long Dream (fic)

1959

DEATHS

Maxwell Anderson
Bernard Berenson
Raymond Chandler
Octavus Roy Cohen
Edgar Albert Guest
Wallace Admah Irwin

LITERATURE

George Abbott. Fiorello! (dr)
Samuel Hopkins Adams. Tenderloin (fic, pub)
Edward Albee. The Zoo Story (dr)
Robert Woodruff Anderson. Silent Night, Lonely Night (dr)
Louis Stanton Auchincloss. Pursuit of the Prodigal (fic)
Margaret Culkin Banning. Echo Answers (fic)
Jacques Barzun. The House of Intellect (e)
Joseph Hamilton Basso. Light Infantry Ball (fic)
Saul Bellow. Henderson the Rain King (fic)
Bernard Berenson. Essays in Appreciation (e)
Edmund J.M. Berrigan, Jr. A Lily for My Love (po)
Ray Douglas Bradbury. A Medicine for Melancholy (fic)
John Malcolm Brinnin. The Third Rose (e, biog)
Van Wyck Brooks. Howells: His Life and World (biog)
Norman Oliver Brown. Life against Death: The Psychoanalytic Meaning
    of History (e)
Pearl Sydenstricker Buck. Command the Morning (fic)
Ben Lucien Burman. The Street of the Laughing Camel (fic)
William Riley Burnett. Mi Amigo (fic)
William Seward Burroughs (William Lee). The Naked Lunch (fic)
Erskine Preston Caldwell. When You Think of Me (fic)
Janet Taylor Caldwell. Dear and Glorious Physician (fic)
Hayden Carruth. The Crow and the Heart (po)
John Chamberlain. The Roots of Capitalism (e)
William Henry Chamberlain. Evolution of a Conservative (e)
Paddy Chayefsky. The Tenth Man (dr)
Marquis William Childs and James Reston. Walter Lippmann and His
    Times (e, ed)
James Bryant Conant. The American High School Today (e)
_____. The Child, the Parent, and the State (e)
Evan Shelby Connell, Jr. Mrs. Bridge (fic)
Thomas Bertram Costain. The Darkness and the Dawn (fic)
Russel Crouse and Howard Lindsay. Tall Story (dr)
Harold Lenoir Davis. Kettle of Fire (e)
David Cornel DeJong. The Unfairness of Easter (fic)
Babette Deutsch. Coming of Age (po)
Peter DeVries. The Tests of Wickedness (dr)
John Roderigo Dos Passos. Prospect of a Golden Age (biog)
Allen Stuart Drury. Advise and Consent (fic)
William Edward Burghardt DuBois. Mansart Builds a School (fic)
Max Forrester Eastman. Great Companions (e)
Paul Hamilton Engle. Poems in Praise (po)
William Everson (Brother Antoninus). The Crooked Lines of God (po)

Howard Melvin Fast. The Winston Affair (fic)
Peter Steinham Feibleman. The Daughters of Necessity (fic)
Frederick Feikema (Frederick Manfred/Feike Feikema). Conquering Horse
    (fic)
Vardis Alvero Fisher. Love and Death (fic)
Dudley Fitts. Ladies' Day (trans)
George Palmer Garrett, Jr. The Finished Man (fic)
Jean Garrigue. A Water Walk by Villa d'Este (po)
Jack Gelber. The Connection (dr)
Martha Gellhorn. The Face of War (nar)
Herbert Gold. The Optimist (fic)
Paul Eliot Green. The Stephen Foster Story (dr)
Horace Victor Gregory. The World of James MacNeill Whistler (biog,
    hist)
Nancy Hale. Dear Beast (fic)
Lorraine Hansberry. A Raisin in the Sun (dr)
Mark Harris. Wake Up, Stupid (fic)
Moss Hart. Act One (auto)
Ben Hecht. The Sensualists (fic)
James Leo Herlihy. The Sleep of Baby Filberton (fic)
John Richard Hersey. The Child Buyer (sat)
_____. The War Lover (fic)
Chester Bomar Himes. The Crazy Kill (fic)
_____. The Real Cool Killers (fic)
Barbara Howes. Light and Dark (po)
James Langston Hughes. Selected Poems (pub)
_____. Shakespeare in Harlem (dr)
Harold Louis Humes. Men Die (fic)
William Inge. A Loss of Roses (dr)
Shirley Hardie Jackson. The Bad Children (juv, dr)
_____. The Haunting of Hill House (fic)
_____. The Lottery (fic)
James Jones. The Pistol (fic)
Garson Kanin. Blow up a Storm (fic)
Bob Kaufman. Abomunist Manifesto (po)
_____. Does the Secret Wind Whisper (po)
_____. Second April (po)
Jack Kerouac. Doctor Sax (fic)
_____. Maggie Cassidy (fic)
_____. Mexico City Blues (po)
Arthur Kober. A Mighty Man Is He (dr)
Philip Lamantia. Ekstasis (po)
Denise Levertov. With Eyes at the Back of Our Heads (po)
Meyer Levin. Eva (fic)
Janet Lewis. The Ghost of Monsieur Scarron (fic)
Robert Traill Spence Lowell, Jr. Life Studies, to 1968 (po)
Norman Mailer. Advertisements for Myself (fic, e)
David Meltzer. Rogas (po)
Michael Thomas McClure. For Artaud (po)
_____. Hymns to St. Geryon (po)
Phyllis McGinley. Province of the Heart (e)
James Ingram Merrill. The Country of a Thousand Years of Peace (po)
Thomas Merton. Secular Journal (nar)
James Albert Michener. Hawaii (fic)
Kenneth Millar (Ross MacDonald). The Galton Case (fic)
Marianne Craig Moore. O To Be a Dragon (po)

Samuel Eliot Morison. John Paul Jones (biog, hist)
Vladimir Nabokov. Poems (pub)
Howard Nemerov. A Commodity of Dreams (fic)
John Frederick Nims. Poems of St. John of the Cross (trans)
Anais Nin. Cities of the Interior (fic)
Robert Pack. A Stranger's Privilege (po)
Grace Paley. The Little Disturbances of Man: Stories of Women and
    Men at Love (fic)
Louis Paul. Dara, the Cypriot (fic)
Joseph Stanley Pennell. Darksome House (po)
Ezra Weston Loomis Pound. Thrones: 96-109 de los Cantares (po)
James Purdy. Malcolm (fic)
Elmer Reizenstein (Elmer Rice). The Living Theatre (e)
Kenneth Rexroth. Bird in the Bush (e)
Charles Reznikoff. Inscriptions (po)
Leo Calvin Rosten (Leonard Q. Ross). The Return of Hyman Kaplan (fic)
Philip Roth. Goodbye, Columbus (fic)
Delmore Schwartz. Summer Knowledge (po)
Louis Aston Marantz Simpson. A Dream of Governors (po)
Isaac Bashevis Singer. The Magician of Lublin (fic)
William DeWitt Snodgrass. Heart's Needle (po)
Gary Sherman Snyder. Riprap (po)
Jack Spicer. Billy the Kid (po)
William Strunk, Jr. and Elwyn Brooks White. The Elements of Style
    (e, ref)
Ruth Suckow. The John Wood Case (fic)
Harvey Swados. False Coin (fic)
John Orley Allen Tate. Collected Essays (pub)
Peter Hillsman Taylor. Happy Families Are All Alike (fic)
Studs Lewis Terkel. Amazing Grace (dr)
John Hoyer Updike. The Poorhouse Fair (fic)
James Grover Thurber. The Years with Ross (nar)
John Hoyer Updike. The Same Door (fic)
Mark Albert Van Doren. The Last Days of Lincoln (dr)
Kurt Vonnegut, Jr. Sirens of Titan (fic)
Irving Wallace. The Sins of Phillip Fleming (fic)
Robert Penn Warren. The Cave (fic)
Jessamyn West. Love, Death, and the Ladies' Drill Team (fic)
_____. Love Is Not What You Think (e)
Philip Whalen. Self-Portrait from Another Direction (po)
Edward Reed Whittemore II. The Self-Made Man (po)
Thomas Lanier (Tennessee) Williams. Sweet Bird of Youth (dr)
_____. Triple Play (dr)
Frances Winwar. The Haunted Palace (biog)
Herman Wouk. This Is My God (e)
James Arlington Wright. Saint Judas (po)
Louis Zukofsky. A 1-2 (po)

1960

DEATHS

    Franklin Pierce Adams
    Harold Lenoir Davis
    Zora Neale Hurston

Hibbard (Harry) Kemp
John Phillips Marquand
Emily Post
Arthur Hobson Quinn
Ruth Suckow
Richard Nathaniel Wright
Audrey Wurdemann

EVENTS

Noble Savage, New York, New York, to 1962 (per)

LITERATURE

Herbert Sebastian Agar. The Saving Remnant (e)
James Agee. Agee on Film: II (e, dr, pub)
Edward Albee. The Death of Bessie Smith (dr)
_____. The Sandbox (dr)
Roger Angell. The Stone Arbor, and Other Stories (fic)
John Lawrence Ashbery. The Poems (pub)
Louis Stanton Auchincloss. The House of Five Talents (fic)
Wystan Hugh Auden. Homage to Clio (po)
John Barth. The Sot-Weed Factor (fic)
John Hamilton Basso. A Quota of Seaweed (nar)
Joseph Warren Beach. Obsessive Images: Symbolism in the Poetry of the
    1930's and 1940's (e, pub)
Peter Soyer Beagle. A Fine and Private Place (fic)
Carleton Beals. Brass-Knuckle Crusade (e)
Samuel Nathaniel Behrman. Portrrait of Max (biog)
Bernard Berenson. The Passionate Sight-Seer (e, nar)
Don Berry. Trask (fic)
Morris Gilbert Bishop. History of Cornell (hist)
Paul Blackburn. Brooklyn-Manhattan Transit (po)
Vance Nye Bourjaily. Confessions of a Spent Youth (fic)
Catherine Shober Drinker Bowen. Adventures of a Biographer (nar, e)
Kay Boyle. Generation without Farewell (fic)
Gerald Warner Brace. Winter Solstice (fic)
Gwendolyn Brooks. The Bean Eaters (po)
Charles Bukowski. Flower Fist and Bestial Wail (po)
William Seward Burroughs. The Exterminator (fic)
Morley Callaghan. The Many-Colored Coat (fic)
Melville Henry Cane. Bullet-Hunting (po)
Mary Ellen Chase. Lovely Ambition (fic)
Stuart Chase. Live and Let Live (e)
Robert Myron Coates. The View from Here (nar, auto)
James Bryant Conant. Education in the Junior High Years (e)
Evan Shelby Connell. The Patriot (fic)
Gregory Nunzio Corso. The Happy Birthday of Death (po)
Thomas Bertram Costain. The Chord of Steel (biog)
Norman Cousins. The Last Defense in a Nuclear Age (e)
Louis Osborne Coxe. The Middle Passage (po)
Marcia Davenport. Constant Image (fic)
Clyde Brion Davis. The Big Pink Kite (fic)
August William Derleth. The Hills Stand Watch (fic)
James Lafayette Dickey. Into the Stone (po)
Pietro DiDonato. Immigrant Saint: The Life of Mother Cabrini (biog)

_____. Three Circles of Light (fic)
Edgar Lawrence Doctorow. Welcome to Hard Times (fic)
Hilda Doolittle. Bid Me To Live (fic)
Edward Merton Dorn. What I See in the Maximus Poems (e)
Robert Edward Duncan. Faust Foutou (dr)
_____. The Opening of the Field (po)
Paul Hamilton Engle. A Prairie Christmas (po)
William Harrison Faulkner. The Mansion (fic)
Kenneth Fearing. The Crozart Story (fic)
Lawrence Ferlinghetti. Her (fic)
Leslie Aaron Fiedler. Love and Death in the American Novel (e)
Vardis Alvero Fisher. Orphans in Gethsemane (fic)
William Gibson. The Miracle Worker (dr)
Allen Ginsberg. Empty Mirror (po)
Herbert Gold. Love and Like (fic)
_____. Therefore Be Bold (fic)
Charles William Goyen. The Faces of Blood Kindred (fic)
_____. The Diamond Rattler (dr)
Alfred Bertram Guthrie, Jr. The Big It (fic)
Nancy Hale. The Pattern of Perfection (fic)
Alfred Hayes. The Temptation of Don Volpi (fic)
Anthony Evan Hecht. A Bestiary (po)
Lillian Hellman. Toys in the Attic (dr)
James Leo Herlihy. All Fall Down (fic)
Robert Silliman Hillyer. In Pursuit of Poetry (e)
Chester Bomar Himes. All Shot Up (fic)
_____. The Big Gold Dream (fic)
Edward Hoagland. The Circle Home (fic)
Daniel Gerard Hoffman. A Little Geste (po)
Paul Horgan. A Distant Trumpet (fic)
James Langston Hughes. Port Town (dr)
Fanny Hurst. Family! (fic)
Randall Jarrell. The Woman at the Washington Zoo: Poems and Transla-
    tions (pub)
Donald Rodney Justice. The Summer Anniversaries (po)
Jack Kerouac. Tristessa (fic)
Galway Kinnell. What a Kingdom It Was (po)
John Knowles. A Separate Peace (fic)
Kenneth Jay Koch. Ko, or a Season on Earth (po)
Arthur L. Kopit. Oh Dad, Poor Dad, Mama's Hung You in the Closet and
    I'm Feelin' So Sad (dr)
Josephine Lawrence. Hearts Do Not Break (fic)
Nelle Harper Lee. To Kill a Mockingbird (fic)
Ira Levin. Critic's Choice (dr)
John Logan. Ghosts of the Heart (po)
Archibald MacLeish. Poetry and Experience (e)
Peter Matthiessen. Raditzer (fic)
Phyllis McGinley. Times Three: Selected Verse from Three Decades (po,
    pub)
Peter McNab, Jr. (Harry Brown). The Stars in Their Courses (fic)
James Ingram Merrill. The Bait (dr)
William Stanley Merwin. The Drunk in the Furnace (po)
Josephine Miles. Poems, 1930-1960 (pub)
_____. Renaissance, Eighteenth-Century, and Modern Lang-
    uage in Poetry (e)
Henry Miller. The Rosy Crucifixion: Nexus (nar)

Wright Morris. Ceremony in Lone Tree (fic)
Howard Moss. A Winter Come, a Summer Gone (po)
Ogden Nash. Scrooge Rides Again (po)
Robert Gruntal Nathan. The Color of Evening (fic)
John Frederick Nims. Knowledge of the Evening (po)
Flannery O'Connor. The Violent Bear It Away (fic)
Frank O'Hara. Odes (po)
_____. Second Avenue (po)
John Henry O'Hara. Ourselves To Know (fic)
_____. Sermons and Soda-Water (fic)
Charles Olson. The Distances (po)
Kenneth Patchen. Because It Is (po)
Ezra Weston Loomis Pound. Essays on Ignorance and the Decline of
    American Civilization (e)
Frederick Prokosch. The Seven Sisters (fic)
James Purdy. The Nephew (fic)
Jack Carter Richardson. The Prodigal (dr)
Conrad Michael Richter. The Waters of Kronos (fic)
Howard Sackler. Mr. Welk and Jersey Jim (dr)
Carl August Sandburg. Harvest Poems, 1910-1960 (po, pub)
_____. Wind Song (po)
Mari Sandoz. Son of the Gamblin' Man (fic)
James Marcus Schuyler. Salute (po)
Allen Seager. Death of Anger (fic)
Anne Sexton. To Bedlam and Part Way Back (po)
Karl Jay Shapiro. In Defense of Ignorance (e)
Irwin Shaw. Two Weeks in Another Town (fic)
William Lawrence Shirer. The Rise and Fall of the Third Reich (hist,
    nar)
Lillian Eugenia Smith. One Hour (fic)
Gary Sherman Snyder. Myths and Texts (po)
Gilbert Sorrentino. The Darkness Surrounds Us (po)
Virginia Sorensen. Kingdom Come (fic)
Elizabeth Spencer. The Light in the Piazza (fic)
David Derek Stacton. A Dancer in Darkness (fic)
_____. The Invincible Question: A Signal Victory (fic)
William Edgar Stafford. West of Your City (po)
George Edwin Starbuck. Bone Thoughts (po)
Richard Gustave Stern. Golk (fic)
Jesse Hilton Stuart. God's Oddling (fic)
William Styron. Set This House on Fire (fic)
Louis Untermeyer. Lives of the Poets (biog)
John Hoyer Updike. Rabbit, Run (fic)
Mark Albert Van Doren. Morning Worship (po)
Gore Vidal. The Best Man (dr)
Irving Wallace. The Chapman Report (fic)
Edward Lewis Wallant. The Human Season (fic)
Robert Penn Warren. You, Emperors, and Others (po)
Jerome Weidman. Before You Go (fic)
_____ and George Abbott. Fiorello! rev (dr)
Jessamyn West. South of the Angels (fic)
Philip Whalen. Like I Say (po)
_____. Memoirs of an Inter-Glacial Age (po)
Theodore Harold White. The View from the Fortieth Floor (fic)
John Alfred Williams. The Angry Ones (fic)
Thomas Lanier (Tennessee) Williams. Period of Adjustment (dr)

Edmund Wilson. Apologies to the Iriquois (e)
Arthur Yvor Winters. Collected Poems (pub)
Frances Winwar. Jean-Jacques Rousseau, Conscience of an Era (biog)
Marya Zaturenska. Terraces of Light (po)

1961

DEATHS

Konrad Bercovici
Henry Seidel Canby
Hilda Doolittle
Jessie Redmon Fauset
Kenneth Fearing
Samuel Dashiell Hammett
Moss Hart
Ernest Miller Hemingway
Robert Silliman Hillyer
George Simon Kaufman
Julia Mood Peterkin
James Grover Thurber
Thyra Samter Winslow

EVENTS

Bollingen Poetry Translation Prize (est)
Floating Bear, New York, New York, to 1969 (per)
John Fitzgerald Kennedy, 35th President of the United States, to
    1963

LITERATURE

Mortimer Jerome Adler. Great Ideas from the Great Books (e)
Conrad Porter Aiken. Selected Poems (po)
Edward Albee. The American Dream (dr)
Benjamin Appel. A Big Man, a Fast Man (fic)
Louis Stanton Auchincloss. Reflections of a Jacobite (biog, e)
James Baldwin. Nobody Knows My Name (e)
Stringfellow Barr. The Will of Zeus (hist)
Jacques Barzun. Classic, Romantic, and Modern (e)
Thomas Louis Berger. Reinhart in Love (fic)
Don Berry. A Majority of Scoundrels (hist)
Paul Blackburn. The Nets (po)
Arno Wendell Bontemps. One Hundred Years of Negro Freedom (hist)
Philip Booth. The Islanders (po)
Van Wyck Brooks. From the Shadow of the Mountain: My Post-Meridian
    Years (auto)
Kenneth Duva Burke. The Rhetoric of Religion (e)
Ben Lucien Burman. It's a Big Continent (trav)
_____. The Owl Hoots Twice at Catfish Bend (fic)
William Seward Burroughs. The Soft Machine (fic)
Erskine Preston Caldwell. Jenny by Nature (fic)
Janet Taylor Caldwell. A Prologue to Love (fic)
Hortense Calisher. False Entry (fic)
Morley Callaghan. A Passion in Rome (fic)

Gladys Hasty Carroll. Come with Me Home (fic)
Ronald Verlin Cassill. Clem Anderson (fic)
Paddy Chayefsky. Gideon (dr)
John Cheever. Some People, Places, and Things That Will Not Appear
    in My Next Novel (fic)
Marquis William Childs. The Peacemakers (fic)
James Bryant Conant. Slums and Suburbs (e)
Gregory Nunzio Curso. The American Express (fic)
Edward Dahlberg. Truth Is More Sacred (e)
Donald Grady Davidson. The Long Street (po)
Vina Delmar. The Big Family (fic)
Peter DeVries. Through the Fields of Clover (fic)
James Patrick Donleavy. Fairy Tales of New York (dr)
Hilda Doolittle. Helen in Egypt (po, pub)
John Roderigo Dos Passos. Midcentury (fic)
William Edward Burghardt DuBois. Worlds of Color (fic)
Alan Dugan. Poems (pub)
George Paul Elliott. Among the Dangs (fic)
_____. Fever and Chills (po)
James Thomas Farrell. Boarding House Blues (fic)
_____. Side Street (fic)
Howard Melvin Fast. April Morning (fic)
Frederick Feikema (Frederick Manfred/Feike Feikema). Arrow of Love
    (fic)
Lawrence Ferlinghetti. Starting from San Francisco (po)
Irving Fineman. Woman of Valor (biog)
Waldo David Frank. Cuba: Prophetic Island (des, e)
Ernest Kellogg Gann. Fate Is the Hunter (nar, auto)
Isabella Stewart Gardner. The Looking Glass (po)
John Champlin Gardner, Jr. The Forms of Fiction (e)
George Palmer Garrett, Jr. Abraham's Knife (po)
_____. In the Briar Patch (fic)
_____. Which Ones Are the Enemy? (fic)
Jack Gelber. The Apple (dr)
Shirley Ann Grau. The House on Coliseum Street (fic)
Julian Green. Each in His Darkness (fic)
Horace Victor Gregory. The Dying Gladiators (e)
_____. Medusa in Gramercy Park (po)
John Clendennin Burne Hawkes, Jr. The Lime Twig (fic)
Ben Hecht. Perfidy (e)
Robert Anson Heinlein. Stranger in a Strange Land (fic)
Joseph Heller. Catch-22 (fic)
Robert Silliman Hillyer. Collected Poems (pub)
Chester Bomar Himes. Pinktoes (fic)
John Hollander. The Untuning of the Sky: Ideas of Music in English
    Poetry, 1500-1700 (hist, e)
Paul Horgan. Citizen of New Salem (e)
James Langston Hughes. Ask Your Mama: 12 Moods for Jazz (po)
_____. The Best of Simple (fic)
_____. Black Nativity (dr)
Richard Franklin Hugo. A Run of Jacks (po)
Fanny Hurst. God Must Be Sad (fic)
Le Roi Jones (Imamu Amiri Baraka). Preface to a Twenty-Volume Suicide
    Note (po)
MacKinlay Kantor. Spirit Lake (fic)
Jean Collins Kerr. Mary, Mary (dr)

Louis Kronenberger. A Month of Sundays (fic)
Maxine Winoker Kumin. Halfway (po)
Denise Levertov. The Jacob's Ladder (po)
Abbott Joseph Liebling. The Earl of Louisiana (biog)
Anita Loos. No Mother To Guide Her (fic)
Robert Traill Spence Lowell, Jr. Imitations (po)
Bernard Malamud. A New Life (fic)
William Maxwell. The Chateau (fic)
Michael Thomas McClure. Dark Brown (po)
Carson Smith McCullers. Clock without Hands (fic)
William Stanley Merwin. The Gilded West (dr)
James Albert Michener. Report of the County Chairman (nar)
Arthur Miller. The Misfits (fic, dr)
Edwin O'Connor. The Edge of Sadness (fic)
John Henry O'Hara. Assembly (fic)
_____. Five Plays (dr, pub)
Elder James Olson. Tragedy and the Theory of Drama (e)
Walker Percy. The Moviegoer (fic)
Sidney Joseph Perelman. The Rising Gorge (sat, nar)
Ayn Rand. For the New Intellectual (fic, e)
Kenneth Rexroth. Assays (e)
Jack Carter Richardson. Gallows Humor (dr)
Theodore Roethke. I Am! Says the Lamb (po)
Leo Calvin Rosten. Captain Newman, M.D. (fic)
Jerome David Salinger. Franny and Zooey (fic)
Eleanor May Sarton. Cloud, Stone, Sun, Vine (po)
_____. The Small Room (fic)
Gladys Schmitt. Rembrandt (fic)
Mark Schorer. Sinclair Lewis: An American Life (biog)
Delmore Schwartz. Successful Love (fic)
Wilfred John Joseph Sheed. A Middle Class Education (fic)
William Lawrence Shirer. The Rise and Fall of Adolph Hitler (biog,
   hist)
Isaac Bashevis Singer. The Spinoza of Market Street (fic)
William Jay Smith. The Spectra Hoax (e)
David Derek Stacton. The Judges of the Secret Court (fic)
Francis Steegmuller. The Christening Party (fic)
Wallace Erle Stegner. A Shooting Star (fic)
John Ernst Steinbeck. The Winter of Our Discontent (fic)
Richard Gustave Stern. Europe; or, Up and Down with Baggish and
   Schreiber (fic)
Irving Stone. The Agony and the Ecstasy (fic)
Harvey Swados. Nights in the Gardens of Brooklyn (fic)
Robert Lewis Taylor. A Journey to Matecumbe (fic)
James Grover Thurber. Lanterns and Lances (e)
Leon Uris. Mila 18 (fic)
Mark Albert Van Doren. The Happy Critic (e)
Peter Viereck. The Tree Witch (po, dr)
Kurt Vonnegut, Jr. Mother Night (fic)
Diane Wakowski. Coins and Coffins (po)
Edward Lewis Wallant. The Pawnbroker (fic)
Robert Penn Warren. Who Speaks for the Negro? (e)
_____. Wilderness (fic)
Jerome Weidman. Tenderloin (dr)
John Hall Wheelock. The Gardener (po)
Richard Purdy Wilbur. Advice to a Prophet, and Other Poems (po)

John Alfred Williams. Night Song (fic)
William Carlos Williams. Many Loves (dr)
Edmund Wilson. Night Thoughts (po)
Mitchell Wilson. Meeting at a Far Meridian (fic)
Richard Nathaniel Wright. Eight Men (fic, pub)
Frank Garvin Yerby. The Garfield Honor (fic)
Louis Zukofsky. It Was (fic)

1962

DEATHS

Charles William Beebe
Ludwig Bemelmans
William Stanley Beaumont Braithwaite
Edward Estlin Cummings
Clyde Brion Davis
William Harrison Faulkner
Francis Hackett
John Robinson Jeffers
George Sylvester Viereck
Edward Lewis Wallant

EVENTS

Dwight David Eisenhower Library, Abilene, Kansas (est)

LITERATURE

James Agee. Letters to Father Flye (nar, pub)
Edward Albee. Who's Afraid of Virginia Woolf? (dr)
John Lawrence Ashbery. The Philosopher (dr)
_____. The Tennis Court Oath (po)
Louis Stanton Auchincloss. Portrait in Brownstone (fic)
Wystan Hugh Auden. The Dyer's Hand (e)
Dorothy Baker. Cassandra at the Wedding (fic)
James Baldwin. Another Country (fic)
Carleton Beals. Cyclone Carry (biog)
Samuel Nathaniel Behrman. Lord Pengo (dr)
Ludwig Bemelmans. On Board Noah's Ark (nar)
Don Berry. Moontrap (fic)
Burt Blechman. How Much? (fic)
Robert Elwood Bly. Silence in the Snowy Fields (po)
Kay Boyle. Collected Poems (pub)
Ray Douglas Bradbury. The Anthem Sprinters (dr)
_____. R. Is for Rocket, S. Is for Space (fic)
Van Wyck Brooks. Fenollosa and His Circle (biog)
Pearl Sydenstricker Buck. A Bridge for Passing (auto, nar)
William Seward Burroughs. The Ticket That Exploded (fic)
James Branch Cabell. Between Friends (let)
James Mallahan Cain. Mignon (fic)
Hortense Calisher. Tale for the Mirror (fic)
Gladys Hasty Carroll. Only Fifty Years Ago (auto)
John Chamberlain. The Enterprising Americans (hist)
Henry Steele Commager and Samuel Eliot Morison. The Growth of the

American Republic, 2 vols, rev ed (hist)
Gregory Nunzio Corso. Long Live Man (po)
Thomas Bertram Costain. The Last Plantagenets (hist)
Robert White Creeley. For Love (po)
Olive Tilford Dargan. Innocent Bigamy (fic)
Peter DeVries. The Blood of the Lamb (fic)
James Lafayette Dickey. Drowning with Others (po)
Pietro Di Donato. The Penitent (biog)
Allen Stuart Drury. A Shade of Difference (fic)
Richard Ghormley Eberhart. Collected Verse Plays (po, dr, pub)
George Paul Elliott. David Knudsen (fic)
Paul Hamilton Engle. Golden Child (fic)
William Everson (Brother Antoninus). The Hazards of Holiness (po)
James Thomas Farrell. Sound of the City (fic)
William Harrison Faulkner. Early Prose and Poetry (pub)
_____. The Reivers (fic)
Frederick Feikema (Frederick Manfred/Feike Feikema). Wanderlust
   (fic)
Lawrence Ferlinghetti. Unfair Arguments with Existence (dr)
Francis Scott Key Fitzgerald. The Pat Hobby Stories (fic, pub)
Jessie Hill Ford. Mountains of Gilead (fic)
William Price Fox. Southern Fried (fic)
Bruce Jay Friedman. Stern (fic)
Robert Lee Frost. In the Clearing (po)
George Palmer Garrett, Jr. Sir Slob and the Princess (dr, juv)
Frank Daniel Gilroy. Who'll Save the Plowboy? (dr)
Herbert Gold. The Age of Happy Problems (e)
Elizabeth Hardwick. A View of My Own (e)
Mark Harris. Friedman and Son (dr)
Robert Hayden. A Ballad of Remembrance (po)
Hiram Haydn. The Hands of Esau (fic)
John Hollander. Movie-Going (po)
Richard Joseph Howard. Quantities (po)
James Langston Hughes. Gospel Glow (dr)
David Ignatow. Say Pardon (po)
Shirley Hardie Jackson. We Have Always Lived in the Castle (fic)
Randall Jarrell. A Sad Heart at the Supermarket (e, fic)
James Jones. The Thin Red Line (fic)
Elia Kazan. America, America (fic)
Alfred Kazin. Contemporaries (e)
William Melvin Kelley. A Different Drummer (fic)
Jack Kerouac. Big Sur (fic)
Ken Kesey. One Flew over the Cuckoo's Nest (fic)
Sidney Kingsley. Night Life (dr)
John Knowles. Morning in Antibes (fic)
Kenneth Jay Koch. Thank You (po)
Joseph Kramm. Giants, Sons of Giants (dr)
Anne Morrow Lindbergh. Dearly Beloved (fic)
Robert James Collas Lowry. Party of Dreamers (fic)
_____. The Snowbird (po)
Grace Lumpkin. Full Circle (fic)
Alison Lurie. Love and Friendship (fic)
Norman Mailer. Death for the Ladies, and Other Disasters (po)
Harry Mathews. The Conversions (fic)
David Meltzer. We All Have Something To Say to Each Other (e, po)
James Ingram Merrill. Water Street (po)

Henry Miller. Stand Still Like a Hummingbird (e)
Samuel Eliot Morison and Henry Steele Commager. The Growth of the
   American Republic, 2 vols, rev ed (hist)
Wright Morris. What a Way To Go (fic)
Theodore Morrison. The Whole Creation (fic)
Vladimir Nabokov. Pale Fire (fic)
Ogden Nash. Everyone But Thee and Me (po)
Robert Gruntal Nathan. A Star in the Wind (fic)
John Henry O'Hara. The Big Laugh (fic)
_____. The Cape Cod Lighter (fic)
Tillie Olsen. Tell Me a Riddle (fic)
George Oppen. The Materials (po)
Sylvia Plath. The Colossus (po)
Katherine Anne Porter. Ship of Fools (fic)
James Farl Powers. Morte d'Urban (fic)
Reynolds Price. A Long and Happy Life (fic)
James Purdy. Children Is All (fic, dr)
Charles Reznikoff. By the Waters of Manhattan (po)
Conrad Michael Richter. A Simple Honorable Man (fic)
Philip Roth. Letting Go (fic)
Muriel Rukeyser. Waterlily Fire (po)
William Saroyan. Here Comes, There Goes, You Know Who (nar)
Winfield Townley Scott. Collected Poems (pub)
Anya Seton. Devil Water (fic)
Anne Sexton. All My Pretty Ones (po)
Karl Jay Shapiro. Prose Keys to Modern Poetry (e)
Louis Aston Marantz Simpson. Riverside Drive (fic)
Isaac Bashevis Singer. The Slave (fic)
Jack Spicer. The Heads of the Town Up to the Aether (po)
David Derek Stacton. Old Acquaintance (fic)
_____. Tom Fool (fic)
William Edgar Stafford. Traveling through the Dark (po)
John Ernst Steinbeck. Travels with Charley in Search of America
   (nar)
Grace Zaring Stone. Althea (fic)
Jesse Hilton Stuart. Hold April (po)
Harvey Swados. A Radical's America (e)
James Grover Thurber. Credos and Curios (fic, nar, pub)
Lionel Trilling. The Life and Work of Sigmund Freud (biog, e)
Barbara Wertheim Tuchman. The Guns of August (hist)
Louis Untermeyer. Long Feud: Selected Poems (pub)
John Hoyer Updike. Pigeon Feathers (fic)
Mark Albert Van Doren. Collected Stories (fic, pub)
Gore Vidal. Rocking the Boat (e)
Irving Wallace. The Prize (fic)
Jerome Weidman. The Sound of Bow Bells (fic)
Glenway Wescott. Images of Truth: Remembrances and Criticism (e)
Elwyn Brooks White. The Points of My Compass (e)
Edward Reed Whittemore II. The Boy from Iowa: Poems and Essays (pub)
Thornton Niven Wilder. Plays for Bleecker Street (dr)
Thomas Lanier (Tennessee) Williams. The Night of the Iguana (dr)
William Carlos Williams. The Farmers' Daughters (fic)
_____. Pictures from Brueghel (po)
Edmund Wilson. Patriotic Gore (hist)
Herman Wouk. Youngblood Hawke (fic)
James Arlington Wright. The Lion's Tale and Eyes (po)

1963

DEATHS

Van Wyck Brooks
William Edward Burghardt DuBois
Robert Lee Frost
Oliver Hazard Perry LaFarge
Abbott Joseph Liebling
Clifford Odets
Martha Ostenso
Joseph Stanley Pennell
Sylvia Plath
Theodore Roethke
Evelyn Scott
William Carlos Williams
Stark Young

EVENTS

Center for Editions of American Authors, Modern Language Association
   (est)
Lyndon Baines Johnson, 36th President of the United States, to 1969
New York Review of Books (per, f)
North American Review, 2nd series, Cedar Falls, Iowa (per)

LITERATURE

George Abbott. Mister Abbott (auto)
Conrad Potter Aiken. The Morning of Lord Zero (po)
Nelson Algren. Who Lost an American? (nar)
Benjamin Appel. With Many Voices (e)
Justin Brooks Atkinson. Tuesdays and Fridays (e)
Louis Stanton Auchincloss. Powers of Attorney (fic)
Richard David Bach. Stranger to the Ground (fic)
James Baldwin. The Fire Next Time (e, nar)
Walter Jackson Bate. John Keats (biog)
Don Berry. To Build a Ship (fic)
Burt Blechman. The War of Camp Omongo (fic)
Arna Wendell Bontemps. Personals (fic)
Vance Nye Bourjaily. The Unnatural Enemy (e, nar)
Catherine Shober Drinker Bowen. Francis Bacon: The Temper of a Man
   (biog)
Claude Gernade Bowers. My Life (auto)
Paul Bowles. Their Heads Are Green and Their Hands Are Blue (nar)
Ray Douglas Bradbury. Something Wicked This Way Comes (fic)
Gwendolyn Brooks. Selected Poems (pub)
John Brooks. The Fate of the Edsel and Other Business Adventures
   (e, nar)
John Mason Brown. Dramatis Personae (e)
Pearl Sydenstricker Buck. The Living Reed (fic)
Charles Bukowski. It Catches My Heart in Its Hands (po)
William Seward Burroughs. The Yage Letters (let)
Hortense Calisher. Textures of Life (fic)

Morley Callaghan. That Summer in Paris (nar)
Hayden Carruth. Appendix A (fic)
Rachel Carson. Silent Spring (e)
John Ciardi. Dialogue with an Audience (e)
_____. In Fact (po)
James Bryant Conant. The Education of American Teachers (e)
Evan Shelby Connell, Jr. Notes from a Bottle Found on the Beach at
    Carmel (po)
Thomas Bertram Costain. The Last Love (fic)
Robert White Creeley. The Island (fic)
Edward Estlin Cummings. 73 Poems (pub)
Merle Eugene Curti. American Philanthropy Abroad (hist)
Donald Grady Davidson. The Spyglass (e)
Clyde Brion Davis. Shadow of a Tiger (fic)
Joan Didion. Run River (fic)
James Patrick Donleavy. A Singular Man (fic)
John Roderigo Dos Passos. Brazil on the Move (trav)
_____. Mr. Wilson's War (hist)
Alan Dugan. Poems 2 (po, pub)
William Eastlake. Portrait of an Artist with Twenty-Six Horses
    (fic)
James Thomas Farrell. The Silence of History (fic)
Peter Steinham Feibleman. Tiger Tiger Burning Bright (dr)
Edna Ferber. A Kind of Magic (auto)
Jessie Hill Ford. The Conversion of Buster Drumwright (dr)
William Price Fox. Dr. Golf (nar)
Bruce Jay Friedman. Far from the City of Class (fic)
Allen Ginsberg. Reality Sandwiches (po)
_____. The Yage Letters (let)
Herbert Gold. Salt (fic)
Paul Goodman. Making Do (fic)
Caroline Gordon. Old Red (fic)
Charles William Goyen. The Fair Sister (fic)
Paul Eliot Green. Plough and Furrow (e)
Albert Joseph Guerard. The Exiles (fic)
Oakley Hall. The Downhill Races (fic)
Shirley Hazzard. Cliffs of Fall (fic)
Ben Hecht. Gaily, Gaily (nar)
Robert Anson Heinlein. Orphans of the Sky (fic)
Lillian Hellman. My Mother, My Father and Me (dr)
John Richard Hersey. Here To Stay (fic)
Eric Hoffer. The Ordeal of Change (e)
John Hollander. Various Owls (po, juv)
Paul Horgan. Conquistadores in North American History (hist)
Irving Howe. Politics and the Novel: A World More Attractive (e)
James Langston Hughes. Five Plays (dr, pub)
_____. Jericho-Jim Crow (dr)
_____. Something in Common, and Other Stories (fic)
_____. Tambourines to Glory (dr)
William Inge. Natural Affection (dr)
Shirley Hardie Jackson. Nine Magic Wishes (juv)
John Robinson Jeffers. The Beginning and the End and Other Poems
    (po, pub)
Josephine Winslow Johnson. The Dark Traveler (fic)
Jack Kerouac. Visions of Gerard (fic)
Philip Levine. On the Edge (po)

John Logan. Spring of the Thief (po)
Norman Mailer. The Presidential Papers of Norman Mailer (e)
Bernard Malamud. Idiots First (fic)
Mary Therese McCarthy. The Group (fic)
Thomas Merton. Life and Holiness (e)
William Stanley Merwin. The Moving Target (po)
James Albert Michener. Caravans (fic)
Henry Miller. Just Wild about Harry (dr)
Wright Morris. Cause for Wonder (fic)
Willard Motley. Soon, One Morning (fic)
Robert Gruntal Nathan. The Devil with Love (fic)
Howard Nemerov. Poetry and Fiction (e)
Joyce Carol Oates. By the North Gate (fic)
John Henry O'Hara. Elizabeth Appleton (fic)
_____. The Hat on the Bed (fic)
Elder James Olson. Collected Poems (pub)
Robert Pack. Guarded by Women (po)
Sidney Joseph Perelman. The Beauty Part (dr)
Sylvia Plath. The Bell Jar (fic)
Reynolds Price. A Generous Man (fic)
_____. The Names and Faces of Heroes (fic)
Thomas Pynchon. V (fic)
John Crowe Ransom. Selected Poems (pub)
John Francisco Rechy. City of Night (fic)
Elmer Reizenstein (Elmer Rice). Minority Report (auto)
Kenneth Rexroth. Natural Numbers (po)
Adrienne Cecile Rich. Snapshots of a Daughter-in-Law (po)
Jack Carter Richardson. Lorenzo (dr)
_____. The Prison Life of Harris Fillmore (fic)
Jerome David Salinger. Raise High the Roof-Beam, Carpenters (fic)
_____. Seymour: An Introduction (fic)
Carl August Sandburg. Honey and Salt (po)
William Saroyan. Boys and Girls Together (fic)
_____. Not Dying (nar)
Irwin Shaw. Children from Their Games (dr)
Susan Sontag. The Benefactor (fic)
James Vincent Sheean. Dorothy and Red (biog)
Wilfred John Joseph Sheed. The Hack (fic)
Louis Aston Marantz Simpson. At the End of the Open Road (po)
Charles Wilbert Snow. Collected Poems (pub)
David Derek Stacton. Sir William (fic)
Richard Gustave Stern. In Any Case (fic)
Harvey Swados. The Will (fic)
May Swenson. To Mix with Time (po)
Peter Hillsman Taylor. Miss Leonora When Last Seen (fic)
Alice Babette Toklas. What Is Remembered (nar)
John Hoyer Updike. The Centaur (fic)
_____. Telephone Poles (po)
Mark Albert Van Doren. Collected and New Poems, 1924-1963 (po, pub)
Kurt Vonnegut, Jr. Cat's Cradle (fic)
David Russell Wagoner. The Nesting Ground (po)
Irving Wallace. The Three Sirens (fic)
Edward Lewis Wallant. The Tenants of Moonbloom (fic, pub)
Jerome Weidman. Back Talk (nar)
John Hall Wheelock. What Is Poetry? (e)
Edward Reed Whittemore II. The Fascination of the Abomination (po,

fic, e)
Richard Purdy Wilbur. The Poems (pub)
_____. Prince Souvanna Phouma: An Exchange between
    Richard Wilbur and William Jay Smith (po)
_____. Tartuffe (dr, trans)
John Alfred Williams. Sissie (fic)
Calder Baynard Willingham, Jr. Eternal Fire (fic)
Edmund Wilson. The Cold War and the Income Tax (e)
Lanford Wilson. So Long at the Fair (dr)
James Arlington Wright. The Branch Will Not Break (po)
Richard Nathaniel Wright. Lawd Today (fic, pub)
Louis Zukofsky. Bottom: On Shakespeare, 2 vols (e)

1964

DEATHS

Nathan Asch
Joseph Hamilton Basso
Rachel Carson
Hermann Hagedorn
Ben Hecht
Clarence Budington Kelland
Flannery O'Connor
Donald Culross Peattie
Carl Van Vechten

LITERATURE

Nelson Algren. Conversations (nar)
Archie Randolph Ammons. Expressions of Sea Level (po)
Louis Stanton Auchincloss. The Rector of Justin (fic)
James Baldwin. The Amen Corner (dr)
_____. Blues for Mister Charley (dr)
Margaret Culkin Banning. The Vine and the Olive (fic)
Donald Barthelme. Come Back, Dr. Caligari (fic)
Jacques Barzun. Science: The Glorious Entertainment (e)
Joseph Hamilton Basso. A Touch of the Dragon (fic)
Samuel Nathaniel Behrman. But for Whom, Charlie (dr)
Ben Belitt. The Enemy Joy (po)
Saul Bellow. Herzog (fic)
_____. The Last Analysis (dr)
Thomas Louis Berger. Little Big Man (fic)
Edmund J.M. Berrigan, Jr. Galileo; or, Finksville (dr)
_____. The Sonnets (po)
John Berryman. 77 Dream Songs (po)
Richard Palmer Blackmur. Eleven Essays in the European Novel (e)
Burt Blechman. Stations (fic)
Paul Bowles. A Life Full of Holes (fic, trans)
Ray Douglas Bradbury. The Machineries of Joy (fic)
Richard Brautigan. A Confederate General from Big Sur (fic)
Kenneth Duva Burke. Perspectives by Incongruity (e)
William Seward Burroughs. Nova Express (fic)
Erskine Preston Caldwell. Around about America (e)
Hortense Calisher. Extreme Magic (fic)

Ronald Verlin Cassill. The President (fic)
Stuart Chase. Money To Grow On (e)
Paddy Chayefsky. The Passion of Joseph D (dr)
John Cheever. The Brigadier and the Golf Widow (fic)
_____. The Wapshot Scandal (fic)
Eleanor Clark. The Oysters of Locmariaquer (des)
James Gould Cozzins. Children and Others (fic)
Edward Dahlberg. Because I Was Flesh (auto)
Peter Hubert Davison. The Breaking of the Day (po)
Peter DeVries. Reuben, Reuben (fic)
James Lafayette Dickey. Helmets (po)
_____. The Suspect in Poetry (e)
James Patrick Donleavy. Meet My Maker the Mad Molecule (fic)
John Roderigo Dos Passos. Occasions and Protests (e)
Robert Edward Duncan. Roots and Branches (po)
Richard Ghormley Eberhart. The Quarry (po)
Stanley Lawrence Elkin. Boswell (fic)
George Paul Elliott. A Piece of Lettuce (e)
Ralph Waldo Ellison. Shadow and Act (e)
William Everson (Brother Antoninus). The Poet Is Dead (po)
James Thomas Farrell. What Time Collects (fic)
Howard Melvin Fast. Agrippa's Daughter (fic)
Frederick Feikema (Frederick Manfred/Feike Feikema). Scarlet Plume
   (fic)
Leslie Aaron Fiedler. Waiting for the End (e)
Shelby Foote. Jordan County (dr)
Bruce Jay Friedman. A Mother's Kisses (fic)
Ernest J. Gaines. Catherine Carmier (fic)
George Palmer Garrett, Jr. Cold Ground Was My Bed Last Night (fic)
Jean Garrigue. Country without Maps (po)
Jack Gelber. On Ice (fic)
Frank Daniel Gilroy. The Subject Was Roses (dr)
Charles William Goyen. Christy (dr)
Shirley Ann Grau. The Keepers of the House (fic)
Horace Victor Gregory. Collected Poems (pub)
Donald Andrew Hall. A Roof of Tiger Lilies (po)
Lorraine Hansberry. The Sign in Sidney Brustein's Window (dr)
Mark Harris. Mark the Glove Boy, or the Last Days of Richard Nixon
   (fic, nar)
John Clendennin Burne Hawkes, Jr. Second Skin (fic)
Ben Hecht. Letters from Bohemia (let)
Ernest Miller Hemingway. A Moveable Feast (nar, pub)
Laura Zametkin Hobson. First Papers (fic)
John Clellon Holmes. Get Home Free (fic)
Paul Horgan. Things As They Are (fic)
David Ignatow. Figures of the Human (po)
Randall Jarrell. Selected Poems (pub)
Le Roi Jones (Imamu Amiri Baraka). The Dead Lecturer (po)
_____. Dutchman (dr)
_____. A Recent Killing (dr)
_____. The Slave (dr)
_____. The Toilet (dr)
William Melvin Kelley. Dancers on the Shore (fic)
Jean Collins Kerr. Poor Richard (dr)
Ken Kesey. Sometimes a Great Notion (fic)
Galway Kinnell. Flower Herding on Mount Monadnock (po)

John Knowles. Double Vision (trav)
Louis Kronenberger. The Cart and the Horse (e)
Jeremy Larner. Drive, He Said (fic)
Josephine Lawrence. Not a Cloud in the Sky (fic)
Tom Lea. The Hands of Cantu (fic)
Ursula K. LeGuin. Rocannon's World (fic)
Denise Levertov. City Psalm (po)
_____. O Taste and See: New Poems (po)
Meyer Levin. The Fanatic (fic)
Robert Traill Spence Lowell, Jr. For the Union Dead (po)
Helen MacInnes. Home Is the Hunter (dr)
Wallace Markfield. To an Early Grave (fic)
Phyllis McGinley. Sixpence in Her Shoe (e)
William Morris Meredith. The Wreck of the Thresher (po)
Thomas Merton. Seeds of Destruction (e)
Kenneth Millar (Ross Macdonald). The Goodbye Look (fic)
Arthur Miller. After the Fall (dr)
Ogden Nash. Marriage Lines: Notes of a Student Husband (po)
Robert Gruntal Nathan. The Fair (fic)
Howard Nemerov. The Next Room of the Dream (po)
Anais Nin. Collages (des, fic)
Joyce Carol Oates. With Shuddering Fall (fic)
Edwin O'Connor. I Was Dancing (fic)
Frank O'Hara. Lunch Poems (po, pub)
John Henry O'Hara. The Horse Knows the Way (fic)
Charles Olson. A Bibliography on America for Ed Dorn (e)
Eugene Gladstone O'Neill. More Stately Mansions (dr, pub)
Ann Petry. Tituba of Salem Village (juv)
Frederick Prokosch. The Dark Dancer (fic)
James Purdy. Cabot Wright Begins (fic)
Conrad Michael Richter. The Grandfathers (fic)
Theodore Roethke. The Far Field (po, pub)
Samuel Shepard Rogers, Jr. (Sam Shepard). Cowboys (dr)
_____. The Rock Garden (dr)
Theodore Roethke. Sequence, Sometimes Metaphysical (po, pub)
Leo Calvin Rosten. The Many Worlds of Leo Rosten (nar, fic)
Jane Rule. The Desert of the Heart (fic)
William Saroyan. One Day in the Afternoon of the World (fic)
Gladys Schmitt. Electra (fic)
Hubert Selby. Last Exit to Brooklyn (fic)
Karl Jay Shapiro. The Bourgeois Poet (po, e)
Isaac Bashevis Singer. Short Friday (fic)
Betty Wehner Smith. Joy in the Morning (fic)
Gilbert Sorrentino. Black and White (po)
Jean Stafford. Bad Characters (fic)
Richard Gustave Stern. Teeth, Dying, and Other Matters (fic)
Mark Strand. Sleeping with One Eye Open (po)
Jesse Hilton Stuart. Save Every Lamb (fic)
Robert Lewis Taylor. Two Roads to Guadalupe (fic)
Dana Trilling. Claremont Essays (e)
Leon Uris. Armageddon (fic)
Mark Albert Van Doren. The Narrative Poems (po)
Gore Vidal. Julian (fic)
Irving Wallace. The Man (fic)
Edward Lewis Wallant. The Children at the Gate (fic, pub)
Robert Penn Warren. Flood (fic)

Joseph Wechsberg. The Best Things of Life (e)
Jerome Weidman. Word of Mouth (fic)
Eudora Welty. The Shoe Bird (juv, fic)
Philip Whalen. Monday in the Evening (po)
Thomas Lanier (Tennessee) Williams. The Eccentricities of a Nightin-
   gale (dr)
Lanford Wilson. Balm in Gilead (dr)
_____ . Home Free (dr)
_____ . The Madness of Lady Bright (dr)

1965

DEATHS

Joseph Auslander
Richard Palmer Blackmur
Thornton Wald Burgess
Thomas Bertram Costain
Thomas Stearns Eliot
Joseph Freeman
Lorraine Hansberry
Shirley Hardie Jackson
Randall Jarrell
Willard Motley
Jack Spicer
Thomas Sigismund Stribling
Harold Vinal

EVENTS

National Endowment for the Humanities (est)
Salmagundi, Saratoga Springs, New York (per, f)
The Southern Review, Baton Rouge, Louisiana, 2nd series (per, f)

LITERATURE

Edward Albee. Tiny Alice (dr)
Nelson Algren. Notes from a Sea Diary (fic, e)
Archie Randolph Ammons. Corsons Inlet (po)
_____ . Tape for the Turn of the Year (po)
Robert Woodruff Anderson. The Days Between (dr)
Wystan Hugh Auden. About the House (po)
James Baldwin. To Meet the Man (fic)
Peter Soyer Beagle. I See by My Outfit (fic)
Samuel Nathaniel Berhman. The Suspended Drawing Room (biog, nar)
Saul Bellow. Under the Weather (dr)
Wendell Berry. Openings (po)
Elizabeth Bishop. A Question of Travel (po)
Burt Blechman. The Octapus Papers (fic)
Daniel J. Boorstin. The Americans. The National Experience (hist)
Ray Douglas Bradbury. The Wonderful Ice Cream Suit (dr)
Van Wyck Brooks. An Autobiography (pub)
Courtlandt Dixon Barnes Bryan. P.S. Wilkinson (fic)
Carl Frederick Buechner. The Final Beast (fic)
Charles Bukowski. Confessions of a Man Insane Enough To Live with

Beasts (auto)
Erskine Preston Caldwell. In Search of Bisco (nar)
Janet Taylor Caldwell. A Pillar of Iron (fic)
Hortense Calisher. Journal from Ellipsia (fic)
Hayden Carruth. Nothing for Tigers (po)
Ronald Verlin Cassill. The Father (fic)
Evan Shelby Connell. At the Crossroads (fic)
Marcus Cook Connelly. A Souvenir from Qam (fic)
Robert Lowell Coover. The Origin of the Brunists (fic)
Gregory Nunzio Curso. There Is Yet Time To Run Back through Life and
    Expiate All That's Been Sadly Done (po)
Louis Osborne Coxe. The Last Hero (po)
William Demby. The Catacombs (fic)
Peter DeVries. Let Me Count the Ways (fic)
James Lafayette Dickey. Buckdancer's Choice (po)
Robert Edward Duncan. Medea at Kolchis (dr)
William Eastlake. Castle Keep (fic)
George Paul Elliott. In the World (fic)
Paul Hamilton Engle. A Woman Unashamed (po)
James Thomas Farrell. Collected Poems (pub)
William Harrison Faulkner. Essays, Speeches, and Public Letters
    (pub)
Vardis Alvero Fisher. Mountain Man (fic)
Jessie Hill Ford. The Liberation of Lord Byron Jones (fic)
Isabella Stewart Gardner. West of Childhood (po)
George Palmer Garrett, Jr. Do, Lord, Remember Me (fic)
Martha Gellhorn. Pretty Tales for Tired People (fic)
Alex Palmer Haley. The Autobiography of Malcolm X (biog)
James Leo Herlihy. Midnight Cowboy (fic)
John Richard Hersey. White Lotus (fic)
Chester Bomar Himes. Cotton Comes to Harlem (fic)
_____. A Rage in Harlem (fic)
Edward Hoagland. The Peacock's Tail (fic)
John Hollander. Visions from the Ramble (po)
Paul Horgan. Songs after Lincoln (po)
James Langston Hughes. The Prodigal Son (dr)
_____. Simple's Uncle Sam (fic)
Richard Franklin Hugo. Death of the Kapowsin Tavern (po)
William Humphrey. The Ordways (fic)
George Rolfe Humphries. Collected Poems (po, pub)
Randall Jarrell. The Lost World: New Poems (po)
Diane Lain Johnson. Fair Game (fic)
Josephine Winslow Johnson. The Sorcerer's Son (fic)
LeRoi Jones (Imamu Amiri Baraka). The System of Dante's Hell (fic)
Bob Kaufman. Solitiudes Crowded with Loneliness (po)
Alfred Kazin. Starting Out in the Thirties (auto)
William Melvin Kelley. A Drop of Patience (fic)
Jack Kerouac. Desolation Angels (fic)
Arthur L. Kopit. The Day the Whores Came Out to Play Tennis (dr)
Jerzy Nikodem Kosinski. The Painted Bird (fic)
Maxine Winoker Kumin. Through Dooms of Love (fic)
_____. The Privilege (po)
Jeremy Larner. The Addict in the Street (fic)
Meyer Levin. The Stronghold (fic)
Robert Traill Spence Lowell, Jr. Selected Poems (pub)
Alison Lurie. The Nowhere City (fic)

Norman Mailer. An American Dream (fic)
Peter Matthiessen. At Play in the Fields of the Lord (fic)
Cormac McCarthy. The Orchard Keeper (fic)
David Meltzer. The Process (po)
James Ingram Merrill. The (Diblos) Notebook (fic)
James Albert Michener. The Source (fic)
Kenneth Millar (Ross Macdonald). The Far Side of the Dollar (fic)
Arthur Miller. Incident at Vichy (dr)
Samuel Eliot Morison. The Oxford History of the American People
   (hist)
Wright Morris. One Day (fic)
Howard Moss. Finding Them Lost (po)
Vladimir Nabokov. The Eye (fic)
Ogden Nash. The Mysterious Ouphe (po)
Robert Gruntal Nathan. The Mallot Diaries (fic)
Flannery O'Connor. Everything That Rises Must Converge (fic, pub)
John Henry O'Hara. The Lockwood Concern (fic)
Charles Olson. Human Universe (e)
George Oppen. This in Which (po)
Katherine Anne Porter. Collected Stories (fic, pub)
Philip Rahv. The Myth and the Powerhouse (e)
Charles Reznikoff. Testimony: The United States, 1885-1915 (po)
Jack Carter Richardson. Xmas in Las Vegas (dr)
Theodore Roethke. On the Poet and His Craft (e, pub)
Howard Sackler. The Nine O'Clock Mail (dr)
Jerome David Salinger. Hapworth 16, 1924 (fic)
Eleanor May Sarton. Mrs. Stevens Hears the Mermaids Singing (fic)
_____. A Private Mythology (po)
Anya Seton. Avalon (fic)
Irwin Shaw. Voices of a Summer Day (fic)
_____. Love on a Dark Street (fic)
James Vincent Sheean. Beware of Caesar (fic)
Wilfred John Joseph Sheed. Square's Progress (fic)
Louis Aston Marantz Simpson. Selected Poems (pub)
Gary Sherman Snyder. Six Sections from Mountains and Rivers without
   End (po)
Elizabeth Spencer. Knights and Dragons (fic)
Jack Spicer. Language (po)
David Derek Stacton. People of the Book (fic)
Richard Gustav Stern. Stitch (fic)
Harvey Swados. A Story for Teddy (fic)
Melvin Beaunorus Tolson. Harlem Gallery: Book 1, The Curator (po)
Lionel Trilling. Beyond Culture (e)
Barbara Wertheim Tuchman. The Proud Tower (hist)
Frederick Goddard Tuckerman. Complete Poems (pub)
Anne Tyler. If Morning Ever Comes (fic)
John Hoyer Updike. Of the Farm (fic)
Mark Albert Van Doren. Never Ask His Name (dr)
Gore Vidal. The City and the Pillar, rev ed (fic)
_____. The Judgment of Paris, rev ed (fic)
_____. Messiah, rev ed (fic)
Kurt Vonnegut, Jr. God Bless You, Mr. Rosewater (fic)
David Russell Wagoner. The Escape Artist (fic)
Jerome Weidman. The Death of Dickie Draper (fic)
Philip Whalen. Every Day (po)
John Alfred Williams. This Is My Country Too (nar)

Thomas Lanier (Tennessee) Williams. Slapstick Tragedy (dr)
Edmund Wilson. The Bit between My Teeth (e, nar)
_____. O Canada (e)
Lanford Wilson. The Rimers of Eldritch (dr)
_____. This Is the Rill Speaking (dr)
Thomas Clayton Wolfe. The Lost Boy (fic, pub)
Herman Wouk. Don't Stop the Carnival (fic)
Frank Garvin Yerby. An Odor of Sanctity (fic)
Marya Zaturenska. Collected Poems (pub)
Louis Zukofsky. All the Collected Short Poems, 1923-1958 (po, pub)

                          1966

DEATHS

    John Cournos
    Russel Crouse
    Alfred Kreymborg
    Mina Gertrude Lowry (Mina Loy)
    William Morley Punshon McFee
    Anne Nichols
    Kathleen Norris
    Frank O'Hara
    Mari Sandoz
    Delmore Schwartz
    Lillian Eugenia Smith
    Melvin Beaunorus Tolson
    Mary Marvin Heaton Vorse

EVENTS

    International John Steinbeck Society (f)
    Western American Literature, Fort Collins, Colorado (per, f)

LITERATURE

    Alice Adams. Careless Love (fic)
    Herbert Sebastian Agar. The Perils of Democracy (e)
    Edward Albee. Delicate Balance (dr)
    William Alfred. Hogan's Goat (dr, po)
    Archie Randolph Ammons. Northfield Poems (po)
    John Lawrence Ashbery. Rivers and Mountains (po)
    Isaac Asimov. Fantastic Voyage (fic)
    Justin Brooks Atkinson. Brief Chronicles (e)
    Louis Stanton Auchincloss. The Embezzler (fic)
    Richard David Bach. Biplane (fic)
    Leonard Stanley Baker. The Johnson Eclipse (hist)
    John Barth. Giles Goat-Boy (fic)
    Paul Blackburn. El Cid Campeador (po, trans)
    _____. Sing-Song (po)
    Philip Booth. North by East (po)
    _____. Weathers and Edges (po)
    Jane Bowles. Plain Pleasures (fic)
    Kay Boyle. Nothing Ever Breaks Except the Heart (fic)
    Gerald Warner Brace. Between Wind and Water (fic)

Ray Douglas Bradbury. Twice Twenty-Two (fic)
Norman Oliver Brown. Love's Body (e)
Carl Frederick Buechner. The Magnificent Defeat (ser)
Kenneth Duva Burke. Language As Symbolic Action (e)
Hortense Calisher. The Railway Police and the Last Trolly Ride (fic)
Truman Capote. A Christmas Memory (fic)
_____. In Cold Blood (nar)
Evan Shelby Connell, Jr. The Diary of a Rapist (fic)
Clark Coolidge. Flag Flutter and U.S. Electric (po)
Louis Osborne Coxe. Nikal Seyn and Decoration Day (po)
Edward Dahlberg. Cipango's Hinder Door (po)
Jonathan Worth Daniels. The Time between the Wars (hist)
Donald Grady Davidson. Poems (pub)
David Brion Davis. The Problem of Slavery in Western Culture (hist)
Peter Hubert Davison. The City and the Island (po)
James Patrick Donleavy. The Saddest Summer of Samuel S. (fic)
John Roderigo Dos Passos. The Best Times (nar)
Allen Stuart Drury. Capable of Honor (fic)
Robert Edward Duncan. Passages 22-27 (po)
_____. The Years As Catches (po)
Stanley Lawrence Elkin. Criers and Kibitzers, Kibitzers and Criers
   (fic)
William Everson (Brother Antoninus). Single Source (po)
James Thomas Farrell. Lonely Future (fic)
Howard Melvin Fast. Torquemada (fic)
Peter Steinham Feibleman. Strangers and Graves (fic)
Frederick Feikema (Frederick Manfred/Feike Feikema). King of Spades
   (fic)
_____. Winter Count
   (po)
Leslie Aaron Fiedler. The Last Jew in America (fic)
Bruce Jay Friedman. Black Angels (fic)
John Champlin Gardner, Jr. The Resurrection (fic)
Jean Garrigue. The Animal Hotel (fic)
William Howard Gass. Omensetter's Luck (fic)
Jack Gelber. Square in the Eye (dr)
Albert Halper. The Fourth Horseman of Miami Beach (fic)
Mark Harris. Twentyone Twice (nar)
John Clendennin Burne Hawkes, Jr. The Innocent Party (dr)
Robert Hayden. Selected Poems (pub)
Shirley Hazzard. The Evening of the Holiday (fic)
John Richard Hersey. Too Far To Walk (fic)
Chester Bomar Himes. The Heat's On (fic)
_____. Run Man Run (fic)
John Hollander. The Quest of the Gole (po, juv)
Barbara Howes. Looking Up at Leaves (po)
William Inge. Where's Daddy? (dr)
LeRoi Jones (Imamu Amiri Baraka). Home (e)
Bob Kaufman. Golden Sardine (po)
Galway Kinnell. Black Light (fic)
_____. Body Rags (po)
John Knowles. Indian Summer (fic)
Kenneth Jay Koch. Bertha, and Other Plays (dr)
Allen Stewart Konigsberg (Woody Allen). Don't Drink the Water (dr)
Philip Lamantia. Touch of the Marvelous (po)
Denise Levertov. Psalm Concerning the Castle (po)

Andrew Nelson Lytle. The Hero with the Private Parts (e)
Norman Mailer. Cannibals and Christians (e)
Albert Maltz. A Tale of One January (fic)
Harry Matthews. Tlooth (fic)
William Maxwell. The Old Man at the Railroad Crossing (fic)
Rod McKuen. Stanyan Street and Other Sorrows (po)
James Ingram Merrill. Nights and Days (po)
Thomas Merton. Conjectures of a Guilty Bystander (e)
Marianne Craig Moore. Tell Me, Tell Me (po, e)
Willard Motley. Let Noon Be Fair (fic)
Vladimir Nabokov. Despair (fic)
_____. Speak, Memory (nar, des)
_____. The Waltz Invention (dr)
Robert Gruntal Nathan. Juliet in Mantua (dr)
Joyce Carol Oates. Upon the Sweeping Flood (fic)
Cynthia Ozick. Trust (fic)
Walker Percy. The Last Gentleman (fic)
Sidney Joseph Perelman. Chicken Inspector No. 23 (sat, nar)
Robert Phillips. Inner Weather (po)
Sylvia Plath. Ariel (po, pub)
Frederic Prokosch. The Wreck of the Cassandra (fic)
Thomas Pynchon. The Crying of Lot 49 (fic)
Kenneth Rexroth. An Autobiographical Novel (fic, auto)
_____. Shorter Poems (po)
Adrienne Cecile Rich. Necessities of Life (po)
Judith Perelman Rossner. To the Precipice (fic)
Howard Sackler. Skippy (dr)
_____. The Pastime of Monsieur Robert (dr)
William Saroyan. Short Drive, Sweet Chariot (nar)
James Marcus Schuyler. May 24th or So (po)
Anne Sexton. Live or Die (po)
Wilfred John Joseph Sheed. Office Politics (fic)
Isaac Bashevis Singer. In My Father's Court (nar)
_____. Zlateh the Goat (fic)
William Jay Smith. The Tin Can (po)
Gary Sherman Snyder. A Range of Poems (po)
Susan Sontag. Against Interpretation (e)
Gilbert Sorrentino. The Sky Changes (fic)
Jack Spicer. Book of Magazine Verse (po)
David Derek Stacton. The Bonapartes (hist)
Jean Stafford. A Mother in History (biog, hist)
William Edgar Stafford. The Rescued Year (po)
George Edwin Starbuck. White Paper (po)
Rex Todhunter Stout. Death of a Doxy (fic)
May Swenson. Poems To Solve (po, juv)
Robert Lewis Taylor. Vessel of Wrath (biog)
Studs Lewis Terkel. Division Street: America (nar)
Paul Edward Theroux. Waldo (fic)
Anne Tyler. The Tin Can Tree (fic)
John Hoyer Updike. The Music School (fic)
Mark Albert Van Doren. Three Plays (dr, pub)
David Russell Wagoner. Staying Alive (po)
Diane Wakowski. Discrepancies and Apparitions (po)
Jessamyn West. A Matter of Time (fic)
Philip Whalen. Highgrade (po)
_____. You Didn't Even Try (fic)

John Hall Wheelock. Dear Men and Women (po)
Thomas Lanier (Tennessee) Williams. The Knightly Quest (fic)
Edmund Wilson. Europe without Baedeker, rev (trav)
Arthur Yvor Winters. The Early Poems (po, pub)
_____. Forms of Discovery (e)
Louis Zukofsky. All the Collected Short Poems, 1956-1964 (po, pub)

1967

DEATHS

Margaret Ayer Barnes
David Cornel DeJong
Martin Archer Flavin
Esther Forbes
Waldo David Frank
James Langston Hughes
Carson Smith McCullers
Dorothy Rothschild Parker
Elmer Reizenstein (Elmer Rice)
Carl August Sandburg
Odell Shepard
Alice Babette Toklas
Jean Toomer

EVENTS

James Branch Cabell Society (f)
Case Western Reserve University, Cleveland, Ohio (est)

LITERATURE

Robert Woodruff Anderson. You Know I Can't Hear You When the Water's
    Running (dr)
Benjamin Appel. Man and Magic (e, hist)
John Lawrence Ashbery. Selected Poems (pub)
William Attaway. Hear America Singing (juv)
Donald Barthelme. Snow White (fic)
Thomas Louis Berger. Killing Time (fic)
Edmund J.M. Berrigan, Jr. and Ron Padgett. Bean Spasms (po, fic)
John Berryman. Berryman's Sonnets (po, pub)
Paul Blackburn. The Cities (po)
Burt Blechman. Maybe (fic)
Robert Elwood Bly. The Light Around the Body (po)
Philip Booth. Beyond Our Fears (po)
Vance Nye Bourjaily. The Man Who Knew Kennedy (fic)
Richard Brautigan. Trout Fishing in America (fic)
Janet Taylor Caldwell. Dialogues with the Devil (fic)
Clark Coolidge. Clark Coolidge (po)
Norman Cousins. Present Tense (e, nar)
Malcolm Cowley. Think Back on Us (e)
Robert White Creeley. Words (po)
Michael Cristofer. The Mandala (dr)
Edward Dahlberg. Epitaphs of Our Times (let)
Marcia Davenport. Too Strong for Fantasy (auto)

Peter DeVries. The Vale of Laughter (fic)
James Lafayette Dickey. Poems (pub)
Andre Dubus. The Lieutenant (fic)
John Gregory Dunne. Delano (e)
Richard Ghormley Eberhart. Thirty-One Sonnets (po)
Stanley Lawrence Elkin. A Bad Man (fic)
William Everson (Brother Antoninus). The Rose of Solitude (po)
James Thomas Farrell. New Year's Eve, 1929 (fic)
_____. When Time Was Born (fic)
Lawrence Ferlinghetti. After the Cries of the Birds (po)
Jessie Hill Ford. Fishes, Birds and Sons of Men (fic)
Paula Fox. Poor George (fic)
William Price Fox. Moonshine Light, Moonshine Bright (fic)
Ernest J. Gaines. Of Love and Dust (fic)
George Palmer Garrett, Jr. For a Bitter Season (po)
Jean Garrigue. New and Selected Poems (po, pub)
Frank Daniel Gilroy. That Summer--That Fall (dr)
Herbert Gold. Fathers (fic)
Horace Victor Gregory. Dorothy Richardson (biog)
Hiram Haydn. Report from the Red Windmill (fic)
Shirley Hazzard. People in Glass Houses (fic)
Anthony Evan Hecht. The Hard Hours (po)
Robert Anson Heinlein. The Moon Is a Harsh Mistress (fic)
James Leo Herlihy. A Story That Ends with a Scream (fic)
John Richard Hersey. Under the Eye of the Storm (fic)
John Hollander and Anthony Hecht. Jiggery Pokery (po)
Paul Horgan. The Peach Stone (fic)
Richard Joseph Howard. The Damages (po)
Irving Howe. Thomas Hardy (e, biog)
James Langston Hughes. The Panther and the Lash: Poems of Our Times
   (po)
James Jones. Go to the Widow-Maker (fic)
LeRoi Jones (Imamu Amiri Baraka). Tales (fic)
Donald Rodney Justice. Night Light (po)
MacKinlay Kantor. Storyteller (fic)
Elia Kazan. The Arrangement (fic)
William Melvin Kelley. dem (fic)
Jonathan Kozol. Death at an Early Age: The Destruction of the Hearts
   and Minds of Negro Children in the Boston Public Schools (e, nar)
Denise Levertov. The Sorrow Dance (po)
Ira Levin. Rosemary's Baby (fic)
Robert Traill Spence Lowell, Jr. Near the Ocean (po)
Alison Lurie. Imaginary Friends (fic)
Archibald MacLeish. Herakles (po, dr)
Norman Mailer. Why Are We in Vietnam? (fic)
_____. Short Fiction (fic, pub)
Bernard Malamud. The Fixer (fic)
Michael Thomas McClure. The Beard (dr)
Rod McKuen. Listen to the Warm (po)
David Meltzer. The Dark Continent (po)
William Stanley Merwin. The Lice (po)
Josephine Miles. Kinds of Affection (po)
Arthur Miller. I Don't Need You Anymore (fic)
Marianne Craig Moore. Complete Poems (pub)
Wright Morris. In Orbit (fic)
Ogden Nash. A Nash Omnibook (po)

_____. Santa Go Home: A Case History for Parents (po)
Robert Gruntal Nathan. Stonecliff (fic)
Howard Nemerov. The Blue Swallows (po)
John Frederick Nims. Of Flesh and Bone (po)
Joyce Carol Oates. A Garden of Earthly Delights (fic)
John Henry O'Hara. The Instrument (fic)
James Purdy. Eustace Chisholm and the Works (fic)
John Francisco Rechy. Numbers (fic)
Ishmael Scott Reed. The Free-Lance Pallbearers (fic)
Adrienne Cecile Rich. Selected Poems (pub)
Samuel Shepard Rogers, Jr. (Sam Shepard). La Turista (dr)
Leo Calvin Rosten. A Most Private Intrigue (fic)
Philip Roth. When She Was Good (fic)
Howard Sackler. The Great White Hope (dr)
William Saroyan. I Used To Believe I Had Forever, Now I'm Not So
    Sure (fic, e, po)
Isaac Bashevis Singer. The Manor (fic)
William DeWitt Snodgrass. Gallows Songs of Christian Morgenstern
    (po, trans)
Susan Sontag. Death Kit (fic)
Wallace Earle Stegner. All the Little Live Things (fic)
Robert Anthony Stone. A Hall of Mirrors (fic)
William Styron. The Confessions of Nat Turner (fic)
May Swenson. Half Sun Half Sleep (po)
James Vincent Tate. The Lost Pilot (po)
Leon Uris. Topaz (fic)
Gore Vidal. Washington, D.C. (fic)
Peter Viereck. New and Selected Poems (po, pub)
Diane Wakowski. The George Washington Poems (po)
Irving Wallace. The Plot (fic)
Jessamyn West. Leafy Rivers (fic)
Edward Reed Whittemore II. From Zero to the Absolute (po)
_____. Poems, New and Selected (pub)
John Edgar Wideman. A Glance Away (fic)
John Wieners. Jive Shoelaces and Anklesox (dr)
Thornton Niven Wilder. The Eighth Day (fic)
John Alfred Williams. The Man Who Cried I Am (fic)
Edmund Wilson. I Thought of Daisy, rev (fic)
_____. A Prelude (nar)
Frank Garvin Yerby. Goat Song: A Novel of Ancient Greece (fic)
Louis Zukofsky. Prepositions (e)

1968

DEATHS

    Dorothy Baker
    Harry Elmer Barnes
    Harold Witter Bynner
    Olive Tilford Dargan
    Donald Grady Davidson
    George Dillon
    Edna Ferber
    Vardis Alvero Fisher
    Dudley Fitts

Fannie Hurst
Howard Lindsay
Charles Reginald Jackson
Edwin O'Connor
Conrad Michael Richter
Winfield Townley Scott
Allen Seager
Upton Beall Sinclair
David Derek Stacton
Laurence Stallings
John Ernst Steinbeck
Arthur Yvor Winters

EVENTS

Society for the Study of Southern Literature (f)

LITERATURE

Robert Woodruff Anderson. I Never Sang for My Father (dr)
Benjamin Appel. The Age of Dictators (hist)
John Lawrence Ashbery. Sunrise in Suburbia (po)
_____. Three Madrigals (po)
Louis Stanton Auchincloss. A World of Profit (fic)
Wystan Hugh Auden. The Dyer's Hand, and Other Essays (e)
James Baldwin. Tell Me How Long the Train's Been Gone (fic)
John Barth. Lost in the Funhouse (fic)
Donald Barthelme. Unspeakable Practices, Unnatural Acts (fic)
Jacques Barzun. The American University (e)
Walter Jackson Bate. Coleridge (e)
Peter Soyer Beagle. The Last Unicorn (fic)
Samuel Nathaniel Behrman. The Burning Glass (fic)
Saul Bellow. Mosby's Memories (fic)
John Berryman. His Toy, His Dream, His Rest (po)
Paul Blackburn. In, On, or About the Premises (po)
Philip Booth. Beyond Our Fears (po)
Gerald Warner Brace. The Department (fic)
Ray Douglas Bradbury. Any Friend of Nicholas Nickleby's Is a Friend
    of Mine (fic)
_____. The Halloween Tree (dr)
Richard Brautigan. In Watermelon Sugar (fic)
_____. The Pill Versus the Springfield Mine Disaster
    (po)
Gwendolyn Brooks. In the Mecca (po)
Kenneth Duva Burke. Collected Poems (pub)
Erskine Preston Caldwell. Deep South (nar)
_____. Sometimes Island (fic)
Melville Henry Cane. All and Sundry (auto)
Raymond Carver. Near Klamath (po)
Ronald Verlin Cassill. La Vie Passionee of Rodney Buckthorne (fic)
Stuart Chase. The Most Probable World (e)
Paddy Chayefsky. The Latent Heterosexual (dr)
Marcus Cook Connelly. Voices Offstange (auto)
Robert Lowell Coover. The Universal Baseball Association, Inc., J.
    Henry Waugh, Prop. (fic)
James Gould Cozzens. Morning, Noon, and Night (fic)

Harry Crews. The Gospel Singer (fic)
Michael Cristofer. Rienzi (dr)
Edward Dahlberg. The Carnal Myth (e)
Robert Choate Darnton. Mesmerism and the End of Enlightenment in France (hist)
Vina Delmar. The Becker Scandal (nar)
Peter DeVries. The Cat's Pajamas and Witch's Milk (fic)
James Lafayette Dickey. Babel to Byzantium (e)
Joan Didion. Slouching towards Bethlehem (e)
James Patrick Donleavy. The Beastly Beatitudes of Balthazar B. (fic)
Allen Stuart Drury. Preserve and Protect (fic)
Alan Dugan. Poems 3 (po, pub)
Robert Edward Duncan. Bending the Bow (po)
Richard Ghormley Eberhart. Shifts of Being (po)
George Paul Elliott. An Hour of Last Things (fic)
William Everson (Brother Antoninus). Robinson Jeffers: Fragments of an Older Fury (e)
Frederick Feikema (Frederick Manfred/Feike Feikema). Apples of Paradise (fic)
_____. Eden Prairie (fic)
Leslie Aaron Fiedler. The Return of the Vanishing American (e)
William Price Fox. Southern Fried Plus Six (fic)
Bruce Jay Friedman. Scuba Duba (dr)
Ernest J. Gaines. Bloodline (fic)
William Howard Gass. In the Heart of the Heart of the Country (fic)
Frank Daniel Gilroy. The Only Game in Town (dr)
Allen Ginsberg. Ankor Wat (po)
_____. Planet News (po)
_____. T.V. Baby Poems (po)
Nikki Giovanni. Black Feeling, Black Talk (po)
_____. Black Judgement (po)
Alfred Hayes. The End of Me (fic)
_____. Just before the Divorce (po)
Joseph Heller. We Bombed in New Haven (dr)
James Leo Herlihy. Stop, You're Killing Me (dr)
John Richard Hersey. The Algiers Motel Incident (nar)
Daniel Gerard Hoffman. Striking the Stones (po)
John Hollander. Types of Shape (po)
Paul Horgan. Everything To Live For (fic)
William Humphrey. A Time and a Place (fic)
David Ignatow. Earth Hard (po)
_____. Rescue the Dead (po)
John Winslow Irving. Setting Free the Beans (fic)
Shirley Hardie Jackson. Come Along with Me (fic, pub)
Diane Lain Johnson. Loving Hands at Home (fic)
James Jones. The Ice-Cream Headache (fic)
MacKinlay Kantor. Beauty Beast (fic)
Jack Kerouac. Vanity of Duluoz (fic)
John Knowles. Phineas (fic)
Jerzy Nikodem Kosinski. Steps (fic)
Maxine Winokur Kumin. Passions of Uxport (fic)
Jeremy Larner. The Answer (fic)
Tom Lea. A Picture Gallery (fic)
Ursula K. LeGuin. The Wizard of Earthsea (fic)
Denise Levertov. The Cold Spring, and Other Poems (po)

_____. In the Night: A Story (fic)
_____. A Marigold from North Vietnam (po)
_____. Three Poems (po)
_____. A Tree Telling of Orpheus (po)
Meyer Levin. Gore and Igor (fic)
Robert Traill Spence Lowell, Jr. The Voyage, and Other Versions of
   Poems by Baudelaire (po, trans)
Norman Mailer. The Armies of the Night (nar)
_____. The Idol and the Octopus (e, nar)
_____. Miami and the Siege of Chicago (nar, e)
Cormac McCarthy. Outer Dark (fic)
James Rodney McConkey. Crossroads (fic)
Helen MacInnes. The Salzburg Connection (fic)
Archibald MacLeish. A Continuing Journey (e)
Thomas Merton. Cables to the Ace (po)
Josephine Miles. Fields of Learning (po)
Arthur Miller. The Price (dr)
Howard Moss. Second Nature (po)
_____. The Oedipus Mah-Jongg Scandal (dr)
Ogden Nash. There's Always Another Windmill (po)
Anais Nin. The Novel of the Future (e)
Joyce Carol Oates. Expensive People (fic)
_____. Women in Love (po)
John Henry O'Hara. And Other Stories (fic)
Charles Olson. Maximus IV, V, VI (po)
Elder James Olson. The Theory of Comedy (e)
George Oppen. Of Being Numerous (po)
Kenneth Patchen. But Even So (po)
Marge Piercy. Breaking Camp (po)
Robert Pinsky. Landor's Poetry (e)
Reynolds Price. Love and Work (fic)
Frederic Prokosch. The Missolonghi Manuscript (fic)
Kenneth Rexroth. Longer Poems (po)
Jack Carter Richardson. As Happy As Kings (dr)
Muriel Rukeyser. The Speed of Darkness (po)
Mark Schorer. The World We Imagine (e)
Michael Joseph Shaara, Jr. The Broken Place (fic)
Karl Jay Shapiro. To Abolish Children (e, fic)
Wilfred John Joseph Sheed. The Blacking Factory and Pennsylvania Go-
   thic (fic)
Isaac Bashevis Singer. The Seance (fic)
_____. When Shlemihl Went to Warsaw (juv, fic)
William Jay Smith. Mr. Smith (po)
William DeWitt Snodgrass. After Experience (po)
Gary Sherman Snyder. The Back Country (po)
Susan Sontag. Trip to Hanoi (e, nar)
Gilbert Sorrentino. The Perfect Fiction (po)
Elizabeth Spencer. Ship Island (fic)
William Edgar Stafford. Friends to This Ground (e)
Grace Zaring Stone. Dear Deadly Cara (fic)
Mark Strand. Reasons for Moving (po)
Ronald Sukenick. Up (fic)
Peter Hillsman Taylor. A Stand in the Mountains (dr)
Paul Edward Theroux. Fong and the Indians (fic)
John Hoyer Updike. Couples (fic)
Gore Vidal. Myra Breckenridge (fic)

Kurt Vonnegut, Jr. Welcome to the Monkey House (fic, e)
David Russell Wagoner. Come On Inside (fic)
Diane Wakowski. Inside the Blood Factory (po)
Alice Walker. Once (po)
Robert Penn Warren. Incarnations (po)
Jerome Weidman. Other People's Money (fic)
Theodore Harold White. Caesar at the Rubicon (dr)
Richard Purdy Wilbur. Complaint (po)
Thomas Lanier (Tennessee) Williams. Kingdom of Earth (dr)
Lanford Wilson. The Gingham Dog (dr)
Herman Wouk. The Lomokome Papers (fic)
James Arlington Wright. Shall We Gather at the River? (po)
Frank Garvin Yerby. Judas, My Brother (fic)
Louis Zukofsky. Ferdinand (fic)

1969

DEATHS

John Mason Brown
William Henry Chamberlain
Floyd Dell
Max Forrester Eastman
Josephine Frey Herbst
Maurice Gerschon Hindus
George Rolfe Humphries
Jack Kerouac
Thomas Merton
John Kennedy Toole
Leane Zugsmith

EVENTS

Bibliographical Society of Northern Illinois (f)
Richard Milhous Nixon, 37th President of the United States, to 1974
Popular Culture Association (f)

LITERATURE

John Lawrence Ashbery. 77, Fragment (po)
                        and James Schuyler. A Nest of Ninnies (fic)
Isaac Asimov. Nightfall, and Other Stories (fic)
Margaret Culkin Banning. Mesabi (fic)
Peter Soyer Beagle. The California Feeling (nar, des)
John Berryman. The Dream Songs (po)
Elizabeth Bishop. Complete Poems (po, pub)
Judy Sussman Blume. The One in the Middle is the Green Kangaroo
   (juv, fic)
Gerald Warner Brace. The Stuff of Fiction (e)
Ray Douglas Bradbury. I Sing the Body Electric (fic)
Gwendolyn Brooks. Riot (po)
Carl Frederick Buechner. The Hungering Defeat (med, pra)
Charles Bukowski. Notes of a Dirty Old Man (fic)
Erskine Preston Caldwell. The Weather Shelter (fic)
Truman Capote. The Thanksgiving Visitor (fic)

Gladys Hasty Carroll. Man on the Mountain (fic)
Mary Coyle Chase. Mickey (dr)
Stuart Chase. Danger--Men Talking! (e)
John Cheever. Bullet Park (fic)
Mary Higgins Clark. Aspire to the Heavens (biog)
Lucille Clifton. Good Times (po)
Evan Shelby Connell, Jr. Mr. Bridge (fic)
Clark Coolidge. Ing (po)
Robert Lowell Coover. Pricksongs and Descants (fic)
Louis Osborne Coxe. Edwin Arlington Robinson (e)
Robert White Creeley. Pieces (po)
Harry Crews. Naked in Garden Hills (fic)
John Michael Crichton. The Andromeda Strain (fic)
Michael Cristofer. Dorian (dr)
Merle Eugene Curti. Human Nature in American Historical Thought (e,
    hist)
Babette Deutsch. Collected Poems (pub)
John Gregory Dunne. The Studio (e)
George Paul Elliott. From the Berkeley Hills (po)
Paul Hamilton Engle. Embraced (po)
William Everson (Brother Antoninus). The Last Crusade (po)
John Fante. Bravo Burro (fic)
James Thomas Farrell. Childhood Is Not Forever (fic)
Lawrence Ferlinghetti. The Secret Meaning of Things (po)
_____. Tyrannus Nix (fic)
Leslie Aaron Fiedler. Being Busted (nar)
_____. Nude Croquet (fic)
Jessie Hill Ford. The Feast of St. Barnabas (fic)
George Palmer Garrett, Jr. A Wreath for Garibaldi (fic)
Jack Gelber. The Cuban Thing (dr)
Martha Gellhorn. The Lowest Trees Have Tops (fic)
Herbert Gold. The Great American Jackpot (fic)
Louise Gluck. Firstborn (po)
Charles Gordone. No Place To Be Somebody (dr)
Paul Eliot Green. Home to My Valley (fic)
Nancy Hale. The Life in the Studio (auto)
Donald Andrew Hall. The Alligator Bride (po)
John Clendennin Burne Hawkes, Jr. Lunar Landscapes (fic)
Lillian Hellman. An Unfinished Workman (auto)
Chester Bomar Himes. Blind Man with a Pistol (fic)
Edward Hoagland. Notes from the Century Before (trav)
Eric Hoffer. Working and Thinking on the Waterfront: A Journal, June
    1958--May 1959 (nar, e)
John Hollander. Images of Voice (e)
Richard Joseph Howard. Alone with America (e)
_____. Untitled Subjects (po)
Irving Howe. The Decline of the New (e)
James Langston Hughes. Don't You Turn Back: Poems (po, juv, pub)
Richard Franklin Hugo. Good Luck in Cracked Italian (po)
George Rolfe Humphries. Coat on a Stick (po)
Randall Jarrell. The Third Book of Criticism (e)
_____. The Three Sisters (dr)
Josephine Winslow Johnson. The Inland Island (e)
LeRoi Jones (Imamu Amiri Baraka). Black Magic (po)
_____. Four Black Revolutionary Plays
    (dr)

William Kennedy. The Ink Truck (fic)
Kenneth Jay Koch. The Pleasures of Peace (po)
Allen Stewart Konigsberg (Woody Allen). Play It Again, Sam (dr)
Arthur L. Kopit. Indians (dr)
Louis Kronenberger. The Polished Surface (e)
Ursula K. LeGuin. The Left Hand of Darkness (fic)
Denise Levertov. Embroideries (po)
Anne Morrow Lindbergh. Earth Shine (e)
John Logan. The Zig-Zag Walk (po)
Robert Traill Spence Lowell, Jr. Notebook 1967-1968 (po)
Alison Lurie. Real People (fic)
Bernard Malamud. Pictures of Fidelman (fic)
Thomas Francis McGuane III. The Sporting Club (fic)
James Alan McPherson. Hue and Cry (fic)
James Ingram Merrill. The Fire Screen (po)
Thomas Merton. Mystic and Zen Masters (e)
Leonard Michaels. Going Places (fic)
Navarre Scott Momaday. House Made of Dawn (fic)
_____. The Way to Rainy Mountain (fic)
Robert Morgan. Zirconia Poems (po)
Vladimir Nabokov. Ada or Ardor (fic)
Joyce Carol Oates. Anonymous Sins (po)
_____. Them (fic)
Flannery O'Connor. Mystery and Manners (e, pub)
Charles Olson. Casual Mythology (e)
_____. Letters for Origin (e)
Robert Pack. Home from the Cemetary (po)
Kenneth Patchen. Collected Poems (pub)
Marge Piercy. Hard Loving (po)
Philip Rahv. Literature and the Sixth Sense (e)
Ayn Rand. The Romantic Manifesto (e)
John Crowe Ransom. Selected Poems (pub)
Ishmael Scott Reed. Yellow Black Radio Broke Down (fic)
Kenneth Rexroth. Classics Revisited (e)
Charles Reznikoff. Family Chronicle (nar)
Adrienne Cecile Rich. Leaflets (po)
William Pitt Root. The Storm, and Other Poems (po)
Judith Perelman Rossner. Nine Months in the Life of an Old Maid (fic)
Philip Roth. Portnoy's Complaint (fic)
Budd Wilson Schulberg. Sanctuary V (fic)
James Marcus Schuyler. Freely Espousing (po)
_____ and John Lawrence Ashbery. A Nest of Ninnies
    (fic)
Anne Sexton. Love Poems (po)
William Lawrence Shirer. The Collapse of the Third Republic (hist)
Isaac Bashevis Singer. The Estate (fic)
Gary Sherman Snyder. Earth House Hold (e)
Susan Sontag. Styles of Radical Will (e)
Jean Stafford. Collected Stories (pub)
Ronald Sukenick. The Death of the Novel (fic)
John Orley Allen Tate. Essays of Four Decades (pub)
Peter Hillsman Taylor. Collected Stories (pub)
Paul Edward Theroux. Girls at Play (fic)
Calvin Trillin. Barnett Frummer Is an Unbloomed Flower (fic)
John Hoyer Updike. Midpoint (po)
Mark Albert Van Doren. That Shining Place: New Poems (po)

Gore Vidal. Reflections on a Sinking Ship (e)
Kurt Vonnegut, Jr. Slaughterhouse-Five; or, the Children's Crusade
    (fic)
David Russell Wagoner. New and Selected Poems (pub)
Irving Wallace. The Seven Minutes (fic)
Robert Penn Warren. Audubon: A Vision (po)
Jerome Weidman. Asterisk (dr)
                 . The Center of the Action (fic)
                 . Ivory Tower (dr)
Jessamyn West. Except for Me and Thee (fic)
Philip Whalen. On Bear's Head (po)
Richard Purdy Wilbur. Walking to Sleep: New Poems and Translations
    (po, trans)
Kate Wilhelm. Orbit 2 (fic)
C.K. Williams. Lies (po)
John Alfred Williams. Sons of Darkness, Sons of Light (fic)
Thomas Lanier (Tennessee) Williams. In the Bar of a Tokyo Hotel (dr)
                                    . The Two-Character Play (dr)
Calder Baynard Willingham, Jr. Providence Island (fic)
Edmund Wilson. The Dead Sea Scrolls, 1947-1969 (hist)
              . The Duke of Palermo (dr)
Larry Alfred Woiwode. What I'm Going To Do, I Think (fic)
Geoffrey Ansell Wolff. Bad Debts (fic)
Albert James Young. Dancing (po)
Louis Zukofsky. A 13-21 (po)
               . The Gas Age (e)
               . Little; for Careenagers (fic)

                        1970

DEATHS

    Louise Bogan
    John Roderigo Dos Passos
    Erle Stanley Gardner
    Joseph Wood Krutch
    John Henry O'Hara
    Charles Olson
    Louis Paul
    Gilbert Vivian Seldes
    Wilbur Daniel Steele
    Jean Starr Untermeyer
    Anzia Yezierska

LITERATURE

    Mortimore Jerome Adler. The Time of Our Lives: The Ethics of Common
        Sense (e)
    Renata Adler. Toward a Radical Middle (e)
                 . A Year in the Dark (e)
    Archie Randolph Ammons. Uplands (po)
    Roger Angell. A Day in the Life of Roger Angell (nar)
    Benjamin Appel. The Fantastic Mirror (e)
    Harriette Arnow. The Weedkiller's Daughter (fic)
    John Lawrence Ashbery. The Double Dream of Spring (po)

Wystan Hugh Auden. City without Walls (po)
Richard David Bach. Jonathan Livingston Seagull (fic)
Leonard Stanley Baker. Roosevelt and Pearl Harbor (hist)
Donald Barthelme. City Life (fic)
Ben Belitt. Nowhere but Light (po)
Saul Bellow. Mr. Sammler's Planet (fic)
Thomas Louis Berger. Vital Parts (fic)
Wendell Berry. A Continuous Harmony (po)
John Berryman. Love and Fame (po)
Judy Sussman Blume. Are You There, God? It's Me, Margaret (juv, fic)
_____. Iggie's House (juv, fic)
Louise Bogan. Poet's Alphabet (e)
Philip Booth. Margins (po)
Vance Nye Bourjaily. Brill among the Ruins (fic)
Kay Boyle. The Long Walk at San Francisco State (e)
_____. Testament for My Students (fic)
Richard Brautigan. Rommel Drives on Deep into Egypt (po)
John Malcolm Brinnin. Skin Diving in the Virgins (po)
Gwendolyn Brooks. Family Pictures (po)
Courtlandt Dixon Barnes Bryan. The Great Dethriffe (fic)
Carl Frederick Buechner. The Alphabet of Grace (med, pra)
_____. The Entrance to Porlock (fic)
Carl Lamson Carmer. The Farm Boy and the Angel (hist)
Hayden Carruth. For You (po)
Raymond Carver. Winter Insomnia (po)
Ronald Verlin Cassill. Dr. Cobb's Game (fic)
James Bryant Conant. My Several Lives (auto)
Clark Coolidge. Space (po)
Sidney (Cid) Corman. Livingdying (po)
Gregory Nunzio Corso. Elegiac Feelings American (po)
Malcolm Cowley. A Many-Windowed House (e)
Robert White Creeley. The Finger (po)
_____. A Quick Graph (e)
Harry Crews. This Thing Don't Lead to Heaven (fic)
Peter Hubert Davison. Pretending To Be Asleep (po)
Peter DeVries. Mrs. Wallop (fic)
James Lafayette Dickey. Blood (po)
_____. Buckhead and Mercy (po)
_____. Deliverance (fic)
_____. The Eye-Beaters (po)
_____. Madness (po)
_____. Self Interviews (e)
_____. Victory (po)
Joan Didion. Play It As It Lays (fic)
Pietro DiDonato. Naked Author (fic)
Alan Dugan. Collected Poems (pub)
Gretel Ehrlich. Geode/Rock Body (po)
Theodore Vernon Enslin. Forms, to 1974 (po)
Nora Ephron. Wallflower at the Orgy (e)
Paula Fox. Desperate Characters (fic)
Bruce Jay Friedman. The Dick (fic)
_____. Steambath (dr)
John Champlin Gardner, Jr. The Wreckage of Agathon (fic)
William Howard Gass. Fiction and the Figures of Life (e)
William Howard Gass. Willie Master's Lonesome Wife (fic)
Allen Ginsberg. Indian Journals (nar)

Nikki Giovanni. Poem of Angela Yvonne Davis (po)
_____. Re: Creation (po)
Gail Godwin. The Perfectionists (fic)
Charles Gordone. Gordone Is Muthah (dr)
Albert Halper. Good-Bye, Union Square (nar, auto)
Joseph Hansen. Fadeout (fic)
Michael S. Harper. Dear John, Dear Coltrane (po)
Mark Harris. The Goy (fic)
Robert Hayden. Words in the Mourning Time (po)
Shirley Hazzard. The Bay of Noon (fic)
Ernest Miller Hemingway. Islands in the Stream (fic, pub)
John Richard Hersey. Letter to the Alumni (e)
William Heyen. Depth of Field (po)
Granville Hicks. Literary Horizons (e)
David Ignatow. Poems, 1934-1969 (pub)
William Inge. Good Luck, Miss Wyckoff (fic)
Marguerite Johnson (Maya Angelou). I Know Why the Caged Bird Sings
   (auto)
William Melvin Kelley. Dunfords Travels Everywhere (fic)
Galway Kinnell. First Poems, 1946-1954 (po, pub)
Maxine Winokur Kumin. The Nightmare Factory (po)
Philip Lamantia. The Blood of the Air (po)
Jeremy Larner. Nobody Knows (fic)
Ella Lefland. Mrs. Munck (fic)
Ursula K. LeGuin. The Lathe of Heaven (fic)
Denise Levertov. A New Year's Garland for My Students, MIT 1969-1970
   (po)
_____. Relearning the Alphabet (po)
_____. Summer Poems 1969 (po)
Ira Levin. The Perfect Day (fic)
Robert Traill Spence Lowell, Jr. Notebook (po)
Clare Boothe Luce. Slam the Door Softly (dr)
Norman Mailer. Of a Fire on the Moon (e)
Albert Maltz. Afternoon in the Jungle (fic)
Wallace Markfield. Teitlebaum's Window (fic)
Harry Mathews. The Ring (po)
William Matthews. Running the New Road (po)
Sandra McPherson. Elegies for the Hot Season (po)
William Morris Meredith. Earth Walk (po)
William Stanley Merwin. The Carriers of Ladders (po)
_____. The Miner's Pale Children (fic, misc)
Jason Miller. Nobody Hears a Broken Drum (dr)
Toni Morrison. The Bluest Eye (fic)
Albert Murray. The Omni-Americans (fic)
Ogden Nash. Bed Riddance: A Posy for the Indisposed (po)
Robert Gruntal Nathan. Mia (fic)
Joyce Carol Oates. Love and Its Derangements (po)
_____. The Wheel of Love (fic)
John Henry O'Hara. Lovey Childs (fic)
Sidney Joseph Perelman. Baby, It's Cold Inside (sat, nar)
Robert Phillips. The Land of Lost Content (fic)
Stanley Plumly. In the Outer Dark (po)
Ezra Weston Loomis Pound. Cantos (po)
Reynolds Price. Permanent Errors (fic)
James Purdy. Jeremy's Version (fic)
John Francisco Rechy. This Day's Death (fic)

Ishmael Scott Reed. <u>Catechism of the Neo-American Hoo Doo Church</u>
   (po)
Laura Reichenthal (Laura Riding). <u>Selected Poems</u> (pub)
Howard Sackler. <u>A Few Enquiries</u> (dr)
Carl August Sandburg. <u>Complete Poems</u> (pub)
William Saroyan. <u>Days of Life and Death and Escape to the Moon</u> (nar)
Irwin Shaw. <u>Rich Man, Poor Man</u> (fic)
Wilfred John Joseph Sheed. <u>Max Jamison</u> (fic)
Isaac Bashevis Singer. <u>A Day of Pleasure</u> (nar)
_____. <u>Enemies</u> (fic)
_____. <u>A Friend of Kafka</u> (fic)
Gary Sherman Snyder. <u>Regarding Wave</u> (po)
Gilbert Sorrentino. <u>Steelwork</u> (fic)
William Edgar Stafford. <u>Allegiances</u> (po)
Richard Gustave Stern. <u>1968: A Short Novel</u> (fic)
Mark Strand. <u>Darker</u> (po)
Jesse Hilton Stuart. <u>To Teach, To Love</u> (nar)
Harvey Swados. <u>Standing Fast</u> (fic)
May Swenson. <u>Iconographs</u> (po)
James Vincent Tate. <u>The Oblivion Ha-Ha</u> (po)
Studs Lewis Turkel. <u>Hard Times</u> (nar)
Anne Tyler. <u>A Slipping Down Life</u> (fic)
Gore Vidal. <u>Two Sisters</u> (fic)
Kurt Vonnegut, Jr. <u>Happy Birthday, Wanda June</u> (dr)
David Russell Wagoner. <u>Where Is My Wondering Boy Tonight?</u> (fic)
_____. <u>Working against Time</u> (po)
Alice Walker. <u>The Third Life of George Copeland</u> (fic)
Eudora Welty. <u>Losing Battles</u> (fic)
Jessamyn West. <u>Crimson Ramblers of the World, Farewell</u> (fic)
John Hall Wheelock. <u>By Daylight and in Dream</u> (po)
Edward Reed Whittemore II. <u>50 Poems 50</u> (po)
John Edgar Wideman. <u>Hurry Home</u> (fic)
John Wieners. <u>Nerves</u> (po)
Richard Purdy Wilbur. <u>Digging to China</u> (po)
John Alfred Williams. <u>The King God Didn't Save</u> (biog)
Lanford Wilson. <u>Lemon Sky</u> (dr)
_____. <u>Serenading Louie</u> (dr)
Albert James Young. <u>Snakes</u> (fic)
Paul Zindel. <u>The Effect of Gamma Rays on Man-in-the-Moon Marigolds</u>
   (dr)

1971

DEATHS

   Archie Binns
   Paul Blackburn
   Walter Van Tilburg Clark
   August William Derleth
   Harvey Fergusson
   Manfred Lee
   Ogden Nash
   James Floyd Stevens

EVENTS

New Catholic World (per, f)
The Saturday Evening Post, 2nd series (per, est)

LITERATURE

Edward Albee. All Over (dr)
Archie Randolph Ammons. Briefings (po)
_____. Collected Poems (pub)
Robert Woodruff Anderson. Solitaire/Double Solitaire (dr)
James Baldwin and Margaret Mead. A Rap on Race (e, dia)
Margaret Culkin Banning. Lifeboat Number Two (fic)
Stringfellow Barr. Voices That Endured (e)
Edmund J.M. Berrigan, Jr. The Early Morning Rain (po)
Judy Sussman Blume. Freckle Juice (juv, fic)
_____. Then Again, Maybe I Won't (juv, fic)
Richard Brautigan. The Abortion: An Historical Romance (fic)
_____. Revenge of the Lawn (fic)
Gwendolyn Brooks. Aloneness (po)
James Richard Broughton. A Long Undressing (po)
Rita Mae Brown. The Hand That Cradles the Rock (po)
_____. Hrotsvitra: Six Medieval Latin Plays (dr, trans)
Carl Frederick Buechner. Lion Country (fic)
Charles Bukowski. Post Office (fic)
William Seward Burroughs. The Job (nar, e)
_____. The Wild Boys (fic)
Hortense Calisher. Queenie (fic)
John Ciardi. Lives of X (po)
Eleanor Clark. Baldur's Gate (fic)
Clark Coolidge. The So (po)
Robert White Creeley. St. Martin's (po)
John Michael Crichton. Dealing: or, the Berkeley-to-Boston Forty-
   Brick Lost-Boy Blues (fic)
Michael Cristofer. Plot Counter Plot (dr)
James Vincent Cunningham. Collected Poems and Epigrams (pub)
Edward Dahlberg. Confessions (nar)
Peter Hubert Davison. Dark Houses (po)
Peter DeVries. Into Your Tent I'll Creep (fic)
James Lafayette Dickey. Sorties (nar, e)
Edgar Lawrence Doctorow. The Book of Daniel (fic)
James Patrick Donleavy. The Onion Eaters (fic)
Allen Stuart Drury. The Throne of Saturn (fic)
Stanley Lawrence Elkin. The Dick Gibson Show (fic)
George Paul Elliott. Conversions (e)
James Thomas Farrell. Invisible Swords (fic)
Howard Melvin Fast. The Crossing (fic)
Leslie Aaron Fiedler. Collected Essays (pub)
Robert Stuart Fitzgerald. Spring Shade (po)
William Price Fox. Ruby Red (fic)
Daniel Fuchs. West of the Rockies (fic)
Ernest J. Gaines. The Autobiography of Miss Jane Pitman (fic)
John Champlin Gardner, Jr. Grendel (fic)
George Palmer Garrett, Jr. Death of the Fox (fic)
Nikki Giovanni. Gemini (e)
_____. Spin a Soft Black Song (po)

Herbert Gold. The Magic Will (fic)
Caroline Gordon. The Glory of Hera (fic)
Charles William Goyen. The House of Breath Black/White (dr)
Shirley Ann Grau. The Condor Passes (fic)
Alfred Bertram Guthrie, Jr. Arfive (fic)
Nancy Hale. Secrets (fic)
Donald Andrew Hall. The Yellow Room (po)
Oakley Hall. Report from Beau Harbor (fic)
John Clendennin Burne Hawkes, Jr. The Blood Oranges (fic)
James Leo Herlihy. The Season of the Witch (fic)
Edward Hoagland. The Courage of Turtles (e)
Laura Zametkin Hobson. The Tenth Man (fic)
Eric Hoffer. First Things, Last Things (e)
John Hollander. The Night Mirror (po)
Richard Joseph Howard. Findings (po)
William Humphrey. The Spawning Run (nar)
William Inge. My Son Is a Splendid Driver (fic)
Randall Jarrell. Jerome: The Biography of a Poem (po, pub)
Diane Lain Johnson. Burning (fic)
Marguerite Johnson (Maya Angelou). Just Give Me a Cool Drink of Wa-
    ter 'fore I Diiie (po)
James Jones. The Merry Month of May (fic)
LeRoi Jones (Imamu Amiri Baraka). In Our Trembleness (po)
Erica Mann Jong. Fruits and Vegetables (po)
Bob Kaufman. Watch My Tracks (po)
Jack Kerouac. Pic (fic, pub)
Galway Kinnell. The Book of Nightmares (po)
_____. The Lackawanna Elegy (po)
John Knowles. The Paragon (fic)
Allen Stewart Konigsberg (Woody Allen). Getting Even (nar)
Jerzy Nikodem Kosinski. Being There (fic)
Maxine Winoker Kumin. The Abduction (fic)
Stanley Jasspon Kunitz. The Testing-Tree (po)
Ursula K. LeGuin. The Tombs of Atuan (fic)
Denise Levertov. To Stay Alive (po)
Philip Levine. Red Dust (po)
Robert Ludlum. The Scarlatti Inheritance (fic)
Archibald MacLeish. Scratch (dr)
Norman Mailer. The Prisoner of Sex (e)
Bernard Malamud. The Tenants (fic)
Mary Therese McCarthy. Birds of America (fic)
Michael Thomas McClure. The Adept (fic)
James Rodney McConkey. A Journey to Sahalin (fic)
Carson Smith McCullers. The Mortgaged Heart (fic, pub)
Thomas Francis McGuane III. The Backwashed Piano (fic)
James Albert Michener. The Drifters (fic)
_____. Kent State: What Happened and Why (nar, e)
Kenneth Millar (Ross Macdonald). The Underground Man (fic)
Samuel Eliot Morison. The European Discovery of America, 2 vols, to
    1974 (hist)
Wright Morris. Fire Sermon (fic)
Howard Moss. Selected Poems (pub)
Vladimir Nabokov. Poems and Problems (po)
Robert Gruntal Nathan. The Elixer (fic)
John Frederick Nims. Sappho to Valery (trans)
Joyce Carol Oates. The Edge of Impossibility (e)

_____. Wonderland (fic)
Flannery O'Connor. Complete Stories (fic, pub)
Charles Olson. The Archaeologist of Morning (po)
_____. Poetry and Truth (e, pub)
Cynthia Ozick. The Pagan Rabbi, and Other Stories (fic)
Walker Percy. Love in the Ruins (fic)
Ann Petry. Miss Muriel (fic)
Sylvia Plath. Crossing the Water (po, pub)
James Purdy. The Running Sun (po)
David William Rabe. The Basic Training of Pavlo Hummel (dr)
_____. Sticks and Bones (dr)
John Francisco Rechy. The Vampires (fic)
Kenneth Rexroth. The Alternative Society (e)
_____. With Eye and Ear (e)
Adrienne Cecile Rich. The Will To Change (po)
Tomas Rivera. And the Earth Did Not Part (fic)
Tom Robbins. Another Roadside Attraction (fic)
Philip Roth. Our Gang (sat, fic)
Hubert Selby. The Room (fic)
Anne Sexton. Transformations (po)
Karl Jay Shapiro. Edsel (fic)
Wilfred John Joseph Sheed. The Morning After (e)
Charles Simic. Dismantling the Silence (po)
Louis Aston Marantz Simpson. Adventures of the Letter I (po)
Gilbert Sorrentino. Corrosive Sublimate (po)
_____. Imaginary Qualities of Actual Things (fic)
Wallace Earle Stegner. Angle of Repose (fic)
Wallace Stevens. The Palm at the End of the Mind (po, dr, pub)
Irving Stone. Passions of the Mind (fic)
May Swenson. More Poems To Solve (po, juv)
John Orley Allen Tate. The Swimmers (po)
Paul Edward Theroux. Jungle Lovers (fic)
John Hoyer Updike. Rabbit Redux (fic)
Diane Wakowski. Motorcycle Betrayal Poems (po)
Robert Penn Warren. Homage to Theodore Dreiser (e)
_____. John Greenleaf Whittier (e)
_____. Meet Me in the Green Glen (fic)
Jerome Weidman. Fourth Street East (fic)
_____. Last Respects (fic)
John Hall Wheelock. In Love and Song (po)
John Wieners. Selected Poems (pub)
Richard Purdy Wilbur. School for Wives (dr)
Edmund Wilson. Upstate (nar)
Herman Wouk. The Winds of War (fic)
Charles Wright. Hard Freight (po)
James Arlington Wright. Collected Poems (pub)
Albert James Young. The Song Turning Back into Itself (po)

1972

DEATHS

    Sara Mahala Redway Smith Benson
    John Berryman
    Norman Foerster

Jean Garrigue
Paul Goodman
Ruth McKenney
Marianne Craig Moore
Kenneth Patchen
Ezra Weston Loomis Pound
Gladys Schmitt
Betty Wehner Smith
Harvey Swados
Mark Albert Van Doren
Edmund Wilson

EVENTS

Center for Southern Folklore, Memphis, Tennessee (f)
Poe Studies Association (f)
Yardbird Reader, Berkeley, California, to 1978 (per, ed)

LITERATURE

Roger Angell. The Summer Game (nar)
John Lawrence Ashbery. Three Poems (po, pub)
James Baldwin. No Name in the Street (e)
Toni Cade Bambara. Gorilla, My Love (fic)
John Barth. Chimera (fic)
Donald Barthelme. Sadness (fic)
Samuel Nathaniel Behrman. People in a Diary (auto)
Wendell Berry. The Country of Marriage (po)
John Berryman. Delusions, etc. (po)
Judy Sussman Blume. It's Not the End of the World (juv, fic)
_____. Otherwise Known As Sheila the Great (juv, fic)
_____. Tales of a Fourth Grade Nothing (juv, fic)
Paul Bowles. The Thicket of Spring (po)
_____. Without Stopping (auto)
Gwendolyn Brooks. Report from Part One (auto)
Carl Frederick Buechner. Open Heart (fic)
Charles Bukowski. Erections, Ejaculations, Exhibitions, and General
    Tales of Ordinary Madness (fic)
Kenneth Duva Burke. Dramatism and Development (e)
Hortense Calisher. Herself (auto)
Robert Emmet Cantwell. The Hidden Northwest (hist)
Gladys Hasty Carroll. Years Away from Home (auto)
Lucille Clifton. Good News about the Earth (po)
Robert Lowell Coover. A Theological Position (dr)
_____. The Water Pourer (dr)
Robert White Creeley. A Day Book (po)
Harry Crews. CAR (fic)
John Michael Crichton. Westworld (fic)
Michael Cristofer. Americomedia (dr)
Jonathan Worth Daniels. The Randolphs of Virginia (biog)
Peter DeVries. Without a Stitch in Time (fic)
Hilda Doolittle. Hermetic Definition (e, pub)
Richard Ghormley Eberhart. Fields of Grace (po)
George Paul Elliott. Muriel (fic)
James Thomas Farrell. A Brand New Life (fic)
Howard Melvin Fast. The Hessian (fic)

Peter Steinham Feibleman. The Columbus Tree (fic)
Leslie Aaron Fiedler. The Stranger in Shakespeare (e)
Paula Fox. The Western Coast (fic)
John Champlin Gardner, Jr. The Sunlight Dialogues (fic)
Frank Daniel Gilroy. Present Tense (dr)
Jack Gelber. Sleep (dr)
Nikki Giovanni. My House (po)
Gail Godwin. Glass People (fic)
Herbert Gold. My Last Two Thousand Years (auto)
Ernest Miller Hemingway. The Nick Adams Stories (fic, pub)
John Richard Hersey. The Conspiracy (fic)
Edward Hoagland. Walking the Dead Diamond River (trav, e)
John Hollander. An Entertainment for Elizabeth (po, dr)
_____. Town and Country Matters: Erotica and Satirica (po)
Barbara Howes. The Blue Garden (po)
John Winslow Irving. The Water-Method Man (fic)
Diane Lain Johnson. The Shadow Knows (fic)
Roger Kahn. The Boys of Summer (nar)
Elia Kazan. The Assassins (fic)
Norma Klein. Love and Other Euphemisms (fic)
Jonathan Kozol. Free Schools (e, ref)
Maxine Winokur Kumin. Up Country: Poems of New England (po)
Arthur Laurents. The Way We Were (dr)
Ursula K. LeGuin. The Farthest Shore (fic)
Denise Levertov. Footprints (po)
Ira Levin. The Stepford Wives (fic)
Meyer Levin. The Settlers (fic)
Philip Levine. They Feed, They Lion (po)
Robert Ludlam. The Chancellor Manuscript (fic)
_____. The Osterman Weekend (fic)
Norman Mailer. Existential Errands (e, nar)
William Matthews. Sleek for the Long Flight (po)
James Ingram Merrill. Braving the Elements (po)
Arthur Miller. The Creation of the World, and Other Business (fic)
Jason Miller. The Championship Season (dr)
Steven Millhauser. Edwin Mullhouse: The Life and Death of an American
    Writer, 1943-1954, by Jeffrey Cartwright (fic)
Czeslaw Milosz. Selected Poems (pub)
George Frederick Morgan. A Book of Change (po)
Robert Morgan. Red Owl (po)
Howard Moss. The Palace at 4 a.m. (dr)
Albert Murray. South to a Very Old Place (fic)
Vladimir Nabokov. Transparent Things (fic)
Ogden Nash. The Old Dog Barks Backwards (po, pub)
Howard Nemerov. Reflections on Poetry and Poetics (e)
Joyce Carol Oates. Marriages and Infidelities (fic)
John Henry O'Hara. The Ewings (fic, pub)
_____. The Time Element (fic, pub)
Sylvia Plath. Winter Trees (po, pub)
Reynolds Price. Things Themselves (e)
Frederic Prokosch. My Wilderness (fic)
James Purdy. I Am Elijah Thrush (fic)
John Crowe Ransom. Beating the Bushes (e)
Ishmael Scott Reed. Conjure (po)
_____. Mumbo Jumbo (fic)
Samuel Shepard Rogers, Jr. (Sam Shepard). Hawk Moon (fic)

               . The Tooth of Crime (dr)
Judith Perelman Rossner. Any Minute I Can Split (fic)
Philip Roth. The Breast (fic)
William Saroyan. Places Where I've Done Time (nar)
Budd William Schulberg. The Four Seasons of Success (e)
James Marcus Schuyler. The Crystal Lithium (po)
Anne Sexton. The Book of Folly (po, fic)
William Jay Smith. Poems from Italy (po, trans)
               . The Streaks of the Tulip (e)
Gary Sherman Snyder. Manzanita (po)
Elizabeth Spencer. The Snare (fic)
Francis Steegmuller. Stories and True Stories (fic)
William Styron. In the Clap Shack (dr)
May Swenson. Windows and Stones (po, trans)
James Vincent Tate. Absences (po)
Lionel Trilling. Sincerity and Authenticity (e)
Paul Edward Theroux. Sinning with Annie (fic)
Estela Portillo Trambley. Days of the Swallow (dr)
Barbara Wertheim Tuchman. Notes from China (hist)
               . Stilwell and the American Experience in
   China, 1911-1945 (hist)
John Hoyer Updike. Museums and Women (fic)
               . Seventy Poems (po)
David Russell Wagoner. Riverbed (po)
Irving Wallace. The Word (fic)
Eudora Welty. The Optimist's Daughter (fic)
C.K. Williams. I Am the Bitter Name (po)
John Alfred Williams. Captain Blackman (fic)
Thomas Lanier (Tennessee) Williams. Small Craft Warnings (dr)
Calder Baynard Willingham, Jr. Rambling Rose (fic)
Edmund Wilson. A Window on Russia (e)
Helen Yglesias. How She Died (fic)

1973

DEATHS

    Conrad Potter Aiken
    Wystan Hugh Auden
    Samuel Nathaniel Behrman
    Samuel Flagg Bemis
    Morris Gilbert Bishop
    Arna Wendell Bontemps
    Catherine Shober Drinker Bowen
    Jane Bowles
    Pearl Sydenstricker Buck
    Mary Ellen Chase
    Robert Myron Coates
    Hiram Haydn
    William Inge
    John Gneisenau Neihardt
    Philip Rahv
    William Lindsay White
    Margaret Wilson
    Mitchell Wilson

LITERATURE

Herbert Sebastian Agar. The Darkest Hour (hist)
Nelson Algren. The Last Carousel (fic, po)
Robert Woodruff Anderson. After (fic)
Florence Anthony (Ai). Cruelty (po)
Wystan Hugh Auden. Forewards and Afterwords (e)
Thomas Louis Berger. Regiment of Women (fic)
John Berryman. Recovery (fic, pub)
Frank Bidart. Golden State (po)
Judy Sussman Blume. Deenie (juv, fic)
Rita Mae Brown. Rubyfruit Jungle (fic)
_____. Songs to a Handsome Woman (po)
Robert Elwood Bly. Sleepers Joining Hands (po)
Louise Bogan. What the Woman Lived (let, pub)
Arna Wendell Bontemps. The Old South (fic)
Daniel J. Boorstin. The Americans: The Democratic Experience (hist)
Vance Nye Bourjaily. Country Matters (e, nar)
Ray Douglas Bradbury. When Elephants Last in the Dooryard Bloomed
    (po)
Norman Oliver Brown. Closing Time (e)
Carl Frederick Buechner. Wishful Thinking (med, pra)
Charles Bukowski. Life and Death in the Charity Ward (fic)
_____. South of No North (fic)
Ben Lucien Burman. Look Down That Winding River (nar)
William Seward Burroughs. Exterminator! (fic)
Erskine Preston Caldwell. Annette (fic)
Hortense Calisher. Eagle Eye (fic)
Truman Capote. The Dogs Bark (e)
Hayden Carruth. From Snow and Rock, for Chaos (po)
John Cheever. The World of Apples (fic)
Evan Shelby Connell, Jr. Points for a Compass Rose (po)
John Wesley Conroy. Writers in Revolt (e)
Clark Coolidge. Suite V (po)
Malcolm Cowley. A Second Flowering (e)
Harry Crews. The Hawk Is Dying (fic)
Peter Hubert Davison. Half Remembered (auto)
John Roderigo Dos Passos. The Fourteenth Chronicle (nar)
Stanley Lawrence Elkin. Searches and Seizures (fic)
William Harrison Faulkner. Flags in the Dust (fic, pub)
Lawrence Ferlinghetti. Open Eye, Open Heart (po)
John Champlin Gardner, Jr. Jason and Medeia (po)
_____. Nickel Mountain (fic)
George Palmer Garrett, Jr. The Magic Striptease (fic)
Jean Garrigue. Studies for an Actress (po, pub)
Allen Ginsberg. The Fall of America: Poems of These States (po)
_____. The Gates of Wrath (po)
Nikki Giovanni. Ego Tripping (po)
Albert Goldbarth. Opticks (po)
Shirley Ann Grau. The Wind Shifting West (fic)
Alfred Bertram Guthrie, Jr. Wild Pitch (fic)
Joseph Hansen. Death Claims (fic)
Mark Harris. Killing Everybody (fic)
Robert Hass. Field Guide (po)
Alfred Hayes. The Stockbroker, the Bitter Young Man, and the Beauti-
    ful Girl (fic)

Anthony Evan Hecht and Helen Bacon. Seven against Thebes (trans)
Robert Anson Heinlein. Time Enough for Love (fic)
Lillian Hellman. Pentimento (biog, nar)
Chester Bomar Himes. Black on Black (fic)
Eric Hoffer. Reflections on the Human Condition (e)
John Hollander. The Head of the Bed (po)
Irving Howe. The Critical Point (e)
Richard Franklin Hugo. The Lady in Kicking Horse Reservoir (po)
William Humphrey. Proud Flesh (fic)
Josephine Winslow Johnson. Seven Houses (auto)
James Jones. A Touch of Danger (fic)
Erica Mann Jong. Fear of Flying (fic)
_____. Half-Lives (po)
Donald Rodney Justice. Departures (po)
Roger Kahn. How the Weather Was (nar)
Garson Kanin. A Thousand Summers (fic)
Alfred Kazin. Bright Book of Life (e)
Kenneth Jay Koch. A Change of Hearts (dr)
Jerzy Nikodem Kosinski. The Devil Tree (fic)
Josephine Lawrence. Retreat with Honor (fic)
Denise Levertov. The Poet in the World (e)
Meyer Levin. The Obsession (fic)
John Logan. The Anonymous Lover (po)
Robert Traill Spence Lowell, Jr. The Dolphin (po)
_____. For Lizzie and Harriet (po)
_____. History (po)
Robert Ludlum. The Matlock Paper (fic)
_____. Trevayne (fic)
Norman Mailer. Marilyn (biog)
Bernard Malamud. Rembrandt's Hat (fic)
Thomas Francis McGuane III. Ninety-Two in the Shade (fic)
Rod McKuen. Come to Me in Silence (po)
Peter McNab, Jr. (Harry Brown). The Wild Hunt (fic)
Sandra McPherson. Radiation (po)
David Meltzer. Tens (po)
William Stanley Merwin. Writings to an Unfinished Accompaniment (po)
Jason Miller. Three One-Act Plays (dr, pub)
Judith Minty. Lake Songs and Other Fears (po)
Navarre Scott Momaday. Angel of Geese (po)
Wright Morris. Here Is Einbaum (fic)
_____. A Life (fic)
Toni Morrison. Sula (fic)
Albert Murray. The Hero and the Blues (fic)
Vladimir Nabokov. Strong Opinions (e)
Robert Gruntal Nathan. Evening Song (po)
Howard Nemerov. Gnomes (po)
Joyce Carol Oates. Angel Fire (po)
_____. Do with Me What You Will (fic)
_____. Dreaming America (po)
_____. The Hostile Sun (e)
Frank O'Hara. Selected Poems (pub)
George Oppen. Seascape (po)
Gregory Orr. Burning the Empty Nests (po)
Robert Pack. Nothing but Light (po)
Stanley Plumly. Giraffe (po)
James Purdy. Sunshine Is an Only Child (po)

Thomas Pynchon. Gravity's Rainbow (fic)
David William Rabe. In the Boom Boom (dr)
_____. The Orphan (dr)
John Francisco Rechy. The Fourth Angel (fic)
Ishmael Scott Reed. Chattanooga (po)
Adrienne Cecile Rich. Diving into the Wreck (po)
William Pitt Root. Striking the Dark Air for Music (po)
Philip Roth. The Great American Novel (fic)
Muriel Rukeyser. Breaking Open (po)
Eleanor May Sarton. As We Are Now (fic)
Robert Siegel. The Beasts and the Elders (po)
Anya Seton. Green Darkness (fic)
Irwin Shaw. Evening in Byzantium (fic)
_____. God Was Here But He Left Early (fic)
Wilfred John Joseph Sheed. People Will Always Be Kind (fic)
Alice H.B. Sheldon. Ten Thousand Light Years from Home (fic)
Isaac Bashevis Singer. A Crown of Feathers (fic)
Gilbert Sorrentino. Splendide-Hotel (e)
William Edgar Stafford. Someday, Maybe (po)
Richard Gustave Stern. The Books in Fred Hampton's Apartment (e)
_____. Other Men's Daughters (fic)
Mark Strand. The Story of Our Lives (po)
Ronald Sukenick. Out (fic)
Peter Hillsman Taylor. Presences (dr)
Paul Edward Theroux. Saint Jack (fic)
Joyce Carol Thomas. Bittersweet (po)
Alice Babette Toklas. Staying On Alone (let)
Lionel Trilling. Mind in the Modern World (e)
Anne Tyler. The Clock Winder (fic)
Mark Albert Van Doren. Good Morning: Last Poems (po, pub)
Gore Vidal. Burr (fic)
_____. Homage to Daniel Shays (e)
Kurt Vonnegut, Jr. Between Time and Timbuktu (dr)
_____. Breakfast of Champions: or, Goodbye Blue Monday!
(fic)
Alice Walker. In Love and Trouble (fic)
_____. Revolutionary Petunias (auto)
John Edgar Wideman. The Lynchers (fic)
Thornton Niven Wilder. Theophilus North (fic)
Thomas Lanier (Tennessee) Williams. Outcry (dr)
Edmund Wilson. The Devils and Canon Barham (e, pub)
Lanford Wilson. The Hot 1 Baltimore (dr)
Arthur Yvor Winters. Uncollected Essays (pub)
James Arlington Wright. Two Citizens (po)

1974

DEATHS

    George Edward Kelly
    Arthur Kober
    Manuel Komroff
    Margaret Kernochan Leech
    Charles Augustus Lindbergh
    Michele Murray

John Crowe Ransom
Anne Sexton

EVENTS

Gerald Rudolph Ford, 38th President of the United States, to 1977
Nathaniel Hawthorne Society (f)
National Book Critics Circle (f)

LITERATURE

Alice Adams. Families and Survivors (fic)
Archie Randolph Ammons. Sphere: The Form of a Motion (po)
Harriette Arnow. The Kentucky Trace: A Novel of the American Revolu-
    tion (fic)
Louis Stanton Auchincloss. A Writer's Capital (fic)
Richard David Bach. A Gift of Wings (e)
Leonard Stanley Baker. John Marshall: A Life in Law (biog)
James Baldwin. If Beale Street Could Talk (fic)
Donald Barthelme. Guilty Pleasures (fic)
Jacques Barzun. The Use and Abuse of Art (e)
Peter Bradford Benchley. Jaws (fic)
Judy Sussman Blume. Blubber (juv, fic)
Richard Brautigan. The Hawkins Monster: A Gothic Western (fic)
Carl Frederick Buechner. The Faces of Jesus (e)
_____. Love Feast (fic)
Charles Bukowski. Burning in Water, Drowning in Flame (po)
Melville Henry Cane. Snow toward Evening (po)
Gladys Hasty Carroll. Next of Kin (fic)
Ronald Verlin Cassill. The Goss Women (fic)
Mary Coyle Chase. Cocktails with Mimi (dr)
Lucille Clifton. An Ordinary Woman (po)
Evan Shelby Connell, Jr. The Connoisseur (fic)
Clark Coolidge. The Mountains (po)
Norman Cousins. The Celebration of Life (e)
Robert White Creeley. Thirty Things (po)
Harry Crews. The Gypsy's Curse (fic)
Michael Cristofer. Ice (dr)
Peter Hubert Davison. Walking the Boundaries (po)
Vina Delmar. A Time for Titans (fic)
Peter DeVries. The Glory of the Hummingbird (fic)
Annie Dillard. Pilgrim at Tinker Creek (des, e)
_____. Tickets for a Prayer Wheel (po)
Alan Dugan. Poems 4 (po, pub)
John Gregory Dunne. Vegas (des)
William Everson. Man-Fate (po)
James Thomas Farrell. Judith (fic)
Leslie Aaron Fiedler. The Messengers Will Come No More (fic)
Bruce Jay Friedman. About Harry Towns (fic)
Charles Fuller. In the Deepest Part of Sleep (dr)
John Champlin Gardner, Jr. The King's Indian (fic)
Allen Ginsberg. Allen Verbatim (e)
Gail Godwin. The Odd Woman (fic)
Herbert Gold. Swiftie the Magician (fic)
Albert Goldbarth. Jan. 31 (po)
Paul Goodman. Collected Poems (pub)

Charles William Goyen. Come the Restorer (fic)
Shirley Ann Grau. Evidence of Love (fic)
Elizabeth Hardwick. Seduction and Betrayal (e)
John Clendennin Burne Hawkes, Jr. Sleep and the Traveler (fic)
Joseph Heller. Clevinger's Trial (dr)
_____. Something's Happened (fic)
John Richard Hersey. My Petition for More Space (fic)
Richard Joseph Howard. Preferences (po, ed)
_____. Two-Part Inventions (po, fic)
John Winslow Irving. The 158-Pound Marriage (fic)
Charles Richard Johnson. Faith and the Good Thing (fic)
Marguerite Johnson (Maya Angelou). Gather Together in My Name (auto)
James Jones. Viet Journal (nar)
Elia Kazan. The Understudy (fic)
Edith Summers Kelley. The Devil's Hand (fic, pub)
Faye Kicknosway. A Man Is a Hook. Trouble (po)
Galway Kinnell. The Avenue Bearing the Initial of Christ into the
   New World (po)
John Knowles. Spreading Fires (fic)
Maxine Winokur Kumin. The Designated Heir (fic)
Stanley Jasspon Kunitz. The Terrible Threshold: Selected Poems, 1940-
   1970 (po, pub)
Tom Lea. In the Crucible of the Sun (fic)
Ella Lefland. Love Out of Season (fic)
Meyer Levin. The Spell of Time (fic)
Philip Levine. 1933 (po)
Robert Ludlam. The Cry of the Halidon (fic)
_____. The Rhineman Exchange (fic)
Alison Lurie. The War between the Tates (fic)
David Alan Mamet. Duck Variations (dr)
_____. Sexual Perversity in Chicago (dr)
Wallace Markfield. You Could Live If They Let You (fic)
Harry Mathews. The Planisphere (po)
Cormac McCarthy. Child of God (fic)
Michael Thomas McClure. Ghost Tantras (po)
James Ingram Merrill. The Yellow Pages (po)
James Albert Michener. Centennial (fic)
Josephine Miles. Poetry and Change (e)
_____. To All Appearances (po)
Albert Murray. Train Whistle Guitar (fic)
Michele Murray. The Great Mother, and Other Poems (po)
Vladimir Nabokov. Look at the Harlequins! (fic)
Joyce Carol Oates. The Goddess and Other Women (fic)
_____. The Hungry Ghosts (fic)
_____. New Heaven, New Earth (e)
_____. Where Are You Going, Where Have You Been? (fic)
John Henry O'Hara. Good Samaritan (fic, pub)
Tillie Olsen. Yonnondio (fic)
Grace Paley. Enormous Changes at the Last Minute (fic)
James Purdy. The House of the Solitary Maggot (fic)
Ishmael Scott Reed. The Last Days of Louisiana Red (fic)
Kenneth Rexroth. The Elastic Retort (e)
_____. New Poems (po)
Charles Reznikoff. By the Well of Living and Seeing (po, pub)
Selden Rodman. Tongues of Fallen Angels (nar)
Philip Roth. My Life As a Man (fic)

Eleanor May Sarton. Collected Poems (pub)
Gladys Schmitt. The Godforgotten (fic, pub)
James Marcus Schuyler. Hymn to Life (po)
Richard Selzer. Rituals of Surgery (fic)
Anne Sexton. The Death Notebooks (nar)
Michael Joseph Shaara, Jr. Killer Angels (fic)
Charles Simic. Return to a Place Lit by a Glass of Milk (po)
David Smith. The Fisherman's Whore (po)
Gary Sherman Snyder. Turtle Island (po, e)
Robert Anthony Stone. Dog Soldiers (fic)
Studs Lewis Turkel. Working (nar)
Paul Edward Theroux. The Black House (fic)
Joyce Carol Thomas. Crystal Breezes (po)
Lewis Thomas. The Lives of a Cell (e)
Calvin Trillin. American Fried (nar)
John Hoyer Updike. Buchanan Dying (dr)
Gore Vidal. Myron (fic)
Kurt Vonnegut, Jr. Wampeters, Foma and Granfalloons (e)
David Russell Wagoner. The Road to Many a Wonder (fic)
          . Sleeping in the Woods (po)
Irving Wallace. The Fan Club (fic)
Jerome Weidman. Tiffany Street (fic)
Jessamyn West. The Secret Look (po)
Edward Reed Whittemore II. The Mother's Breast and the Father's
    House (po)
Richard Purdy Wilbur. Seed Leaves: Homage to R.F. (po)
Thomas Lanier (Tennessee) Williams. Eight Mortal Ladies Possessed
    (fic)
Geoffrey Ansell Wolff. The Sightseer (fic)
Marya Zaturenska. The Hidden Waterfall (po)

1975

DEATHS

Hannah Arendt
James Vincent Sheean
Rex Todhunter Stout
Lionel Trilling
Thornton Niven Wilder

LITERATURE

Edward Albee. Seascape (dr)
Archie Randolph Ammons. Diversifications (po)
John Lawrence Ashbery. Self-Portrait in a Convex Mirror (po)
Djuna Barnes. Vagaries Malicieux (e)
Donald Barthelme. The Dead Father (fic)
Saul Bellow. A Collection of Critical Essays, ed Earl Rovit (e, pub)
          . Humboldt's Gift (fic)
Nathaniel Benchley. Humphrey Bogart (biog)
Thomas Louis Berger. Sneaky People (fic)
Paul Blackburn. The Journals (po, nar, pub)
Judy Sussman Blume. Forever (juv, fic)
Robert Elwood Bly. Leaping Poetry (e)

_____. The Morning Glory (po)
_____. Old Man Rubbing His Eyes (po)
Kay Boyle. The Underground Woman (fic)
Ray Douglas Bradbury. Pillar of Fire (dr)
Richard Brautigan. Willard and His Bowling Trophies: A Perverse Mystery (fic)
Charles Bukowski. Factotum (fic)
William Seward Burroughs. The Last Words of Dutch Schultz (fic_
James Mallahan Cain. Rainbow's End (fic)
Morley Callaghan. A Fine and Private Place (fic)
Hayden Carruth. The Bloomingdale Papers (po)
Paddy Chayefsky. Network (dr)
Jerome Chodorov and Joseph Fields. Culture Caper (dr)
John Ciardi. Fast and Slow (e)
Mary Higgins Clark. Where Are the Children (fic)
Clark Coolidge. Polaroid (po)
John Michael Crichton. The Great Train Robbery (fic, hist)
Jonathan Worth Daniels. White House Witness (nar)
David Brion Davis. The Problem of Slavery in the Age of Revolution, 1770-1823 (hist)
Peter DeVries. Forever Panting (fic)
Edgar Lawrence Doctorow. Ragtime (fic)
James Patrick Donleavy. The Unexpurgated Code (sat)
Edward Merton Dorn. Gunslinger (po)
Allen Stuart Drury. The Promise of Joy (fic)
Norman Dubie. In the Dead of Night (po)
Andre Dubus. Separate Flights (fic)
Nora Ephron. Crazy Salad (e)
William Harrison Faulkner. Marionettes: A Play in One Act (dr, pub)
Jesse Hill Ford. The Raider (fic)
John Champlin Gardner, Jr. Dragon, Dragon (fic, juv)
Allen Ginsberg. First Blues (po)
Nikki Giovanni. The Women and the Men (po)
Louise Gluck. The House on Marshland (po)
Alfred Bertram Guthrie, Jr. The Last Valley (fic)
Donald Andrew Hall. A Blue Wing Tilts at the Edge of the Sea (po)
_____. The Town of Hell (po)
Oakley Hall. The Adelita (fic)
Joseph Hansen. Troublemaker (fic)
Mark Helprin. A Dove of the East and Other Stories (fic)
John Hollander. Tales Told of the Father (po)
Paul Horgan. Lamy of Sante Fe (Biog)
Richard Franklin Hugo. What Thou Lovest Well, Remains American (po)
David Ignatow. Facing the Tree (po)
_____. Selected Poems (pub)
Marguerite Johnson (Maya Angelou). Oh Pray My Wings Are Gonna Fit Me Well (po)
Erica Mann Jong. Loveroot (po)
MacKinlay Kantor. Valley Forge (fic)
William Kennedy. Legs (fic)
Kenneth Jay Koch. The Art of Love (po)
Allen Stewart Konigsberg (Woody Allen). Without Feathers (nar)
Jerzy Nikodem Kosinski. Cockpit (fic)
Jonathan Kozol. The Night Is Dark and I Am Far from Home (e)
Maxine Winokur Kumin. House, Bridge, Fountain, Gate (po)
Stanley Jasspon Kunitz. A Kind of Order, a Kind of Folly (e)

Josephine Lawrence. Under One Roof (fic)
Ursula K. LeGuin. The Wind's Twelve Quarters (fic)
Denise Levertov. The Freeing of the Dust (po)
Archibald MacLeish. The Great American Fourth of July Parade (po, dr)
Norman Mailer. The Fight (e)
_____. Some Honorable Men (e, nar)
Harry Matthews. The Sinking of the Odradek Stadium (fic)
William Matthews. Sticks and Stones (po)
Donald McCaig. Caleb, Who Is Hotter Than a Two-Dollar Pistol (fic)
_____. Last Poems (po, pub)
William Morris Meredith. Hazard, the Painter (po)
Leonard Michaels. I Would Have Saved Them If I Could (fic)
Howard Moss. Burned City (po)
Anais Nin. A Woman Speaks (e)
Joyce Carol Oates. The Assassins (fic)
_____. The Poisoned Kiss (fic)
_____. The Seduction (fic)
Frank O'Hara. Art Chronicles (e, pub)
_____. Standing Still and Walking in New York (e, pub)
Charles Olson. The Maximus Poems (po, pub)
Elder James Olson. Olson's Penny Arcade (po)
George Oppen. Collected Poems (pub)
Gregory Orr. Gathering the Bones Together (po)
Linda Pastan. Aspects of Eve (po)
Walker Percy. The Message in the Bottle (fic)
Sidney Joseph Perelman. Vinegar Pass (sat, nar)
Robert Pinsky. Sadness and Happiness (po)
James Farl Powers. Look How the Fish Live (fic, dr)
Reynolds Price. The Surface of the Earth (fic)
James Purdy. In a Shallow Grave (fic)
Laura Reichenthal (Laura Riding). The Telling (e)
Kenneth Rexroth. Communalism (e)
Charles Reznikoff. Holocaust (po)
Adrienne Cecile Rich. Poems Selected and New (pub)
Judith Perelman Rossner. Looking for Mr. Goodbar (fic)
Philip Roth. Reading Myself (e)
Eleanor May Sarton. Crucial Conversations (fic)
Anne Sexton. The Awful Rowing toward God (po, pub)
Karl Jay Shapiro. The Poetry Wreck (e)
Irwin Shaw. Nightwork (fic)
Alice H.B. Sheldon. Warm Worlds and Otherwise (fic)
William Jay Smith. Venice in the Fog (po)
William DeWitt Snodgrass. In Radical Pursuit (e)
Gilbert Sorrentino. Flawless Play Restored (dr)
Jack Spicer. The Collected Books (po, pub)
George Edwin Starbuck. Elegy in a Country Church Yard (po)
Irving Stone. The Greek Treasure (fic)
Rex Todhunter Stout. A Family Affair (fic)
Ronald Sukenick. 98.6 (fic)
Harvey Swados. Celebration (fic, pub)
John Orley Allen Tate. Memoirs and Opinions (nar, e)
Joyce Carol Thomas. Blessing (po)
Estela Portillo Trambley. Rain of Scorpions (fic)
Anne Tyler. Celestial Navigation (fic)
John Hoyer Updike. A Month of Sundays (fic)
_____. Picked Up Pieces (e)

David Russell Wagoner. Tracker (fic)
Robert Penn Warren. Democracy and Poetry (e)
_____. Or Else-Poem (po)
Michael Waters. Fish Light (po)
Jerome Weidman. The Temple (fic)
Jessamyn West. The Massacre at Fall Creek (fic)
Edward Reed Whittemore II. The Poet As Journalist (e)
_____. William Carlos Williams (biog, e)
John Alfred Williams. Mothersill and the Foxes (fic)
Thomas Lanier (Tennessee) Williams. Moise and the World of Reason
    (fic)
Calder Baynard Willingham, Jr. The Big Nickel (fic)
Edmund Wilson and Leon Edel. The Twenties (nar, pub)
Lanford Wilson. The Mound Builders (dr)
Larry Alfred Woiwode. Beyond the Bedroom Wall: A Family Album (fic)
Bari Wood. The Killing Gift (fic)
Helen Yglesias. Family Feeling (fic)
Albert James Young. Who Is Angelina? (fic)

1976

DEATHS

    Carl Lamson Carmer
    Samuel Eliot Morison
    Vladimir Nabokov
    Charles Reznikoff
    Charles Wilbert Snow
    Dan Totheroh

EVENTS

    American Academy and Institute of Arts and Letters (f)
    National Humanities Center, Research Triangle Park, North Carolina
        (est)

LITERATURE

    Renata Adler. Speedboat (fic)
    Lisa Alther. Kinflicks (fic)
    David Antin. Talking (po)
    _____. Talking at the Boundaries (po)
    Isaac Asimov. The Bicentennial Man, and Other Stories (fic, pub)
    Wystan Hugh Auden. Collected Poems, ed. Edward Mendelson (po, pub)
    James Baldwin. The Devil Finds Work (e)
    Margaret Culkin Banning. The Splendid Torments (fic)
    Donald Barthelme. Amateurs (fic)
    Ann Beattie. Chilly Scenes of Winter (fic)
    _____. Distortions (fic)
    Saul Bellow. Jerusalem and Back (nar)
    Peter Bradford Benchley. The Deep (fic)
    Edmund J.M. Berrigan, Jr. Red Wagon (po)
    John Berryman. The Freedom of the Poet (fic, e)
    Elizabeth Bishop. Geography III (po)
    Philip Booth. Available Light (po)

Vance Nye Bourjaily. Now Playing at Canterbury (fic)
Jane Bowles. Feminine Wiles (fic, nar, dr, pub)
Gerald Warner Brace. Days That Were (auto)
Richard Brautigan. Loading Mercury with a Pitchfork (po)
_____. Sombrero Fallout: A Japanese Novel (fic)
Rita Mae Brown. In Her Day (fic)
_____. A Plain Brown Rapper (e)
Courtlandt Dixon Barnes Bryan. Friendly Fire (nar)
James Mallahan Cain. The Institute (fic)
Erskine Preston Caldwell. Afternoons in Mid-America (e)
Truman Capote. Then It All Came Down (nar, e)
Raymond Carver. At Night the Salmon Move (po)
_____. Will You Please Be Quiet, Please? (fic)
Ronald Verlin Cassill. Hoyt's Child (fic)
Lucille Clifton. Generations: A Memoir (nar)
Elizabeth Jane Coatsworth. Personal Geography (auto)
Donald Lee Coburn. The Gin Game (dr)
Evan Shelby Connell, Jr. Double Honeymoon (fic)
Louis Osborne Coxe. Enabling Acts (e)
Robert White Creeley. Away (po)
Harry Crews. A Feast of Snakes (fic)
John Michael Crichton. Eaters of the Dead: The Manuscript of Ibn
    Fadlan Relating His Experiences with the Northmen in A.D. 922 (fic)
Michael Cristofer. Black Angel (dr)
Edward Dahlberg. The Olive of Minerva (fic)
Peter DeVries. I Hear America Swinging (fic)
James Lafayette Dickey. The Zodiac (po)
Stephen Dixon. No Relief (fic)
Allen Stuart Drury. A God against the Gods (fic)
_____. Return to Thebes (fic)
Richard Ghormley Eberhart. Collected Poems (pub)
_____. Poems to Poets (po)
Stanley Lawrence Elkin. The Franchiser (fic)
William Everson. River-Root (po)
James Thomas Farrell. The Dunne Family (fic)
Frederick Feikema (Frederick Manfred/Feike Feikema). The Manly-Hear-
    ted Woman (fic)
_____. Milk of Wolves
    (fic)
Lawrence Ferlinghetti. Who Are We Now (po)
Paula Fox. The Widow's Children (fic)
Marilyn French. The Book As World--James Joyce's "Ulysses" (e)
Charles Fuller. The Brownsville Raid (dr)
Tess Gallagher. Instructions to the Double (po)
John Champlin Gardner, Jr. October Light (fic)
Jack Gelber. Rehearsal (dr)
Gail Godwin. Dream Children (fic)
Albert Goldbarth. Comings Back (po)
Charles Gordone. The Lost Chord (dr)
Paul Eliot Green. Land of Nod (fic)
Horace Victor Gregory. Another Look (po)
Albert Joseph Guerard. The Triumph of the Novel (e)
Judith Ann Guest. Ordinary People (fic)
Alex Palmer Haley. Roots (fic)
Mark Harris. Best Father Ever Invented (nar)
John Clendennin Bourne Hawkes, Jr. Travesty (fic)

Lillian Hellman. Scoundrel Time (nar)
Edward Hoagland. Red Wolves and Black Bears (e)
Eric Hoffer. In Our Time (e)
John Hollander. Reflections on Espionage (e)
Richard Joseph Howard. Fellow Feelings (po)
Marguerite Johnson (Maya Angelou). Singin' and Swingin' and Gettin'
    Merry Like Christmas (auto)
Maxine Hong Kingston. The Woman Warrior (fic)
Ursula K. LeGuin. Orsinian Tales (fic)
Ira Levin. The Boys from Brazil (fic)
Philip Levine. The Names of the Lost (po)
Robert Traill Spence Lowell, Jr. Selected Poems (pub)
Robert Ludlam. The Gemini Contenders (fic)
Helen MacInnes. Agent in Place (fic)
_____. Snare of the Hunter (fic)
Archibald MacLeish. New and Collected Poems (po, pub)
Donald McCaig. Stalking Blind (fic)
Michael Thomas McClure. Gorf (dr)
Rod McKuen. Finding My Father (nar)
James Ingram Merrill. Divine Comedies (po)
Navarre Scott Momaday. The Gourd Dancer (po)
_____. The Names (nar)
Robert Morgan. Land Diving (po)
Wright Morris. Real Losses, Imaginary Gains (fic)
Howard Moss. A Swim Off the Rocks (po)
Howard Nemerov. The Western Approaches (po)
Anais Nin. In Favor of the Sensitive Man (e)
Joyce Carol Oates. The Childworld (fic)
_____. Crossing the Border (fic)
Robert Pack. Keeping Watch (po)
Marge Piercy. Living in the Open (po)
_____. Woman on the Edge of Time (fic)
David William Rabe. Streamers (dr)
Ishmael Scott Reed. Flight to Canada (fic)
Adrienne Cecile Rich. Of Woman Born (e, hist)
Tom Robbins. Even Cowgirls Get the Blues (fic)
Leo Calvin Rosten (Leonard Q. Ross). O Kaplan! My Kaplan! (fic)
Muriel Rukeyser. The Gates (po)
William Saroyan. Sons Come and Go, Mothers Hang In Forever (nar)
Hubert Selby. The Demon (fic)
Anne Sexton. 45 Mercy Street (po, pub)
Karl Jay Shapiro. Adult Bookstore (po)
William Lawrence Shirer. 20th Century Journey (nar)
Louis Aston Marantz Simpson. Searching for the Ox (po)
Isaac Bashevis Singer. A Little Boy in Search of God (nar)
Wallace Earle Stegner. The Spectator Bird (fic)
John Ernst Steinbeck. The Acts of King Arthur and His Noble Knights
    (fic, pub)
Mark Strand. The Late Hour (po)
Jesse Hilton Stuart. The Seasons (auto, po)
James Vincent Tate. Viper Jazz (po)
Paul Edward Theroux. The Family Arsenal (fic)
Joyce Carol Thomas. Look! What a Wonder! (dr)
_____. A Song in the Sky (dr)
Anne Tyler. Searching for Caleb (fic)
John Hoyer Updike. Marry Me (fic)

Leon Uris. Trinity (fic)
Gore Vidal. 1876 (fic)
Kurt Vonnegut, Jr. Slapstick; or, Lonesome No More! (fic)
David Russell Wagoner. Collected Poems (pub)
_____. Whole Hog (fic)
Diane Wakowski. Virtuoso Literature for Two and Four Hands (po)
Alice Walker. Meredian (fic)
Irving Wallace. The R Document (fic)
Philip Whalen. The Kindness of Strangers (po)
Richard Purdy Wilbur. The Mind-Reader: New Poems (po)
John Alfred Williams. The Junior Bachelor Society (fic)
Sherley Anne Williams. The Peacock Poems (po)
James Arlington Wright. Moments of the Italian Summer (po)
Albert James Young. Geography of the Near Past (po)

1977

DEATHS

James Mallahan Cain
Edward Dahlberg
James Jones
MacKinlay Kantor
John Howard Lawson
Robert Traill Spence Lowell, Jr.
Joseph Moncure March
Anais Nin
Mark Schorer
Chard Powers Smith
Louis Untermeyer

EVENTS

American Culture Association (f)
James Earl Carter, Jr., 39th President of the United States, to 1981
National Women's Studies Association (f)

LITERATURE

Mortimore Jerome Adler. Philosopher at Large: An Intellectual Auto-
    biography (auto, e)
Edward Albee. Counting the Ways (dr)
_____. Listening (dr)
Archie Randolph Ammons. Highgate Road (po)
_____. The Snow Poems (po)
John Lawrence Ashbery. Houseboat Days (po)
James Atlas. Delmore Schwartz: The Life of an American Poet (biog)
Louis Stanton Auchincloss. The Dark Lady (fic)
Wystan Hugh Auden. The English Auden: Poems, Essays, and Dramatic
    Writings, 1927-1939, ed Edward Mendelson (misc, pub)
Jane Augustine. Lit by the Earth's Dark Blood (po)
Richard David Bach. Illusions: The Adventures of a Reluctant Messiah
    (fic)
Toni Cade Bambara. The Sea Birds Are Still Alive: Collected Stories
    (fic, pub)

Walter Jackson Bate. Samuel Johnson (biog)
Ben Belitt. Adam's Dream (e)
_____. The Double Witness (po)
Thomas Louis Berger. Who Is Teddy Villanova (fic)
John Berryman. Henry's Fate (po, pub)
Frank Bidart. The Book of the Body (po)
Judy Sussman Blume. Starring Sally. J. Freedman As Herself (juv, fic)
_____. Wifey (fic)
Robert Elwood Bly. This Body Is Made of Camphor and Gopherwood (po)
Ray Douglas Bradbury. Where Robot Men and Robot Women Run Round Ro-
     bot Towns (po)
Richard Brautigan. Dreaming of Babylon: A Private Eye Novel (fic)
John Brooks. Showing Off in America (e)
James Richard Broughton. Seeing the Light (po)
Olga Broumas. O (po)
Carl Frederick Buechner. Telling the Truth (e)
_____. Treasure Hunt (fic)
Charles Bukowski. Love Is a Dog from Hell (po)
Hortense Calisher. On Keeping Women (fic)
Morley Callaghan. Close to the Sun Again (fic)
Raymond Carver. Furious Seasons (fic)
John Cheever. Falconer (fic)
Eleanor Clark. Eyes, Etc (nar, auto)
Lucille Clifton. Amifka (po)
Henry Steele Commager. The Empire of Reason (e)
Robert Lowell Coover. The Public Burning (fic)
Michael Cristofer. The Shadow Box (dr)
James Vincent Cunningham. Collected Essays (pub)
Peter Herbert Davison. A Voice in the Mountain (po)
Peter DeVries. Madder Music (fic)
Joan Didion. A Book of Common Prayer (fic)
Annie Dillard. Holy the Firm (e)
Stephen Dixon. Work (fic)
James Patrick Dunleavy. The Destinies of Darcy Dancer (fic)
Norman Dubie. The Illustrations (po)
Andre Dubus. Adultery and Other Poems (fic)
John Gregory Dunne. True Confessions (fic)
Howard Melvin Fast. The Immigrants (fic)
Frederick Feikema (Frederick Manfred/Feike Feikema). Green Earth
     (fic)
Marilyn French. The Women's Room (fic)
John Champlin Gardner, Jr. A Child's Bestiary (po, juv)
_____. In the Suicide Mountains (fic)
William Gibson. Golda (dr)
Allen Ginsberg. As Ever (let)
_____. Journals (nar)
_____. Mind Breaths (po)
Herbert Gold. Waiting for Cordelia (fic)
Alfred Bertram Guthrie, Jr. The Genuine Article (fic)
Michael S. Harper. Images of Kin: New and Selected Poems (po)
Anthony Evan Hecht. Millions of Strange Shadows (po)
Mark Helprin. Refiner's Fire: The Life and Adventures of Marshall
     Pearl, a Foundling (fic)
Lamar Herrin. The Rio Loja Ringmaster (fic)
John Richard Hersey. The Walnut Door (fic)
John Clellon Holmes. The Bowling Green Poems (po)

Paul Horgan. The Thin Mountain Air (fic)
Barbara Howes. A Private Signal (po)
Richard Franklin Hugo. 31 Letters and 13 Dreams (po)
William Humphrey. Farther Off (auto)
Erica Mann Jong. How To Save Your Own Life (fic)
Roger Kahn. A Season in the Sun (nar)
Garson Kanin. A Hell of an Actor (fic)
Kenneth Jay Koch. The Duplications (po)
Jerzy Nokodem Kosinski. Blind Date (fic)
Arthur Laurents. The Turning Point (fic)
Robert Traill Spence Lowell, Jr. Day by Day (po)
David Alan Mamet. American Buffalo (dr)
_____. A Life in the Theatre (dr)
Harry Mathews. Selected Declarations of Dependence (fic)
_____. Trial Impressions (po)
William Maxwell. Over by the River (fic)
David Thompson Watson McCord. One at a Time (po, juv)
Heather McHugh. Dangers (po)
Peter McNab, Jr. (Harry Brown). The Gathering (fic)
James Alan McPherson. Elbow Room (fic)
William Stanley Merwin. The Compass Flower (po)
Steven Millhauser. Portrait of a Romantic (fic)
George Frederick Morgan. Poems of the Two Worlds (po)
Wright Morris. The Fork River Space Project (fic)
Toni Morrison. Song of Solomon (fic)
Howard Nemerov. Collected Poems (pub)
Joyce Carol Oates. Night-Side (fic)
_____. The Triumph of the Spider Monkey (fic)
Kenneth Patchen. Patchen's Lost Plays (dr, pub)
Walker Percy. Lancelot (fic)
Sidney Joseph Perelman. Eastward Ha! (trav)
Robert Pinsky. The Situation of Poetry (e)
Sylvia Plath. Johnny Panic and the Bible of Dreams (fic, nar, e,pub)
Stanley Plumly. Out-of-the-Body Travel (po)
Katherine Anne Porter. The Never-Ending Wrong (nar, auto)
Reynolds Price. Early Dark (dr)
James Purdy. A Day after the Fair (dr, po)
Judith Perelman Rossner. Attachments (fic)
Philip Roth. The Professor of Desire (fic)
John W. Saul III. Suffer the Children (fic)
Mark Schorer. Pieces of Life (nar, fic)
James Marcus Schuyler. The Home Book (e, po)
Irwin Shaw. Beggarman, Thief (fic)
Charles Simic. Charon's Cosmology (po)
William DeWitt Snodgrass. The Fuhrer's Bunker (po)
_____. Six Troubadour Songs (po, trans)
Gary Sherman Snyder. The Old Ways (e)
Susan Sontag. On Photography (e)
William Edgar Stafford. That Could Be True (po)
George Edwin Starbuck. Desperate Measures (po)
Whitley Strieber. The Wolfen (fic)
John Orley Allen Tate. Collected Poems (pub)
Peter Hillsman Taylor. In the Miro District (fic)
Studs Lewis Turkel. Talking to Myself (nar)
Paul Edward Theroux. The Consul's File (fic, juv)
_____. Picture Palace (fic)

Joyce Carol Thomas. Magnolia (dr)
Calvin Trillin. Runestruck (fic)
Diana Trilling. We Must March, My Darlings (e)
Anne Tyler. Earthly Possessions (fic)
John Hoyer Updike. Tossing and Turning (po)
Gore Vidal. Matters of Fact and Fiction (e)
Diane Wakowski. Waiting for the King of Spain (po)
Robert Penn Warren. A Place To Come To (fic)
C.K. Williams. With Ignorance (po)
Thomas Lanier (Tennessee) Williams. Androgyne, Mon Amour (po)
Larry Alfred Woiwode. Even Tide (po)
Geoffrey Ansell Wolff. Inklings (fic)
Bari Wood and Jack Geasland. Twins (fic)
Charles Wright. China Trace (po)
James Arlington Wright. To a Blossoming Pear Tree (po)
Richard Nathaniel Wright. American Hunger (auto, pub)
Albert James Young. Sitting Pretty (fic)

1978

DEATHS

Faith Baldwin
Gerald Warner Brace
Robert Emmett Cantwell
James Bryant Conant
James Gould Cozzens
Janet Flanner
Josephine Lawrence
Phyllis McGinley
John Hall Wheelock
Margaret Widdemer
Louis Zukofsky

EVENTS

Life, 3rd series (per, est)
Y'Bird Magazine, Berkeley, California (per, f)

LITERATURE

Alice Adams. Listening to Billie (fic)
Mortimore Jerome Adler. Aristotle for Everybody (e)
Conrad Potter Aiken. Selected Letters (pub)
Edward Albee. The Lady from Dubuque (dr)
Robert Woodruff Anderson. Getting Up and Going Home (fic)
Max Apple. Zip (fic)
Leonard Stanley Baker. Days of Sorrow and Pain: Leo Baeck and the
   Berlin Jews (hist)
Ann Beattie. Secrets and Surprises (fic)
Thomas Louis Berger. Arthur Rex (fic)
Ray Douglas Bradbury. The Mummies of Guomajuato (fic)
Richard Brautigan. June 30th, June 30th (po)
Rita Mae Brown. Six of One (fic)
Charles Bukowski. Women (fic)

William Seward Burroughs and Brion Gysin. The Third Mind (e)
Paddy Chayefsky. Altered State (fic)
Mary Higgins Clark. A Stranger Is Waiting (fic)
Malcolm Cowley. And I Worked at the Writer's Trade (e)
Robert White Creeley. Later (po)
William Demby. Love Story Black (fic)
Stephen Dixon. Too Late (fic)
Edward Merton Dorn. Selected Poems (pub)
John Gregory Dunne. Quintana and Friends (e)
Richard Ghormley Eberhart. Selected Prose (e, pub)
James Thomas Farrell. The Death of Nora Ryan (fic)
Howard Melvin Fast. Second Generation (fic)
Leslie Aaron Fiedler. Freaks (hist, e)
Shelby Foote. September September (fic)
Bruce Jay Friedman. The Lonely Guy's Book of Life (hum)
Ernest J. Gaines. In My Father's House (fic)
Tess Gallagher. Under Stars (po)
John Champlin Gardner, Jr. On Moral Fiction (e)
George Palmer Garrett, Jr. Welcome to the Medicine Show (po)
William Howard Gass. The World within the Word (e)
Nikki Giovanni. Cotton Candy on a Rainy Day (po)
Gail Godwin. Violet Clay (fic)
Elizabeth Forsythe Hailey. A Woman of Independent Means (fic)
Donald Andrew Hall. Kicking the Leaves (po)
Oakley Hall. The Bad Lands (fic)
Patricia Hampl. Woman before an Aquarium (po)
Joseph Hansen. The Man Everybody Was Afraid Of (fic)
Barbara Grizzuti Harrison. Visions of Glory: A History and a Memory
    of Jehovah's Witnesses (hist, nar)
Robert Hayden. American Journal (po)
John Hollander. Spectral Emanations (po)
Maureen Howard. Facts of Life (auto)
William Humphrey. My Moby Dick (nar)
David Ignatow. Tread the Dark (po)
John Winslow Irving. The World According to Garp (fic)
Diane Lain Johnson. Lying Low (fic)
Marguerite Johnson (Maya Angelou). And Still I Rise (po)
James Jones. Whistle (fic, pub)
Roger Kahn. But Not To Keep (nar)
Elia Kazan. Acts of Love (fic)
Alfred Kazin. New York Jew (auto)
William Kennedy. Billy Phelan's Greatest Game (fic)
Galway Kinnell. Walking Down the Stairs (e)
Jonathan Kozol. Children of the Revolution (e)
Judith Krantz. Scruples (fic)
Maxine Winokur Kumin. The Retrieval System (po)
Meyer Levin. The Harvest (fic)
Morgan Llywelyn. The Wind from Hastings (fic)
Helen MacInnes. Prelude to Terror (fic)
Archibald MacLeish. Riders on the Earth (e)
Norman Mailer. A Transit to Narcissus (fic, pub)
Sandra McPherson. The Year of Our Birth (po)
James Ingram Merrill. Mirabell (po)
James Albert Michener. Chesapeake (fic)
Arthur Miller. Theatre Essays (e)
Czeslaw Milosz. Bells in Winter (po)

George Frederick Morgan. The Tarot of Cornelius Agrippa (po)
Robert Morgan. Trunk and Thicket (po)
Howard Nemerov. Figures of Thought (e)
Joyce Carol Oates. Song of the Morning (fic)
_____. Women Whose Lives Are Food, Men Whose Lives Are
   Money (po)
Tillie Olsen. Silences (e)
Charles Olson. The Fiery Hunt (po, dr, pub)
George Oppen. Primitive (po)
Linda Pastan. The Five Stages of Grief (po)
Robert Phillips. The Pregnant Man (po)
Reynolds Price. A Palpable God (e, trans)
James Purdy. Narrow Rooms (fic)
Philip Rahv. Essays on Literature and Politics (e, pub)
John Francisco Rechy. The Sexual Outlaw (nar)
Ishmael Scott Reed. Secretary to the Spirits (po)
_____. Shrovetide in Old New Orleans (nar)
Adrienne Cecile Rich. The Dream of a Common Language (po)
Conrad Michael Richter. The Rawhide Knot (fic, pub)
Samuel Shepard Rogers, Jr. (Sam Shepard). Buried Child (dr)
_____. The Starving Class (dr)
Leo Calvin Rosten. Passions and Prejudices (e)
William Saroyan. Chance Meetings (nar)
Eleanor May Sarton. A Reckoning (fic)
John W. Saul III. Punish the Sinners (fic)
Hubert Selby. Requiem for a Dream (fic)
Anne Sexton. Words for Dr. Y (po, pub)
Karl Jay Shapiro. Collected Poems (po)
Irwin Shaw. Five Decades (fic)
Wilfred John Joseph Sheed. Transatlantic Blues (fic)
Alice H.B. Sheldon. Star-Songs of an Old Primate (fic)
_____. Up the Walls of the World (fic)
Isaac Bashevis Singer. Passions (fic)
_____. Shoska (fic)
_____. A Young Man in Search of Love (nar)
William Jay Smith. The Telephone (po)
Susan Sontag. I, etcetera (fic)
_____. Illness As Metaphor (e)
Gilbert Sorrentino. The Orangery (po)
William Edgar Stafford. Writing the Australian Crawl (e)
Francis Steegmuller. Silence at Salerno (fic)
Richard Gustave Stern. Natural Shocks (fic)
Mark Strand. The Late Hour (po)
_____. The Monument (e)
Robert Lewis Taylor. A Roaring in the Wind (fic)
Joyce Carol Thomas. Ambrosia (dr)
Alvin Trillin. Alice, Let's Eat (nar)
Dana Trilling. Reviewing the Forties (e)
Lionel Trilling. Collected Works, 12 vols, to 1980 (misc, pub)
Barbara Wertheim Tuchman. A Distant Mirror (hist)
Gore Vidal. Kalki (fic)
David Russell Wagoner. Who Shall Be the Sun? (po)
Diane Wakowski. The Man Who Shook Hands (po)
Robert Penn Warren. Now and Then (po)
Jerome Weidman. A Family Fortune (fic)
Eudora Welty. The Eye of the Story (e)

John Hall Wheelock. This Blessed Earth (po)
Richard Purdy Wilbur. The Learned Ladies (dr)
Lanford Wilson. Fifth of July (dr)
Herman Wouk. War and Remembrance (fic)
Helen Yglasias. Starting: Early, Anew, Over, and Late (nar, auto)

1979

DEATHS

Benjamin Appel
Elizabeth Bishop
James Thomas Farrell
Sidney Joseph Perelman
Cornelia Otis Skinner
Jean Stafford
John Orley Allen Tate

EVENTS

The Henry James Society (f)
Kenyon Review, 2nd series (per, f)
Library of America, New York, New York (f)

LITERATURE

George Abbott. Tryout (fic)
Alice Adams. Beautiful Girl (fic)
Edward Albee. The Lady from Dubuque (dr)
Florence Anthony (Ai). Killing Floor (po)
John Lawrence Ashbery. As We Know (po)
Isaac Asimov. In Memory Yet Green (auto)
_____. Opus 200 (fic)
Louis Stanton Auchincloss. Life, Law, and Letters (e, nar)
Richard David Bach. There's No Such Place As Far Away (fic)
James Baldwin. Just above My Head (fic)
Margaret Culkin Banning. Such Interesting People (fic)
John Barth. Letters (fic)
Donald Barthelme. Great Days (fic)
Peter Bradford Benchley. The Island (fic)
Robert Elwood Bly. This Tree Will Be Here for a Thousand Years (po)
Paul Bowles. Collected Stories (fic, pub)
Charles Bukowski. Shakespeare Never Did This (auto)
John Cheever. The Stories of John Cheever (fic, pub)
Eleanor Clark. Gloria Mundi (fic)
Jan Clausen. Waking at the Bottom of the Dark (po)
Evan Shelby Connell, Jr. A Long Desire (e)
Norman Cousins. Anatomy of an Illness (auto)
John P. Coyne. The Legacy (fic)
_____. The Piercing (fic)
Robert White Creeley. Was That a Real Poem (e)
Robert Choate Darnton. The Business of Enlightenment: A Publishing
    History of the Encyclopedie, 1775-1800 (hist)
James Lafayette Dickey. The Strength of Fields (po)
Joan Didion. The White Album (e)

Stephen Dixon. Quite Contrary (fic)
Edgar Lawrence Doctorow. Drinks before Dinner (dr)
James Patrick Donleavy. Schultz (fic)
Norman Dubie. The City of Olesha Fruit (po)
Richard Ghormley Eberhart. Of Poetry and Poets (e)
Stanley Lawrence Elkin. The Living End (fic)
Joseph Epstein. Familiar Territory (e)
Howard Melvin Fast. The Establishment (fic)
William Harrison Faulkner. Uncollected Stories (fic, pub)
Bruce Jay Friedman. Foot in the Door (dr)
Daniel Fuchs. The Apathetic Bookie Joint (fic, nar)
Martha Gellhorn. Travels with Myself and Another (auto)
Ellen Gilchrist. The Land Surveyor's Daughter (po)
Albert Goldbarth. Different Fleshes (po)
Barbara Gordon. I'm Dancing As Fast As I Can (auto)
Joseph Hansen. Skinflick (fic)
Elizabeth Hardwick. Sleepless Nights (fic)
Mark Harris. It Looked Like Forever (fic)
Robert Hass. Praise (po)
John Clendennin Bourne Hawkes, Jr. The Passion Artist (fic)
Anthony Evan Hecht. The Venetian Vespers (po)
Joseph Heller. Good As Gold (fic)
Lillian Hellman. Three (nar)
Ernest Miller Hemingway. 88 Poems (pub)
Benth Henley. Crimes of the Heart (dr)
William Heyen. Long Island Light (po)
Eric Hoffer. Before the Sabbath (e)
Richard Joseph Howard. Misgivings (fic, po)
Irving Howe. Celebrations and Attacks (e)
Richard Franklin Hugo. Selected Poems (pub)
_____. The Triggering Town (e)
Rona Jaffe. Class Reunion (fic)
LeRoi Jones (Imamu Amiri Baraka). Selected Plays and Prose (misc, pub)
_____. Selected Poetry (pub)
Erica Mann Jong. At the Edge of the Body (po)
Donald Rodney Justice. Selected Poems (pub)
Garson Kanin. Maviola (fic)
Faye Kicknosway. Nothing Wakes Her (po)
John Knowles. A Vein of Riches (fic)
Kenneth Jay Koch. The Burning Mystery of Anna in 1951 (po, fic)
Jerzy Nikodem Kosinski. Passion Play (fic)
Jonathan Kozol. Prisoners of Silence: Breaking the Bonds of Adult
   Illiteracy in the United States (e)
Maxine Winokur Kumin. To Make a Prairie (e)
Ella Lefland. Rumors of Peace (fic)
Ira Levin. Break a Leg (dr)
Philip Levine. Ashes (po)
_____. Seven Years from Somewhere (po)
Morgan Llywelyn. Lion of Ireland: The Legend of Brian Boru (fic, biog)
Alison Lurie. Only Children (fic)
Norman Mailer. The Executioner's Song (fic, biog)
Bernard Malamud. Dubin's Lives (fic)
Paul Mariani. Timing Devices (po)
William Matthews. Rising and Falling (po)

William Maxwell. So Long, See You Tomorrow (fic)
Mary Therese McCarthy. Cannibals and Missionaries (fic)
Cormac McCarthy. Sultree (fic)
James Rodney McConkey. The Tree House Confessions (fic)
Thomas Francis McGuane III. Panama (fic)
James Albert Michener. The Watermen (fic)
Josephine Miles. Coming to Terms (po)
Arthur Miller. The American Clock (dr)
Judith Minty. Yellow Dog Journal (po)
George Frederick Morgan. Death Mother (po)
Robert Morgan. Groundwork (po)
Howard Moss. Notes from the Castle (po)
Jayne Anne Phillips. Black Tickets (fic)
Robert Pinsky. An Explanation of America (po)
John Francisco Rechy. Rushes (fic)
Mary Robison. Days (fic)
Samuel Shepard Rogers, Jr. (Sam Shepard). True West (dr)
Philip Roth. The Ghost Writer (fic)
Muriel Rukeyser. Collected Poems (pub)
William Saroyan. Obituaries (nar)
John W. Saul III. Cry for the Strangers (fic)
James Marcus Schuyler. What's for Dinner? (fic)
Delmore Schwartz. Last and Lost Poems (po, pub)
Irwin Shaw. The Top of the Hill (fic)
Wilfred John Joseph Sheed. The Good Word and Other Words (e)
David Smith. Goshawk, Antelope (po)
Gilbert Sorrentino. Mulligan Stew (fic)
Wallace Earle Stegner. Recapitulation (fic)
Jesse Hilton Stuart. Lost Sandstones and Lonely Skies (e)
William Styron. Sophie's Choice (fic)
May Swenson. New and Selected Things Taking Place (po)
James Vincent Tate. Riven Doggeries (po)
Lewis Thomas. The Medusa and the Snail: More Notes of a Biology Watcher (e)
Jean Thompson. Gasoline Wars (fic)
John Hoyer Updike. Bech: A Book (fic)
_____. The Coup (fic)
_____. Problems (fic)
_____. Too Far To Go (fic)
Kurt Vonnegut, Jr. Jailbird (fic)
David Russell Wagoner. In Broken Country (po)
Irving Wallace. The Pigeon Project (fic)
Robert Penn Warren. Brother to Dragons, rev ed (po)
Michael Waters. Not Just Any Death (po)
Jessamyn West. The Life I Really Lived (fic)
Thornton Niven Wilder. American Characteristics (e, pub)
Lanford Wilson. Talley's Folly (dr)
Frank Garvin Yerby. A Darkness at Ingraham's Crest (fic)
Anzia Yezierska. The Open Cage (fic, pub)
Louis Zukofsky. A (po, pub)

1980

DEATHS

Herbert Sebastian Agar
Melville Henry Cane
Marcus Cook Connelly
John Wesley Conroy
George Paul Elliott
Robert Hayden
Louis Kronenberger
Henry Miller
Katherine Anne Porter
Muriel Rukeyser
Donald Ogden Stewart
George Rippey Stewart
James Arlington Wright

EVENTS

Hemingway Society (f)
The Times-Picayune and the States-Item, New Orleans, Louisiana (per,
   f)

LITERATURE

Alice Adams. Rich Rewards (fic)
Isaac Asimov. In Joy Still Felt (auto)
_____. Microcosmic Tales (fic)
Jean Marie Auel. The Clan of the Cave Bear (fic)
Ann Beattie. Falling in Place (fic)
Thomas Louis Berger. Neighbors (fic)
Edmund J.M. Berrigan, Jr. So Going around Cities (po)
Wendell Berry. A Part (po)
Elizabeth Bishop. That Was Then (po, pub)
Richard Palmer Blackmur. Henry Adams (e, pub)
Judy Sussman Blume. Superjudge (juv, fic)
Michael Blumenthal. Sympathetic Magic (po)
Philip Booth. Before Sleep (po)
Vance Nye Bourjaily. A Game Men Play (fic)
Kay Boyle. Fifty Stories (pub)
Ray Douglas Bradbury. The Stories of Ray Bradbury (pub)
Olga Broumas. Soie Sauvage (po)
Sterling Allan Brown. Collected Poems (pub)
Ben Lucien Burman. The Strange Invasion of Catfish Bend (fic)
William Seward Burroughs. Port of Saints (fic)
Truman Capote. Music for Cameleons (fic, e, nar)
Ronald Verlin Cassill. Labors of Love (fic)
Mary Higgins Clark. The Cradle Will Fall (fic)
Jan Clausen. Mother, Sister, Daughter, Lover (fic)
Lucille Clifton. Two-Headed Woman (po)
Evan Shelby Connell, Jr. St. Augustine's Pigeon (fic)
_____. The White Lantern (e)
John Wesley Conroy. The Jack Conroy Reader (pub)
Robert Lowell Coover. A Political Fable (fic)
Malcolm Cowley. The Dream of the Golden Mountains (nar)
John P. Coyne. The Searing (fic)
John Michael Crichton. Congo (fic)
William Demby. Blueboy (fic)
Peter DeVries. Consenting Adults, or, the Duchess Will Be Furious

(fic)
James Lafayette Dickey. The Early Motion: "Drowning with Others" and
   "Hamlets" (po, pub)
Stephen Dixon. 14 Stories (fic, pub)
Edgar Lawrence Doctorow. Loon Lake (fic)
Rita Dove. The Yellow House on the Corner (po)
Norman Dubie. The Everlastings (po)
Andre Dubus. Finding a Girl in America (fic)
Andrea Dworkin. The New Woman's Broken Heart (fic)
Richard Ghormley Eberhart. Ways of Light (po)
Joseph Epstein. Ambition: The Secret Passion (e)
Frederick Feikema (Frederick Manfred/Feike Feikema). Sons of Adam
   (fic)
Lawrence Ferlinghetti and Nancy Peters. Literary San Francisco (hist)
Marilyn French. The Bleeding Heart (fic)
Charles Fuller. Zooman and the Sign (dr)
John Champlin Gardner, Jr. Freddy's Book (fic)
Martha Gellhorn. The Weather in Africa (fic)
Louise Gluck. Descending Figure (po)
Herbert Gold. He/She (fic)
Alfred Bertram Guthrie, Jr. No Second Wind (fic)
Mark Harris. Saul Bellow, Drumlin Woodchuck (biog)
_____. Short Work of It (e)
Barbara Grizzuti Harrison. Off Center: Essays (e)
Shirley Hazzard. The Transit of Venus (fic)
Robert Anson Heinlein. The Number of the Beast (fic)
Lillian Hellman. Maybe (nar)
Mark Helprin. Ellis Island and Other Stories (fic)
Beth Henley. The Miss Firecracker Contest (dr)
William Heyen. The City Parables (po)
Daniel Gerard Hoffman. Brotherly Love (po)
Mary Greay Hughes. The Calling (fic)
Richard Franklin Hugo. The Right Madness on Skye (po)
Rona Jaffe. Mr. Right Is Dead (fic)
Randall Jarrell. Kipling, Auden, and Company (e, pub)
Erica Mann Jong. Fanny (fic)
Maxine Hong Kingston. China Men (fic)
Galway Kinnell. Mortal Acts, Mortal Words (po)
John Knowles. Peace Breaks Out (fic)
Kenneth Jay Koch. Red Robbins (fic)
Judith Krantz. Princess Daisy (fic)
Ella Lefland. Last Courtesies (fic)
Ursula K. LeGuin. The Beginning Place (fic)
Helen MacInnes. The Hidden Target (fic)
Norman Mailer. Of Women and Their Elegance (biog, fic)
Donald McCaig. The Butte Polka (fic)
Thomas Francis McGuane III. An Outside Chance (e)
Rod McKuen. Looking for a Friend (po)
Sandra McPherson. Sensing (po)
William Morris Meredith. The Cheer (po)
James Ingram Merrill. Scripts for the Pageant (po)
James Albert Michener. The Covenant (fic)
Judith Minty. My Daughters (po)
Wright Morris. Plains Song: For Female Voices (fic)
Vladimir Nabokov. Lectures on Literature (e, pub)
Joyce Carol Oates. Bellefleur (fic)

Sharon Olds. Satan Says (po)
Gregory Orr. The Red House (po)
Eugene Gladstone O'Neill. Poems (pub)
Walker Percy. The Second Coming (fic)
Marge Piercy. Vida (fic)
Jack Carter Richardson. Memoir of a Gambler (nar)
Tom Robbins. Still Life with Woodpecker (fic)
Judith Perelman Rossner. Emmeline (fic)
John W. Saul III. Comes the Blind Fury (fic)
Budd Wilson Schulberg. Everything That Moves (fic)
James Marcus Schuyler. The Morning of the Poet (po)
Robert Siegal. Alpha Centauri (fic)
_____. In a Pig's Eye (po)
Charles Simic. Classic Ballroom Dances (po)
Louis Aston Marantz Simpson. Caviare at the Funeral (po)
William Jay Smith. The Traveler's Tree (po)
Susan Sontag. Under the Sign of Saturn (e)
Gilbert Sorrentino. Aberration of Starlight (fic)
Richard Gustave Stern. Packages (fic)
Irving Stone. The Origin (fic)
Mark Strand. Selected Poems (po)
Robert Lewis Taylor. Niagara (fic)
Studs Lewis Terkel. American Dreams: Lost and Found (nar)
Paul Edward Theroux. World's End (fic)
John Kennedy Toole. A Confederacy of Dunces (fic, pub)
Calvin Trillin. Floater (fic)
Lionel Trilling. Speaking of Literature and Society (e, pub)
Anne Tyler. Morgan's Passing (fic)
David Russell Wagoner. The Hanging Garden (fic)
Diane Wakowski. Cap of Darkness (po)
Irving Wallace. The Second Lady (fic)
Robert Penn Warren. Being Here (po)
Eudora Welty. Moon Lake (fic)
Jessamyn West. Double Discovery (nar, trav)
John Edgar Wideman. Damballah (fic)
_____. Hiding Place (fic)
Helen Yglasias. Sweetsir (fic)
Albert James Young. Ask Me Now (fic)

1981

DEATHS

Nelson Algren
Carleton Beals
Nathaniel Benchley
Mary Coyle Chase
Paddy Chayefsky
Jonathan Worth Daniels
Ketti Frings
Isabella Stewart Gardner
Caroline Gordon
Paul Eliot Green
Meyer Levin
Victoria Lincoln

Anita Loos
William Saroyan

EVENTS

National Humanities Alliance, Washington, D.C. (est)
Ronald Wilson Reagan, 40th President of the United States, to 1989

LITERATURE

Alice Adams. You Can't Keep a Good Woman Down (fic)
Lisa Alther. Original Sins (fic)
Archie Randolph Ammons. A Coast of Trees (po)
Max Apple. The Oranging of America (fic)
John Lawrence Ashbery. Shadow Train (po)
Donald Barthelme. Sixty Stories (pub)
Thomas Louis Berger. Reinhart's Women (fic)
Wendell Berry. Recollected Essays, 1965-1980 (e, pub)
Judy Sussman Blume. The One in the Middle Is the Green Kangaroo,
     rev ed (juv, fic)
_____. Tiger Eyes (juv, fic)
Robert Elwood Bly. The Man in the Black Coat Turns (po)
David Bradley. The Chaneysville Incident (fic)
John Malcolm Brinnin. Sextet: T.S. Eliot and Truman Capote and
     Others (e)
Gwendolyn Brooks. To Disembark (po)
Rita Mae Brown. Southern Discomfort (fic)
Charles Bukowski. Dangling in the Tournefortia (po)
William Seward Burroughs. Cities of the Red Night (fic)
James Mallahan Cain. The Baby in the Icebox (fic, pub)
Janet Taylor Caldwell. Answer As a Man (fic)
Raymond Carver. What We Talk about When We Talk about Love (fic)
Lucille Clifton. Source Beautiful (po)
Malcolm Cowley. The View from 80 (e, auto)
John P. Coyne. Hobgoblin (fic)
Peter DeVries. Sauce for the Goose (fic)
Hilda Doolittle. HERmoione (fic)
Allen Stuart Drury. The Hill of Summer (fic)
Gretel Ehrlich. To Touch the Water (po)
Howard Melvin Fast. The Legacy (fic)
Lawrence Ferlinghetti. Endless Life (po)
Francis Scott Key Fitzgerald. Poems (pub)
Charles Fuller. A Soldier's Play (dr)
Ernest J. Gaines. Catherine Carmier (fic)
John Champlin Gardner, Jr. The Art of Living (fic)
George Palmer Garrett, Jr. Love's Shining Child (po)
Ellen Gilchrist. In the Land of Dreamy Dreams (fic)
Allen Ginsberg. Plutonian Ode (po)
Gail Godwin. A Mother and Two Daughters (fic)
Herbert Gold. Family (fic)
_____. A Walk on the West Side (e, fic)
Caroline Gordon. Collected Stories (pub)
Donald Andrew Hall. The Oxford Book of American Literary Anecdotes
     (ed)
Joseph Hansen. A Smile in His Lifetime (fic)
Lamar Herrin. American Baroque (fic)

William Heyen. Lord Dragonfly: Five Sequences (po)
John Hollander. The Figures of Echo (e)
_____. Rhyme's Reason (ref)
Richard Franklin Hugo. Death and the Good Life (fic)
David Ignatow. Whisper to the Earth (po)
John Winslow Irving. The Hotel New Hampshire (fic)
Marguerite Johnson (Maya Angelou). The Heart of a Woman (auto, nar)
Faye Kicknosway. Asparagus, Asparagus, Ah Sweet Asparagus (po)
Allen Stewart Konigsberg (Woody Allen). The Floating Lightbulb (e)
Jonathan Kozol. On Being a Teacher (e, nar)
Philip Lamantia. Becoming Visible (po)
Ursula K. LeGuin. Hard Words, and Other Poems (po)
Denise Levertov. Light Up the Cave (po)
Philip Levine. One for the Rose (po)
Janet Lewis. Poems Old and New, 1918-1978 (po, pub)
Heather McHugh. A World of Difference (po)
Leonard Michaels. The Men's Club (fic)
Judith Minty. In the Presence of Mothers (po)
Robert Morgan. Bronze Age (po)
Toni Morrison. Tar Baby (fic)
Vladimir Nabokov. Lectures on Russian Literature (e, pub)
Joyce Carol Oates. Contraries (e)
Linda Pastan. Waiting for My Life (po)
Sidney Joseph Perelman. The Last Laugh (auto, nar, sat)
Robert Phillips. Running on Empty: New Poems (po)
Sylvia Plath. Collected Poems (pub)
Reynolds Price. The Source of Light (fic)
James Purdy. Mourners Below (fic)
Kenneth Rexroth. Excerpts from a Life (auto)
Adrienne Cecile Rich. A Wild Patience Has Taken Me This Far (po)
John Rollin Ridge. A Trumpet of Our Own (e, pub)
Marilynne Robinson. Housekeeping (fic)
Mary Robison. Oh! (fic)
William Pitt Root. In the World's Common Grasses (po)
_____. Reasons for Going It On Foot (po)
Sheldon Rosen. Ned and Jack (dr)
Philip Roth. Zuckerman Unbound (fic)
John W. Saul III. When the Wind Blows (fic)
Richard Selzer. Letters to a Young Doctor (e)
Anne Sexton. The Complete Poems (pub)
Irwin Shaw. Bread upon the Waters (fic)
Alice H.B. Sheldon. Out of Everywhere, and Other Extraordinary Vi-
    sions (fic)
Robert Siegel. Whalesong (fic)
Isaac Bashevis Singer. Lost in America (nar)
David Smith. Dream Flights (po)
_____. Homage to Edgar Allan Poe (po)
_____. Onliness (fic)
Gilbert Sorrentino. Crystal Vision (fic)
_____. Selected Poems (pub)
Elizabeth Spencer. Marilee (fic)
_____. The Stories of Elizabeth Spencer (fic, pub)
Mark Strand. The Planet of Lost Things (po)
Whitley Strieber. The Hunger (fic)
Joyce Carol Thomas. Black Child (po)
_____. Gospel Roots (dr)

Dana Trilling. Mrs. Harris (e)
Barbara Wertheim Tuchman. Practicing History (e)
John Hoyer Updike. Rabbit Is Rich (fic)
Gore Vidal. Creation (fic)
Kurt Vonnegut, Jr. Palm Sunday (e)
David Russell Wagoner. Landfall (po)
Robert Penn Warren. Rumor Verified (po)
Elwyn Brooks White. Poems and Sketches (misc, pub)
Richard Purdy Wilbur. Seven Poems (po, pub)
Lanford Wilson. A Tale Told (dr)
Larry Alfred Woiwode. Pappa John (fic)
Bari Wood. The Tribe (fic)
Charles Wright. The Southern Cross (po)

1982

DEATHS

Margaret Culkin Banning
Djuna Barnes
Stringfellow Barr
William Riley Burnett
John Cheever
Frederick Dannay
Babette Deutsch
John Champlin Gardner, Jr.
Horace Victor Gregory
Granville Hicks
Richard Franklin Hugo
Archibald MacLeish
Ayn Rand
Kenneth Rexroth
Howard Sackler
Marya Zaturenska

EVENTS

The Library of America (misc, ed)

LITERATURE

Alice Adams. To See You Again (fic)
William Alfred. The Curse of an Aching Heart (dr)
Archie Randolph Ammons. Worldly Hopes (po)
Louis Stanton Auchincloss. Watchfires (fic)
Djuna Barnes. Smoke, and Other Early Stories (fic, pub)
John Barth. Sabbatical: A Romance (fic)
Peter Soyer Beagle. The Garden of Earthly Delights (e)
Ann Beattie. The Burning House (fic)
Saul Bellow. The Dean's December (fic)
Wendell Berry. The Wheel (po)
Peter Bradford Benchley. The Girl of the Sea of Cortez (fic)
Ray Douglas Bradbury. Poems (pub)
Richard Brautigan. So the Wind Wont Blow It All Away (fic)
Courtlandt Dixon Barnes Bryan. Beautiful Women; Ugly Scenes (fic)

Carl Frederick Buechner. The Sacred Journey (nar, e)
Charles Bukowski. Ham on Rye (fic)
Hayden Carruth. Working Papers (e)
Raymond Carver. Two Poems (po)
John Chamberlain. A Life with the Printed Word (auto)
John Cheever. What a Paradise It Seems (fic)
Mary Higgins Clark. A Cry in the Night (fic)
Robert Lowell Coover. Spanking the Maid (fic)
Norman Cousins. Human Options (e, auto)
John P. Cpyne. The Shroud (fic)
Robert White Creeley. Collected Poems (pub)
Robert Choate Darnton. The Literary Underground of the Old Regime
     (hist)
James Lafayette Dickey. Puella (po)
Annie Dillard. Teaching a Stone To Talk (e)
John Gregory Dunne. Dutch Shea, Jr. (fic)
Stanley Lawrence Elkin. George Mills (fic)
Howard Melvin Fast. Max (fic)
Leslie Aaron Fiedler. What Was Literature? (e)
John Champlin Gardner, Jr. Mickelsson's Ghosts (fic)
Gail Godwin. A Mother and Two Daughters (fic)
Herbert Gold. True Love (fic)
Barbara Gordon. Defects of the Heart (fic)
Judith Ann Guest. Second Heaven (fic)
Alfred Bertram Guthrie, Jr. Fair Land, Fair Land (fic)
Elizabeth Forsythe Hailey. Life Sentences (fic)
Oakley Hall. Lullaby (fic)
Joseph Hansen. Backtrack (fic)
_____. Gravedigger (fic)
John Clendennin Burne Hawkes, Jr. Virginie (fic)
Robert Anson Heinlein. Friday (fic)
Edward Hoagland. The Tugman's Passage (e)
Eric Hoffer. Between the Devil and the Dragon: Thoughts of Men and
     Nature (e)
Mary Gray Hughes. My Wisdom (fic)
Rona Jaffe. Away from Home (fic)
Charles Richard Johnson. Oxherding Tale (fic)
Diane Lain Johnson. Terrorists and Novelists (e)
Roger Kahn. The Seventh Game (nar)
Garrison Keillor. Happy To Be Here (fic)
Galway Kinnell. Selected Poems (pub)
Norma Klein. Wives and Other Women (fic)
Elaine Loble Konigsburg. Journey to an 800 Number (juv)
Jerzy Nikodem Kosinski. Pinball (fic)
Jonathan Kozol. Alternative Schools: A Guide for Educators and Pa-
     rents (e, ref)
Judith Krantz. Mistral's Daughter (fic)
Maxine Winokur Kumin. Our Ground Time Here Will Be Brief (po)
_____. Why Can't We Live Together Like Civilized Hu-
     man Beings (fic)
Meridel LeSueur. Ripening (fic)
Denise Levertov. Candles in Babylon (po)
Meyer Levin. The Architect (fic, pub)
Morgan Llywelyn. The Horse Goddess (fic)
Mina Gertrude Lowy (Mina Loy). The Last Lunar Baedecker (po, pub)
Norman Mailer. Pieces and Pontifications (nar, e)

Bernard Malamud. God's Grace (fic)
David Alan Mamet. Edmond (dr)
Paul Mariani. Crossing Cocytus (po)
Bobbie Ann Mason. Shiloh and Other Stories (fic)
William Matthews. Flood (po)
Thomas Francis McGuane III. Nobody's Angel (fic)
James Ingram Merrill. The Changing Light at Sandover (po)
             . From the First Nine Poems (po)
William Stanley Merwin. Finding the Islands (po)
James Albert Michener. Space (fic)
Kenneth Millar. Self-Portrait (e)
Czeslaw Milosz. Visions from San Francisco (e)
George Frederick Morgan. Northbook (po)
John Frederick Nims. The Kiss (po)
Joyce Carol Oates. A Bloodsmoor Romance (fic)
             . Invisible Woman: New and Selected Poems, 1970-
1982 (po, pub)
Linda Pastan. New and Selected Poems (po, pub)
Marge Piercy. Braided Lives (fic)
             . Circles in the Water (po)
             . Parti-Colored Blocks for a Quilt (e)
Reynolds Price. Vital Provisions (po)
Ishmael Scott Reed. The Terrible Twos (fic)
John W. Saul III. The God Project (fic)
Robert Siegel. The Kingdom of Wundle (fic)
Laura Reichenthal (Laura Riding). Progress of Stories, rev ed (fic)
Eleanor May Sarton. Anger (fic)
Irwin Shaw. Acceptable Losses (fic)
Charles Simic. Austerities (po)
Isaac Bashevis Singer. Collected Stories (fic, pub)
Wallace Earle Stegner. One Way To Spell Man (e)
Richard Gustav Stern. The Invention of the Real (e, po)
Robert Anthony Stone. A Flag for Sunrise (fic)
Whitley Strieber. Black Magic (fic)
William Styron. This Quiet Dust (e, nar)
Paul Edward Theroux. The Mosquito Coast (fic)
Joyce Carol Thomas. Inside the Rainbow (po)
             . Marked by Fire (juv, fic)
Calvin Trillin. Uncivil Liberties (e)
Anne Tyler. Dinner at the Homesick Restaurant (fic)
John Hoyer Updike. Bech Is Back (fic)
Gore Vidal. The Second American Revolution (e)
Kurt Vonnegut, Jr. Deadeye Dick (fic)
Richard Purdy Wilbur. Andromache (trans)
Kate Wilhelm. Oh! Susanna (fic)
Sherley Anne Williams. Some Sweet Angel Chile (po)
Lanford Wilson. Angels Fall (dr)
Tobias Wolff. In the Garden of the North American Martyrs (fic)
James Arlington Wright. This Journey (po, pub)
Charles Wright. Country Music (po)
Frank Garvin Yerby. Western: A Saga of the Great Plains (fic)
Albert James Young. The Blues Don't Change (po)

1983

DEATHS

John Fante
Eric Hoffer
Kenneth Millar (Ross MacDonald)
Joseph Wechsberg
Thomas Lanier (Tennessee) Williams

LITERATURE

Roger Angell. Five Seasons (nar)
_____. Last Innings (nar)
Donald Barthelme. Overnight to Many Distant Cities (fic)
Frank Bidart. The Sacrifice (po)
Elizabeth Bishop. Complete Poems, 1927-1979 (pub)
Ray Douglas Bradbury. Dinosaur Tales (fic)
Olga Broumas. Pastoral Jazz (po)
Rita Mae Brown. Sudden Death (fic)
Hortense Calisher. Standard Dreaming (fic)
Raymond Carver. Fires: Essays, Poems, Stories, 1966-1982 (pub)
Amy Clampitt. The Kingfisher (po)
James Vincent Cunningham. Two Poems (po)
Janet Ann Dailey. Best Way To Lose (fic)
_____. Calder Born, Calder Bred (fic)
_____. Separate Cabins (fic)
_____. Stands a Calder Man (fic)
_____. Western Man (fic)
Stephen Dixon. Movies (fic)
Rita Dove. Museum (po)
Allen Stuart Drury. Decision (fic)
Norman Dubie. Selected and New Poems (pub)
Andre Dubus. The Times Are Never So Bad (fic)
Joseph Epstein. The Middle of My Tether (e)
Ernest J. Gaines. A Gathering of Old Men (fic)
Ellen Gilchrist. The Annunciation (fic)
Nikki Giovanni. Those Who Ride the Night Winds (po)
Gail Godwin. Mr. Bedford and the Muses (fic)
Albert Goldbarth. Original Light: New and Selected Poems, 1973-1983
  (po, pub)
Jorie Graham. Erosion (po)
Patricia Hampl. Resort, and Other Poems (pub)
Joseph Hansen. Job's Year (fic)
Mark Helprin. Winter's Tale (fic)
Laura Zamatkin Hobson. Laura Z (auto)
Eric Hoffer. Truth Imagined (e)
Erica Mann Jong. Ordinary Miracles (po)
William Kennedy. Ironweed (fic)
Faye Kicknosway. She Wears Him Fancy in Her Right Braid (po)
Norma Klein. Sextet in a Mirror (fic)
Gordon Lish. Dear Mr. Capote (fic)
Norman Mailer. Ancient Evenings (fic)
Bernard Malamud. The Stories of Bernard Malamud (fic, pub)
David Alan Mamet. Glengarry Glen Ross (dr)
Michael Thomas McClure. Fragments of Perseus (po)

James Rodney McConkey. Court of Memory (auto, nar)
Michael McFee. Plain Air (po)
Sandra McPherson. Patron Happiness (po)
William Stanley Merwin. Opening the Hand (po)
Cynthia Ozick. Art and Ardor (e)
Linda Pastan. PM/AM: New and Selected Poems (po, pub)
Marge Piercy. Stone, Paper, Knife (po)
Stanley Plumly. Summer Celestial (po)
Mary Robison. An Amateur's Guide to the Night (fic)
Judith Perelman Rossner. August (fic)
Philip Roth. The Anatomy Lesson (fic)
James Scully. Apollo Helmet (po)
David Smith. In the House of the Judge (po)
Gilbert Sorrentino. Blue Pastoral (fic)
Whitley Strieber. The Night Church (fic)
Joyce Carol Thomas. Bright Shadow (juv, fic)
Lewis Thomas. Late Night Thoughts on Listening to Mahler's Ninth
    Symphony (e)
_____. The Youngest Science: Notes of a Medicine Watcher
    (auto)
Calvin Trillin. Third Helpings (des, nar)
Gore Vidal. Duluth (fic)
Alice Walker. The Color Purple (fic)
_____. In Search of Our Mothers' Gardens: Womanist Prose (e,
    misc, pub)
Robert Penn Warren. Chief Joseph of the Nez Perce (po)
John Edgar Wideman. I Sent for You Yesterday (fic)
_____. Sent for You Yesterday (fic)
Kate Wilhelm. Welcome, Chaos (fic)
C.K. Williams. Tar (po)
Robley Wilson, Jr. Dancing for Men (fic)
Tobias Wolff. Matters of Life and Death: New American Stories (fic,
    ed)
James Arlington Wright. Complete Poems (pub)

1984

DEATHS

    Justin Brooks Atkinson
    Paul Bowles
    Ben Lucien Burman
    Truman Capote
    Albert Halper
    Lillian Hellman
    Chester Bomar Himes
    Richmond Alexander Lattimore
    Albert Maltz
    George Oppen
    Tomas Rivera
    Irwin Shaw
    Jesse Hilton Stuart

LITERATURE

Alice Adams. Superior Women (fic)
David Antin. Tuning (po)
Max Apple. Free Agents (fic, nar)
John Lawrence Ashbery. A Wave (po)
Richard David Bach. The Bridge across Forever: A Lovestory (fic)
Elizabeth Bishop. Collected Prose (misc, pub)
Judy Sussman Blume. The Pain and the Great One (juv, fic)
_____ . Smart Women (fic)
Michael Blumenthal. Days We Would Rather Know (po)
_____ . Laps (po)
Ray Douglas Bradbury. A Memory of Murder (fic)
Raymond Carver. Cathedral (fic)
Tom Clancy. The Hunt for Red October (fic)
Mary Higgins Clark. Stillwatch (fic)
Janet An Dailey. Leftover Love (fic)
_____ . Silver Wings, Santiago Blue (fic)
Robert Choate Darnton. The Great Cat Massacre and Other Episodes in
    French Cultural History (hist)
Joan Didion. Democracy (fic)
Stephen Dixon. Time To Go (fic)
Edgar Lawrence Doctorow. Lives of the Poets (fic)
Allen Stuart Drury. The Roads of Earth (fic)
Andre Dubus. Land Where My Fathers Died (fic)
_____ . We Don't Live Here Anymore (fic)
_____ and David R. Godine. Voices from the Moon (fic)
Tess Gallagher. Willingly (po)
Ellen Gilchrist. Victory over Japan (fic)
Herbert Gold. Mister White Eyes (fic)
Joseph Hansen. Brandstetter and Others (fic)
_____ . Nightwork (fic)
Michael S. Harper. Healing Song for the Inner Ear (po)
Barbara Grizzuti Harrison. Foreign Bodies (fic)
Robert Hass. Twentieth-Century Poetry: Prose on Poetry (e)
William Heyen. Erika: Poems of the Holocaust (po)
Mary Gray Hughes. Little Faces, and Other Stories (fic)
Richard Franklin Hugo. Making Certain It Goes On: The Collected Po-
    ems of Richard Hugo (po, pub)
Jamaica Kincaid. At the Bottom of the River (fic)
Norma Klein. Lovers (fic)
Arthur Kopit. End of the World (dr)
David Leavitt. Family Dancing (fic)
Denise Levertov. Oblique Players (po)
Gordon Lish. What I Know So Far (fic)
Morgan Llywelyn. Bard: The Odyssey of the Irish (fic)
Alison Lurie. Foreign Affairs (fic)
Thomas McGuane. Something To Be Desired (fic)
Norman Mailer. Tough Guys Don't Dance (fic)
David Alan Mamet. Warm and Cold (juv)
William Matthews. A Happy Childhood (po)
Donald McCaig. Nop's Trials (fic)
Howard Nemerov. Inside the Onion (po)
_____ . Last Things/First Light (po)
Sharon Olds. The Dead and the Living (po)
Tillie Olsen. Mother of a Daughter, Daughter of a Mother (po)
Jayne Anne Phillips. Machine Dreams (fic)
Marge Piercy. Fly Away Home (po)

Kenneth Rexroth. Selected Poems (pub)
Adrienne Cecile Rich. The Fact of a Doorframe: Poems Selected and
    New (po)
Jane Rule. Against the Season (fic)
_____. The Young in One Another's Arms (fic)
Eleanor May Sarton. At Seventy: A Journal (pub)
Reg Saver. Essay on Air (po)
John W. Saul III. Nathaniel (fic)
Janet Beeler Shaw. Some of the Things I Did Not Do (fic)
Gilbert Sorrentino. Something Said: Essays (e)
_____. Splendide-Hotel (po)
Whitley Strieber and James Kunteka. Warday: And the Journey Onward
    (fic)
Studs Louis Terkel. The Good War: An Oral History of World War II
    (hist, nar, e)
Calvin Trillin. Killings (nar)
John Hoyer Updike. The Witches of Eastwick (fic)
Eudora Welty. One Writer's Beginnings (e, nar)
John Edgar Wideman. Brothers and Keepers (nar, auto)
Tobias Wolff. The Barracks Thief (fic)
Bari Wood. Lightsource (fic)
Charles Wright. The Other Side of the River (po)
Frank Garvin Yerby. Devilseed (fic)

1985

DEATHS

Janet Taylor Caldwell
Stuart Chase
Robert Stuart Fitzgerald
Alfred Hayes
Helen MacInnes
Albert Maltz
Robert Gruntal Nathan
John Wexley
Elwyn Brooks White

LITERATURE

John Ashbery. Selected Poems (pub)
Louis Stanton Auchincloss. Honorable Men (fic)
Jean Marie Auel. The Mammoth Hunters (fic)
James Baldwin. The Price of the Ticket: Collected Nonfiction, 1948-
    1985 (e)
Russell Banks. Continental Drift (fic)
Ann Beattie. Love Always (fic)
Ray Douglas Bradbury. Death Is a Lonely Business (fic)
Raymond Carver. The Stories of Raymond Carver (fic, pub)
_____. Where Water Comes Together with Other Water (po)
Amy Clampitt. What the Light Was Like (po)
Jan Clausen. Sinking Stealing (fic)
Marcelle Clements. The Dog Is Us (e)
Martha Collins. A Catastrophe of Rainbows (po)
Jane Ann Dailey. The Glory Game (fic)

_____. The Pride of Hannah Wade (fic)
Stephen Dixon. Fall and Rise (fic)
Edgar Lawrence Doctorow. World's Fair (fic)
Gretel Ehrlich. The Solace of Open Spaces (e, nar, des)
Joseph Epstein. Plausible Prejudices (e)
Richard Ford. The Sportswriter (fic)
Ellen Gilchrist. In the Land of Dreamy Dreams, new ed (fic)
Molly Giles. Rough Translation (fic)
Allen Ginsberg. Collected Poems (pub)
Gail Godwin. The Finishing School (fic)
Herbert Gold. Stories of Misbegotten Love (fic)
Joseph Hansen. Steps Going Down (fic)
Robert Hayden. Complete Poems (pub)
Robert Anson Heinlein. The Cat Who Walks through Walls: A Comedy of
   Manners (fic)
Amy Hempel. Reasons To Live (fic)
John Richard Hersey. The Call (fic)
John Winslow Irving. Cider House Rules (fic)
Roger Kahn. Good Enough To Dream (nar)
Garrison Keillor. Lake Wobegon Days (fic)
Jamaica Kincaid. Annie John (fic)
Norma Klein. Give and Take (fic)
Jonathan Kozol. Illiterate America (e)
Helen MacInnes. Ride a Pale Horse (fic)
Maynard Mack. Alexander Pope: A Life (biog)
Mary Therese McCarthy. Occasional Prose (misc, pub)
Michael Thomas McClure. The Beard and VKTMS (dr)
_____. Fleas (180-186) (po)
James Albert Michener. Texas (fic)
Joyce Carol Oates. Solstice (fic)
Linda Pastan. A Fraction of Darkness: Poems (po)
Jane Rule. A Hot-Eyed Moderate (e)
_____. Inland Passage (fic)
Carl Sagan. Contact (fic)
John W. Saul III. Brainchild (fic)
Charles (Charlie) Smith. Canaan (fic)
Irving Stone. Depths of Glory (fic)
Jean Thompson. The Woman Driver (fic)
Anne Tyler. The Accidental Tourist (fic)
John Hoyer Updike. Facing Nature (po)
Leon Uris. The Haj (fic)
Gore Vidal. Vidal in Venice (trav, e)
Kurt Vonnegut, Jr. Galapagos (fic)
Eudora Welty. One Writer's Beginnings (fic)
Herman Wouk. Inside Outside (fic)
Frank Garvin Yerby. McKenzie's Hundred (fic)

1986

DEATHS

Hariette Simpson Arnow
John Ciardi
Laura Zametkin Hobson
Bob Kaufman

Bernard Malamud
Theodore Harold White

EVENTS

Robert Penn Warren, Poet Laureate of the United States

LITERATURE

Mortimore Jerome Adler. A Guidebook to Learning (e, ref)
Renata Adler. Reckless Disregard (hist, nar)
Sandra Alcosser. A Fish To Feed All Hunger (po)
James Applewhite. Ode to the Chinaberry Tree, and Other Poems (po)
Anthony Ardizzone. Heart of the Order (fic)
Brooke Astor. The Last Blossom on the Plum Tree (fic)
James Atlas. The Great Pretender (fic)
Louis Stanton Auchincloss. Diary of a Yuppie (fic)
Russell Banks. Success Stories (fic)
Peter Bradford Benchley. Q Clearance (fic)
Judy Sussman Blume. Letters to Judy: What Your Kids Wish They Could
    Tell You (nar)
Robert Elwood Bly. Selected Poems (po, e, pub)
Philip Booth. Relations: Selected Poems, 1950-1985 (po, pub)
James Breslin. Table Money (fic)
Joseph Brodsky. Less Than One (e)
Jared Brown. The Fabulous Lunts (biog, hist)
Rita Mae Brown. High Hearts (fic)
Jan Harold Brunvand. The Mexican Pet (fic)
William F. Buckley, Jr. High Jinx (fic)
William Seward Burroughs. The Adding Machine: Collected Essays (e,
Hortense Calisher. The Bobby-Soxer (fic)
Truman Capote. Answered Prayers: The Partial Manuscript (fic, pub)
Raymond Carver. Ultramarine (po)
Tom Clancy. Red Storm Rising (fic)
Eleanor Clark. Camping Out (fic)
Linda Collins. Going To See the Leaves (fic)
Pat Conroy. The Prince of Tides (fic)
John Byrne Cook. The Snowblind Bird, 3 vols (fic)
Clark Coolidge. Solution Passage: Poems, 1978-1981 (po, pub)
Gwen Davis. Silk Lady (fic)
Peter DeVries. Peckham's Marbles (fic)
Allen Stuart Drury. Pentagon (fic)
Andre Dubus. The Last Worthless Evening (fic)
Andrea Dworkin. Ice and Fire (fic)
Deborah Eisenberg. Transactions in a Foreign Country (fic)
David Eisenhower. Eisenhower (biog)
Ralph Waldo Ellison. Going to the Territory (e)
Louise Erdich. The Beet Queen (fic)
Dave Etter. Live at the Silver Dollar (po)
Laura Furman. Tuxedo Park (fic)
Ernest Kellogg Gann. The Triumph (fic)
John Champlin Gardner, Jr. Shadows (fic, pub)
                          . Stillness (fic, pub)
Herbert Gold. A Girl of Forty (fic)
Shirley Ann Grau. Nine Women (fic)
Andrew Greely. Confessions of a Parish Priest (auto)

Rachel Hadas. A Son from Sleep (po)
Elizabeth Forsythe Hailey. Joanna's Husband and David's Wife (fic)
Daniel Halpern. Tango (po)
Joseph Hansen. The Little Dog Laughed (fic)
Ernest Miller Hemingway. The Garden of Eden (fic, pub)
Dorothy Herrmann. S.J. Perelman: A Life (biog)
Edward Hoagland. Seven Rivers West (fic)
Thomas Hoving. Masterpiece (fic)
Maureen Howard. Expensive Habits (fic)
Evan Hunter (Ed McBain). Another Part of the City (fic)
_____. Cinderella (fic)
David Ignatow. New and Collected Poems, 1970-1985 (po, pub)
Charles Richard Johnson. The Sorcerer's Apprentice (fic)
Marguerite Johnson (Maya Angelou). All God's Children Need Traveling
    Shoes (auto)
Roger Kahn. Joe and Marilyn (biog)
Ken Kesey. Demon Box (fic, auto)
Richard Kluger. The Paper: The Life and Death of the New York Herald
    Tribune (hist)
John Knowles. The Private Life of Axie Reed (fic)
Kenneth Koch. On the Edge (po)
Elaine Lobl Konigsburg. Up from Jericho Tel (juv)
William Kotzwinkle. Jewell of the Moon (fic)
Judith Krantz. I'll Take Manhattan (fic)
Philip Lamantia. Meadowlark West (po)
Elmore Leonard. Double Dutch Treat: Three Novels (fic, pub)
Richard Lingeman. Theodore Dreiser: At the Gates of the City, 1871-
    1907 (biog)
Gordon Lish. Peru (fic)
Morgan Llywelyn. Grania (fic)
Robert Ludlum. The Bourne Conspiracy (fic)
Peter Matthiessen. Men's Lives (nar, hist)
Michael McClure. Selected Poems (po, pub)
Rod McKuen. Valentines (po)
Marianne Craig Moore. The Complete Prose, ed. Patricia C. Willis
    (e, nar)
Robert Morgan. At the Edge of the Orchard Country (po)
Anais Nin. Henry and June (nar, pub)
Joyce Carol Oates. Marya: A Life (fic)
Robert Brown Parker. Taming a Sea-Horse (fic)
T.R. Pearson. Off for the Sweet Hereafter (fic)
Cathie Pelletier. The Funeral Makers (fic)
Ron Powers. White Town Drowsing (fic)
Reynolds Price. Kate Vaiden (fic)
Ishmael Scott Reed. Reckless Eyeballing (fic)
Ruth Rendell. The New Girl Friend (fic)
Norman Rush. Whites (fic)
J.R. Salamanca. Southern Light (fic)
Arthur Meier Schlessinger, Jr. The Cycles of American History (hist)
Carolyn See. Golden Days (fic)
Vikram Seth. The Golden Gate (fic)
John Smith. The Complete Works of Captain John Smith, 1580-1631, 3
    vols (misc, pub)
Robert Anthony Stone. Children of Light (fic)
Peter Hillsman Taylor. A Summons to Memphis (fic)
Studs Louis Terkel. Chicago (nar, des)

Paul Theroux. O-Zone (fic)
Joyce Carol Thomas. Amber (fic)
_____. The Golden Pasture (fic)
_____. Water Girl (fic)
John Hoyer Updike. Roger's Version (fic)
Irving Wallace. The Seventh Secret (fic)
James Melvin Washington. A Testament of Hope: The Essential Writings
   of Martin Luther King, Jr. (e, ed)
Thomas Williams. The Moon Pinnace (fic)
Edmund Wilson. The Fifties, ed. Leon Edel (nar, e, pub)
Geoffrey Ansell Wolff. Providence (fic)
Richard Yates. Cold Spring Harbor (fic)
William Zinsser. Extraordinary Lives: The Art and Craft of American
   Biography (e, biog, ed)

Index of Authors and Events

( ) following the page number indicates multiple reference on that page

A

About the Author

SAMUEL J. ROGAL is Chairman of the Division of Humanities and Fine Arts at Illinois Valley Community College, Oglesby, Illinois. He has written numerous scholarly papers and essays, has contributed widely to literary journals, and is the author of many books, including *A Chronological Outline of British Literature* (Greenwood Press, 1980), *The Children's Jubilee* (Greenwood Press, 1983), and *Guide to the Hymns and Tunes of American Methodism, 1878-1964* (Greenwood Press, 1986).